WRITING FICTION
A Guide to Narrative Craft

Sixth Edition

JANET BURROWAY

Florida State University

with

SUSAN WEINBERG

Appalachian State University

New York   San Francisco   Boston
London   Toronto   Sydney   Tokyo   Singapore   Madrid
Mexico City   Munich   Paris   Cape Town   Hong Kong   Montreal

Vice President and Editor-in-Chief: Joseph Terry
Acquisitions Editor: Erika Berg
Associate Editor: Barbara Santoro
Senior Marketing Manager: Melanie Craig
Production Manager: Donna DeBenedictis
Project Coordination, Text Design, and Electronic Page Makeup: Elm Street
    Publishing Services, Inc.
Senior Cover Design Manager: Nancy Danahy
Cover Designer: Neil Flewellyn
Cover Image: Background image: © Don Bishop/Artville LLC; Montage images:
    © PhotoDisc, Inc.
Manufacturing Buyer: Roy Pickering
Printer and Binder: The Maple-Vail Book Manufacturing Group
Cover Printer: Phoenix Color Corporation

For permission to use copyrighted material, grateful acknowledgment is made to the copyright holders on pages 422–423, which are hereby made part of this copyright page.

Library of Congress Cataloging-in-Publication Data

Burroway, Janet.
    Writing fiction : a guide to narrative craft / Janet Burroway.—6th ed.
        p.   cm.
    Includes bibliographical references and index.
    ISBN 0-321-11795-6
        1. Fiction—Technique.   2. Fiction—Authorship.   3. Narrative (Rhetoric).
    4. Creative writing.   I. Title.
    PN3355 .B79   2003
    808.3—dc21   2002016220
                                                                        CIP

Please visit our website at http://www.ablongman.com

ISBN 0-321-11795-6

4 5 6 7 8 9 10—MA—05 04

For David Daiches, mentor and friend

CONTENTS

PREFACE

To Instructors: About This Book

The sixth edition of *Writing Fiction*, like its previous manifestations, attempts to guide the student writer from first impulse to final revision, employing concepts of fiction's elements familiar from literature study, but shifting the perspective toward that of the practicing writer. I have wanted to address the student, however inexperienced, as a fellow artist, whose concerns are both frightening and, often, also, a question of understanding and developing technique.

As experienced instructors are aware, the idea of a text for writing fiction is itself problematic. Unlike such subjects as math and history, where a certain mass of information needs to be organized and conveyed, the writing of fiction is more often a process of trial and error—the learning is perpetual, and, paradoxically, the writer needs to know everything at once. If a text is too prescriptive, it's not true to the immense variety of possibilities; if it's too anecdotal, it may be cheering but is unlikely to be of use.

I'm also aware that *Writing Fiction* is used by many instructors in both beginning and advanced writing courses and for students at very different levels of understanding. I've tried therefore to make it practical, comprehensive, and flexible, and to keep the focus on the student writer and the process of the writing. My means of doing this is to cover discrete elements in separate chapters, yet to build in each chapter on what has been covered earlier. Focus on the writing process and suggestions for getting started have seemed to me a logical place to begin, but I have tried to keep subsequent chapters sufficiently self-contained that teachers may assign them in any order they prefer.

More than any previous edition, the sixth edition attempts to respond to teachers who use it in the classroom, those who write or email spontaneously throughout the life of the edition, colleagues in universities and the Associated Writing Programs, and those asked by the publisher to engage in a formal process of review. There is really no appropriate term for these people. A "reviewer" usually makes a take-it-or-leave-it judgment, whereas the reviewers of a text are collaborators in an ongoing attempt to keep the book vital among the changing needs of students, teachers, and the academic zeitgeist. Naturally these teacher/writers tend to nudge the new edition in the direction of their own pedagogical needs and methods, and inevitably some advice conflicts with other.

Nevertheless, reviewers are surprisingly often in agreement and often thorough, thoughtful, practical, and inspired. One such writer/teacher is Susan Weinberg of Appalachian State University. When asked to review the fourth edition, Susan in effect produced a workable plan for a revision. I therefore requested that she be involved in the review of following edition and again found her response so apt, engaged, and comprehensive that I asked her to take a much more substantial role in the edition you now hold. Susan was responsible for the sometimes daunting task of receiving, researching, collating, and incorporating hundreds of suggestions for both the substance of the book and its apparatus, considering and selecting from among many dozen suggested readings, updating some sections of the book, and introducing new passages in others.

FEATURES OF THE SIXTH EDITION

The sixth edition includes a significant expansion of readings, almost doubling the number of stories in order to function both as a course anthology and as a writing manual. These stories have been chosen primarily from contemporary American fiction with attention to increased variety in form, mood, and content and emphasis on multicultural representation of authors and experiences. A number of short-short stories are used to offer quick illustrations of concepts.

Discussion of key issues has been enhanced, including character growth and change, portrayal of emotion, subtext in dialogue, dialogue format, characterization through setting, and use of the workshop process to aid revision.

Examples of the revision process include comments by several authors of the anthologized stories on their revision of those works.

Expanded supplements of writing exercises follow each chapter, including Individual, Development/Revision, and Collaborative assignments.

There are new question sets for discussion of anthologized stories, focusing on issues of craft.

Boxed quotations from established authors—on topics such as writing from experience, story structure, openings and endings, and revision—offer students a quick and encouraging reminder of key chapter concepts.

Above all, for the new edition both Susan Weinberg and I have kept the exigencies of the creative writing classroom in mind, intending to be catalytic rather than prescriptive, hoping to encourage both students and teachers to feel comfortable with themselves and the writing process.

ACKNOWLEDGMENTS

Many people have helped with the sixth edition of *Writing Fiction*. Thanks go to my students and colleagues in the Writing Program at Florida State University. At Appalachian State University, Susan Weinberg would like to thank graduate research assistants Sharon Price, Sara Littlejohn, Laurin Blanks, and Natalie Serriani; visiting writers Robert Morgan and Stephen Fischer; students Kim Zdanowicz, Amber Thompson, Todd Atchison, and members of the Fall 2000 Senior Seminar in Creative Writing; and colleagues Lynn Doyle and Joseph Bathanti. Much appreciation is also due to John L'Heureux, Nancy Huddleston Packer, and Gay Pierce of Stanford University's Creative Writing Program.

I am also grateful to the following writers/teachers who have reviewed this edition: Robert C. Adams, Community College of Southern Nevada; C. D. Albin, Southwest Missouri State University, West Plains; Cathleen Calbert, Rhode Island College; George Clark, University of Louisiana at Lafayette; Lawrence Coates, Southern Utah University; Becky Hagenston, Mississippi State University; Robin Hemley, Western Washington University; Colleen McElroy, University of Washington; Michael McFarland, North Harris College; Alyce Miller, Indiana University; Amanda Moore, Cornell University; Gary L. Myers, Mississippi State University; John Peterson, University of Washington, Tacoma; James Plath, Illinois Wesleyan University; Sheryl St. Germain, Iowa State University; Heather L. Sellers, Hope College; Maura Stanton, Indiana University; Susan Swartwout, Southeast Missouri State University; Jeffery R. White, Bellevue Community College; and Marilyn Wilton, Clovis Community College.

We would like to acknowledge the writers Simone Poirier-Bures, Judith Slater, Anne Giles Rimbey, Gerald Shapiro, B. W. Jorgensen, Gordon Johnson, Tobey Kaplan, and Rachel Hall whose exercises, which have appeared in The Associated Writing Programs' publication entitled *Pedagogy Papers*, have been adapted within this text. We would also like to acknowledge the writers Robert Olen Butler, Doug Bauer, Lee Smith, Jill McCorkle, Ron Hansen, Tom Batt, Wally Lamb, and Alan Gurganus whose insightful words from interviews published in the Associated Writing Programs' publication *The Writer's Chronicle* have been quoted in this text. Among the many others who have shared exercises over the years, special thanks go to Nancy Huddleston Packer, John L'Heureux, Alice La Plante, Erin McGraw, Brad Owens, Rick Hillis, Bo Caldwell, Michelle Carter, and Leslee Becker.

—J. B.

A Note from the Publisher

SUPPLEMENTS AVAILABLE WITH WRITING FICTION, SIXTH EDITION

- **A Workshop Guide for Creative Writing** (0-321-09539-1) is a laminated reference tool that includes guidelines for criticism, workshop etiquette, and more. Free when packaged with *Writing Fiction*, Sixth Edition.
- **The Longman Journal for Creative Writing** (0-321-09540-5) helps students explore and discover their own writing habits and styles. Free when packaged with *Writing Fiction*, Sixth Edition.
- **Penguin Discount Novel Program.** A variety of Penguin paperbacks are offered at a significant discount when packaged with *Writing Fiction*, Sixth Edition. To review the complete list of titles available, please visit: http://www.ablongman.com/penguin.
- *Merriam Websters Reader's Handbook: Your Complete Guide to Literary Terms* (0-321-10541-9) includes nearly 2,000 entries including descriptions for every major genre, style, and era of writing. Available at a significant discount when packaged with *Writing Fiction*, Sixth Edition.
- **Course Compass.** This customizable course management program enables professors to tailor content and functionality to meet individual course needs. For more information, or to see a demo, visit http://www.coursecompass.com/, or contact your local Longman sales representative.

To Students: About the Writing Workshop

Writing Fiction is primarily intended for use in the college-level writing workshop—a phenomenon now so firmly established that nearly every higher institution in America offers some form of workshop-based creative writing course or program, and sufficiently evolved that it has given rise to a new verb—"to workshop."

To workshop is much more than to discuss. It implies a commitment on the part of everyone concerned to give close attention to work that is embryonic. The atmosphere of such a group is intense and personal in a way that other college classes are not, since a major text of the course is also the raw effort of its participants. At the same time, unlike the classic model of the artist's atelier or the music conservatory, the instruction is assumed to come largely from the group rather than from a single master of technical expertise. Thus the workshop represents a democratization of both the material for college study and its teaching.

Although workshops inevitably vary, a basic pattern has evolved in which twelve to twenty students are led by an instructor who is also a published writer. The students take turns writing, copying, and distributing stories, which the others take away, read, and critique. What is sought in such a group is mutual goodwill—the desire to make the story under scrutiny the best that it can be—together with an agreed-to toughness on the part of writer and readers.

This sounds simple enough, but as with all democratization, the perceived danger is that the process will flatten out the story's edge and originality, and that the result will be a homogenized "revision by committee." The danger is partly real and deserves attention. Partly, however, such fear masks protectiveness toward the image—solitary, remote, romantic—of the writer's life.

But those who have taken part in the process tend to champion it. John Gardner asserted that not only could writing be taught, but that "writing ability is mainly a product of good teaching supported by a deep-down love of writing." John Irving says of his instructors, "they clearly saved me valuable time . . . [and] time is precious for a young writer." Isabel Allende says, "The process is lonely, but the response connects you with the world." Novelist and teacher Robert Morgan explains that "writing can't be taught as a body of knowledge to be passed from instructor to students, as with history or physics, say, because the young writer only really learns from practice." But, comparing writers to athletes, Morgan suggests that "We teach ourselves to write by doing it again and again, learning from our successes and mistakes . . . The writing teacher mostly builds up the confidence of the students that they can teach themselves, and tell when they are doing it right."

There are, I think, three questions about the workshop endeavor that have to be asked: Is it good for the most startlingly talented, those who will go on to "become" published professional writers? Is it good for the majority who will not publish, but will instead become (as some of my most gifted students have) restaurateurs, photographers, technical writers, high-school teachers? And is it good for literature and literacy generally to have students of all fields struggle toward this play and this craft? My answer must in all cases be a vigorous yes. The workshop aids both the vocation and the avocation. Writing is a solitary struggle, and from the beginning writers have sought relief in the company and understanding of other writers. At its best the workshop provides an intellectual, emotional, and social (and some argue a spiritual) discipline. For the potential professionals there is the important focus on craft; course credit is a form of early pay-for-writing; deadlines help you find the time and discipline to do what you really want to; and above all, the workshop offers attention in an area where attention is hard to command. For those who will not be professionals, a course in writing fiction can be a valuable part of a liberal arts education, making for better readers, better letters home, better company reports, and better private memoirs. For everyone, the workshop can help develop critical thinking, a respect for craft, and important social skills.

There are also some pitfalls in the process: that students will develop unrealistic expectations of their chances in a chancy profession; that they will dull or provincialize their talents by trying to please the teacher or the group; that they will be buoyed into self-satisfaction by too-lavish praise or that they will be crushed by too-harsh criticism. On the other hand, workshop peers recognize and revere originality, vividness, and truth at least as often as professional critics. Hard work counts for more than anyone but writers realize, and facility with the language can be learned out of obsessive attention to it. The driven desire is no guarantee of talent, but it is an annealing force. And amazing transformations can and do occur in the creative writing class. Sometimes young writers who exhibit only a propensity for cliché and the most hackneyed initial efforts make sudden, breathtaking progress. Sometimes the leap of imaginative capacity is inexplicable, like a sport of nature.

The appropriate atmosphere in which to foster this metamorphosis is a balance constructed of right-brain creative play and left-brain crafted language, and of obligations among readers, writers, and teachers. Of these obligations, a few seem to me worth noting.

HOW WORKSHOPS WORK

The most basic expectation is that the manuscript itself should be professionally presented—that is, double-spaced on one side of white 8½-by-11-inch paper, with generous margins, in clear copies, proofread for grammar, spelling, and punctuation. In most workshops the content is left entirely to the writer, with no censorship of subject. The reader's obligation is to read the story twice, once for its sense and story, a second time with pen in hand to make marginal comments, observations, suggestions. A summarizing end note is usual and helpful. This should be done with the understanding—on the parts of both writer and reader—that the work at hand is by definition a work in progress. If it were finished then there would be no reason to bring it into workshop. Workshop readers should school themselves to identify the successes that are in every story: the potential strength, the interesting subject matter, the pleasing shape, or the vivid detail.

It's my experience that the workshop itself proceeds most usefully to the writer if each discussion begins with a critically neutral description and interpretation of the story. This is important because workshopping can descend into a litany of *I like, I don't like*, and it's the responsibility of the first speaker to provide a coherent reading as a basis for discussion. It's often a good idea to begin with a detailed summary of the narrative action—useful because if class members understand the events of the story differently, or are unclear about what happens, this is important information for the author, a signal that she has not revealed what, or all, she meant. The interpretation might then address such questions as: *What kind of story is this? What defining choices do the characters face? What is its conflict-crisis-resolution structure? What is it about? What does it say about what it is about? How sympathetic should the reader feel with the main character? How does its imagery relate to its theme?*

Only after some such questions are addressed should the critique begin to deal with whether the story is successful in its effects. The first speaker should try to close with two or three questions that, in his/her opinion, the story raises, and invite the class to consider these. Most of the questions will be technical: *Is the point of view consistent, are the characters fully drawn, is the imagery vivid and specific?* But now and again it is well to pause and return to more substantive matters: *What's the spirit of this story, what is it trying to say, what does it make me feel?*

THE WRITER'S ROLE

For the writer, the obligations are more emotionally strenuous, but the rewards are great. The hardest part of being a writer in a workshop is to learn this: Be still, be greedy for suggestions, take everything in, and don't defend.

This is difficult because the story under discussion is still new and may feel highly personal. The author has a strong impulse to explain and plead. If the criticism is "this isn't clear," it's hard not to feel "you didn't read it right"—even if you understand that it is not up to the workshop to "get it" but up to the author to be clear. If the reader's complaint is "this isn't credible," it's very hard not to respond "but it really happened!"—even though you know perfectly well that credibility is a different sort of fish than fact, and that autobiography is irrelevant. There is also a self-preservative impulse to keep from changing the core of what you've done: "Don't they realize how much time and effort I've already put in?"

But only the author's attempt at complete receptivity will make the workshop work. The chances are that your first draft really does not say the most meaningful thing inherent in the story, and that most meaningful thing may announce itself sideways, in a detail, within parentheses, an afterthought, a slip. Somebody else may see the design before you do. Sometimes the best advice comes from the most surprising source. The thing you resist the hardest may be exactly what you need.

After the workshop, the writer's obligation alters slightly. It's important to take the written critiques and take them seriously, let them sink in with as good a will as you brought to the workshop. But part of the need is also not to let them sink in too far. Reject without regret whatever seems on reflection wrongheaded, dull, destructive, or irrelevant to your vision. It's just as important to be able to discriminate between helpful and unhelpful criticism as it is to be able to write. More often than not, the most useful criticism will simply confirm what you already suspected yourself. So listen to everything and receive all criticism as if it were golden. Then listen to yourself and toss the dross.

(For further discussion of giving and receiving workshop feedback, please see Chapter 11, "Play It Again, Sam: Revision.")

J. B.

1

WHATEVER WORKS
The Writing Process

• *Get Started*

• *Keep Going*

• *A Word about Theme*

You want to write. Why is it so hard?

There are a few lucky souls for whom the whole process of writing is easy, for whom the smell of fresh paper is better than air, whose minds chuckle over their own agility, who forget to eat, and who consider the world at large an intrusion on their good time at the keyboard. But you and I are not among them. We are in love with words except when we have to face them. We are caught in a guilty paradox in which <u>we grumble over our lack</u> of time, and when we have the time, we sharpen pencils, check e-mail, or clip the hedges.

Of course, there's also joy. We write for the satisfaction of having wrestled a sentence to the page, for the rush of discovering an image, for the excitement of seeing a character come alive. Even the most successful writers will sincerely say that these pleasures—not money, fame, or glamour—are the real rewards of writing. Fiction writer Alice Munro concedes:

> It may not look like pleasure, because the difficulties can make me morose and distracted, but that's what it is—the pleasure of telling the story I mean to tell as wholly as I can tell it, of finding out in fact what the story is, by working around the different ways of telling it.

Nevertheless, writers may forget what such pleasure feels like when confronting a blank page, like the heroine of Anita Brookner's novel *Look at Me:*

Sometimes it feels like a physical effort simply to sit down at the desk and pull out the notebook. . . . Sometimes the effort of putting pen to paper is so great that I literally feel a pain in my head. . .

It helps to know that most writers share the paradox of least wanting to do what we most want to do. It also helps to know some of the reasons for our reluctance. Fear of what could emerge on the page, and what it may reveal about our inner lives, can keep us from getting started. Dorothy Allison, author of *Bastard Out of Carolina*, describes the necessity of breaking through this form of self-censorship:

> I believe the secret of writing is that fiction never exceeds the reach of the writer's courage. The best fiction comes from the place where the terror hides, the edge of our worst stuff. I believe, absolutely, that if you do not break out in that sweat of fear when you write, then you have not gone far enough. And I know you can fake that courage when you don't think of yourself as coura-geous—because I have done it. And that is not a bad thing, to fake it until you can make it. I know that until I started pushing on my own fears, telling the sto-ries that were hardest for me, writing about exactly the things I was most afraid of and unsure about, I wasn't writing worth a damn.

There's another impediment to beginning, expressed by a writer character in Lawrence Durrell's *Alexandria Quartet*. Durrell's Pursewarden broods over the illu-sory significance of what he is about to write, unwilling to begin in case he spoils it. Many of us do this: The idea, whatever it is, seems so luminous, whole, and fragile, that to begin to write about that idea is to commit it to rubble. "The paradox of writ-ing," says screenwriter Stephen Fischer, "is that you're trying to use words to express what words can't express." Knowing in advance that words will never exactly cap-ture what we mean or intend, we must gingerly and gradually work ourselves into a state of accepting what words can do instead. No matter how many times we find out that what words can do is quite all right, we still shy again from the next begin-ning. Against this wasteful impulse I have a motto over my desk that reads: "Don't Dread; Do." It's a fine motto, and I contemplated it for several weeks before I began writing this chapter.

The mundane daily habits of writers are apparently fascinating. No author offers to answer questions at the end of a public reading without being asked: *Do you write in the morning or at night? Do you write every day? Do you compose longhand or on a computer?* Sometimes such questions show a reverent interest in the workings of ge-nius. More often, I think, they are a plea for practical help: *Is there something I can do to make this job less horrific? Is there a trick that will unlock my words?*

Get Started

The variety of authors' habits suggests that there is no magic to be found in any par-ticular one. Donald Hall will tell you that he spends a dozen hours a day at his desk, moving back and forth between as many projects. Philip Larkin said that he wrote a poem only every eighteen months or so and never tried to write one that was not a gift. Gail Godwin goes to her workroom every day "because what if the angel came and I wasn't there?" Julia Alvarez begins the day by reading first poetry, then prose, by her favorite writers "to remind me of the quality of writing I am aiming for." Like Hemingway, the late Andre Dubus advised students to stop writing midsentence in order to begin the next day by completing the thought, thereby reentering the creative flow more easily. Dickens could not deal with people when he was working: "The mere consciousness of an engagement will worry a whole day." Thomas Wolfe wrote standing up. Some writers can plop at the kitchen table without clearing the breakfast dishes; others need total seclusion, a beach, a cat, a string quartet.

There is something to be learned from all this, though. It is not an "open sesame" but a piece of advice older than fairy tales: Know thyself. The bottom line is that if you do not at some point write your story down, it will not get written. Having decided that you will write it, the question is not "How do you get it done?" but "How do *you* get it done?" Any discipline or indulgence that actually helps nudge you into

I do not sit down at my desk to put into verse something that is already clear in my mind. If it were clear in my mind, I should have no incentive or need to think about it. . . . We do not write in order to be understood; we write in order to understand.

C. Day Lewis

If you haven't surprised yourself, you haven't written.

Eudora Welty

Forget *inspiration*. Habit is more dependable. Habit will sustain you whether you're inspired or not. Habit will help you finish and polish your stories. Inspiration won't. Habit is persistence in practice.

Octavia Butler

All water has a perfect memory and is forever trying to get back to where it was. Writers are like that: remembering where we were, what valley we ran through, what the banks were like, the light that was there, and the route back to our original place. It is emotional memory—what the nerves and the skin remember as well as how it appeared. And a rush of imagination is our "flooding."

Toni Morrison

position facing the page is acceptable and productive. If jogging after breakfast energizes your mind, then jog before you sit. If you have to pull an all-nighter on a coffee binge, do that. Some schedule, regularity, pattern in your writing day (or night) will always help, but only you can figure out what that pattern is for you.

JOURNAL KEEPING

There are, though, a number of tricks you can teach yourself in order to free the writing self, and the essence of these is to give yourself permission to fail. The best place for such permission is a private place, and for that reason a writer's journal is an essential, likely to be the source of originality, ideas, experimentation, and growth.

Keep a journal. A journal is an intimate, a friend that will accept you as you are. Pick a notebook you like the look of, one you feel comfortable with, as you would pick a friend. I find a bound blank book too elegant to live up to, preferring instead a loose-leaf because I write my journal mainly at the computer and can stick anything in at the flip of a three-hole punch. But you can glue scribbled napkins into a spiral, too.

Keep the journal regularly, at least at first. It doesn't matter what you write and it doesn't matter very much how much, but it does matter that you make a steady habit of the writing. A major advantage of keeping a journal regularly is that it will put you in the habit of observing in words. If you know at dawn that you are committed to writing so many words before dusk, you will half-consciously tell the story of your day to yourself as you live it, finding a phrase to catch whatever catches your eye. When that habit is established, you'll begin to find that whatever invites your attention or sympathy, your anger or curiosity, may be the beginning of invention. *Whoever* catches your attention may be the beginning of a character.

But before the habit is developed, you may find that even a blank journal page has the awesome aspect of a void, and you may need some tricks of permission to let yourself start writing there. The playwright Maria Irene Fornes says that there are two of you: one who wants to write and one who doesn't. The one who wants to write had better keep tricking the one who doesn't. Or another way to think of this conflict is between right brain and left brain—the playful, detail-loving creator, and the linear critic. The critic is an absolutely essential part of the writing process. The trick is to shut him or her up until there is something to criticize.

FREEWRITING

Freewriting is a technique that allows you to take very literally the notion of getting something down on paper. It can be done whenever you want to write, or just to free up the writing self. The idea is to put

> anything on paper and I mena anything, it doesn't matter as long as it's coming out of your head nad hte ends of your fingers, down ont the page I wonder if;m improving, if this process gets me going better now than it did all those—hoew-

ever many years ago? I know my typing is geting worse, deteriorating even as we speak (are we speaking? to whom? IN what forM? I love it when i hit the caps button by mistake, it makes me wonder whether there isn;t something in the back or bottom of the brain that sez PAY ATTENTION now, which makes me think of a number of things, freud and his slip o tonuge, self-deception, the myriad way it operates in everybody's life, no not everybody's but in my own exp. llike Aunt Ch. mourniong for the dead cats whenevershe hasn't got her way and can't disconnect one kind of sadness from another, I wonder if we ever disconnect kinds of sadness, if the first homesickness doesn;t operatfor everybody the same way it does for me, grandma's house the site of it, the grass out the window and the dog rolling a tin pie plate under the willow tree, great heavy hunger in the belly, the empty weight of loss, loss, loss

That's freewriting. Its point is to keep going, and that is the only point. When the critic intrudes and tells you that what you're doing is awful, tell the critic to take a dive, or acknowledge her/him (*typing is getting worse*) and keep writing. If you work on a computer, try dimming the screen so you can't see what you're doing. At times, you might find it liberating to freewrite to music, random or selected. If you freewrite often, pretty soon you'll be bored with writing about how you don't feel like writing (though that is as good a subject as any; the subject is of no importance and neither is the quality of the writing) and you will find your mind and your phrases running on things that interest you. Fine. It doesn't matter. Freewriting is the literary equivalent of scales at the piano or a short gym workout. All that matters is that you do it. The verbal muscles will develop of their own accord.

Though freewriting is mere technique, it can affect the freedom of the content. Many writers feel themselves to be *an instrument through which*, rather than a *creator of*, and whether you think of this possibility as humble or holy, it is worth finding out what you say when you aren't monitoring yourself. Fiction is written not so much to inform as to find out, and if you force yourself into a mode of informing when you haven't yet found out, you're likely to end up pontificating or lying some other way.

In *Becoming a Writer*, a book that only half-facetiously claims to do what teachers of writing claim cannot be done—to teach genius—Dorothea Brande suggests that the way to begin is not with an idea or a form at all, but with an unlocking of your thoughts on paper. She advises that you rise each day and go directly to your desk (if you have to have coffee, put it in a thermos the night before) and begin writing whatever comes to mind, before you are quite awake, before you have read anything or talked to anyone, before reason has begun to take over from the dream-functioning of your brain. Write for twenty or thirty minutes and then put away what you have written without reading it over. After a week or two of this, pick an additional time during the day when you can salvage a half hour or so to write, and when that time arrives, write, even if you "must climb out over the heads of your friends" to do it. It doesn't matter what you write. What does matter is that you develop the habit of beginning to write the moment you sit down to do so.

CLUSTERING

Clustering is a technique, described in full by Gabriele Rico in her book *Writing the Natural Way*, that helps you organize your writing organically rather than sequentially. Usually when we plan a piece of writing in advance, it is in a linear fashion—topic sentences and subheadings in the case of an essay, usually an outline of the action in the case of fiction. Clustering is a way of quite literally making visual the organization of your thoughts.

To practice the technique, choose a word that represents your central subject, write it in the center of the page, and circle it. Then for two or three minutes free-associate by jotting down around it any word—image, action, emotion, or part of speech—that comes to mind. Every now and again, circle the words you have written and draw lines or arrows between words that seem to connect. As with freewriting, it is crucial to keep going, without self-censoring and without worrying about whether you're making sense. What you're doing is *making*; sense will emerge. When you've clustered for two or three minutes, you will have a page that looks like a cobweb with very large dewdrops, and you will probably sense when it is enough. Take a few seconds, no more, to look at what you have done. (*Look at* seems more relevant here than *read over*, because the device does make you see the words as part of a visual composition.) Then start writing. Don't let the critic in yet. (This is called a "focused" freewrite because you have chosen the subject.)

Here is a sample cluster of the preceding passage:

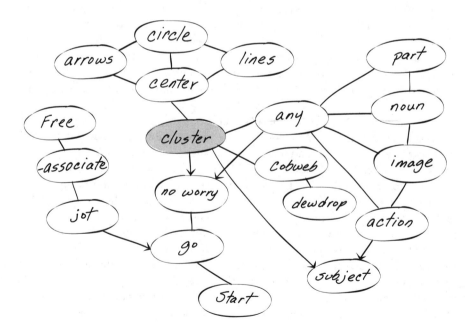

When I first encountered this device, I was aware that it was widely used for English composition classes, but I doubted its usefulness for a fiction writer. I decided to try it, though, so I sat down to the first exercise offered in Rico's book, which was to cluster on the word "fear." I was not very thrilled with the project, but I wrote the word in the center of my page. As soon as I circled it, I realized that in the novel I was then writing, there was a lot of fear in the mind of the heroine, a Baltimore Catholic headed for the desert Southwest in 1914. I started free-associating her fear rather than my own, and images erupted out of nowhere, out of her childhood—a cellar, the smell of rotting apples and mice droppings, old newspapers, my heroine as a little girl squatting in the dank dark, the priest upstairs droning on about the catechism. Where had it all come from? Within fifteen minutes I had a two-paragraph memory for my character that revealed her to me, and to my reader, more clearly than anything I had yet written.

Now I cluster any scene, character, narrative passage, or reflection that presents me with the least hint of resistance. When I have a complicated scene with several characters in it, I cluster each character so I have a clear idea at the beginning how each is feeling in that situation. Even if, as is usually the case, the passage is written from the point of view of only one of them, I will know how to make the other characters react, speak, and move if I've been gathering cobwebs in their minds.

To take a simple example, suppose you are writing a scene in which Karl is furiously berating Liz for being late when an important guest was expected for dinner. The dialogue comes easily. But you're unclear about Liz's reaction. So you cluster what's going on in her mind:

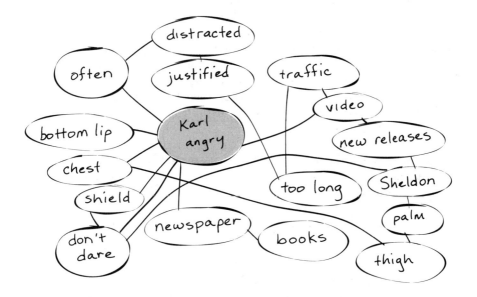

Naturally your cluster would be entirely different from this one and suited to your story. But though I started without any concept of these characters, the clustering tossed up these ideas in a few minutes: Karl is justified, Liz thinks; she got distracted at the video store when she ran into her old boyfriend Sheldon looking through the new releases, and she stopped to talk to him for too long and got caught in rush-hour traffic—none of which she dares say to Karl. She's often distracted these days. Right now she can't concentrate on what Karl is saying because she's so interested in the way his bottom lip shakes when he's angry and the way he holds his newspaper like a shield over his chest—Sheldon always cupped his books in his palm and swung them against his thigh, she remembers. She wouldn't dare mention that either.

If the story were told from inside Liz's mind, then you might use much of this directly. But even if it were told from Karl's angry point of view, it would help you (and him) *see* her—the way she tries to poke the video out of sight in her handbag, the way she seems to be concentrating on his newspaper as if she were trying to read it off his chest. It might also help you hear her, how she mumbles complaining about rush hour, how she starts a sentence and then gives up on it.

Clustering is an excellent technique for journal keeping. It focuses your thoughts, cuts out extraneous material, and reduces writing time. In composing fiction, I recommend frequent clustering, followed by freedrafting and light editing. Then put the passage away for twenty-four hours. Like most recommendations, all this one means is that it seems to work for me.

I instinctively but unhappily followed a similar habit for many years before I discovered that I could make it work for me instead of against me. I would sit at my desk from midmorning to noon paralyzed by the cosmic weight of needing to write something absolutely wonderful. I would lunch at my desk regularly in despair. By midafternoon I would hate myself so thoroughly that I'd decide to splash anything down, any trash at all, just to be free of the blank page and feel justified in fleeing my paper prison. The whole evening would be tainted by the knowledge of having written such garbage. Next morning I would find that although it was mostly orange peels and eggshells, there was a little bit of something salvageable here and there. For a couple of intent hours I would work on that to make it right, feeling better, feeling good. Then I'd be faced with a new passage to begin, which, unlike that mess I'd cleaned up from yesterday, was going to emerge in rough draft as Great Literature. Lunch loomed in gloom.

Now, most days (allowing for a few failures, a few relapses into old habits), I write the junk quite happily straight away. Then I begin to tinker, usually with something I did yesterday or last week—which is where I concentrate, lose myself, and am transported into the word world. Often it's two o'clock before I remember to stop for my apple and chunk of cheese.

Cluster, freedraft, lightly edit, put away. I do urge you to try this, several times.

THE COMPUTER

I think it's important for a writer to try a pencil from time to time so as not to lose the knack of writing by hand, of jotting at the park or the beach without any source of energy but your own hand and mind.

But for most writers, a computer is a great aid to spontaneity. Freewriting frees more freely on a computer. The knowledge that you can so easily delete makes it easier to quiet the internal critic and put down whatever comes. The "wraparound" feature of the computer means that you need never be aware that what you write is chopped into lines of type on the page. Turn down the screen or ignore it, stare out the window into middle space. You can follow the thread of your thought without a pause.

THE CRITIC: A CAUTION

The cautionary note that needs to be sounded regarding all the techniques and technology that free you to write is that the critic is absolutely essential afterwards. Because revision—the heart of the writing process—will continue until you finally finish or abandon a piece of work, exercises for revision follow most chapters of this book. The revising process is continuous and begins as soon as you choose to let your critic in. Clustering and freedrafting allow you to create before you criticize, to do the essential play before the essential work. Don't forget the essential work. The computer lets you write a lot because you can so easily cut. Don't forget to do so.

A short story is a writer's way of thinking through experience. . . . Journalism aims at accuracy, but fiction's aim is truth. The writer distorts reality in the interest of a larger truth.

John L'Heureux

I want hard stories, I demand them from myself. Hard stories are worth the difficulty. It seems to me the only way I have forgiven anything, understood anything, is through that process of opening up to my own terror and pain and reexamining it, re-creating it in the story, and making it something different, making it meaningful—even if the meaning is only in the act of the telling.

Dorothy Allison

The great Japanese film director Akira Kurosawa said that to be an artist means never to avert your eyes. And that's the hardest thing, because we want to flinch. The artist must go into the white hot center of himself, and our impulse when we get there is to look away and avert our eyes.

Robert Olen Butler

CHOOSING A SUBJECT

Some writers are lucky enough never to be faced with the problem of choosing a subject. The world presents itself to them in terms of conflict, crisis, and resolution. Ideas for stories pop into their heads day after day; their only difficulty is choosing among them. In fact, the habit of mind that produces stories is a habit and can be cultivated, so that the more and the longer you write, the less likely you are to run out of ideas.

But sooner or later you may find yourself faced with the desire (or the deadline necessity) to write a story when your mind is a blank. The sour and untrue impulse crosses your thoughts: Nothing has ever happened to me. The task you face then is to recognize among all the paraphernalia of your mind a situation, idea, perception, or character that you can turn into a story.

Some teachers and critics advise beginning writers to write only from their personal experience, but I feel that this is a misleading and demeaning rule. If your imagination never gets beyond your age group or off campus, never tackles issues larger than dormitory life, then you are severely underestimating the range of your imagination. It is certainly true that you must draw on your own experience (including your experience of the shape of sentences). But the trick is to identify what is interesting, unique, and original in that experience (including your experience of the shape of sentences), which will therefore surprise and attract the reader.

The kind of "writing what you know" that is *least* likely to produce good fiction is trying to tell just exactly what happened to you at such and such a time. Probably all good fiction is "autobiographical" in some way, but the awful or hilarious or tragic thing you went through may offer as many problems as possibilities when you start to turn it into fiction. The first of these is that to the extent you want to capture "what really happened," you remove your focus from what will work as narrative. Young writers, offended by being told that a piece is unconvincing, often defend themselves by declaring that it *really happened*. But credibility in words has almost nothing to do with fact. Aristotle went so far as to say that a "probable impossibility" made a better story than an "improbable possibility," meaning that a skillful author can sell us glass mountains, UFOs, and hobbits, whereas a less skilled writer may not be able to convince us that Mary Lou has a crush on Sam.

The first step toward using autobiography in fiction is to accept this: Words are not experience. Even the most factual account of a personal experience involves choices and interpretations—your sister's recollection of the same event might be entirely different. If you are writing a memoir or personal essay, then it is important to maintain a basis in fact because, as Annie Dillard says, "that is the convention and the covenant between the nonfiction writer and his reader." But between fiction writer and reader it is the revelation of meaning through the creation of character, the vividness of scene, the effect of action that take priority over ordinary veracity. The test of this other truth is at once spiritual and visceral; its validity has nothing to do with whether such things did, or could, occur. Lorrie Moore says:

. . . the proper relationship of a writer to his or her own life is similar to a cook with a cupboard. What the cook makes from the cupboard is not the same thing as what's in the cupboard . . .

Dorothy Allison strives to tell "the emotional truth of people's lives, not necessarily the historical truth"; similarly, Craig Nova stresses that

The truth for a novelist isn't the same as the facts. . . . When a writer is successful in using a story taken from experience, it is not told exactly the way it happened, but in the way that reveals, through all one's beliefs, hopes, and fear, how the event should have happened.

Good. Now: what was it about this experience that made it matter to you? Try writing a *very* brief summary of what happened—no more than a hundred words. What kind of story might this be? Can the raw material of incident, accident, and choice be reshaped, plumped up, pared to the bone, refleshed, differently spiced? You experienced whatever it was chronologically—but is that the best way to tell it so as to bring its meaning out? Perhaps you experienced it over a period of months or years; what are the *fewest* scenes in the *least* amount of time that could contain the action? If "you" are at the center of the action then "you" must be thoroughly characterized, and that may be difficult. Can you augment some revealing aspect of yourself, change yourself so you are forced to see anew, even make someone else altogether the central character? Use some of the suggestions in this chapter. Try freewriting moments from your memory in no particular order. Or freewrite the last scene first. Pick a single word that sums up the experience and cluster that word. Then write a scene that does not use the word. Describe a place and exaggerate the description: if it's cold, make it murderously cold, if messy, then a disastrous mess. Describe the central character and be at least partly unflattering. All of these are devices to put some distance between you and raw experience so you can begin to shape the different thing that fiction is.

Writer Eudora Welty has suggested writing what you *don't* know about what you know—that is, exploring aspects of experience that remain puzzling or painful. In *Making Shapely Fiction*, Jerome Stern urges a broad interpretation of "writing what you know," recognizing that "the idea of *you* is complex in itself . . . your self is made of many selves . . . not only persons you once were, but also persons you have tried to be, persons you have avoided being, and persons you fear you might be." John Gardner, in *The Art of Fiction*, argues that "nothing can be more limiting to the imagination" than the advice that you write about what you know. He suggests instead that you "write the kind of story you know and like best."

This is a useful idea, because the kind of story you know and like best has also taught you something about the way such stories are told, how they are shaped, what kind of surprise, conflict, and change they involve. Many beginning writers who are not yet avid readers have learned from television more than they realize about struc-

Novelist Lee Smith says that as a young writer in college, "I didn't know what I knew and so wrote about whole-cloth imaginings, alternate universes, and stewardesses in Hawaii" before coming across the book that served as a passport—"*River of Earth*, an Appalachian *Grapes of Wrath*, in which the destination was my hometown of Grundy, Virginia." It was back in this small mining town that she found her own stories and wrote about her family. "The mountains that used to imprison me became my chosen stalking ground," says Smith. "I was writing for memory, for love, for home. . . . We cannot choose our truest material, but sometimes we may be lucky enough to find it."

ture, the way characters behave and talk, how a joke is arranged, how a lie is revealed, and so forth. The trouble is that if you learn fiction from television, or if the kind of story you know and like best is genre fiction—science fiction, fantasy, romance, mystery—you may have learned about technique without having learned anything about the unique contribution you can make to such a story. The result is that you end up writing imitation soap opera or space odyssey, second-rate somebody else instead of first-rate you.

The essential thing is that you write about something you really care about, and the first step is to find out what that is. Playwright Claudia Johnson advises her students to identify their real concerns by making a "menu" of them. Pick the big emotions and make lists in your journal: *What makes you angry? What are you afraid of? What do you want? What hurts?* Or consider the crucial turning points of your life: *What really changed you? Who really changed you?* Those will be the areas to look to for stories, whether or not those stories are autobiographical. Novelist Ron Carlson says, "I always write from my own experiences, whether I've had them or not."

Another journal idea is to jot down the facts of the first seven years of your life under several categories: *Events, People, Your Self, Inner Life, Characteristic Things.* What from those first seven years still occupies your mind? Underline or highlight the items on your page(s) that you aren't done with yet. Those items are clues to your concerns and a possible source of storytelling.

A related device for your journal might be borrowed from the *Pillow Book* of Sei Shonagun. A courtesan in tenth-century Japan, she kept a diary of the goings-on at court and concealed it in her wooden pillow—hence *pillow book*. Sei Shonagun made lists under various categories of specific, often quirky *Things*. This device is capable of endless variety and can reveal yourself to you as you find out what sort of things you want to list: *Things I wish had never been said. Red things. Things more embarrassing than nudity. Things to put off as long as possible. Things to die for. Acid things. Things that last only a day.*

Such devices may be necessary because identifying what we care about is not always easy. We are surrounded by a constant barrage of information, drama, ideas, and judgments offered to us live, printed, and electronically. It is so much easier to know what we ought to think and feel than what we actually do. Worthy authorities constantly exhort us to care about worthy causes, only a few of which really touch us, whereas what we care about at any given moment may seem trivial, self-conscious, or self-serving.

This, I think, is in large part the value of Brande's first exercise, which forces you to write in the intuitively honest period of first light, when the half-sleeping brain is still dealing with its real concerns. Often what seems unworthy is precisely the thing that contains a universal, and by catching it honestly, then stepping back from it, you may achieve the authorial distance that is an essential part of significance. (All you really care about this morning is how you'll look at the dance tonight? This is a trivial obsession that can hit anyone, at any age, anywhere. Write about it as honestly as you can. Now who else might have felt this way? Someone you hate? Someone remote in time from you? Look out: You're on your way to a story.)

Brande advises that once you have developed the habit of regular freewriting, you should read your pages over and pick a passage that seems to suggest a simple story. Muse on the idea for a few days, find its shape, and then fill that shape with people, settings, details from your own experience, observation, and imagination. Turn the story over in your mind. Sleep on it—more than once. Finally, pick a time when you are going to write the story, and when that time comes, go to the desk and write a complete first draft as rapidly as possible. Then put it away, at least overnight. When you take it out again, you will have something to work with, and the business of shaping the story may begin.

Eventually you will learn what sort of experience sparks ideas for your sort of story—and you may be astonished at how such experiences accumulate, as if your life were arranging itself to produce material for you. In the meantime, here are a half dozen suggestions for the kind of idea that may be fruitful.

The Dilemma, or Catch-22.   You find yourself facing—or know someone who is facing—a situation that offers no solution. Any action taken would be painful and costly. You have no chance of solving this dilemma in real life, but you're a writer, and it costs nothing to explore it with imaginary people in an imaginary setting, even if the outcome is a tragic one. Some writers use newspaper stories to generate this sort of idea. The situation is there in the bland black and white of this morning's news. But who are these people, and how did they come to be in such a mess? Make it up, think it through.

The Incongruity.   Something comes to your attention that is interesting precisely because you can't figure it out. It doesn't seem to make sense. Someone is breeding pigs in the backyard of a mansion. Who is it? Why is she doing it? Your inventing mind can find the motives and the meanings. An example from my own experience: Once when my phone was out of order, I went out very late at night to make a call from a public phone at a supermarket plaza. At something like two in the morning all the stores were closed but the plaza was not empty. There were three women there, one of them with a baby in a stroller. What were they doing there? It was several years before I figured out a possible answer, and that answer was a short story.

The Connection.   You notice a striking similarity in two events, people, places, or periods that are fundamentally unlike. The more you explore the similarity, the more striking it becomes. My novel *The Buzzards* came from such a connection: The daughter of a famous politician was murdered, and I found myself in the position of comforting the dead girl's fiancé. At the same time I was writing lectures on the Agamemnon of Aeschylus. Two politicians, two murdered daughters—one in ancient Greece and one in contemporary America. The connection would not let go of me until I had thought it through and set it down.

The Memory.   Certain people, places, and events stand out in your memory with an intensity beyond logic. There's no earthly reason you should remember the smell of Aunt K's rouge. It makes no sense that you still flush with shame at the thought of that ball you "borrowed" when you were in fourth grade. But for some reason these things are still vivid in your mind. That vividness can be explored, embellished, given form. Stephen Minot in *Three Genres* wisely advises, though, that if you are going to write from a memory, *it should be a memory more than a year old*. Otherwise you are likely to be unable to distinguish between what happened and what must happen in the story or between what is in your mind and what you have conveyed on the page.

The Transplant.   You find yourself having to deal with a feeling that is either startlingly new to you or else obsessively old. You feel incapable of dealing with it. As a way of distancing yourself from that feeling and gaining some mastery over it, you write about the feeling as precisely as you can, but giving it to an imaginary someone in an imaginary situation. What situation other than your own would produce such a feeling? Who would be caught in that situation? Think it through.

The Revenge.   An injustice has been done, and you are powerless to do anything about it. But you're not really, because you're a writer. Reproduce the situation with another set of characters, in other circumstances or another setting. Cast the outcome to suit yourself. Punish whomever you choose. Even if the story ends in a similar injustice, you have righted the wrong by enlisting your reader's sympathy on the side of right. (Dante was particularly good at this: He put his enemies in the inferno and his friends in paradise.) Remember too that as human beings we are intensely, sometimes obsessively, interested in our boredom, and you can take revenge against the things that bore you by making them absurd or funny on paper.

Keep Going

A story idea may come from any source at any time. You may not know you have an idea until you spot it in the random jottings of your journal. Once you've identified the idea, the process of thinking it through begins and doesn't end until you finish (or abandon) the story. Most writing is done between the mind and the hand, not between the hand and the page. It may take a fairly competent typist about three hours to type a twelve-page story. It may take days or months to write it. It follows that, even when you are writing well, most of the time spent writing is not spent putting words on the page. If the story idea grabs hard hold of you, the process of thinking through may be involuntary, a gift. If not, you need to find the inner stillness that will allow you to develop your characters, get to know them, follow their actions in your mind—and it may take an effort of the will to find such stillness.

The metamorphosis of an idea into a story has many aspects, some deliberate and some mysterious. "Inspiration" is a real thing, a gift from the subconscious to the conscious mind. Still, perhaps influenced by the philosophy (although it was not always the practice) of the Beat authors, some new writers may feel that "forcing" words is aesthetically false—and yet few readers can tell which story "flowed" from the writer's pen and which was set down one hard-won word at a time. Toni Morrison has said that she will frequently rewrite a passage eight times, simply to create the impression of an unbroken, inspired flow; Cynthia Ozick often begins with "simple forcing" until the breakthrough comes, and so bears with the "fear and terror until I've pushed through to joy."

Over and over again, successful writers attest that unless they prepare the conscious mind with the habit of work, the gift does not come. Writing is mind-farming. You have to plow, plant, weed, and hope for growing weather. Why a seed turns into a plant is something you are never going to understand, and the only relevant response to it is gratitude. You may be proud, however, of having plowed.

Many writers besides Dorothea Brande have observed that it is ideal, having turned your story over in your mind, to write the first draft at one sitting, pushing on through the action to the conclusion, no matter how dissatisfied you are with this paragraph, that character, this phrasing, or that incident. There are two advantages

---

At its best, the sensation of writing is that of any unmerited grace. It is handed to you, but only if you look for it. You search, you break your heart, your back, your brain, and then—and only then—is it handed to you. From the corner of your eye, you see motion. Something is moving through the air and headed your way. It is a parcel bound in ribbons and bows; it has two white wings. It flies directly at you; you can read your name on it. If it were a baseball, you would hit it out of the park. It is that one pitch in a thousand you see in slow motion; its wings beat slowly as a hawk's.

Annie Dillard

to doing this. The first is that you are more likely to produce a coherent draft when you come to the desk in a single frame of mind with a single vision of the whole, than when you write piecemeal, having altered ideas and moods. The second is that fast writing tends to make for fast pace in the story. It is always easier, later, to add and develop than it is to sharpen the pace. If you are the sort of writer who stays on page one for days, shoving commas around and combing the thesaurus for a word with slightly better connotations, then you should probably force yourself to try this method (more than once). A note of caution, though: If you write a draft at one sitting, it will not be the draft you want to show anyone, so schedule the sitting well in advance of whatever deadline you may have.

It may happen—always keeping in mind that a single-sitting draft is the ideal—that as you write, the story will take off of its own accord in some direction totally other than you intended. You thought you knew where you were going and now you don't, and you know that unless you stop for a while and think it through again, you'll go wrong. You may find that although you are doing precisely what you had in mind, it doesn't work—Brian Moore calls this "the place where the story gets sick," and often found he had to retrace his steps from an unlikely plot turn or unnatural character action. At such times, the story needs more imaginative mulching before it will bear fruit. Or you may find, simply, that your stamina gives out, and that though you have done your exercises, been steadfast, loyal, and practiced every writerly virtue known, you're stuck. You have writer's block.

Writer's block is not so popular as it was a few years ago. I suspect people got tired of hearing or even talking about it—sometimes writers can be sensitive even to their own clichés. But it may also be that writers began to understand and accept their difficulties. Sometimes the process seems to require working yourself into a muddle and past the muddle to despair; until you have done this, it may be impossible suddenly to see what the shape of a thing ought to be. When you're writing, this feels terrible. You sit spinning your wheels, digging deeper and deeper into the mental muck. You decide you are going to trash the whole thing and walk away from it—only you can't, and you keep coming back to it like a tongue to an aching tooth. Or you decide you are going to sit there until you bludgeon it into shape—and as long as you sit there it remains recalcitrant. W. H. Auden observed that the hardest part of writing is not knowing whether you are procrastinating or must wait for the words to come.

"What's called writer's block," claims novelist Tom Wolfe, "is almost always ordinary fear." Indeed, whenever I ask a group of writers what they find most difficult, a significant number answer that they feel they aren't good enough, that the empty page intimidates them, that they are in some way afraid. Many complain of their own laziness, but laziness, like money, doesn't really exist except to represent something else—in this case fear, severe self-judgment, or what Natalie Goldberg calls "the cycle of guilt, avoidance, and pressure."

I know a newspaper editor who says that writer's block always represents a lack of information. I thought this inapplicable to fiction until I noticed that I was mainly frustrated when I didn't know enough about my characters, the scene, or the action—when I had not gone to the imaginative depth where information lies.

Encouragement comes from the poet William Stafford, who advised his students always to write to their lowest standard. Somebody always corrected him: "You mean your highest standard." No, he meant your lowest standard. Jean Cocteau's editor gave him the same advice. "The thought of having to produce a masterpiece is giving you writer's cramp. You're paralysed at the sight of a blank sheet of paper. So begin any old way. Write: 'One winter evening . . .'" In *On Writer's Block: A New Approach to Creativity*, Victoria Nelson points out that "there is an almost mathematical ratio between soaring, grandiose ambition . . . and severe creative block." More writers prostitute themselves "up" than "down"; more are false in the determination to write great literature than to throw off a romance.

A rough draft is rough; that's its nature. Let it be rough. Think of it as making clay. The molding and the gloss come later.

And remember: Writing is easy. Not writing is hard.

A Word about Theme

The process of discovering, choosing, and revealing the theme of your story begins as early as a first freewrite and continues, probably, beyond publication. The theme is what your story is about and what you think about it, its core and the spin you put on it. John Gardner points out that theme "is not imposed on the story but evoked from within it—initially an intuitive but finally an intellectual act on the part of the writer."

What your story has to say will gradually reveal itself to you and to your reader through every choice you as a writer make—the actions, characters, setting, dialogue, objects, pace, metaphors and symbols, viewpoint, atmosphere, style, even syntax and punctuation, and even in some cases typography.

Because of this comprehensive nature of theme, I have placed the discussion of it in chapter 10, after the individual story elements have been addressed. But this is not entirely satisfactory, since each of those elements contribute to the theme as it unfolds. You may want to skip ahead to take a look at that chapter, or you may want to anticipate the issue by asking at every stage of your manuscript: What really interests me about this? How does this (image, character, dialogue, place . . .) reveal what I care about? What connections do I see between one image and another? How can I strengthen those connections? Am I saying what I really mean, telling my truth about it?

All the later chapters in this book include short stories or excerpts that operate as examples of the elements of fiction under consideration. What follows here, however, is an excerpt from a book about the writing process that takes a reassuring, "just do it" approach to getting started; the second selection, "American History," offers one example of a fictional story with recognizable roots in real-life experience.

Shitty First Drafts

ANNE LAMOTT
FROM *BIRD BY BIRD*

Now, practically even better news than that of short assignments is the idea of shitty first drafts. All good writers write them. This is how they end up with good second drafts and terrific third drafts. People tend to look at successful writers, writers who are getting their books published and maybe even doing well financially, and think that they sit down at their desks every morning feeling like a million dollars, feeling great about who they are and how much talent they have and what a great story they have to tell; that they take in a few deep breaths, push back their sleeves, roll their necks a few times to get all the cricks out, and dive in, typing fully formed passages as fast as a court reporter. But this is just the fantasy of the uninitiated. I know some very great writers, writers you love who write beautifully and have made a great deal of money, and not *one* of them sits down routinely feeling wildly enthusiastic and confident. Not one of them writes elegant first drafts. All right, one of them does, but we do not like her very much. We do not think that she has a rich inner life or that God likes her or can even stand her. (Although when I mentioned this to my priest friend Tom, he said you can safely assume you've created God in your own image when it turns out that God hates all the same people you do.)

Very few writers really know what they are doing until they've done it. Nor do they go about their business feeling dewy and thrilled. They do not type a few stiff warm-up sentences and then find themselves bounding along like huskies across the snow. One writer I know tells me that he sits down every morning and says to himself nicely, "It's not like you don't have a choice, because you do—you can either type or kill yourself." We all often feel like we are pulling teeth, even those writers whose prose ends up being the most natural and fluid. The right words and sentences just do not come pouring out like ticker tape most of the time. Now, Muriel Spark is said to have felt that she was taking dictation from God every morning—sitting there, one supposes, plugged into a Dictaphone, typing away, humming. But this is a very hostile and aggressive position. One might hope for bad things to rain down on a person like this.

For me and most of the other writers I know, writing is not rapturous. In fact, the only way I can get anything written at all is to write really, really shitty first drafts.

The first draft is the child's draft, where you let it all pour out and then let it romp all over the place, knowing that no one is going to see it and that you can shape it later. You just let this childlike part of you channel whatever voices and visions come through and onto the page. If one of the characters wants to say, "Well, so what, Mr. Poopy Pants?" you let her. No one is going to see it. If the kid wants to get into really sentimental, weepy, emotional territory, you let him. Just get it all down on paper, because there may be something great in those six crazy pages that you would never have gotten to by more rational, grown-up means. There may be something in the very last line of the very last paragraph on page six that you just love, that is so beautiful or wild that you now know what you're supposed to be writing about, more or less, or in what direction you might go—but there was no way to get to this without first getting through the first five and a half pages.

I used to write food reviews for *California* magazine before it folded. (My writing food reviews had nothing to do with the magazine folding, although every single review did cause a couple of canceled subscriptions. Some readers took umbrage at my comparing mounds of vegetable puree with various ex-presidents' brains.) These reviews always took two days to write. First I'd go to a restaurant several times with a few opinionated, articulate friends in tow. I'd sit there writing down everything anyone said that was at all interesting or funny. Then on the following Monday I'd sit down at my desk with my notes, and try to write the review. Even after I'd been doing this for years, panic would set in. I'd try to write a lead, but instead I'd write a couple of dreadful sentences, xx them out, try again, xx everything out, and then feel despair and worry settle on my chest like an x-ray apron. It's over I'd think, calmly. I'm not going to be able to get the magic to work this time. I'm ruined. I'm through. I'm toast. Maybe, I'd think, I can get my old job back as a clerk-typist. But probably not. I'd get up and study my teeth in the mirror for a while. Then I'd stop, remember to breathe, make a few phone calls, hit the kitchen and chow down. Eventually I'd go back and sit down at my desk, and sigh for the next ten minutes. Finally I would pick up my one-inch picture frame, stare into it as if for the answer, and every time the answer would come: all I had to do was to write a really shitty first draft of, say, the opening paragraph. And no one was going to see it.

So I'd start writing without reining myself in. It was almost just typing, just making my fingers move. And the writing would be *terrible*. I'd write a lead paragraph that was a whole page, even though the entire review could only be three pages long, and then I'd start writing up descriptions of the food, one dish at a time, bird by bird, and the critics would be sitting on my shoulders, commenting like cartoon characters. They'd be pretending to snore, or rolling their eyes at my overwrought descriptions, no matter how hard I tried to tone those descriptions down, no matter how conscious I was of what a friend said to me gently in my early days of restaurant reviewing. "Annie," she said, "it is just a piece of *chicken*. It is just a bit of *cake*."

But because by then I had been writing for so long, I would eventually let myself trust the process—sort of, more or less. I'd write a first draft that was maybe twice as long as it should be, with a self-indulgent and boring beginning, stupefying descriptions of the meal, lots of quotes from my black-humored friends that made them sound more like the Manson girls than food lovers, and no ending to speak of. The whole thing would be so long and incoherent and hideous that for the rest of the day I'd obsess about getting creamed by a car before I could write a decent second draft. I'd worry that people would read what I'd written and believe that the accident had really been a suicide, that I had panicked because my talent was waning and my mind was shot.

The next day, though, I'd sit down, go through it all with a colored pen, take out everything I possibly could, find a new lead somewhere on the second page, figure out a kicky place to end it, and then write a second draft. It always turned out fine, sometimes even funny and weird and helpful. I'd go over it one more time and mail it in.

Then, a month later, when it was time for another review, the whole process would start again, complete with the fears that people would find my first draft before I could rewrite it.

Almost all good writing begins with terrible first efforts. You need to start somewhere. Start by getting something—anything—down on paper. A friend of mine says that the first draft is the down draft—you just get it down. The second draft is the up draft—you fix it up. You try to say what you have to say more accurately. And the third draft is the dental draft, where you check every tooth, to see if it's loose or cramped or decayed, or even, God help us, healthy.

What I've learned to do when I sit down to work on a shitty first draft is to quiet the voices in my head. First there's the vinegar-lipped Reader Lady, who says primly, "Well, *that's* not very interesting, is it?" And there's the emaciated German male who writes these Orwellian memos detailing your thought crimes. And there are your parents, agonizing over your lack of loyalty and discretion; and there's William Burroughs, dozing off or shooting up because he finds you as bold and articulate as a houseplant; and so on. And there are also the dogs: let's not forget the dogs, the dogs in their pen who will surely hurtle and snarl their way out if you ever *stop* writing, because writing is, for some of us, the latch that keeps the door of the pen closed, keeps those crazy ravenous dogs contained.

Quieting these voices is at least half the battle I fight daily. But this is better than it used to be. It used to be 87 percent. Left to its own devices, my mind spends much of its time having conversations with people who aren't there. I walk along defending myself to people, or exchanging repartee with them, or rationalizing my behavior, or seducing them with gossip, or pretending I'm on their TV talk show or whatever. I speed or run an aging yellow light or don't come to a full stop, and one nanosecond later am explaining to imaginary cops exactly why I had to do what I did, or insisting that I did not in fact do it.

I happened to mention this to a hypnotist I saw many years ago, and he looked at me very nicely. At first I thought he was feeling around on the floor for the silent alarm button, but then he gave me the following exercise, which I still use to this day.

Close your eyes and get quiet for a minute, until the chatter starts up. Then isolate one of the voices and imagine the person speaking as a mouse. Pick it up by the tail and drop it into a mason jar. Then isolate another voice, pick it up by the tail, drop it in the jar. And so on. Drop in any high-maintenance parental units, drop in any contractors, lawyers, colleagues, children, anyone who is whining in your head. Then put the lid on, and watch all these mouse people clawing at the glass, jabbering away, trying to make you feel like shit because you won't do what they want—won't give them more money, won't be more successful, won't see them more often. Then imagine that there is a volume-control button on the bottle. Turn it all the way up for a minute, and listen to the stream of angry, neglected, guilt-mongering voices. Then turn it all the way down and watch the frantic mice lunge at the glass, trying to get to you. Leave it down, and get back to your shitty first draft.

A writer friend of mine suggests opening the jar and shooting them all in the head. But I think he's a little angry, and I'm sure nothing like this would ever occur to you.

🖋 🖋 🖋

Suggestions for Discussion

1. Do you relate to the experience of writing that Anne Lamott describes? How?

2. A key writing question is "How do *you* get it done?" (page 3) Compare your answers and suggestions with others, aiming to find the widest possible range of successful approaches.

3. Find a short fiction annual, such as *Best American Short Stories* or *The O'Henry Awards*, that features an appendix of authors' notes on the genesis of their stories. Read through a number of these "seeds" and the resulting stories to get a sense of the diverse ways in which stories may be generated. How apparent or invisible is that seed in the finished product?

4. What is the book or story that you wish you had written? How does it inspire you to write?

🖋

American History

JUDITH ORTIZ COFER

I once read in a "Ripley's Believe It or Not" column that Paterson, New Jersey, is the place where the Straight and Narrow (streets) intersect. The Puerto Rican tenement known as *El Building* was one block up from Straight. It was, in fact, the corner of Straight and Market; not "at" the corner, but *the* corner. At almost any hour of the day, El Building was like a monstrous jukebox, blasting out *salsas* from open windows as the residents, mostly new immigrants just up from the island, tried to drown out whatever they were currently enduring with loud music. But the day President Kennedy was shot there was a profound silence in El Building; even the abusive tongues of viragoes, the cursing of the unemployed, and the screeching of small children had been somehow muted. President Kennedy was a saint to these people. In fact, soon his photograph would be hung alongside the Sacred Heart and over the spiritist altars that many women kept in their apartments. He would become part of the hierarchy of martyrs they prayed to for favors that only one who had died for a cause would understand.

On the day that President Kennedy was shot, my ninth grade class had been out in the fenced playground of Public School Number 13. We had been given "free" exercise time and had been ordered by our P.E. teacher, Mr. DePalma, to "keep moving." That meant that the girls should jump rope and the boys toss basketballs through a hoop at the far end of the yard. He in the meantime would "keep an eye" on us from just inside the building.

It was a cold gray day in Paterson. The kind that warns of early snow. I was miserable, since I had forgotten my gloves, and my knuckles were turning red and raw from the jump rope. I was also taking a lot of abuse from the black girls for not turning the rope hard and fast enough for them.

"Hey, Skinny Bones, pump it, girl. Ain't you got no energy today?" Gail, the biggest of the black girls had the other end of the rope, yelled, "Didn't you eat your rice and beans and pork chops for breakfast today?"

The other girls picked up the "pork chop" and made it into a refrain: "pork chop, pork chop, did you eat your pork chop?" They entered the double ropes in pairs and exited without tripping or missing a beat. I felt a burning on my cheeks and then my glasses fogged up so that I could not manage to coordinate the jump rope with Gail. The chill was doing to me what it always did; entering my bones, making me cry, humiliating me. I hated the city, especially in winter. I hated Public School Number 13. I hated my skinny flatchested body, and I envied the black girls who could jump rope so fast that their legs became a blur. They always seemed to be warm while I froze.

There was only one source of beauty and light for me that school year. The only thing I had anticipated at the start of the semester. That was seeing Eugene. In August, Eugene and his family had moved into the only house on the block that had a yard and trees. I could see his place from my window in El Building. In fact, if I sat on the fire escape I was literally suspended above Eugene's backyard. It was my favorite spot to read my library books in the summer. Until that August the house had been occupied by an old Jewish couple. Over the years I had become part of their family, without their knowing it, of course. I had a view of their kitchen and their backyard, and though I could not hear what they said, I knew when they were arguing, when one of them was sick, and many other things. I knew all this by watching them at mealtimes. I could see their kitchen table, the sink, and the stove. During good times, he sat at the table and read his newspapers while she fixed the meals. If they argued, he would leave and the old woman would sit and stare at nothing for a long time. When one of them was sick, the other would come and get things from the kitchen and carry them out on a tray. The old man had died in June. The last week of school I had not seen him at the table at all. Then one day I saw that there was a crowd in the kitchen. The old woman had finally emerged from the house on the arm of a stocky, middle-aged woman, whom I had seen there a few times before, maybe her daughter. Then a man had carried out suitcases. The house had stood empty for weeks. I had had to resist the temptation to climb down into the yard and water the flowers the old lady had taken such good care of.

By the time Eugene's family moved in, the yard was a tangled mass of weeds. The father had spent several days mowing, and when he finished, from where I sat, I didn't see the red, yellow, and purple clusters that meant flowers to me. I didn't see this family sit down at the kitchen table together. It was just the mother, a red-headed tall woman who wore a white uniform—a nurse's, I guessed it was; the father was gone before I got up in the morning and was never there at dinner time. I only saw him on weekends when they sometimes sat on lawn-chairs under the oak tree, each hidden behind a section of the newspaper; and there was Eugene. He was tall and blond, and he wore glasses. I liked him right away because he sat at the kitchen table and read books for hours. That summer, before we had even spoken one word to each other, I kept him company on my fire escape.

Once school started I looked for him in all my classes, but P.S. 13 was a huge, over-populated place and it took me days and many discreet questions to discover that Eugene was in honors classes for all his subjects; classes that were not open to me because English was not my first language, though I was a straight A student. After much maneuvering I managed "to run into him" in the hallway where his locker was—on the other side of the building from mine—and in study hall at the library where he first seemed to notice me, but did not speak; and finally, on the way home after school one day when I decided to approach him directly, though my stomach was doing somersaults.

I was ready for rejection, snobbery, the worst. But when I came up to him, practically panting in my nervousness, and blurted out: "You're Eugene. Right?" he smiled, pushed his glasses up on his nose, and nodded. I saw then that he was blushing deeply. Eugene liked me, but he was shy. I did most of the talking that day. He nodded and smiled a lot. In the weeks that followed, we walked home together. He would linger at the corner of El Building for a few minutes then walk down to his two-story house. It was not until Eugene moved into that house that I noticed that El Building blocked most of the sun, and that the only spot that got a little sunlight during the day was the tiny square of earth the old woman had planted with flowers.

I did not tell Eugene that I could see inside his kitchen from my bedroom. I felt dishonest, but I liked my secret sharing of his evenings, especially now that I knew what he was reading since we chose our books together at the school library.

One day my mother came into my room as I was sitting on the window sill staring out. In her abrupt way she said: "Elena, you are acting 'moony'." *Enamorada* was what she really said, that is—like a girl stupidly infatuated. Since I had turned fourteen and started menstruating my mother had been more vigilant than ever. She acted as if I was going to go crazy or explode or something if she didn't watch me and nag me all the time about being a *señorita* now. She kept talking about virtue, morality, and other subjects that did not interest me in the least. My mother was unhappy in Paterson, but my father had a good job at the bluejeans factory in Passaic and soon, he kept assuring us, we would be moving to our own house there. Every Sunday we drove out to the suburbs of Paterson, Clifton, and Passaic, out to where people mowed grass on Sundays in the summer, and where children made snowmen in the winter from pure white snow, not like the gray slush of Paterson which seemed to fall from the sky in that hue. I had learned to listen to my parents' dreams, which were spoken in Spanish, as fairy tales, like the stories about life in the island paradise of Puerto Rico before I was born. I had been to the island once as a little girl, to grandmother's funeral, and all I remembered was wailing women in black, my mother becoming hysterical and being given a pill that made her sleep two days, and me feeling lost in a crowd of strangers all claiming to be my aunts, uncles, and cousins. I had actually been glad to return to the city. We had not been back there since then, though my parents talked constantly about buying a house on the beach someday, retiring on the island—that was a common topic among the residents of El Building. As for me, I was going to college and become a teacher.

But after meeting Eugene I began to think of the present more than of the future. What I wanted now was to enter that house I had watched for so many years. I wanted to see the other rooms where the old people had lived, and where the boy spent his time. Most of all, I wanted to sit at the kitchen table with Eugene like two adults, like the old man and his wife had done, maybe drink some coffee and talk about books. I had started reading *Gone With the Wind*. I was enthralled by it, with the daring and the passion of the beautiful girl living in a mansion, and with her devoted parents and the slaves who did everything for them. I didn't believe such a world had ever really existed, and I wanted to ask Eugene some questions since he and his parents, he had told me, had come up from Georgia, the same place where the novel was set. His father worked for a company that had transferred him to Paterson. His mother was very unhappy, Eugene said, in his beautiful voice that rose and fell over words in a strange, lilting way. The kids at school called him "the hick" and made fun of the way he talked. I knew I was his only friend so far, and I liked that, though I felt sad for him sometimes. "Skinny Bones" and the "Hick" was what they called us at school when we were seen together.

The day Mr. DePalma came out into the cold and asked us to line up in front of him was the day that President Kennedy was shot. Mr. DePalma, a short, muscular man with slicked-down black hair, was the science teacher, P.E. coach, and disciplinarian at P.S. 13. He was the teacher to whose homeroom you got assigned if you were a troublemaker, and the man called out to break up playground fights, and to escort violently angry teen-agers to the office. And Mr. DePalma was the man who called your parents in for "a conference."

That day, he stood in front of two rows of mostly black and Puerto Rican kids, brittle from their efforts to "keep moving" on a November day that was turning bitter cold. Mr. DePalma, to our complete shock, was crying. Not just silent adult tears, but really sobbing. There were a few titters from the back of the line where I stood shivering.

"Listen," Mr. DePalma raised his arms over his head as if he were about to conduct an orchestra. His voice broke, and he covered his face with his hands. His barrel chest was heaving. Someone giggled behind me.

"Listen," he repeated, "something awful has happened." A strange gurgling came from his throat, and he turned around and spat on the cement behind him.

"Gross," someone said, and there was a lot of laughter.

"The President is dead, you idiots. I should have known that wouldn't mean anything to a bunch of losers like you kids. Go home." He was shrieking now. No one moved for a minute or two, but then a big girl let out a "Yeah!" and ran to get her books piled up with the others against the brick wall of the school building. The others followed in a mad scramble to get to their things before somebody caught on. It was still an hour to the dismissal bell.

A little scared, I headed for El Building. There was an eerie feeling on the streets. I looked into Mario's drugstore, a favorite hangout for the high school crowd, but there were only a couple of old Jewish men at the soda-bar talking with the short order cook in tones that sounded almost angry, but they were keeping their voices low. Even the traffic on one of the busiest intersections in Paterson—Straight Street and Park Avenue—seemed to be moving slower. There were no horns blasting that day. At El Building, the usual little group of unemployed men were not hanging out on the front stoop making it difficult for women to enter the front door. No music spilled out from open doors in the hallway. When I walked into our apartment, I found my mother sitting in front of the grainy picture of the television set.

She looked up at me with a tear-streaked face and just said: "Dios mio," turning back to the set as if it were pulling at her eyes. I went into my room.

Though I wanted to feel the right thing about President Kennedy's death, I could not fight the feeling of elation that stirred in my chest. Today was the day I was to visit Eugene at his house. He had asked me to come over after school to study for an American History test with him. We had also planned to walk to the public library together. I looked down into his yard. The oak tree was bare of leaves and the ground looked gray with ice. The light through the large kitchen window of his house told me that El Building blocked the sun to such an extent that they had to turn lights on in the middle of the day. I felt ashamed about it. But the white kitchen table with the lamp hanging just above it looked cozy and inviting. I would soon sit there, across from Eugene, and I would tell him about my perch just above his house. Maybe I should.

In the next thirty minutes I changed clothes, put on a little pink lipstick, and got my books together. Then I went to tell my mother that I was going to a friend's house to study. I did not expect her reaction.

"You are going out *today?*" The way she said "today" sounded as if a storm warning had been issued. It was said in utter disbelief. Before I could answer, she came toward me and held my elbows as I clutched my books.

"*Hija*, the President has been killed. We must show respect. He was a great man. Come to church with me tonight."

She tried to embrace me, but my books were in the way. My first impulse was to comfort her, she seemed so distraught, but I had to meet Eugene in fifteen minutes.

"I have a test to study for, Mama. I will be home by eight."

"You are forgetting who you are, *Niña*. I have seen you staring down at that boy's house. You are heading for humiliation and pain." My mother said this in Spanish and in a resigned tone that surprised me, as if she had no intention of stopping me from "heading for humiliation and pain." I started for the door. She sat in front of the TV holding a white handkerchief to her face.

I walked out to the street and around the chain-link fence that separated El Building from Eugene's house. The yard was neatly edged around the little walk that led to the door. It always amazed me how Paterson, the inner core of the city, had no apparent logic to its architecture. Small, neat, single residences like this one could be found right next to huge, dilapidated apartment buildings like El Building. My guess was that the little houses had been there first, then the immigrants had come in droves, and the monstrosities had been raised for them—the Italians, the Irish, the Jews, and now us, the Puerto Ricans and the blacks. The door was painted a deep green: *verde*, the color of hope, I had heard my mother say it: *Verde-Esperanza*.

I knocked softly. A few suspenseful moments later the door opened just a crack. The red, swollen face of a woman appeared. She had a halo of red hair floating over a delicate ivory face—the face of a doll—with freckles on the nose. Her smudged eye make-up made her look unreal to me, like a mannequin seen through a warped store window.

"What do you want?" Her voice was tiny and sweet-sounding, like a little girl's, but her tone was not friendly.

"I'm Eugene's friend. He asked me over. To study." I thrust out my books, a silly gesture that embarrassed me almost immediately.

"You live there?" She pointed up to El Building, which looked particularly ugly, like a gray prison with its many dirty windows and rusty fire escapes. The woman had stepped halfway out and I could see that she wore a white nurse's uniform with St. Joseph's Hospital on the name tag.

"Yes. I do."

She looked intently at me for a couple of heartbeats, then said as if to herself, "I don't know how you people do it." Then directly to me: "Listen. Honey. Eugene doesn't want to study with you. He is a smart boy. Doesn't need help. You understand me. I am truly sorry if he told you you could come over. He cannot study with you. It's nothing personal. You understand? We won't be in this place much longer, no need for him to get close to people—it'll just make it harder for him later. Run back home now."

I couldn't move. I just stood there in shock at hearing these things said to me in such a honey-drenched voice. I had never heard an accent like hers, except for Eugene's softer version. It was as if she were singing me a little song.

"What's wrong? Didn't you hear what I said?" She seemed very angry, and I finally snapped out of my trance. I turned away from the green door, and heard her close it gently.

Our apartment was empty when I got home. My mother was in someone else's kitchen, seeking the solace she needed. Father would come in from his late shift at midnight. I would hear them talking softly in the kitchen for hours that night. They would not discuss their dreams for the future, or life in Puerto Rico, as they often did; that night they would talk sadly about the young widow and her two children, as if they were family. For the next few days, we would observe *luto* in our apartment; that is, we would practice restraint and silence—no loud music or laughter. Some of the women of El Building would wear black for weeks.

That night, I lay in my bed trying to feel the right thing for our dead President. But the tears that came up from a deep source inside me were strictly for me. When my mother came to the door, I pretended to be sleeping. Sometime during the night, I saw from my bed the streetlight come on. It had a pink halo around it. I went to my window and pressed my face to the cool glass. Looking up at the light I could see the white snow falling like a lace veil over its face. I did not look down to see it turning gray as it touched the ground below.

𐑀 𐑀 𐑀
Suggestions for Discussion

1. "American History" takes place as a public crisis intersects with a personal one. If you were to select a significant public event from your lifetime as the background for a story with autobiographical roots, which event would you choose?

2. Ernest Hemingway spoke of the importance of "knowing what you really felt, rather than what you were supposed to feel, or had been taught to feel." What details does the author use to show the two sorts of "feeling"?

3. How would you describe the difference between a memoir and a short story? How do you feel when you "improve" upon a story that has its roots in real-life events?

🐦 🐦 🐦

Writing Exercises

INDIVIDUAL

Keep a journal for two weeks. Decide on a comfortable amount to write daily, and then determine not to let a day slide. To get started, refer to the journal suggestions in this chapter—freewriting, pages 4–5; the Dorothea Brande exercise, page 5; clustering, pages 6–8; a menu of concerns, page 12; a review of your first seven years, page 12; and a set of *Pillow Book* lists, page 12. At the end of the two weeks, assess yourself and decide what habit of journal keeping you can develop and stick to. A page a day? A paragraph a day? Three pages a week? Then do it. Probably at least once a day you have a thought worth wording, and sometimes it's better to write one sentence a day than to let the habit slide. Like exercise and piano practice, a journal is most useful when it's kept up regularly and frequently. If you pick an hour during which you write each day, no matter how much or how little, you may find yourself looking forward to, and saving things up for, that time.

In addition to keeping a journal, you might try some of these story triggers:

1. Latin American magical realist Gabriel García Márquez has said that his stories evolve from a mysterious image rather than a plot idea. "The image grows in my head," he said, "until the whole story takes shape as it might in real life." Similarly, another Nobel Prize winner, Toni Morrison, says that in her early drafts, "the image comes first and tells me what the 'memory' is about." Put an image from a dream at the center of the page and cluster from it. Like García Márquez and Morrison, experiment with allowing a story to arise intuitively from the image rather than first planning the story and finding the central image to fit it.

2. Sketch a floor plan of the first house or apartment you remember. Place an X on the spots in the plan where significant events happened to you. Write a tour of the house as if you were a guide, pointing out its features and its history.

3. Identify the kernel of a short story from your experience of one of the following.
   - an early memory
   - an unfounded fear
   - a scar
   - a bad haircut
   - yesterday
   - a sudden change in a relationship
   - the loss of a small object
   - conflict over a lesson you were taught or never taught
   - an experience you still do not fully understand

   Cluster the word and freedraft a passage about it. Outline a story based on it. Write the first page of the story.

4. *Writing with Music:*
   a. For help in finding a flow, try freewriting to instrumental music, such as jazz, swing, newgrass, or classical. Let the music suggest a memory of a person, mood, or landscape.
   b. Record dramatically different pieces of music, changing selections every two to three minutes. Freewrite as you play the tape or CD back, letting the changes in mood and tempo guide your writing.
   c. List five songs that you associate with your high school years. Write notes about events, people, and a possible conflict that you associate with each one. Choose the one that interests you most, and if possible, listen to the song to further jog memories of details and relationships. Then write a scene between two or three characters in which the song is heard in the background.

COLLABORATIVE

5. Bring in a photograph, art print, postcard, or advertisement that suggests an intriguing situation. Put all the pictures on a table and have each class member

choose one. Write for ten minutes, through a pictured character's viewpoint, allowing yourself to discover the thread of a story. In small groups, show the picture, read your writing back to your small group, and together brainstorm possible directions for the story. Variations:

a. With three others, individually write the exercise about the same picture. Then read your pieces back to observe the common and original elements that emerged.

b. If you wish to write a fantastic or surreal story, try using as your source the paintings of George Tooker, René Magritte, or Salvador Dalí or the photographs of Jerry Uelsmann.

6. Read the short-short story "Girl," by Jamaica Kincaid, that comes at the end of chapter 2.

a. List five *specific* things your family members or best friend taught you to do (for example, to drive a stick shift, sneak into R-rated movies, build a fire in the rain). Then, list five specific things they *never* taught you to do (jump from a speeding Jeep, lock my mother's boss in his office, write Valentines).

b. Exchange your list with someone else. On the list you receive, mark one or two lessons that suggest a larger story or evoke a vivid picture. Check for any lessons that might be usefully combined (for example, my brother taught me how to tie a tie/My brother never taught me what *not* to say on a first date).

c. Notice how the exercise asks you to put abstract feelings (love, guilt, rage, etc.) into specific, dramatic circumstances.

d. Follow-up: Write the opening paragraph of a story that starts with a scene related to the lesson or its consequences. Then, at the bottom of the page, make a note of one past and one future scene that could help readers see the episode in its larger context. Finally, describe one thing you still do not fully understand about that episode–something you might discover if you continue to write this story.

2

THE TOWER AND THE NET
Story Form, Plot, and Structure

- *Conflict, Crisis, and Resolution*
- *The Arc of the Story*
- *Patterns of Power*
- *Connection and Disconnection*
- *Story Form as a Check Mark*
- *Story and Plot*
- *The Short Story and the Novel*
- *Reading as Writers*

What makes you want to write?

It seems likely that the earliest storytellers—in the tent or the harem, around the campfire or on the Viking ship—told stories out of an impulse to tell stories. They made themselves popular by distracting their listeners from a dull or dangerous evening with heroic exploits and a skill at creating suspense: What happened next? And after that? And then what happened?

Natural storytellers are still around, and a few of them are very rich. Some are on the best-seller list; more are in television and film. But it's probable that your impulse to write has little to do with the desire or the skill to work out a plot. On the contrary, you want to write because you are a sensitive observer. You have something to say that does not answer the question, *What happened next?* You share with most—

30

> A story has to be a good date, because the reader can stop at any time. . . .
> Remember, readers are selfish and have no compulsion to be decent about
> anything.
>
> Kurt Vonnegut

and the best—contemporary fiction writers a sense of the injustice, the absurdity, and the beauty of the world; and you want to register your protest, your laughter, and your affirmation.

Yet readers still want to wonder what happened next, and unless you make them wonder, they will not turn the page. You must master plot, because no matter how profound or illuminating your vision of the world may be, you cannot convey it to those who do not read you.

When editors take the trouble to write a rejection letter to a young author (and they do so only when they think the author talented), the gist of the letter most frequently is: "This piece is sensitive (perceptive, vivid, original, brilliant, funny, moving), but it is not a *story*."

How do you know when you have written a story? And if you're not a natural-born wandering minstrel, can you go about learning to write one?

It's interesting that we react with such different attitudes to the words "formula" and "form" as they apply to a story. A formula story is hackwork: to write one, you read three dozen copies of *Cosmopolitan* or *Amazing Stories*, make a list of what kinds of characters and situations the editors buy, shuffle nearly identical characters around in slightly altered situations, and sit back to hope for a check. Whereas form is a term of the highest artistic approbation, even reverence, with overtones of *order, harmony, model, archetype*.

And "story" is a "form" of literature. Like a face, it has necessary features in a necessary harmony. We're aware of the infinite variety of human faces, aware of their unique individuality, which is so powerful that you can recognize a face you know even after twenty years of age and fashion have done their work on it. We're aware that minute alterations in the features can express grief, anger, or joy. If you place side by side two photographs of, say, Julia Roberts and Geronimo, you are instantly aware of the fundamental differences of age, race, sex, class, and century; yet these two faces are more like each other than either is like a foot or a fern, both of which have their own distinctive forms. Every face has two eyes, a nose between them, a mouth below, a forehead, two cheeks, two ears, and a jaw. If a face is missing one of these features, you may say, "I love this face in spite of its lacking a nose," but you must acknowledge the *in spite of*. You can't simply say, "This is a wonderful face."

The same is true of a story. You might say, "I love this piece even though there's no crisis action in it." You can't simply say, "This is a wonderful *story*."

Conflict, Crisis, and Resolution

One of the useful ways of describing the necessary features of story form is to speak of *conflict, crisis,* and *resolution.*

Conflict is the first encountered and the fundamental element of fiction. Playwright Elia Kazan describes it simply as "two dogs fighting over a bone"; William Faulkner reminds us that in addition to a conflict of wills, fiction also shows "the heart in conflict with itself," so that conflict seethes both within and between characters. In life, "conflict" often carries negative connotations, yet in fiction, be it comic or tragic, dramatic conflict is fundamental because in literature only trouble is interesting.

Only trouble is interesting. This is not so in life. Life offers periods of comfortable communication, peaceful pleasure, and productive work, all of which are extremely interesting to those involved. But passages about such times by themselves make for dull reading; they can be used as lulls in an otherwise tense situation, as a resolution, even as a hint that something awful is about to happen. They cannot be used as a whole plot, as Margaret Atwood sardonically illustrates in her story "Happy Endings," which appears at the end of this chapter.

Suppose, for example, you go on a picnic. You find a beautiful deserted meadow with a lake nearby. The weather is splendid and so is the company. The food's delicious, the water's fine, and the insects have taken the day off. Afterward, someone asks you how your picnic was. "Terrific," you reply, "really perfect." No story.

But suppose the next week you go back for a rerun. You set your picnic blanket on an anthill. You all race for the lake to get cold water on the bites, and one of your friends goes too far out on the plastic raft, which deflates. He can't swim and you have to save him. On the way in you gash your foot on a broken bottle. When you get back to the picnic, the ants have taken over the cake and a possum has demolished the chicken. Just then the sky opens up. When you gather your things to race for the car, you notice an irritated bull has broken through the fence. The others run for it, but because of your bleeding heel the best you can do is hobble. You have two choices: try to outrun him or stand perfectly still and hope he's interested only in a moving target. At this point, you don't know if your friends can be counted on for help, even the nerd whose life you saved. You don't know if it's true that a bull is attracted by the smell of blood.

A year later, assuming you're around to tell about it, you are still saying, "Let me *tell* you what happened last year." And your listeners are saying, "What a story!"

As Charles Baxter, in *Burning Down the House,* more vividly puts it:

Say what you will about it, Hell is story-friendly. If you want a compelling story, put your protagonist among the damned. The mechanisms of hell are nicely attuned to the mechanisms of narrative. Not so the pleasures of Paradise. Paradise is not a story. It's about what happens when the stories are over.

If it takes trouble to make a picnic into a story, this is equally true of the great themes of life: birth, love, sex, work, and death. Here is a very interesting love story to live: Jan and Jon meet in college. Both are beautiful, intelligent, talented, popular, and well adjusted. They're of the same race, class, religion, and political persuasion. They are sexually compatible. Their parents become fast friends. They marry on graduating, and both get rewarding work in the same city. They have three children, all of whom are healthy, happy, beautiful, intelligent, and popular; the children love and respect their parents to a degree that is the envy of everyone. All the children succeed in work and marriage. Jan and Jon die peacefully, of natural causes, at the same moment, at the age of eighty-two, and are buried in the same grave.

No doubt this love story is very interesting to Jan and Jon, but you can't make a novel of it. Great love stories involve intense passion and a monumental impediment to that passion's fulfillment. So: They love each other passionately, but their parents are sworn enemies (*Romeo and Juliet*). Or: They love each other passionately, but he's black and she's white, and he has an enemy who wants to punish him (*Othello*). Or: They love each other passionately, but she's married (*Anna Karenina*). Or: He loves her passionately, but she falls in love with him only when she has worn out his passion ("Frankly, my dear, I don't give a damn").

In each of these plots, there is both intense desire and great danger to the achievement of that desire; generally speaking, this shape holds good for all plots. It can be called 3-D: *Drama* equals *desire* plus *danger*. One common fault of talented young writers is to create a main character who is essentially passive. This is an understandable fault; as a writer you are an observer of human nature and activity, and so you identify easily with a character who observes, reflects, and suffers. But such a character's passivity transmits itself to the page, and the story also becomes passive. Charles Baxter regrets that, "In writing workshops, this kind of story is often the rule rather than the exception." He calls it:

> the fiction of finger-pointing . . . In such fiction, people and events are often accused of turning the protagonist into the kind of person the protagonist is, usually an unhappy person. That's the whole story. When blame has been assigned, the story is over.

In such flawed stories, the central character (and by implication, the story's author) seems to take no responsibility for what that character wants to have happen. This is quite different from Aristotle's rather startling claim that a man *is* his desire.

In fiction, in order to engage our attention and sympathy, the protagonist must *want*, and want intensely. The thing that the character wants need not be violent or spectacular; it is the intensity of the wanting that introduces an element of danger. She may want, like *The Suicide's Wife* in David Madden's novel, no more than to get her driver's license, but if so she must feel that her identity and her future depend on her getting a driver's license, while a corrupt highway patrolman tries to manipulate her. He may want, like Samuel Beckett's Murphy, only to tie himself to his rocking chair and rock, but if so he will also want a woman who nags him to get up and get a job. She may want, like the heroine of Margaret Atwood's *Bodily Harm*, only to get away from it all for a rest, but if so she must need rest for her survival, while tourists

Fiction is the art form of human yearning. That is absolutely essential to any work of fictional narrative art—a character who yearns. And that is not the same as a character who simply has problems. . . . The yearning is also the thing that generates what we call plot, because the elements of the plot come from thwarted or blocked or challenged attempts to fulfill that yearning.

Robert Olen Butler

and terrorists involve her in machinations that begin in discomfort and end in mortal danger.

It's important to realize that the great dangers in life and in literature are not necessarily the most spectacular. Another mistake frequently made by young writers is to think that they can best introduce drama into their stories by way of murderers, chase scenes, crashes, and vampires, the external stock dangers of pulp and TV. In fact, all of us know that the most profound impediments to our desire usually lie close to home, in our own bodies, personalities, friends, lovers, and families. Fewer people have cause to panic at the approach of a stranger with a gun than at the approach of Mama with the curling iron. More passion is destroyed at the breakfast table than in a time warp.

A frequently used critical tool divides possible conflicts into several basic categories: man against man, man against nature, man against society, man against machine, man against God, man against himself. Most stories fall into these categories, and in a literature class they can provide a useful way of discussing and comparing works. But the employment of categories can be misleading to new writers, insofar as it suggests that literary conflicts take place in these abstract, cosmic dimensions. A writer needs a specific story to tell, and if you sit down to pit "man" against "nature," you will have less of a story than if you pit seventeen-year-old James Tucker of Weehawken, New Jersey, against a two-and-a-half-foot bigmouth bass in the backwoods of Toomsuba, Mississippi. (The value of specificity is a point to which we will return again and again.)

Once conflict is established and developed in a story, the conflict must come to a crisis—the final turning point—and a resolution. Order is a major value that literature offers us, and order implies that the subject has been brought to closure. In life this never quite happens, but whether or not the lives of fictional characters end, the story does, and we are left with a satisfying sense of completion.

What I want to do now is to present several ways—they are all essentially metaphors—of seeing this pattern of *conflict-crisis-resolution* in order to make the shape and its variations clearer, and particularly to indicate what a crisis action is.

Art is pleasing yourself . . . But you can please yourself and it won't be art. Art is having the mastery to take your experience, whether it's visual or mental, and make meaningful shapes that convey a reality to others.

Gail Godwin

The Arc of the Story

Novelist John L'Heureux says that a story is about a single moment in a character's life that culminates in a defining choice—such as the life-or-death choice Violet makes in "Silver Water" at the end of this chapter—after which nothing will be the same again. Plotting is a matter of finding the decision points that lead to this final choice and choosing the best scenes through which to dramatize them.

The editor and teacher Mel McKee states flatly that "a story is a war. It is sustained and immediate combat." He offers four imperatives for the writing of this "war" story.

(1) get your fighters fighting, (2) have something—the stake—worth their fighting over, (3) have the fight dive into a series of battles with the last battle in the series the biggest and most dangerous of all, (4) have a walking away from the fight.

The stake over which wars are fought is usually a territory, and it's important that this "territory" in a story be as tangible and specific as the Gaza Strip. For example, in William Carlos Williams's story "The Use of Force," found at the end of this chapter, the war is fought over the territory of the little girl's mouth, and the fight begins narrowing to that territory from the first paragraph. As with warring nations, the story territory itself can come to represent all sorts of serious abstractions—self-determination, domination, freedom, dignity, identity—but the soldiers fight yard by yard over a particular piece of grass or sand.

Just as a minor "police action" may gradually escalate into a holocaust, story form follows its most natural order of "complications" when each battle is bigger than the last. It begins with a ground skirmish, which does not decide the war. Then one side brings in spies, and the other, guerrillas; these actions do not decide the war. So one side brings in the air force, and the other answers with antiaircraft. One side takes to missiles, and the other answers with rockets. One side has poison gas, and the other has a hand on the nuclear button. Metaphorically, this is what happens in a story. As long as one antagonist can recoup enough power to counterattack, the conflict goes on. But, at some point in the story, one of the antagonists will produce a weapon from which the other cannot recover. *The crisis action is the last battle and makes the outcome inevitable;* there can no longer be any doubt who wins the particular territory—though there can be much doubt about moral victory. When this has happened the conflict ends with a significant and permanent *change*—which is the definition, in fiction, of a resolution.

Notice that although a plot involves a desire and a danger to that desire, it does not necessarily end happily if the desire is achieved, nor unhappily if it is not. The more morally complex the story, the less straightforward the idea of winning and losing becomes. In *Hamlet,* Hamlet's desire is to kill King Claudius, and he is prevented from doing so for most of the play by other characters, intrigues, and his own mental state. When he finally succeeds, it is at the cost of every significant life in the play, including his own. Although the hero "wins" his particular "territory," the play is a tragedy. In Margaret Atwood's *Bodily Harm,* on the other hand, the heroine ends up in a political prison. Yet the discovery of her own strength and commitment is such that we know she has achieved salvation. *What does my character win by losing his struggle, or lose by winning?* John L'Heureux suggests the writer ask himself or herself.

Patterns of Power

Novelist Michael Shaara described a story as a power struggle between equal forces. It is imperative, he argued, that each antagonist have sufficient power that the reader is left in doubt about the outcome. We may be wholly in sympathy with one character and even reasonably confident that she or he will triumph. But the antagonist must represent a real and potent danger, and the pattern of the story's complications will be achieved by *shifting the power back and forth from one antagonist to the other.* Finally, an action will occur that will shift the power irretrievably in one direction.

"Power" takes many forms—physical strength, charm, knowledge, moral power, wealth, ownership, rank, and so on. Most obvious is the power of brute force, as wielded by mobster Max Blue in Leslie Marmon Silko's epic novel *Almanac of the Dead:*

> . . . Max thinks of himself as an executive producer of one-night-only performances, dramas played out in the warm California night breezes, in a phone booth in downtown Long Beach. All Max had done was dial a phone number and listen while the pigeon repeats, "Hello? Hello? Hello? Hello?" until .22-pistol shots snap *pop!pop!* and Max hangs up.

A character who blends several types of power—good looks, artistic talent, social privilege and the self-assurance that stems from it—is Zavier Chalfant, son of a furniture factory owner in Donald Secreast's story "Summer Help." Zavier is seen through the eyes of Wanda, a longtime employee assigned the coveted job of painting designs on the most expensive pieces. As the plant supervisor introduces them

> . . . Zavier Chalfant was letting his gaze rest lightly on Wanda. Most boys—and that's what Zavier was, after all, a boy of about twenty-one—were very embar-

rassed their first day on the job. Zavier, in contrast, seemed more amused than embarrassed . . . His thick blond hair covered the collar of his jacket but was clean and expertly cut so he looked more like a knight than a hippie . . . his face looked like a Viking's face; she'd always been partial to Vikings. Of course, Zavier was too thin to be a Viking all the way down, but he had the face of an adventurer. Of an artist.

Wanda's awe of Zavier's power is confirmed when he easily paints a design she must labor over.

"Color is my specialty." Zavier deftly added the highlights to the woman's face and hands. "It's everything." He finished the flesh parts in a matter of minutes. He took another brush from Wanda and in six or seven strokes had filled in the woman's robe.

Yet if power is entirely one-sided, suspense will be lost, so it is important to identify a source of power for each character surrounding the story's conflict. Remember that "power" takes many forms, some of which have the external appearance of weakness. Anyone who has ever been tied to the demands of an invalid can understand this: Sickness can be great strength. Weakness, need, passivity, an ostensible desire not to be any trouble to anybody—all these can be used as manipulative tools to prevent the protagonist from achieving his or her desire. Martyrdom is immensely powerful, whether we sympathize with it or not; a dying man absorbs all our energies.

The power of weakness has generated the central conflict in many stories and in such plays as *Uncle Vanya* and *The Glass Menagerie*. Here is a passage in which it is swiftly and deftly sketched:

This sepulchral atmosphere owed a lot to the presence of Mrs. Taylor herself. She was a tall, stooped woman with deep-set eyes. She sat in her living room all day long and chain-smoked cigarettes and stared out the picture window with an air of unutterable sadness, as if she knew things beyond mortal bearing. Sometimes she would call Taylor over and wrap her arms around him, then close her eyes and hoarsely whisper, "Terence, Terence!" Eyes still closed, she would turn her head and resolutely push him away.

Tobias Wolff, *This Boy's Life*

Connection and Disconnection

Some students, as well as critics, object to the description of narrative as a war or power struggle. Seeing the world in terms of conflict and crisis, of enemies and warring factions, not only constricts the possibilities of literature, they argue, but also promulgates an aggressive and antagonistic view of our own lives.

Speaking of the "gladiatorial view of fiction," Ursula Le Guin writes:

People are cross-grained, aggressive, and full of trouble, the storytellers tell us; people fight themselves and one another, and their stories are full of their struggles. But to say that that *is* the story is to use one aspect of existence, conflict, to subsume all other aspects, many of which it does not include and does not comprehend.

Romeo and Juliet is a story of the conflict between two families, and its plot involves the conflict of two individuals with those families. Is that all it involves? Isn't *Romeo and Juliet* about something else, and isn't it the something else that makes the otherwise trivial tale of a feud into a tragedy?

I'm indebted to dramatist Claudia Johnson for this further—and, it seems to me, crucial—insight about that "something else": Whereas the dynamic of the power struggle has long been acknowledged, narrative is also driven by a pattern of connection and disconnection between characters that is the main source of its emotional effect. Over the course a story, and within the smaller scale of a scene, characters make and break emotional bonds of trust, love, understanding, or compassion with one another. A connection may be as obvious as a kiss or as subtle as a glimpse; a connection may be broken with an action as obvious as a slap or as subtle as an arched eyebrow.

In *Romeo and Juliet*, for example, the Montague and Capulet families are fiercely disconnected, but the young lovers manage to connect in spite of that. Throughout the play they meet and part, disconnect from their families in order to connect with each other, finally part from life in order to be with each other eternally. Their ultimate departure in death reconnects the feuding families.

Johnson puts it this way:

. . . underlying any good story, fictitious or true—is a deeper pattern of change, a pattern of connection and disconnection. The conflict and the surface events are like waves, but underneath is an emotional tide, the ebb and flow of human connection. . . .

Patterns of conflict and connection occur in every story, and sometimes they are evident in much smaller compass, as in this scene from Leslee Becker's story "The Personals." The story takes place shortly after the Loma Prieta earthquake, a catastrophe that has united the community, in the eyes of bookshop owner Alice, while reminding her how cut off from others she actually is. The story centers around her nervous first date with Warren, a shoe salesman and widower still grieving his wife Doris. Described by one reviewer as "factory irregulars," the lonely couple end their date with an after-hours visit to Warren's shoe store.

Suddenly, music began, and Warren emerged from the back room, holding liquor, glasses, shoe boxes, and stockings. "For you," he said, spreading the things at her feet. He opened a box and removed shoes with dramatic high heels. "I've got hand bags, too," he said. "For you, Doris."

She knew he had not realized his mistake, and she said nothing as he sat on the floor in front of her. She felt his hand on her heel, her shoe sliding off effortlessly. She watched the back of him in the mirror and did not want to look at herself as he lifted her foot and pressed it against his chest.

"I don't want to be alone anymore," he said.

She felt her foot slipping out of his hand, the stocking rasping under his fingers. He got to his feet immediately and sat next to her. She looked to the mirror and saw him touch his toupee and wince.

"It's all right," she said. "Warren . . ."

"I'll take you home," he said.

The moment she reached for his hand he got up and began replacing the shoes in the box. "Please," she said. "I know what you're feeling."

"How can you? I don't even know. I'll take you back."

He went into the back room, and the music stopped. While she slipped her shoe on, she felt small and dishonest.

As soon as they returned to the car, she told him what she had done after the earthquake. "I was in a huge department store. Nobody was paying attention to me. I stole things."

"Promise me," he said, "you won't tell anyone about tonight."

"But nothing happened."

"Yeah," he said.

In this short excerpt, Warren tries to connect with Alice through a generous display of shoes, only to blunder and break the fragile connection by calling her by his dead wife's name. When he presses further, Alice withdraws, then tries to ease his humiliation by first offering common emotional experience and then admitting a secret. But it is too late, at least for the present, and Warren refuses to reconnect, perhaps ashamed of the neediness he has revealed.

While the pattern of either conflict or connection may dominate in a given work, "stories are about *both* conflict and connection," says novelist and poet Robert Morgan.

> A story which is only about conflict will be shallow. There must be some deepening of our understanding of the characters. Stories are rarely just about conflicts between good and bad. They are more often about conflicts of loyalty, one good versus another: does a man join up to serve his country, or stay home to help protect and raise his children? The writer strives to bring art to a level where a story is not so much a plot as about human connection, and not just about the conflict of good versus bad, but about the conflict of loyalty with loyalty.

Human wills clash; human belonging is necessary. In discussing human behavior, psychologists speak in terms of "tower" and "network" patterns, the need to climb (which implies conflict) and the need for community, the need to win out over others and the need to belong to others; and these two forces also drive fiction. Like conflict and its complications, connection and its complications can produce a pattern of change, and both inform the process of change recorded in scene and story.

Structure is the art that conceals itself—you only *see* the structure in a
badly structured story, and call it formula.

Stephen Fischer

Story Form as a Check Mark

The nineteenth-century German critic Gustav Freitag analyzed plot in terms of a
pyramid of five actions: an exposition, followed by a complication (or *nouement*,
"knotting up," of the situation), leading to a crisis, which is followed by a "falling action" or anticlimax, resulting in a resolution (or *dénouement*, "unknotting").

In the compact short story form, the falling action is likely to be very brief or
nonexistent, and often the crisis action itself implies the resolution, which is not
necessarily stated but exists as an idea established in the reader's mind.

So for our purposes it is probably more useful to think of story shape not as a pyramid
with sides of equal length but as an inverted check mark. If we take the familiar tale of
Cinderella and diagram it on such a shape in terms of the power struggle, we can see
how the various elements reveal themselves even in this simple children's story.

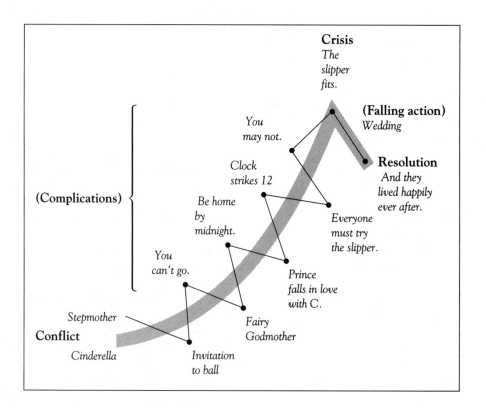

At the opening of the tale we're given the basic conflict: Cinderella's mother has died, and her father has married a brutal woman with two waspish daughters. Cinderella is made to do all the dirtiest and most menial work, and she weeps among the cinders. The Stepmother has on her side the strength of ugliness and evil (two very powerful qualities in literature as in life). With her daughters she also has the strength of numbers, and she has parental authority. Cinderella has only beauty and goodness, but (in literature and life) these are also very powerful.

At the beginning of the struggle in "Cinderella," the power is very clearly on the Stepmother's side. But the first event (action, battle) of the story is that an invitation arrives from the Prince, which explicitly states that *all* the ladies of the land are invited to a ball. Notice that Cinderella's desire is not to triumph over her Stepmother (though she eventually will, much to our satisfaction); such a desire would diminish her goodness. She simply wants to be relieved of her mistreatment. She wants equality, so that the Prince's invitation, which specifically gives her a right equal to the Stepmother's and Stepdaughters' rights, shifts the power to her.

The Stepmother takes the power back by blunt force: You may not go; you must get us ready to go. Cinderella does so, and the three leave for the ball.

Then what happens? The Fairy Godmother appears. It is *very* powerful to have magic on your side. The Fairy Godmother offers Cinderella a gown, glass slippers, and a coach with horses and footmen, giving her more force than she has yet had.

But the magic is not all-potent. It has a qualification that portends bad luck. It will last only until midnight (unlike the Stepmother's authority), and Cinderella must leave the ball before the clock strikes twelve or risk exposure and defeat.

What happens next? She goes to the ball and the Prince falls in love with her—and love is an even more powerful weapon than magic in a literary war. In some versions of the tale, the Stepmother and Stepsisters are made to marvel at the beauty of the Princess they don't recognize, pointing to the irony of Cinderella's new power.

And then? The magic quits. The clock strikes twelve, and Cinderella runs down the steps in her rags to her rats and pumpkin, losing a slipper, bereft of her power in every way.

But after that, the Prince sends out a messenger with the glass slipper and a dictum (a dramatic repetition of the original invitation in which all ladies were invited to the ball) that every female in the land is to try on the slipper. Cinderella is given her rights again by royal decree.

What happens then? In most good retellings of the tale, the Stepmother also repeats her assumption of brute authority by hiding Cinderella away, while our expectation of triumph is tantalizingly delayed with grotesque comedy: one sister cuts off a toe, the other a heel, trying to fit into the heroine's rightful slipper.

After that, Cinderella tries on the slipper and it fits. *This is the crisis action.* Magic, love, and royalty join to recognize the heroine's true self; evil, numbers, and authority are powerless against them. At this point, the power struggle has been decided; the outcome is inevitable. When the slipper fits, no further action can occur that will deprive Cinderella of her desire. Nothing will be the same again: the change in the lives of all concerned is significant and permanent.

The tale has a brief "falling action" or "walking away from the fight": the Prince sweeps Cinderella up on his white horse and gallops away to their wedding. The story comes to closure with the classic resolution of all comedy: They lived happily ever after.

If we also look at "Cinderella" in terms of connection/disconnection, we see a pattern as clear as that represented by the power struggle. The first painful disconnection is that Cinderella's mother has died; her father has married (connected with) a woman who spurns (disconnects from) her; the Prince's invitation offers connection; the Stepmother's cruelty alienates again. The Fairy Godmother connects as a magical friend, but the disappearance of the coach and gown disconnect Cinderella temporarily from that grand and glorious fairy-tale union, marriage to the Prince. If we consult the emotions that this tale engenders—pity, anger, hope, fear, romance, anticipation, disappointment, triumph—we see that both the struggle between antagonist/protagonist and the pattern of alienation/connectedness is necessary to ensure, not only that there is an action, but also that we care about its outcome. The traditional happy ending is the grand connection, marriage; the traditional tragic outcome is the final disconnection, death.

In the *Poetics*, the first extensive work of extant Western literary criticism, Aristotle referred to the crisis action of a tragedy as a *peripeteia*, or reversal of the protagonist's fortunes. Critics and editors agree that a reversal of some sort is necessary to all story structure, comic as well as tragic. Although the protagonist need not lose power, land, or life, he or she must in some significant way be changed or moved by the action. Aristotle specified that this reversal came about because of *hamartia*, which has for centuries been translated as a "tragic flaw" in the protagonist's character, usually assumed to be, or defined as, pride. But more recent critics have defined and translated *hamartia* much more narrowly as a "mistake in identity" with the reversal coming about in a "recognition."

It is true that recognition scenes have played a disproportionately large role in the crisis actions of plots both comic and tragic, and that these scenes frequently stretch credibility. In real life, you are unlikely to mistake the face of your mother, son, uncle, or even friend, and yet such mistakes have provided the turning point of many a plot. If, however, the notion of "recognition" is extended to more abstract and subtle realms, it becomes a powerful metaphor for moments of "realization." In other words, the "recognition scene" in literature may stand for that moment in life when we "recognize" that the man we have considered good is evil, the event we have considered insignificant is crucial, the woman we have thought out of touch with reality is a genius, the object we have thought desirable is poison. There is in this symbolic way a recognition in "Cinderella." We knew that she was essentially a princess, but until the Prince recognizes her as one, our knowledge must be frustrated.

James Joyce developed a similar idea when he spoke of, and recorded both in his notebooks and in his stories, moments of what he called *epiphany*. As Joyce saw it, epiphany is a crisis action in the mind, a moment when a person, an event, or a thing is seen in a light so new that it is as if it has never been seen before. At this recognition, the mental landscape of the viewer is permanently changed.

In many of the finest modern short stories and novels, the true territory of struggle is the main character's mind, and so the real crisis action must occur there. Yet it
is important to grasp that Joyce chose the word *epiphany* to represent this moment of
reversal, and that the word means "a *manifestation* of a supernatural being"; specifically, in Christian doctrine, "the manifestation of Christ to the gentiles." By extension, then, in a short story any mental reversal that takes place in the crisis of a story
must be *manifested*; it must be triggered or shown by an action. The slipper must fit.
It would not do if the Stepmother just happened to change her mind and give up the
struggle; it would not do if the Prince just happened to notice that Cinderella looked
like his love. The moment of recognition must be manifested in an action.

This point, that the crisis must be manifested or externalized in an action, is absolutely central, although sometimes difficult to grasp when the struggle of the story
takes place in a character's mind. In the upcoming story "The Things They Carried,"
for example, the young lieutenant's mental determination to change himself into a
hardened leader is manifested in the action of burning photographs, letters, and finally a village.

In a revenge story, it is easy to see how the conflict must come to crisis. The common revenge plot, from *Hamlet* to *Traffic*, takes this form: Someone important to the
hero (father, sister, lover, friend) is killed, and for some reason the authorities who
ought to be in charge of justice can't or won't avenge the death. The hero must do
so, then, and the crisis action is manifested in the swing of the dagger, the blast of
the gun, the swallowing of the poison, whatever.

But suppose the story is about a struggle between two brothers on a fishing trip,
and the change that takes place is that the protagonist, believing for most of the action that he holds his older brother in contempt, discovers at the end of the story
that they are deeply bound by love and family history. Clearly this change is an
epiphany, a mental reversal. A writer insufficiently aware of the nature of crisis action might signal the change in a paragraph that begins "Suddenly Larry remembered their father and realized that Jeff was very much like him." Well, unless that
memory and that realization are manifested in an action, the reader is unable to
share them, and therefore cannot be moved with the character.

> Jeff reached for the old net and neatly bagged the trout, swinging round to offer
> it with a triumphant, "Got it! We got it, didn't we?" The trout flipped and strug-
> gled, giving off a smell of weed and water and fecund mud. Jeff's knuckles were
> lined with grime. The knuckles and the rich river smell filled him with a
> memory of their first fishing trip together, the sight of their father's hands on the
> same scarred net. . . .

Here the epiphany, a memory leading to a realization, is triggered by an action
and sensory details that the reader can share; the reader now has a good chance of
also being able to share the epiphany. Less commonly, a story may offer readers an
epiphany the main character neglects to see, as in the short-short story "No One's a

Mystery," which appears at the end of this chapter. Such characters are often on the verge of great change, yet lack the maturity or courage to take that difficult leap to recognition.

Much great fiction, and the preponderance of serious modern fiction, echoes life in its suggestion that there are no clear or permanent solutions, that the conflicts of character, relationship, and the cosmos cannot be permanently resolved. Most of the stories in this volume end, in Vladimir Nabokov's words, "with no definite full-stop, but with the natural motion of life." None could end "they lived happily ever after" or even "they lived unhappily ever after."

Yet the story form demands a resolution. Is there such a thing as a no-resolution resolution? Yes, and it has a very specific form. Go back to the metaphor that "a story is a war." After the skirmish, after the guerrillas, after the air strike, after the poison gas and the nuclear holocaust, imagine that the two surviving combatants, one on each side, emerge from their fallout shelters. They crawl, then stumble to the fence that marks the border. Each possessively grasps the barbed wire with a bloodied fist. The "resolution" of this battle is that neither side will ever give up and that no one will ever win; *there will never be a resolution*. This is a distinct reversal (the recognition takes place in the reader's mind) of the opening scene, in which it seemed eminently worthwhile to open a ground skirmish. In the statement of the conflict was an inherent possibility that one side or the other could win. Inherent in the resolution is a statement that no one can ever win. That is a distinct reversal and a powerful change.

Story and Plot

So far, I have used the words "story" and "plot" interchangeably. The equation of the two terms is so common that they are often comfortably understood as synonyms. When an editor says, "This is not a story," the implication is not that it lacks character, theme, setting, or even incident, but that it has no plot.

Almost all good stories are sad because it is the human struggle that engages us readers and listeners the most. To watch characters confront their hardships and uncertainties makes us feel better about our own conflicts and confusions and fears. We have a sense of community, of sympathy, a cleansing sympathy, as Aristotle said, and relief that we are safe in our room only reading the story. A story of sadness, even tragedy, makes us feel, paradoxically, better, as though we are confronting our own conflicts and fears, and have endured.

Robert Morgan

Yet there is a distinction frequently drawn between the two terms, a distinction that although simple in itself, gives rise to manifold subtleties in the craft of narrative and that also represents a vital decision that you as a writer must make: Where should your narrative begin?

The distinction is easily made. A *story* is a series of events recorded in their chronological order. A *plot* is a series of events deliberately arranged so as to reveal their dramatic, thematic, and emotional significance. A story gives us only "what happened next," whereas plot's concern is "what, how, and why," with scenes ordered to highlight the workings of cause and effect.

Here, for example, is a fairly standard story: A sober, industrious, and rather dull young man meets the woman of his dreams. She is beautiful, brilliant, passionate, and compassionate; more wonderful still, she loves him. They plan to marry, and on the eve of their wedding his friends give him a stag party in the course of which they tease him, ply him with liquor, and drag him off to a whorehouse for a last fling. There he stumbles into a cubicle . . . to find himself facing his bride-to-be.

Where does this story become interesting? Where does the *plot* begin?

You may start, if you like, with the young man's *Mayflower* ancestry. But if you do, it's going to be a very long story, and we're likely to close the book about the middle of the nineteenth century. You may begin with the first time he meets the extraordinary woman, but even then you must cover at least weeks, probably months, in a few pages; and that means you must summarize, skip, and generalize, and you'll have a hard time both maintaining your credibility and holding our attention. Begin at the stag party? Better. If you do so, you will somehow have to let us know all that has gone before, either through dialogue or through the young man's memory, but you have only one evening of action to cover, and we'll get to the conflict quickly. Suppose you begin instead the next morning, when the man wakes with a hangover in bed in a brothel with his bride on his wedding day. Is that, perhaps, the best of all? An immediate conflict that must lead to a quick and striking crisis?

E. M. Forster, author of *Aspects of the Novel*, distinguishes between plot and story by describing story as

> the chopped off length of the tape worm of time . . . a narrative of events arranged in their time sequence. A plot is also a narrative of events, the emphasis falling on causality. "The king died, and then the queen died," is a story. "The king died, and then the queen died of grief," is a plot. The time sequence is preserved, but the sense of causality overshadows it. Or again: "The queen died, no one knew why, until it was discovered that it was through grief at the death of the king." This is a plot with a mystery in it, a form capable of high development. It suspends the time sequence, it moves as far away from the story as its limitations will allow. Consider the death of the queen. If it is in a story we say, "and then?" If it is in a plot we ask, "why?"

The human desire to know *why* is as powerful as the desire to know what happened next, and it is a desire of a higher order. Once we have the facts, we inevitably look for the links between them, and only when we find such links are we satisfied that we "understand." Rote memorization in a science class bores almost everyone. Grasp and a sense of discovery begin only when we perceive *why* "a body in motion tends to remain in motion" and what an immense effect this actuality has on the phenomena of our lives.

The same is true of the events of a story. Random incidents neither move nor illuminate; we want to know why one thing leads to another and to feel the inevitability of cause and effect.

Here is a series of uninteresting events chronologically arranged.

> Ariadne had a bad dream.
> She woke up tired and cross.
> She ate breakfast
> She headed for class.
> She saw Leroy.
> She fell on the steps and broke her ankle.
> Leroy offered to take notes for her.
> She went to a hospital.

This series of events does not constitute a plot, and if you wish to fashion it into a plot, you can do so only by letting us know the meaningful relations among the events. We first assume that Ariadne woke in a temper because of her bad dream, and that Leroy offered to take notes for her because she broke her ankle. But why did she fall? Perhaps because she saw Leroy? Does that suggest that her bad dream was about him? Was she, then, thinking about his dream-rejection as she broke her egg irritably on the edge of the frying pan? What is the effect of his offer? Is it a triumph or just another polite form of rejection when, really, he could have missed class once to drive her to the x-ray lab? The emotional and dramatic significance of these ordinary events emerges in the relation of cause to effect, and where such relation can be shown, a possible plot comes into existence. Notice also that in this brief attempt to form the events into a plot, I have introduced both conflict and a pattern of connection/disconnection.

Ariadne's is a story you might very well choose to tell chronologically: it needs to cover only an hour or two, and that much can be handled in the compressed form of the short story. But such a choice of plot is not inevitable even in this short compass. Might it be more gripping to begin with the wince of pain as she stumbles? Leroy comes to help her up and the yolk yellow of his T-shirt fills her field of vision. In the shock of pain she is immediately back in her dream. . . .

When "nothing happens" in a story, it is because we fail to sense the causal relation between what happens first and what happens next. When something does "happen," it is because the resolution of a short story or a novel describes a change in the character's life, an effect of the events that have gone before. This is why Aristotle insisted with such apparent simplicity on "a beginning, a middle, and an end." A story is capable of many meanings, and it is first of all in the choice of structure—which portion of the story forms the plot—that you offer us the gratifying sense that we "understand."

It's commonly said that there are only two plots: a person leaves home and a stranger comes to town. If you think about it, both of those are really the same story seen from two different points of view. In both cases, what causes the "story" to occur is that something has happened to throw out of balance the relative calm or homeostasis of a person or community.

In the person-goes-on-a-journey story, the person's quest and the ultimate conclusion of that quest (that is, returning home with whatever grail he's found), is what achieves his personal re-balancing, or homeostasis.

In the second storyline, the chemistry of the town is thrown out of whack by the stranger's arrival, and not until they either incorporate him or reject him or kill him is their old order re-established. This desire to "get my old life back" seems to propel a great deal of fiction. To me, getting your old life back suggests regaining some balance, harmony and homeostasis in your life.

James Hall

The Short Story and the Novel

Many editors and writers insist that the short story and the novel are vastly different creatures. It is my belief, however, that, like the distinction between story and plot, the distinction between the two forms is very simple, and the many and profound possibilities of difference proceed from that simple source: A short story is short, and a novel is long.

Because of this, a short story can waste no words. It usually features the perspective of one, or at most, a very few characters. It may recount only one central action and one major change in the life of the central character or characters. It can afford no digression that does not directly affect the action. A short story strives to create what Edgar Allan Poe called "the single effect"—a single emotional impact that imparts a flash of understanding, though both impact and understanding may be complex. The virtue of a short story is its density, for it raises a single "what if" question, while a novel may raise many. If it is tight, sharp, economic, well knit, and charged, then it is a good short story because it has exploited a central attribute of the form— that it is short.

Occasionally in workshops, a new writer struggling to craft the shape of conflict-crisis-resolution may wonder if a story's lack of one of these elements means the work "must be a novel." Tempting as this hope may be, it only sidesteps the inevitable challenge of plotting, for not only must a novel have a large-scale plot structure, but individual chapters or episodes frequently are shaped around a pattern of conflict-crisis-incremental change that impels the novel onward.

Further, while no literary form is superior to another, few novelists achieve publication without first having crafted any number of short stories. The greater the limitation of space, the greater the necessity for pace, sharpness, and density. Short stories ask the writer to rise to the challenges of shaping, "showing," and making significance again and again, experiences that later may save that writer countless hours and pages when the time to tackle a novel comes along.

The form of the novel is an expanded story form. It asks for a conflict, a crisis, and a resolution, and no technique described in this book is irrelevant to its effectiveness.

Reading as Writers

Each story in this book will be followed by a few suggestions for discussion that ask not *What does this story mean?* but *How does this story work?* Learning to read as a writer involves focusing on craft, the choices and the techniques of the author. In *On Becoming A Novelist*, John Gardner urges young writers to read "the way a young architect looks at a building, or a medical student watches an operation, both devotedly, hoping to learn from a master, and critically alert for any possible mistake." "Bad poets imitate; good poets steal," was T. S. Eliot's advice.

Ask yourself as you read: what is memorable, effective, moving? Reread, if possible, watching for the techniques that produced those reactions in you. *Why did the author choose to begin at this point? Why did s/he make this choice of imagery, setting, ending? What gives this scene its tension; what makes me feel sympathetic?* You can also learn from stories that don't personally move you—how would you have handled the same material, and what would have changed with that approach? Be greedy from your own viewpoint as an author: *What, from this story, can I learn/imitate/steal?*

The Use of Force

WILLIAM CARLOS WILLIAMS

They were new patients to me, all I had was the name, Olson. Please come down as soon as you can, my daughter is very sick.

When I arrived I was met by the mother, a big startled looking woman, very clean and apologetic who merely said, Is this the doctor? and let me in. In the back, she added. You must excuse us, doctor, we have her in the kitchen where it is warm. It is very damp here sometimes.

The child was fully dressed and sitting on her father's lap near the kitchen table. He tried to get up, but I motioned for him not to bother, took off my overcoat and started to look things over. I could see that they were all very nervous, eyeing me up and down distrustfully. As often, in such cases, they weren't telling me more than they had to, it was up to me to tell them; that's why they were spending three dollars on me.

The child was fairly eating me up with her cold, steady eyes, and no expression to her face whatever. She did not move and seemed, inwardly, quiet; an unusually attractive little thing, and as strong as a heifer in appearance. But her face was flushed, she was breathing rapidly, and I realized that she had a high fever. She had magnificent blonde hair, in profusion. One of those picture children often reproduced in advertising leaflets and the photogravure sections of the Sunday papers.

She's had a fever for three days, began the father, and we don't know what it comes from. My wife has given her things, you know, like people do, but it don't do no good. And there's been a lot of sickness around. So we tho't you'd better look her over and tell us what is the matter.

As doctors often do I took a trial shot at it as a point of departure. Has she had a sore throat?

Both parents answered me together, No . . . No, she says her throat don't hurt her.

Does your throat hurt you? added the mother to the child. But the little girl's expression didn't change, nor did she move her eyes from my face.

Have you looked?

I tried to, said the mother, but I couldn't see.

As it happens, we had been having a number of cases of diphtheria in the school to which this child went during that month and we were all, quite apparently, thinking of that, though no one had as yet spoken of the thing.

Well, I said, suppose we take a look at the throat first. I smiled in my best professional manner and asking for the child's first name I said, come on, Mathilda, open your mouth and let's take a look at your throat.

Nothing doing.

Aw, come on, I coaxed, just open your mouth wide and let me take a look. Look, I said opening both hands wide, I haven't anything in my hands. Just open up and let me see.

Such a nice man, put in the mother. Look how kind he is to you. Come on, do what he tells you to. He won't hurt you.

At that I ground my teeth in disgust. If only they wouldn't use the word "hurt" I might be able to get somewhere. But I did not allow myself to be hurried or disturbed, but speaking quietly and slowly I approached the child again.

As I moved my chair a little nearer, suddenly with one catlike movement both her hands clawed instinctively for my eyes and she almost reached them too. In fact she knocked my glasses flying and they fell, though unbroken, several feet away from me on the kitchen floor.

Both the mother and father almost turned themselves inside out in embarrassment and apology. You bad girl, said the mother, taking her and shaking her by one arm. Look what you've done. The nice man.

For heaven's sake, I broke in. Don't call me a nice man to her. I'm here to look at her throat on the chance that she might have diphtheria and possibly die of it. But that's nothing to her. Look here, I said to the child, we're going to look at your throat. You're old enough to understand what I'm saying. Will you open it now by yourself or shall we have to open it for you?

Not a move. Even her expression hadn't changed. Her breaths however were coming faster and faster. Then the battle began. I had to do it. I had to have a throat culture for her own protection. But first I told the parents that it was entirely up to them. I explained the danger but said that I would not insist on a throat examination so long as they would take the responsibility.

If you don't do what the doctor says you'll have to go to the hospital, the mother admonished her severely.

Oh yeah? I had to smile to myself. After all, I had already fallen in love with the savage brat, the parents were contemptible to me. In the ensuing struggle they grew more and more abject, crushed, exhausted while she surely rose to magnificent heights of insane fury of effort bred of her terror of me.

The father tried his best, and he was a big man but the fact that she was his daughter, his shame at her behavior and his dread of hurting her made him release her just at the critical moment several times when I had almost achieved success, till I wanted to kill him. But his dread also that she might have diphtheria made him tell me to go on, go on though he himself was almost fainting, while the mother moved back and forth behind us raising and lowering her hands in an agony of apprehension.

Put her in front of you on your lap, I ordered, and hold both her wrists.

But as soon as he did the child let out a scream. Don't, you're hurting me. Let go of my hands. Let them go I tell you. Then she shrieked terrifyingly, hysterically. Stop it! Stop it! You're killing me!

Do you think she can stand it, doctor! said the mother.

You get out, said the husband to his wife. Do you want her to die of diphtheria? Come on now, hold her, I said.

Then I grasped the child's head with my left hand and tried to get the wooden tongue depressor between her teeth. She fought, with clenched teeth, desperately! But now I also had grown furious—at a child. I tried to hold myself down but I couldn't. I know how to expose a throat for inspection. And I did my best. When finally I got the wooden spatula behind the last teeth and just the point of it into the mouth cavity, she opened up for an instant but before I could see anything she came down again and gripping the wooden blade between her molars she reduced it to splinters before I could get it out again.

Aren't you ashamed, the mother yelled at her. Aren't you ashamed to act like that in front of the doctor?

Get me a smooth-handled spoon of some sort, I told the mother. We're going through with this. The child's mouth was already bleeding. Her tongue was cut and she was screaming in wild hysterical shrieks. Perhaps I should have desisted and come back in an hour or more. No doubt it would have been better. But I have seen at least two children lying dead in bed of neglect in such cases, and feeling that I must get a diagnosis now or never I went at it again. But the worst of it was that I too had got beyond reason. I could have torn the child apart in my own fury and enjoyed it. It was a pleasure to attack her. My face was burning with it.

The damned little brat must be protected against her own idiocy, one says to one's self at such times. Others must be protected against her. It is social necessity. And all these things are true. But a blind fury, a feeling of adult shame, bred of a longing for muscular release are the operatives. One goes on to the end.

In a final unreasoning assault I overpowered the child's neck and jaws. I forced the heavy silver spoon back of her teeth and down her throat till she gagged. And there it was—both tonsils covered with membrane. She had fought valiantly to keep me from knowing her secret. She had been hiding that sore throat for three days at least and lying to her parents in order to escape just such an outcome as this.

Now truly she was furious. She had been on the defensive before but now she attacked. Tried to get off her father's lap and fly at me while tears of defeat blinded her eyes.

✿ ✿ ✿
Suggestions for Discussion

1. What kinds of power would you ascribe to each of the characters? Where does power shift from one character to another?
2. Identify the central conflict, the crisis, and the resolution in "The Use of Force." Can it be positioned like "Cinderella" on the diagram?
3. How does the author show the doctor's inner conflict?
4. What does the doctor lose by winning? What does the girl win even in losing?

How Far She Went
MARY HOOD

They had quarreled all morning, squalled all summer about the incidentals: how tight the girl's cut-off jeans were, the "Every Inch a Woman" T-shirt, her choice of music and how loud she played it, her practiced inattention, her sullen look. Her granny wrung out the last boiled dishcloth, pinched it to the line, giving the basin a sling and a slap, the water flying out in a scalding arc onto the Queen Anne's lace by the path, never mind if it bloomed, that didn't make it worth anything except to chiggers, but the girl would cut it by the everlasting armload and cherish it in the old churn, going to that much trouble for a week but not bending once—unbegged—to pick the nearest bean; she was sulking now. Bored. Displaced.

"And what do you think happens to a chigger if nobody ever walks by his weed?" her granny asked, heading for the house with that sidelong uneager unanswered glance, hoping for what? The surprise gift of a smile? Nothing. The woman shook her head and said it. "Nothing." The door slammed behind her. Let it.

"I hate it here!" the girl yelled then. She picked up a stick and broke it and threw the pieces—one from each hand—at the laundry drying in the noon. Missed. Missed.

Then she turned on her bare, haughty heel and set off high-shouldered into the heat, quick but not far, not far enough—no road was *that* long—only as far as she dared. At the gate, a rusty chain swinging between two lichened posts, she stopped, then backed up the raw drive to make a run at the barrier, lofting, clearing it clean, her long hair wild in the sun. Triumphant, she looked back at the house where she caught at the dark window her granny's face in its perpetual eclipse of disappointment, old at fifty. She stepped back, but the girl saw her.

"You don't know me!" the girl shouted, chin high, and ran till her ribs ached.

As she rested in the rattling shade of the willows, the little dog found her. He could be counted on. He barked all the way, and squealed when she pulled the burr from his ear. They started back to the house for lunch. By then the mailman had long come and gone in the old ruts, leaving the one letter folded now to fit the woman's apron pocket.

If bad news darkened her granny's face, the girl ignored it. Didn't talk at all, another of her distancings, her defiances. So it was as they ate that the woman summarized, "Your daddy wants you to cash in the plane ticket and buy you something. School clothes. For here."

Pale, the girl stared, defenseless only an instant before blurting out, "You're lying."

The woman had to stretch across the table to leave her handprint on that blank cheek. She said, not caring if it stung or not, "He's been planning it since he sent you here."

"I could turn this whole house over, dump it! Leave you slobbering over that stinking jealous dog in the dust!" The girl trembled with the vision, with the strength it gave her. It made her laugh. "Scatter the Holy Bible like confetti and ravel the crochet into miles of stupid string! I could! I will! I won't stay here!" But she didn't move, not until her tears rose to meet her color, and then to escape the shame of minding so much she fled. Just headed away, blind. It didn't matter, this time, how far she went.

The woman set her thoughts against fretting over their bickering, just went on unalarmed with chores, clearing off after the uneaten meal, bringing in the laundry, scattering corn for the chickens, ladling manure tea onto the porch flowers. She listened though. She always had been a listener. It gave her a cocked look. She forgot why she had gone into the girl's empty room, that ungirlish, tenuous lodging place with its bleak order, its ready suitcases never unpacked, the narrow bed, the contested radio on the windowsill. The woman drew the cracked shade down between the radio and the August sun. There wasn't anything else to do.

It was after six when she tied on her rough oxfords and walked down the drive and dropped the gate chain and headed back to the creosoted shed where she kept her tools. She took a hoe for snakes, a rake, shears to trim the grass where it grew, and seed in her pocket to scatter where it never had grown at all. She put the tools and her gloves and the bucket in the trunk of the old Chevy, its prime and rust like an Appaloosa's spots through the chalky white finish. She left the trunk open and the tool handles sticking out. She wasn't going far.

The heat of the day had broken, but the air was thick, sultry, weighted with honeysuckle in second bloom and the Nu-Grape scent of kudzu. The maple and poplar leaves turned over, quaking, silver. There wouldn't be any rain. She told the dog to stay, but he knew a trick. He stowed away when she turned her back, leaped right into the trunk with the tools, then gave himself away with exultant barks. Hearing him, her court jester, she stopped the car and welcomed him into the front seat beside her. Then they went on. Not a mile from her gate she turned onto the blue gravel of the cemetery lane, hauled the gearshift into reverse to whoa them, and got out to take the idle walk down to her buried hopes, bending all along to rout out a handful of weeds from between the markers of old acquaintance. She stood there and read, slow. The dog whined at her hem; she picked him up and rested her chin on his head, then he wriggled and whined to run free, contrary and restless as a child.

The crows called strong and bold MOM! MOM! A trick of the ear to hear it like that. She knew it was the crows, but still she looked around. No one called her that now. She was done with that. And what was it worth anyway? It all came to this: solitary weeding. The sinful fumble of flesh, the fear, the listening for a return that never came, the shamed waiting, the unanswered prayers, the perjury on the certificate—hadn't she lain there weary of the whole lie and it only beginning? and a voice telling her, "Here's your baby, here's your girl," and the swaddled package meaning no more to her than an extra anything, something store-bought, something she could take back for a refund.

"Tie her to the fence and give her a bale of hay," she had murmured, drugged, and they teased her, excused her for such a welcoming, blaming the anesthesia, but it went deeper than that; *she* knew, and the *baby* knew: there was no love in the begetting. That was the secret, unforgivable, that not another good thing could ever make up for, where all the bad had come from, like a visitation, a punishment. She knew that was why Sylvie had been wild, had gone to earth so early, and before dying had made this child in sudden wedlock, a child who would be just like her, would carry the hurting on into another generation. A matter of time. No use raising her hand. But she *had* raised her hand. Still wore on its palm the memory of the sting of the collision with the girl's cheek; had she broken her jaw? Her heart? Of course not. She said it aloud: "Takes more than that."

She went to work then, doing what she could with her old tools. She pecked the clay on Sylvie's grave, new-looking, unhealed after years. She tried again, scattering seeds from her pocket, every last possible one of them. Off in the west she could hear the pulpwood cutters sawing through another acre across the lake. Nearer, there was the racket of motorcycles laboring cross-country, insect-like, distracting.

She took her bucket to the well and hung it on the pump. She had half filled it when the bikers roared up, right down the blue gravel, straight at her. She let the bucket overflow, staring. On the back of one of the machines was the girl. Sylvie's girl! Her bare arms wrapped around the shirtless man riding between her thighs. They were first. The second biker rode alone. She studied their strangers' faces as they circled her. They were the enemy, all of them. Laughing. The girl was laughing too, laughing like her mama did. Out in the middle of nowhere the girl had found these two men, some moth-musk about her drawing them (too soon!) to what? She shouted it: "What in God's—" They roared off without answering her, and the bucket of water tipped over, spilling its stain blood-dark on the red dust.

The dog went wild barking, leaping after them, snapping at the tires, and there was no calling him down. The bikers made a wide circuit of the churchyard, then roared straight across the graves, leaping the ditch and landing upright on the road again, heading off toward the reservoir.

Furious, she ran to her car, past the barking dog, this time leaving him behind, driving after them, horn blowing nonstop, to get back what was not theirs. She drove after them knowing what they did not know, that all the roads beyond that point dead-ended. She surprised them, swinging the Impala across their path, cutting them off; let them hit it! They stopped. She got out, breathing hard, and said, when she could, "She's underage." Just that. And put out her claiming hand with an authority that made the girl's arms drop from the man's insolent waist and her legs tremble.

"I was just riding," the girl said, not looking up.

Behind them the sun was heading on toward down. The long shadows of the pines drifted back and forth in the same breeze that puffed the distant sails on the lake. Dead limbs creaked and clashed overhead like the antlers of locked and furious beasts.

"Sheeeut," the lone rider said. "I told you." He braced with his muddy boot and leaned out from his machine to spit. The man the girl had been riding with had the invading sort of eyes the woman had spent her lifetime bolting doors against. She met him now, face to face.

"Right there, missy," her granny said, pointing behind her to the car.

The girl slid off the motorcycle and stood halfway between her choices. She started slightly at the poosh! as he popped another top and chugged the beer in one uptilting of his head. His eyes never left the woman's. When he was through, he tossed the can high, flipping it end over end. Before it hit the ground he had his pistol out and, firing once, winged it into the lake.

"Freaking lucky shot," the other one grudged.

"I don't need luck," he said. He sighted down the barrel of the gun at the woman's head. "POW!" he yelled, and when she recoiled, he laughed. He swung around to the girl; he kept aiming the gun, there, high, low, all around. "Y'all settle it," he said, with a shrug.

The girl had to understand him then, had to know him, had to know better. But still she hesitated. He kept looking at her, then away.

"She's fifteen," her granny said. "You can go to jail."

"You can go to hell," he said.

"Probably will," her granny told him. "I'll save you a seat by the fire." She took the girl by the arm and drew her to the car; she backed up, swung around, and headed out the road toward the churchyard for her tools and dog. The whole way the girl said nothing, just hunched against the far door, staring hard-eyed out at the pines going past.

The woman finished watering the seed in, and collected her tools. As she worked, she muttered, "It's your own kin buried here, you might have the decency to glance this way one time . . ." The girl was finger-tweezing her eyebrows in the side mirror. She didn't look around as the dog and the woman got in. Her granny shifted hard, sending the tools clattering in the trunk.

When they came to the main road, there were the men. Watching for them. Waiting for them. They kicked their machines into life and followed, close, bumping them, slapping the old fenders, yelling. The girl gave a wild glance around at the one by her door and said, "Gran'ma?" and as he drew his pistol, "Gran'ma!" just as the gun nosed into the open window. She frantically cranked the glass up between her and the weapon, and her granny, seeing, spat, "Fool!" She never had been one to pray for peace or rain. She stamped the accelerator right to the floor.

The motorcycles caught up. Now she braked, hard, and swerved off the road into an alley between the pines, not even wide enough for the school bus, just a fire scrape that came out a quarter mile from her own house, if she could get that far. She slewed on the pine straw, then righted, tearing along the dark tunnel through the woods. She had for the time being bested them; they were left behind. She was winning. Then she hit the wallow where the tadpoles were already five weeks old. The Chevy plowed in and stalled. When she got it cranked again, they were stuck. The tires spattered mud three feet up the near trunks as she tried to spin them out, to rock them out. Useless. "Get out and run!" she cried, but the trees were too close on the passenger side. The girl couldn't open her door. She wasted precious time having to crawl out under the steering wheel. The woman waited but the dog ran on.

They struggled through the dusky woods, their pace slowed by the thick straw and vines. Overhead, in the last light, the martins were reeling free and sure after their prey.

"Why? Why?" the girl gasped, as they lunged down the old deer trail. Behind them they could hear shots, and glass breaking as the men came to the bogged car. The woman kept on running, swatting their way clear through the shoulder-high weeds. They could see the Greer cottage, and made for it. But it was ivied-over, padlocked, the woodpile dry-rotting under its tarp, the electric meterbox empty on the pole. No help there.

The dog, excited, trotted on, yelping, his lips white-flecked. He scented the lake and headed that way, urging them on with thirsty yips. On the clay shore, treeless, deserted, at the utter limit of land, they stood defenseless, listening to the men coming on, between them and home. The woman pressed her hand to her mouth, stifling her cough. She was exhausted. She couldn't think.

"We can get under!" the girl cried suddenly, and pointed toward the Greers' dock, gap-planked, its walkway grounded on the mud. They splashed out to it, wading in, the woman grabbing up the telltale, tattletale dog in her arms. They waded out to the far end and ducked under. There was room between the foam floats for them to crouch neck-deep.

The dog wouldn't hush, even then, never had yet, and there wasn't time to teach him. When the woman realized that, she did what she had to do. She grabbed him, whimpering; held him; held him under till the struggle ceased and the bubbles rose silver from his fur. They crouched there then, the two of them, submerged to the shoulders, feet unsteady on the slimed lake bed. They listened. The sky went from rose to ocher to violet in the cracks over their heads. The motorcycles had stopped now. In the silence there was the glissando of locusts, the dry crunch of boots on the flinty beach, their low man-talk drifting as they prowled back and forth. One of them struck a match.

"—they in these woods we could burn 'em out."

The wind carried their voices away into the pines. Some few words eddied back.

"—lippy old smartass do a little work on her knees besides praying—"

Laughter. It echoed off the deserted house. They were getting closer.

One of them strode directly out to the dock, walked on the planks over their heads. They could look up and see his boot soles. He was the one with the gun. He slapped a mosquito on his bare back and cursed. The carp, roused by the troubling of the waters, came nosing around the dock, guzzling and snorting. The girl and her granny held still, so still. The man fired his pistol into the shadows, and a wounded fish thrashed, dying. The man knelt and reached for it, chuffing out his beery breath. He belched. He pawed the lake for the dead fish, cursing as it floated out of reach. He shot it again, firing at it till it sank and the gun was empty. Cursed that too. He stood then and unzipped and relieved himself of some of the beer. They had to listen to that. To know that about him. To endure that, unprotesting.

Back and forth on shore the other one ranged, restless. He lit another cigarette. He coughed. He called, "Hey! They got away, man, that's all. Don't get your shorts in a wad. Let's go."

"Yeah." He finished. He zipped. He stumbled back across the planks and leaped to shore, leaving the dock tilting amid widening ripples. Underneath, they waited.

The bike cranked. The other ratcheted, ratcheted, then coughed, caught, roared. They circled, cut deep ruts, slung gravel, and went. Their roaring died away and away. Crickets resumed and a near frog bic-bic-bicked.

Under the dock, they waited a little longer to be sure. Then they ducked below the water, scraped out from under the pontoon, and came up into free air, slogging toward shore. It had seemed warm enough in the water. Now they shivered. It was almost night. One streak of light still stood reflected on the darkening lake, drew itself thinner, narrowing into a final cancellation of day. A plane winked its way west.

The girl was trembling. She ran her hands down her arms and legs, shedding water like a garment. She sighed, almost a sob. The woman held the dog in her arms; she dropped to her knees upon the random stones and murmured, private, haggard, "Oh, honey," three times, maybe all three times for the dog, maybe once for each of them. The girl waited, watching. Her granny rocked the dog like a baby, like a dead child, rocked slower and slower and was still.

"I'm sorry," the girl said then, avoiding the dog's inert, empty eye.

"It was him or you," her granny said, finally, looking up. Looking her over. "Did they mess with you? With your britches? Did they?"

"No!" Then, quieter, "No, ma'am."

When the woman tried to stand up she staggered, lightheaded, clumsy with the freight of the dog. "No, ma'am," she echoed, fending off the girl's "Let me." And she said again, "It was him or you. I know that. I'm not going to rub your face in it." They saw each other as well as they could in that failing light, in any light.

The woman started toward home, saying, "Around here, we bear our own burdens." She led the way along the weedy shortcuts. The twilight bleached the dead limbs of the pines to bone. Insects sang in the thickets, silencing at their oncoming.

"We'll see about the car in the morning," the woman said. She bore her armful toward her own moth-ridden dusk-to-dawn security light with that country grace she had always had when the earth was reliably progressing underfoot. The girl walked close behind her, exactly where she walked, matching her pace, matching her stride, close enough to put her hand forth (if the need arose) and touch her granny's back where the faded voile was clinging damp, the merest gauze between their wounds.

🍂 🍂 🍂

Suggestions for Discussion

1. What early moment of tension sets the rest of the story in motion? Where is the final crisis, and what begins to change as a result of the grandmother's action?

2. The bikers have the obvious physical power in this story. But with what kinds of power does the grandmother counter them? What kind of power does she have over her granddaughter?

3. Where does the author show the girl making an emotional connection with her grandmother? Where are other moments of connection placed?

4. How, literally, is the situation at the end of this story the reverse of the situation at the beginning? How does Hood signal this?

🍂

Silver Water

AMY BLOOM

My sister's voice was like mountain water in a silver pitcher; the clear, blue beauty of it cools you and lifts you up beyond your heat, beyond your body. After we went to see *La Traviata*, when she was fourteen and I was twelve, she elbowed me in the parking lot and said, "Check this out." And she opened her mouth unnaturally wide and her voice came out, so crystalline and bright, that all the departing operagoers stood frozen by their cars, unable to take out their keys or open their doors until she had finished and then they cheered like hell.

That's what I like to remember and that's the story I told to all of her therapists. I wanted them to know her, to know that who they saw was not all there was to see. That before the constant tinkling of commercials and fast-food jingles, there had been Puccini and Mozart and hymns so sweet and mighty, you expected Jesus to come down off his cross and clap. That before there was a mountain of Thorazined fat, swaying down the halls in nylon maternity tops and sweatpants, there had been the prettiest girl in Arrandale Elementary School, the belle of Landmark Junior High. Maybe there were other pretty girls, but I didn't see them. To me, Rose, my beautiful blond defender, my guide to Tampax and my mother's moods, was perfect.

She had her first psychotic break when she was fifteen. She had been coming home moody and tearful, then quietly beaming, then she stopped coming home. She would go out into the woods behind our house and not come in until my mother would go out at dusk, and step gently into the briars and saplings and pull her out, blank-faced, her pale blue pullover covered with crumbled leaves, her white jeans smeared with dirt. After three weeks of this, my mother, who is a musician and widely regarded as eccentric, said to my father, who is a psychiatrist and a kind, sad man, "She's going off."

"What is that, your professional opinion?" He picked up the newspaper and put it down again, sighing. "I'm sorry, I didn't mean to snap at you. I know something's bothering her. Have you talked to her?"

"What's there to say? David, she's going crazy, she doesn't need a heart-to-heart talk with Mom, she needs a hospital."

They went back and forth and my father sat down with Rose for a few hours and she sat there, licking the hairs on her forearm, first one way, then the other. My mother stood in the hallway, dry-eyed and pale, watching the two of them. She had already packed Rose's bag and when three of my father's friends dropped by to offer free consultations and recommendations, my mother and Rose's suitcase were already in the car. My mother hugged me and told me that they would be back that night, but not with Rose. She also said, divining my worst fear, "It won't happen to you, honey. Some people go crazy and some never do. You never will." She smiled and stroked my hair. "Not even when you want to."

Rose was in hospitals, great and small, for the next ten years. She had lots of terrible therapists and a few good ones. One place had no pictures on the walls, no windows, and the patients all wore slippers with the hospital crest on them. My mother didn't even bother to go to Admissions. She turned Rose around and the two of them marched out, my father, trailing behind them, apologizing to his colleagues. My mother ignored the psychiatrists, the social workers and the nurses and she played Handel and Bessie Smith for the patients on whatever piano was available. At some places, she had a Steinway donated by a grateful, or optimistic family; at others she banged out "Gimme a Pigfoot" on an old, scarred box that hadn't been tuned since there'd been English-speaking physicians on the grounds. My father talked in serious, appreciative voices to the administrators and unit chiefs and tried to be friendly with whoever was managing Rose's case. We all hated the family therapists.

The worst family therapist we ever had sat in a pale green room with us, visibly taking stock of my mother's ethereal beauty and her faded blue T-shirt and girl-sized jeans, my father's rumpled suit and stained tie and my own unreadable, sixteen-year-old fashion statement. Rose was beyond fashion that year, in one of her dancing teddy-bear smocks and extra-extra-large Celtics sweatpants. Mr. Walker read Rose's file in front of us and then watched, in alarm, as Rose began crooning, beautifully, and slowly massaging her breasts. My mother and I started to laugh and even my father started to smile. This was Rose's usual opening salvo for new therapists.

Mr. Walker said, "I wonder why it is that everyone is so entertained by Rose behaving inappropriately."

Rose burped and then we all laughed. This was the seventh family therapist we had seen and none of them had lasted very long. Mr. Walker, unfortunately, was determined to do right by us.

"What do you think of Rose's behavior, Violet?" They did this sometimes. In their manual, it must say, if you think the parents are too weird, try talking to the sister.

"I don't know. Maybe she's trying to get you to stop talking about her in the third person."

"Nicely put," my father said.

"Indeed," my mother said.

"Fuckin' A," Rose said.

"Well, this is something that the whole family agrees upon," Mr. Walker said, trying to act as if he understood, or even liked us.

"That was not a successful intervention, Ferret Face." Rose tended to function better when she was angry. He did look like a blond ferret and we all laughed again. Even my father, who tried to give these people a chance out of some sense of collegiality, had given it up.

Mr. Walker decided, after fourteen minutes, that our time was up and walked out, leaving us grinning at each other. Rose was still nuts, but at least we'd all had a little fun.

Our best family therapist started out almost as badly. We scared off a resident and then scared off her supervisor, who sent us Dr. Thorne. Three hundred pounds of Texas chili, cornbread and Lone Star beer, finished off with big black cowboy boots and a little string tie around the area of his neck.

"Oh, frabjous day, it's Big Nut." Rose was in heaven and stopped massaging her breasts immediately.

"Hey, Little Nut." You have to understand how big a man would have to be to call my sister "little." He christened us all, right away. "And it's the good Doctor Nut, and Madame Hickory Nut, 'cause they are the hardest damn nuts to crack, and over here in the overalls and not much else, is No One's Nut"—a name which summed up both my sanity and my loneliness. We all relaxed.

Dr. Thorne was good for us. Rose moved into a halfway house, whose director loved Big Nut so much she kept Rose even when Rose went through a period of having sex with everyone who passed her door. She was in a fever for a while, trying to still the voices by fucking her brains out.

Big Nut said, "Darlin', I can't. I cannot make love to every beautiful woman I meet and, furthermore, I can't do that and be your therapist, too. It's a great shame, but I think you might be able to find a really nice guy, someone who treats you just as sweet and kind as I would, if I were lucky enough to be your beau. I don't want you to settle for less." And she stopped propositioning the crack addicts and the alcoholics and the guys at the shelter. We loved Dr. Thorne.

My father cut back on seeing rich neurotics and helped out one day a week at Dr. Thorne's walk-in clinic. My mother finished a record of Mozart concerti and played at fund-raisers for Rose's halfway house. I went back to college and found a wonderful linebacker from Texas to sleep with. In the dark, I would make him call me "darlin'." Rose took her meds, lost about fifty pounds and began singing at the A.M.E. Zion Church, down the street from the halfway house.

At first, they didn't know what to do with this big, blonde lady, dressed funny and hovering wistfully in the doorway during rehearsals, but she gave them a few bars of "Precious Lord" and the choir director felt God's hand and saw that, with the help of His sweet child, Rose, the Prospect Street Choir was going all the way to the Gospel Olympics.

Amidst a sea of beige, umber, cinnamon and espresso faces, there was Rose, bigger, blonder and pinker than any two white women could be. And Rose and the choir's contralto, Addie Robicheaux, laid their gold and silver voices and wove them together in strands as fine as silk, as strong as steel. And we wept as Rose and Addie, in their billowing garnet robes, swayed together, clasping hands until the last perfect note floated up to God and then they smiled down at us.

Rose would still go off from time to time and the voices would tell her to do bad things, but Dr. Thorne or Addie or my mother could usually bring her back. After five good years, Big Nut died. Stuffing his face with a chili dog, sitting in his un-air-conditioned office in the middle of July, he had one big, Texas-sized aneurism and died.

Rose held on tight for seven days; she took her meds, went to choir practice and rearranged her room about a hundred times. His funeral was a Lourdes for the mentally ill. If you were psychotic, borderline, bad-off neurotic, or just very hard to get along with, you were there. People shaking so bad from years of heavy meds that they fell out of the pews. People holding hands, crying, moaning, talking to themselves; the crazy and the not-so-crazy were all huddled together, like puppies at the pound.

Rose stopped taking her meds and the halfway house wouldn't keep her after she pitched another patient down the stairs. My father called the insurance company and found out that Rose's new, improved psychiatric coverage wouldn't begin for forty-five days. I put all of her stuff in a garbage bag and we walked out of the halfway house, Rose winking at the poor, drooling boy on the couch.

"This is going to be difficult—not all bad, but difficult—for the whole family and I thought we should discuss everybody's expectations. I know I have some concerns."

My father had convened a family meeting as soon as Rose had finished putting each one of her thirty stuffed bears in its own special place.

"No meds," Rose said, her eyes lowered, her stubby fingers, those fingers that had braided my hair and painted tulips on my cheeks, pulling hard on the hem of her dirty smock.

My father looked in despair at my mother.

"Rosie, do you want to drive the new car?" my mother asked.

Rose's face lit up. "I'd love to drive that car. I'd drive to California, I'd go see the bears at the San Diego Zoo. I would take you, Violet, but you always hated the zoo. Remember how she cried at the Bronx Zoo when she found out that the animals didn't get to go home at closing?" Rose put her damp hand on mine and squeezed it, sympathetically. "Poor Vi."

"If you take your medication, after a while, you'll be able to drive the car. That's the deal. Meds, car." My mother sounded accommodating but unenthusiastic, careful not to heat up Rose's paranoia.

"You got yourself a deal, darlin'."

I was living about an hour away then, teaching English during the day, writing poetry at night. I went home every few days, for dinner. I called every night.

My father said, quietly, "It's very hard. We're doing all right, I think. Rose has been walking in the mornings with your mother and she watches a lot of TV. She won't go to the day hospital and she won't go back to the choir. Her friend, Mrs. Robicheaux, came by a couple of times. What a sweet woman. Rose wouldn't even talk to her; she just sat there, staring at the wall and humming. We're not doing all that well, actually, but I guess we're getting by. I'm sorry, sweetheart, I don't mean to depress you."

My mother said, emphatically, "We're doing fine. We've got our routine and we stick to it and we're fine. You don't need to come home so often, you know. Wait till Sunday, just come for the day. Lead your life, Vi. She's leading hers."

I stayed away until Sunday, afraid to pick up my phone, grateful to my mother for her harsh calm and her reticence, the qualities that had enraged me throughout my childhood.

I came on a Sunday, in the early afternoon, to help my father garden, something we had always enjoyed together. We weeded and staked tomatoes and killed aphids while my mother and Rose were down at the lake. I didn't even get into the house until four, when I needed a glass of water.

Someone had broken the piano bench into five neatly stacked pieces and placed them where the piano bench usually was.

"We were having such a nice time, I couldn't bear to bring it up," my father said, standing in the doorway, carefully keeping his gardening boots out of the kitchen.

"What did Mommy say?"

"She said, 'Better the bench than the piano.' And your sister lay down on the floor and just wept. Then, your mother took her down to the lake. This can't go on, Vi. We have twenty-seven days left, your mother gets no sleep because Rose doesn't sleep and if I could just pay twenty-seven thousand dollars to keep her in the hospital until the insurance takes over, I'd do it."

"All right. Do it. Pay the money and take her back to Hartley-Rees. It was the prettiest place and she liked the art therapy there."

"I would if I could. The policy states that she must be symptom-free for at least forty-five days before her coverage begins. Symptom-free means no hospitalization."

"Jesus, Daddy, how could you get that kind of policy? She hasn't been symptom-free for forty-five minutes."

"It's the only one I could get for long-term psychiatric." He put his hand over his mouth to block whatever he was about to say and went back out to the garden. I couldn't see if he was crying.

He stayed outside and I stayed inside, until Rose and my mother came home from the lake. Rose's soggy sweatpants were rolled up to her knees and she had a bucketful of shells and gray stones, which my mother persuaded her to leave on the back porch. My mother kissed me lightly and told Rose to go up to her room and change out of her wet pants.

Rose's eyes grew very wide. "Never. I will never . . ." she began banging her head with rhythmic intensity, against the kitchen floor, throwing all of her weight behind each attack. My mother put her arms around Rose's waist and tried to hold her back. Rose shook her off, not even looking around to see what was slowing her down. My mother crumpled next to the refrigerator.

"Violet, please . . ."

I threw myself onto the kitchen floor, becoming the spot that Rose was smacking her head against. She stopped a fraction of an inch short of my stomach.

"Oh, Vi, Mommy, I'm sorry. I'm sorry, don't hate me." She staggered to her feet and ran, wailing, to her room.

My mother got up and washed her face, brusquely rubbing it dry with a dishcloth. My father heard the wailing and came running in, slipping his long bare feet out of his rubber boots.

"Galen, Galen, let me see." He held her head and looked closely for bruises on her pale, small face. "What happened?" My mother looked at me. "Violet, what happened? Where's Rose?"

"Rose got upset and when she went running upstairs, she pushed Mommy out of the way." I've only told three lies in my life and that was my second.

"She must feel terrible, pushing you, of all people. It would have to be you, but I know she didn't want it to be." He made my mother a cup of tea and all the love he had for her, despite her silent rages and her vague stares, came pouring through the teapot, warming her cup, filling her small, long-fingered hands. He stood by her and she rested her head against his hip. I looked away.

"Let's make dinner, then I'll call her. Or you call her, David, maybe she'd rather see your face first."

Dinner was filled with all of our starts and stops and Rose's desperate efforts to control herself. She could barely eat and hummed the McDonald's theme song over and over again, pausing only to spill her juice down the front of her smock and begin weeping. My father looked at my mother and handed Rose his napkin. She dabbed at herself, listlessly, but the tears stopped.

"I want to go to bed. I want to go to bed and be in my head. I want to go to bed and be in my bed and in my head and just wear red. For red is the color that my baby wore and once more, it's true, yes, it is, it's true. Please don't wear red tonight, ohh, ohh, please don't wear red tonight, for red is the color—"

"Okay, okay, Rose. It's okay. I'll go upstairs with you and you can get ready for bed. Then Mommy will come up and say good night, too. It's okay, Rose." My father reached out his hand and Rose grasped it and they walked out of the dining room together, his long arm around her middle.

My mother sat at the table for a moment, her face in her hands and then she began clearing the table. We cleared without talking, my mother humming Schubert's "Schlummerlied," a lullaby about the woods and the river calling to the child to go to sleep. She sang it to us every night, when we were small.

My father came back into the kitchen and signaled to my mother. She went upstairs and they came back down together, a few minutes later.

"She's asleep," they said and we went to sit on the porch and listen to the crickets. I don't remember the rest of the evening, but I remember it as quietly sad and I remember the rare sight of my parents holding hands, sitting on the picnic table, watching the sunset.

I woke up at three o'clock in the morning, feeling the cool night air through my sheet. I went down the hall for another blanket and looked into Rose's room, for no reason. She wasn't there. I put on my jeans and a sweater and went downstairs. I could feel her absence. I went outside and saw her wide, draggy footprints darkening the wet grass, into the woods.

"Rosie," I called, too softly, not wanting to wake my parents, not wanting to startle Rose, "Rosie, it's me. Are you here? Are you all right?"

I almost fell over her. Huge and white in the moonlight, her flowered smock bleached in the light and shadow, her sweatpants now completely wet. Her head, was flung back, her white, white neck exposed like a lost Greek column.

"Rosie, Rosie—" Her breathing was very slow and her lips were not as pink as they usually were. Her eyelids fluttered.

"Closing time," she whispered. I believe that's what she said.

I sat with her, uncovering the bottle of white pills by her hand, and watched the stars fade.

When the stars were invisible and the sun was warming the air, I went back to the house. My mother was standing on the porch, wrapped in a blanket, watching me. Every step I took overwhelmed me; I could picture my mother slapping me, shooting me for letting her favorite die.

"Warrior queens," she said, wrapping her thin strong arms around me. "I raised warrior queens." She kissed me fiercely and went into the woods by herself.

A little later, she woke my father, who could not go into the woods, and still later she called the police and the funeral parlor. She hung up the phone, lay down, and didn't get back out of bed until the day of the funeral. My father fed us both and called the people who needed to be called and picked out Rose's coffin by himself.

My mother played the piano and Addie sang her pure gold notes and I closed my eyes and saw my sister, fourteen years old, lion's mane thrown back and her eyes tightly closed against the glare of the parking lot lights. That sweet sound held us tight, flowing around us, eddying through our hearts, rising, still rising.

🖋 🖋 🖋

Suggestions for Discussion

1. Although Rose seems to occupy center stage, what makes this the narrator's story?
2. What conflicting pressures does Violet feel when she discovers Rose in the woods? Why has the author chosen to give Violet the final decision over Rose's life or death?
3. Why has the author of "Silver Water" placed a comic scene within this serious story? Is there a point in one of your own stories where a comic or absurd moment could make the situation seem more lifelike?
4. The story's crisis, at which Violet discovers Rose with the pill bottle, is reported sparely. Why does the author depict the story's most dramatic moment in this manner?

Happy Endings

MARGARET ATWOOD

John and Mary meet.
What happens next?
If you want a happy ending, try A.

A

John and Mary fall in love and get married. They both have worthwhile and remunerative jobs which they find stimulating and challenging. They buy a charming house. Real estate values go up. Eventually, when they can afford live-in help, they have two children, to whom they are devoted. The children turn out well. John and Mary have a stimulating and challenging sex life and worthwhile friends. They go on fun vacations together. They retire. They both have hobbies which they find stimulating and challenging. Eventually they die. This is the end of the story.

B

Mary falls in love with John but John doesn't fall in love with Mary. He merely uses her body for selfish pleasure and ego gratification of a tepid kind. He comes to her apartment twice a week and she cooks him dinner, you'll notice that he doesn't even consider her worth the price of a dinner out, and after he's eaten the dinner he fucks her and after that he falls asleep, while she does the dishes so he won't think she's untidy, having all those dirty dishes lying around, and puts on fresh lipstick so she'll look good when he wakes up, but when he wakes up he doesn't even notice, he puts on his socks and his shorts and his pants and his shirt and his tie and his shoes, the reverse order from the one in which he took them off. He doesn't take off Mary's clothes, she takes them off herself, she acts as if she's dying for it every time, not because she likes sex exactly, she doesn't, but she wants John to think she does because if they do it often enough surely he'll get used to her, he'll come to depend on her and they will get married, but John goes out the door with hardly so much as a good-night and three days later he turns up at six o'clock and they do the whole thing over again.

Mary gets run-down. Crying is bad for your face, everyone knows that and so does Mary but she can't stop. People at work notice. Her friends tell her John is a rat, a pig, a dog, he isn't good enough for her, but she can't believe it. Inside John, she thinks, is another John who is much nicer. This other John will emerge like a butterfly from a cocoon, a Jack from a box, a pit from a prune, if the first John is only squeezed enough.

One evening John complains about the food. He has never complained about the food before. Mary is hurt.

Her friends tell her they've seen him in a restaurant with another woman, whose name is Madge. It's not even Madge that finally gets to Mary: it's the restaurant. John has taken Mary to a restaurant. Mary collects all the sleeping pills and aspirins she can find, and takes them and a half a bottle of sherry. You can see what kind of a woman she is by the fact that it's not even whiskey. She leaves a note for John. She hopes he'll discover her and get her to the hospital in time and repent and then they can get married, but this fails to happen and she dies.

John marries Madge and everything continues as in A.

C

John, who is an older man, falls in love with Mary, and Mary, who is only twenty-two, feels sorry for him because he's worried about his hair falling out. She sleeps with him even though she's not in love with him. She met him at work. She's in love with someone called James, who is twenty-two also and not yet ready to settle down.

John on the contrary settled down long ago: this is what is bothering him. John has a steady, respectable job and is getting ahead in his field, but Mary isn't impressed by him, she's impressed by James, who has a motorcycle and a fabulous record collection. But James is often away on his motorcycle, being free. Freedom isn't the same for girls, so in the meantime Mary spends Thursday evenings with John. Thursdays are the only days John can get away.

John is married to a woman called Madge and they have two children, a charming house which they bought just before the real estate values went up, and hobbies which they find stimulating and challenging, when they have the time. John tells Mary how important she is to him, but of course he can't leave his wife because a commitment is a commitment. He goes on about this more than is necessary and

Mary finds it boring, but older men can keep it up longer so on the whole she has a fairly good time.

One day James breezes in on his motorcycle with some top-grade California hybrid and James and Mary get higher than you'd believe possible and they climb into bed. Everything becomes very underwater, but along comes John, who has a key to Mary's apartment. He finds them stoned and entwined. He's hardly in any position to be jealous, considering Madge, but nevertheless he's overcome with despair. Finally he's middle-aged, in two years he'll be bald as an egg and he can't stand it. He purchases a handgun, saying he needs it for target practice—this is the thin part of the plot, but it can be dealt with later—and shoots the two of them and himself.

Madge, after a suitable period of mourning, marries an understanding man called Fred and everything continues as in A, but under different names.

D
Fred and Madge have no problems. They get along exceptionally well and are good at working out any little difficulties that may arise. But their charming house is by the seashore and one day a giant tidal wave approaches. Real estate values go down. The rest of the story is about what caused the tidal wave and how they escape from it. They do, though thousands drown, but Fred and Madge are virtuous and lucky. Finally on high ground they clasp each other, wet and dripping and grateful, and continue as in A.

E
Yes, but Fred has a bad heart. The rest of the story is about how kind and understanding they both are until Fred dies. Then Madge devotes herself to charity work until the end of A. If you like, it can be "Madge," "cancer," "guilty and confused," and "bird watching."

F
If you think this is all too bourgeois, make John a revolutionary and Mary a counterespionage agent and see how far that gets you. Remember, this is Canada. You'll still end up with A, though in between you may get a lustful brawling saga of passionate involvement, a chronicle of our times, sort of.

You'll have to face it, the endings are the same however you slice it. Don't be deluded by any other endings, they're all fake, either deliberately fake, with malicious intent to deceive, or just motivated by excessive optimism if not by downright sentimentality.

The only authentic ending is the one provided here:
John and Mary die. John and Mary die. John and Mary die.

So much for endings. Beginnings are always more fun. True connoisseurs, however, are known to favor the stretch in between, since it's the hardest to do anything with.

That's about all that can be said for plots, which anyway are just one thing after another, a what and a what and a what.

Now try How and Why.

𝒷 𝒷 𝒷
Suggestions for Discussion

1. How does this story dramatize the notion that "only trouble is interesting"?

2. "Happy Endings" is more of an idea-based story than a character-driven one. Can you think of any other idea-based stories you may have read? What are some common differences between idea-based and character-driven stories?

3. How does the author use fiction as a metaphor for life? What is being suggested by the title and the ending?

Girl

JAMAICA KINCAID

Wash the white clothes on Monday and put them on the stone heap; wash the color clothes on Tuesday and put them on the clothesline to dry; don't walk barehead in the hot sun; cook pumpkin fritters in very hot sweet oil; soak your little cloths right after you take them off; when buying cotton to make yourself a nice blouse, be sure that it doesn't have gum on it, because that way it won't hold up well after a wash; soak salt fish overnight before you cook it; is it true that you sing benna in Sunday school?; always eat your food in such a way that it won't turn someone else's stomach; on Sundays try to walk like a lady and not like the slut you are so bent on becoming; don't sing benna in Sunday school; you mustn't speak to wharf-rat boys, not even to give directions; don't eat fruits on the street—flies will follow you; *but I don't sing benna on Sundays at all and never in Sunday school*; this is how to sew on a button; this is how to make a buttonhole for the button you have just sewed on; this is how to hem a dress when you see the hem coming down and so to prevent yourself from looking like the slut I know you are so bent on becoming; this is how you iron your father's khaki shirt so that it doesn't have a crease; this is how you iron your father's khaki pants so that they don't have a crease; this is how you grow okra—far from the house, because okra tree harbors red ants; when you are growing dasheen, make sure it gets plenty of water or else it makes your throat itch when you are eating it; this is how you sweep a corner; this is how you sweep a whole house; this is how you sweep a yard; this is how you smile to someone you don't like too much; this is how you smile to someone you don't like at all; this is how you smile to someone you like completely; this is how you set a table for tea; this is how you set a table for dinner; this is how you set a table for dinner with an important guest; this is how you set a table for lunch; this is how you set a table for breakfast; this is how to behave in the presence of men who don't know you very well, and this way they won't recognize immediately the slut I have warned you against becoming; be sure to wash every day, even if it is with your own spit; don't squat down to play marbles—you are not a boy, you know; don't pick people's flowers—you might catch something; don't throw stones at blackbirds, because it might not be a blackbird at all; this is how to make a bread pudding; this is how to make doukona; this is how to make pepper pot; this is how to make a good medicine for a cold; this is how to make a good medicine to throw away a child before it even becomes a child; this is how to catch a fish; this is how to throw back a fish you don't like, and that way something bad won't fall on you; this is how to bully a man; this is how a man bullies you; this is how to love a man, and if this doesn't work there are other ways, and if they don't work don't feel too bad about giving up; this is how to spit up in the air if you feel like it, and this is how to move quick so that it doesn't fall on you; this is how to make ends meet; always squeeze bread to make sure it's fresh; *but what if the baker won't let me feel the bread?*; you mean to say that after all you are really going to be the kind of woman who the baker won't let near the bread?

No One's a Mystery

ELIZABETH TALLENT

For my eighteenth birthday Jack gave me a five-year diary with a latch and a little key, light as a dime. I was sitting beside him scratching at the lock, which didn't want to work, when he thought he saw his wife's Cadillac in the distance, coming toward us. He pushed me down onto the dirty floor of the pickup and kept one hand on my head while I inhaled the musk of his cigarettes in the dashboard ashtray and sang along with Rosanne Cash on the tape deck. We'd been drinking tequila and the bottle was between his legs, resting up against his crotch, where the seam of his Levi's was bleached linen-white, though the Levi's were nearly new. I don't know why his Levi's always bleached like that, along the seams and at the knees. In a curve of cloth his zipper glinted, gold.

"It's her," he said. "She keeps the lights on in the daytime. I can't think of a single habit in a woman that irritates me more than that." When he saw that I was going to stay still he took his hand from my head and ran it through his own dark hair.

"Why does she?" I said.

"She thinks it's safer. Why does she need to be safer? She's driving exactly fifty-five miles an hour. She believes in those signs: 'Speed Monitored by Aircraft.' It doesn't matter that you can look up and see that the sky is empty."

"She'll see your lips move, Jack. She'll know you're talking to someone."

"She'll think I'm singing along with the radio."

He didn't lift his hand, just raised the fingers in salute while the pressure of his palm steadied the wheel, and I heard the Cadillac honk twice, musically; he was driving easily eighty miles an hour. I studied his boots. The elk heads stitched into the

leather were bearded with frayed thread, the toes were scuffed, and there was a compact wedge of muddy manure between the heel and the sole—the same boots he'd
been wearing for the two years I'd known him. On the tape deck Rosanne Cash
sang, "Nobody's into me, no one's a mystery."

"Do you think she's getting famous because of who her daddy is or for herself?"
Jack said.

"There are about a hundred pop tops on the floor, did you know that? Some little
kid could cut a bare foot on one of these, Jack."

"No little kids get into this truck except for you."

"How come you let it get so dirty?"

"'How come,'" he mocked. "You even sound like a kid. You can get back into the
seat now, if you want. She's not going to look over her shoulder and see you."

"How do you know?"

"I just know," he said. "Like I know I'm going to get meat loaf for supper. It's in
the air. Like I know what you'll be writing in that diary."

"What will I be writing?" I knelt on my side of the seat and craned around to look
at the butterfly of dust printed on my jeans. Outside the window Wyoming was daz-
zling in the heat. The wheat was fawn and yellow and parted smoothly by the thin
dirt road. I could smell the water in the irrigation ditches hidden in the wheat.

"Tonight you'll write, 'I love Jack. This is my birthday present from him. I can't
imagine anybody loving anybody more than I love Jack.'"

"I can't."

"In a year you'll write, 'I wonder what I ever really saw in Jack. I wonder why I
spent so many days just riding around in his pickup. It's true he taught me something
about sex. It's true there wasn't ever much else to do in Cheyenne.'"

"I won't write that."

"In two years you'll write, 'I wonder what that old guy's name was, the one with
the curly hair and the filthy dirty pickup truck and time on his hands.'"

"I won't write that."

"No?"

"Tonight I'll write, 'I love Jack. This is my birthday present from him. I can't
imagine anybody loving anybody more than I love Jack.'"

"No, you can't," he says. "You can't imagine it."

"In a year I'll write, 'Jack should be home any minute now. The table is set—my
grandmother's linen and her old silver and the yellow candles left over from the
wedding—but I don't know if I can wait until after the trout *a la Navarra* to make
love to him.'"

"It must have been a fast divorce."

"In two years I'll write, 'Jack should be home by now. Little Jack is hungry for his
supper. He said his first word today besides "Mama" and "Papa." He said, "Caca."'"

Jack laughed. "He was probably trying to fingerpaint with caca on the bathroom
wall when you heard him say it."

"In three years I'll write, 'My nipples are a little sore from nursing Eliza
Rosamund.'"

"Rosamund. Every little girl should have a middle name she hates."

"'Her breath smells like vanilla and her eyes are just Jack's color of blue.'"

"That's nice," Jack said.

"So? Which one do you like?"

"I like yours," he said. "But I believe mine."

"It doesn't matter. I believe mine."

"Not in your heart of hearts, you don't."

"You're wrong."

"I'm not wrong," he said. "And her breath would smell like your milk, and it's kind of a bittersweet smell, if you want to know the truth."

🐎 🐎 🐎

Suggestions for Discussion

Although perhaps the most difficult fictional form, short-short stories offer an instant glimpse of the elements of fiction.

1. Think back to the phrase "Drama equals desire plus danger." What is the source of danger in each story? What does each young woman want intensely enough to risk that danger?

2. Does one character "win" outright?

3. "Girl" is experimental in form, while "No One's a Mystery" is told in a realistic style. Despite these differences, how does the pattern of conflict-crisis-resolution apply to each?

4. Often an epiphany—a clear moment of insight—is shared by the character and the reader. Yet sometimes a reader has an epiphany about the situation, while the character remains in the dark. Do you find an epiphany in these stories? If so, is it shared by reader and character, or is it recognized only by the reader?

🐎

20/20

LINDA BREWER

By the time they reached Indiana, Bill realized that Ruthie, his driving companion, was incapable of theoretical debate. She drove okay, she went halves on gas, etc., but she refused to argue. She didn't seem to know how. Bill was used to East Coast women who disputed everything he said, every step of the way. Ruthie stuck to simple observations, like "Look, cows." He chalked it up to the fact that she was from rural Ohio and thrilled to death to be anywhere else.

She didn't mind driving into the setting sun. The third evening out, Bill rested his eyes while she cruised along making the occasional announcement.

"Indian paintbrush. A golden eagle."

Miles later he frowned. There was no Indian paintbrush, that he knew of, near Chicago.

The next evening, driving, Ruthie said, "I never thought I'd see a Bigfoot in real life." Bill turned and looked at the side of the road streaming innocently out behind them. Two red spots winked back—reflectors nailed to a tree stump.

"Ruthie, I'll drive," he said. She stopped the car and they changed places in the light of the evening star.

"I'm so glad I got to come with you," Ruthie said. Her eyes were big, blue, and capable of seeing wonderful sights. A white buffalo near Fargo. A UFO above Twin Falls. A handsome genius in the person of Bill himself. This last vision came to her in Spokane and Bill decided to let it ride.

🐾 🐾 🐾
Suggestions for Discussion

1. Paraphrase a definition of "epiphany" and apply it to the last paragraph of this story.

🐾 🐾 🐾
Writing Exercises

INDIVIDUAL

1. Write a short story on a postcard. Send it. Notice that if you're going to manage a conflict, crisis, and resolution in this small space, you'll have to introduce the conflict immediately.

2. A character's decision at the crisis point is usually confirmed in action (such as the doctor's prying the child's mouth open in "The Use of Force"). Choose three of the story seeds you generated with chapter 1 assignments: What is the crisis of each event? What action expresses this crisis?

3. Write a scene (dialogue and action between two or more characters in a specific place and time) placing two characters in this very fundamental conflict: One wants something that the other does not want to give. The something may be anything—money, respect, jewelry, sex, information, a match—but be sure to focus on the one desire.

4. A slightly more complicated variation on the same theme: Each of two characters has half of something that is no good without the other half. Neither wants to give up his or her half.

5. Write a very short story, no longer than three pages, in which the protagonist does *not* get what s/he wants, but which nevertheless ends in a satisfying way.

6. Write a scene in which a character is in a restaurant and, in going from the table to the restroom, passes his or her old love on a date with a new love.

DEVELOPMENT/REVISION

7. Look back at an autobiographical freewrite or draft based on a chapter 1 exercise.
   - What choice did "you" have to make at some point in that episode?
   - What made it a difficult choice? Could those pressures be intensified to create a more dramatic story?
   - How were "you" changed by it, even in a small way?

8. How does the phrase "only trouble is interesting" apply to your story-in-progress?

9. "Change" can be easier to measure than "plot," especially when you are close to the first draft of your story. Early on, it may be more helpful to ask yourself "does my character/situation change?" than "does my story have a plot?"

10. Once you've written a draft of a dialogue scene, go back and "ground" it in the physical world by adding:
    a. two actions or gestures that will help us see another important character
    b. two physical descriptions of another character that will help us visualize him or her
    c. two setting or atmosphere details that will help put readers in the scene

11. The dramatic elements of a full-length story—crisis, power shifts, emotional connections, and withdrawals—are often mirrored on a smaller scale within a scene. Try analyzing one of your own scenes, asking yourself:
    - What kind of power does each of the main characters have?
    - Where is there at least one shift in power—or even a failed attempt to take power?
    - Where is there at least one moment of making or breaking the emotional connection between the characters? Does it raise the emotional temperature?
    - Is there a mini-crisis or turning point? Something that is said or done, however minor, after which things cannot go back to quite the way they were before?

COLLABORATIVE

12. Most writers create stories intuitively, without a "game plan." Nonetheless, at some point you may get an idea for a story from its crisis, which will require plotting backwards to find out how the character reached such an extreme point. This group exercise adapted from John Gardner's *The Art of Fiction* allows you to work through an example of plotting backwards:

    > A man (or woman) sets his house on fire, but insurance money is not the motive. Working in a small group, plot the story that led him to this point. Then choose three scenes that should be dramatized, in addition to the crisis scene of setting the fire.

    Compare your stories and scenes with those of the other groups.

13. With a partner, describe your story-in-progress first in terms of a power struggle, and then in terms of the network pattern of making and breaking emotional connections.

14. Think back to the statement that "the thing the character wants need not be violent or spectacular: it is the intensity of the wanting that introduces an element of danger." Find a word or phrase that represents what the character desires intensely. Cluster this central phrase and draw the connections between elements. At the end of five minutes, read over the cluster, then explain its significance to a partner, along with any new insights the writing revealed to you.

15. Exchange scenes with a partner. Put an X by the line where you hear a turning point in the scene. Go around the room reading only these lines aloud to get a sense of what a turning point might sound like. How many of these turning points were also power shifts or moments of connection?

16. In front of the class, try an improvisation. Two women or two men play roommates and best friends. Friend One has just decided to break up with a long-term boyfriend or girlfriend. In the first improvisation, Friend Two thinks this is a great idea and agrees with every reason that Friend One mentions. Let this run for a few minutes and see what happens. Then repeat the situation, but this time Friend Two thinks breaking up is the worst possible thing Friend One could do and argues with every justification offered.

    Afterwards, have the actors and class audience discuss the differences. Which scene was more interesting? Which was harder to act and might therefore be harder to write?

3

SEEING IS BELIEVING
Showing and Telling

- *Significant Detail*

- *Filtering*

- *The Active Voice*

- *Prose Rhythm*

- *Mechanics*

Literature offers feelings for which we do not have to pay. It allows us to love, condemn, condone, hope, dread, and hate without any of the risks those feelings ordinarily involve, for even good feelings—intimacy, power, speed, drunkenness, passion—have consequences, and powerful feelings may risk powerful consequences. Fiction also must contain ideas, which give significance to characters and events. If the ideas are shallow or untrue, the fiction will be correspondingly shallow or untrue. But the ideas must be experienced through or with the characters; they must be felt or the fiction will fail also.

Much nonfiction writing, from editorials to advertising, also tries to persuade us to feel one way rather than another, but nonfiction works largely by means of logic and reasoning. Fiction tries to reproduce the emotional impact of experience. And this is a more difficult task, because unlike the images of film and drama, which directly strike the eye and ear, words are transmitted first to the mind, where they must be translated into images.

In order to move your reader, the standard advice runs, "Show, don't tell." This dictum can be confusing, considering that words are all a writer has to work with. What it means is that your job as a fiction writer is to focus attention not on the words, which are inert, nor on the thoughts these words produce, but through these to felt experience, where the vitality of understanding lies. There are techniques for accomplishing this—for making narrative vivid, moving, and resonant—which can be partly learned and always strengthened.

Significant Detail

In *The Elements of Style*, William Strunk, Jr., writes:

> If those who have studied the art of writing are in accord on any one point, it is on this: the surest way to arouse and hold the attention of the reader is by being specific, definite and concrete. The greatest writers . . . are effective largely because they deal in particulars and report the details that matter.

Specific, definite, concrete, particular details—these are the life of fiction. Details (as every good liar knows) are the stuff of persuasiveness. Mary is sure that Ed forgot to go pay the gas bill last Tuesday, but Ed says, "I know I went, because this old guy in a knit vest was in front of me in the line, and went on and on about his twin granddaughters"—and it is hard to refute a knit vest and twins even if the furnace doesn't work. John Gardner in *The Art of Fiction* speaks of details as "proofs," rather like those in a geometric theorem or a statistical argument. The novelist, he says, "gives us such details about the streets, stores, weather, politics, and concerns of Cleveland (or wherever the setting is) and such details about the looks, gestures, and experiences of his characters that we cannot help believing that the story he tells us is true."

A detail is "definite" and "concrete" when it appeals to the senses. It should be seen, heard, smelled, tasted, or touched. The most superficial survey of any bookshelf of published fiction will turn up dozens of examples of this principle. Here is a fairly obvious one.

> It was a narrow room, with a rather high ceiling, and crowded from floor to ceiling with goodies. There were rows and rows of hams and sausages of all shapes and colors—white, yellow, red and black; fat and lean and round and long—rows of canned preserves, cocoa and tea, bright translucent glass bottles of honey, marmalade and jam.
>
> I stood enchanted, straining my ears and breathing in the delightful atmosphere and the mixed fragrance of chocolate and smoked fish and earthy truffles. I spoke into the silence, saying: "Good day" in quite a loud voice; I can still remember how my strained, unnatural tones died away in the stillness. No one answered. And my mouth literally began to water like a spring. One quick, noiseless step and I was beside one of the laden tables. I made one rapturous grab into the nearest glass urn, filled as it chanced with chocolate creams, slipped a fistful into my coat pocket, then reached the door, and in the next second was safely round the corner.

Thomas Mann, *Confessions of Felix Krull, Confidence Man*

The shape of this passage is a tour through the five senses. Mann lets us see: *narrow room, high ceiling, hams, sausages, preserves, cocoa, tea, glass bottles, honey, marmalade, jam.* He lets us smell: *fragrance of chocolate, smoked fish, earthy truffles.* He lets us hear: *"Good day," unnatural tones, stillness.* He lets us taste: *mouth, water like a spring.* He lets us touch: *grab, chocolate creams, slipped, fistful into my coat pocket.* The writing is alive because we do in fact live through our sense perceptions, and Mann takes us past words and through thought to let us perceive the scene in this way.

In this process, a number of ideas not stated reverberate off the sense images, so that we are also aware of a number of generalizations the author might have made but does not need to make; we will make them ourselves. Mann could have had his character "tell" us: *I was quite poor, and I was not used to seeing such a profusion of food, so that although I was very afraid there might be someone in the room and that I might be caught stealing, I couldn't resist taking the risk.*

Such a version would be very flat, and none of that telling is necessary as all these points are "shown." The character's relative poverty is inherent in the tumble of images of sight and smell; if he were used to such displays, his eyes and nose would not dart about as they do. His fear is inherent in the "strained, unnatural tones" and their dying away in the stillness. His desire is in his watering mouth, his fear in the furtive speed of "quick" and "grab" and "slipped."

The points to be made here are two, and they are both important. The first is that the writer must deal in sense detail. The second is that these must be details "that matter." As a writer of fiction you are at constant pains not simply to say what you mean, but to mean more than you say. Much of what you mean will be an abstraction or a judgment—*love requires trust, children can be cruel.* But if you write in abstractions or judgments, you are writing an essay, whereas if you let us use our senses and form our own interpretations, we will be involved as participants in a real way. Much of the pleasure of reading comes from the egotistical sense that we are clever enough to understand. When the author explains to us or interprets for us, we suspect that he or she doesn't think us bright enough to do it for ourselves.

A detail is *concrete* if it appeals to one of the five senses; it is *significant* if it also conveys an idea or a judgment or both. *The windowsill was green* is concrete, because we can see it. *The windowsill was shedding flakes of fungus-green paint* is concrete and also significant because it conveys the idea that the paint is old and suggests the judgment that the color is ugly. The second version can also be seen more vividly. (For further discussion of selecting detail, see chapter 10, "How Fictional Elements Contribute to Theme," page 360.)

Here is a passage from a young writer, which fails through lack of appeal to the senses.

Debbie was a very stubborn and completely independent person and was always doing things her way despite her parents' efforts to get her to conform. Her father was an executive in a dress manufacturing company and was able to afford his family all the luxuries and comforts of life. But Debbie was completely indifferent to her family's affluence.

This passage contains a number of judgments we might or might not share with the author, and she has not convinced us that we do. What constitutes stubbornness? Independence? Indifference? Affluence? Further, since the judgments are supported by generalizations, we have no sense of the individuality of the characters, which alone would bring them to life on the page. What things was she always doing? What efforts did her parents make to get her to conform? What level of executive? What dress manufacturing company? What luxuries and comforts?

> Debbie would wear a tank top to a tea party if she pleased, with fluorescent earrings and ankle-strap sandals.
> "Oh, sweetheart," Mrs. Chiddister would stand in the doorway wringing her hands. "It's not *nice*."
> "Not who?" Debbie would say, and add a fringed belt.
> Mr. Chiddister was Artistic Director of the Boston branch of Cardin and had a high respect for what he called "elegant textures," which ranged from handwoven tweed to gold filigree, and which he willingly offered his daughter. Debbie preferred her laminated wrist bangles.

We have not passed a final judgment on the merits of these characters, but we know a good deal more about them, and we have drawn certain interim conclusions that are our own and not forced on us by the author. Debbie is independent of her parents' values, rather careless of their feelings, energetic, and possibly a tart. Mrs. Chiddister is quite ineffectual. Mr. Chiddister is a snob, though perhaps Debbie's taste is so bad we'll end up on his side.

But maybe that isn't at all what the author had in mind. The point is that we weren't allowed to know what the author did have in mind. Perhaps it was more like this version:

> One day Debbie brought home a copy of *Ulysses*. Mrs. Strum called it "filth" and threw it across the sunporch. Debbie knelt on the parquet and retrieved her bookmark, which she replaced. "No, it's not," she said.
> "You're not so old I can't take a strap to you!" Mr. Strum reminded her.
> Mr. Strum was controlling stockholder of Readywear Conglomerates and was proud of treating his family, not only on his salary, but also on his expense account. The summer before, he had justified their company on a trip to Belgium, where they toured the American Cemetery and the torture chambers of Ghent Castle. Entirely ungrateful, Debbie had spent the rest of the trip curled up in the hotel with a shabby copy of some poet.

Now we have a much clearer understanding of *stubbornness, independence, indifference,* and *affluence,* both their natures and the value we are to place on them. This time our judgment is heavily weighed in Debbie's favor—partly because people who read books have a sentimental sympathy with people who read books—but also because we hear hysteria in "filth" and "take a strap to you," whereas Debbie's resistance is quiet and strong. Mr. Strum's attitude toward his expense account suggests that he's corrupt, and his choice of "luxuries" is morbid. The passage does contain two overt judgments, the first being that Debbie was "entirely ungrateful." Notice that by the time we get to this, we're aware that the judgment is Mr. Strum's and that Debbie has little enough to be grateful for. We understand not only what the author says but also that she means the opposite of what she says, and we feel doubly clever to get it; that is the pleasure of irony. Likewise, the judgment that the poet's book is "shabby" shows Mr. Strum's crass materialism toward what we know to be the finer things. At the very end of the passage, we are denied a detail that we might very well be given: *What* poet did Debbie curl up with? Again, by this time we understand that we are being given Mr. Strum's view of the situation and that it's Mr. Strum (not Debbie, not the author, and certainly not us) who wouldn't notice the difference between John Keats and Stanley Kunitz.

It may be objected that both rewrites of the passage are longer than the original. Doesn't "adding" so much detail make for long writing? The answer is yes and no. No, because in the rewrites we know so much more about the values, activities, lifestyles, attitudes, and personalities of the characters that it would take many times the length of the original to "tell" it all in generalizations. Yes, in the sense that detail requires words, and if you are to realize your characters through detail, then you must be careful to select the details that convey the characteristics essential to our understanding. You can't convey a whole person, or a whole action, or everything there is to be conveyed about a single moment of a single day. You must select the significant.

In fact, the greater significance of realistic details may emerge only as you continue to develop and revise your story, for, as Flannery O'Connor says, "the longer you look at one object, the more of the world you see in it." Just as in the story "Linoleum Roses" that comes near the end of this chapter, where roses imprisoned in the patterned floor mirror the image of the child bride trapped in her apartment and the too-hasty marriage, certain details "tend to accumulate meaning from the action of the story itself" becoming "symbolic in the way they work," O'Connor notes. "While having their essential place in the literal level of the story, [details] operate in depth as well as on the surface, increasing the story in every direction."

No amount of concrete detail will move us, therefore, unless it also implicitly suggests meaning and value. Following is a passage that fails, not because it lacks detail, but because those details lack significance.

> Terry Landon, a handsome young man of twenty-two, was six foot four and broad-shouldered. He had medium-length thick blond hair and a natural tan, which set off the blue of his intense and friendly long-lashed eyes.

Here we have a good deal of generic sensory information, but we still know very little about Terry. There are so many broad-shouldered twenty-two-year-olds in the world, so many blonds, and so on. This sort of cataloging of characteristics suggests an all-points bulletin: *Male Caucasian, medium height, dark hair, last seen wearing gray raincoat.* Such a description may help the police locate a suspect in a crowd, but the assumption is that the identity of the person is not known. As an author you want us to know the character individually and immediately.

The fact is that all our ideas and judgments are formed through our sense perceptions, and daily, moment by moment, we receive information that is not merely sensuous in this way. Four people at a cocktail party may *do* nothing but stand and nibble canapés and may *talk* nothing but politics and the latest films. But you feel perfectly certain that X is furious at Y, who is flirting with Z, who is wounding Q, who is trying to comfort X. You have only your senses to observe with. How do you reach these conclusions? By what gestures, glances, tones, touches, choices of words?

It may be that this constant emphasis on judgment makes the author, and the reader, seem opinionated or self-righteous. "I want to present my characters objectively/neutrally. I'm not making any value judgments. I want the reader to make up his or her own mind." Yet human beings are constantly judging: *How was the film? He seemed friendly. What a boring class! Do you like it here? She's very thin. That's fascinating. I'm so clumsy. You're gorgeous tonight. Life is crazy, isn't it?*

The fact is that when we are not passing such judgments, it's because we aren't much interested; we are indifferent. Although you may not want to sanctify or damn your characters, you do want us to care about them, and if you refuse to direct our judgment, you may be inviting our indifference. Usually, when you "don't want us to judge," you mean that you want our feelings to be mixed, paradoxical, complex. *She's horribly irritating, but it's not her fault. He's sexy, but there's something cold about it underneath.* If this is what you mean, then you must direct our judgment in both or several directions, not in no direction.

Even a character who doesn't exist except as a type or function will come to life if presented through significant detail, as in this portrait of an aunt in Dorothy Allison's story "Don't Tell Me You Don't Know." Like many of the female relatives the adult narrator mentions, the aunt embodies a powerful, nurturing force that nonetheless failed to protect the narrator from childhood abuse.

> My family runs to heavy women, gravy-fed working women, the kind usually seen in pictures taken at mining disasters. Big women, all of my aunts move under their own power and stalk around telling everybody else what to do. But Aunt Alma was the prototype, the one I had loved most, starting back when she had given us free meals in the roadhouse she'd run for awhile . . . Once there, we'd be fed on chicken gravy and biscuits, and Mama would be fed from the well of her sister's love and outrage.

For a character who is a "prototype," we have a remarkably clear image of this woman. Notice how Allison moves us from generalization toward sharpness of image, gradually bringing the character into focus. First she has only a size and gender, then a certain abstract "power" and an appeal to our visual memory of the grieving, tough women seen in documentary photographs; then a distinct role as the one who "had given us free meals" when the family hit hard times. Once in focus as manager of a particular roadhouse "on the Eustis Highway," Alma's qualities again become generalized to the adult women of the family.

Good writers may "tell" about almost anything in fiction except the characters' feelings. One may tell the reader that the character went to a private school . . . or one may tell the reader that the character hates spaghetti; but with rare exceptions the characters' feelings must be demonstrated: fear, love, excitement, doubt, embarrassment, despair become real only when they take the form of events—action (or gesture), dialogue, or physical reaction to setting. Detail is the lifeblood of fiction.

John Gardner

The power in them, the strength and the heat! . . . How could my daddy, my uncles, ever stand up to them, dare to raise hand or voice to them? They were a power on the earth.

Finally, the focus narrows to the individual again, whose body has been formed by the starchy foods that poverty made a necessity and that at least kept hunger temporarily at bay: "My aunt always made biscuits. What else stretched so well? Now those starch meals shadowed her loose shoulders and dimpled her fat white elbows."

The point is not that an author must never express an idea, general quality, or judgment. But, in order to carry the felt weight of fiction, these abstractions must be realized through the senses—"I smelled chicken gravy and hot grease, the close thick scent of love and understanding." Through details these abstract qualities live.

WRITING ABOUT EMOTION

Fiction offers feelings for which the reader doesn't pay–and yet to evoke those feelings, it is often necessary to re-create through detail sensations that the reader may have experienced. Simply labeling a character's emotion as love or hatred will have little effect, for such abstraction operates solely on a vague, intellectual level; rather, emotion is the body's physical reaction to information the senses receive. The great Russian director Stanislavski, originator of realistic "Method" acting, urged his students to abandon the clichéd emotive postures of the nineteenth-century stage in favor of emotions evoked by the actor's recollection of sensory details connected with a personal past trauma. By recalling such details as the tingling of fingertips, the smell of singed hair, and the tensing of calf muscles, an emotion such as anger might naturally be induced within the actor's body.

Similarly, in written fiction, if the writer depicts the precise physical sensations experienced by the character, a particular emotion may be triggered by the reader's own sense memory. For example, in the story "Where Are You Going, Where Have You Been?" at the end of this chapter, the reader may reflexively identify with the

> The past is beautiful because one never realizes an emotion at the time. It expands later, and thus we don't have complete emotions about the present, only about the past . . . That is why we dwell on the past, I think.
>
> Virginia Woolf

protagonist's terror through a personal memory of fear in which vision became blurred and a pumping heart felt too big for its chest, or perhaps from a nightmare in which fingers were too weak to dial a telephone. To simply state that the main character is afraid would keep her at a dispassionate distance, but to dramatize her fear through physical detail allows a reader to share the experience.

In his story "The Easy Way," author Tom Perrotta describes the moment in which a lottery winner learns of a jealous friend's death: "I stood perfectly still and let the news expand inside of me, like a bubble in my chest that wouldn't rise or pop. I waited for anger or grief to fill the space it opened, but all I felt just then was an unsteadiness in my legs, a faulty connection with the ground." By tracing the physical reaction and staying true to the shock of the moment, Perrotta conveys the initial impact of this loss.

"Get control of emotion by avoiding the *mention* of the emotion," urges John L'Heureux. "To avoid melodrama, aim for a restrained tone rather than an exaggerated one. A scene with hysteria needs more, not less control in the writing: keep the language deflated and rooted in action and sensory detail. Don't reach for dramatic language but for what's implied," as is illustrated by the muted crisis of "Silver Water."

There are further reasons to avoid labeling emotion: emotion is seldom pure. Conflicting feelings often run together; we rarely stop to analyze our passions as we're caught up in them; and the reader may cease to participate when a label is simply given.

Filtering

John Gardner, in *The Art of Fiction*, points out that in addition to the faults of insufficient detail and excessive use of abstraction, there's a third failure:

> . . . the needless filtering of the image through some observing consciousness. The amateur writes: "Turning, she noticed two snakes fighting in among the rocks." Compare: "She turned. In among the rocks, two snakes were fighting . . ." Generally speaking—though no laws are absolute in fiction—vividness urges that almost every occurrence of such phrases as "she noticed" and "she saw" be suppressed in favor of direct presentation of the thing seen.

The filter is a common fault and often difficult to recognize—although once the principle is grasped, cutting away filters is an easy means to more vivid writing. As a fiction writer you will often be working through "some observing consciousness." Yet when you step back and ask readers to observe the observer—to look *at* rather than *through* the character—you start to tell-not-show and rip us briefly out of the scene. Here, for example, is a student passage quite competent except for the filtering:

> Mrs. Blair made her way to the chair by the window and sank gratefully into it. *She looked out the window* and *there*, across the street, *she saw* the ivory BMW parked in front of the fire plug once more. *It seemed to her, though,* that something was wrong with it. *She noticed* that it was listing slightly toward the back and side, and *then saw* that the back rim was resting almost on the asphalt.

(handwritten margin note: Reportage (too wordy))

Remove the filters from this paragraph and we are allowed to stay in Mrs. Blair's consciousness, watching with her eyes, sharing understanding as it unfolds for her:

> Mrs. Blair made her way to the chair by the window and sank gratefully into it. Across the street the ivory BMW was parked in front of the fire plug again. Something was wrong with it, though. It was listing toward the back and side, the back rim resting almost on the asphalt.

A similar filtering occurs when the writer chooses to begin a flashback and mistakenly supposes that the reader is not clever enough to follow this technique without a guiding transition:

> Mrs. Blair *thought back to* the time that she and Henry had owned an ivory car, though it had been a Chevy. *She remembered clearly* that it had a hood shaped like a sugar scoop, and chrome bumpers that stuck out a foot front and back. And there was that funny time, *she recalled*, when Henry had to change the flat tire on Alligator Alley, and she'd thought the alligators would come up out of the swamp.

Just as the present scene will be more present to the reader without a filter, so we will be taken more thoroughly back to the time of the memory without a filter:

> She and Henry had owned an ivory car once, though it had been a Chevy, with a hood shaped like a sugar scoop and chrome bumpers that stuck out a foot front and back. And there was that funny time Henry had to change the flat tire on Alligator Alley, and she'd thought the alligators would come up out of the swamp.

Observe that the pace of the reading is improved by the removal of the filters—at least partly, literally, because one or two lines of type have been removed.

The Active Voice

If your prose is to be vigorous as well as vivid, if your characters are to be people who do rather than people to whom things are done, if your descriptions are to "come to life," you must make use of the active voice.

The active voice occurs when the subject of a sentence performs the action described by the verb of that sentence: *She spilled the milk.* When the passive voice is used, the object of the active verb becomes the subject of the passive verb: *The milk was spilled by her.* The passive voice is more indirect than the active; the subject is acted upon rather than acting, and the effect is to weaken the prose and to distance the reader from the action.

The passive voice does have an important place in fiction, precisely because it expresses a sense that the character is being acted upon. If a prison guard is kicking the hero, then *I was slammed into the wall; I was struck blindingly from behind and forced to the floor* appropriately carries the sense of his helplessness.

In general, however, you should seek to use the active voice in all prose and use the passive only when the actor is unknown or insignificant or when you want to achieve special stylistic effects like the one above.

But there is one other common grammatical construction that is *in effect* passive and can distance the reader from a sense of immediate experience. The verbs that we learn in school to call *linking verbs* are effectively passive because verbs with auxiliaries suggest an indefinite time and are never as sharply focused as active verbs. (Further editing his example cited above, Gardner contrasts the phrase "two snakes were fighting" with the improved "two snakes fought," which pinpoints a specific moment; he further suggests substitution of active verbs, as in "two snakes whipped and lashed, striking at each other.")

Linking verbs also invite complements that tend to be generalized or judgmental: *Her hair* looked *beautiful. He was very happy. The room* seemed *expensively furnished. They* became *morose.* Let her hair bounce, tumble, cascade, or swing; we'll see better. Let him laugh, leap, cry, or hug a tree; we'll experience his joy.

The following is a passage with very little action, nevertheless made vital by the use of active verbs:

> At Mixt she neither drinks nor eats. Each of the sisters furtively stares at her as she tranquilly sits in post-Communion meditation with her hands immersed in her habit. *Lectio* has been halted for the morning, so there is only the Great Silence and the tinks of cutlery, but handsigns are being traded as the sisters lard their hunks of bread or fold and ring their dinner napkins. When the prioress stands, all rise up with her for the blessing, and then Sister Aimee gives Mariette the handsigns. *You, infirmary.*
>
> Ron Hansen, *Mariette in Ecstasy*

Here, though the convent meal is silent and action is minimal, a number of the verbs suggest suppressed power: *stares, sits, lard, fold, ring, stands, rise, gives.*

On Active Verbs

A general verb creates a general impression, but a precise, active verb conveys the exact picture in the writer's mind. For example:

General	Specific
walk	does the waiter *scurry* or *amble?*
yell	does the coach *demand* or *bellow?*
swim	does the child *splash* or *glide?*
climb	does the hiker *stumble up the hill?* or *stride?*

Compare the first passage about Debbie on page 76 with the second of the rewrites on page 77. In the generalized original we have *was stubborn, was doing things, was executive, was able, was indifferent.* Apart from the compound verb *was doing,* all these are linking verbs. In the rewrite the characters *brought, called, threw, knelt, retrieved, replaced, said, reminded, justified, toured, spent,* and *curled up.* What energetic people! The rewrite contains two linking verbs: Mr. Strum *was stockholder* and *was proud;* these properly represent static states, a position and an attitude.

One beneficial side effect of active verbs is that they tend to call forth significant details. If you say "she was shocked," you are telling us; but if you are to show us that she was shocked through an action, you are likely to have to search for an image as well. "She clenched the arm of the chair so hard that her knuckles whitened." *Clenched* and *whitened* actively suggest shock, and at the same time we see her knuckles on the arm of the chair.

To be is the most common of the linking verbs and also the most overused, but all the linking verbs invite generalization and distance. *To feel, to seem, to look, to appear, to experience, to express, to show, to demonstrate, to convey, to display*—all these suggest in fiction that the character is being acted upon or observed by someone rather than doing something. She felt *happy/sad/amused/mortified* does not convince us. We want to see her and infer her emotion for ourselves. *He very clearly conveyed his displeasure.* It isn't clear to us. How did he convey it? To whom?

Linking verbs, like the passive voice, can appropriately convey a sense of passivity or helplessness when that is the desired effect. Notice that in the passage by Mann quoted earlier in this chapter, where Felix Krull is momentarily stunned by the sight of the food before him, linking verbs are used: *It was a narrow room, there were rows and rows,* while all the colors and shapes buffet his senses. Only as he gradually recovers can he *stand, breathe, speak,* and eventually *grab.*

I don't mean to suggest that as an author you should analyze your grammar as you go along. Most word choice is instinctive, and instinct is often the best guide. However, I do mean to suggest that you should be aware of the vigor and variety of available verbs, and that if a passage lacks energy, it may be because your instinct has let you down. How often *are* things or are they acted *upon*, when they could more forcefully *do*?

A note of caution about active verbs: Make sparing use of what John Ruskin called the "pathetic fallacy"—the attributing of human emotions to natural and man-made objects. Even a description of a static scene can be invigorated if the houses *stand*, the streets *wander*, and the trees *bend*. But if the houses *frown*, the streets *stagger drunkenly*, and the trees *weep*, we will feel more strain than energy in the writing.

Prose Rhythm

Novelists and short story writers are not under the same obligation as poets to reinforce sense with sound. In prose, on the whole, the rhythm is all right if it isn't clearly wrong. But it can be wrong if, for example, the cadence contradicts the meaning; on the other hand, rhythm can greatly enhance the meaning if it is sensitively used.

> The river moved slowly. It seemed sluggish. The surface lay flat. Birds circled lazily overhead. Jon's boat slipped forward.

In this extreme example, the short, clipped sentences and their parallel structures—subject, verb, modifier—work against the sense of slow, flowing movement. The rhythm could be effective if the character whose eyes we're using is not appreciating or sharing the calm; otherwise it needs recasting.

> The surface lay flat on the sluggish, slow-moving river, and the birds circled lazily overhead as Jon's boat slipped forward.

There is nothing very striking about the rhythm of this version, but at least it moves forward without obstructing the flow of the river.

> The first impression I had as I stopped in the doorway of the immense City Room was of extreme rush and bustle, with the reporters moving rapidly back and forth in the long aisles in order to shove their copy at each other or making frantic gestures as they shouted into their many telephones.

This long and leisurely sentence cannot possibly provide a sense of rush and bustle. The phrases need to move as fast as the reporters; the verbiage must be pared down because it slows them down.

I stopped in the doorway. The City Room was immense, reporters rushing down the aisles, shoving copy at each other, bustling back again, flinging gestures, shouting into telephones.

The poet Rolfe Humphries remarked that "*very* is the least very word in the language." It is frequently true that adverbs expressing emphasis or suddenness—*extremely, rapidly, suddenly, phenomenally, quickly, immediately, instantly, definitely, terribly, awfully*—slow the sentence down so as to dilute the force of the intended meaning. "'It's a very nice day,'" said Humphries, "is not as nice a day as 'It's a day!'" Likewise, "They stopped very abruptly" is not as abrupt as "They stopped."

The rhythm of an action can be imitated by the rhythm of a sentence in a rich variety of ways. In the previous example, simplifying the clauses helped create a sense of rush. James Joyce, in the short story "The Dead," structures a long sentence with a number of prepositional phrases so that it carries us headlong.

Lily, the caretaker's daughter, was literally run off her feet. Hardly had she brought one gentleman into the little pantry behind the office on the ground floor and helped him off with his overcoat than the wheezy hall-door bell clanged and she had to scamper along the bare hallway to let in another guest.

Lily's haste is largely created by beginning the sentence, "Hardly had she brought," so that we anticipate the clause that will finish the meaning, "than the bell clanged." Our anticipation forces us to scamper like Lily through the intervening actions.

Not only action but also character can be revealed and reinforced by sensitive use of rhythm. In Tillie Olsen's "Tell Me a Riddle," half a dozen grown children of a couple who have been married for forty-seven years ask each other what, after all this time, could be tearing their parents apart. The narrative answers:

Something tangible enough.
    Arthritic hands, and such work as he got, occasional. Poverty all his life, and there was little breath left for running. He could not, could not turn away from this desire: to have the troubling of responsibility, the fretting with money, over and done with; to be free, to be *care*free where success was not measured by accumulation, and there was use for the vitality still in him.

The old man's anguished irritability is conveyed by syncopation, the syntax wrenched, clauses and qualifiers erupting out of what would be their natural place in the sentence, just as they would erupt in the man's mind. Repetition conveys his frustration: "He could not, could not" and "to be free, to be *care*free."

Just as action and character can find an echo in prose rhythm, so it is possible to help us experience a character's emotions and attitudes through control of the starts and stops of prose tempo. In the following passage from *Persuasion*, Jane Austen combines generalization, passive verbs, and a staccato speech pattern to produce a kind of breathless blindness in the heroine.

. . . a thousand feelings rushed on Anne, of which this was the most consoling, that it would soon be over. And it was soon over. In two minutes after Charles's preparation, the others appeared; they were in the drawing room. Her eye half met Captain Wentworth's, a bow, a courtesy passed; she heard his voice; he talked to Mary, said all that was right, said something to the Miss Musgroves, enough to mark an easy footing; the room seemed full, full of persons and voices, but a few minutes ended it.

Often an abrupt change in the prose rhythm will signal a discovery or change in mood; such a shift can also reinforce a contrast in characters, actions, and attitudes. In this passage from Frederick Busch's short story "Company," a woman whose movements are relatively confined watches her husband move, stop, and move again.

Every day did not start with Vince awake that early, dressing in the dark, moving with whispery sounds down the stairs and through the kitchen, out into the autumn morning while groundfog lay on the milkweed burst open and on the stumps of harvested corn. But enough of them did.

I went to the bedroom window to watch him hunt in a business suit.

He moved with his feet in the slowly stirring fog, moving slowly himself with the rifle held across his body and his shoulders stiff. Then he stopped in a frozen watch for woodchucks. His stillness made the fog look faster as it blew across our field behind the barn. Vince stood. He waited for something to shoot. I went back to bed and lay between our covers again. I heard the bolt click. I heard the unemphatic shot, and then the second one, and after a while his feet on the porch, and soon the rush of water, the rattle of the pots on top of the stove, and later his feet again, and the car starting up as he left for work an hour before he had to.

The long opening sentence is arranged in a series of short phrases to move Vince forward. By contrast, "But enough of them did" comes abruptly, its abruptness as well as the sense of the words suggesting the woman's alienation. When Vince starts off again more slowly, the repetition of "moved, slowly stirring, moving slowly," slows down the sentence to match his strides. "Vince stood" again stills him, but the author also needs to convey that Vince stands for a long time, waiting, so we have the repetitions "he stopped, his stillness, Vince stood, he waited." As his activity speeds up again, the tempo of the prose speeds up with another series of short phrases, of which only the last is drawn out with a dependent clause, "as he left for work an hour before he had to," so that we feel the retreat of the car in the distance. Notice that Busch chooses the phrase "the rush of water," not the flow or splash of water, as the sentence and Vince begin to rush. Here, meaning reinforces a tempo that, in turn, reinforces meaning. (An added bonus is that variety in sentence lengths and rhythms helps to hold readers' attention.)

"The Things They Carried" by Tim O'Brien, at the end of this chapter, demonstrates a range of rhythms with a rich variation of effects. Here is one:

The things they carried were largely determined by necessity. Among the necessities or near-necessities were P-38 can openers, pocket knives, heat tabs, wristwatches, dog tags, mosquito repellent, chewing gum, candy, cigarettes, salt
tablets, packets of Kool-Aid, lighters, matches, sewing kits, Military Payment
Certificates, C rations, and two or three canteens of water. Together, these items
weighed between 15 and 20 pounds . . .

In this passage the piling of items one on the other has the effect of loading the
men down and at the same time increasingly suggests the rhythm of their marching
as they "hump" their stuff. Similar lists through the story create a rhythmic thread,
while variations and stoppages underlie shifts of emotion and sudden crises.

Mechanics

Significant detail, the active voice, and prose rhythm are techniques for achieving
the sensuous in fiction, means of helping the reader "sink into the dream" of the
story, in John Gardner's phrase. Yet no technique is of much use if the reader's eye is
wrenched back to the surface by misspellings or grammatical errors, for once the
reader has been startled out of the story's "vivid and continuous dream," that reader
may not return.

Spelling, grammar, paragraphing, and punctuation are a kind of magic; their purpose is to be invisible. If the sleight of hand works, we will not notice a comma or a
quotation mark but will translate each instantly into a pause or an awareness of
voice; we will not focus on the individual letters of a word but extract its sense
whole. When the mechanics are incorrectly used, the trick is revealed and the magic
fails; the reader's focus is shifted from the story to its surface. The reader is irritated
at the author, and of all the emotions the reader is willing to experience, irritation at
the author is not one.

There is no intrinsic virtue in standardized mechanics, and you can depart from
them whenever you produce a result that adequately compensates for a distracting
effect. But only then. Poor mechanics signal amateurism to an editor and suggest
that the story itself may be flawed. Unlike the techniques of narrative, the rules of

---

The difference between the right word and the almost right word . . . is
the difference between lightning and the lightning bug.

Mark Twain

---

spelling, grammar, and punctuation can be coldly learned anywhere in the English-speaking world—and they should be learned by anyone who aspires to write.

Linoleum Roses

SANDRA CISNEROS

Sally got married like we knew she would, young and not ready but married just the same. She met a marshmallow salesman at a school bazaar, and she married him in another state where it's legal to get married before eighth grade. She has her husband and her house now, her pillowcases and her plates. She says she is in love, but I think she did it to escape.

Sally says she likes being married because now she gets to buy her own things when her husband gives her money. She is happy, except sometimes her husband gets angry and once he broke the door where his foot went through, though most days he is okay. Except he won't let her talk on the telephone. And he doesn't let her look out the window. And he doesn't like her friends, so nobody gets to visit her unless he is working.

She sits at home because she is afraid to go outside without his permission. She looks at all the things they own: the towels and the toaster, the alarm clock and the drapes. She likes looking at the walls, at how neatly their corners meet, the linoleum roses on the floor, the ceiling smooth as wedding cake.

Suggestions for Discussion

1. Reread the final paragraph and paraphrase what is suggested by the details. Compare the number of words used to list the details to the number of words needed to paraphrase their meanings.

2. Some new writers feel the impulse to end with a final, editorializing comment that explains the story. Rarely, if ever, is this needed. Imagine that you had written "Linoleum Roses" and initially felt nervous about whether readers would "get it." What "telling" last line might you be tempted to add? How would it affect the impact of the story?

3. In the final version of a story, every detail "counts" toward illuminating the meaning of the story. Try changing some seemingly minor details in this story to see how the significance changes. For example, what makes a marshmallow salesman a better choice for this story than a class ring salesman or a yearbook photographer?

The Things They Carried

TIM O'BRIEN

First Lieutenant Jimmy Cross carried letters from a girl named Martha, a junior at Mount Sebastian College in New Jersey. They were not love letters, but Lieutenant Cross was hoping, so he kept them folded in plastic at the bottom of his rucksack. In the late afternoon, after a day's march, he would dig his foxhole, wash his hands under a canteen, unwrap the letters, hold them with the tips of his fingers, and spend the last hour of light pretending. He would imagine romantic camping trips into the White Mountains in New Hampshire. He would sometimes taste the envelope flaps, knowing her tongue had been there. More than anything, he wanted Martha to love him as he loved her, but the letters were mostly chatty, elusive on the matter of love. She was a virgin, he was almost sure. She was an English major at Mount Sebastian, and she wrote beautifully about her professors and roommates and midterm exams, about her respect for Chaucer and her great affection for Virginia Woolf. She often quoted lines of poetry; she never mentioned the war, except to say, Jimmy, take care of yourself. The letters weighed 10 ounces. They were signed Love, Martha, but Lieutenant Cross understood that Love was only a way of signing and did not mean what he sometimes pretended it meant. At dusk, he would carefully return the letters to his rucksack. Slowly, a bit distracted, he would get up and move among his men, checking the perimeter, then at full dark he would return to his hole and watch the night and wonder if Martha was a virgin.

The things they carried were largely determined by necessity. Among the necessities or near-necessities were P-38 can openers, pocket knives, heat tabs, wristwatches, dog tags, mosquito repellent, chewing gum, candy, cigarettes, salt tablets, packets of Kool-Aid, lighters, matches, sewing kits, Military Payment Certificates, C rations, and two or three canteens of water. Together, these items weighed between 15 and 20 pounds, depending upon a man's habits or rate of metabolism. Henry Dobbins, who was a big man, carried extra rations; he was especially fond of canned peaches in heavy syrup over pound cake. Dave Jensen, who practiced field hygiene, carried a toothbrush, dental floss, and several hotel-sized bars of soap he'd stolen on R&R in Sydney, Australia. Ted Lavender, who was scared, carried tranquilizers until he was shot in the head outside the village of Than Khe in mid-April. By necessity, and because it was SOP, they all carried steel helmets that weighed 5 pounds including the liner and camouflage cover. They carried the standard fatigue jackets and trousers. Very few carried underwear. On their feet they carried jungle boots—2.1 pounds— and Dave Jensen carried three pairs of socks and a can of Dr. Scholl's foot powder as a precaution against trench foot. Until he was shot, Ted Lavender carried six or seven ounces of premium dope, which for him was a necessity. Mitchell Sanders, the RTO, carried condoms. Norman Bowker carried a diary. Rat Kiley carried comic books. Kiowa, a devout Baptist, carried an illustrated New Testament that had been presented to him by his father, who taught Sunday school in Oklahoma City, Oklahoma. As a hedge against bad times, however, Kiowa also carried his grandmother's distrust of the white man, his grandfather's old hunting hatchet. Necessity dictated. Because the land was mined and booby-trapped, it was SOP for each man to carry a steel-centered, nylon-covered flak jacket, which weighed 6.7 pounds, but which on hot days seemed much heavier. Because you could die so quickly, each man carried at least one large compress bandage, usually in the helmet band for easy access. Because the nights were cold, and because the monsoons were wet, each carried a green plastic poncho that could be used as a raincoat or groundsheet or makeshift tent. With its quilted liner, the poncho weighed almost two pounds, but it was worth every ounce. In April, for instance, when Ted Lavender was shot, they used his poncho to wrap him up, then to carry him across the paddy, then to lift him into the chopper that took him away.

They were called legs or grunts.

To carry something was to hump it, as when Lieutenant Jimmy Cross humped his love for Martha up the hills and through the swamps. In its intransitive form, to hump meant to walk, or to march, but it implied burdens far beyond the intransitive.

Almost everyone humped photographs. In his wallet, Lieutenant Cross carried two photographs of Martha. The first was a Kodacolor snapshot signed Love, though he knew better. She stood against a brick wall. Her eyes were gray and neutral, her lips slightly open as she stared straight-on at the camera. At night, sometimes, Lieutenant Cross wondered who had taken the picture, because he knew she had boyfriends, because he loved her so much, and because he could see the shadow of the picture-taker spreading out against the brick wall. The second photograph had been clipped from the 1968 Mount Sebastian yearbook. It was an action shot—women's volleyball—and Martha was bent horizontal to the floor, reaching, the palms of her hands in sharp focus, the tongue taut, the expression frank and competitive. There was no visible sweat. She wore white gym shorts. Her legs, he thought, were almost certainly the legs of a virgin, dry and without hair, the left knee cocked and carrying her entire weight, which was just over one hundred pounds. Lieutenant Cross remembered touching that left knee. A dark theater, he remembered, and the movie was *Bonnie and Clyde*, and Martha wore a tweed skirt, and during the final scene, when he touched her knee, she turned and looked at him in a sad, sober way that made him pull his hand back, but he would always remember the feel of the tweed skirt and the knee beneath it and the sound of the gunfire that killed Bonnie and Clyde, how embarrassing it was, how slow and oppressive. He remembered kissing her good night at the dorm door. Right then, he thought, he should've done something brave. He should've carried her up the stairs to her room and tied her to the bed and touched that left knee all night long. He should've risked it. Whenever he looked at the photographs, he thought of new things he should've done.

What they carried was partly a function of rank, partly of field specialty.

As a first lieutenant and platoon leader, Jimmy Cross carried a compass, maps, code books, binoculars, and a .45-caliber pistol that weighed 2.9 pounds fully loaded. He carried a strobe light and the responsibility for the lives of his men.

As an RTO, Mitchell Sanders carried the PRC-25 radio, a killer, 26 pounds with its battery.

As a medic, Rat Kiley carried a canvas satchel filled with morphine and plasma and malaria tablets and surgical tape and comic books and all the things a medic must carry, including M&M's for especially bad wounds, for a total weight of nearly 20 pounds.

As a big man, therefore a machine gunner, Henry Dobbins carried the M-60, which weighed 23 pounds unloaded, but which was almost always loaded. In addition, Dobbins carried between 10 and 15 pounds of ammunition draped in belts across his chest and shoulders.

As PFCs or Spec 4s, most of them were common grunts and carried the standard M-16 gas-operated assault rifle. The weapon weighed 7.5 pounds unloaded, 8.2 pounds with its full 20-round magazine. Depending on numerous factors, such as topography and psychology, the riflemen carried anywhere from 12 to 20 magazines, usually in cloth bandoliers, adding on another 8.4 pounds at minimum, 14 pounds at maximum. When it was available, they also carried M-16 maintenance gear—rods and steel brushes and swabs and tubes of LSA oil—all of which weighed about a pound. Among the grunts, some carried the M-79 grenade launcher, 5.9 pounds unloaded, a reasonably light weapon except for the ammunition, which was heavy. A single round weighed 10 ounces. The typical load was 25 rounds. But Ted Lavender, who was scared, carried 34 rounds when he was shot and killed outside Than Khe, and he went down under an exceptional burden, more than 20 pounds of ammunition, plus the flak jacket and helmet and rations and water and toilet paper and tranquilizers and all the rest, plus the unweighed fear. He was dead weight. There was no twitching or flopping. Kiowa, who saw it happen, said it was like watching a rock fall, or a big sandbag or something—just boom, then down—not like the movies where the dead guy rolls around and does fancy spins and goes ass over teakettle— not like that, Kiowa said, the poor bastard just flat-fuck fell. Boom. Down. Nothing else. It was a bright morning in mid-April. Lieutenant Cross felt the pain. He blamed himself. They stripped off Lavender's canteens and ammo, all the heavy things, and Rat Kiley said the obvious, the guy's dead, and Mitchell Sanders used his radio to report one U.S. KIA and to request a chopper. Then they wrapped Lavender in his poncho. They carried him out to a dry paddy, established security, and sat smoking the dead man's dope until the chopper came. Lieutenant Cross kept to himself. He pictured Martha's smooth young face, thinking he loved her more than anything, more than his men, and now Ted Lavender was dead because he loved her so much and could not stop thinking about her. When the dustoff arrived, they carried Lavender aboard. Afterward they burned Than Khe. They marched until dusk, then dug their holes, and that night Kiowa kept explaining how you had to be there, how fast it was, how the poor guy just dropped like so much concrete. Boom-down, he said. Like cement.

In addition to the three standard weapons—the M-60, M-16, and M-79—they carried whatever presented itself, or whatever seemed appropriate as a means of killing or staying alive. They carried catch-as-catch-can. At various times, in various situations, they carried M-14s and CAR-15s and Swedish Ks and grease guns and captured AK-47s and Chi-Coms and RPGs and Simonov carbines and black market Uzis and .38-caliber Smith & Wesson handguns and 66 mm LAWs and shotguns and silencers and blackjacks and bayonets and C-4 plastic explosives. Lee Strunk carried a sling-shot; a weapon of last resort, he called it. Mitchell Sanders carried brass knuckles. Kiowa carried his grandfather's feathered hatchet. Every third or fourth man carried a Claymore antipersonnel mine—3.5 pounds with its firing device. They all carried fragmentation grenades—14 ounces each. They all carried at least one M-18 colored smoke grenade—24 ounces. Some carried CS or tear gas grenades. Some carried white phosphorus grenades. They carried all they could bear, and then some, includ-ing a silent awe for the terrible power of the things they carried.

In the first week of April, before Lavender died, Lieutenant Jimmy Cross received a good-luck charm from Martha. It was a simple pebble, an ounce at most. Smooth to the touch, it was a milky white color with flecks of orange and violet, oval-shaped, like a miniature egg. In the accompanying letter, Martha wrote that she had found the pebble on the Jersey shoreline, precisely where the land touched water at high tide, where things came together but also separated. It was this sepa-rate-but-together quality, she wrote, that had inspired her to pick up the pebble and to carry it in her breast pocket for several days, where it seemed weightless, and then to send it through the mail, by air, as a token of her truest feelings for him. Lieutenant Cross found this romantic. But he wondered what her truest feel-ings were, exactly, and what she meant by separate-but-together. He wondered how the tides and waves had come into play on that afternoon along the Jersey shoreline when Martha saw the pebble and bent down to rescue it from geology. He imagined bare feet. Martha was a poet, with the poet's sensibilities, and her feet would be brown and bare, the toenails unpainted, the eyes chilly and somber like the ocean in March, and though it was painful, he wondered who had been with her that afternoon. He imagined a pair of shadows moving along the strip of sand where things came together but also separated. It was phantom jealousy, he knew, but he couldn't help himself. He loved her so much. On the march, through the hot days of early April, he carried the pebble in his mouth, turning it with his tongue, tasting sea salt and moisture. His mind wandered. He had difficulty keep-ing his attention on the war. On occasion he would yell at his men to spread out the column, to keep their eyes open, but then he would slip away into daydreams, just pretending, walking barefoot along the Jersey shore, with Martha, carrying nothing. He would feel himself rising. Sun and waves and gentle winds, all love and lightness.

What they carried varied by mission.

When a mission took them to the mountains, they carried mosquito netting, ma-chetes, canvas tarps, and extra bug juice.

If a mission seemed especially hazardous, or if it involved a place they knew to be bad, they carried everything they could. In certain heavily mined AOs, where the land was dense with Toe Poppers and Bouncing Betties, they took turns humping a 28-pound mine detector. With its headphones and big sensing plate, the equipment was a stress on the lower back and shoulders, awkward to handle, often useless be-cause of the shrapnel in the earth, but they carried it anyway, partly for safety, partly for the illusion of safety.

On ambush, or other night missions, they carried peculiar little odds and ends. Kiowa always took along his New Testament and a pair of moccasins for silence. Dave Jensen carried night-sight vitamins high in carotene. Lee Strunk carried his slingshot; ammo, he claimed, would never be a problem. Rat Kiley carried brandy and M&M's candy. Until he was shot, Ted Lavender carried the starlight scope, which weighed 6.3 pounds with its aluminum carrying case. Henry Dobbins carried his girlfriend's pantyhose wrapped around his neck as a comforter. They all carried ghosts. When dark came, they would move out single file across the meadows and paddies to their ambush coordinates, where they would quietly set up the Claymores and lie down and spend the night waiting.

Other missions were more complicated and required special equipment. In mid-April, it was their mission to search out and destroy the elaborate tunnel complexes in the Than Khe area south of Chu Lai. To blow the tunnels, they carried one-pound blocks of pentrite high explosives, four blocks to a man, 68 pounds in all. They carried wiring, detonators, and battery-powered clackers. Dave Jensen carried earplugs. Most often, before blowing the tunnels, they were ordered by higher command to search them, which was considered bad news, but by and large they just shrugged and carried out orders. Because he was a big man, Henry Dobbins was excused from tunnel duty. The others would draw numbers. Before Lavender died there were 17 men in the platoon, and whoever drew the number 17 would strip off his gear and crawl in headfirst with a flashlight and Lieutenant Cross's .45-caliber pistol. The rest of them would fan out as security. They would sit down or kneel, not facing the hole, listening to the ground beneath them, imagining cobwebs and ghosts, whatever was down there—the tunnel walls squeezing in—how the flashlight seemed impossibly heavy in the hand and how it was tunnel vision in the very strictest sense, compression in all ways, even time, and how you had to wiggle in— ass and elbows—a swallowed-up feeling—and how you found yourself worrying about odd things: Will your flashlight go dead? Do rats carry rabies? If you screamed, how far would the sound carry? Would your buddies hear it? Would they have the courage to drag you out? In some respects, though not many, the waiting was worse than the tunnel itself. Imagination was a killer.

On April 16, when Lee Strunk drew the number 17, he laughed and muttered something and went down quickly. The morning was hot and very still. Not good, Kiowa said. He looked at the tunnel opening, then out across a dry paddy toward the village of Than Khe. Nothing moved. No clouds or birds or people. As they waited, the men smoked and drank Kool-Aid, not talking much, feeling sympathy for Lee Strunk but also feeling the luck of the draw. You win some, you lose some, said Mitchell Sanders, and sometimes you settle for a rain check. It was a tired line and no one laughed.

Henry Dobbins ate a tropical chocolate bar. Ted Lavender popped a tranquilizer and went off to pee.

After five minutes, Lieutenant Jimmy Cross moved to the tunnel, leaned down, and examined the darkness. Trouble, he thought—a cave-in maybe. And then suddenly, without willing it, he was thinking about Martha. The stresses and fractures, the quick collapse, the two of them buried alive under all that weight. Dense, crushing love. Kneeling, watching the hole, he tried to concentrate on Lee Strunk and the war, all the dangers, but his love was too much for him, he felt paralyzed, he wanted to sleep inside her lungs and breathe her blood and be smothered. He wanted her to be a virgin and not a virgin, all at once. He wanted to know her. Intimate secrets: Why poetry? Why so sad? Why that grayness in her eyes? Why so alone? Not lonely, just alone—riding her bike across campus or sitting off by herself in the cafeteria—even dancing, she danced alone—and it was the aloneness that filled him with love. He remembered telling her that one evening. How she nodded and looked away. And how, later, when he kissed her, she received the kiss without returning it, her eyes wide open, not afraid, not a virgin's eyes, just flat and uninvolved.

Lieutenant Cross gazed at the tunnel. But he was not there. He was buried with Martha under the white sand at the Jersey shore. They were pressed together, and the pebble in his mouth was her tongue. He was smiling. Vaguely, he was aware of how quiet the day was, the sullen paddies, yet he could not bring himself to worry about matters of security. He was beyond that. He was just a kid at war, in love. He was twenty-four years old. He couldn't help it.

A few moments later Lee Strunk crawled out of the tunnel. He came up grinning, filthy but alive. Lieutenant Cross nodded and closed his eyes while the others clapped Strunk on the back and made jokes about rising from the dead.

Worms, Rat Kiley said. Right out of the grave. Fuckin' zombie.

The men laughed. They all felt great relief.

Spook city, said Mitchell Sanders.

Lee Strunk made a funny ghost sound, a kind of moaning, yet very happy, and right then, when Strunk made that high happy moaning sound, when he went *Ahhooooo,* right then Ted Lavender was shot in the head on his way back from peeing. He lay with his mouth open. The teeth were broken. There was a swollen black bruise under his left eye. The cheekbone was gone. Oh shit, Rat Kiley said, the guy's dead. The guy's dead, he kept saying, which seemed profound—the guy's dead. I mean really.

The things they carried were determined to some extent by superstition. Lieutenant Cross carried his good-luck pebble. Dave Jensen carried a rabbit's foot. Norman Bowker, otherwise a very gentle person, carried a thumb that had been presented to him as a gift by Mitchell Sanders. The thumb was dark brown, rubbery to the touch, and weighed four ounces at most. It had been cut from a VC corpse, a boy of fifteen or sixteen. They'd found him at the bottom of an irrigation ditch, badly burned, flies in his mouth and eyes. The boy wore black shorts and sandals. At the time of his death he had been carrying a pouch of rice, a rifle, and three magazines of ammunition.

You want my opinion, Mitchell Sanders said, there's a definite moral here.

He put his hand on the dead boy's wrist. He was quiet for a time, as if counting a pulse, then he patted the stomach, almost affectionately, and used Kiowa's hunting hatchet to remove the thumb.

Henry Dobbins asked what the moral was.

Moral?

You know. *Moral.*

Sanders wrapped the thumb in toilet paper and handed it across to Norman Bowker. There was no blood. Smiling, he kicked the boy's head, watched the flies scatter, and said, It's like what that old TV show—Paladin. Have gun, will travel.

Henry Dobbins thought about it.

Yeah, well, he finally said. I don't see no moral.

There it is, man.

Fuck off.

They carried USO stationery and pencils and pens. They carried Sterno, safety pins, trip flares, signal flares, spools of wire, razor blades, chewing tobacco, liberated joss sticks and statuettes of the smiling Buddha, candles, grease pencils, *The Stars and Stripes*, fingernail clippers, Psy Ops leaflets, bush hats, bolos, and much more. Twice a week, when the resupply choppers came in, they carried hot chow in green mermite cans and large canvas bags filled with iced beer and soda pop. They carried plastic water containers, each with a two-gallon capacity. Mitchell Sanders carried a set of starched tiger fatigues for special occasions. Henry Dobbins carried Black Flag insecticide. Dave Jensen carried empty sandbags that could be filled at night for added protection. Lee Strunk carried tanning lotion. Some things they carried in common. Taking turns, they carried the big PRC–77 scrambler radio, which weighed 30 pounds with its battery. They shared the weight of memory. They took up what others could no longer bear. Often, they carried each other, the wounded or weak. They carried infections. They carried chess sets, basketballs, Vietnamese-English dictionaries, insignia of rank, Bronze Stars and Purple Hearts, plastic cards imprinted with the Code of Conduct. They carried diseases, among them malaria and dysentery. They carried lice and ringworm and leeches and paddy algae and various rots and molds. They carried the land itself—Vietnam, the place, the soil—a powdery orange-red dust that covered their boots and fatigues and faces. They carried the sky. The whole atmosphere, they carried it, the humidity, the monsoons, the stink of fungus and decay, all of it, they carried gravity. They moved like mules. By daylight they took sniper fire, at night they were mortared, but it was not battle, it was just the endless march, village to village, without purpose, nothing won or lost. They marched for the sake of the march. They plodded along slowly, dumbly, leaning forward against the heat, unthinking, all blood and bone, simple grunts, soldiering with their legs, toiling up the hills and down into the paddies and across the rivers and up again and down, just humping, one step and then the next and then another, but no volition, no will, because it was automatic, it was anatomy, and the war was entirely a matter of posture and carriage, the hump was everything, a kind of inertia, a kind of emptiness, a dullness of desire and intellect and conscience and hope and human sensibility. Their principles were in their feet. Their calculations were biological. They had no sense of strategy or mission. They searched the villages without knowing what to look for, not caring, kicking over jars of rice, frisking children and old men, blowing tunnels, sometimes setting fires and sometimes not, then forming up and moving on to the next village, then other villages, where it would always be the same. They carried their own lives. The pressures were enormous. In the heat of early afternoon, they would remove their helmets and flak jackets, walking bare, which was dangerous but which helped ease the strain. They would often discard things along the route of march. Purely for comfort, they would throw away rations, blow their Claymores and grenades, no matter, because by nightfall the resupply choppers would arrive with more of the same, then a day or two later still more, fresh watermelons and crates of ammunition and sunglasses and woolen sweaters—the resources were stunning—sparklers for the Fourth of July, colored eggs for Easter. It was the great American war chest—the fruits of science, the smokestacks, the canneries, the arsenals at Hartford, the Minnesota forests, the machine shops, the vast fields of corn and wheat—they carried like freight trains; they carried it on their backs and shoulders—and for all the ambiguities of Vietnam, all the mysteries and unknowns, there was at least the single abiding certainty that they would never be at a loss for things to carry.

After the chopper took Lavender away, Lieutenant Jimmy Cross led his men into the village of Than Khe. They burned everything. They shot chickens and dogs, they trashed the village well, they called in artillery and watched the wreckage, then they marched for several hours through the hot afternoon, and then at dusk, while Kiowa explained how Lavender died, Lieutenant Cross found himself trembling.

He tried not to cry. With his entrenching tool, which weighed five pounds, he began digging a hole in the earth.

He felt shame. He hated himself. He had loved Martha more than his men, and as a consequence Lavender was now dead, and this was something he would have to carry like a stone in his stomach for the rest of the war.

All he could do was dig. He used his entrenching tool like an ax, slashing, feeling both love and hate, and then later, when it was full dark, he sat at the bottom of his foxhole and wept. It went on for a long while. In part, he was grieving for Ted Lavender, but mostly it was for Martha, and for himself, because she belonged to another world, which was not quite real, and because she was a junior at Mount Sebastian College in New Jersey, a poet and a virgin and uninvolved, and because he realized she did not love him and never would.

Like cement, Kiowa whispered in the dark. I swear to God—boom, down. Not a word.

I've heard this, said Norman Bowker.

A pisser, you know? Still zipping himself up. Zapped while zipping.

All right, fine. That's enough.

Yeah, but you had to see it, the guy just—

I heard, man. Cement. So why not shut the fuck up?

Kiowa shook his head sadly and glanced over at the hole where Lieutenant Jimmy Cross sat watching the night. The air was thick and wet. A warm dense fog had settled over the paddies and there was the stillness that precedes rain.

After a time Kiowa sighed.

One thing for sure, he said. The lieutenant's in some deep hurt. I mean that crying jag—the way he was carrying on—it wasn't fake or anything, it was real heavy-
duty hurt. The man cares.

Sure, Norman Bowker said.

Say what you want, the man does care.

We all got problems.

Not Lavender.

No, I guess not, Bowker said. Do me a favor, though.

Shut up?

That's a smart Indian. Shut up.

Shrugging, Kiowa pulled off his boots. He wanted to say more, just to lighten up
his sleep, but instead he opened his New Testament and arranged it beneath his
head as a pillow. The fog made things seem hollow and unattached. He tried not to
think about Ted Lavender, but then he was thinking how fast it was, no drama,
down and dead, and how it was hard to feel anything except surprise. It seemed
unchristian. He wished he could find some great sadness, or even anger, but the
emotion wasn't there and he couldn't make it happen. Mostly he felt pleased to be
alive. He liked the smell of the New Testament under his cheek, the leather and ink
and paper and glue, whatever the chemicals were. He liked hearing the sounds of
night. Even his fatigue, it felt fine, the stiff muscles and the prickly awareness of his
own body, a floating feeling. He enjoyed not being dead. Lying there, Kiowa admired
Lieutenant Jimmy Cross's capacity for grief. He wanted to share the man's pain, he
wanted to care as Jimmy Cross cared. And yet when he closed his eyes, all he could
think was Boom-down, and all he could feel was the pleasure of having his boots off
and the fog curling in around him and the damp soil and the Bible smells and the
plush comfort of night.

After a moment Norman Bowker sat up in the dark.

What the hell, he said. You want to talk, *talk*. Tell it to me.

Forget it.

No, man, go on. One thing I hate, it's a silent Indian.

For the most part they carried themselves with poise, a kind of dignity. Now and
then, however, there were times of panic, when they squealed or wanted to squeal
but couldn't, when they twitched and made moaning sounds and covered their
heads and said Dear Jesus and flopped around on the earth and fired their weapons
blindly and cringed and sobbed and begged for the noise to stop and went wild and
made stupid promises to themselves and to God and to their mothers and fathers,
hoping not to die. In different ways, it happened to all of them. Afterward, when the
firing ended, they would blink and peek up. They would touch their bodies, feeling
shame, then quickly hiding it. They would force themselves to stand. As if in slow
motion, frame by frame, the world would take on the old logic—absolute silence,
then the wind, then sunlight, then voices. It was the burden of being alive. Awkwardly, the men would reassemble themselves, first in private, then in groups, becoming soldiers again. They would repair the leaks in their eyes. They would check
for casualties, call in dustoffs, light cigarettes, try to smile, clear their throats and spit

and begin cleaning their weapons. After a time someone would shake his head and say, No lie, I almost shit my pants, and someone else would laugh, which meant it was bad, yes, but the guy had obviously not shit his pants, it wasn't that bad, and in any case nobody would ever do such a thing and then go ahead and talk about it. They would squint into the dense, oppressive sunlight. For a few moments, perhaps, they would fall silent, lighting a joint and tracking its passage from man to man, inhaling, holding in the humiliation. Scary stuff, one of them might say. But then someone else would grin or flick his eyebrows and say, Roger-dodger, almost cut me a new asshole, *almost*.

There were numerous such poses. Some carried themselves with a sort of wistful resignation, others with pride or stiff soldierly discipline or good humor or macho zeal. They were afraid of dying but they were even more afraid to show it.

They found jokes to tell.

They used a hard vocabulary to contain the terrible softness. *Greased* they'd say. *Offed, lit up, zapped while zipping.* It wasn't cruelty, just stage presence. They were actors. When someone died, it wasn't quite dying, because in a curious way it seemed scripted, and because they had their lines mostly memorized, irony mixed with tragedy, and because they called it by other names, as if to encyst and destroy the reality of death itself. They kicked corpses. They cut off thumbs. They talked grunt lingo. They told stories about Ted Lavender's supply of tranquilizers, how the poor guy didn't feel a thing, how incredibly tranquil he was.

There's a moral here, said Mitchell Sanders.

They were waiting for Lavender's chopper, smoking the dead man's dope.

The moral's pretty obvious, Sanders said, and winked. Stay away from drugs. No joke, they'll ruin your day every time.

Cute, said Henry Dobbins.

Mind blower, get it? Talk about wiggy. Nothing left, just blood and brains.

They made themselves laugh.

There it is, they'd say. Over and over—there it is, my friend, there it is—as if the repetition itself were an act of poise, a balance between crazy and almost crazy, knowing without going, there it is, which meant be cool, let it ride, because Oh yeah, man, you can't change what can't be changed, there it is, there it absolutely and positively and fucking well is.

They were tough.

They carried all the emotional baggage of men who might die. Grief, terror, love, longing—these were intangibles, but the intangibles had their own mass and specific gravity, they had tangible weight. They carried shameful memories. They carried the common secret of cowardice barely restrained, the instinct to run or freeze or hide, and in many respects this was the heaviest burden of all, for it could never be put down, it required perfect balance and perfect posture. They carried their reputations. They carried the soldier's greatest fear, which was the fear of blushing. Men killed, and died, because they were embarrassed not to. It was what had brought them to the war in the first place, nothing positive, no dreams of glory or honor, just to avoid the blush of dishonor. They died so as not to die of embarrassment. They crawled into tunnels and walked point and advanced under fire. Each morning, despite the unknowns, they made their legs move. They endured. They kept humping, they did not submit to the obvious alternative, which was simply to close the eyes and fall. So easy, really. Go limp and tumble to the ground and let the muscles unwind and not speak and not budge until your buddies picked you up and lifted you into the chopper that would roar and dip its nose and carry you off to the world. A mere matter of falling, yet no one ever fell. It was not courage, exactly; the object was not valor. Rather, they were too frightened to be cowards.

By and large they carried these things inside, maintaining the masks of composure. They sneered at sick call. They spoke bitterly about guys who had found release by shooting off their own toes or fingers. Pussies, they'd say. Candy-asses. It was fierce, mocking talk, with only a trace of envy or awe, but even so the image played itself out behind their eyes.

They imagined the muzzle against flesh. So easy: squeeze the trigger and blow away a toe. They imagined it. They imagined the quick, sweet pain, then the evacuation to Japan, then a hospital with warm beds and cute geisha nurses.

And they dreamed of freedom birds.

At night, on guard, staring into the dark, they were carried away by jumbo jets. They felt the rush of takeoff. *Gone!* they yelled. And then velocity—wings and engines—a smiling stewardess—but it was more than a plane, it was a real bird, a big sleek silver bird with feathers and talons and high screeching. They were flying. The weights fell off; there was nothing to bear. They laughed and held on tight, feeling the cold slap of wind and altitude, soaring, thinking *It's over, I'm gone!*—they were naked, they were light and free—it was all lightness, bright and fast and buoyant, light as light, a helium buzz in the brain, a giddy bubbling in the lungs as they were taken up over the clouds and the war, beyond duty, beyond gravity and mortification and global entanglements—*Sin loi!* they yelled. *I'm sorry, motherfuckers, but I'm out of it, I'm goofed, I'm on a space cruise, I'm gone!*—and it was a restful, unencumbered sensation, just riding the light waves, sailing that big silver freedom bird over the mountains and oceans, over America, over the farms and great sleeping cities and cemeteries and highways and the golden arches of McDonald's, it was flight, a kind of fleeing, a kind of falling, falling higher and higher, spinning off the edge of the earth and beyond the sun and through the vast, silent vacuum where there were no burdens and where everything weighed exactly nothing—Gone! they screamed. I'm sorry but I'm gone!—and so at night, not quite dreaming, they gave themselves over to lightness, they were carried, they were purely borne.

On the morning after Ted Lavender died, First Lieutenant Jimmy Cross crouched at the bottom of his foxhole and burned Martha's letters. Then he burned the two photographs. There was a steady rain falling, which made it difficult, but he used heat tabs and Sterno to build a small fire, screening it with his body, holding the photographs over the tight blue flame with the tips of his fingers.

He realized it was only a gesture. Stupid, he thought. Sentimental, too, but mostly just stupid.

Lavender was dead. You couldn't burn the blame.

Besides, the letters were in his head. And even now, without photographs, Lieutenant Cross could see Martha playing volleyball in her white gym shorts and yellow T-shirt. He could see her moving in the rain.

When the fire died out, Lieutenant Cross pulled his poncho over his shoulders and ate breakfast from a can.

There was no great mystery, he decided.

In those burned letters Martha had never mentioned the war, except to say, Jimmy, take care of yourself. She wasn't involved. She signed the letters "Love," but it wasn't love, and all the fine lines and technicalities did not matter. Virginity was no longer an issue. He hated her. Yes, he did. He hated her. Love, too, but it was a hard, hating kind of love.

The morning came up wet and blurry. Everything seemed part of everything else, the fog and Martha and the deepening rain.

He was a soldier, after all.

Half smiling, Lieutenant Jimmy Cross took out his maps. He shook his head hard, as if to clear it, then bent forward and began planning the day's march. In ten minutes, or maybe twenty, he would rouse the men and they would pack up and head west, where the maps showed the country to be green and inviting. They would do what they had always done. The rain might add some weight, but otherwise it would be one more day layered upon all the other days.

He was realistic about it. There was that new hardness in his stomach. He loved her but he hated her.

No more fantasies, he told himself.

Henceforth, when he thought about Martha, it would be only to think that she belonged elsewhere. He would shut down the daydreams. This was not Mount Sebastian, it was another world, where there were no pretty poems or mid-term exams, a place where men died because of carelessness and gross stupidity. Kiowa was right. Boom-down, and you were dead, never partly dead.

Briefly, in the rain, Lieutenant Cross saw Martha's gray eyes gazing back at him. He understood.

It was very sad, he thought. The things men carried inside. The things men did or felt they had to do.

He almost nodded at her, but didn't.

Instead he went back to his maps. He was now determined to perform his duties firmly and without negligence. It wouldn't help Lavender, he knew that, but from this point on he would comport himself as an officer. He would dispose of his good-luck pebble. Swallow it, maybe, or use Lee Strunk's slingshot, or just drop it along the trail. On the march he would impose strict field discipline. He would be careful to send out flank security, to prevent straggling or bunching up, to keep his troops moving at the proper pace and at the proper interval. He would insist on clean weapons. He would confiscate the remainder of Lavender's dope. Later in the day, perhaps, he would call the men together and speak to them plainly. He would accept the blame for what had happened to Ted Lavender. He would be a man about it. He would look them in the eyes, keeping his chin level, and he would issue the new

SOPs in a calm, impersonal tone of voice, a lieutenant's voice, leaving no room for argument or discussion. Commencing immediately, he'd tell them, they would no longer abandon equipment along the route of march. They would police up their acts. They would get their shit together, and keep it together, and maintain it neatly and in good working order.

He would not tolerate laxity. He would show strength, distancing himself.

Among the men there would be grumbling, of course, and maybe worse, because their days would seem longer and their loads heavier, but Lieutenant Jimmy Cross reminded himself that his obligation was not to be loved but to lead. He would dispense with love; it was not now a factor. And if anyone quarreled or complained, he would simply tighten his lips and arrange his shoulders in the correct command posture. He might give a curt little nod. Or he might not. He might just shrug and say, Carry on, then they would saddle up and form into a column and move out toward the villages west of Than Khe.

🖎 🖎 🖎

Suggestions for Discussion

1. Why does the narrator insist on the exact weight of things?
2. Name two concrete objects that help to characterize the individual soldiers (such as the photo or the Bible). Explain what these details imply.
3. Find one passage where the prose rhythm mirrors the rhythm of the action described and another where it reinforces the emotion depicted.
4. Typically, writing teachers suggest avoiding abstract terms, such as love, injustice, and beauty. Yet here, in addition to their gear, the soldiers carry such abstract qualities as *distrust of the white man, all they could bear, grief, terror, love, fear.* How does O'Brien use so many grand abstractions successfully in this story?

Retrospect

5. How would you describe the way the story is told? What advantages are there to telling the story this way rather than in a more traditional, chronological form?
6. What choice does Jimmy Cross make on the first page of the story? The last page? How would you describe the change in Jimmy from beginning to end?

Where Are You Going, Where Have You Been?

JOYCE CAROL OATES

for Bob Dylan

Her name was Connie. She was fifteen and she had a quick nervous giggling habit of craning her neck to glance into mirrors, or checking other people's faces to make sure her own was all right. Her mother, who noticed everything and knew everything and who hadn't much reason any longer to look at her own face, always scolded Connie about it. "Stop gawking at yourself, who are you? You think you're so pretty?" she would say. Connie would raise her eyebrows at these familiar complaints and look right through her mother, into a shadowy vision of herself as she was right at that moment: she knew she was pretty and that was everything. Her mother had been pretty once too, if you could believe those old snapshots in the album, but now her looks were gone and that was why she was always after Connie.

"Why don't you keep your room clean like your sister? How've you got your hair fixed—what the hell stinks? Hair spray? You don't see your sister using that junk."

Her sister June was twenty-four and still lived at home. She was a secretary in the high school Connie attended, and if that wasn't bad enough—with her in the same building—she was so plain and chunky and steady that Connie had to hear her praised all the time by her mother and her mother's sisters. June did this, June did that, she saved money and helped clean the house and cooked and Connie couldn't do a thing, her mind was all filled with trashy daydreams. Their father was away at work most of the time and when he came home he wanted supper and he read the newspaper at supper and after supper he went to bed. He didn't bother talking much to them, but around his bent head Connie's mother kept picking at her until Connie wished her mother was dead and she herself was dead and it was all over. "She makes me want to throw up sometimes," she complained to her friends. She had a high, breathless, amused voice which made everything she said a little forced, whether it was sincere or not.

There was one good thing: June went places with girl friends of hers, girls who were just as plain and steady as she, and so when Connie wanted to do that her mother had no objections. The father of Connie's best girl friend drove the girls the three miles to town and left them off at a shopping plaza, so that they could walk through the stores or go to a movie, and when he came to pick them up again at eleven he never bothered to ask what they had done.

They must have been familiar sights, walking around that shopping plaza in their shorts and flat ballerina slippers that always scuffed the sidewalk, with charm bracelets jingling on their thin wrists; they would lean together to whisper and laugh secretly if someone passed by who amused or interested them. Connie had long dark blond hair that drew anyone's eye to it, and she wore part of it pulled up on her head and puffed out and the rest of it she let fall down her back. She wore a pullover jersey blouse that looked one way when she was at home and another way when she was away from home. Everything about her had two sides to it, one for home and one for anywhere that was not home: her walk that could be childlike and bobbing, or languid enough to make anyone think she was hearing music in her head, her mouth which was pale and smirking most of the time, but bright and pink on these evenings out, her laugh which was cynical and drawling at home—"Ha, ha, very funny"—but high-pitched and nervous anywhere else, like the jingling of the charms on her bracelet.

Sometimes they did go shopping or to a movie, but sometimes they went across the highway, ducking fast across the busy road, to a drive-in restaurant where older kids hung out. The restaurant was shaped like a big bottle, though squatter than a real bottle, and on its cap was a revolving figure of a grinning boy who held a hamburger aloft. One night in midsummer they ran across, breathless with daring, and right away someone leaned out a car window and invited them over, but it was just a boy from high school they didn't like. It made them feel good to be able to ignore him. They went up through the maze of parked and cruising cars to the bright-lit, fly-infested restaurant, their faces pleased and expectant as if they were entering a sacred building that loomed out of the night to give them what haven and what blessing they yearned for. They sat at the counter and crossed their legs at the ankles, their thin shoulders rigid with excitement and listened to the music that made everything so good: the music was always in the background like music at a church service, it was something to depend upon.

A boy named Eddie came in to talk with them. He sat backwards on his stool, turning himself jerkily around in semi-circles and then stopping and turning again, and after a while he asked Connie if she would like something to eat. She said she did and so she tapped her friend's arm on her way out—her friend pulled her face up into a brave droll look—and Connie said she would meet her at eleven, across the way. "I just hate to leave her like that," Connie said earnestly, but the boy said that she wouldn't be alone for long. So they went out to his car and on the way Connie couldn't help but let her eyes wander over the windshields and faces all around her, her face gleaming with the joy that had nothing to do with Eddie or even this place; it might have been the music. She drew her shoulders up and sucked in her breath with the pure pleasure of being alive, and just at that moment she happened to glance at a face just a few feet from hers. It was a boy with shaggy black hair, in a convertible jalopy painted gold. He stared at her and then his lips widened into a grin. Connie slit her eyes at him and turned away, but she couldn't help glancing back and there he was still watching her. He wagged a finger and laughed and said, "Gonna get you, baby," and Connie turned away again without Eddie noticing anything.

She spent three hours with him, at the restaurant where they ate hamburgers and drank Cokes in wax cups that were always sweating, and then down an alley a mile or so away, and when he left her off at five to eleven only the movie house was still open at the plaza. Her girl friend was there, talking with a boy. When Connie came up the two girls smiled at each other and Connie said, "How was the movie?" and the girl said, "*You* should know." They rode off with the girl's father, sleepy and pleased, and Connie couldn't help but look at the darkened shopping plaza with its big empty parking lot and its signs that were faded and ghostly now, and over at the drive-in restaurant where cars were still circling tirelessly. She couldn't hear the music at this distance.

Next morning June asked her how the movie was and Connie said, "So-so."

She and that girl and occasionally another girl went out several times a week that way, and the rest of the time Connie spent around the house—it was summer vacation—getting in her mother's way and thinking, dreaming, about the boys she met. But all the boys fell back and dissolved into a single face that was not even a face, but an idea, a feeling, mixed up with the urgent insistent pounding of the music and the humid night air of July. Connie's mother kept dragging her back to the daylight by finding things for her to do or saying suddenly, "What's this about the Pettinger girl?"

And Connie would say nervously, "Oh, her. That dope." She always drew thick clear lines between herself and such girls, and her mother was simple and kindly enough to believe her. Her mother was so simple, Connie thought, that it was maybe cruel to fool her so much. Her mother went scuffling around the house in old bedroom slippers and complained over the telephone to one sister about the other, then the other called up and the two of them complained about the third one. If June's name was mentioned her mother's tone was approving, and if Connie's name was mentioned it was disapproving. This did not really mean she disliked Connie and actually Connie thought that her mother preferred her to June because she was prettier, but the two of them kept up a pretense of exasperation, a sense that they were tugging and struggling over something of little value to either of them. Sometimes, over coffee, they were almost friends, but something would come up—some vexation that was like a fly buzzing suddenly around their heads—and their faces went hard with contempt.

One Sunday Connie got up at eleven—none of them bothered with church—and washed her hair so that it could dry all day long, in the sun. Her parents and sister were going to a barbecue at an aunt's house and Connie said no, she wasn't interested, rolling her eyes, to let mother know just what she thought of it. "Stay home alone then," her mother said sharply. Connie sat out back in a lawn chair and watched them drive away, her father quiet and bald, hunched around so that he could back the car out, her mother with a look that was still angry and not at all softened through the windshield, and in the back seat poor old June all dressed up as if she didn't know what a barbecue was, with all the running yelling kids and the flies. Connie sat with her eyes closed in the sun, dreaming and dazed with the warmth about her as if this were a kind of love, the caresses of love, and her mind slipped over onto thoughts of the boy she had been with the night before and how nice he had been, how sweet it always was, not the way someone like June would suppose but sweet, gentle, the way it was in movies and promised in songs; and when she opened her eyes she hardly knew where she was, the back yard ran off into weeds and a fenceline of trees and behind it the sky was perfectly blue and still. The asbestos "ranch house" that was now three years old startled her—it looked small. She shook her head as if to get awake.

It was too hot. She went inside the house and turned on the radio to drown out the quiet. She sat on the edge of her bed, barefoot, and listened for an hour and a half to a program called XYZ Sunday Jamboree, record after record of hard, fast, shrieking songs she sang along with, interspersed by exclamations from "Bobby King": "An' look here you girls at Napoleon's—Son and Charley want you to pay real close attention to this song coming up!"

And Connie paid close attention herself, bathed in a glow of slow-pulsed joy that seemed to rise mysteriously out of the music itself and lay languidly about the airless little room, breathed in and breathed out with each gentle rise and fall of her chest.

After a while she heard a car coming up the drive. She sat up at once, startled, because it couldn't be her father so soon. The gravel kept crunching all the way in from the road—the driveway was long—and Connie ran to the window. It was a car she didn't know. It was an open jalopy, painted a bright gold that caught the sun opaquely. Her heart began to pound and her fingers snatched at her hair, checking it, and she whispered "Christ. Christ," wondering how bad she looked. The car came to a stop at the side door and the horn sounded four short taps as if this were a signal Connie knew.

She went into the kitchen and approached the door slowly, then hung out the screen door, her bare toes curling down off the step. There were two boys in the car and now she recognized the driver: he had shaggy, shabby black hair that looked crazy as a wig and he was grinning at her.

"I ain't late, am I?" he said.

"Who the hell do you think you are?" Connie said.

"Toldja I'd be out, didn't I?"

"I don't even know who you are."

She spoke sullenly, careful to show no interest or pleasure, and he spoke in a fast bright monotone. Connie looked past him to the other boy, taking her time. He had fair brown hair, with a lock that fell onto his forehead. His sideburns gave him a fierce, embarrassed look, but so far he hadn't even bothered to glance at her. Both boys wore sunglasses. The driver's glasses were metallic and mirrored everything in miniature.

"You wanta come for a ride?" he said.

Connie smirked and let her hair fall loose over one shoulder.

"Don'tcha like my car? New paint job," he said. "Hey."

"What?"

"You're cute."

She pretended to fidget, chasing flies away from the door.

"Don't cha believe me, or what?" he said.

"Look, I don't even know who you are," Connie said in disgust.

"Hey, Ellie's got a radio, see. Mine's broke down." He lifted his friend's arm and showed her the little transistor the boy was holding, and now Connie began to hear the music. It was the same program that was playing inside the house.

"Bobby King?" she said.

"I listen to him all the time. I think he's *great*."

"He's kind of great," Connie said reluctantly.

"Listen, that guy's *great*. He knows where the action is."

Connie blushed a little, because the glasses made it impossible for her to see just what this boy was looking at. She couldn't decide if she liked him or if he was just a jerk, and so she dawdled in the doorway and wouldn't come down or go back inside. She said, "What's all that stuff painted on your car?"

"Can'tcha read it?" He opened the door very carefully, as if he was afraid it might fall off. He slid out just as carefully, planting his feet firmly on the ground, the tiny metallic world in his glasses slowing down like gelatine hardening and in the midst of it Connie's bright green blouse. "This here is my name, to begin with," he said. ARNOLD FRIEND was written in tar-like black letters on the side, with a drawing of a round grinning face that reminded Connie of a pumpkin, except it wore sun-glasses. "I wanta introduce myself, I'm Arnold Friend and that's my real name and I'm gonna be your friend, honey, and inside the car's Ellie Oscar, he's kinda shy." Ellie brought his transistor up to his shoulder and balanced it there. "Now these numbers are a secret code, honey," Arnold Friend explained. He read off the num-bers 33, 19, 17 and raised his eyebrows at her to see what she thought of that, but she didn't think much of it. The left rear fender had been smashed and around it was written, on the gleaming gold background: DONE BY CRAZY WOMAN DRIVER. Connie had to laugh at that. Arnold Friend was pleased at her laughter and looked up at her. "Around the other side's a lot more—you wanta come and see them?"

"No."

"Why not?"

"Why should I?"

"Don'tcha wanta see what's on the car? Don'tcha wanta go for a ride?"

"I don't know."

"Why not?"

"I got things to do."

"Like what?"

"Things."

He laughed as if she had said something funny. He slapped his thighs. He was standing in a strange way, leaning back against the car as if he were balancing him-self. He wasn't tall, only an inch or so taller than she would be if she came down to him. Connie liked the way he was dressed, which was the way all of them dressed: tight faded jeans stuffed into black, scuffed boots, a belt that pulled his waist in and showed how lean he was, and a white pull-over shirt that was a little soiled and showed the hard small muscles of his arms and shoulders. He looked as if he probably did hard work, lifting and carrying things. Even his neck looked muscular. And his face was a familiar face, somehow: the jaw and chin and cheeks slightly darkened, because he hadn't shaved for a day or two, and the nose long and hawk-like, sniffing as if she were a treat he was going to gobble up and it was all a joke.

"Connie, you ain't telling the truth. This is your day set aside for a ride with me and you know it," he said, still laughing. The way he straightened and recovered from his fit of laughing showed that it had been all fake.

"How do you know what my name is?" she said suspiciously.

"It's Connie."

"Maybe and maybe not."

"I know my Connie," he said, wagging his finger. Now she remembered him even better, back at the restaurant, and her cheeks warmed at the thought of how she sucked in her breath just at the moment she passed him—how she must have looked to him. And he had remembered her. "Ellie and I come out here especially for you," he said. "Ellie can sit in back. How about it?"

"Where?"

"Where what?"

"Where're we going?"

He looked at her. He took off the sunglasses and she saw how pale the skin around his eyes was, like holes that were not in shadow but instead in light. His eyes were like chips of broken glass that catch the light in an amiable way. He smiled. It was as if the idea of going for a ride somewhere, to some place, was a new idea to him.

"Just for a ride, Connie sweetheart."

"I never said my name was Connie," she said.

"But I know what it is. I know your name and all about you, lots of things," Arnold Friend said. He had not moved yet but stood still leaning back against the side of his jalopy. "I took a special interest in you, such a pretty girl, and found out all about you like I know your parents and sister are gone somewheres and I know where and how long they're going to be gone, and I know who you were with last night, and your best friend's name is Betty. Right?"

He spoke in a simple lilting voice, exactly as if he were reciting the words to a song. His smile assured her that everything was fine. In the car Ellie turned up the volume on his radio and did not bother to look around at them.

"Ellie can sit in the back seat," Arnold Friend said. He indicated his friend with a casual jerk of his chin, as if Ellie did not count and she should not bother with him.

"How'd you find out all that stuff?" Connie said.

"Listen: Betty Schultz and Tony Fitch and Jimmy Pettinger and Nancy Pettinger," he said, in a chant. "Raymond Stanley and Bob Hutter—"

"Do you know all those kids?"

"I know everybody."

"Look, you're kidding. You're not from around here."

"Sure."

"But—how come we never saw you before?"

"Sure you saw me before," he said. He looked down at his boots, as if he were a little offended. "You just don't remember."

"I guess I'd remember you," Connie said.

"Yeah?" He looked up at this, beaming. He was pleased. He began to mark time with the music from Ellie's radio, tapping his fists lightly together. Connie looked away from his smile to the car, which was painted so bright it almost hurt her eyes to look at it. She looked at that name, ARNOLD FRIEND. And up at the front fender was an expression that was familiar—MAN THE FLYING SAUCERS. It was an expression kids had used the year before, but didn't use this year. She looked at it for a while as if the words meant something to her that she did not yet know.

"What're you thinking about? Huh?" Arnold Friend demanded. "Not worried about your hair blowing around in the car, are you?"

"No."

"Think I maybe can't drive good?"

"How do I know?"

"You're a hard girl to handle. How come?" he said. "Don't you know I'm your friend? Didn't you see me put my sign in the air when you walked by?"

"What sign?"

"My sign." And he drew an X in the air, leaning out toward her. They were maybe ten feet apart. After his hand fell back to his side the X was still in the air, almost visible. Connie let the screen door close and stood perfectly still inside it, listening to the music from her radio and the boy's blend together. She stared at Arnold Friend. He stood there so stiffly relaxed, pretending to be relaxed, with one hand idly on the door handle as if he were keeping himself up that way and had no intention of ever moving again. She recognized most things about him, the tight jeans that showed his thighs and buttocks and the greasy leather boots and the tight shirt, and even that slippery friendly smile of his, that sleepy dreamy smile that all the boys used to get across ideas they didn't want to put into words. She recognized all this and also the singsong way he talked, slightly mocking, kidding, but serious and a little melancholy, and she recognized the way he tapped one fist against the other in homage to the perpetual music behind him. But all these things did not come together.

She said suddenly, "Hey, how old are you?"

His smile faded. She could see then that he wasn't a kid, he was much older— thirty, maybe more. At this knowledge her heart began to pound faster.

"That's a crazy thing to ask. Can'tcha see I'm your own age?"

"Like hell you are."

"Or maybe a coupla years older, I'm eighteen."

"Eighteen?" she said doubtfully.

He grinned to reassure her and lines appeared at the corners of his mouth. His teeth were big and white. He grinned so broadly his eyes became slits and she saw how thick the lashes were, thick and black as if painted with a black tar-like material. Then he seemed to become embarrassed, abruptly, and looked over his shoulder at Ellie. "*Him*, he's crazy," he said. "Ain't he a riot, he's a nut, a real character." Ellie was still listening to the music. His sunglasses told nothing about what he was thinking. He wore a bright orange shirt unbuttoned halfway to show his chest, which was a pale, bluish chest and not muscular like Arnold Friend's. His shirt collar was turned up all around and the very tips of the collar pointed out past his chin as if they were protecting him. He was pressing the transistor radio up against his ear and sat there in a kind of daze, right in the sun.

"He's kinda strange," Connie said.

"Hey, she says you're kinda strange! Kinda strange!" Arnold Friend cried. He pounded on the car to get Ellie's attention. Ellie turned for the first time and Connie saw with shock that he wasn't a kid either—he had a fair, hairless face, cheeks reddened slightly as if the veins grew too close to the surface of his skin, the face of a forty-year-old baby. Connie felt a wave of dizziness rise in her at this sight and she stared at him as if waiting for something to change the shock of the moment, make it all right again. Ellie's lips kept shaping words, mumbling along with the words blasting his ear.

"Maybe you two better go away," Connie said faintly.

"What? How come?" Arnold Friend cried. "We come out here to take you for a ride. It's Sunday." He had the voice of the man on the radio now. It was the same voice, Connie thought. "Don'tcha know it's Sunday all day and honey, no matter who you were with last night today you're with Arnold Friend and don't you forget it!—Maybe you better step out here," he said, and this last was in a different voice. It was a little flatter, as if the heat was finally getting to him.

"No. I got things to do."

"Hey."

"You two better leave."

"We ain't leaving until you come with us."

"Like hell I am—"

"Connie, don't fool around with me. I mean—I mean, don't fool *around*," he said, shaking his head. He laughed incredulously. He placed his sunglasses on top of his head, carefully, as if he were indeed wearing a wig, and brought the stems down behind his ears. Connie stared at him, another wave of dizziness and fear rising in her so that for a moment he wasn't even in focus but was just a blur, standing there against his gold car, and she had the idea that he had driven up the driveway all right but had come from nowhere before that and belonged nowhere and that everything about him and even the music that was so familiar to her was only half real.

"If my father comes and sees you—"

"He ain't coming. He's at a barbecue."

"How do you know that?"

"Aunt Tillie's. Right now they're—uh—they're drinking. Sitting around," he said vaguely, squinting as if he were staring all the way to town and over to Aunt Tillie's back yard. Then the vision seemed to clear and he nodded energetically. "Yeah. Sitting around. There's your sister in a blue dress, huh? And high heels, the poor sad bitch—nothing like you, sweetheart! And your mother's helping some fat woman with the corn, they're cleaning the corn—husking the corn—"

"What fat woman?" Connie cried.

"How do I know what fat woman. I don't know every goddam fat woman in the world!" Arnold Friend laughed.

"Oh, that's Mrs. Hornby. . . . Who invited her?" Connie said. She felt a little light-headed. Her breath was coming quickly.

"She's too fat. I don't like them fat. I like them the way you are, honey," he said, smiling sleepily at her. They stared at each other for a while, through the screen door. He said softly, "Now what you're going to do is this: you're going to come out that door. You're going to sit up front with me and Ellie's going to sit in the back, the hell with Ellie, right? This isn't Ellie's date. You're my date. I'm your lover, honey."

"What? You're crazy—"

"Yes, I'm your lover. You don't know what that is but you will," he said. "I know that too. I know all about you. But look: it's real nice and you couldn't ask for nobody better than me, or more polite. I always keep my word. I'll tell you how it is, I'm always nice at first, the first time. I'll hold you so tight you won't think you have to try to get away or pretend anything because you'll know you can't. And I'll come inside you where it's all secret and you'll give in to me and you'll love me—"

"Shut up! You're crazy!" Connie said. She backed away from the door. She put her hands against her ears as if she'd heard something terrible, something not meant for her. "People don't talk like that, you're crazy," she muttered. Her heart was almost too big now for her chest and its pumping made sweat break out all over her. She looked out to see Arnold Friend pause and then take a step toward the porch lurching. He almost fell. But, like a clever drunken man, he managed to catch his balance. He wobbled in his high boots and grabbed hold of one of the porch posts.

"Honey?" he said. "You still listening?"

"Get the hell out of here!"

"Be nice, honey. Listen."

"I'm going to call the police—"

He wobbled again and out of the side of his mouth came a fast spat curse, an aside not meant for her to hear. But even this "Christ!" sounded forced. Then he began to smile again. She watched this smile come, awkward as if he were smiling from inside a mask. His whole face was a mask, she thought wildly, tanned down onto his throat but then running out as if he had plastered make-up on his face but had forgotten about his throat.

"Honey—? Listen, here's how it is. I always tell the truth and I promise you this: I ain't coming in that house after you."

"You better not! I'm going to call the police if you—if you don't—"

"Honey," he said, talking right through her voice, "honey, I'm not coming in there but you are coming out here. You know why?"

She was panting. The kitchen looked like a place she had never seen before, some room she had run inside but which wasn't good enough, wasn't going to help her. The kitchen window had never had a curtain, after three years, and there were dishes in the sink for her to do—probably—and if you ran your hand across the table you'd probably feel something sticky there.

"You listening, honey? Hey?"

"—going to call the police—"

"Soon as you touch the phone I don't need to keep my promise and can come inside. You won't want that."

She rushed forward and tried to lock the door. Her fingers were shaking. "But why lock it," Arnold Friend said gently, talking right into her face. "It's just a screen door. It's just nothing." One of his boots was at a strange angle, as if his foot wasn't in it. It pointed out to the left, bent at the ankle. "I mean, anybody can break through a screen door and glass and wood and iron or anything else if he needs to, anybody at all and specially Arnold Friend. If the place got lit up with a fire, honey, you'd come running out into my arms, right into my arms and safe at home—like you knew I was your lover and'd stopped fooling around. I don't mind a nice shy girl but I don't like no fooling around." Part of those words were spoken with a slight rhythmic lilt, and Connie somehow recognized them—the echo of a song from last year, about a girl rushing into her boy friend's arms and coming home again—

Connie stood barefoot on the linoleum floor, staring at him. "What do you want?" she whispered.

"I want you," he said.

"What?"

"Seen you that night and thought, that's the one, yes sir. I never needed to look any more."

"But my father's coming back. He's coming to get me. I had to wash my hair first—" She spoke in a dry, rapid voice, hardly raising it for him to hear.

"No, your daddy is not coming and yes, you had to wash your hair and you washed it for me. It's nice and shining and all for me, I thank you, sweetheart," he said, with a mock bow, but again he almost lost his balance. He had to bend and adjust his boots. Evidently his feet did not go all the way down; the boots must have been stuffed with something so that he would seem taller. Connie stared out at him and behind him Ellie in the car, who seemed to be looking off toward Connie's right, into nothing. This Ellie said, pulling the words out of the air one after another as if he were just discovering them, "You want me to pull out the phone?"

"Shut your mouth and keep it shut," Arnold Friend said, his face red from bending over or maybe from embarrassment because Connie had seen his boots. "This ain't none of your business."

"What—what are you doing? What do you want?" Connie said. "If I call the police they'll get you, they'll arrest you—"

"Promise was not to come in unless you touch that phone, and I'll keep that promise," he said. He resumed his erect position and tried to force his shoulders back. He sounded like a hero in a movie, declaring something important. He spoke too loudly and it was as if he were speaking to someone behind Connie. "I ain't made plans for coming in that house where I don't belong but just for you to come out to me, the way you should. Don't you know who I am?"

"You're crazy," she whispered. She backed away from the door but did not want to go into another part of the house, as if this would give him permission to come through the door. "What do you. . . . You're crazy, you. . . ."

"Huh? What're you saying, honey?"

Her eyes darted everywhere in the kitchen. She could not remember what it was, this room.

"This is how it is, honey: you come out and we'll drive away, have a nice ride. But if you don't come out we're gonna wait till your people come home and then they're all going to get it."

"You want that telephone pulled out?" Ellie said. He held the radio away from his ear and grimaced, as if without the radio the air was too much for him.

"I toldja shut up, Ellie." Arnold Friend said, "You're deaf, get a hearing aid, right? Fix yourself up. This little girl's no trouble and's gonna be nice to me, so Ellie keep to yourself, this ain't your date—right? Don't hem in on me. Don't hog. Don't crush. Don't bird dog. Don't trail me," he said in a rapid meaningless voice, as if he were running through all the expressions he'd learned but was no longer sure which one of them was in style, then rushing on to new ones, making them up with his eyes closed, "Don't crawl under my fence, don't squeeze in my chipmunk hole, don't sniff my glue, suck my popsicle, keep your own greasy fingers on yourself!" He shaded his eyes and peered in at Connie, who was backed against the kitchen table. "Don't mind him, honey, he's just a creep. He's a dope. Right? I'm the boy for you and like I said you come out here nice like a lady and give me your hand, and nobody else gets hurt, I mean, your nice old bald-headed daddy and your mummy and your sister in her high heels. Because listen: why bring them in this?"

"Leave me alone," Connie whispered.

"Hey, you know that old woman down the road, the one with the chickens and stuff—you know her?"

"She's dead!"

"Dead? What? You know her?" Arnold Friend said.

"She's dead—"

"Don't you like her?"

"She's dead—she's—she isn't here any more—"

"But don't you like her, I mean, you got something against her? Some grudge or something?" Then his voice dipped as if he were conscious of rudeness. He touched the sunglasses on top of his head as if to make sure they were still there. "Now you be a good girl."

"What are you going to do?"

"Just two things, or maybe three," Arnold Friend said. "But I promise it won't last long and you'll like me that way you get to like people you're close to. You will. It's all over for you here, so come on out. You don't want your people in any trouble, do you?"

She turned and bumped against a chair or something, hurting her leg, but she ran into the back room and picked up the telephone. Something roared in her ear, a tiny roaring, and she was so sick with fear that she could do nothing but listen to it—the telephone was clammy and very heavy and her fingers groped down to the dial but were too weak to touch it. She began to scream into the phone, into the roaring. She cried out, she cried for her mother, she felt her breath start jerking back and forth in her lungs as if it were something Arnold Friend were stabbing her with again and again with no tenderness. A noisy sorrowful wailing rose all about her and she was locked inside it the way she was locked inside this house.

After a while she could hear again. She was sitting on the floor, with her wet back against the wall.

Arnold Friend was saying from the door, "That's a good girl. Put the phone back."

She kicked the phone away from her.

"No, honey. Pick it up. Put it back right."

She picked it up and put it back. The dial tone stopped.

"That's a good girl. Now you come outside."

She was hollow with what had been fear, but what was now just an emptiness. All that screaming had blasted it out of her. She sat, one leg cramped under her, and deep inside her brain was something like a pinpoint of light that kept going and would not let her relax. She thought, I'm not going to see my mother again. She thought, I'm not going to sleep in my bed again. Her bright green blouse was all wet.

Arnold Friend said, in a gentle-loud voice that was like a stage voice, "The place where you came from ain't there any more, and where you had in mind to go is cancelled out. This place you are now—inside your daddy's house—is nothing but a cardboard box I can knock down any time. You know that and always did know it. You hear me?"

She thought, I have got to think. I have to know what to do.

"We'll go out to a nice field, out in the country here where it smells so nice and it's sunny," Arnold Friend said. "I'll have my arms tight around you so you won't need to try to get away and I'll show you what love is like, what it does. The hell with this house! It looks solid all right," he said. He ran a fingernail down the screen and the noise did not make Connie shiver, as it would have the day before. "Now put your hand on your heart, honey. Feel that? That feels solid too but we know better, be nice to me, be sweet like you can because what else is there for a girl like you but to be sweet and pretty and give in?—and get away before her people come back?"

She felt her pounding heart. Her hands seemed to enclose it. She thought for the first time in her life that it was nothing that was hers, that belonged to her, but just a pounding, living thing inside this body that wasn't hers either.

"You don't want them to get hurt," Arnold Friend went on. "Now get up, honey. Get up all by yourself."

She stood.

"Now turn this way. That's right. Come over here to me—Ellie, put that away, didn't I tell you? You dope. You miserable creepy dope," Arnold Friend said. His words were not angry but only part of an incantation. The incantation was kindly. "Now come out through the kitchen to me honey and let's see a smile, try it, you're a brave sweet little girl and now they're eating corn and hotdogs cooked to bursting over an outdoor fire, and they don't know one thing about you and never did and honey you're better than them because not one of them would have done this for you."

Connie felt the linoleum under her feet; it was cool. She brushed her hair back out of her eyes. Arnold Friend let go of the post tentatively and opened his arms for her, his elbows pointing up toward each other and his wrists limp, to show that this was an embarrassed embrace and a little mocking, he didn't want to make her self-conscious.

She put out her hand against the screen. She watched herself push the door slowly open as if she were safe back somewhere in the other doorway, watching this body and this head of long hair moving out into the sunlight where Arnold Friend waited.

"My sweet little blue-eyed girl," he said, in a half-sung sigh that had nothing to do with her brown eyes but was taken up just the same by the vast sunlit reaches of the land behind him and on all sides of him—so much land that Connie had never seen before and did not recognize except to know that she was going to it.

🦜 🦜 🦜

Suggestions for Discussion

1. Find passages where Connie's fear is described though physical sensations.
2. What specific things make Arnold Friend frightening? As the writer attempting to create a frightening, original character, what kinds of clichés would it have been too easy to use?
3. What is shown by Connie's habit of checking her reflection? By the "two sides" of her appearance?

Retrospect

4. How does Arnold Friend maintain power over Connie?
5. Find three dialogue lines that show different kinds of persuasion used by Arnold Friend. Why has the author portrayed him as trying to persuade rather than force Connie to leave?
6. What seems to be implied in the final paragraph? Why does the author end the story at that point?

🦜 🦜 🦜

Writing Exercises

INDIVIDUAL

1. *Story Trigger.* One way to test your skill in the use of concrete, significant detail is to create a reality that is convincing—and yet literally impossible. To begin, draft a three-to-five-page story in which a single impossible event happens in the everyday world. (For example, a dog tells fortunes, a secret message appears on a pizza, the radio announcer speaks in an ex-husband's voice—supermarket tabloids can be a good source of ideas.) First, focus on using detail to create the reality of both the normal world and the impossible event—the more believable the reality is, the more seamlessly readers will accept the magic. After

you've drafted the story, focus on the character and why that person has somehow earned or deserved this miracle.

2. Describe an object of great importance to a character: a car, trophy, dress, or ring, for example. First, write a paragraph using details that portray the object as sensuous, beautiful, and tempting. Then write a second paragraph in which the same object is described through details that make it seem repellent.

DEVELOPMENT/REVISION

3. Write down three adjectives (*beautiful, aggressive, haughty*) that describe a character in your story-in-progress. (Be sure the adjectives describe *different* qualities, not the same ones. For instance, *handsome, well groomed, muscular* are too similar, as opposed to *handsome, talkative,* and *mechanically inclined,* which show different aspects of the character.)
   a. Without using any of these adjectives (or synonyms), write a half-page scene or passage that shows the character engaged in action and perhaps speaking some dialogue that will suggest the selected qualities.
   b. Exchange exercises and read them over. Based on this depiction of the character, guess which three qualities your partner wished to convey. Point out the specific lines that created these impressions.

4. Brainstorm details for your story-in-progress. Begin by putting yourself in the mind of your character and focusing on the setting. Take one to two minutes to make notes in response to each question.
   a. What sounds can you hear in this place?
   b. What is the most distant sound you can hear, the sound that you might not notice if you weren't paying special attention?
   c. What smells do you associate with this place?
   d. What are you wearing? How does it feel against your skin?
   e. What else can you touch? Not only with your fingertips, but with your whole body—the small of your back, for instance, or the soles of your feet.
   f. What can you taste?
   g. What colors do you associate with this place?
   h. What do you see to the left, overhead, on the horizon?
   i. What emotions does this place evoke in you?

COLLABORATIVE

5. Select one scent associated with your story-in-progress. Then go around the classroom, having each writer give a one-sentence summary of his or her story and describing the related scent to see how effective the addition of this sense can be.

6. Choose a well-known fairy tale, such as "Hansel and Gretel," "Cinderella," or "Snow White." Take two minutes for each class member to freewrite a list of details associated with that fairy tale. (Avoid adjectives, such as "ugly," in favor of concrete descriptions, such as "chin like a turnip root.") When time is up, review your partner's list and choose the most striking detail. Then go around the classroom, listing the most effective details to see how even a familiar story may be enlivened with fresh and precise description.

7. As a class, pick four emotions and make two lists for each (eight lists in all)— one that describes the body language of a person experiencing that emotion (external), and the other describing that person's physical sensations (internal). Review the lists: which symptoms seem overly familiar (his hair stood on end; her heart was racing) and which seem fresh and original?

   Follow-up: Circle a passage of high emotion in your own story and exchange manuscripts with a partner. Do you see a place where emotion could be physically shown rather than labeled? Do you see a clichéd or melodramatic description that could be replaced with a more precise and original physical detail?

4

BUILDING CHARACTER
Characterization, Part I

- ◆ Credibility

- ◆ Purpose

- ◆ Complexity

- ◆ Change

- ◆ The Indirect Methods of Character Presentation

Human character is in the foreground of all fiction, however the humanity might be disguised. Anthropomorphism may be a scientific sin, but it is a literary necessity. Bugs Bunny isn't a rabbit; he's a plucky youth in ears. Peter Rabbit is a mischievous boy. Brer Rabbit is a sassy rebel. The romantic heroes of *Watership Down* are out of the Arthurian tradition, not out of the hutch.

Henri Bergson, in his essay "On Laughter," observes:

> . . . the comic does not exist outside the pale of what is strictly human. A landscape may be beautiful, charming or sublime, or insignificant and ugly; it will never be laughable.

Bergson is right, but it is just as true that only the human is tragic. We may describe a landscape as "tragic" because nature has been devastated by industry, but the tragedy lies in the cupidity of those who wrought the havoc, in the dreariness, poverty, or disease of those who must live there. A conservationist or ecologist (or a novelist) may care passionately about nature and dislike people because they pollute oceans and cut down trees. Then we say he or she "identifies" with nature (a wholly human capacity) or "respects the natural unity" (of which humanity is a part) or wants to keep the earth habitable (for whom?) or "values nature for its own sake" (using standards of value that nature does not share). By all available evidence, the universe is indifferent to the destruction of trees, property, peoples, and planets. Only people care.

If this is so, then your fiction can be only as successful as the characters who move it and move within it. Whether they are drawn from life or are pure fantasy— and all fictional characters lie somewhere between the two—we must find them interesting, we must find them believable, and we must care about what happens to them.

The Character Journal.   As a writer you may have the lucky, facile sort of imagination to which characters spring full-blown, complete with gestures, histories, and passions. Or it may be that you need to explore in order to exploit, to draw your characters out gradually and coax them into being. That can be lucky, too.

For either kind of writer, but especially the latter, the journal is an invaluable help. A journal lets you coax and explore without committing yourself to anything or anyone. It allows you to know everything about your character whether you use it or not. Before you put a character in a story, know how well that character sleeps. Know what the character eats for lunch and how much it matters, what he buys and how the bills get paid, how she spends what we call working hours. Know how your character would prefer to spend evenings and weekends and why such plans get thwarted. Know what memories the character has of pets and parents, cities, snow, or school. You may end up using none of this information in the brief segment of your character's life that is your plot, but knowing it may teach you how your bookperson taps a pencil or twists a lock of hair, and when and why. When you know these things, you will have taken a step past invention toward the moment of imagination in which you become your character, live in his or her skin, and produce an action that, for the reader, rings universally true.

Use the journal to note your observations of people. Try clustering your impressions of the library assistant who annoys you or the loner at the bar who intrigues you. Try to capture a gesture or the messages that physical features and clothing send. Invent a reason for that harshness or that loneliness; invent a past. Then try taking the character out of context and setting her or him in another. Get your character in trouble, and you may be on your way to a short story.

It is interesting and relevant that actors schooled in the Stanislavski Method write biographies of the characters they must play. Adherents of "The Method" believe that in the process of inventing a dramatic character's past, the actor will find points of emotional contact with that role and so know how to make the motives and actions prescribed by the script natural and genuine. As a writer you can also use "The Method," imagining much that you will not bring specifically to "the script" but that will enrich your sense of that character until you know with absolute certainty how he or she will move, act, react, and speak.

You are going to love some of your characters, because they are you or some facet of you, and you are going to hate some of your characters for the same reason. But no matter what, you are probably going to have to let bad things happen to some of the characters you love or you won't have much of a story. Bad things happen to good characters, because our actions have consequences, and we do not all behave perfectly all the time.

Anne Lamott

The Universal Paradox.   In any case, the key to rich characterization is the same as that outlined in the preceding chapter, an attention to detail that is significant. Though critics often praise literature for exhibiting characteristics of the *individual,* the *typical,* and the *universal* all at the same time, I don't think this is of much use to the practicing writer. For though you may labor to create an individual character, and you may make that character a credible example of type, I don't think you can *set out to be* "universal."

It is true, I believe, that if literature has any social justification or use it is that readers can identify the common humanity in, and can therefore identify with, characters vastly different from themselves in century, geography, gender, culture, and beliefs; and that this enhances the scope of the reader's sympathy. It is also true that if the fiction does not have this universal quality—if a middle-class American male author creates as protagonist a middle-class American male with whom only middle-class American male readers can sympathize—then the fiction is thin and small. William Sloane voices the "frightening" demand of the reader in his book *The Craft of Writing:* "Tell me about me. I want to be more alive. Give me me." Yet, paradoxically, if you aim for the universal, you're likely to achieve the pompous, whereas if you aim for the individual, you're more apt to create a character in whom a reader can see aspects of himself or herself.

Imagine this scene: The child chases a ball into the street. The tires screech, the bumper thuds, the blood geysers into the air, the pulp of the small body lies inert on the asphalt. How would a bystander react? (Is it universal?) How would a passing doctor react? (Is it typical?) How would Dr. Henry Lowes, just coming from the maternity ward of his own hospital, where his wife has had her fourth miscarriage, react? (Is it individual?) Each question narrows the range of convincing reaction, and as a writer you want to convince in each range. If you succeed in the third, you are likely to have succeeded in the other two.

My advice then is to labor in the range of the particular. If you aim for a universal character you may end up with a vague or dull or windy one. On the other hand, if you set out to write a typical character you're likely to produce a caricature, because people are typical only in the generalized qualities that lump them together. *Typical* is the most provincial adjective in a writer's vocabulary, signaling that you're writing only for those who share your assumptions. A "typical" schoolgirl in Dar es Salaam is a very different type from one in San Francisco. Furthermore, every person is typical of many things successively or simultaneously. She may be in turn a "typical" schoolgirl, bride, divorcée, and feminist. He may be at one and the same time a "typical" New Yorker, math professor, doting father, and adulterer. It is in the confrontation and convolution of types that much of our individuality is produced.

Writing in generalities and typicalities is akin to bigotry—we see only what's alike about people, not what's unique. When effective, a description of type blames the character for the failure to individualize, and if an author sets out deliberately to produce types rather than individuals, then that author invariably wants to condemn or ridicule those types. Joyce Carol Oates illustrates the technique in "How I Contemplated the World from the Detroit House of Corrections and Began My Life Over Again":

> George, Clyde G. 240 Sioux. A manufacturer's representative; children, a dog, a wife. Georgian with the usual columns. You think of the White House, then of Thomas Jefferson, then your mind goes blank on the white pillars and you think of nothing.

Mark Helprin, in "The Schreuderspitze," takes the ridicule of type to comic extreme:

> In Munich are many men who look like weasels. Whether by genetic accident, meticulous crossbreeding, an early and puzzling migration, coincidence, or a reason that we do not know, they exist in great numbers. Remarkably, they accentuate this unfortunate tendency by wearing mustaches, Alpine hats, and tweed. A man who resembles a rodent should never wear tweed.

This is not to say that all characters must be fully drawn or "*round.*" *Flat* characters—who exist only to exhibit a function or a single characteristic—are useful and necessary. Eric Bentley suggests in *The Life of the Drama* that if a messenger's function in a play is to deliver his message, it would be very tedious to stop and learn about his psychology. The same is true in fiction: in Margaret Atwood's "Happy Endings" (near the end of chapter 2), the character of James, "who has a motorcycle and a fabulous record collection" exists for no purpose other than to make Mary's adulterous lover John jealous, and we do not want to hear about his adventures "away on his motorcycle, being free." Nevertheless, onstage even a flat character has a face and a costume, and in fiction detail can give even a flat character a few angles and contours. The servant classes in the novels of Henry James are notoriously absent as individuals because they exist only in their functions (*that excellent creature had already assembled the baggage,* etc.), whereas Charles Dickens, who peoples his novels with dozens of flat characters, brings even these alive in detail.

> And Mrs. Miff, the wheezy little pew opener—a mighty dry old lady, sparely dressed, with not an inch of fullness anywhere about her—is also here.
>
> *Dombey and Son*

To borrow a notion from George Orwell's *Animal Farm*, all good characters are created round, but some are created rounder than others.

Credibility

Though you aim at individuality and not typicality in characters, your characters will exhibit typicality in the sense of "appropriateness." A Baptist Texan behaves differently from an Italian nun; a rural schoolboy behaves differently from a professor emeritus at Harvard. If you are to succeed in creating an individual character, particular and alive, you will also inevitably know what is appropriate to that sort of person and will let us know as much as we need to know to feel the appropriateness of the behavior.

For instance, we need to know soon, preferably in the first paragraph, the character's gender, age, and race or nationality. We need to know something of his or her class, period, and region. A profession (or the clear lack of it) and a marital status help, too. *Almost any reader can identify with almost any character; what no reader can identify with is confusion.* When some or several of the fundamentals of type are withheld from us—when we don't know whether we're dealing with a man or a woman, an adult or a child—the process of identifying cannot begin, and the story is slow to move us.

None of the information need come as information; it can be implied by appearance, tone, action, or detail. In the next example Barbara Kingsolver plunges the character of Leah Price and her family into a new life for which they are clearly ill-prepared, practically and politically. Although they are focused on their destination, by the end of the first two paragraphs, we know a lot about the family and the culture they carry with them.

> We came from Bethlehem, Georgia, bearing Betty Crocker cake mixes into the jungle. My sisters and I were all counting on having one birthday apiece during our twelve-month mission. "And heaven knows," our mother predicted, "they won't have Betty Crocker in the Congo."
>
> "Where we are headed, there will *be* no buyers and sellers at all," my father corrected. His tone implied that Mother failed to grasp our mission, and that her concern with Betty Crocker confederated her with the coin-jingling sinners who vexed Jesus till he pitched a fit and threw them out of the church. "Where we are headed," he said, to make things perfectly clear, "not so much as a Piggly Wiggly." Evidently Father saw this as a point in the Congo's favor. I got the most spectacular chills, just from trying to imagine.
>
> *The Poisonwood Bible*

We know that the family is Southern, not only because their town of origin is named, but also from expressions such as "vexed" and "pitched a fit," as well as from mention of the Piggly Wiggly grocery chain. Not only do we know that they are missionaries, but further, we hear the father's sermonizing voice through his repetition of the phrase "where we are headed," preaching that is echoed in the implication that the mother is "confederated" with "the coin-jingling sinners." We also hear hints of the harsh pleasure the father will take in the family's hardship. The Betty Crocker mixes tell us that the women are trying to hang on to a little bit of home comfort, yet at the same time they are taking all-American '50s culture to a place where it is irrelevant and ultimately destructive—indeed, the cake mixes are quickly ruined by jungle humidity. And although we don't know the exact age of the narrator, she seems to be a teenager old enough to hear the subtext of her father's reprovals and to relish the false sophistication of phrases like "the most spectacular chills" and "imagine." In a very short space, Kingsolver has sketched the family, their dangerous ignorance, and the father's divisive, single-minded determination.

The following passage is an even more striking example of implied information.

> Every time the same story. Your Barbie is roommates with my Barbie, and my Barbie's boyfriend comes over and your Barbie steals him, okay? Kiss kiss kiss. Then the two Barbies fight. You dumbbell! He's mine. Oh no he's not, you stinky! Only Ken's invisible, right? Because we don't have money for a stupid-looking boy doll when we'd both rather ask for a new Barbie outfit next Christmas. We have to make do with your mean-eyed Barbie and my bubblehead Barbie and our one outfit apiece not including the sock dress.
>
> Sandra Cisneros, "Barbie-Q"

Here there is no description whatever of the characters, and no direct reference to them except for the designations *you* and *I*. What do we nevertheless know about their gender, their age, their financial status, the period in which they live, their personalities, their attitudes, their relationship, the narrator's emotions?

Students of writing are sometimes daunted by the need to give so much information immediately. The thing to remember is that credibility consists in the combination of appropriateness and specificity. The trick is to find telling details that will convey the information while our attention remains on the desire or emotion of the character. Nobody wants to read a story that begins:

> She was a twenty-eight-year-old suburban American woman, relatively affluent, who was extremely distressed when her husband, Peter, left her.

But most of that, and much more besides, could be contained in a few details.

> After Peter left with the VCR, the microwave, and the key to the garage, she went down to the kitchen and ate three jars of peanut butter without tasting a single spoonful.

I don't mean to imply that it is necessarily easy to signal the essentials of type immediately. It would be truer to say that it is necessary and hard. The opening paragraph of a story is its second strongest statement (the final paragraph is the strongest) and sets the tone for all that follows. If the right words don't come to you as a gift, you may have to sit sifting and discarding the inadequate ones for a long time before you achieve both clarity and interest.

Purpose

Your character's purpose—that is, the desire that impels her or him to action—will determine our degree of identification and sympathy on the one hand, or judgment on the other.

Aristotle, in *The Poetics*, says that "there will be an element of character if what a person says or does reveals a certain moral purpose; and a good element of character, if the purpose so revealed is good." It might seem that the antiheroes, brutes, hoods, whores, perverts, and bums who people modern literature do very little in the way of revealing good moral purpose. The history of Western literature shows a movement downward and inward: downward through society from royalty to gentry to the middle classes to the lower classes to the dropouts; inward from heroic action to social drama to individual consciousness to the subconscious to the unconscious. What has remained consistent is that, for the time spent in an author's world, we understand and identify with the protagonist or protagonists, we "see their point of view"; and the fiction succeeds largely because we are willing to grant them a goodness that we would not grant them in life. While you read, you expand your mental scope by identifying with, temporarily "becoming," a character, borrowing a different mind. Fiction, as critic Laurence Gonzales says of rock music, "lets you wander around in someone else's hell for a while and see how similar it is to your own."

Obviously we don't identify with all characters, and those whose purpose is revealed as ambiguous or evil will invite varying degrees of judgment. When on page 109 of the story "Where Are You Going, Where Have You Been?" Arnold Friend is described as "stiffly relaxed," with a "slippery friendly smile" and a series of familiar styles that "did not come together," we are immediately skeptical of him; because we suspect his purpose toward Connie, we pass judgment on his fundamental character.

Complexity

If the characters of your story are credible through being appropriate and individual, and if they invite identification or judgment through a sense of their purpose, they also need to be complex. They need to exhibit enough conflict and contradiction that we can recognize them as belonging to the contradictory human race; and they should exhibit a range of possibility so that a shift of power in the plot can also produce a shift of purpose or morality. That is, they need to be capable of change.

Conflict is at the core of character as it is of plot. If plot begins with trouble, then character begins with a person in trouble; and trouble most dramatically occurs because we all have traits, tendencies, and desires that are at war, not simply with the world and other people, but with other traits, tendencies, and desires of our own. All of us probably know a woman of the strong, striding, independent sort, attractive only to men who like a strong and striding woman. And when she falls in love? She becomes a clinging sentimentalist. All of us know a father who is generous, patient, and dependable. And when the children cross the line? He smashes crockery and wields a strap. All of us are gentle, violent; logical, schmaltzy; tough, squeamish; lusty, prudish; sloppy, meticulous; energetic, apathetic; manic, depressive. Perhaps you don't fit that particular list of contradictions, but you are sufficiently in conflict with yourself that as an author you have characters enough in your own psyche to people the work of a lifetime if you will identify, heighten, and dramatize these conflicts within character, which Aristotle called "consistent inconsistencies."

If you think of the great characters of literature, you can see how inner contradiction—consistent inconsistency—brings each to a crucial dilemma. Hamlet is a strong and decisive man who procrastinates. Dorothea Brooke of *Middlemarch* is an idealistic and intellectual young woman, a total fool in matters of the heart. Ernest Hemingway's Francis Macomber wants to test his manhood against a lion and cannot face the test. Here, in a moment of crisis from *Mom Kills Self and Kids*, Alan Saperstein reveals with great economy the consistent inconsistency of his protagonist, a man who hadn't much time for his family until their absence makes clear how dependent he has been on them.

> When I arrived home from work I found my wife had killed our two sons and taken her own life.
>
> I uncovered a blast of foul, black steam from the pot on the stove and said, "Hi, hon, what's for dinner?" But she did not laugh. She did not bounce to her feet and pirouette into the kitchen to greet me. My little one didn't race into my legs and ask what I brought him. The seven-year-old didn't automatically beg me to play a game knowing my answer would be a tired, "Maybe later."

In "The Self as Source," Cheryl Moskowitz proposes a fiction technique that relies specifically on identifying conflicting parts of the writer's personality. She points to Robert Louis Stevenson's *The Strange Case of Dr. Jekyll and Mr. Hyde* as a fairly blatant model for such fiction, and quotes from Dr. Jekyll:

> . . . I thus drew steadily nearer to that truth . . . that man is not truly one, but two. I say two, because the state of my own knowledge does not pass beyond that point. . . . I hazard the guess that man will ultimately be known for a mere polity of multifarious, incongruous and independent denizens.

Moskowitz suggests "character imaging," making lists of the qualities, images, and actions that describe such incongruities in the writer's personality. Here is a sample list from a student exercise:

Elegant	**Vulgar**
silk scarf to the knees	sequins on a fringed cowhide vest
still	laughing
frowns at library noise	hands out candy
startled gazelle	slobbering puppy
Waterford crystal	souvenir plate made in Mexico
a single white rosebud	two dozen overblown red roses
walks alone into the woods	throws a costume party

What's vital for the fiction writer to remember is that the wicked, the violent, and the stupid do also love, in their way. Just as humble and loving and thoughtful people also hate. Hate humbly, hate lovingly, hate thoughtfully, and so on.

Doug Bauer

At this point the contradictory lists could be transformed into two separate, named characters. Then, where might they meet? In what situation might they find themselves? How would a confrontation between these two play out?

It is, of course, impossible to know to what degree Shakespeare, Eliot, Hemingway, or Saperstein self-consciously used their own inner contradictions to build and dramatize their characters. An author works not only from his or her own personality but also from observation and imagination, and I fully believe that you are working at full stretch only when all three are involved. The question of autobiography is a complicated one, and as writer you frequently won't know yourself how much you have experienced, how much you have observed, and how much you have invented. Actress Mildred Dunnock once observed that drama is possible "because people can feel what they haven't experienced," an observation that surely extends to the writing and reading of fiction. If you push yourself to write at the outer edge of your emotional experience—what you can imagine yourself doing, even if you might not risk such actions in life—then all your writing is autobiographical in the sense that it must have passed through your mind.

Change

In a story, as opposed to a sketch or anecdote, says poet and novelist Al Young, "stuff happens, people *change*, situations *change*, there is no standing still." Certainly the easiest way to check the plot of your story is to ask, "Does my character change from opening to end? Do I give the sense that his or her life will never be quite the same again?"

Often the notion of change is mistaken by new writers to mean change that is abrupt and contrived, from Scrooge to St. Nick—yet this rarely happens in life or in realistic fiction. Rather, change can be as subtle as a step in a new direction, a slight shift in belief, or a willingness to question a rigid view or recognize unseen value in a person or situation. Our society's belief in the power of change is reaffirmed each New Year's Day, and one of the vicarious pleasures fiction offers is the chance to experience the workings of change within a character's consciousness.

John L'Heureux offers a psychological framework for viewing change: "A story is about a single moment in a character's life when a definitive choice is made, after which nothing is the same." The moments in "Where Are You Going, Where Have You Been?" when Connie hears the implied threat to her family and goes out to the waiting Arnold Friend and in "Silver Water" when Violet sees the pills in her sister's

If you take two sticks and hold them parallel, you can capture that image in a photograph because it doesn't change. But if you rub those two sticks together, harder and harder, faster and faster, they will burst into flame—that's the kind of change you can capture in a story or on film. Friction is necessary for change to occur. But without the friction of conflict, there is no change. And without change, there is no story. A body at rest remains at rest unless it enters into conflict.

Stephen Fischer

hand and takes no action are both moments of choice that lead to life-or-death change. By contrast, in the upcoming story "Wave," Ray's quick salute to his fellow highway driver confirms his nonetheless significant choice to reconnect with the human world.

The "integrity" of fiction is a concept John L'Heureux emphasizes, for in good fiction incidents lead to a single moment when the main character makes a decision that regards—and determines—his or her essential integrity, after which nothing will ever be the same. He uses integrity in its primal sense of "wholeness," since at the moment of choice the character elects to live either more in harmony or more at odds with his or her best self. The decision made in that moment affects the character's relationship with the self forever.

"What we do determines what we become," fiction writer Nancy Huddleston Packer affirms. "Because character and event are interlocked, stories don't end in accident; rather, the consequences of the story come from the character who determines events. Our decisions make us who we are forever afterward."

The Indirect Methods of Character Presentation

There are six basic *methods of character presentation*. The indirect methods of authorial interpretation and interpretation by another character will be discussed below. The four direct methods—*appearance*, *action*, *speech*, and *thought*—will be discussed in chapter 5. Employing a variety of these methods can help you draw a full character.

AUTHORIAL INTERPRETATION

The first indirect method of presenting a character is authorial interpretation—"telling" us the character's background, motives, values, virtues, and the like. The advantages of the indirect method are enormous, for its use leaves you free to move in time and space; to know anything you choose to know whether the character knows it or not; and, godlike, to tell us what we are to feel. The indirect method allows you to convey a great deal of information in a short time.

The most excellent Marquis of Lumbria lived with his two daughters, Caroline, the elder, and Luisa; and his second wife, Doa Vicenta, a woman with a dull brain, who, when she was not sleeping, was complaining of everything, especially the noise . . .

The Marquis of Lumbria had no male children, and this was the most painful thorn in his existence. Shortly after having become a widower, he had married Doa Vicenta, his present wife, in order to have a son, but she proved sterile.

The Marquis' life was as monotonous and as quotidian, as unchanging and regular, as the murmur of the river below the cliff or as the liturgic services in the cathedral.

Miguel De Unamuno, The Marquis of Lumbria

The disadvantages of this indirect method are outlined in chapter 3. Indeed, in the passage above, it may well be part of Unamuno's purpose to convey the "monotonous and quotidian" quality of the Marquis's life by this summarized and distanced rehearsal of facts, motives, and judgments. Nearly every author will use the indirect method occasionally, and you may find it useful when you want to cover the exposition quickly. However, direct presentation of the characters—showing them in action and allowing readers to draw their own conclusions—is much more likely to please a modern audience.

INTERPRETATION BY ANOTHER CHARACTER

A character may also be presented through the opinions of other characters, which may be considered a second indirect method. When this method is employed, however, the second character must give his or her opinions in speech, action, or thought. In the process, the observing character is inevitably also characterized. Whether we accept the opinion depends on what we think of that character as he or she is thus directly characterized. In this scene from Jane Austen's *Mansfield Park*, for example, the busybody Mrs. Norris gives her opinion of the heroine.

". . . there is something about Fanny, I have often observed it before,—she likes to go her own way to work; she does not like to be dictated to; she takes her own independent walk whenever she can; she certainly has a little spirit of secrecy, and independence, and nonsense, about her, which I would advise her to get the better of."

As a general reflection on Fanny, Sir Thomas thought nothing could be more unjust, though he had been so lately expressing the same sentiments himself, and he tried to turn the conversation, tried repeatedly before he could succeed.

Here Mrs. Norris's opinion is directly presented in her speech and Sir Thomas's in his thoughts, each of them being characterized in the process. It is left to the reader to decide (without much difficulty) whose view of Fanny is the more reliable.

Similarly, in Clyde Edgerton's contemporary novel *Raney*, the opposing outlooks of a newlywed "odd couple" are dramatized through their contradictory characterizations of a lonely and preoccupied neighbor.

> "Charles," I said, "you'd rather sit down back there in the bedroom and read a book than talk to a live human being like Mrs. Moss."
>
> "I'm not so sure I agree with your assessment of Mrs. Moss," he says.
>
> "What do you mean by that?"
>
> "It means I have had one conversation with Mrs. Moss and one conversation with Mrs. Moss is enough. I am not interested in her falling off the commode and having a hairline rib fracture. I am not interested in her cataract operation. Mrs. Moss is unable to comprehend anything beyond her own problems and you know it."
>
> .... Mrs. Moss does talk about herself right much. She'll come over in her apron to borrow a cup of something. One Sunday she borrowed a cup of flour after I saw a bag of Red Band in her shopping cart—on top—at the Piggly Wiggly on Saturday. But the way I figure it is this: Mrs. Moss has had a lifetime of things happening to her and all along she's had these other people—her husband and children—to watch these things happen. So she didn't ever have to *tell* anybody. Then her husband died and her children left and there was nobody around to watch these things happen anymore, so she don't have any way to share *except* to tell. So the thing to do is listen. It's easy to cut her off when she just goes on and on. You just start talking about something else. She follows right along.
>
> "She's given me several pints of preserves and one quart of chow-chow," I said. "She can comprehend that."
>
> "Raney, that has nothing to do with the fact that she is senile and self-centered. There are old people who aren't self-centered, you know."
>
> "Charles, she also showed me how to keep applesauce from turning brown in the jar, and she's going to give me some cactus seeds and she said she'd help me dig up a circle and plant them. And give me some big rocks to go around that. If she's so self-centered, why is she giving me preserves and chow-chow and seeds?"
>
> "Because it's a habit. A life-long habit. If you were Atilla the Hun she'd give you preserves and chow-chow and seeds."
>
> "Charles. Sometimes I wonder about your heart."

Set halfway through the novel, this argument confirms the reader's view of Charles as an urban liberal who is broad-minded in abstract principles yet impatient with actual people, while Raney, the small-town narrator, tends to be narrow-minded in the abstract but compassionate with individuals, at least those long-familiar to her. What is crystallized about this couple through their argument is even more important than what is learned about the incidental character of the neighbor.

Whether indirect, direct, or, most commonly, both direct and indirect methods are used, a full and rich fictional character will need to be both credible and complex, will show purpose (and that purpose will reveal something about his or her morality), and in the course of the story will undergo some, perhaps small but nonetheless significant, change. In order to explore these elements of character, your journal can be an invaluable help. Character will be best presented through individualizing detail, though such detail will inevitably reveal something about the character's type and perhaps also something universal about the human condition.

But what are the means of presenting a character *in detail*? How is individuality achieved? The direct means of presenting character through appearance, action, dialogue, and thought will be taken up in chapter 5.

Yours

MARY ROBISON

Allison struggled away from her white Renault, limping with the weight of the last of the pumpkins. She found Clark in the twilight on the twig-and-leaf-littered porch, behind the house. He wore a tan wool shawl. He was moving up and back in a cushioned glider, pushed by the ball of his slippered foot.

Allison lowered a big pumpkin and let it rest on the porch floor.

Clark was much older than she—seventy-eight to Allison's thirty-five. They had been married for four months. They were both quite tall, with long hands, and their faces looked something alike. Allison wore a natural-hair wig. It was a thick blond hood around her face. She was dressed in bright-dyed denims today. She wore durable clothes, usually, for she volunteered afternoons at a children's day-care center.

She put one of the smaller pumpkins on Clark's long lap. "Now, nothing surreal," she told him. "Carve just a *regular* face. These are for kids."

In the foyer, on the Hepplewhite desk, Allison found the maid's chore list, with its cross-offs, which included Clark's supper. Allison went quickly through the day's mail: a garish coupon packet, a flyer advertising white wines at Jamestown Liquors, November's pay-TV program guide, and—the worst thing, the funniest—an already opened, extremely unkind letter from Clark's married daughter, up North. "You're an old fool," Allison read, and "You're being cruelly deceived." There was a gift check for twenty-five dollars, made out to Clark, enclosed—his birthday had just passed—but it was uncashable. It was signed "Jesus H. Christ."

Late, late into this night, Allison and Clark gutted and carved the pumpkins together, at an old table set out on the back porch. They worked over newspaper after soggy newspaper, using paring knives and spoons and a Swiss Army knife Clark liked for the exact shaping of teeth and eyes and nostrils. Clark had been a doctor—an internist—but he was also a Sunday watercolor painter. His four pumpkins were expressive and artful. Their carved features were suited to the sizes and shapes of the pumpkins. Two looked ferocious and jagged. One registered surprise. The last was serene and beaming.

Allison's four faces were less deftly drawn, with slits and areas of distortion. She had cut triangles for noses and eyes. The mouths she had made were all just wedges—two turned up and two turned down.

By 1 A.M., they were finished. Clark, who had bent his long torso forward to work, moved over to the glider again and looked out sleepily at nothing. All the neighbors' lights were out across the ravine. For the season and time, the Virginia night was warm. Most of the leaves had fallen and blown away already, and the trees stood unbothered. The moon was round, above them.

Allison cleaned up the mess.

"Your jack-o'-lanterns are much much better than mine," Clark said to her.

"Like hell," Allison said.

"Look at me," Clark said, and Allison did. She was holding a squishy bundle of newspapers. The papers reeked sweetly with the smell of pumpkin innards. "Yours are *far* better," he said.

"You're wrong. You'll see when they're lit," Allison said.

She went inside, came back with yellow vigil candles. It took her a while to get each candle settled into a pool of its own melted wax inside the jack-o'-lanterns, which were lined up in a row on the porch railing. Allison went along and relit each candle and fixed the pumpkin lids over the little flames. "See?" she said. They sat together a moment and looked at the orange faces.

"We're exhausted. It's good-night time," Allison said. "Don't blow out the candles. I'll put in new ones tomorrow."

In her bedroom, a few weeks earlier in her life than had been predicted, she began to die. "Don't look at me if my wig comes off," she told Clark. "Please." Her pulse cords were fluttering under his fingers. She raised her knees and kicked away the comforter. She said something to Clark about the garage being locked.

At the telephone, Clark had a clear view out back and down to the porch. He wanted to get drunk with his wife once more. He wanted to tell her, from the greater perspective he had, that to own only a little talent, like his, was an awful, plaguing thing; that being only a little special meant you expected too much, most of the time, and liked yourself too little. He wanted to assure her that she had missed nothing.

Clark was speaking into the phone now. He watched the jack-o'-lanterns. The jack-o'-lanterns watched him.

🍂 🍂 🍂

Suggestions for Discussion

1. Most of the story's elements are left to speak for themselves. Where, however, does the narrator use the indirect method to "tell" us information?

2. Which details give clues to the characters' ages, Allison's illness, and her impending death? Which actions? What unexpected traits of character emerge?

Retrospect

3. Where do you see conflict in this story? If it is not between Allison and Clark, where is it?

4. The subject of the story is deeply serious, yet the tone of the writing is low-key and somewhat light. How would the story change if its tone were as serious and sad as its subject?

Gryphon

CHARLES BAXTER

On Wednesday afternoon, between the geography lesson on ancient Egypt's hand-operated irrigation system and an art project that involved drawing a model city next to a mountain, our fourth-grade teacher, Mr. Hibler, developed a cough. This cough began with a series of muffled throat clearings and progressed to propulsive noises contained within Mr. Hibler's closed mouth. "Listen to him," Carol Peterson whispered to me. "He's gonna blow up." Mr. Hibler's laughter—dazed and infrequent—sounded a bit like his cough, but as we worked on our model cities we would look up, thinking he was enjoying a joke, and see Mr. Hibler's face turning red, his cheeks puffed out. This was not laughter. Twice he bent over, and his loose tie, like a plumb line, hung down straight from his neck as he exploded himself into a Kleenex. He would excuse himself, then go on coughing. "I'll bet you a dime," Carol Peterson whispered, "we get a substitute tomorrow."

Carol sat at the desk in front of mine and was a bad person—when she thought no one was looking she would blow her nose on notebook paper, then crumble it up and throw it into the wastebasket—but at times of crisis she spoke the truth. I knew I'd lose the dime.

"No deal," I said.

When Mr. Hibler stood us up in formation at the door just prior to the final bell, he was almost incapable of speech. "I'm sorry, boys and girls," he said. "I seem to be coming down with something."

"I hope you feel better tomorrow, Mr. Hibler," Bobby Kryzanowicz, the faultless brown-noser said, and I heard Carol Peterson's evil giggle. Then Mr. Hibler opened the door and we walked out to the buses, a clique of us starting noisily to hawk and cough as soon as we thought we were a few feet beyond Mr. Hibler's earshot.

Five Oaks being a rural community, and in Michigan, the supply of substitute teachers was limited to the town's unemployed community college graduates, a pool of about four mothers. These ladies fluttered, provided easeful class days, and nervously covered material we had mastered weeks earlier. Therefore it was a surprise when a woman we had never seen came into the class the next day, carrying a purple purse, a checkerboard lunchbox, and a few books. She put the books on one side of Mr. Hibler's desk and the lunchbox on the other, next to the Voice of Music phonograph. Three of us in the back of the room were playing with Heever, the chameleon that lived in the terrarium and on one of the plastic drapes, when she walked in.

She clapped her hands at us. "Little boys," she said, "why are you bent over together like that?" She didn't wait for us to answer. "Are you tormenting an animal? Put it back. Please sit down at your desks. I want no cabals this time of the day." We just stared at her. "Boys," she repeated, "I asked you to sit down."

I put the chameleon in his terrarium and felt my way to my desk, never taking my eyes off the woman. With white and green chalk, she had started to draw a tree on the left side of the blackboard. She didn't look usual. Furthermore, her tree was outsized, disproportionate, for some reason.

"This room needs a tree," she said, with one line drawing the suggestion of a leaf. "A large, leafy, shady, deciduous . . . oak."

Her fine, light hair had been done up in what I would learn years later was called a chignon, and she wore gold-rimmed glasses whose lenses seemed to have the faintest blue tint. Harold Knardahl, who sat across from me, whispered "Mars," and I nodded slowly, savoring the imminent weirdness of the day. The substitute drew another branch with an extravagant arm gesture, then turned around and said, "Good morning. I don't believe I said good morning to all you yet."

Facing us, she was no special age—an adult is an adult—but her face had two prominent lines, descending vertically from the sides of her mouth to her chin. I knew where I had seen those lines before: *Pinocchio*. They were marionette lines. "You may stare at me," she said to us, as a few more kids from the last bus came into the room, their eyes fixed on her, "for a few more seconds, until the bell rings. Then I will permit no more staring. Looking I will permit. Staring, no. It is impolite to stare, and a sign of bad breeding. You cannot make a social effort while staring."

Harold Knardahl did not glance at me, or nudge, but I heard him whisper "Mars" again, trying to get more mileage out of his single joke with the kids who had just come in.

When everyone was seated, the substitute teacher finished her tree, put down her chalk fastidiously on the phonograph, brushed her hands, and faced us. "Good morning," she said. "I am Miss Ferenczi, your teacher for the day. I am fairly new to your community, and I don't believe any of you know me. I will therefore start by telling you a story about myself."

While we settled back, she launched into her tale. She said her grandfather had been a Hungarian prince; her mother had been born in some place called Flanders, had been a pianist, and had played concerts for people Miss Ferenczi referred to as "crowned heads." She gave us a knowing look. "Grieg," she said, "the Norwegian master, wrote a concerto for piano that was," she paused, "my mother's triumph at her debut concert in London." Her eyes searched the ceiling. Our eyes followed. Nothing up there but ceiling tile. "For reasons that I shall not go into, my family's fortunes took us to Detroit, then north to dreadful Saginaw, and now here I am in Five Oaks, as your substitute teacher, for today, Thursday, October the eleventh. I believe it will be a good day: All the forecasts coincide. We shall start with your reading lesson. Take out your reading book. I believe it is called *Broad Horizons*, or something along those lines."

Jeannie Vermeesch raised her hand. Miss Ferenczi nodded at her. "Mr. Hibler always starts the day with the Pledge of Allegiance," Jeannie whined.

"Oh, does he? In that case," Miss Ferenczi said, "you must know it *very* well by now, and we certainly need not spend our time on it. No, no allegiance pledging on the premises today, by my reckoning. Not with so much sunlight coming into the room. A pledge does not suit my mood." She glanced at her watch. "Time is flying. Take out *Broad Horizons*."

She disappointed us by giving us an ordinary lesson, complete with vocabulary word drills, comprehension questions, and recitation. She didn't seem to care for the material, however. She sighed every few minutes and rubbed her glasses with a frilly perfumed handkerchief that she withdrew, magician style, from her left sleeve.

After reading we moved on to arithmetic. It was my favorite time of the morning, when the lazy autumn sunlight dazzled its way through ribbons of clouds past the windows on the east side of the classroom, and crept across the linoleum floor. On the playground the first group of children, the kindergartners, were running on the quack grass just beyond the monkey bars. We were doing multiplication tables. Miss Ferenczi had made John Wazny stand up at his desk in the front row. He was supposed to go through the tables of six. From where I was sitting, I could smell the Vitalis soaked into John's plastered hair. He was doing fine until he came to six times eleven and six times twelve. "Six times eleven," he said, "is sixty-eight. Six times twelve is . . ." He put his fingers to his head, quickly and secretly sniffed his fingertips, and said, "seventy-two." Then he sat down.

"Fine," Miss Ferenczi said. "Well now. That was very good."

"Miss Ferenczi!" One of the Eddy twins was waving her hand desperately in the air. "Miss Ferenczi! Miss Ferenczi!"

"Yes?"

"John said that six times eleven is sixty-eight and you said he was right!"

"*Did* I?" She gazed at the class with a jolly look breaking across her marionette's face. "Did I say that? Well, what *is* six times eleven?"

"It's sixty-six!"

She nodded. "Yes. So it is. But, and I know some people will not entirely agree with me, at some times it is sixty-eight."

"When? When is it sixty-eight?"

We were all waiting.

"In higher mathematics, which you children do not yet understand, six times eleven can be considered to be sixty-eight." She laughed through her nose. "In higher mathematics numbers are . . . more fluid. The only thing a number does is contain a certain amount of something. Think of water. A cup is not the only way to measure a certain amount of water, is it?" We were staring, shaking our heads. "You could use saucepans or thimbles. In either case, the water *would be the same*. Perhaps," she started again, "it would be better for you to think that six times eleven is sixty-eight only when I am in the room."

"Why is it sixty-eight," Mark Poole asked, "when you're in the room?"

"Because it's more interesting that way," she said, smiling very rapidly behind her blue-tinted glasses. "Besides, I'm your substitute teacher, am I not?" We all nodded. "Well, then, think of six times eleven equals sixty-eight as a substitute fact."

"A substitute fact?"

"Yes." Then she looked at us carefully. "Do you think," she asked, "that anyone is going to be hurt by a substitute fact?"

We looked back at her.

"Will the plants on the windowsill be hurt?" We glanced at them. There were sensitive plants thriving in a green plastic tray, and several wilted ferns in small clay pots. "Your dogs and cats, or your moms and dads?" She waited. "So," she concluded, "what's the problem?"

"But it's wrong," Janice Weber said, "isn't it?"

"What's your name, young lady?"

"Janice Weber."

"And you think it's wrong, Janice?"

"I was just asking."

"Well, all right. You were just asking. I think we've spent enough time on this matter by now, don't you, class? You are free to think what you like. When your teacher, Mr. Hibler, returns, six times eleven will be sixty-six again, you can rest assured. And it will be that for the rest of your lives in Five Oaks. Too bad, eh?" She raised her eyebrows and glinted herself at us. "But for now, it wasn't. So much for that. Let us go to your assigned problems for today, as painstakingly outlined, I see, in Mr. Hibler's lesson plan. Take out a sheet of paper and write your names in the upper left-hand corner."

For the next half hour we did the rest of our arithmetic problems. We handed them in and went on to spelling, my worst subject. Spelling always came before lunch. We were taking spelling dictation and looking at the clock. "Thorough," Miss Ferenczi said. "Boundary." She walked in the aisles between the desks, holding the spelling book open and looking down at our papers. "Balcony." I clutched my pencil. Somehow, the way she said those words, they seemed foreign, Hungarian, mis-voweled and mis-consonanted. I stared down at what I had spelled. *Balconie.* I turned my pencil upside down and erased my mistake. *Balconey.* That looked better, but still incorrect. I cursed the world of spelling and tried erasing it again and saw the paper beginning to wear away. *Balkony.* Suddenly I felt a hand on my shoulder.

"I don't like that word either," Miss Ferenczi whispered, bent over, her mouth near my ear. "It's ugly. My feeling is, if you don't like a word, you don't have to use it." She straightened up, leaving behind a slight odor of Clorets.

At lunchtime we went out to get our trays of sloppy joes, peaches in heavy syrup, coconut cookies, and milk, and brought them back to the classroom, where Miss Ferenczi was sitting at the desk, eating a brown sticky thing she had unwrapped from tightly rubber-banded wax paper. "Miss Ferenczi," I said, raising my hand. "You don't have to eat with us. You can eat with the other teachers. There's a teachers' lounge," I ended up, "next to the principal's office."

"No, thank you," she said. "I prefer it here."

"We've got a room monitor," I said. "Mrs. Eddy." I pointed to where Mrs. Eddy, Joyce and Judy's mother, sat silently at the back of the room, doing her knitting.

"That's fine," Miss Ferenczi said. "But I shall continue to eat here, with you children. I prefer it," she repeated.

"How come?" Wayne Razmer asked without raising his hand.

"I talked with the other teachers before class this morning," Miss Ferenczi said, biting into her brown food. "There was a great rattling of the words for the fewness of ideas. I didn't care for their brand of hilarity. I don't like ditto machine jokes."

"Oh," Wayne said.

"What's that you're eating?" Maxine Sylvester asked, twitching her nose. "Is it food?"

"It most certainly *is* food. It's a stuffed fig. I had to drive almost down to Detroit to get it. I also bought some smoked sturgeon. And this," she said, lifting some green leaves out of her lunchbox, "is raw spinach, cleaned this morning before I came out here to the Garfield-Murry School."

"Why're you eating raw spinach?" Maxine asked.

"It's good for you," Miss Ferenczi said. "More stimulating than soda pop or smelling salts." I bit into my sloppy joe and stared blankly out the window. An almost invisible moon was faintly silvered in the daytime autumn sky. "As far as food is concerned," Miss Ferenczi was saying, "you have to shuffle the pack. Mix it up. Too many people eat . . . well, never mind."

"Miss Ferenczi," Carol Peterson said, "what are we going to do this afternoon?"

"Well," she said, looking down at Mr. Hibler's lesson plan, "I see that your teacher, Mr. Hibler, has you scheduled for a unit on the Egyptians." Carol groaned. "Yessss," Miss Ferenczi continued, "that is what we will do: the Egyptians. A remarkable people. Almost as remarkable as the Americans. But not quite." She lowered her head, did her quick smile, and went back to eating her spinach.

After noon recess we came back into the classroom and saw that Miss Ferenczi had drawn a pyramid on the blackboard, close to her oak tree. Some of us who had been playing baseball were messing around in the back of the room, dropping the bats and the gloves into the playground box, and I think that Ray Schontzeler had just slugged me when I heard Miss Ferenczi's high-pitched voice quavering with emotion. "Boys," she said, "come to order right this minute and take your seats. I do not wish to waste a minute of class time. Take out your geography books." We trudged to our desks and, still sweating, pulled out *Distant Lands and Their People*. "Turn to page forty-two." She waited for thirty seconds, then looked over at Kelly Munger. "Young man," she said, "why are you still fossicking in your desk?"

Kelly looked as if his foot had been stepped on. "Why am I what?"

"Why are you . . . burrowing in your desk like that?"

"I'm lookin' for the book, Miss Ferenczi."

Bobby Kryzanowicz, the faultless brown-noser who sat in the first row by choice, softly said, "His name is Kelly Munger. He can't ever find his stuff. He always does that."

"I don't care what his name is, especially after lunch," Miss Ferenczi said. "*Where is your book?*"

"I just found it." Kelly was peering into his desk and with both hands pulled at the book, shoveling along in front of it several pencils and crayons, which fell into his lap and then to the floor.

"I hate a mess," Miss Ferenczi said. "I hate a mess in a desk or a mind. It's . . . unsanitary. You wouldn't want your house at home to look like your desk at school, now, would you?" She didn't wait for an answer. "I should think not. A house at home should be as neat as human hands can make it. What were we talking about? Egypt. Page forty-two. I note from Mr. Hibler's lesson plan that you have been discussing the modes of Egyptian irrigation. Interesting, in my view, but not so interesting as what we are about to cover. The pyramids and Egyptian slave labor. A plus on one side, a minus on the other." We had our books open to page forty-two, where there was a picture of a pyramid, but Miss Ferenczi wasn't looking at the book. Instead, she was staring at some object just outside the window.

"Pyramids," Miss Ferenczi said, still looking past the window. "I want you to think about the pyramids. And what was inside. The bodies of the pharaohs, of course, and their attendant treasures. Scrolls. Perhaps," Miss Ferenczi said, with something gleeful but unsmiling in her face, "these scrolls were novels for the pharaohs, helping them to pass the time in their long voyage through the centuries. But then, I am joking." I was looking at the lines on Miss Ferenczi's face. "Pyramids," Miss Ferenczi went on, "were the repositories of special cosmic powers. The nature of a pyramid is to guide cosmic energy forces into a concentrated point. The Egyptians knew that; we have generally forgotten it. Did you know," she asked, walking to the side of the room so that she was standing by the coat closet, "that George Washington had Egyptian blood, from his grandmother? Certain features of the Constitution of the United States are notable for their Egyptian ideas."

Without glancing down at the book, she began to talk about the movement of souls in Egyptian religion. She said that when people die, their souls return to Earth in the form of carpenter ants, or walnut trees, depending on how they behaved—"well or ill"—in life. She said that the Egyptians believed that people act the way they do because of magnetism produced by tidal forces in the solar system, forces produced by the sun and by its "planetary ally," Jupiter. Jupiter, she said, was a planet, as we had been told, but had "certain properties of stars." She was speaking very fast. She said that the Egyptians were great explorers and conquerors. She said that the greatest of all the conquerors, Genghis Khan, had had forty horses and forty young women killed on the site of his grave. We listened. No one tried to stop her. "I myself have been in Egypt," she said, "and have witnessed much dust and many brutalities." She said that an old man in Egypt who worked for a circus had personally shown her an animal in a cage, a monster, half bird and half lion. She said that this monster was called a gryphon and that she had heard about them but never seen them until she traveled to the outskirts of Cairo. She said that Egyptian astronomers had discovered the planet Saturn, but had not seen its rings. She said that the Egyptians were the first to discover that dogs, when they are ill, will not drink from rivers, but wait for rain, and hold their jaws open to catch it.

"She lies."

We were on the school bus home. I was sitting next to Carl Whiteside, who had bad breath and a huge collection of marbles. We were arguing. Carl thought she was lying. I said she wasn't, probably.

"I didn't believe that stuff about the bird," Carl said, "and what she told us about the pyramids? I didn't believe that either. She didn't know what she was talking about."

"Oh, yeah?" I had liked her. She was strange. I thought I could nail him. "If she was lying," I said, "what'd she say that was a lie?"

"Six times eleven isn't sixty-eight. It isn't ever. It's sixty-six, I know for a fact."

"She said so. She admitted it. What else did she lie about?"

"I don't know," he said. "Stuff."

"What stuff?"

"Well." He swung his legs back and forth. "You ever see an animal that was half lion and half bird?" He crossed his arms. "It sounded real fakey to me."

"It could happen," I said. I had to improvise, to outrage him. "I read in this newspaper my mom bought in the IGA about this scientist, this mad scientist in the Swiss Alps, and he's been putting genes and chromosomes and stuff together in test tubes, and he combined a human being and a hamster." I waited, for effect. "It's called a humster."

"You never." Carl was staring at me, his mouth open, his terrible bad breath making its way toward me. "What newspaper was it?"

"The *National Enquirer*," I said, "that they sell next to the cash registers." When I saw his look of recognition, I knew I had bested him. "And this mad scientist," I said, "his name was, um, Dr. Frankenbush." I realized belatedly that this name was a mistake and waited for Carl to notice its resemblance to the name of the other famous mad master of permutations, but he only sat there.

"A man and a hamster?" He was staring at me, squinting, his mouth opening in distaste. "Jeez. What'd it look like?"

When the bus reached my stop, I took off down our dirt road and ran up through the back yard, kicking the tire swing for good luck. I dropped my books on the back steps so I could hug and kiss our dog, Mr. Selby. Then I hurried inside. I could smell Brussels sprouts cooking, my unfavorite vegetable. My mother was washing other vegetables in the kitchen sink, and my baby brother was hollering in his yellow playpen on the kitchen floor.

"Hi, Mom," I said, hopping around the playpen to kiss her, "Guess what?"

"I have no idea."

"We had this substitute today, Miss Ferenczi, and I'd never seen her before, and she had all these stories and ideas and stuff."

"Well. That's good." My mother looked out the window behind the sink, her eyes on the pine woods west of our house. Her face and hairstyle always reminded other people of Betty Crocker, whose picture was framed inside a gigantic spoon on the side of the Bisquick box; to me, though, my mother's face just looked white. "Listen, Tommy," she said, "go upstairs and pick your clothes off the bathroom floor, then go outside to the shed and put the shovel and ax away that your father left outside this morning."

"She said that six times eleven was sometimes sixty-eight!" I said. "And she said she once saw a monster that was half lion and half bird." I waited. "In Egypt, she said."

"Did you hear me?" my mother asked, raising her arm to wipe her forehead with the back of her hand. "You have chores to do."

"I know," I said. "I was just telling you about the substitute."

"It's very interesting," my mother said, quickly glancing down at me, "and we can talk about it later when your father gets home. But right now you have some work to do."

"Okay, Mom." I took a cookie out of the jar on the counter and was about to go outside when I had a thought. I ran into the living room, pulled out a dictionary next to the TV stand, and opened it to the G's. *Gryphon:* "variant of griffin." *Griffin:* "a fabulous beast with the head and wings of an eagle and the body of a lion." Fabulous was right. I shouted with triumph and ran outside to put my father's tools back in their place.

Miss Ferenczi was back the next day, slightly altered. She had pulled her hair down and twisted it into pigtails, with red rubber bands holding them tight one inch from the ends. She was wearing a green blouse and pink scarf, making her difficult to look at for a full class day. This time there was no pretense of doing a reading lesson or moving on to arithmetic. As soon as the bell rang, she simply began to talk.

She talked for forty minutes straight. There seemed to be less connection between her ideas, but the ideas themselves were, as the dictionary would say, fabulous. She said she had heard of a huge jewel, in what she called the Antipodes, that was so brilliant that when the light shone into it at a certain angle it would blind whoever was looking at its center. She said that the biggest diamond in the world was cursed and had killed everyone who owned it, and that by a trick of fate it was called the Hope diamond. Diamonds are magic, she said, and this is why women wear them on their fingers, as a sign of the magic of womanhood. Men have strength, Miss Ferenczi said, but no true magic. That is why men fall in love with women but women do not fall in love with men: they just love being loved. George Washington had died because of a mistake he made about a diamond. Washington was not the first *true* President, but she did not say who was. In some places in the world, she said, men and women still live in the trees and eat monkeys for breakfast. Their doctors are magicians. At the bottom of the sea are creatures thin as pancakes which have never been studied by scientists because when you take them up to the air, the fish explode.

There was not a sound in the classroom, except for Miss Ferenczi's voice, and Donna DeShano's coughing. No one even went to the bathroom.

Beethoven, she said, had not been deaf; it was a trick to make himself famous, and it worked. As she talked, Miss Ferenczi's pigtails swung back and forth. There are trees in the world, she said, that eat meat: their leaves are sticky and close up on bugs like hands. She lifted her hands and brought them together, palm to palm.

Venus, which most people think is the next closest planet to the sun, is not always closer, and, besides, it is the planet of greatest mystery because of its thick cloud cover. "I know what lies underneath those clouds," Miss Ferenczi said, and waited. After the silence, she said, "Angels. Angels live under those clouds." She said that angels were not invisible to everyone and were in fact smarter than most people. They did not dress in robes as was often claimed but instead wore formal evening clothes, as if they were about to attend a concert. Often angels *do* attend concerts and sit in the aisles where, she said, most people pay no attention to them. She said the most terrible angel had the shape of the Sphinx. "There is no running away from that one," she said. She said that unquenchable fires burn just under the surface of the earth in Ohio, and that the baby Mozart fainted dead away in his cradle when he first heard the sound of a trumpet. She said that someone named Narzim al Harrardim was the greatest writer who ever lived. She said that planets control behavior, and anyone conceived during a solar eclipse would be born with webbed feet.

"I know you children like to hear these things," she said, "these secrets, and that is why I am telling you all this." We nodded. It was better than doing comprehension questions for the readings in *Broad Horizons*.

"I will tell you one more story," she said, "and then we will have to do some arithmetic." She leaned over, and her voice grew soft. "There is no death," she said. "You must never be afraid. Never. That which is, cannot die. It will change into different earthly and unearthly elements, but I know this as sure as I stand here in front of you, and I swear it: you must not be afraid. I have seen this truth with these eyes. I know it because in a dream God kissed me. Here." And she pointed with her right index finger to the side of her head, below the mouth, where the vertical lines were carved into her skin.

Absent-mindedly we all did our arithmetic problems. At recess the class was out on the playground, but no one was playing. We were all standing in small groups, talking about Miss Ferenczi. We didn't know if she was crazy, or what. I looked out beyond the playground, at the rusted cars piled in a small heap behind a clump of sumac, and I wanted to see shapes there, approaching me.

On the way home, Carl sat next to me again. He didn't say much, and I didn't either. At last he turned to me. "You know what she said about the leaves that close up on bugs?"

"Huh?"

"The leaves," Carl insisted. "The meat-eating plants. I know it's true. I saw it on television. The leaves have this icky glue that the plants have got smeared all over them and the insects can't get off 'cause they're stuck. I saw it." He seemed demoralized. "She's tellin' the truth."

"Yeah."

"You think she's seen all those angels?"

I shrugged.

"I don't think she has," Carl informed me. "I think she made that part up."

"There's a tree," I suddenly said. I was looking out the window at the farms along County Road H. I knew every barn, every broken windmill, every fence, every anhydrous ammonia tank, by heart. "There's a tree that's . . . that I've seen . . ."

"Don't you try to do it," Carl said. "You'll just sound like a jerk."

I kissed my mother. She was standing in front of the stove. "How was your day?" she asked.

"Fine."

"Did you have Miss Ferenczi again?"

"Yeah."

"Well?"

"She was fine, Mom," I asked, "can I go to my room?"

"No," she said, "not until you've gone out to the vegetable garden and picked me a few tomatoes." She glanced at the sky. "I think it's going to rain. Skedaddle and do it now. Then you come back inside and watch your brother for a few minutes while I go upstairs. I need to clean up before dinner." She looked down at me. "You're looking a little pale, Tommy." She touched the back of her hand to my forehead and I felt her diamond ring against my skin. "Do you feel all right?"

"I'm fine," I said, and went out to pick the tomatoes.

Coughing mutedly, Mr. Hibler was back the next day, slipping lozenges into his mouth when his back was turned at forty-five minute intervals and asking us how much of the prepared lesson plan Miss Ferenczi had followed. Edith Atwater took the responsibility for the class of explaining to Mr. Hibler that the substitute hadn't always done exactly what he would have done, but we had worked hard even though she talked a lot. About what? he asked. All kinds of things, Edith said. I sort of forgot. To our relief, Mr. Hibler seemed not at all interested in what Miss Ferenczi had said to fill the day. He probably thought it was woman's talk; unserious and not suited for school. It was enough that he had a pile of arithmetic problems from us to correct.

For the next month, the sumac turned a distracting red in the field, and the sun traveled toward the southern sky, so that its rays reached Mr. Hibler's Halloween display on the bulletin board in the back of the room, fading the scarecrow with a pumpkin head from orange to tan. Every three days I measured how much farther the sun had moved toward the southern horizon by making small marks with my black Crayola on the north wall, ant-sized marks only I knew were there, inching west.

And then in early December, four days after the first permanent snowfall, she appeared again in our classroom. The minute she came in the door, I felt my heart begin to pound. Once again, she was different: this time, her hair hung straight down and seemed hardly to have been combed. She hadn't brought her lunchbox with her, but she was carrying what seemed to be a small box. She greeted all of us and talked about the weather. Donna DeShano had to remind her to take her overcoat off.

When the bell to start the day finally rang, Miss Ferenczi looked out at all of us and said, "Children, I have enjoyed your company in the past, and today I am going to reward you." She held up the small box. "Do you know what this is?" She waited. "Of course you don't. It is a tarot pack."

Edith Atwater raised her hand. "What's a tarot pack, Miss Ferenczi?"

"It is used to tell fortunes," she said. "And that is what I shall do this morning. I shall tell your fortunes, as I have been taught to do."

"What's fortune?" Bobby Kryzanowicz asked.

"The future, young man. I shall tell you what your future will be. I can't do your whole future, of course. I shall have to limit myself to the five-card system, the wands, cups, swords, pentacles, and the higher arcanes. Now who wants to be first?"

There was a long silence. Then Carol Peterson raised her hand.

"All right," Miss Ferenczi said. She divided the pack into five smaller packs and walked back to Carol's desk, in front of mine. "Pick one card from each of these packs," she said. I saw that Carol had a four of cups, a six of swords, but I couldn't see the other cards. Miss Ferenczi studied the cards on Carol's desk for a minute. "Not bad," she said. "I do not see much higher education. Probably an early marriage. Many children. There's something bleak and dreary here, but I can't tell you what. Perhaps just the tasks of a housewife life. I think you'll do very well, for the most part." She smiled at Carol, a smile with a certain lack of interest. "Who wants to be next?"

Carl Whiteside raised his hand slowly.

"Yes," Miss Ferenczi said, "let's do a boy." She walked over to where Carl sat. After he picked his five cards, she gazed at them for a long time. "Travel," she said. "Much distant travel. You might go into the Army. Not too much romantic interest here. A late marriage, if at all. Squabbles. But the Sun is in your major arcana, here, yes, that's a very good card." She giggled. "Maybe a good life."

Next I raised my hand, and she told me my future. She did the same with Bobby Kryzanowicz, Kelly Munger, Edith Atwater, and Kim Foor. Then she came to Wayne Razmer. He picked his five cards, and I could see that the Death card was one of them.

"What's your name?" Miss Ferenczi asked.

"Wayne."

"Well, Wayne," she said, "you will undergo a *great* metamorphosis, the greatest, before you become an adult. Your earthly element will leap away, into thin air, you sweet boy. This card, this nine of swords here, tells of suffering and desolation. And this ten of wands, well, that's certainly a heavy load."

"What about this one?" Wayne pointed to the Death card.

"That one? That one means you will die soon, my dear." She gathered up the cards. We were all looking at Wayne. "But do not fear," she said. "It's not really death, so much as change." She put the cards on Mr. Hibler's desk. "And now, let's do some arithmetic."

At lunchtime Wayne went to Mr. Faegre, the principal, and told him what Miss Ferenczi had done. During the noon recess, we saw Miss Ferenczi drive out of the parking lot in her green Rambler. I stood under the slide, listening to the other kids coasting down and landing in the little depressive bowl at the bottom. I was kicking stones and tugging at my hair right up to the moment when I saw Wayne come out to the playground. He smiled, the dead fool, and with the fingers of his right hand he was showing everyone how he had told on Miss Ferenczi.

I made my way toward Wayne, pushing myself past two girls from another class. He was watching me with his little pinhead eyes.

"You told," I shouted at him. "She was just kidding."

"She shouldn't have," he shouted back. "We were supposed to be doing arithmetic."

"She just scared you," I said. "You're a chicken. You're a chicken, Wayne. You are. Scared of a little card," I singsonged.

Wayne fell at me, his two fists hammering down on my nose. I gave him a good one in the stomach and then I tried for his head. Aiming my fist, I saw that he was crying. I slugged him.

"She was right," I yelled. "She was always right! She told the truth!" Other kids were whooping. "You were just scared, that's all!"

And then large hands pulled at us, and it was my turn to speak to Mr. Faegre.

In the afternoon Miss Ferenczi was gone, and my nose was stuffed with cotton clotted with blood, and my lip had swelled, and our class had been combined with Mrs. Mantei's sixth-grade class for a crowded afternoon science unit on insect life in ditches and swamps. I knew where Mrs. Mantei lived: she had a new house trailer just down the road from us, at the Clearwater Park. She was no mystery. Somehow she and Mr. Bodine, the other fourth-grade teacher, had managed to fit forty-five desks into the room. Kelly Munger asked if Miss Ferenczi had been arrested, and Mrs. Mantei said, no, of course not. All that afternoon, until the buses came to pick us up, we learned about field crickets and two-striped grasshoppers, water bugs, cicadas, mosquitoes, flies, and moths. We learned about insects' hard outer shell, the exoskeleton, and the usual parts of the mouth, including the labrum, mandible, maxilla, and glossa. We learned about compound eyes and the four-stage metamorphosis from egg to larva to pupa to adult. We learned something, but not much, about mating. Mrs. Mantei drew, very skillfully, the internal anatomy of the grasshopper on the blackboard. We learned about the dance of the honeybee, directing other bees in the hive to pollen. We found out about which insects were pests to man, and which were not. On lined white pieces of paper we made lists of insects we might actually see, then a list of insects too small to be clearly visible, such as fleas; Mrs. Mantei said that our assignment would be to memorize these lists for the next day, when Mr. Hibler would certainly return and test us on our knowledge.

🕭 🕭 🕭

Suggestions for Discussion

1. What details describing Miss Ferenczi show us why the narrator is drawn to her? How does he change in response to her lessons?

2. "Bobby Kryzanowicz, the faultless brown-noser," is an example of a "flat" character. How do details and dialogue create this effect?

Retrospect

3. What is the story's crisis? What action does the narrator take there and why?

The Visible Man

ELIZABETH STUCKEY-FRENCH

By the time Rona Arbuckle arrived to pick Althea Fish up for lunch, Althea had almost given up. She was sitting in the lobby of the Sycamore Retirement Villas, and had just decided to walk back to her room and go back to bed when she spotted Rona's Saab idling in front of the building. In the pale spring light the red car looked like a glaring mistake. Althea closed her eyes. She didn't want to see Rona, but she hadn't had the energy to call and decline her invitation, delivered yesterday by mail, a silly little YOU ARE INVITED card. Earlier that morning it had taken all of Althea's willpower to lift the spoon and eat her Bran Buds, peel off her flaccid nightgown, and rake a comb through her hair, which used to be silvery blond but was now the color of a used cigarette filter.

"Hey there!" She felt talons gripping her shoulder. "Thea. You asleep?" Rona was sixty years old but still had the look and demeanor of a cheerleader, one who'd seen too much overtime but felt obligated to keep on cheering. On weekdays she wore business suits, but today she wore what she called "play clothes"—white shorts, a navy cotton sweater with a white sailboat on it, white socks, and navy tennis shoes. Althea had never realized till this moment how much she disliked nauticalia—was there such a word?

Rona sat down in a turquoise chair that matched Althea's. Sycamore Villas had recently been redone in Southwestern style, even though this was Indiana. They'd painted everything peach and turquoise, hung paintings off cliff-dwelling Indians on the walls, and propped a withered cactus up in the corner of the lobby. "You didn't tell me you'd be waiting down here," said Rona. "Are you hiding something in your room? Like a dead body?" This was Rona's idea of a joke. Althea had endured jokes like this for the fifteen years she'd cleaned Rona's house. Every Friday, over lunch, she'd listened politely to stories about severed heads and ghosts and killer bees.

"I'm not hiding anything," Althea told Rona, but in a way, she was. Her room was as institutional and barren-looking as this waiting room, and she was ashamed of it. Most of the things she'd kept when she moved to Sycamore Villas nearly a year ago were still in boxes underneath her bed. Rona would insist on helping her unpack everything. For some reason, Rona wouldn't leave Althea alone. She'd visited her in the hospital and took her out to Wendy's on her seventieth birthday. She called every week to ask how Althea was feeling. How would anyone feel? Max was dead and she was living in a state nursing home.

"I talked to your psychiatrist yesterday. Dr. Wong?" Rona patted her knee. "I told him that if your new medication doesn't work, he should try shock treatment. But *don't* worry about it. Shock treatment's a lot less brutal than it used to be. Plus, it works!"

Rona would never understand that things like medication, shock treatment, and foreign doctors went right through Althea without causing a ripple. What worried her were the small things, like the red thread now dangling from her skirt. "Do you have scissors?" she asked Rona.

Rona gave her a sideways, calculating look. "You mean on me?"

Althea lifted the string to show her why she need them.

"Sharp objects are probably not a good idea," Rona said. "When you're feeling so bad." She stood up, grabbed Althea's hand, and jerked her to her feet as if she wanted to surprise her into action. "My chariot awaits," she said, and began pulling Althea toward the door. "Oh my God, you forgot your shoes!"

Althea wore an old pair of Max's argyle socks. She hadn't forgotten shoes—they were just too much trouble to put on. And why bother, when she was just going from the lobby to Rona's car, into her house for an hour, and then back here again?

She could almost hear Rona's mind working. *It might take a good thirty minutes to get a pair of shoes and convince Althea to put them on.* Rona bent over and untied her own tennis shoes, pulled them off and then her socks. Her feet looked dingy after the sparkling white socks. "I'll keep you company," said Rona. "If they arrest one for indecent exposure, they'll have to arrest both of us."

Soon they were zipping down the bypass in Rona's car. It was a sunny, peppy day, the trees sporting brand-new leaves. Rona looked like a child behind the wheel, and her bare feet only magnified this illusion. She'd always given Althea a ride home on Fridays, and she always drove too fast and hit the brakes too hard, which made Althea queasy, but it was better than taking the bus. Now Rona was talking about what she'd be serving for lunch—chicken salad and brownies with vanilla icing. And coffee. She said she knew how much Althea liked coffee, when actually, Althea only drank it to distract herself from Rona's incessant chatter. Rona always served it with horrible-tasting evaporated milk. "I'm evaporating," Althea said.

"What?" Rona stepped on the brakes and then on the gas. "Of course you're not!" she said. "That's just your depression talking." Rona gave Althea's arm a squeeze. "We're going to have a nice lunch, like in the old days, just the two of us. There's something I want to talk to you about, because *you* never tell me to stop imagining things."

Uh-oh. This wasn't good. Althea felt down around her knee for the thread, wrapping it around her finger. The car swung right onto Park Street, a narrow street lined with bungalows and picket fences, the street Althea and Max had once lived on.

"Want to see your old house?" Rona asked.

That would mean making a U-turn, which Rona would do in a gleeful, reckless manner, so Althea said no, even though she desperately missed her former home, a craftsman-style house she'd been forced to sell before she went into Sycamore Villas. By the time Max died of brain cancer, all their savings were gone, even though they'd had insurance through the university, where Max had worked for thirty years on the buildings and grounds crew.

"Take me to the cemetery," Althea said.

"Now now," said Rona. "You're not dead yet."

"I have to get out of that place," Althea said.

"I know you. You'll grow to love it there!" said Rona. "And you've got that nice blind friend."

Althea didn't have a blind friend, but she didn't bother to correct Rona, who would only insist that she did. Dr. Wong was no help either. Yesterday, when she'd said the same thing to him, "Get me out of that place," he'd just laughed like she was telling a joke, scribbled out her new prescription, and ushered her to the door.

Rona was still talking. "I knew women who had shock treatment just for fun. Back in my hometown." Rona was from Alabama somewhere, and Althea wasn't surprised to hear about anything people did down there. "You know, Seth has been seeing Dr. Wong too," said Rona, as if this would be a comfort to Althea. "He's on antidepressants now."

Last Althea remembered, Rona's son Seth still lived in town and did some sort of clerical work at the hospital. Rona'd been divorced since Seth was little, and often complained about it—"We single moms have a tough time"—putting herself in the same category as the welfare moms down on Fourth Street, even though she was a dean at the university. Max and Althea had never been able to have children, which sometimes felt to Althea like a terrible loss and sometimes like a ghastly fate barely avoided.

Rona made a left turn in front of an oncoming pickup truck, which blared its horn in protest. "Seth just moved out, into his own apartment," said Rona. "I've given up on him going to medical school. But he's got a new girlfriend, an anesthesiologist. Can you beat that?"

"No," said Althea. She'd suspected for years that Seth was a homosexual. Even in high school, he never seemed to have any interest in impressing girls. Rona was always talking about some girl or other who was *after* Seth, so Althea sensed that Rona knew too, but would never admit it.

Rona said, "Seth brought his new gal by the house last week. Her name's Serenity. Isn't that a hoot? Seth and Serenity. She's got a big mouth. I don't mean she talks a lot, I mean her mouth's big." Rona took her hands off the wheel and stretched her lips wide. The car drifted toward a telephone pole till Rona finally caught it. "I'm already planning their wedding!" Rona said. "I can't say that to anybody but you. Isn't it funny how I can talk to my *cleaning* lady better than my friends?"

Who was she kidding? Althea thought. Rona didn't have friends. She and Althea certainly weren't friends, but what were they? There wasn't a word for it. Althea had become one of Rona's projects, like curbside recycling or Mothers Without Partners. And Rona was Althea's ticket out of Sycamore Villas, if only for a few hours.

The car was now winding down Highland Avenue, a wide brick street of mostly Victorians. As the familiar houses slid past, Althea greeted them one by one.

"There's something that bothers me about Seth's wedding," Rona said. "I'll have to dance at the reception. I'm a terrible dancer. I'll look like a fool! The thought of it makes my skin crawl." Rona wheeled into her driveway and slammed on the brakes. "Here we are," she said.

Althea looked around. She hadn't seen Rona's house for two years, and she realized she'd never said a proper good-bye to it. The place looked peaceful as always, a two-story Colonial made of white limestone bricks, surrounded by tall maple and oak trees. The same green haze of mold lined the house. The little pond was still there in the front yard, but now it was empty. Seth used to fill it full of various creatures—mostly tropical fish that died or frogs that hopped away. But the grass was newly mowed, and the pink peony bushes were in full sugary bloom. "I'm just going to sit here," Althea said.

Rona sighed, her irritation finally showing. "You walked out to the car just fine. Do you want me to take you back?"

Althea thought about this. She didn't want to walk inside, but she also wasn't quite ready for another car ride with Rona. Strangely enough, she felt as if she and Rona had just arrived home after a long journey together. Before she knew it, she'd opened up the car door and was standing in the driveway. Her finger ached, and she lifted her hand and noticed the red string wrapped tightly around it. She hadn't needed scissors after all.

"Your medication must be working," said Rona. "What are you taking now?"

"Can't remember," said Althea. But she did feel sprightly, walking toward the door. How many times had she walked to this door from the bus stop, slipping on ice, sweating in the humidity? She'd always told herself she merely tolerated the job and found Rona profoundly irritating, so why was she now feeling a trickle of anticipation? Maybe it was just the medication.

Inside, the house smelled and looked the same. If Althea was placed blindfolded in the living room of this house—unlikely, but you never know—she'd recognize her surroundings by the smell: a closed-up, sweetish, antiseptic kind of smell. The furniture was still the same, the impractical white couch and citrus-colored silk chairs. Everything looked clean, even the pale green carpet had no footprints in it. Just looking at the carpet made Althea want to lie down. It was a leftover feeling from her cleaning days, when she spent much of her time alone, fighting to keep from sinking down onto beds and couches and nice soft carpets. Now she unwound the thread from her finger and dropped it. Who was vacuuming now? Was there a new Althea? She thought about asking, but Rona had her by the shoulders.

"Let's go right on in and I'll serve you up some lunch," Rona said. They crossed the foyer and stumbled into a mound of laundry on the floor. "Seth," said Rona, kicking the clothes down the stairs. "I guess Serenity's too busy knocking people out to do his laundry. Did I tell you she's an anesthesiologist?" Rona steered Althea up to the kitchen table and into a chair. "We're in for a treat," she said. "Any excuse for chocolate. You know me."

The kitchen floor looked dull—wax buildup—but there was a new tablecloth on the table, a festive print of Parisian street scenes. Somebody else must've picked it out, Althea decided. She was pleased to see that the sink was full of dirty dishes. Rona's rebellion.

Rona opened the refrigerator door and began rummaging around. "I've lost touch with the contents of my refrigerator," she muttered.

On the tablecloth, Althea noticed, it was the same little street scene repeated over and over again. The same little Eiffel Tower, over and over. She stood up, feeling woozy. "I'm going to the bathroom," she announced, and started out of the room, pleased with the way her sock feet took her smoothly along, out of the kitchen, moving under their own power. In the foyer, she paused. The bathroom she'd be expected to use, the guest bathroom, was downstairs, but she decided to go upstairs instead.

Upstairs, she stood for a minute in the bathroom, flushed the toilet, then peeked into Seth's room.

Everything was just as she remembered it. Seth's posters of constellations and fossils still hung on the walls, his encyclopedias still lined the bookshelf, his scien-tific toys were still stacked on the desk. When Seth was a kid he'd pestered Althea while she was working, following her from room to room asking her idiotic ques-tions—Would she care for a *delicious bar of Ex-Lax?* Would she like to play *52 Pickup?* But as he grew older he became silent and almost wary, lying on his bed pretending to read *Scientific American* while Althea cleaned his room. Every week she enjoyed dusting his microscope, his junior chemistry set, and the glass cover of this insect collection, which had earned an A-plus in ninth grade. He also had an anatomy kit called the Visible Man, a model of a human figure with clear plastic skin so you could view his skeleton and color-coded organs. She could still see Seth bent over his desk, diligently assembling the Visible Man, painting the veins blue, the rectum green, the liver red, the brain white, then hooking the bones to-gether, slipping the organs into their correct cavities, snapping the breastplate on. When he finished, he stuck the man back in his box—even though there was a display stand included—which struck Althea as disrespectful. Sometimes, when Seth wasn't around, Althea would open the box, detach and examine the organs, and then try to replace them without consulting the instruction manual, feeling a strange thrill when she could. She loved the scientific names, the thin rivers of blood, the clarity.

Now Althea tiptoed over to the desk and began pawing through the toys, looking for the Visible Man. There was his cardboard coffin, on the bottom of the stack. Hands shaking, she pulled out the box and peeked inside. Underneath his sheer skin, his organs were all in their proper places. Liver, colon, testes. His penis was just part of the clear outer shell, which Althea felt was cheating. She gave his penis a little squeeze, but it didn't seem to bother him. His skeleton face grinned away at nothing; his red eyeballs stared. She'd remembered him as a proud and splendid creature—a Wall Street tycoon—but today he looked more like the victim of a plague. A jaunty victim. Typhoid Larry. All he needed was a bandanna and a jug of rum.

"Thea! What on God's earth?"

Althea closed the box and turned around. Rona stood in the doorway. "Are you all right? Did you forget what you're doing?"

"I came in here to clean," said Althea, shaking her head as if it were fuzzy. "But I forgot my dust rag." She set the box back on the desk.

"Honey, you don't work here anymore," said Rona, marching over to escort her back downstairs. "You are here as my guest."

Althea stole a look back at the box and wished she'd thought to bring her purse up here with her, her purse which was really a big string shopping bag. Rona'd never miss him, she decided. And he'd be much happier with her.

Down in the kitchen, Rona had laid out chicken salad on beds of lettuce and served it on glass plates with the outlines of grape leaves on them. The veins of the leaves reminded Althea of the veins in the Visible Man.

Rona speared a hunk of chicken salad. She frowned and spoke slowly. "Are you having trouble with your memory?"

"What memory?"

Rona barked with laughter. "Have you told your Dr. Wong about it? He might have to adjust those meds."

Althea took a nibble of the salad. "Too much mayo," she said, without realizing she was speaking aloud.

"Oh well," said Rona, her feelings clearly hurt. "It came from Marsh deli." She lowered her head and began to shovel it in. After a moment she bobbed back up. "Met another PH last Saturday at the car wash," she said. "False teeth, but he drives a Jeep." PH meant Potential Honey, an expression she'd picked up on campus.

Althea wished she didn't know Rona's vulnerabilities so well. Even though Rona had a Ph.D. and an important job, her life was barely in control. She was always trying to diet. She couldn't cook or clean, and she was always flailing out against loneliness. "I asked him to teach me how to dance," Rona went on. "He said 'no can do.' Don't you just *hate* that expression? 'No can do.' What a fuddy-duddy." She sighed melodramatically, gazing heavenward. "I'll never learn to dance," she said.

"Take a dance class," said Althea, knowing Rona never would.

"Good idea!" said Rona. "Althea, you're a genius." She nibbled on some lettuce. "Where would I do that?"

"How about Arthur Murray's?" said Althea. When they were first married, she and Max had lived in a tiny apartment above the Arthur Murray Dance Studio. On weeknights Althea would come home from her job at Loeb's Department Store, kick off her pumps, toss her red wool coat on the bed, and she and Max, who was usually still in his sweaty work clothes, would dance along with the big band music coming up through their floorboards, Count Basie or Duke Ellington, following the dance instructor's directions as best they could, often falling into a laughing heap on the floor. "Look at me!" the dance instructor would shout at his students. "Look at me!" Little Brown Jug. Chattanooga Choo-Choo.

"Is Arthur Murray's still in business?" Rona said. She wiped her lips and folded her napkin. "Arthur Murray. Now there was a homely man. People on TV were uglier back then, don't you think? Not just him and his wife. Red Skelton, Milton Berle, Sid Caesar. All hideous."

Rona went on talking, and Althea found herself thinking about the Visible Man, imprisoned in his dusty box, and how she was going to manage to get back upstairs, with her purse, and slip him inside. In all her years of cleaning houses, she'd never had the desire to take anything before now, in part because she'd always thought of the houses she cleaned, and their contents, as belonging, in a way, to her. She was like the poor sister who popped in and out of her stepsisters' lives and carried the details back to Max. He loved hearing about the cat couple, who scolded her if she turned on the vacuum cleaner without first calling out, "Kitties! Althea's gonna make a vroom-vroom!" And the family of tall, handsome tennis players who held belching contests and had dock spiders in their basement. Without Max at home to help her put Rona in perspective she felt vulnerable, endangered. The Visible Man seemed like something to cling to, a familiar plank to keep her afloat.

"I hope Serenity wants to have children," Rona was saying, "but I hope they look like Seth. Do you think it would be premature for me to buy a crib? Not to give them. I'd put it in Seth's room. For when they visit. Who could take offense at that?"

"Seth could."

Rona blinked, startled, and went back to her salad. Althea wondered why she rarely told Rona what she really thought. For some reason, she felt more like being honest since she'd decided to steal something. She said, "I *like* it when people say 'no can do.'"

"Huh?"

"No can do. One of my favorite expressions."

"Okay. Sure. Well. Anyway." Rona pushed her plate impatiently aside, as though it were imposing on her. "I've got something to tell you," she said, glancing quickly around the room. "*My house is haunted.*"

Althea said nothing, so Rona continued. "I don't even believe in ghosts, but I've got one. A mean one. When it's quiet I can hear him breathing. Last week I found all my black socks wadded into one big ball. Isn't that creepy? Sometimes I can smell waffles, and I haven't fixed waffles in years. I *despise* waffles. And this morning I almost slipped in a puddle of water in the hallway. At least I think it was water. *And I don't know how it got there.*" Rona gazed at Althea intently. "But here's the worst thing. Know how you feel pressure when someone sits down on your bed? Sometimes I feel his hand on my knee. Not a friendly feeling. It's like he's planning to attack me." She pursed her lips. "*Rape me.*"

Althea forced herself to keep chewing the tasteless chicken. She did a quick mental inventory of Rona's obsessions over the years—was this one the most absurd ever? Yup. She pulled her purse up into her lap. "How could a ghost rape?" she asked Rona.

"Good question," Rona said. "But I feel like this one could manage it." She popped out of her chair and opened the cardboard carton on the counter. "I'm going to start on dessert!" She cut herself a large slab of brownie, poured herself a cup of coffee, and sat back down. "I'm too scared to sleep at night," she said. She tried to smile as she chewed. "I finally got your Wong to prescribe me some knockout pills."

"He's not *my* Wong," Althea said. "And he's a scumbucket."

"Well," said Rona. "I don't know about that." She took a dainty, professional-woman sip of coffee.

Underneath the table, Althea began fumbling around in her purse, wondering if the Visible Man would fit inside. She could dump the contents of her purse into the wastebasket if she needed to. It would be worth it. "I think I'll go right to dessert too," she said.

"Oh. Sure." Rona hopped up to cut Althea some brownie.

"Could I have some of that delicious evaporated milk with my coffee?"

"Why certainly!" Rona disappeared into the pantry.

Althea leaned over the huge Rubbermaid wastebasket, opened her purse, emptied it, and sat back down before Rona returned, triumphantly bearing a can of milk.

Rona served Althea coffee with yellow milk curdling in the center, and a hunk of brownie, and Althea said, "Thanks so much." She had no idea what she'd just thrown away. The only thing she might miss was her Social Security card. But how was she going to get back upstairs and rescue the Visible Man?

Rona dropped heavily into her chair. "I keep on thinking," she said, "of this religious pamphlet I once got handed on campus, asking 'Are you bugged with fear?'" She swung her arms out, knocking over her coffee cup, spilling coffee all over the table. "Phooey," she said, and jumped up, fumbling at the roll of paper towels. "I'm hoping you can help me."

"Me?" said Althea, squeezing her empty purse. "I'm a certified basket case."

Rona laughed gaily, blotted coffee into a Parisian street scene, and tossed the wad of paper towels onto the counter. "I've got to get rid of this ghost." She gazed beseechingly at Althea. "I thought we could have a little séance thing."

"A séance thing?"

"Just a quickie," Rona said. "Ask him to tell us what he wants."

Althea had never been in a séance before, only seen them on TV. She had no idea how to conduct a séance. "How about Seth's room?" she said.

"Seth's room?"

"I think the conditions are good in there."

Rona clapped her hands. "I knew I was asking the right person. Finish your brownie and let's go."

Upstairs, Rona lit two candles and placed them on Seth's bedside table—white candles in brass candleholders. Vanilla-scented. They sat down across from each other on Seth's twin beds, which were neatly made with red corduroy spreads. His Boy Scout sash, thick with badges, was slung over one bedpost.

"Wouldn't it be better in my room?" said Rona.

"No," said Althea, looking over at the Visible Man. "You'd better pull the blinds." The box was far too big for her purse, she realized. What had she been thinking? Her purse lay on her lap, empty but useless.

When the room was dimmer they sat there foolishly, waiting for something to begin.

"Hear him breathing?" whispered Rona.

"I think that's the central air."

"No it's not," Rona snapped, and then, more plaintively, "Listen. It's deep, like a growl."

Althea did hear something now, something like breathing, soft and steady. She pictured the Visible Man's lungs rising and deflating.

Rona whispered, "What's next?"

"We close our eyes," said Althea, who opened hers to make sure Rona had obeyed. She had.

"Yes?" said Rona, as if she were in a trance.

Althea glanced at the Visible Man. Then she sat up as straight as she could. "I'm getting a message," she said.

Rona wrinkled her nose. "What's it want?"

"No talking," said Althea. "It's not an it. It's a person. A man."

"A young man?" said Rona.

"No," Althea said sternly. "An old man. Very old."

"Can I say something?"

"Make it quick."

Rona's eyes popped open. She was sweating, wisps of blond hair curling up around her face. "Why's he so angry at me?"

"Silence," said Althea. "Close your eyes."

Rona did as she was told, and Althea suddenly knew two things—first, she'd only been invited to lunch today because of the ghost, only because Rona wouldn't parade her neuroses in front of anyone else; and second, she would not be invited back again.

"I can see the ghost now," said Althea. "He's sitting there beside you, on the bed."

"Where?" Rona stiffened up like a charmed cobra. "What's he doing?"

"Drinking rum, from a jug. He has the other hand on your knee."

"Make him stop," said Rona. She let out a little whimper.

"Okay, he stopped," said Althea. "Now he's wiping his eyes with his handkerchief. He's sad because he misses Seth. He only came here because he was attracted to Seth. Being a homosexual himself. He'd never rape you."

Rona sighed. "That's a relief," she said.

Althea felt a stirring in her chest like a swarm of bees. Something was happening. When she spoke again, her voice sounded deeper and louder, like Typhoid Larry's voice would sound, if he had one. "There is something you should know."

"What's that?"

"Your son is a homosexual."

Rona hunched her shoulders and screwed up her face as if it had started raining, hard, right into her eyes. Acid rain. "But he's going to get married," she said. "In the arboretum."

The buzzing in Althea's chest stopped abruptly and she felt her body sag. It's no use, she thought. Then she heard footsteps coming down the hall. There *was* a ghost!

The door swung open and Seth stuck his head inside. He needed a haircut. "What are you doing in here?"

"Want some lunch?" said Rona.

Seth stepped into the room. He looked as handsome as ever, with his dark eyes and square chin, but over his T-shirt he wore a pale blue down vest. Althea had always wondered who would wear such a useless and ugly piece of clothing. "Hello, Seth," she said.

"You remember Mrs. Fish?"

"Of course. Hello." He didn't smile. "Why are you in my room?"

"We just now came in," said Rona, clasping her hands together as if she were going to pray.

Seth flipped on the light and glanced at the candles. "You were having a séance. You were trying to contact that damn ghost. Don't deny it." He folded his arms on his chest.

Rona smiled her cheerleader smile but said nothing.

Althea said, "We did contact the ghost." She blew out the vanilla candles with great gusto.

"Honey, the ghost is a *pirate*," said Rona.

"His name's Typhoid Larry." Althea tried to speak casually, like she was introducing the mailman. "He's gone now. He had things to do—murders, plundering."

Seth frowned at Althea, looking her up and down, his eyes finally resting on her argyle socks.

"Seth," said Althea. "I hear we have the same doctor now. Good old Dr. Wong. Isn't he a card?"

Seth turned back to his mother. "Do you tell *everyone?*"

"Only her. Swear on a Bible."

"I practically forced it out of her," Althea said.

Seth waved his hand. "Listen. I just came by to give you some news. I'm going to take a job in Brisbane, at the Royal Victoria Hospital. That's in Australia." He nodded as if confirming his good sense of geography. "It starts in two months."

Rona said, "I can't believe it."

"Well, you better believe it," said Seth, with the bluster, Althea thought, of someone who doesn't know what the hell he's doing.

Rona seemed to have shrunk into a smaller version of herself. "What about Serenity?" she said in her new small voice.

"What about her?"

"You'll break her heart."

"How many times do I have to tell you? We are *just friends*."

"Good friends?"

Seth shook his head and his neck turned red.

"Listen," said Althea. "Isn't it too warm out for the vest? It's such a warm day."

Seth looked down and plucked at his vest as if he were surprised to see it. "It's not that warm," he said.

Rona took a deep breath, inflating herself back up to normal size. "Honey. That ghost said you were a homosexual!"

Seth opened his mouth, made a sound like a horse snorting, turned, and left the room, stomping off down the hallway. *"I am not!"* he yelled, thumping down the stairs.

"Don't forget your laundry!" Rona called, but the back door slammed shut.

Rona and Althea smiled wanly at each other.

"I already bought a dress for their wedding," said Rona. "Lavender with yellow blossoms." Her expression was one Althea'd never seen on her face before—empty, as if she'd gone and checked into a new hotel, into a room where no one could reach her.

Come back here, Althea wanted to say.

Rona sank back on the bed and lay stiff and unmoving, gazing at the ceiling.

After a while Althea said, "Can I get you something? Coffee? Another brownie?"

Rona curled up her toes. "No. Thank you."

It wasn't just that Seth was moving halfway around the world, Althea realized. Rona saw Serenity as her last chance. Her only chance.

"I'm sure Seth will meet another girl," said Althea. "A nice Australian girl."

Rona sniffled and covered her face with her hands.

"He'll find one prettier than Serenity," Althea went on, feeling like a fool but quickly warming to the feeling. "A girl with a small mouth. Who loves to do laundry." And so he might, Althea thought. So what if he is a homosexual? What did it matter? A lot of those marriages seemed to work out anyway.

Rona wouldn't say anything. The sailboat on her chest rose and fell too quickly.

"They'll get married in the arboretum," Althea said, "and it will be a sunny day, like today, and you'll be standing under the gazebo in your lavender dress, sipping champagne with your new PH. One who has a Jeep *and* teeth. You'll be watching Seth dance with his beautiful Australian bride. His already pregnant Australian bride."

Rona still didn't respond, and Althea feared she'd gone too far. Then Rona uncovered her face and wiped tears into her hair. "Will you be there?"

"Of course," said Althea. She too would be standing under the gazebo, also wearing a new dress, but instead of enjoying the spectacle of Seth dancing with his pregnant bride, she would be furtively watching the male guests, scrutinizing the way they watched Seth, straining to detect the narrowing of jealous eyes, an angry hand clutching a cocktail napkin. Looking for clues. Evidence. She wouldn't be able to report her findings to Max, but the Visible Man would be waiting for her back in her room at Sycamore Villas, lounging against his display stand. She would simply tell Rona that she wanted him, and Rona would give him to her.

She stood up. "Come on, mother of the groom," she said, pulling Rona to her feet. Rona stood before her, impotent, damp-haired, eyes downcast.

Althea had no idea what she was going to do until she did it. "Let's dance," she said. She placed one hand in the small of Rona's back and with the other she clasped Rona's hand. She'd forgotten she was so much taller than Rona.

"With you?" said Rona. "Now?"

"I'll teach you the swing." Althea began to hum "A String of Pearls" and guided Rona around the room, stepping left, right, back, pretending she knew what she was doing. She could still see the Arthur Murray sign that hung outside their kitchen window, she could still hear it buzzing—a neon outline of a dancing couple, the woman's yellow skirt blinking on and off, on and off.

She was leading perfectly, but Rona kept tripping. "Look at me!" said Althea. "I'm your dance partner, not your feet."

They ran into the rocking chair. "Ouch!" Rona yelped, but Althea kept them moving.

Rona wheezed with laughter. "We're clumsier than cows on ice," she said. Color had drained back into her face. "Is this really how you do it?"

"It's close enough," Althea said.

🐚 🐚 🐚

Suggestions for Discussion

1. How are the "typical" characteristics of Althea's aging made unique?

2. What does Rona's clothing say about her? Her car and driving? Her dialogue? Her fascination with the bizarre?

3. Find a passage where Rona is "indirectly" characterized through Althea's opinions.

Retrospect

4. What is "shown not told" through the various settings: the nursing home, Althea's own room, Seth's room, and Rona's living room and kitchen?

5. How does the dancing in the final scene serve as a resolution?

🍃 🍃 🍃

Writing Exercises

INDIVIDUAL

1. Find a painting or photograph that shows a group of characters, and take a few minutes to imagine the relationships among them. Assume the role of one of the pictured figures and write a dramatic monologue. What do you understand that no one else does? What will you do next?

DEVELOPMENT/REVISION

2. Name the most significant choice that your main character must make in the course of the story; then list in your journal the pressures that make that choice a difficult one.

3. Take an earlier assignment you have written and give the main character a contradictory aspect—a "consistent inconsistency."

4. Write a paragraph describing a memory that will help readers better understand why the character responds as he or she does to a certain story situation.

5. In the present tense, write out your main character's recurring dream.

COLLABORATIVE

6. Recall three anecdotes you've heard about family members. Tell them to a partner and explain what each one captures about the personality of that relative.

7. Choose a character from a story-in-progress and list four objects that character would carry in a purse, backpack, briefcase, etc. One should be a secret object. Then choose a fifth, intangible thing the character carries, just as the soldiers carried the sky, their reputations, their fear, and so forth in "The Things They

Carried." Review your list with a partner and explain what each thing carried reveals about the character. Discuss where one or more of these might be worked into the story.

8. Look through a page of newspaper want ads. Imagine the person who placed the ad to sell the ticket, car, unused wedding dress, etc. As a group, conjure up that character and the story line that might have led him or her to do this. A second group should brainstorm the character that wants to buy the advertised object, along with that person's motive. Individually, write the scene of a meeting between these two characters.

5

THE FLESH MADE WORD
Characterization, Part II

• *The Direct Methods of Character Presentation*

• *Conflict Between Methods of Presentation*

• *Reinventing Character*

• *Creating a Group or Crowd*

• *Character: A Summary*

Credibility, purpose, complexity, and the drive toward (or away from) change form the unseen skeleton of a character. Indirect characterization—"telling" by the author or another speaker—may put that character in a context that begins to shape our view, but it is through the four methods of direct characterization—*appearance, action, dialogue,* and *thought*—that a character is captured in print and transformed from a concept in the writer's mind to a living presence in the reader's. While each method will be examined separately, it is their combination that convinces, for while appearance and action convey a strong impression, characters reveal themselves most profoundly in the ways they speak and think. Like every other kind of "showing," the techniques explored in this chapter appeal to the senses, allowing readers to draw their own conclusions and to either accept or resist the narrator's judgment.

Unlike even those closest to us in real life—our spouses, our lovers, our kin, whom we can never know completely—fictional people retain only as much privacy and secrecy as those who create them decide to let them keep.

Doug Bauer

The Direct Methods of Character Presentation

APPEARANCE

Of the four methods of direct presentation, appearance is especially important because our eyes are our most highly developed means of perception, and we therefore receive more nonsensuous information by sight than by any other sense. Beauty is only skin deep, but people are embodied, and whatever beauty—or ugliness—there is in them must somehow surface in order for us to perceive it. Such surfacing involves speech and action as well as appearance, but it is appearance that prompts our first reaction to people, and everything they wear and own bodies forth some aspect of their inner selves.

Concerned to see beyond mere appearances, writers are sometimes inclined to neglect this power of the visible. In fact, much of the tension and conflict in character does proceed from the truth that appearance is not reality. But in order to know this, we must see the appearance first. Features, shape, style, clothing, and objects can make statements of internal values that are political, religious, social, intellectual, and essential. The man in the Ultrasuede jacket is making a different statement from the one in the holey sweatshirt. The woman with the cigarette holder is telling us something different from the one with the palmed joint. Even a person who has forsaken our materialistic society altogether, sworn off supermarkets, and gone to the country to grow organic potatoes has a special relationship with his or her hoe. However indifferent we may be to our looks, that indifference is the result of experiences with our bodies. A twenty-two-year-old Apollo who has been handsome since he was six is a very different person from the man who spent his childhood cocooned in fat and burst the chrysalis at age sixteen.

Following are four very brief portraits of women. Each is mainly characterized by such trivialities as fabric, hairdo, and cosmetics. It would nevertheless be impossible to mistake the essential nature of any one of them for that of any of the others.

> Mrs. Withers, the dietician, marched in through the back door, drew up, and scanned the room. She wore her usual Betty Grable hairdo and open-toed pumps, and her shoulders had an aura of shoulder pads even in a sleeveless dress.
>
> Margaret Atwood, *The Edible Woman*

> My grandmother had on not just one skirt, but four, one over the other. It should not be supposed that she wore one skirt and three petticoats; no, she wore four skirts; one supported the next, and she wore the lot of them in accordance with a definite system, that is, the order of the skirts was changed from day to day . . . The one that was closest to her yesterday clearly disclosed its pattern today, or rather its lack of pattern: all my grandmother Anna Bronski's skirts favored the same potato color. It must have been becoming to her.
>
> Günter Grass, *The Tin Drum*

How beautiful Helen is, how elegant, how timeless: how she charms Esther Songford and how she flirts with Edwin, laying a scarlet fingernail on his dusty lapel, mesmerizing.

She comes in a chauffeured car. She is all cream and roses. Her stockings are purest silk; her underskirt, just briefly showing, is lined with lace.

Fay Weldon, *Female Friends*

As soon as I entered the room, a pungent odor of phosphorus told me she'd taken rat poison. She lay groaning between the quilts. The tatami by the bed was splashed with blood, her waved hair was matted like rope waste, and a bandage tied round her throat showed up unnaturally white . . . The painted mouth in her waxen face created a ghastly effect, as though her lips were a gash open to the ears.

Masuji Ibuse, "Tajinko Village"

Vividness and richness of character are created in these four passages, which use nothing more than appearance to characterize.

Note that sense impressions other than sight are still a part of the way a character "appears." A limp handshake or a soft cheek; an odor of Chanel, oregano, or decay—if we are allowed to taste, smell, or touch a character through the narrative, then these sense impressions characterize much the way looks do.

The sound and associations of a character's name, too, can give a clue to personality: The affluent Mr. Chiddister in chapter 3 is automatically a more elegant sort than the affluent Mr. Strum; Huck Finn must have a different life from that of the Marquis of Lumbria. Although names with a blatant meaning—Joseph Surface, Billy Pilgrim, Martha Quest—tend to stylize a character and should be used sparingly, if at all, ordinary names can hint at traits you mean to heighten, and it is worth combing any list of names, including the telephone book, to find suggestive sounds. My own telephone book yields, at a glance this morning, Linda Holladay, Marvin Entzminger, and Melba Peebles, any one of which might set me to speculating on a character.

Sound also characterizes as a part of "appearance" insofar as sound represents timbre, tenor, or quality of noise and speech, the characterizing reediness or gruffness of a voice, the lift of laughter or stiffness of delivery.

The way a character physically moves is yet another form of "appearance." The almost feral nature of the sick child in "The Use of Force" is reinforced when "suddenly with one catlike movement both her hands clawed instinctively for my eyes and she almost reached them too." In "Gryphon," Mr. Hibler's rigidity and inane way of stifling imagination is shown even in the way he reacts to a terrible cold: "Twice he bent over, and his loose tie, like a plumb line, hung straight down from his neck as he exploded himself into a Kleenex."

It is important to understand the difference between *movement* and *action*, however, for these terms are not synonymous. Physical movement—the way he crosses his legs, the way she charges down the hall—characterizes without necessarily moving the plot forward. Often movement is part of the setup of the scene, a way of establishing the situation before change-producing action begins.

ACTION

The significant characters of a fiction must be both capable of causing an action and capable of being changed by it.

If we accept that a story records a process of change, how is this change brought about? Basically, human beings face chance and choice, or discovery and decision—the first involuntary and the second voluntary. Translated into action, this means that a character driven by desire takes an action with an expected result, but something intervenes. Some force outside the character presents itself, in the form of information or accident or the behavior of others or the elements. The unknown becomes known, and then the discoverer must either take action or deliberately not take action, involving readers in the tension of the narrative query: and then what happens?

Here is a passage from Toni Morrison's "Recitatif" that demonstrates first movement, then discovery, then decision:

> It was August and a bus crowd was just unloading. They would stand around a long while: going to the john, and looking at gifts and junk-for-sale machines, reluctant to sit down so soon. Even to eat. I was trying to fill the coffeepots and get them all situated on the electric burners when I saw her. She was sitting in a booth smoking a cigarette with two guys smothered in head and facial hair. Her own hair was so big and wild I could hardly see her face. But the eyes. I would know them anywhere. She had on a powder-blue halter and shorts outfit and earrings the size of bracelets. Talk about lipstick and eyebrow pencil. She made the big girls look like nuns. I couldn't get off the counter until seven o'clock, but I kept watching the booth in case they got up to leave before that. My replacement was on time for a change, so I counted and stacked my receipts as fast as I could and signed off. I walked over to the booth . . .

Here, unloading, milling around, and filling coffeepots is *movement* that represents scene-setting and characterization. The significant *action* begins with the discovery, "I saw her." Notice that "she" is characterized directly by appearance whereas the narrator is mainly characterized by her movements (expressed in active verbs)—watching, counting, stacking, signing off—until the moment when she acts on her decision. At the points of both the discovery and the decision we anticipate the possibility of change: what happens next?

In the next passage the movement is even blander before the moment that involves us in suspense:

> I turned on a light in the living room and looked at Rachel's books. I chose one by an author named Lin Yutang and sat down on a sofa under a lamp. Our living room is comfortable. The book seemed interesting. I was in a neighborhood

where most of the front doors were unlocked, and on a street that is very quiet on a summer night. All the animals are domesticated, and the only night birds that I've ever heard are some owls way down by the railroad track. So it was very quiet. I heard the Barstows' dog bark, briefly, as if he had been waked by a nightmare, and then the barking stopped. Everything was quiet again. Then I heard, very close to me, a footstep and a cough.

I felt my flesh get hard—you know that feeling—but I didn't look up from my book, although I felt that I was being watched.

John Cheever, "The Cure"

This scene is set with movement and one choice—that book—that offers no particular opportunity for change and no particular dramatic force. With the moment "Then I heard," however, a discovery or realization of a different sort occurs, and there is suddenly the possibility of real change and so, suddenly, real dramatic tension. Notice that in the second paragraph the narrator discovers a familiar and entirely involuntary reaction—"I felt my flesh get hard"—followed by the decision *not* to take what would be the instinctive action. In fiction as in life, restraint, the decision to do nothing, is fraught with possible tension.

You don't want your technique to show, however, so once you're sure of your decision-and-discovery structure, you need to bury it. In the next example, from Raymond Carver's "Neighbors," the pattern of change—Bill Miller's gradual intrusion into his neighbor's house—is based on a series of decisions that Carver does not explicitly state. The passage ends with a turning point, a moment of discovery.

When he returned to the kitchen the cat was scratching in her box. She looked at him steadily for a minute before she turned back to the litter. He opened all the cupboards and examined the canned goods, the cereals, the packaged foods, the cocktail and wine glasses, the china, the pots and pans. He opened the refrigerator. He sniffed some celery, took two bites of cheddar cheese, and chewed on an apple as he walked into the bedroom. The bed seemed enormous, with a fluffy white bedspread draped to the floor. He pulled out a nightstand drawer, found a half-empty package of cigarettes and stuffed them into his pocket. Then he stepped to the closet and was opening it when the knock sounded at the front door.

There is hardly grand larceny being committed here, but the actions build toward tension through two distinct techniques. The first is that they do actually "build": At first Bill only "examines." The celery he only sniffs, whereas he takes two bites of the cheese, then a whole apple, then half a pack of cigarettes. He moves from the kitchen to the bedroom, which is a clearer invasion of privacy, and from cupboard to refrigerator to nightstand to closet, each a more intimate intrusion than the last.

The second technique is that the narrative subtly hints at Bill's own sense of stealth. It would be easy to imagine a vandal who performed the same actions with complete indifference. But Bill thinks the cat looks "steadily" at him, which is hardly of any importance except that he feels it to be. His awareness of the enormous white bed hints at sexual guilt. When the knock at the front door sounds, we start, as he must, in a clear sense of getting caught.

Thus it turns out that the internal or mental moment of change is where the action lies. Much movement in a story is mere event, and this is why descriptions of actions, like stage directions in a dull play, sometimes add little or nothing. When the wife picks up a cup of coffee, that is mere event. If she finds that the lipstick on the cup is not her shade, that is a dramatic event, a discovery; it makes a difference. She makes a decision to fling it at the woman with the Cherry Ice mouth. Flinging it is an action, but the dramatic change occurs with the second character's realization (discovery) that she has been hit—and so on.

Every story is a pattern of change (events connected, as Forster observed, primarily by cause and effect) in which small and large changes are made through decision and discovery.

DIALOGUE

Speech characterizes in a way that is different from appearance, because speech represents an effort, mainly voluntary, to externalize the internal and to manifest not merely taste or preference but also deliberated thought. Like fiction itself, human dialogue attempts to marry logic to emotion.

Summary, Indirect, and Direct Dialogue   Speech can be conveyed in fiction with varying degrees of directness. It can be *summarized* as part of the narrative so that a good deal of conversation is condensed:

> At home in the first few months, he and Maizie had talked brightly about changes that would make the company more profitable and more attractive to a prospective buyer: new cuts, new packaging, new advertising, new incentives to make supermarkets carry the brand.
>
> Joan Wickersham, "Commuter Marriage"

It can be reported in the third person as *indirect speech* so that it carries, without actual quotation, the feel of the exchange:

> Had he brought the coffee? She had been waiting all day long for coffee. They had forgot it when they ordered at the store the first day.
>
> Gosh, no, he hadn't. Lord, now he'd have to go back. Yes, he would if it killed him. He thought, though, he had everything else. She reminded him it was only because he didn't drink coffee himself. If he did he would remember it quick enough.
>
> Katherine Anne Porter, "Rope"

But usually when the exchange contains the possibility of discovery or decision, and therefore of dramatic action, it will be presented in *direct quotation*:

> "But I thought you hardly knew her, Mr. Morning."
> He picked up a pencil and began to doodle on a notebook page. "Did I tell you that?"
> "Yes, you did."
> "It's true. I didn't know her well."
> "What is it you're after, then? Who was this person you're investigating?"
> "I would like to know that too."
>
> Siri Hustvedt, "Mr. Morning"

These three methods of presenting speech can be used in combination to take advantage of the virtues of each:

> They differed on the issue of the holiday, and couldn't seem to find a common ground. (*Summary.*) She had an idea: why not some Caribbean island over Christmas? Well, but his mother expected them for turkey. (*Indirect.*)
> "Oh, lord, yes, I wouldn't want to go without a yuletide gizzard." (*Direct.*)

Summary and indirect speech are often useful to get us quickly to the core of the scene, or when, for example, one character has to inform another of events that we already know, or when the emotional point of a conversation is that it has become tedious.

> Carefully, playing down the danger, Len filled her in on the events of the long night.

> Samantha claimed to be devastated. It was all very well if the Seversons wanted to let their cats run loose, but she certainly wasn't responsible for Lisbeth's parakeets, now was she?

But nothing is more frustrating to a reader than to be told that significant events are taking place in talk and to be denied the drama of the dialogue.

> They whispered to each other all night long, and as he told her all about his past, she began to realize that she was falling in love with him.

Such a summary—it's *telling*—is a stingy way of treating the reader, who wants the chance to fall in love, too: Give me me!

Economy in Dialogue   Because direct dialogue has a dual nature—emotion within a logical structure—its purpose in fiction is never merely to convey information. Dialogue may do that (although information often is more naturally conveyed in narration), but it needs simultaneously to characterize, provide exposition, set the scene, advance the action, foreshadow, and/or remind. William Sloane, in *The Craft of Writing*, says:

> There is a tentative rule that pertains to all fiction dialogue. It must do more than one thing at a time or it is too inert for the purposes of fiction. This may sound harsh, but I consider it an essential discipline.

In considering Sloane's "tentative rule," I place the emphasis on *rule*. With dialogue as with significant detail, when you write you are constantly at pains to mean more than you say. If a significant detail must both call up a sense image and *mean*, then the character's words, which presumably mean something, should simultaneously suggest image, personality, or emotion.

Dialogue, therefore, is not simply transcribed speech, but distilled speech—the "filler" and inert small talk of real conversation is edited away, even as the weight of implication is increased. "You don't simply copy what you heard on the street," says fiction writer Alice LaPlante. "You want to make it *sound* natural, but that doesn't mean it *is* natural. It takes careful editing to create natural-sounding dialogue. Generally, that means keeping things brief, and paying attention to the rhythm of the sentences. Sentences are short. They're not particularly grammatically correct, but rather quirky and characteristic of the speaker."

Characterizing Dialogue Even rote exchanges, however, can call up images. A character who says, "It is indeed a pleasure to meet you" carries his back at a different angle, dresses differently, from a character who says, "Hey, man, what's up?"

In the three very brief speeches that follow are three fictional men, sharply differentiated from each other not only by the content of what they say, but also by their diction (choice and use of words) and their syntax (the ordering of words in a sentence). Like appearance, these choices convey attributes of class, period, ethnicity, and so forth, as well as political or moral attitudes. How much do you know about each? How does each look?

> "I had a female cousin one time—a Rockefeller, as it happened—" said the Senator, "and she confessed to me that she spent the fifteenth, sixteenth and seventeenth years of her life saying nothing but, No, thank you. Which is all very well for a girl of that age and station. But it would have been a damned unattractive trait in a male Rockefeller."
>
> Kurt Vonnegut, *God Bless You, Mr. Rosewater*

> "You think you the only one ever felt this way?" he asked. "You think I never felt this way? You think she never felt this way? Every last one of them back there one time in they life wanted to give up. She want to give up now. You know that? You got any idea how sick she is? Soon after he go, she's going too. I won't

give her another year. I want her to believe he'll be up there waiting for her. And you can help me do it. And you the only one."

Ernest Gaines, A Lesson Before Dying

The Knight looked surprised at the question. "What does it matter where my body happens to be?" he said. "My mind goes on working all the same. In fact, the more head downward I am, the more I keep inventing new things.

"Now, the cleverest thing of the sort that I ever did," he went on after a pause, "was inventing a new pudding during the meat course."

Lewis Carroll, Through the Looking Glass

There are forms of insanity that condemn people to hear voices against their will, but as writers we invite ourselves to hear voices without relinquishing our hold on reality or our right to control. The trick to writing good dialogue is hearing voice. The question is, what would he or she say? The answer is entirely in language. The choice of language reveals content, character, and conflict, as well as type.

It's logical that if you must develop voices in order to develop dialogue, you'd do well to start with monologue and develop voices one by one. Use your journal to experiment with speech patterns that will characterize. Some people speak in telegraphically short sentences missing various parts of speech. Some speak in convoluted eloquence or in rhythms tedious with qualifying phrases. Some rush headlong without a pause for breath until they're breathless; others are measured or terse or begrudge even forming a sentence. Trust your "inner ear" and use your journal to practice catching voices. Freewriting is invaluable to dialogue writing because it is the manner of composition closest to speech. There is no time to mull or edit. Any qualifications, corrections, and disavowals must be made part of the process and the text.

To increase your ability to "hear" dialogue, try carrying a small pocket notebook with you and noting vivid lines or exchanges of eavesdropped dialogue verbatim. At home, look back through your notebook for speech that interests you and freedraft a monologue passage of that speech in your writing journal. Don't look for words that seem right; just listen to the voice and let it flow. You'll begin to develop your own range of voices whether you catch a particular voice or not, and may even develop your ear by the very process of "hearing" it go wrong at times.

Other Uses of Dialogue   You can also limber up in your journal by setting yourself deliberate exercises in making dialogue—or monologue—do more than one thing at a time. In addition to revealing character, dialogue can *set the scene.*

"We didn't know no one was here. We thought hit a summer camp all closed up. Curtains all closed up. Nothing here. No cars or gear nor nothing. Looks closed to me, don't hit to you, J.J.?"

Joy Williams, "Woods"

Dialogue can *set the mood.*

"I have a lousy trip to Philadelphia, lousy flight back, I watch my own plane blow a tire on closed-circuit TV, I go to my office, I find Suzy in tears because Warren's camped in her one-room apartment. I come home and I find my wife hasn't gotten dressed in two days."

Joan Didion, *Book of Common Prayer*

Dialogue can *reveal the theme* because, as William Sloane says, the characters talk about what the story is about.

"You feel trapped, don't you?"
   Jane looks at her.
   "Don't you?"
   "No."
   "O.K.—You just have a headache."
   "I do." . . .
Milly waits a moment and then clears her throat and says, "You know, for a while there after Wally and I were married, I thought maybe I'd made a mistake. I remember realizing that I didn't like the way he laughed. I mean, let's face it, Wally laughs like a hyena . . ."

Richard Bausch, "The Fireman's Wife"

In all of the preceding passages, the dialogue fulfills Sloane's rule because in addition to conveying its content, the dialogue either moves the story forward or enriches our understanding.

Dialogue is also one of the simplest ways to *reveal the past* (a fundamental play-writing device is to have a character who knows tell a character who doesn't know); and it is one of the most effective, because we get both the drama of the memory and the drama of the telling. Here is a passage from Toni Morrison's *The Bluest Eye* in which the past is evoked, the speaker characterized, the scene and mood set, and the theme revealed, all at the same time and in less than a dozen lines.

"The onliest time I be happy seem like was when I was in the picture show. Every time I got, I went. I'd go early, before the show started. They'd cut off the lights, and everything be black. Then the screen would light up, and I'd move right on in them pictures. White men taking such good care of they women, and they all dressed up in big clean houses with the bathtubs right in the same room with the toilet. Them pictures gave me a lot of pleasure, but it made coming home hard, and looking at Cholly hard. I don't know."

Dialogue as Action   If the telling of a memory *changes the relationship* between the teller and the listener, then you have a scene of high drama, and the dialogue can *advance the action*.

This is an important device, because dialogue is most valuable to fiction when it is itself a means of telling the story.

In the following passage, for example, the mother of a seriously ill toddler looks anxiously to a radiologist for information:

> "The surgeon will speak to you," says the Radiologist.
> "Are you finding something?"
> "The surgeon will speak to you," the Radiologist says again. "There seems to be something there, but the surgeon will talk to you about it."
> "My uncle once had something on his kidney," says the Mother. "So they removed the kidney and it turned out the something was benign."
> The Radiologist smiles a broad, ominous smile. "That's always the way it is," he says. "You don't know exactly what it is until it's in the bucket."
> "In the bucket," the Mother repeats.
> "That's doctor talk," the Radiologist says.
> "It's very appealing," says the Mother. "It's a very appealing way to talk."
>
> Lorrie Moore, "People Like That Are the Only People Here"

Here the radiologist's speech alters the mother's feeling toward him from hopeful to hostile in one short exchange. The level of fear for the child rises, and the dialogue itself has effected change.

A crucial (and sometimes difficult) distinction to make is between speech that is mere discussion or debate and speech that is drama or action. If in doubt, ask yourself: Can this conversation between characters really change anything? *Dialogue is action when it contains the possibility of change.* When two characters have made up their minds and know each other's positions on some political or philosophical matter, for instance, they may argue with splendid eloquence but there will be no discovery and nothing to decide, and therefore no option for change. No matter how significant their topic, we are likely to find them wooden and uninteresting. The story's question *what happened next?* will suggest only *more talk:*

> "This has been the traditional fishing spot of the river people for a thousand years, and we have a moral responsibility to aid them in preserving their way of life. If you put in these rigs, it may undermine the ecosystem and destroy the aquifer of the entire county!"
> "Join the real world, Sybil. Free enterprise is based on this kind of technological progress, and without it we would endanger the economic base."

Ho-hum. In order to engage us emotionally in a disagreement, the characters must have an emotional stake in the outcome; we need to feel that, even if it's unlikely they would change their minds, they might change their lives.

> "If you sink that drill tomorrow morning, I'll be gone by noon."
> "Sybil, I have no choice."

Further, if you find your characters getting stuck in a repetitive conflict ("yes-you-are, no-I'm-not"), you can jump-start the action if you remember that people generally change their tactics—become charming, threatening, seductive, guilt-inducing, and so on—when they are not succeeding in getting what they badly want. And if *each* character in the scene wants something from the other, although it probably won't be the same thing, the momentum will build. It's much harder (although not impossible) to maintain dramatic energy when one of the characters simply wants to get off stage.

Text and Subtext   Often the most forceful dialogue can be achieved by *not* having the characters say what they mean. People in extreme emotional states—whether of fear, pain, anger, or love—are at their least articulate. There is more narrative tension in a love scene where the lovers make anxious small talk, terrified of revealing their feelings, than in one where they hop into bed. A character who is able to say "I hate you!" hates less than one who bottles the fury and pretends to submit, unwilling to expose the truth.

Dialogue can fall flat if characters define their feelings too precisely and honestly, because often the purpose of human exchange is to conceal as well as to reveal—to impress, hurt, protect, seduce, or reject. Anton Chekhov believed that a line of dialogue should always leave the sense that more could have been said. Playwright David Mamet suggests that people may or may not say what they mean, but always say something designed to get what they want.

In this example from Alice Munro's "Before the Change," the daughter of a doctor who performed illegal abortions up until his recent death takes a phone call:

A woman on the phone wants to speak to the doctor.
"I'm sorry. He's dead."
"Dr. Strachan. Have I got the right doctor?"
"Yes but I'm sorry, he's dead."
"Is there anyone—does he by any chance have a partner I could talk to? Is there anybody else there?"
"No. No partner."
"Could you give me any other number I could call? Isn't there some other doctor that can—"
"No. I haven't any number. There isn't anybody that I know of."
"You must know what this is about. It's very crucial. There are very special circumstances—"
"I'm sorry."

It's clear here that neither woman is willing to mention abortion, and that the daughter will also not (and probably could not) speak about her complicated feelings toward her father and his profession. The exchange is rich with irony in that both women and also the reader know the "special circumstance" they are guardedly referring to; only the daughter and the reader are privy to the events surrounding the doctor's death and to the daughter's feelings.

Notice that this is not a very articulate exchange, but it does represent dramatic action, because for both women the stakes are high; they are both emotionally involved, but in ways that put them at cross-purposes.

The idea of "reading between the lines" of dialogue is familiar to most people, for in life we tend to react more to what is implied in dialogue than to what is actually said. The linkage of text and subtext—that is, the surface, plot-related dialogue and its emotional undercurrent—was famously described by Ernest Hemingway with the analogy of an iceberg: "There is seven-eighths of it under water for every part that shows. Anything you know you can eliminate and it only strengthens your iceberg. It is the part that doesn't show."

When an unspoken subject remains unspoken, tension continues to build in a story. Often the crisis of a story occurs when the unspoken tension comes to the surface and an explosion results. "If you're trying to build pressure, don't take the lid off the pot," Jerome Stern suggests in his book *Making Shapely Fiction*. "Once people are really candid, once the unstated becomes stated, the tension is released and the effect is cathartic. . . . you want to give yourself the space for a major scene. Here you do want to describe setting and action vividly, and render what they say fully. You've taken the lid off the pot and we want to feel the dialogue boil over."

"No" Dialogue The Munro passage above also illustrates an essential element of conflict in dialogue: Tension and drama are heightened when characters are constantly (in one form or another) saying no to each other. In the following exchange from Ernest Hemingway's *The Old Man and the Sea*, the old man feels only love for his young protégé, and their conversation is a pledge of affection. Nevertheless, it is the old man's steady denial that lends the scene tension.

"Can I go out and get sardines for you tomorrow?"

"No. Go and play baseball. I can still row and Rogelio will throw the net."

"I would like to go. If I cannot fish with you, I would like to serve in some way."

"You brought me a beer," the old man said. "You are already a man."

"How old was I when you first took me in a boat?"

"Five and you were nearly killed when I brought the fish in too green and he nearly tore the boat to pieces. Can you remember?"

"I can remember the tail slapping and banging and the thwart breaking and the noise of the clubbing. I can remember you throwing me into the bow where the wet coiled lines were and feeling the whole boat shiver and the noise of you clubbing him like chopping a tree down and the sweet blood smell all over me."

"Can you really remember that or did I just tell it to you?"

"I remember everything from when we first went together."

The old man looked at him with his sunburned, confident loving eyes.

"If you were my boy I'd take you out and gamble," he said. "But you are your father's and mother's and you are in a lucky boat."

Neither of these characters is consciously eloquent, and the dialogue is extremely simple. But look how much more it does than "one thing at a time"! It provides exposition on the beginning of the relationship, and it conveys the mutual affection of the two and the conflict within the old man between his love for the boy and his loyalty to the parents. It conveys the boy's eagerness to persuade and carries him into the emotion he had as a small child while the fish was clubbed. The dialogue represents a constant shift of power back and forth between the boy and the old man, as the boy, whatever else he is saying, continues to say *please,* and the old man, whatever else he is saying, continues to say *no.*

Another Hemingway story, "Hills Like White Elephants," which comes near the end of this chapter, as well as the chapter 2 story "No One's a Mystery" also offer clear examples of "no" dialogue. Notice, however, that the conflict does not simply get stuck in a rut, because the characters continue to find new ways to ask and answer the questions as each tries to find the other's vulnerable points.

Specificity   In dialogue, just as in narrative, we will tend to believe a character who speaks in concrete details and to be skeptical of one who generalizes or who delivers judgments unsupported by example. When the boy in the Hemingway passage protests, "I remember everything," we believe him because of the vivid details in his memory of the fish. If one character says, "It's perfectly clear from all his actions that he adores me and would do anything for me," and another says, "I had my hands all covered with the clay slick, and he just reached over to lift a lock of hair out of my eyes and tuck it behind my ear," which character do you believe is the more loved?

Similarly, in conflict dialogue, "details are the rocks characters throw at each other," says Stephen Fischer. Our memories for hurts and slights are sadly long, and an accusation that begins as a general blame—"You never think of my feelings"—is likely to be backed up with specific proof as the argument escalates—"You said you'd pick me up at seven New Year's Eve, but you left me waiting for an hour in the snow." "There's nothing generic in our lives," Fischer explains, "and the sparks given off in conflict may reveal all the facts we need to know about the characters."

It's interesting to observe that whereas in narrative you will demonstrate control if you state the facts and let the emotional value rise off of them, in dialogue you will convey information more naturally if the emphasis is on the speaker's feelings. "My brother is due to arrive at midafternoon and is bringing his four children with him" reads as bald exposition; whereas, "That idiot brother of mine thinks he can walk in in the middle of the afternoon and plunk his four kids in my lap!" or, "I can't wait till my brother gets here at three! You'll see—those are the four sweetest kids this side of the planet"—will sound like talk and will slip us the information sideways.

Examine your dialogue to see if it does more than one thing at a time. Do the sound and syntax characterize by region, education, attitude? Do the choice of words and their syntax reveal that the character is stiff, outgoing, stifling anger, ignorant of the facts, perceptive, bigoted, afraid? Is the conflict advanced by "no" dialogue, in which the characters say no to each other in different ways? Is the drama heightened by the characters' inability or unwillingness to tell the whole truth?

Once you are comfortable with the voice of your character, it is well to acknowledge that everyone has many voices and that what that character says will be, within his or her verbal range, determined by the character *to whom* it is said. All of us have one sort of speech for the vicar and another for the man who pumps the gas. Huck Finn, whose voice is idiosyncratically his own, says, "Yes, sir" to the judge and "Maybe I am, maybe I ain't" to his degenerate dad.

Format and Style   The *format and style of dialogue*, like punctuation, has as its goal to be invisible; and though there may be occasions when departing from the rules is justified by some special effect, it's best to consider such occasions rare. Here are some basic guidelines:

What a character says aloud should be in quotation marks; thoughts should not. This helps clearly differentiate between the spoken and the internal, especially by acknowledging that speech is more deliberately formulated. If you feel that thoughts need to be set apart from narrative, use italics instead of quotation marks.

Begin the dialogue of each new speaker as a new paragraph. This helps orient the reader and keep clear who is speaking. If an action is described between the dialogue lines of two speakers, put that action in the paragraph of the speaker it describes:

> "I wish I'd taken that picture." Larry traced the horizon with his index finger.
>
> Janice snatched the portfolio away. "You've got chicken grease on your hands," she said, "and this is the only copy!"

Notice that the punctuation goes inside the quotation marks.

A dialogue tag tells us who has spoken—*John said, Mary said, Tim announced.* When a tag is used, it is connected to the dialogue line with a comma, even though the dialogue line may sound like a full sentence: *"I'm paying tonight," Mary said.* (Misusing a period in place of the comma with a tag is one of the most common mistakes in dialogue format.)

Like a luggage tag or a name tag, a dialogue tag is for the purpose of identification, and *said* is usually adequate to the task. People also *ask* and *reply* and occasionally *add, recall, remember,* or *remind.* But sometimes an unsure writer will strain for emphatic synonyms: *She gasped, he whined, they chorused, John snarled, Mary spat.* This is unnecessary and obtrusive, because although unintentional repetition usually makes for awkward style, the word *said* is as invisible as punctuation. When reading we're scarcely aware of it, whereas we are forced to be aware of *she wailed.* If it's clear who is speaking without any dialogue tag at all, don't use one. Usually an identification at the beginning of a dialogue passage and an occasional reminder are sufficient. If the speaker is inherently identified in the speech pattern, so much the better.

Similarly, tonal dialogue tags should be used sparingly: *he said with relish; she added limply.* Such phrases are blatant "telling," and the chances are that good dialogue will convey its own tone. *"Get off my case!" she said angrily.* We do not need to be told that she said this angrily. If she said it sweetly, then we would probably need to be told. If the dialogue does not give us a clue to the manner in which it is said, an action will often do so better than an adverb. *"I'll have a word with Mr. Ritter about it," he said with finality* is weaker than *"I'll have a word with Mr. Ritter about it," he said, and picked up his hat.*

It helps to make the dialogue tag unobtrusive if it comes within the spoken line: *"Don't give it a second thought," he said. "I was just going anyway."* (A midline tag has the added benefit of helping readers hear a slight pause or change in the speaker's inflection.) A tag that comes at the beginning of the line may look too much like a play script: *He said, "Don't give it a second thought . . ."* whereas a tag that comes after too much speech becomes confusing or superfluous: *"Don't give it a second thought. I was going anyway, and I'll just take these and drop them at the copy shop on the way," he said.* If we didn't know who was speaking long before this tag appears, it's too late to be of use and simply calls attention to itself.

Dialect   Dialect is a tempting, and can be an excellent, means of characterizing, but it is difficult to do well and easy to overdo. Dialect should always be achieved by word choice and syntax, and misspellings kept to a minimum. They distract and slow the reader, and worse, they tend to make the character seem stupid rather than regional. There is no point in spelling phonetically any word as it is ordinarily pronounced: Almost all of us say things like "fur" for *for*, "uv" for *of*, "wuz" for *was*, "an" for *and*, and "sez" for *says*. It's common to drop the g in words ending in *ing*. When you misspell these words in dialogue, you indicate that the speaker is ignorant enough to spell them that way when writing. Even if you want to indicate ignorance, you may alienate the reader by the means you choose to do so.

These rules for dialect have changed in the past fifty years or so, largely for political reasons. Nineteenth-century authors felt free to misspell the dialogue of foreigners, the lower classes, and racial, regional, and ethnic groups. This literary habit persisted into the first decades of the twentieth century. But the world is considerably smaller now, and its consciousness has been raised. Dialect, after all, is entirely relative, and we disdain the implication that regionality is ignorance. Ignorance itself is a charged issue. If you misspell a foreign accent or black English, the reader is likely to have a political rather than a literary reaction. A line of dialogue that runs "Doan rush me nun, Ah be gwine" reads as caricature, whereas "Don't rush me none, I be going" makes legitimate use of black English syntax and lets us concentrate on the meaning and emotion. John Updike puts this point well when he complains of a Tom Wolfe character:

> "(his) pronunciations are steadfastly spelled out—'sump'm' for 'something,' 'far fat' for 'fire fight'—in a way that a Faulkner character would be spared. For Faulkner, Southern life was life; for Wolfe it is a provincial curiosity . . ."

It is largely to avoid the charge of creating "provincial curiosities" that most fiction writers now avoid misspellings.

It can be even trickier catching the voice of a foreigner with imperfect English, because everyone has a native language, and when someone whose native language is French or Ibu starts to learn English, the grammatical mistakes they make will be based on the grammatical structure of the native language. Unless you know French or Ibu, you will make mistaken mistakes, and your dialogue is likely to sound as if it came from second-rate sitcoms.

In dialect or standard English, the bottom-line rule is that dialogue must be speakable. If it isn't speakable, it isn't dialogue.

> "Certainly I had had a fright I wouldn't soon forget," Reese would say later, "and as I slipped into bed fully dressed except for my shoes, which I flung God-knows-where, I wondered why I had subjected myself to a danger only a fool would fail to foresee for the dubious pleasure of spending one evening in the company of a somewhat less than brilliant coed."

Nobody would say this because it can't be said. It is not only convoluted beyond reason but it also stumbles over its alliteration, "only a fool would fail to foresee for," and takes more breath than the human lungs can hold. Read your dialogue aloud and make sure it is comfortable to the mouth, the breath, and the ear. If not, then it won't ring true as talk.

THOUGHT

Fiction has a flexibility denied to film and drama, where everything the spectator knows must be shown. In fiction you have the privilege of entering a character's mind, sharing at its source internal conflict, reflection, and the crucial processes of decision and discovery. Like speech, a character's thought can be offered in summary (*He hated the way she ate*), or as indirect thought (*Why did she hold her fork straight up like that?*) or directly, as if we are overhearing the character's own mind (*My God, she's going to drop the yolk!*). As with speech, the three methods can be alternated in the same paragraph to achieve at once immediacy and pace.

Methods of presenting a character's thought will be more fully discussed in chapters 7 and 8 on point of view. What's most important to characterization is that thought, like speech, reveals more than information. It can also set mood, reveal or betray desires, develop theme, and so forth.

The territory of a character's mind is above all likely to be the center of the action. Aristotle says, as we have seen, that a man "is his desire," that is, his character is defined by his ultimate purpose, good or bad. *Thought*, says Aristotle, is the process by which a person works backward in his mind from his goal to determine what action he can take toward that goal at a given moment.

It is not, for example, your ultimate desire to read this book. Very likely you don't even "want" to read it; you'd rather be sleeping or jogging or making love. But your ultimate goal is, say, to be a rich, respected, and famous writer. In order to attain this goal, you reason, you must know as much about the craft as you can learn. To do this, you would like to take a graduate degree at the Writer's Workshop in Iowa. To do that, you must take an undergraduate degree in _____, where you now find yourself, and must get an A in Ms. or Mr. _____'s creative writing course. To do that, you must produce a character sketch from one of the assignments at the end of this chapter by a week from Tuesday. To do so, you must sit here reading this chapter now instead of sleeping, jogging, or making love. Your ultimate motive has led you logically backward to a deliberate "moral" decision on the action you can take at this minor crossroad. In fact, it turns out that you want to be reading after all.

The relation that Aristotle perceives among desire, thought, and action seems to me a very useful one for an author, both in structuring plot and in creating character. What does this protagonist want to happen in the last paragraph of this story? What is the particular thought process by which this person works backward to determine what she or he will do now, in the situation that presents itself on page one?

> I was on my way to what I hoped would be *the* romantic vacation of my life, off to Door County for a whole week of sweet sane rest. More rest. I needed more rest.
>
> David Haynes, *All American Girls*

The action, of course, may be the wrong one. Thought thwarts us, because it leads to a wrong choice, or because thought is full of conflicting desires and consistent inconsistencies, or because there is enormous human tension between suppressed thought and expressed thought:

> When he shuts off the shower, the phone is ringing. A sense that it has been ringing for a long time—can a mechanical noise have a quality of desperation?—propels him naked and dripping into the living room. He picks up the phone and his caller, as he has suspected, is Mieko . . . He is already annoyed after the first hello. Mieko's voice is sharp, high, very Japanese, although she speaks superb English. He says, "Hello, Mieko," and he sounds annoyed.
>
> Jane Smiley, "Long Distance"

In "Where Are You Going, Where Have You Been?" at the end of chapter 3, Connie wants to get away every chance she can from a family she despises. From the opening paragraphs, she devises a number of schemes and subterfuges to avoid their company. At the end of the story her success is probably permanent, at a cost she had not figured into her plan. Through the story she is richly characterized, inventing two personalities in order single-mindedly to pursue her freedom, finally caught between conflicting and paralyzing desires.

A person, a character, can't do much about what he or she wants; it just is (which is another way of saying that character is desire). What we can deliberately choose is our behavior, the action we take in a given situation. Achievement of our desire would be easy if the thought process between desire and act were not so faulty and so wayward, or if there were not such an abyss between the thoughts we think and those that we are willing and able to express.

Conflict Between Methods of Presentation

The conflict that is the essence of character can be effectively (and, if it doesn't come automatically, quite consciously) achieved in fiction by producing a conflict between methods of presentation. A character can be directly revealed to us through *appearance, dialogue, action,* and *thought.* If you set one of these methods (most frequently *thought*) at odds with the others, then dramatic tension will be produced. Imagine, for example, a character who is impeccably and expensively dressed, who speaks eloquently, who acts decisively, and whose mind is revealed to us as full of order and determination. He is inevitably a flat character. But suppose that he is impeccable, eloquent, decisive, and that his mind is a mess of wounds and panic. He is at once interesting.

Here is the opening passage of Saul Bellow's *Seize the Day,* in which appearance and action are blatantly at odds with thought. Notice that it is the tension between suppressed thought and what is expressed through appearance and action that produces the rich character conflict.

> When it came to concealing his troubles, Tommy Wilhelm was not less capable than the next fellow. So at least he thought, and there was a certain amount of evidence to back him up. He had once been an actor—no, not quite, an extra— and he knew what acting should be. Also, he was smoking a cigar, and when a man is smoking a cigar, wearing a hat, he has an advantage: it is harder to find out how he feels. He came from the twenty-third floor down to the lobby on the mezzanine to collect his mail before breakfast, and he believed—he hoped—he looked passably well: doing all right.

Tommy Wilhelm is externally composed but mentally anxious, mainly anxious about looking externally composed. By contrast, in the next passage, from Samuel Beckett's *Murphy,* the landlady, Miss Carridge, who has just discovered a suicide in one of her rooms, is anxious in speech and action but is mentally composed.

> She came speeding down the stairs one step at a time, her feet going so fast that she seemed on little caterpillar wheels, her forefinger sawing horribly at her craw for Celia's benefit. She slithered to a stop on the steps of the house and screeched for the police. She capered in the street like a consternated ostrich, with strangled distracted rushes towards the York and Caledonian Roads in turn, embarrassingly equidistant from the tragedy, tossing up her arms, undoing the good work of the samples, screeching for police aid. Her mind was so collected that she saw clearly the impropriety of letting it appear so.

In this third example, from Zora Neale Hurston's "The Gilded Six-Bits," it is the very intensity of the internal that both prevents and dictates action:

> Missie May was sobbing. Wails of weeping without words. Joe stood, and after a while he found out that he had something in his hand. And then he stood and

felt without thinking and without seeing with his natural eyes. Missie May kept on crying and Joe kept on feeling so much, and not knowing what to do with all his feelings, he put Slemmon's watch charm in his pants pocket and took a good laugh and went to bed.

I have said that thought is most frequently at odds with one or more of the other three methods of direct presentation—reflecting the difficulty we have expressing ourselves openly or accurately—but this is by no means always the case. A character may be successfully, calmly, even eloquently expressing fine opinions while betraying himself by pulling at his ear, or herself by crushing her skirt. Captain Queeg of Herman Wouk's *The Caine Mutiny* is a memorable example of this, maniacally clicking the steel balls in his hand as he defends his disciplinary code.

Often we are not privy to the thoughts of a character at all, so that the conflicts must be expressed in a contradiction between the external methods of direct presentation, appearance, speech, and action. Character A may be speaking floods of friendly welcome, betraying his real feeling by backing steadily away. Character B, dressed in taffeta ruffles and ostrich plumes, may wail pityingly over the miseries of the poor. Notice that the notion of "betraying oneself" is important here: We're more likely to believe the evidence unintentionally given than deliberate expression.

A classic example of such self-betrayal is found in Leo Tolstoy's *The Death of Ivan Ilyich*, where the widow confronts her husband's colleague at the funeral.

> . . . Noticing that the table was endangered by his cigarette ash, she immediately passed him an ashtray, saying as she did so: "I consider it an affectation to say that my grief prevents my attending to practical affairs. On the contrary, if anything can—I won't say console me, but—distract me, it is seeing to everything concerning him." She again took out her handkerchief as if preparing to cry, but suddenly, as if mastering her feeling, she shook herself and began to speak calmly. "But there is something I want to talk to you about."

It is no surprise either to the colleague or to us that Praskovya Federovna wants to talk about getting money.

Finally, character conflict can be expressed by creating a tension between the direct and the indirect methods of presentation, and this is a source of much irony. We are presented with a judgment of the character, who then speaks, appears, acts, or thinks in contradiction of this judgment, as in the opening of this story by Tobias Wolff:

> . . . Riley was flashy, so flashy that even his bright red hair seemed an affectation, and it was said that he'd had affairs with some of his students. Brooke did not as a rule give credit to those rumors, but in Riley's case he was willing to make an exception. He had once seen a very pretty girl leaving Riley's office in tears. Students did at times cry over bad grades, but this girl's misery was something else: it looked more like a broken heart than a C–.

They belonged to the same parish, and Brooke, who liked to sit in the back of the church, often saw Riley at Mass with his wife and their four red-haired children. Seeing the children and their father together, like a row of burning candles, always made Brooke feel more kindly toward Riley. Then Riley would turn to his wife or look around, and the handlebars of his unnecessarily large moustache would come into view, and Brooke would dislike him again.

"An Episode in the Life of Professor Brooke"

Given the behavior observed by Brooke, we may begin to share his suspicions, only to see the evidence of Riley at church with his seemingly unified family. When Brooke's dislike returns with a glimpse of the flamboyant moustache, we may well doubt Brooke's objectivity in judging his colleague, whom he dislikes even for the natural color of his hair and later for his "powder-blue suits." In fact, as the story progresses, it is the judgmental Brooke who betrays his own wife, while Riley does nothing more incriminating than rating the faces of women they pass on the road.

Reinventing Character

In addition to providing tension between methods of presentation, you can try a few other ways of making a character fresh and forceful in your mind before you start writing.

If the character is based on you or on someone you know, drastically alter the model in some external way: Change blond hair to dark or thin to thick; imagine the character as the opposite gender or radically alter the setting in which the character must act. Part of the trouble with writing directly from experience is that you know too much about it—what "they" did, how you felt. Under such circumstances it's hard to know whether everything in your mind is getting onto the page. An external alteration forces you to re-see, and so to see more clearly, and so to convey more clearly what you see.

On the other hand, if the character is created primarily out of your observation or invention and is unlike yourself, try to find an internal area that you have in common with the character. If you are a blonde, slender young woman and the character is a fat, balding man, do you nevertheless have in common a love of French *haute cuisine*? Are you haunted by the same sort of dream? Do you share a fear of public performance or a susceptibility to fine weather?

I can illustrate these techniques only from my own writing, because I am the only author whose self I can identify with any certainty in fictional characters. In one novel, I wanted to open with a scene in which the heroine buries a dog in her backyard. I had recently buried a dog in my backyard. I wanted to capture the look and feel of red Georgia earth at sunrise, the tangle of roots, and the smell of decay. But I knew that I was likely to make the experience too much my own, too little my character's. I set about to make her not-me. I have long dark hair and an ordinary figure, and I tend to live in Levi's. I made Shaara Soole

. . . big boned, lanky, melon-breasted, her best feature was a head of rusty barbed-wire hair that she tried to control with a wardrobe of scarves and headband things. Like most costume designers, she dressed with more originality than taste, usually on the Oriental or Polynesian side, sometimes with voluminous loops of thong and matte metal over an ordinary shirt. This was somewhat eccentric in Hubbard, Georgia, but Shaara may have been oblivious to her eccentricity, being so concerned to keep her essential foolishness in check.

Having thus separated Shaara from myself, I was able to bury the dog with her arms and through her eyes rather than my own. On the other hand, a few pages later I was faced with the problem of introducing her ex-husband, Boyd Soole. I had voluminous notes on this character, and I knew that he was almost totally unlike me. A man, to begin with, and a huge man, a theater director with a natural air of power and authority and very little interest in domestic affairs. I sat at my desk for several days, unable to make him move convincingly. My desk oppressed me, and I felt trapped and uncomfortable, my work thwarted, it seemed, by the very chair and typewriter. Then it occurred to me that Boyd was *also* sitting at a desk trying to work.

The dresser at the Travelodge was some four inches too narrow and three inches too low. If he set his feet on the floor his knees would sit free of the drawer but would be awkwardly constricted left and right. If he crossed his legs, he could hook his right foot comfortably outside the left of the kneehole but would bruise his thigh at the drawer. If he shifted back he was placed at an awkward distance from his script. And in this position he could not work.

This passage did not instantly allow me to live inside Boyd Soole's skin, nor did it solve all my problems with his characterization. But it did let me get on with the story, and it gave me a flash of sympathy for him that later grew much more profound than I had foreseen.

Often, identifying what you have in common with the feelings of your character will also clarify what is important about her or him to the story—why, in fact, you chose to write about such a person at all. Even if the character is presented as a villain, you have something in common, and I don't mean something forgivable. If he or she is intolerably vain, watch your own private gestures in front of the mirror and borrow them. If he or she is cruel, remember how you enjoyed hooking the worm.

There is no absolute requirement that a writer need behave honestly in life; there is absolutely no such requirement. Great writers have been public hams, domestic dictators, emotional con artists, and Nazis. What is required for fine writing is honesty on the page—not how the characters *should* react at the funeral, the surprise party, in bed, but how they *would*. In order to develop such honesty of observation on the page, you must begin with a willing honesty of observation (though mercifully not of behavior) in yourself.

The older we get, the more . . . you realize there's a whole range of things that you will never do, of things and people you will never be. As life becomes more and more limiting, there is something wonderful about being able to get inside the skin of people unlike yourself.

Lee Smith

Creating a Group or Crowd

Sometimes it is necessary to introduce several or many people in the same scene, and this needn't present a problem, because the principle is pretty much the same in every case, and is the same as in film: pan, then close-up. In other words, give us a sense of the larger scene first, then a few details to characterize individuals. If you begin by concentrating too long on one character only, we will tend to see that person as being alone.

Herm peered through the windshield and eased his foot up off the gas. Damn, he thought, it's not going to let up. The yellow lights made slick pools along the shoulder. He fiddled with the dial, but all he could get was blabber-radio and somebody selling vinyl siding. His back ached. His eyes itched. A hundred and forty miles to go.

At this point, if you introduce a wife, two children, and a dog to the scene, we will have to make rapid and uncomfortable adjustments in our mental picture. Better to begin with the whole carful and then narrow it down to Herm:

Herm peered through the windshield and glanced over at Inga, who was snoring lightly against the window. The kids hadn't made a sound for about half an hour either, and only Cheza was wheezing dogbreath now and then on the back of his neck. He eased his foot up off the gas. Damn, he thought . . .

If the action involves several characters who therefore need to be seen right away, introduce them as a group and then give us a few characterizing details:

All the same there were four guns on him before he'd focused enough to count. "Peace," he said again. There were three old ones, one of them barely bigger than a midget, and the young one was fat. One of the old ones had on a uniform jacket much too big for him, hanging open on his slack chest. The young one spun a string of their language at him.

If the need is to create a crowd, it is still important, having established that there *is* a crowd, to give us a few details. We will believe more thoroughly in large numbers of people if you offer example images for us. Here, for example, is a passage from *Underworld* in which Don LeLillo introduces two parts of a crowd, the boys who are waiting to sneak into the ballpark and the last legitimate arrivals:

> . . . they have found one another by means of slidy looks that detect the fellow foolhard and here they stand, black kids and white kids up from the subways or off the local Harlem streets, bandidos, fifteen in all, and according to topical legends maybe four will get through for every one that's caught.
>
> They are waiting nervously for the ticket holders to clear the turnstiles, the last loose cluster of fans, the stragglers and loiterers. They watch the late-arriving taxis from downtown and the brilliantined men stepping dapper to the windows, policy bankers and supper club swells and Broadway hotshots, high aura'd, picking lint off their sleeves.

Character: A Summary

It may be helpful to summarize the practical advice on character that this chapter and the previous chapter contain.

1. Keep a journal and use it to explore and build ideas for characters.
2. Know all the influences that go into the making of your character's type: age, gender, race, nationality, marital status, region, education, religion, profession.
3. Know the details of your character's life: what he or she does during every part of the day, thinks about, remembers, wants, likes and dislikes, eats, says, means.
4. Identify, heighten, and dramatize consistent inconsistencies. What does your character want that is at odds with whatever else the character wants? What patterns of thought and behavior work against the primary goal?
5. Focus sharply on how the character looks, on what she or he wears and owns, and on how she or he moves. Let us focus on it, too.
6. Examine the character's speech to make sure it does more than convey information. Does it characterize, accomplish exposition, and reveal emotion, intent, or change? Does it advance the conflict through "no" dialogue? Speak it aloud: Does it "say"?
7. Build action by making your characters discover and decide. Make sure that what happens is action and not mere event or movement, that is, that it contains the possibility for human change.
8. Know what your character wants, both generally out of life, and specifically in the context of the story. Keeping that desire in mind, "think backward" with the character to decide what he or she would do in any situation presented.

9. Be aware of the five methods of character presentation: authorial interpretation, appearance, speech, action, and thought. Reveal the character's conflicts by presenting attributes in at least one of these methods that contrast with attributes you present in the others.

10. If the character is based on a real model, including yourself, make a dramatic external alteration.

11. If the character is imaginary or alien to you, identify a mental or emotional point of contact.

Hills Like White Elephants

ERNEST HEMINGWAY

The hills across the valley of the Ebro were long and white. On this side there was no shade and no trees and the station was between two lines of rails in the sun. Close against the side of the station there was the warm shadow of the building and a curtain, made of strings of bamboo beads, hung across the open door into the bar, to keep out flies. The American and the girl with him sat at a table in the shade, outside the building. It was very hot and the express from Barcelona would come in forty minutes. It stopped at this junction for two minutes and went on to Madrid.

"What should we drink?" the girl asked. She had taken off her hat and put it on the table.

"It's pretty hot," the man said.

"Let's drink beer."

"*Dos cervezas*," the man said into the curtain.

"Big ones?" a woman asked from the doorway.

"Yes. Two big ones."

The woman brought two glasses of beer and two felt pads. She put the felt pads and the beer glasses on the table and looked at the man and the girl. The girl was looking off at the line of hills. They were white in the sun and the country was brown and dry.

"They look like white elephants," she said.

"I've never seen one," the man drank his beer.

"No, you wouldn't have."

"I might have," the man said. "Just because you say I wouldn't have doesn't prove anything."

The girl looked at the bead curtain. "They've painted something on it," she said. "What does it say?"

"Anis del Toro. It's a drink."

"Could we try it?"

The man called "Listen" through the curtain. The woman came out from the bar.

"Four reales."

"We want two Anis del Toro."

"With water?"

"Do you want it with water?"

"I don't know," the girl said. "Is it good with water?"

"It's all right."

"You want them with water?" asked the woman.

"Yes, with water."

It tastes like licorice," the girl said and put the glass down.

"That's the way with everything."

"Yes," said the girl. "Everything tastes of licorice. Especially all the things you've waited so long for, like absinthe."

"Oh, cut it out."

"You started it," the girl said. "I was being amused. I was having a fine time."

"Well, let's try and have a fine time."

"All right. I was trying. I said the mountains looked like white elephants. Wasn't that bright?"

"That was bright."

"I wanted to try this new drink: That's all we do, isn't it—look at things and try new drinks?"

"I guess so."

The girl looked across at the hills.

"They're lovely hills," she said. "They don't really look like white elephants. I just meant the coloring of their skins through the trees."

"Should we have another drink?"

"All right."

The warm wind blew the bead curtain against the table.

"The beer's nice and cool," the man said.

"It's lovely," the girl said.

"It's really an awfully simple operation, Jig," the man said. "It's not really an operation at all."

The girl looked at the ground the table legs rested on.

"I know you wouldn't mind it, Jig. It's really not anything. It's just to let the air in."

The girl did not say anything.

"I'll go with you and I'll stay with you all the time. They just let the air in and then it's all perfectly natural."

"Then what will be do afterward?"

"We'll be fine afterward. Just like we were before."

"What makes you think so?"

"That's the only thing that bothers us. It's the only thing that's made us unhappy."

The girl looked at the bead curtain, put her hand out, and took hold of two strings of beads.

"And you think then we'll be all right and be happy."

"I know we will. You don't have to be afraid. I've known lots of people that have done it."

"So have I," said the girl. "And afterward they were all so happy."

"Well," the man said, "If you don't want to you don't have to. I wouldn't have you do it if you didn't want to. But I know it's perfectly simple."

"And you really want to?"

"I think it's the best thing to do. But I don't want you to do it if you don't really want to."

"And if I do it you'll be happy and things will be like they were and you'll love me?"

"I love you now. You know I love you."

"I know. But if I do it, then it will be nice again if I say things are like white elephants, and you'll like it?"

"I'll love it. I love it now but I just can't think about it. You know how I get when I worry."

"If I do it you won't ever worry?"

"I won't worry about that because it's perfectly simple."

"Then I'll do it. Because I don't care about me."

"What do you mean?"

"I don't care about me."

"Well, I care about you."

"Oh, yes. But I don't care about me. And I'll do it and then everything will be fine."

"I don't want you to do it if you feel that way."

The girl stood up and walked to the end of the station. Across, on the other side, were fields of grain and trees along the banks of the Ebro. Far away, beyond the river, were mountains. The shadow of a cloud moved across the field of grain and she saw the river through the trees.

"And we could have all this," she said. "And we could have everything and every day we make it more impossible."

"What did you say?"

"I said we could have everything."

"We can have everything."

"No, we can't."

"We can have the whole world."

"No, we can't."

"We can go everywhere."

"No, we can't. It isn't ours any more."

"It's ours."

"No, it isn't. And once they take it away, you never get it back."

"But they haven't taken it away."

"We'll wait and see."

"Come on back in the shade," he said. "You mustn't feel that way."

"I don't feel any way," the girl said. "I just know things."

"I don't want you to do anything that you don't want to do—"

"Nor that isn't good for me," she said. "I know. Could we have another beer?"

"All right. But you've got to realize—"

"I realize," the girl said. "Can't we maybe stop talking?"

They sat down at the table and the girl looked across at the hills on the dry side of the valley and the man looked at her and at the table.

"You've got to realize," he said, "that I don't want you to do it if you don't want to. I'm perfectly willing to go through with it if it means anything to you."

"Doesn't it mean anything to you? We could get along."

"Of course it does. But I don't want anybody but you. I don't want any one else. And I know it's perfectly simple."

"Yes, you know it's perfectly simple."

"It's all right for you to say that, but I do know it."

"Would you do something for me now?"

"I'd do anything for you."

"Would you please please please please please please please stop talking?"

He did not say anything but looked at the bags against the wall of the station. There were labels on them from all the hotels where they had spent nights.

"But I don't want you to," he said, "I don't care anything about it."

"I'll scream," the girl said.

The woman came out through the curtains with two glasses of beer and put them down on the damp felt pads. "The train comes in five minutes," she said.

"What did she say?" asked girl.

"That the train is coming in five minutes."

The girl smiled brightly at the woman, to thank her.

"I'd better take the bags over to the other side of the station," the man said. She smiled at him.

"All right. Then come back and we'll finish the beer."

He picked up the two heavy bags and carried them around the station to the other tracks. He looked up the tracks but could not see the train. Coming back, he walked through the barroom, where people waiting for the train were drinking. He drank an Anis at the bar and looked at the people. They were all waiting reasonably for the train. He went out through the bead curtain. She was sitting at the table and smiled at him.

"Do you feel better?" he asked.

"I feel fine," she said. "There's nothing wrong with me. I feel fine."

᠀ ᠀ ᠀

Suggestions for Discussion

1. Abortion is the subject of the argument, yet it is never named in the dialogue. Why has the author made this choice? How does this omission add to the tensions of the story?

2. Find examples of such elements of subtext as "no" dialogue; characters saying the opposite of what they feel; characters saying something designed to get what they want; and lines that imply more than is actually said.

3. Why is the story told through a neutral viewpoint? Why aren't we given access to either character's thoughts?

Retrospect

4. What would the woman lose by winning the argument? What would the man lose by winning? Is there a final winner and loser in the end?

5. What clues do we get to the characters' recent life together through the specifics of their dialogue, luggage, and behavior?

Aren't You Happy for Me?

RICHARD BAUSCH

"William Coombs, with two *o*'s," Melanie Ballinger told her father over long distance. "Pronounced just like the thing you comb your hair with. Say it."

Ballinger repeated the name.

"Say the whole name."

"I've got it, sweetheart. Why am I saying it?"

"Dad, I'm bringing him home with me. We're getting *married*."

For a moment, he couldn't speak.

"Dad? Did you hear me?"

"I'm here," he said.

"Well?"

Again, he couldn't say anything.

"Dad?"

"Yes," he said. "That's—that's some news."

"That's all you can say?"

"Well, I mean—Melanie—this is sort of quick, isn't it?" he said.

"Not that quick. How long did you and Mom wait?"

"I don't remember. Are you measuring yourself by that?"

"You waited six months, and you do remember. And this is five months. And we're not measuring anything. William and I have know each other longer than five months, but we've been together—you know, as a couple—five months. And I'm almost twenty-three, which is two years older than Mom was. And don't tell me it was different when *you* guys did it."

"No," he heard himself say. "It's pretty much the same, I imagine."

"Well?" she said.

"Well," Ballinger said. "I'm—I'm very happy for you."

"You don't sound happy."

"I'm happy. I can't wait to meet him."

"Really? Promise? You're not just saying that?"

"It's good news, darling. I mean I'm surprised, of course. It'll take a little getting used to. The—suddenness of it and everything. I mean, your mother and I didn't even know you were seeing anyone. But no, I'm—I'm glad. I can't wait to meet the young man."

"Well, and now there's something *else* you have to know."

"I'm ready," John Ballinger said. He was standing in the kitchen of the house she hadn't seen yet, and outside the window his wife, Mary, was weeding in the garden, wearing a red scarf and a white muslin blouse and jeans, looking young—looking, even, happy, though for a long while there had been between them, in fact, very little happiness.

"Well, this one's kind of hard," his daughter said over the thousand miles of wire. "Maybe we should talk about it later."

"No, I'm sure I can take whatever it is," he said.

The truth was that he had news of his own to tell. Almost a week ago, he and Mary had agreed on a separation. Some time for them both to sort things out. They had decided not to say anything about it to Melanie until she arrived. But now Melanie had said that she was bringing someone with her.

She was hemming and hawing on the other end of the line: "I don't know, see, Daddy, I—God. I can't find the way to say it, really."

He waited. She was in Chicago, where they had sent her to school more than four years ago, and where after her graduation she had stayed, having landed a job with an independent newspaper in the city. In March, Ballinger and Mary had moved to this small house in the middle of Charlottesville, hoping that a change of scene might help things. It hadn't; they were falling apart after all these years.

"Dad," Melanie said, sounding helpless.

"Honey, I'm listening."

"Okay, look," she said. "Will you promise you won't react?"

"How can I promise a thing like that, Melanie?"

"You're going to react, then. I wish you could just promise me you wouldn't."

"Darling," he said, "I've got something to tell you, too. Promise me *you* won't react."

She said "Promise" in that way the young have of being absolutely certain what their feelings will be in some future circumstance.

"So," he said. "Now, tell me whatever it is." And a thought struck through him like a shock. "Melanie, you're not—you're not pregnant, are you?"

She said, "How did you *know?*"

He felt something sharp move under his heart. "Oh, Lord. Seriously?"

"Jeez," she said. "Wow. That's really amazing."

"You're—*pregnant.*"

"Right. My God. You're positively clairvoyant, Dad."

"I really don't think it's a matter of any clairvoyance, Melanie, from the way you were talking. Are you—is it sure?"

"Of course it's sure. But—well, that isn't the really hard thing. Maybe I should just wait."

"Wait," he said. "Wait for what?"

"Until you get used to everything else."

He said nothing. She was fretting on the other end, sighing and starting to speak and then stopping herself.

"I don't know," she said finally, and abruptly he thought she was talking to someone in the room with her.

"Honey, do you want me to put your mother on?"

"No, Daddy. I wanted to talk to you about this first. I think we should get this over with."

"Get this over with? Melanie, what're we talking about here? Maybe I should put your mother on." He thought he might try a joke. "After all," he added, "I've never been pregnant."

"It's not about being pregnant. You *guessed* that."

He held the phone tight against his ear. Through the window, he saw his wife stand and stretch, massaging the small of her back with one gloved hand. *Oh, Mary.*

"Are you ready?" his daughter said.

"Wait," he said. "Wait a minute. Should I be sitting down? I'm sitting down." He pulled a chair from the table and settled into it. He could hear her breathing on the other end of the line, or perhaps it was the static wind he so often heard when talking on these new phones. "Okay," he said, feeling his throat begin to close. "Tell me."

"William's somewhat older than I am," she said. "There." She sounded as though she might hyperventilate.

He left a pause. "That's it?"

"Well, it's how much."

"Okay."

She seemed to be trying to collect herself. She breathed, paused. "This is even tougher than I thought it was going to be."

"You mean you're going to tell me something harder than the fact that you're pregnant?"

She was silent.

"Melanie?"

"I didn't expect you to be this way about it," she said.

"Honey, please just tell me the rest of it."

"Well, what did you mean by that, anyway?"

"Melanie, *you said* this would be hard."

Silence.

"Tell me, sweetie. Please?"

"I'm going to." She took a breath. "Dad, William's sixty—he's—he's sixty—sixty-three years old."

Ballinger stood. Out in the garden his wife had got to her knees again, pulling crabgrass out of the bed of tulips. It was a sunny near-twilight, and all along the shady street people were working in their little orderly spaces of grass and flowers.

"Did you hear me, Daddy? It's perfectly all right, too, because he's really a *young* sixty-three, and *very* strong and healthy, and look at George Burns."

"George Burns," Ballinger said. "George—Burns? Melanie, I don't understand."

"Come on, Daddy, stop it."

"No, what're you telling me?" His mind went blank.

"I said William is sixty-three."

"William who?"

"Dad. My fiancé."

"Wait, Melanie. You're you saying your fiancé, the man you're going to marry, *he's* sixty-three?"

"A young sixty-three," she said.

"Melanie. Sixty-three?"

"Dad."

"You didn't say six feet three?"

She was silent.

"Melanie?"

"Yes."

"Honey, this is a joke, right? You're playing a joke on me."

"It is not a—it's not that. God," she said. "I don't believe this."

"You don't believe—" he began. "You don't believe—"

"Dad," she said. "I told you—" Again, she seemed to be talking to someone else in the room with her. Her voice trailed off.

"Melanie," he said. "Talk into the phone."

"I know it's hard," she told him. "I know it's asking you to take a lot in."

"Well, no," Ballinger said, feeling something shift inside, a quickening in his blood. "It's—it's a little more than that, Melanie, isn't it? I mean it's not a weather report, for God's sake."

"I should've known," she said.

"Forgive me for it," he said, "but I have to ask you something."

"It's all right, Daddy," she said as though reciting it for him. "I know what I'm doing. I'm not really rushing into anything—"

He interrupted her. "Well, good God, somebody rushed into something, right?"

"Daddy."

"Is that what you call *him?* No, *I'm* Daddy. You have to call him *Grand*daddy."

"That is *not* funny," she said.

"I wasn't being funny, Melanie. And anyway, that wasn't my question." He took a breath. "Please forgive this, but I have to know."

"There's nothing you really *have* to know, Daddy. I'm an adult. I'm telling you out of family courtesy."

"I understand that. Family courtesy exactly. Exactly, Melanie, that's a good phrase. Would you please tell me, out of family courtesy, if the baby is his."

"Yes." Her voice was small now, coming from a long way off.

"I am sorry for the question, but I have to put all this together. I mean you're asking me to take in a whole lot here, you know?"

"I said I understood how you feel."

"I don't think so. I don't think you quite understand how I feel."

"All right," she said. "I don't understand how you feel. But I think I knew how you'd react."

For a few seconds, there was just the low, sea sound of long distance.

"Melanie, have you done any of the math on this?"

"I should've bet money," she said in the tone of a person who has been proven right about something.

"Well, but Jesus," Ballinger said. "I mean he's older than *I* am, kid. He's—a *lot* older than I am." The number of years seemed to dawn on him as he spoke; it filled him with a strange, heart-shaking heat. "Honey, nineteen years. When he was my age, I was only two years older than you are now."

"I don't see what that has to do with anything," she said.

"Melanie, I'll be forty-five *all the way* in December. I'm a *young* forty-four.

"I know when your birthday is, Dad."

"Well, good God, this guy's nineteen years older than your own father."

She said, "I've grasped the numbers. Maybe you should go ahead and put Mom on."

"Melanie, you couldn't pick somebody a little closer to my age? Some snot-nosed forty-year-old?"

"Stop it," she said. "Please, Daddy. I know what I'm doing."

"Do you know how old he's going to be when your baby is ten? Do you? Have you given that any thought at all?"

She was silent.

He said, "How many children are you hoping to have?"

"I'm not thinking about that. Any of that. This is now, and I don't care about anything else."

He sat down in his kitchen and tried to think of something else to say. Outside the window, his wife, with no notion of what she was about to be hit with, looked through the patterns of shade in the blinds and, seeing him, waved. It was friendly, and even so, all their difficulty was in it. Ballinger waved back. "Melanie," he said, "do you mind telling me just where you happened to meet William? I mean how do you meet a person forty years older than you are? Was there a senior citizen-student mixer at the college?"

"Stop it, Daddy."

"No, I really want to know. If I'd just picked this up and read it in the newspaper, I think I'd want to know. I'd probably call the newspaper and see what I could find out."

"Put Mom on," she said.

"Just tell me how you met. You can do that, can't you?"

"Jesus Christ," she said, then paused.

Ballinger waited.

"He's a teacher, like you and Mom, only college. He was my literature teacher. He's a professor of literature. He knows everything that was ever written, and he's the most brilliant man I've ever known. You have no idea how fascinating it is to talk with him."

"Yes, and I guess you understand that over the years that's what you're going to be doing a *lot* of with him, Melanie. A lot of talking."

"I am carrying the proof that disproves *you*," she said.

He couldn't resist saying, "Did *he* teach you to talk like that?"

"I'm gonna hang up."

"You promised you'd listen to something *I* had to tell *you*."

"Okay," she said crisply. "I'm listening."

He could imagine her tapping the toe of one foot on the floor: the impatience of someone awaiting an explanation. He thought a moment. "He's a professor?"

"That's not what you wanted to tell me."

"But you said he's a professor."

"Yes, I said that."

"Don't be mad at me, Melanie. Give me a few minutes to get used to the idea. Jesus. Is he a professor emeritus?"

"If that means distinguished, yes. But I know what you're—"

"No, Melanie. It means *retired*. You went to college."

She said nothing.

"I'm sorry. But for God's sake, it's a legitimate question."

"It's a stupid, mean-spirited thing to ask." He could tell from her voice that she was fighting back tears.

"Is he there with you now?"

"Yes," she said, sniffling.

"Oh, Jesus Christ."

"Daddy, why are you being this way?"

"Do you think maybe we could've had this talk alone? What's he, listening on the other line?"

"No."

"Well, thank God for that."

"I'm going to hang up now."

"No, please don't hang up. Please let's just be calm and talk about this. We have some things to talk about here."

She sniffled, blew her nose. Someone held the phone for her. There was a muffled something in the line, and then she was there again. "Go ahead," she said.

"Is he still in the room with you?"

"Yes." Her voice was defiant.

"Where?"

"Oh, for God's sake," she said.

"I'm sorry, I feel the need to know. Is he sitting down?"

"I *want* him here, Daddy. We both want to be here," she said.

"And he's going to marry you."

"Yes," she said impatiently.

"Do you think I could talk to him?"

She said something he couldn't hear, and then there were several seconds of some sort of discussion, in whispers. Finally she said, "Do you promise not to yell at him?"

"Melanie, he wants me to promise not to *yell* at him?"

"Will you promise?"

"Good God."

"Promise," she said. "Or I'll hang up."

"All right. I promise. I promise not to yell at him."

There was another small scuffing sound, and a man's voice came through the line. "Hello, sir." It was, as far as Ballinger could tell, an ordinary voice, slightly lower than baritone. He thought of cigarettes. "I realize this is a difficult—"

"Do you smoke?" Ballinger interrupted him.

"No, sir."

"All right. Go on."

"Well, I want you to know I understand how you feel."

"Melanie says she does, too," Ballinger said. "I mean I'm certain you both *think* you do."

"It was my idea that Melanie call you about this."

"Oh, really. That speaks well of you. You probably knew I'd find this a little difficult to absorb and that's why you waited until Melanie was pregnant, for Christ's sake."

The other man gave forth a small sigh of exasperation.

"So you're a professor of literature."

"Yes, sir."

"Oh, you needn't 'sir' me. After all, I mean I *am* the goddam kid here."

"There's no need for sarcasm, sir."

"Oh, I wasn't being sarcastic. That was a literal statement of the situation that obtains right here as we're speaking. And, really, Mr. . . . . It's Coombs, right?"

"Yes, sir."

"Coombs, like the thing you comb your hair with."

The other man was quiet.

"Just how long do you think it'll take me to get used to this? You think you might get into your seventies before I get used to this? And how long do you think it'll take my wife who's twenty-one years younger than you are to get used to this?"

Silence.

"You're too old for my *wife*, for Christ's sake."

Nothing.

"What's your first name again?"

The other man spoke through another sigh. "Perhaps we should just ring off."

"Ring off. Jesus. Ring off? Did you actually say 'ring off'? What're you, a goddam limey or something?"

"I am an American. I fought in Korea."

"Not World War One?"

The other man did not answer.

"How many other marriages have you had?" Ballinger asked him.

"That's a valid question. I'm glad you—"

"Thank you for the scholarly observation, *sir*. But I'm not sitting in a class. How many did you say?"

"If you'd give me a chance, I'd tell you."

Ballinger said nothing.

"Two, sir. I've had two marriages."

"Divorces?"

"I have been widowed twice."

"And—oh, I get it. You're trying to make sure that that never happens to you again."

"This is not going well at all, and I'm afraid I—I—" The other man stammered, then stopped.

"How did you expect it to go?" Ballinger demanded.

"Cruelty is not what I'd expected. I'll tell you that."

"You thought I'd be glad my daughter is going to be getting social security before I do."

The other was silent.

"Do you have any other children?" Ballinger asked.

"Yes, I happen to have three." There was a stiffness, an overweening tone, in the voice now.

"And how old are they, if I might ask."

"Yes, you may."

Ballinger waited. His wife walked in from outside, carrying some cuttings. She poured water in a glass vase and stood at the counter arranging the flowers, her back to him. The other man had stopped talking. "I'm sorry," Ballinger said. "My wife just walked in here and I didn't catch what you said. Could you just tell me if any of them are anywhere near my daughter's age?"

"I told you, my youngest boy is thirty-eight."

"And you realize that if *he* wanted to marry my daughter I'd be upset, the age difference there being what it is." Ballinger's wife moved to his side, drying her hands on a paper towel, her face full of puzzlement and worry.

"I told you, Mr. Ballinger, that I understood how you feel. The point is, we have a pregnant woman here and we both love her."

"No," Ballinger said. "That's not the point. The point is that you, sir, are not much more than a goddam statutory rapist. That's the point." His wife took his shoulder. He looked at her and shook his head.

"What?" she whispered. "Is Melanie all right?"

"Well, this isn't accomplishing anything," the voice on the other end of the line was saying.

"Just a minute," Ballinger said. "Let me ask you something else. Really now. What's the policy at that goddam university concerning teachers screwing their students?"

"Oh, my God," his wife said as the voice on the line huffed and seemed to gargle.

"I'm serious," Ballinger said.

"Melanie was not my student when we became involved."

"Is that what you call it? Involved?"

"Let me talk to Melanie," Ballinger's wife said.

"Listen," he told her. "Be quiet."

Melanie was back on the line. "Daddy? Daddy?"

"I'm here," Ballinger said, holding the phone from his wife's attempt to take it from him.

"Daddy, we're getting married and there's nothing you can do about it. Do you understand?"

"Melanie," he said, and it seemed that from somewhere far inside himself he heard that he had begun shouting at her. "Jee-zus good Christ. Your fiancé was almost *my* age *now* the day you were *born.* What the hell, kid. Are you crazy? Are you out of your mind?"

His wife was actually pushing against him to take the phone, and so he gave it to her. And stood there while she tried to talk.

"Melanie," she said. "Honey, listen—"

"Hang up," Ballinger said. "Christ. Hang it up."

"Please. Will you go in the other room and let me talk to her?"

"Tell her I've got friends. All these nice men in their forties. She can marry any one of my friends—they're babies. Forties—cradle fodder. Jesus, any one of them. Tell her."

"Jack, stop it." Then she put the phone against her chest. "Did you tell her anything about us?"

He paused. "That—no."

She turned from him. "Melanie, honey. What is this? Tell me, please."

He left her there, walked through the living room to the hall and back around to the kitchen. He was all nervous energy, crazy with it, pacing. Mary stood very still, listening, nodding slightly, holding the phone tight with both hands, her shoulders hunched as if she were out in cold weather.

"Mary," he said.

Nothing.

He went into their bedroom and closed the door. The light coming through the windows was soft gold, and the room was deepening with shadows. He moved to the bed and sat down, and in a moment he noticed that he had begun a low sort of murmuring. He took a breath and tried to be still. From the other room, his wife's voice came to him. "Yes, I quite agree with you. But I'm just unable to put this . . ."

The voice trailed off. He waited. A few minutes later, she came to the door and knocked on it lightly, then opened it and looked in.

"What," he said.

"They're serious." She stood there in the doorway.

"Come here," he said.

She stepped to his side and eased herself down, and he moved to accommodate her. He put his arm around her, and then, because it was awkward, clearly an embarrassment to her, took it away. Neither of them could speak for a time. Everything they had been through during the course of deciding about each other seemed concentrated now. Ballinger breathed his wife's presence, the odor of earth and flowers, the outdoors.

"God," she said. "I'm positively numb. I don't know what to think."

"Let's have another baby," he said suddenly. "Melanie's baby will need a younger aunt or uncle."

Mary sighed a little forlorn laugh, then was silent.

"Did you tell her about us?" he asked.

"No," she said. "I didn't get the chance. And I don't know that I could have."

"I don't suppose it's going to matter much to her."

"Oh, don't say that. You can't mean that."

The telephone on the bedstand rang, and startled them both. He reached for it, held the handset toward her.

"Hello," she said. Then: "Oh. Hi. Yes, well, here." She gave it back to him.

"Hello," he said.

Melanie's voice, tearful and angry: "You had something you said you had to tell *me*." She sobbed, then coughed. "Well?"

"It was nothing, honey. I don't even remember—"

"Well, I want you to know I would've been better than you were, Daddy, no matter how hard it was. I would've kept myself from reacting."

"Yes," he said. "I'm sure you would have."

"I'm going to hang up. And I guess I'll let you know later if we're coming at all. If it wasn't for Mom, we wouldn't be."

"We'll talk," he told her. "We'll work on it. Honey, you both have to give us a little time."

"There's nothing to work on as far as William and I are concerned."

"Of course there are things to work on. Every marriage—" His voice had caught. He took a breath. "In every marriage there are things to work on."

"I know what I know," she said.

"Well," said Ballinger. "That's—that's as it should be at your age, darling."

"Goodbye," she said. "I can't say any more."

"I understand," Ballinger said. When the line clicked, he held the handset in his lap for a moment. Mary was sitting there at his side, perfectly still.

"Well," he said. "I couldn't tell her." He put the handset back in its cradle. "God. A sixty-three-year-old son-in-law."

"It's happened before." She put her hand on his shoulder, then took it away. "I'm so frightened for her. But she says it's what she wants."

"Hell, Mary. You know what this is. The son of a bitch was her goddam teacher."

"Listen to you—what are you saying about her? Listen to what you're saying about her. That's our daughter you're talking about. You might at least try to give her the credit of assuming that she's aware of what she's doing."

They said nothing for a few moments.

"Who knows," Ballinger's wife said. "Maybe they'll be happy for a time."

He'd heard the note of sorrow in her voice, and thought he knew what she was thinking; then he was certain that he knew. He sat there remembering, like Mary, their early happiness, that ease and simplicity, and briefly he was in another house, other rooms, and he saw the toddler that Melanie had been, trailing through slant-ing light in a brown hallway, draped in gowns she had fashioned from her mother's closet. He did not know why that particular image should have come to him out of the flow of years, but for a fierce minute it was uncannily near him in the breathing silence; it went over him like a palpable something on his skin, then was gone. The ache which remained stopped him for a moment. He looked at his wife, but she had averted her eyes, her hands running absently over the faded denim cloth of her lap. Finally she stood. "Well," she sighed, going away. "Work to do."

"Mary?" he said, low; but she hadn't heard him. She was already out the doorway and into the hall, moving toward the kitchen. He reached over and turned the lamp on by the bed, and then lay down. It was so quiet here. Dark was coming to the win-dows. On the wall there were pictures; shadows, shapes, silently clamoring for his gaze. He shut his eyes, listened to the small sounds she made in the kitchen, arrang-ing her flowers, running the tap. *Mary*, he had said. But he could not imagine what he might have found to say if his voice had reached her.

🦚 🦚 🦚
Suggestions for Discussion

1. Coombs and the adult Melanie are characterized only through dialogue. Which lines create your mental impression of their appearance?

2. What are some of the tactics Ballinger uses to highlight the age difference be-tween Melanie and Coombs?

3. Highlight places where long passages of dialogue are "grounded" with narrative references to physical sensation, setting, or movement.

Retrospect

4. Chart the story's growth in intensity. Identify the major points of discovery and decision, as well as moments where there is a lull in the conflict.

🦚 🦚 🦚
Writing Exercises

INDIVIDUAL

1. Write a scene in which a character is accused of something he or she didn't do.

2. *Without using dialogue*, write a scene in which two persons who live together—parent and child, husband and wife, lovers, roommates—have had a quarrel

and are not speaking. Let the reader *see* them and what they are doing to each other in all their silence. Do not explain.

3. Write a two-page scene that is entirely in dialogue. Have one character try to get something from another character (a daughter begging her mother to buy her a pair of shoes) but create a clear subtext (i.e., the daughter really wants her mother's love and approval).

4. Write a scene in which the central character speaks politely or enthusiastically but whose thoughts run in strong contradiction. Characterize the listener by appearance, action, and dialogue.

5. Two friends are in love with the same person. One describes his or her feelings honestly and well; the other is unwilling or unable to do so, but betrays his or her feelings through appearance and action. Write the scene.

DEVELOPMENT/REVISION

6. Look back over the scene you wrote in chapter 2 (or another drafted scene in a story-in-progress). Where is more implied than is actually said? Is there a line where a character says the opposite of what he or she means? Can you add any gestures, actions, or silences that could make unspoken tensions even more apparent to readers?

7. Write a one- to three-sentence description of two different characters in your story-in-progress, either making pancakes or trying to shoot a basket. Don't worry about why they are doing this action. Focus on choosing active, descriptive verbs over "flat" ones. Go around the class and read back your descriptions. By comparing the different ways a number of characters perform the same actions, you will see how distinctively characters can be drawn through physical action.

   Follow-Up: Write or tune up a short description of a character's physical action that does fit into the context of your story. Be clear about the qualities you wish to portray through the way the action is performed.

COLLABORATIVE

8. Eavesdrop and write a list of five separate sentences from actual conversations in five separate settings. Look for vivid or intriguing sentences, such as *How does a giraffe get loose on I-40?* rather than *I don't know, what do you want to do?*
   a. Back in class, go around the room reading each person's lines of eavesdropped dialogue. Discuss what you learned about qualities of spoken dialogue through observation and transcribing.
   b. With a partner, choose the two lines that seem the most vivid and/or the most challenging to incorporate into one scene.

c. Write a two-page scene using the two stolen sentences somewhere in the scene (not necessarily as dialogue), creating a world and situation in which these sentences sound at home.

d. Read the scenes back in groups and brainstorm about possible directions in which to develop a related story. You may also discover characters around whom you will wish to build a different story.

6

LONG AGO AND FAR AWAY
Fictional Place and Time

• *Setting and Atmosphere*

• *Some Aspects of Narrative Time*

"It's the job of the writer to create a world that entices you in and shows you what's at stake there," says fiction writer Nancy Huddleston Packer. For some writers, that world itself may inspire the story, while others will tend to focus on setting and atmosphere during the revision process. Still, even from the first, raw draft, it is important to remember Elizabeth Bowen's maxim that "nothing happens nowhere" and Jerome Stern's further admonition that a scene that seems to happen nowhere often seems not to happen at all. The failure to create an atmosphere, to establish a sense of where or when the story takes place, will leave readers bored or confused. And just as the rhythm of your prose must work with and not against your intention, so the use of place and time must work with and not against your ultimate meaning. Together, setting and narrative time help define a story's dimensions. Setting grounds a story in place (as that place exists in a particular moment), while time frames the story off within the larger story of a character's life and gives perspective to the events depicted.

Like dialogue, setting must do more than one thing at once, from illuminating the story's symbolic underpinnings to such practical kinds of "showing" as reflecting emotion or revealing subtle aspects of a character's life. Yet just as character and plot are interlinked, so character itself is a product of place and culture. We see that to an absurd degree in the corporate cubicle hell of the chapter 7 story "Orientation"; in "Lectures on How You Never Lived Back Home," also upcoming in chapter 7, M. Evelina Galang's unnamed character internalizes an emotional tug-of-war between the social codes of the American suburbs, in which she was raised, and those of the Philippines, from which her family emigrated. Here, as in all stories, we need not only to know a character's gender, race, and age, but also in what atmosphere she or he operates to understand the significance of the action. Finally, setting may give rise to external conflict, as seen in the story "The Things They Carried" and such novels as *The Grapes of Wrath*, *Storming Heaven*, *One Flew Over the Cuckoo's Nest*, and *The Poisonwood Bible*.

But realistic settings constructed from memory or research are only part of the challenge, for an intensely created fantasy world makes new boundaries for the mind. *Once upon a time, long ago and far away, a dream, hell, heaven, a garbage shaft, Middle Earth, Hogwarts boarding school*, and *the subconscious* all have been the settings of excellent fiction. Even Utopian fiction, set *Nowhere* with a capital *N* (or *nowhere* spelled backward, as Samuel Butler had it in *Erehwon*), happens in a nowhere of which the particular characteristics are the point. Outer space is an exciting setting precisely because its physical boundary is the outer edge of our familiar world. Obviously this does not absolve the writer from the necessity of giving outer space its own characteristics, atmosphere, and logic. If anything, these must be more intensely realized within the fiction, since we have less to borrow from in our own experience.

> The westering sun shining in on his face woke Shevek as the dirigible, clearing the last high pass of the Ne Theras, turned south . . . He pressed his face to the dusty window, and sure enough, down there between two low rusty ridges was a great walled field, the Port. He gazed eagerly, trying to see if there was a spaceship on the pad. Despicable as Urras was, still it was another world; he wanted to see a ship from another world, a voyager across the dry and terrible abyss, a thing made by alien hands. But there was no ship in the Port.
>
> Ursula K. Le Guin, *The Dispossessed*

Setting and Atmosphere

Your fiction must have an *atmosphere* because without it your characters will be unable to breathe.

Part of the atmosphere of a scene or story is its setting, including the locale, period, weather, and time of day. Part of the atmosphere is its *tone*, an attitude taken by the narrative voice that can be described in terms of a quality—sinister, facetious, formal, solemn, wry. The two facets of atmosphere, setting and tone, are often inextricably mixed in the ultimate effect: A sinister atmosphere might be achieved partly by syntax, rhythm, and word choice; partly by darkness, dampness, and a desolated landscape, as is shown in the first line of Edgar Allan Poe's "The Fall of the House of Usher":

> During the whole of a dull, dark, and soundless day in the autumn of the year, when the clouds hung oppressively low in the heavens, I had been passing alone, on horseback, through a singularly dreary tract of country; and at length found

myself, as the shades of the evening drew on, within view of the melancholy House of Usher.

You can orient your reader in place and time with straight information (*On the southern bank of the Bayou Teche in the fall of '69 . . .*), but as with the revelation of character, you may more effectively reveal place and time through concrete detail (*The bugs hung over the black water in clusters of a steady hum*). Here the information is indirect and we may have to wait for some of it, but the details reveal an attitude toward the setting and the reader experiences it seemingly first hand.

HARMONY AND CONFLICT BETWEEN CHARACTER AND BACKGROUND

If character is the foreground of fiction, setting is the background, and as in a painting's composition, the foreground may be in harmony or in conflict with the background. If we think of the Impressionist paintings of the late nineteenth century, we think of the harmony of, say, women with light-scattering parasols strolling against summer landscapes of light-scattering trees. By contrast, the Spanish painter Jose Cortijo has a portrait of a girl on her Communion day; she sits curled and ruffled, in a lace mantilla, on an ornately carved Mediterranean throne against a backdrop of stark, harshly lit, poverty-stricken shacks.

Likewise the setting and characters of a story may be in harmony:

The Bus to St. James's—a Protestant Episcopal school for boys and girls—started its round at eight o'clock in the morning, from a corner of Park Avenue in the Sixties. The earliness of the hour meant that some of the parents who took their children there were sleepy and still without coffee, but with a clear sky the light struck the city at an extreme angle, the air was fresh, and it was an exceptionally cheerful time of day. It was the hour when cooks and door men walk dogs, and when porters scrub the lobby floor mats with soap and water.

John Cheever, "The Bus to St. James's"

Or there can be an inherent conflict between the background and foreground:

. . . He opened the door himself and started down the walk to get her going. The sky was a dying violet and the houses stood out darkly against it, bulbous liver-colored monstrosities of a uniform ugliness though no two were alike. Since this had been a fashionable neighborhood forty years ago, his mother persisted in thinking they did well to have an apartment in it. Each house had a narrow collar of dirt around it in which sat, usually, a grubby child. Julian walked with his hands in his pockets, his head down and thrust forward and his eyes glazed with the determination to make himself completely numb during the time he would be sacrificed to her pleasure.

Flannery O'Connor, "Everything That Rises Must Converge"

Notice how images of the time of day work with concrete details of place to create very different atmospheres—on the one hand *morning, Park Avenue, earliness, clear sky, light, extreme angle, air, fresh, cheerful, dogs, scrub, soap, water;* and on the other *dying violet, darkly, bulbous liver-colored monstrosities, uniform ugliness, narrow, dirt, grubby child.* Notice also that where conflict occurs, there is already "narrative content," or the makings of a story. We might reasonably expect that in the Cheever story, where the characters are in apparent harmony with their background, there is or will be conflict in the foreground between or among those children, parents, and perhaps the servitors who keep their lives so well scrubbed. It won't surprise us, toward the end of the story, to see this contrast between weather and narrative mood: ". . . Mr. Bruce led her out the door into the freshness of a winter evening, holding her, supporting her really, for she might have fallen."

SETTING AND CHARACTER

One of the most economical means of sketching a character is simply to show readers a personal space that the character has created, be it a bedroom, locker, kitchen, hideout, office cubicle, or even the interior of a car. This technique is illustrated in Elizabeth Tallent's story "Prowler," as Dennis, a divorced father, surveys his thirteen-year-old son's bedroom.

> Dennis believes it tells everything about Kenny: photo-realist motorcycles, chrome and highly evolved threat, grace the walls, along with a frail Kafka razor-bladed from a library book, a sin so small and so unprecedented that Dennis uncharacteristically forgot to mention it to him. If Kenny's motorcycle paintings are depressing, surely jug-eared Kafka promises complexity, contradiction, hope?

Through the description of Kenny's room, we see that the boy is making a transition to the rocky years of adolescence, showing both a typical interest in fast, powerful, rebellious vehicles and also signs of more private teenage angst (and what is he doing with razor blades anyway?). Not every parent would interpret a Kafka portrait, much less a stolen one, as a sign of hope—in this case, the reflection may reveal as much about the observing father as about the indirectly observed son, adding a further layer of complexity.

Doug Coupland uses an even more self-conscious version of the same technique to create a quick portrait of the household of fanatical young Microsoft employees featured in his novel *Microserfs.*

> More details about our group house—Our House of Wayward Mobility.
> Because the house receives almost no sun, moss and algae tend to colonize what surfaces they can. There is a cherry tree, crippled by a fungus. The rear verandah, built of untreated 2x4's, has quietly rotted away, and the sliding door in the kitchen has been braced shut with a hockey stick to prevent the unwary from straying into the suburban abyss. . . .

Inside, each of us has a bedroom. Because of the McDonald's-like turnover in the house, the public rooms—the living room, kitchen, dining room, and basement—are bleak to say the least. The dormlike atmosphere precludes heavy-duty interior design ideas. In the living room are two velveteen sofas that were too big and too ugly for some long-gone tenants to take with them. Littered about the Tiki Green shag carpet are:

- Two Microsoft Works PC inflatable beach cushions
- One Mitsubishi 27-inch color TV
- Various vitamin bottles
- Several weight-gaining system cartons (mine)
- 86 copies of MacWEEK arranged in chronological order by Bug Barbecue, who will go berserk if you so much as move one issue out of date
- Bone-shaped chew toys for when Mishka visits
- Two PowerBooks
- Three IKEA mugs encrusted with last month's blender drink sensation
- Two 12.5 pound dumbbells (Susan's)
- A Windows NT box
- Three baseball caps (two Mariners, one A's)
- Abe's Battlestar Galactica trading card album
- Todd's pile of books on how to change your life to win! (*Getting Past OK, 7 Habits of Highly Effective People*...)

The kitchen is stocked with ramshackle 1970s avocado green appliances. You can almost hear the ghost of Emily Hartley yelling "Hi, Bob!" every time you open the fridge door (a sea of magnets and 4 X 6-inch photos of last year's house parties). Our mail is in little piles by the front door: bills, Star Trek junk mail, and the heap-o-catalogues next to the phone.

I think we'd order our lives via 1-800 numbers if we could.

Like their mold-ravaged house, the Microserfs also receive almost no sun as they pursue their project shipping deadlines round the clock; the litter of objects listed give clues to whatever thin slices of personality remain.

SETTING AND EMOTION

Our relation to place, time, and weather, like our relation to clothes and other objects, is charged with emotion more or less subtle, more or less profound. It is filled with judgment mellow or harsh. And it alters according to what happens to us. In some rooms you are always trapped; you enter them with grim purpose and escape them as soon as you can. Others invite you to settle in, to nestle or carouse. Some landscapes lift your spirits; others depress you. Cold weather gives you energy and bounce, or else it clogs your head and makes you huddle, struggling. You describe yourself as a night person or a morning person. The house you loved as a child now makes you, precisely because you were once happy there, think of loss and death. It is central to fiction that all such emotion be used or heightened (or invented) to dramatic effect.

Imagine experiencing a thunderstorm when in the throes of a new love: the rain might seem to glitter, the lightning to sizzle, the thunder to rumble with anticipation. The downpour would refresh and exhilarate, nourishing the newly budding violets. Then imagine how the very same storm would feel in the midst of a lousy romantic breakup: the raindrops would be thick and cold, almost greasy; the lightning would slash at the clouds; the thunder would growl. Torrents of rain would beat the delicate tulips to the ground.

Because we have all had the experience of seeing our inner emotional states reflected by the outer world, we instinctively understand that setting can serve as a mirror of emotion. Seen through the eyes of a character, setting is never neutral.

In the chapter 10 story "Ralph the Duck," the narrator thinks back on a troubling incident that has taken place during his rounds at the local college that evening. He sits with a "king-sized drink composed of sour mash whiskey and ice" and

> In our back room, which is on the northern end of the house, and cold for sitting in that close to dawn, I sat and watched the texture of the sky change. It was going to snow, and I wanted to see the storm come up the valley.

He seems to sense that there is worse trouble to come, and in fact it later arrives in the middle of an ice storm. Yet by the story's end, when he is feeling some relief and hope (to which the laconic narrator himself would never admit), we see these feelings mirrored in a very different view of the same landscape.

> I was at the northern windows, looking through the mullions down the valley to the faint red line along the mounds and little peaks of the ridge beyond the valley. The sun was going to come up, and I was looking for it.

Setting can help to portray a swirl of emotion, as in this moment from "Where Are You Going, Where Have You Been?" in which Arnold Friend's attempts to disorient and terrorize Connie are succeeding, and she is losing her grasp on all that is familiar, even as she feels nostalgic for the home she is leaving:

> The kitchen looked like a place she had never seen before, some room she had run inside but which wasn't good enough, wasn't going to help her. The kitchen window had never had a curtain, after three years, and there were dishes in the sink for her to do—probably—and if you ran your hand across the table you'd probably feel something sticky there.

Emotion is conveyed in these and similar passages, even as the story is being anchored in place. When a reader senses that setting is being used to reveal something important, there is no danger of its being what one student calls "the stuff you skip."

SYMBOLIC AND SUGGESTIVE SETTING

Since the rosy-fingered dawn came over the battlefield of Homer's *Iliad* (and no doubt well before that), poets and writers have used the context of history, night, storm, stars, sea, city, and plain to give their stories a sense of reaching out toward the universe. Sometimes the universe resonates with an answer, and in his plays Shakespeare consistently drew parallels between the conflicts of the heavenly bodies and the conflicts of nations and characters.

In "The Life You Save May Be Your Own," Flannery O'Connor uses the elements in a conscious Shakespearian way, letting the setting reflect and affect the theme.

> The old woman and her daughter were sitting on their own porch when Mr. Shiflet came up their road for the first time. The old woman slid to the edge of her chair and leaned forward, shading her eyes from the piercing sunset with her hand. The daughter could not see far in front of her and continued to play with her fingers. Although the old woman lived in this desolate spot with only her daughter, and she had never seen Mr. Shiflet before, she could tell, even from a distance, that he was a tramp and no one to be afraid of. His left coat sleeve was folded up to show there was only half an arm in it and his gaunt figure listed lightly to the side as if the breeze were pushing him. He had on a black town suit and a brown felt hat that was turned up in the front and down in the back and he carried a tin tool box by a handle. He came on at an amble, up her road, his face turned toward the sun which appeared to be balancing itself on the peak of a small mountain.

The focus in this opening paragraph of the story is on the characters and their actions, and the setting is economically, almost incidentally, established: *porch, road, sunset, breeze, peak, small mountain*. What the passage gives us is a type of landscape, rural and harsh; the only adjectives in the description of the setting are *piercing, desolate,* and *small*. But this general background works together with details of action, thought, and appearance to establish a great deal more that is both informational and emotional. The old woman's peering suggests that people on the road are not only unusual but suspicious. On the other hand, that she is reassured to see a tramp suggests both a period and a set of assumptions about country life. That Mr. Shiflet wears a town suit establishes him as a stranger to this set of assumptions. That the sun appears to be balancing itself (we are not sure whether it is the old woman's observation or the author's) leaves us, at the end of the paragraph, with a sense of anticipation and tension.

Now, what happens in the story is this: Mr. Shiflet repairs the old woman's car and (in order to get the car) marries her retarded daughter. He abandons the daughter on their honeymoon and picks up a hitchhiker who insults both Mr. Shiflet and the memory of his mother. The hitchhiker jumps out. Mr. Shiflet curses and drives on.

Throughout the story, as in the first paragraph, the focus remains on the characters and their actions. Yet the landscape and the weather make their presence felt, subtly commenting on attitudes and actions. As Mr. Shiflet's fortunes wax promising and he expresses satisfaction with his own morality, "A fat yellow moon appeared in the branches of the fig tree as if it were going to roost there with the chickens." When, hatching his plot, he sits on the steps with the mother and daughter, "The old woman's three mountains were black against the sky." Once he has abandoned the girl, the weather grows "hot and sultry, and the country had flattened out. Deep in the sky a storm was preparing very slowly and without thunder." Once more there is a sunset, but this time the sun "was a reddening ball that through his windshield was slightly flat on the bottom and top," and this deflated sun reminds us of the "balanced" one about to be punctured by the peak in its inevitable decline. When the hitchhiker has left him, a cloud covers the sun, and Mr. Shiflet in his fury prays for the Lord to "break forth and wash the slime from this earth!" His prayer is apparently answered.

> After a few minutes there was a guffawing peal of thunder from behind and fantastic raindrops, like tin-can tops, crashed over the rear of Mr. Shiflet's car. Very quickly he stepped on the gas and with his stump sticking out the window he raced the galloping shower to Mobile.

The setting in this story, as this bald summary emphasizes, is deliberately used as a comment on the actions. The behavior of the weather, in ironic juxtaposition to the title, "The Life You Save May Be Your Own," makes clear that the "slime" Mr. Shiflet has damned may be himself. Yet the reader is never aware of this as a symbolic intrusion. The setting remains natural and realistically convincing, an incidental backdrop, until the heavens are ready to make their guffawing comment.

Robert Coover's settings rarely present a symbolic or sentient universe, but they produce in us an emotionally charged expectation of what is likely to happen here. The following passages are the opening paragraphs of three short stories from a single collection, *Pricksongs and Descants*. Notice how the three different settings are achieved not only by imagery and content, but also by the very different rhythms of the sentence structure.

> A pine forest in the midafternoon. Two children follow an old man, dropping breadcrumbs, singing nursery tunes. Dense earthy greens seep into the darkening distance, flecked and streaked with filtered sunlight. Spots of red, violet, pale blue, gold, burnt orange. The girl carries a basket for gathering flowers. The boy is occupied with the crumbs. Their song tells of God's care for little ones.
>
> "The Gingerbread House"

> Situation: television panel game, live audience. Stage strobelit and cameras insecting about. Moderator, bag shape corseted and black suited behind desk/rostrum, blinking mockmodesty at lens and lamps, practised pucker on his soft mouth and brows arched in mild goodguy astonishment. Opposite him, the panel: Aged Clown, Lovely Lady and Mr. America, fat as the continent and bald as an eagle. There is an empty chair between Lady and Mr. A, which is now filled, to the delighted squeals of all, by a spectator dragged protesting from the

Audience, nondescript introduced as Unwilling Participant, or more simply, Bad Sport. Audience: same as ever, docile, responsive, good-natured, terrifying. And the Bad Sport, you ask, who is he? fool! thou art!

"Panel Game"

She arrives at 7:40, ten minutes late, but the children, Jimmy and Bitsy, are still eating supper, and their parents are not ready to go yet. From the other rooms come the sounds of a baby screaming, water running, a television musical (no words: probably a dance number—patterns of gliding figures come to mind). Mrs. Tucker sweeps into the kitchen, fussing with her hair, and snatches a baby bottle full of milk out of a pan of warm water, rushes out again. Harry! she calls. The babysitter's here already!

"The Babysitter"

Here are three quite familiar places: a fairy-tale forest, a television studio, and a suburban house. In at least the first two selections, the locale is more consciously and insistently set than in the O'Connor opening, yet all three remain suggestive backdrops rather than active participants. Coover directs our attitude toward these places through imagery and tone. The forest is a neverland, and the time is once upon a time, though there are grimmer than Grimm hints of violence about it. The television studio is a place of hysteria, chaos, and hypocrisy, whereas the American suburbia, where presumably such television shows are received, is boring rather than chaotic, not hysterical but merely hassled in a predictable sort of way.

In "The Gingerbread House," simple sentence structure helps establish the child-like quality appropriate to a fairy tale. But a more complex sentence intervenes, with surprising intensity of imagery: *dense, earthy, seep, darkening, flecked, streaked, filtered*. Because of this, the innocence of the tone is set askew, so that by the time we hear of God's care for little ones, we fully and accurately expect a brutal disillusionment.

Setting can often, and in a variety of ways, arouse reader expectation and foreshadow events to come. In "The Gingerbread House," there is an implied conflict between character and setting, between the sentimentality of the children's flowers and nursery tunes and the threatening forest, so that we are immediately aware of the central conflict of the story: innocence versus violence.

But as in the Cheever passage quoted earlier, anticipation can also be aroused by an insistent single attitude toward setting, and in this case the reader, being a contrary sort of person, is likely to anticipate a change or paradox. Here, for example, is part of the opening paragraph of E. M. Forster's A *Passage to India*:

Except for Marabar Caves—and they are twenty miles off—the city of Chandrapore presents nothing extraordinary. Edged rather than washed by the River Ganges, it trails for a couple of miles along the bank, scarcely distinguishable from the rubbish it deposits so freely . . . The streets are mean, the temples ineffective, and though a few fine houses exist they are hidden away in gardens or down alleys whose filth deters all but the invited guest.

The narrative continues in this way, creating an unrelenting portrait of the dreariness of Chandrapore—*made of mud, mud moving, abased, monotonous, rotting, swelling, shrinking, low but indestructible form of life.* The images are a little too one-sided, and as we might protest in life against a too fanatical condemnation of a place—isn't there anything good about it?—so we are led to expect (accurately again) that in the pages that follow] somehow beauty and mystery will break forth from the dross. Likewise, but in the opposite way, the opening pages of Woolf's *Mrs. Dalloway* burst with affirmation, the beauty of London and spring, love of life and love of life and love of life again! We suspect (accurately once more) that death and hatred lurk.

Where conflict between character and setting is immediately introduced, as it is in both "The Gingerbread House" and "Panel Game," it is usually because the character is unfamiliar with, or uncomfortable in, the setting. In "Panel Game" it's both. The television studio, which is in fact a familiar and unthreatening place to most of us, has been made mad. This is achieved partly by violating expected grammar. The sentences are not sentences. They are missing vital verbs and logical connectives, so that the images are squashed against each other. The prose is cluttered, effortful, negative; as a result, as reader you know "the delighted squeals of all" do not include your own, and you're ready to sympathize with the unwilling central character (you!).

ALIEN AND FAMILIAR SETTING

Many poets and novelists have observed that the function of literature is to make the ordinary fresh and strange. F. Scott Fitzgerald, on the other hand, advised a young writer that reporting extreme things as if they were ordinary was the starting point of fiction. Both of these views are true, and they are particularly true of setting. Whether a place is familiar or unfamiliar, comfortable or discomfiting in fiction has nothing to do with whether the reader actually knows the place and feels good there. It is an attitude taken, an assumption made. In his detective novels, Ross Macdonald assumes a familiarity toward California that is perfectly translatable into Japanese ("I turned left off the highway and down an old switchback blacktop to a dead end"), whereas even the natives of North Hollywood must feel alien on Tom Wolfe's version of their streets.

> . . . endless scorched boulevards lined with one-story stores, shops, bowling alleys, skating rinks, taco drive-ins, all of them shaped not like rectangles but like trapezoids, from the way the roofs slant up from the back and the plate-glass fronts slant out as if they're going to pitch forward on the sidewalk and throw up.
>
> *The Kandy-Kolored Tangerine-Flake Streamline Baby*

The prose of Tom Wolfe, whether about rural North Carolina, Fifth Avenue, or Cape Kennedy, lives in a tone of constant astonishment. By contrast, Ray Bradbury's outer space is pure down-home.

> It was quiet in the deep morning of Mars, as quiet as a cool black well, with stars shining in the canal waters, and, breathing in every room, the children curled with their spiders in closed hands.

The Martian Chronicles

Returning to the passage from Coover's "The Babysitter," notice that the setting is ordinary and is presented as ordinary. The sentences have standard and rather leisurely syntax; neither form nor image startles. Details are generic, not specific: The house is presented without a style; the children are named but not seen; Mrs. Tucker behaves in a way predictable and familiar to anyone in contemporary America. What Coover has in fact done is to present us with a setting so usual, so "typical," that we begin to suspect that something unusual is afoot.

Indeed, the Tuckers, their house, their children, their car, their night out, and their babysitter remain unvaryingly typical throughout all the external actions in the course of the evening. Against this relentlessly wholesome backdrop play the individual fantasies of the characters—brilliant, brutal, sexual, dangerous, and violent—that provide the conflict of the story.

One great advantage of being a writer is that you may create the world. Places and the elements have the significance and the emotional effect you give them in language. As a person you may be depressed by rain, but as an author you are free to make rain mean freshness, growth, bounty, and God. You may choose; the only thing you are not free to do is not to choose.

As with character, the first requisite of effective setting is to know it fully, to experience it mentally, and the second is to create it through significant detail. What sort of place is this, and what are its peculiarities? What is the weather like, the light, the season, the time of day? What are the contours of the land and architecture? What are the social assumptions of the inhabitants, and how familiar and comfortable are the characters with this place and its lifestyle? These things are not less important in fiction than in life, but more, since their selection inevitably takes on significance. And in stories such as "American History," "The Things They Carried," and "Dark Corner," setting may become a character itself.

AN EXERCISE IN SETTING

Here are a series of passages about war, set in different periods and places. The first is in Russia during the campaign of Napoleon, the second on the island of Pianosa during World War II, and the third in a post-holocaust future.

Compare the settings. How do climate, period, imagery, and language contribute to each? To what degree is setting a sentient force? Is there conflict between character and setting? How does setting affect and/or reveal the attitude taken toward the war? What mood, what emotions are implied?

Several tens of thousands of the slain lay in diverse postures and various uniforms. Over the whole field, previously so gaily beautiful with the glitter of bayonets and cloudlets of smoke in the morning sun, there now spread a mist of damp and smoke and a strange acid smell of saltpeter and blood. Clouds gathered and drops of rain began to fall on the dead and wounded, on the frightened, exhausted, and hesitating men, as if to say: Enough, men! Enough! Cease! Bethink yourselves! What are you doing?

Leo Tolstoy, *War and Peace*

Their only hope was that it would never stop raining, and they had no hope because they all knew it would. When it did stop raining in Pianosa, it rained in Bologna. When it stopped raining in Bologna, it began again in Pianosa. If there was no rain at all, there were freakish, inexplicable phenomena like the epidemic of diarrhea or the bomb line that moved. Four times during the first six days they were assembled and briefed and then sent back. Once, they took off and were flying in formation when the control tower summoned them down. The more it rained, the worse they suffered. The worse they suffered, the more they prayed that it would continue raining.

Joseph Heller, *Catch-22*

She liked the wild, quatrosyllabic lilt of the word, Barbarian. Then, looking beyond the wooden fence, she saw a trace of movement in the fields beyond. It was not the wind among the young corn; or, if it was wind among the young corn, it carried her the whinny of a raucous horse. It was too early for poppies but she saw a flare of scarlet. She ceased to watch the Soldiers; instead she watched the movement flow to the fences and crash through them and across the tender wheat. Bursting from the undergrowth came horseman after horseman. They flashed with curious curved plates of metal dredged up from the ruins. Their horses were bizarrely caparisoned with rags, small knives, bells and chains dangling from manes and tails, and man and horse together, unholy centaurs crudely daubed with paint, looked twice as large as life. They fired long guns. Confronted with the terrors of the night in the freshest hours of the morning, the gentle crowd scattered, wailing.

Angela Carter, *Heroes and Villains*

Some Aspects of Narrative Time

Literature is, by virtue of its nature and subject matter, tied to time in a way the other arts are not. A painting represents a frozen instant, and the viewing time is a matter of the viewer's choice. Music takes a certain time to hear, and the timing of the various parts is of utmost importance, but the time scheme is self-enclosed and makes no reference to time in the world outside itself. In fiction, the concern is *content time*, the period covered in the story. It is quite possible to write a story that takes about twenty minutes to read and covers about twenty minutes of action (Jean-Paul Sartre performed experiments in this *durational realism*), but no one has suggested such a correspondence as a fictional requirement. Sometimes the time period covered is telescoped, sometimes stretched. The history of the world up until now can be covered in a sentence; four seconds of crisis may take a chapter. It's even possible to do both at once: William Golding's entire novel *Pincher Martin* takes place between the time the drowning protagonist begins to take off his boots and the moment he dies with his boots still on. But when asked by a student, "How long does it really take?" Golding replied, "Eternity."

SUMMARY AND SCENE

Summary and *scene* are methods of treating time in fiction. A summary covers a relatively long period of time in relatively short compass; a scene deals at length with a relatively short period of time.

Summary narration is a useful and often necessary device: it may give information, fill in a character's background, let us understand a motive, alter pace, create a transition, leap moments or years. For example, early in *The Poisonwood Bible*, summary is used both to fast-forward through time to the story's present moment and to set the political context:

> In the year of our Lord 1960 a monkey barreled through space in an American rocket; a Kennedy boy took the chair out from under a fatherly general named Ike; and the whole world turned on an axis called the Congo. The monkey sailed right overhead, and on a more earthly plane men in locked rooms bargained for the Congo's treasure. But I was there. Right on the head of that pin.

Scene is to time what concrete detail is to the senses; that is, it is the crucial means of allowing your reader to experience the story with the characters. Basically defined, a scene is dialogue and action that take place between two or more characters over a set period of "real" time. Like a story, on its own small scale, a scene has a turning point or mini-crisis that propels the story forward toward its conclusion. Scene is *always* necessary to fiction, for it allows readers to see, hear, and sense the story's drama moment-to-moment. Jerome Stern, in *Making Shapely Fiction*, astutely observes that like a child in a tantrum, when you want everyone's full attention you "make a scene," using the writer's full complement of "dialogue, physical reactions, gestures, smells, sounds, and thoughts." A confrontation, a turning point, or a crisis occur at given moments that take on significance as moments and cannot be summarized. The form of a story requires confrontation, turning points, and crises, and therefore requires scenes.

It is quite possible to write a short story in a single scene, without any summary at all, as demonstrated by "Hills Like White Elephants" and "No One's a Mystery." It is not possible, however, to write a successful story entirely in summary. One of the most common errors beginning fiction writers make is to summarize events rather than to realize them as moments.

Transitions between summary and scene must also be carefully crafted. In the following paragraph from Margaret Atwood's *Lady Oracle*, the narrator has been walking home from her Brownie troop with older girls who tease and terrify her with threats of a bad man. The first paragraph of this quotation covers the way things were over a period of a few months and then makes a transition to one of the afternoons:

> The snow finally changed to slush and then to water, which trickled down the hill of the bridge in two rivulets, one on either side of the path; the path itself turned to mud. The bridge was damp, it smelled rotten, the willow branches turned yellow, the skipping ropes came out. It was light again in the afternoons, and on one of them, when for a change Elizabeth hadn't run off but was merely discussing the possibilities with the others, a real man actually appeared.

The second paragraph then specifies a particular moment:

> He was standing at the far side of the bridge, a little off the path, holding a bunch of daffodils in front of him. He was a nice-looking man, neither old nor young, wearing a good tweed coat, not at all shabby or disreputable. He didn't have a hat on, his taffy-colored hair was receding and the sunlight gleamed on his high forehead.

Notice that the scene is introduced when an element of conflict and confrontation occurs. That the threatened bad man does appear and that he is surprisingly innocuous promises a turn of events and a change in the relationship among the girls. We need to see the moment when this change occurs.

Throughout *Lady Oracle*, a typical pattern recurs: a summary leading up to, and followed by, a scene that represents a turning point.

> My own job was fairly simple. I stood at the back of the archery range, wearing a red leather change apron, and rented out the arrows. When the barrels of arrows were almost used up, I'd go down to the straw targets. The difficulty was that we couldn't make sure all the arrows had actually been shot before we went down to clear the targets. Rob would shout, Bows DOWN, please, arrows OFF the string, but occasionally someone would let an arrow go, on purpose or by accident. This was how I got shot. We'd pulled the arrows and the men were carrying the barrels back to the line; I was replacing a target face, and I'd just bent over.

To get comfortable with this pattern of storytelling, it may help to think of your own past as a movement through time: *I was born in Arizona and lived there with my parents until I was eighteen; then I spent three years in New York before going on to England.* Or you might instead remember the way things were during a period of that time: *In New York we used to go down Broadway for a midnight snack, and Judy would always dare us to do some nonsense or other before we got back.* But when you think of the events that significantly altered your life, your mind will present you with a scene: *Then one afternoon Professor Bovie stopped me in the hall after class and wagged his glasses at me. "Have you thought about studying in England?"*

REVISING SUMMARY AND SCENE

Some writers have a tendency to oversummarize, racing through more time and more events than necessary to tell the story. The danger here is lack of depth. Other writers undersummarize, finding it difficult to deal with quick leaps and transitions, dwelling at excessive length on every scene, including the scenes of the past. The danger of such writing is that readers may not sense which scenes are more important than others. The writer seems not to have made this decision himself or herself. Reluctant to do the writer's job, a reader may lose patience.

After you have written (and especially workshopped) a few stories, you will know which sort of writer you are, and in which direction you need to work. If people say *you have enough material for a novel*, then you have probably not distilled your material down to the very few scenes that contain the significance you seek. Pick one event of all you have included that contains a moment of crucial change in your character. Write *that* scene in detail, moment by moment. Take time to create the place and the period. Make us see, taste, smell. Let characters speak. Is there a way to indicate, sketch, contain—or simply omit—all that earlier life you raced through in summary? If this proves too difficult, have you really found out yet what your story is about? Explore the scene, rather than the summary, for clues.

If your critics say *you write long* or *your story really begins on page three* (or *six*, or *eleven*), have you indulged yourself in setting things up, or dwelt on the story's past at the expense of its present? Try condensing a scene to a sentence. Try fusing two or even three scenes into one. This sometimes seems impossible at first, and it may involve sacrificing a delicious phrase or a nifty nuance, but it is simply the necessary work of plotting.

In either case, if your readers are *confused by what happens at the end*, it may very well be that you have summarized the crisis instead of realizing it in a scene. The crisis moment in a story *must always be presented as a scene*. This is the moment we have been waiting for. This is the payoff when the slipper fits. We want to be there. We want to feel the moment that change happens, hear it, taste it, see it in color in close-up on the wide screen of our minds. This is also a hard job, sometimes the hardest a writer has to do—it's draining to summon up all that emotion in all its intensity. And there isn't always a glass slipper handy when you need one; it may be difficult enough to identify the moment when you need that scene.

Scene and summary are often intermixed, of course, and summary may serve precisely to heighten scene. Used within a scene, summary can suggest contrast with the past, intensify mood, or delay while creating suspense about what will happen next. This example from Rosellen Brown's *Before and After*—in which a father disturbed by reports of a young girl's murder is checking out his son's car in a dark garage—does all three.

The snow was lavender where the light came down on it, like the weird illumination you see in planetariums that changes every color and makes white electric blue. Jacob and I loved to go to the science museum in Boston—not that long ago he had been at that age when the noisy saga of whirling planets and inexplicable anti-gravitational feats, narrated by a man with a deep official-facts voice, was thrilling. He was easily, unstintingly thrilled, or used to be. Not now, though.

Notice how Brown uses brief summaries both of the way things used to be and the way things have changed over time, as well as images of time, weather, and even the whirling cosmos to rouse our fear toward the "instant" in which major change occurs:

At the last instant I thought I'd look at the trunk. I was beginning to feel relief wash over me like that moon-white air outside—a mystery still, where he might be, but nothing suspicious. The trunk snapped open and rose with the slow deliberation of a drawbridge, and then I thought I'd fall over for lack of breath. Because I knew I was looking at blood.

The moments that altered your life you remember at length and in detail; your memory tells you your story, and it is a great natural storyteller.

FLASHBACK

Flashback is one of the most magical of fiction's contrivances, easier and more effective in this medium than in any other, because the reader's mind is a swifter mechanism for getting into the past than anything that has been devised for stage or even film. All you must do is to give the reader smooth passage into the past, and the force of the story will be time-warped to whenever and wherever you want it.

Nevertheless, many beginning writers use unnecessary flashbacks. While flashback can be a useful way to provide background to character or the history of events—the information that screenwriters call *backstory*—it isn't the only way. Rather, dialogue, brief summary, a reference, or detail can often tell us all we need to know.

If you are tempted to use flashback to fill in the whole past, try using your journal for exploring background. Write down everything, fast. Then take a hard look at it to decide just how *little* of it you can use, how much of it the reader can infer, how you can sharpen an image to imply a past incident or condense a grief into a line of dialogue. Trust the reader's experience of life to understand events from attitudes. And keep the present of the story moving.

Flashback is effectively used in fiction to *reveal* at the *right point*. It does not so much distract us from, as contribute to, the central action of the story, deepening our understanding of character and theme. If you find that you do need to use a flashback to reveal, at some point, why the character reacts as she does, or how totally he is misunderstood by those around him, or some other point of emotional significance, then there are several ways to help the reader make that leap in time.

- Provide some sort of transition. A connection between what's happening in the present and what happened in the past will often best transport the reader, just as it does the character.
- Avoid blatant transitions, such as "Henry thought back to the time" and "I drifted back in memory." Assume the reader's intelligence and ability to follow a leap back.

> The kid in the Converse high-tops lifted off on the tips of his toes and slam-dunked it in.
> Joe'd done that once, in the lot off Seymour Street, when he was still four inches shorter than Ruppert and had already started getting zits. It was early fall, and . . .

A graceful transition to the past allows you to summarize necessary background quickly, as in this example from James W. Hall's *Under Cover of Daylight.*

> Thorn watched as Sugarman made a quick inspection of the gallery. Thorn sat on the couch where he'd done his homework as a boy, the one that looked out across the seawall toward Carysfort light.
> That was how his nights had been once, read a little Thoreau, do some algebra, and look up, shifting his body so he could see through the louvers the fragile pulse of that marker light, and let his mind roam, first out the twelve miles to the reef and then pushing farther, out past the shipping lanes into a world he pictured as gaudy and loud, chaotic. Bright colors and horns honking, exotic vegetables and market stalls, and water, clear and deep and shadowy, an ocean of fish, larger and more powerful than those he had hauled to light. Beyond the reef.

- If you are writing in the past tense, begin the flashback in the past perfect (*she had driven; he had worked*) and use the construction "had + (verb)" two or three times more. Then switch to the simple past (*he raced; she crept*); the reader will be with you. If you are writing in the present tense, you may want to keep the whole flashback in the past tense.
- Try to avoid a flashback within a flashback. If you find yourself tempted by this awkward shape, it probably means you're trying to let flashback carry too much of the story.
- When the flashback ends, be very clear that you are catching up to the present again. Repeat an action or image that the reader will remember belongs to the basic time period of the story. Often simply beginning the paragraph with "Now . . ." will accomplish the reorientation.

SLOW MOTION

Flashback is a term borrowed from film, and I want to borrow another—*slow motion*—to point out a correlation between narrative time and significant detail.

When people experience moments of great intensity, their senses become especially alert and they register, literally, more than usual. In extreme crisis people have the odd sensation that time is slowing down, and they see, hear, smell, and remember ordinary sensations with extraordinary clarity. This psychological fact can work artistically in reverse: If you record detail with special focus and precision, it will create the effect of intensity. The phenomenon is so universal that it has become a standard film technique to register a physical blow, gunshot, sexual passion, or extreme fear in slow motion. The technique works forcefully in fiction. Note in the quotation from Rosellen Brown above how the trunk "snapped open and rose with the slow deliberation of a drawbridge."

Ian McEwan, in *A Child in Time,* demonstrates the technique:

> . . . He was preparing to overtake when something happened—he did not quite see what—in the region of the lorry's wheels, a hiatus, a cloud of dust, and then something black and long snaked through a hundred feet towards him. It slapped the windscreen, clung there a moment and was whisked away before he had time to understand what it was. And then—or did this happen in the same moment?—the rear of the lorry made a complicated set of movements, a bouncing and swaying, and slewed in a wide spray of sparks, bright even in sunshine. Something curved and metallic flew off to one side. So far Stephen had had time to move his foot towards the brake, time to notice a padlock swinging on a loose flange, and 'Wash me please' scrawled in grime. There was a whinnying of scraped metal and new sparks, dense enough to form a white flame which seemed to propel the rear of the lorry into the air.

Anyone who has faced some sort of accident can identify with the experience of sensuous slowdown McEwan records. But the slow-motion technique works also with experiences most of us have not had and to which we must submit in imagination:

> Blood was spurting from an artery in my left leg. I could not see it, and I do not recall how I knew it . . . for a short time I was alone with Patrick. I told myself I was in good hands, but I did not do this with words; I surrendered myself. I focused on breathing. I slowed my breathing, and tried to remain absolutely in the present, in each moment . . . waiting to die or stay alive was like getting an injection as a child, when you first learned not to think, but to gather yourself into the present, to breathe slowly, to relax your muscles, even your arm as the nurse swabbed it with alcohol, to feel the cool alcohol, to smell it, to feel your feet on the floor and see the color of the wall, and nothing else as your slow breathing opened you up to the incredible length and breadth and depth of one second.
>
> Andre Dubus, "Breathing"

And the technique will work when the intensity or trauma of the moment is not physical but emotional:

They were in the deep sleep of midnight when Pauline came quietly into her son's room and saw that there were two in his bed. She turned on the light. The room was cold and stuffy; warm in the core of it was the smell of a body she had known since she gave birth to him, unmistakable to her as the scent that leads a bitch to her puppy, and it was mingled with the scents of sexuality caressed from the female nectary. The cat was a rolled fur glove in an angle made by Sasha's bent knees. The two in the bed opened their eyes; they focussed out of sleep and saw Pauline. She was looking at them, at their naked shoulders above the covers . . .

Nadine Gordimer, A Sport of Nature

Central to this technique are the alert but matter-of-fact acceptance of the event and the observation of small, sometimes apparently random, details. The characters do not say, "Oh my God, we're going to die!" or "What an outrage!" Instead they record a padlock swinging, the cool feel of an alcohol swab, a cat rolled into the angle of bent knees.

Beginning writers often skimp on the elements of setting and time, probably out of dreary memories of long descriptions they have read. Certainly, we yawn over passages in which authors have indulged themselves in plum-colored homilies on the beauties of nature or the wealth of decor. But when atmosphere is well created, we do not experience it as description; we simply experience it. Yet just as dialogue that only offers information is too inert for the purposes of fiction, so too is description that only describes. The full realization of place and period, the revelation of a character through his house or of emotion through weather, the advancement of plot through changes in season and history, are among the pleasures of both writer and reader. Once you become adept at the skill of manipulating atmosphere, you will find that the necessity of setting your story in some particular place at some specific time is a liberating opportunity.

FURTHER THOUGHTS ON OPENINGS AND ENDINGS

The most important decisions regarding narrative time are where a story will begin and end, points that often change from first to final drafts. Originally discussed in relation to plot and story structure in chapter 2, some further reflection on these issues may be helpful at this point in your writing process.

- Where the writer begins writing the story is not necessarily where the final version of the story will begin. Chekhov advised his fellow writers to tear the story in half and begin in the middle; in fact, most stories begin as close to the end as possible.

- The first line of a story should hook readers' attention and pull them into the middle of the action. You want readers to feel like the train is leaving without them, so they'd better get on board and keep reading as fast as they can.

Nancy Huddleston Packer

- These are some first lines that command attention:

  "Call me Ishmael." (*Moby Dick*)

  "When I was little, I would think up ways to kill my daddy." (*Ellen Foster*)

  "In walks these three girls in nothing but bathing suits." ("A & P")

  "Those who had no papers entitling them to live lined up to die." (*Soul of Wood*)

  "I steal." ("Lawns")

  "Mother died today. Or maybe yesterday. I can't be sure." (*The Stranger*)

  "It was a bright cold day in April, and the clocks were striking thirteen." (*1984*)

  "As Gregor Samsa awoke one morning from uneasy dreams he found himself transformed in his bed into a gigantic insect." ("The Metamorphosis")

- Look through the stories anthologized here or elsewhere for first lines that seize your interest. Then try "ruining" a few of these first lines, to see how much difference even small adjustments can make ("My name is Ishmael" hardly has the same effect).

- John Gardner described a story as being a "vivid and continuous dream" that the writer creates in the mind of the reader. John L'Heureux applies this notion to the opening of a story, saying that the first paragraph should be designed to help readers "sink into the dream of the story." Like the opening frame of a movie, the opening paragraph entices readers into the story-dream, economically setting the tone, establishing the world, level of reality, and point of view; indirectly conveying information; and "promising" that certain concerns will be dealt with over the course of the story. Often the possible ground for some change or reversal is established in the opening as well.

- It will turn out that your first page has a lot to do with your last page. Just as in a poem, the first line has a lot to do with the last line, even though you didn't know what it was going to be.

  Doris Betts

- An ending that seems unsatisfactory might actually be fine. The trouble with the ending might be that the beginning or the middle doesn't set up the ending. A problem scene may not be a problem because of the way it is written. The revision of the ending might need to be carried out back in the beginning of the story. . . . You start writing the ending when you write your first word.

  Jerome Stern, *Making Shapely Fiction*

- The climax is that major event, usually toward the end, that brings all the tunes you have been playing so far into one major chord, after which at least one of your people is profoundly changed. If someone isn't changed, then what is the point of your story? For the climax, there must be a killing or a healing or a domination. It can be a real killing, a murder, or it can be a killing of the spirit, or of something terrible inside one's soul, or it can be a killing of a deadness within, after which the person becomes alive again. The healing may be about union, reclamation, the rescue of a fragile prize. But whatever happens, we need to feel that it was inevitable, that even though we may be amazed, it feels absolutely right, that of course things would come to this, of course they would shake down in this way.

  Anne Lamott, *Bird By Bird*

- I don't like endings that feel like they've got a big bow or THE END sign. What I really like in an ending is to feel satisfied that there was completion within the story, and yet, in some way, the story is still open.

  Jill McCorkle

Mount Olive

MONIFA A. LOVE

Mount Olive Primitive Baptist Church is two miles from my home. She is a calla lily growing in deep woods. On the third Sunday of each month, I sit in the middle of the fourth pew beneath the jade shower of the skylight. I join other ample women and our rail-thin sisters in testimony and tears. The hymns are cradles and bayonets— nesting our laments and pressing us on. We sing like we have known each other all of our lives; our voices thickly woven ropes, making ladders. Vaselined children with swinging feet draw on their legs and rock to the rhythm. Thin brown men in thinning brown suits punctuate the preacher's cadence with shouts and the percussion of their canes and polished shoes. The faithful rise and fall in the spirit like dolphin. Guardians in starched white uniforms resuscitate the overwhelmed with gentle, gloved pats to powdered faces. The elder women whisper underground words to call the faint back from their peaceful homes. They wield their fans with the skill of a signal corps. Elation evaporates from our bodies. Mercy rains down. Our tongues capture the tonic and we are saved. The service ends with hummingbirds calling "A-men" and the reverberation of small, powerful wings. We drift out to our cars. Well-worn leather bibles cross our hearts and touch the sky. The children pile into backseats to watch the church disappear through dusty windshields; their minds on early supper.

🎵 🎵 🎵

Suggestions for Discussion

1. Where is emotion conveyed through setting?
2. Why is it important that this story be told in first person? Who is the narrator?

Retrospect

3. Where does the prose rhythm mirror the mood or action?

Dark Corner

ROBERT MORGAN

I would die if anybody around here knowed I was one of the Branch girls that walked through this country back then. I don't think a soul here realizes that was me and my sisters. I sure haven't told them. If people had any hint of such a story it would spread faster than flu germs, narrated around in every baby shower and phone call.

If people knowed I was one of that big family that stopped here like beggars way back yonder I couldn't have married and lived on this creek. Not that these kind of people ever accept anybody that ain't their kinfolks even if they marry kin and live here forty years. I guess I was always meant to be a foreigner, but at least they wasn't no scandal. Nobody had dirt on me. I was lucky that way.

You take the people at the church. Somebody will whisper a person stole something from the building fund, or so and so was stepping out on her husband while he worked at the Du Pont plant, and next thing you know it's gone from one end of the valley to the other as fact. It don't pay to trust nothing you hear, unless you see it with your own eyes. And even then you can't always be sure.

We had got off the train at Greenville. I say got off, but it was more like they throwed us off, Mama and Daddy and me and my five sisters. Daddy had bought us tickets far as Atlanta, and we had come all the way from Brownsville, Texas. I don't know where he got the money for the tickets, except from selling what little we had. And maybe he sold some things we still owed money on. He had done it before.

Our tickets give out in Atlanta, and we was still two hundred miles from Uncle Dave's house west of Asheville. It was a great big train station and we stood around with our cardboard boxes tied up with string and Mama's trunk of clothes with a few pots and pans.

"Let's get on the train," Daddy said.

"We ain't got no tickets," I said.

"You hear what I say. Get on the train," Daddy said.

Crowds was pressing all around us, and my sisters was trying to look unconcerned, like tourists coming back from a month in Florida or a visit to St. Louis.

"They'll put us in jail," I said. I was always the one to argue with Daddy when he concocted his schemes. Not that it ever done any good except to get him riled. Nobody else would face up to him, and it just got me in trouble.

"We'll ride until they throw us off," Daddy said. "And then we'll have to walk."

"You mean they'll throw us off the train while it's moving?" I said.

"Do what your daddy says," Mama said. She was always telling me not to argue. The more she told me the worse I was for arguing. I feared something terrible was about to happen. We'd had hard times in Texas, but we never had been throwed off no train.

"Every mile we ride is one less we have to walk," Daddy said.

We got our things on that train just before it pulled out of the station. I was so worried I couldn't enjoy a minute of the ride. We had craved to get back from Texas to North Carolina. I was homesick to see the mountains, and our kinfolks at Asheville. But I didn't hardly notice the mountain we passed outside Atlanta and the hills and red clay fields. It was beginning to look like home, but all I could think of was what was going to happen.

Daddy told us what to do, and we got further than we ever hoped we would. I don't know if the conductor was just lazy, or we was lucky. It was a crowded train, and we moved around from one car to another. Once when we seen the conductor coming my sisters and me hid in the washroom till he had gone to the next car. Daddy and Mama slipped back into the baggage car once. Daddy had rode the railroads a lot, after the Confederate War, and he knowed all kinds of tricks.

I was sick with worry, and it seemed like the longest train ride I ever took. We made it past one stop in the Georgia hills, and then all the way across the Georgia line. My sisters and me held our boxes tight so we wouldn't lose them when we got caught and throwed off. The train rumbled and lurched along, and we moved from seat to seat and car to car. I felt like I was taking a headache and wanted to throw up.

We crossed a river into South Carolina, and though the hills was no higher the countryside seemed more familiar. The trees looked the way trees was supposed to, not like they did in Texas and Mississippi. It even seemed like the air was different. My hands was sweating so they stuck to the box I was carrying.

"Let's try to get to the back," I said to my oldest sister Katie. When we come out of the washroom the conductor was nowhere in sight. I was looking for Mama and Daddy. Daddy had said we should not stay all together, but I didn't want us to get thrown off the train at different places. I was trying to look down the length of the car when somebody tapped me on the shoulder. I jerked around so quick I dropped my box. It was the conductor. "Come with me," he said.

I felt my whole body go hot with embarrassment. When I bent over to pick up the box my face got even redder. As we followed the conductor through the cars to the front everybody watched us. Shirley, my littlest sister, begun to cry. I took her hand.

The conductor led us to the front of the first car. That surprised me, for I thought they would throw us off from the back, from the porch of the caboose. But Mama and Daddy was standing by the door of the first car. Daddy looked out the window at the passing fields. He did not look at me.

"The law allows us to put you off at the next stop," the conductor said. "That's all we can do to deadbeats and white trash."

Daddy turned to the conductor, then looked away.

"You low-down trash are lucky today," the conductor said. "The next stop is normally Anderson, but this train only slows down there to throw off the mail. You've got a free ride all the way to Greenville. Of course, when we get there I'll have the police arrest you."

Shirley started crying again, and I held her by the shoulders. We had had some bad times in Texas, but we had never been arrested. The sheriff did come to our house and carry all our things out into the road. They made us leave the house, and they dumped all our clothes and furniture out in the sand on the side of the road. That was painful, let me tell you.

And while we was standing there trying to decide what to do, and Daddy was talking about going to borrow a wagon, and to look for accommodations, to telegraph back to Asheville for money, the wind come up. The wind in Texas will hit like a pillow in your face and knock you back with surprise. It will come up out of nowhere and lift everything loose and snatch it away.

Before we knew it our clothes and Mama's bolt of cloth, her box of patterns, and all our magazines and papers got jerked off the pile and flung away. We all grabbed something, but the rest got whipped away. It was like trying to stop a flood with a poker.

"Catch my hatbox," Mama said. But the hatbox tumbled off the pile and went rolling along the dusty road. It broke open and all Mama's scarves and handkerchiefs went flying over the weeds. The wind jerked things out of our hands and sent them swirling up in the air. It wasn't a twister exactly, but it was like a twister.

As our things scattered and went flying Daddy run around trying to catch this and that. But everything he touched got pulled away. Finally he stopped and started laughing. His hat got blowed away and he faced into the wind, his hair pushed back, and laughed. It was a bad laugh. It was a laugh like a curse. He looked at us holding our boxes and dresses like he expected us to laugh too.

And then when the wind died down a little he started stomping and kicking the furniture that was left. He kicked a chair until he broke one of the legs, and then he picked up the chair and beat the other chairs. Mama had a dark green vase she had brought from North Carolina and he banged that till it broke. Everything that was little he stomped on.

When he stopped laughing and kicking we didn't have nothing left except what we held in our hands. In the weeds along the edge of the road we picked up a few stockings and clothes. They was still Mama's trunk left, and one little table we could sell to a second-hand store.

The rest of the way to Greenville we stood up on the train. It was like we didn't have a right to a seat now that we was found out. The conductor didn't say we couldn't set down, but we didn't just the same. I guess we was afraid he would tell us to get back up. Mama stood looking at the floor and Daddy watched out the windows. Shirley quit crying, and then Ella Mae started. I held them both, one on each side of me. Callie and Katie and Rita didn't say nothing.

It must have took another hour to get to the station in Greenville. I didn't hardly notice the little shacks with the rows of collards behind them outside town. We rolled by warehouses and cotton gins, coal yards, and water towers. It was beginning to rain.

The conductor made us stand on the train until everybody else had got off. The other passengers looked at us as they went by and whispered.

"Are they going to put us in jail?" Ella Mae whispered.

"Hush up," Mama said.

Shirley begun to cry again.

"Look what you've brung us to," Mama said to Daddy.

"At least you didn't have to walk all the way from Atlanta to Greenville," Daddy said.

Finally the conductor led us into the station. He took us to this little office where a policeman was waiting. Daddy carried Mama's trunk on his shoulder and set it down by the door.

"These are the people," the conductor said.

"Is the railroad preferring charges?" the policeman said.

"They are thieves," the conductor said.

It was musty in the office. The rainy air made the smell more noticeable. It was raining hard outside now, and you could hear horses and wagons splashing in the street. The conductor left because the train was ready to pull out.

The policeman didn't say nothing to us for a long time. He looked at us like we was stray cats they had picked up. I seen he enjoyed lording it over us, making us feel worser.

"You're hoping I will arrest you," he said finally. "So you'll get to spend a night in jail and get a free meal."

"We just want to be," Mama said.

"Trash like you are hard to break," the policeman said. "To put you in jail would waste the taxpayers' money."

"We didn't hurt nobody," Daddy said. "The train would have come to Greenville anyway, where we was on it or not."

"Shut up," the policeman hollered. He leaned his face about three inches from Daddy's. "You should be horsewhipped."

He made us stand there feeling awful for about half an hour. He called us trash and scum and deadbeats, then told us to get out of his sight and out of town. He said he wouldn't waste a penny of the taxpayers' money feeding us.

We carried our boxes and Daddy carried the trunk to the door of the station. It was raining hard, and we stepped to the side of the entrance under the overhang. The policeman followed us to the door. "Get on away from here," he said.

We started walking out into the rain. We held the boxes over our heads to protect us a little. We didn't even have newspapers to use for umbrellas. It was raining harder than ever. Once Daddy stopped and looked back, but the policeman was still standing at the door and he hollered, "Go on now, get!" like we was stray dogs he was chasing away.

I didn't know what we was going to do. It was pouring cold rain and the wet was beginning to sink under our arms. It had been spring in Texas, but it was late winter here. I just had a little old jacket, and it was already soaked.

Greenville was bigger than it seemed at first. At least it stretched out farther. I figured if we could get out in the country we could stand under a pine tree or maybe crawl into a hayloft. Maybe somebody would let us set on their porch until the rain slacked off.

They was nothing but stores along the street far as I could see. Puddles stood on the bricks, and in places the sidewalk was only mud. My teeth was chattering, and my feet squished inside my shoes.

"Where are we going?" Rita said. "I got rain in my face."

"Hush up," Mama said.

People hurried past us on the street, stepping out of our way. Horse apples stained puddles.

"I'm stopping here," Daddy said. He had to set the trunk down to open the door. It was a dark little store with "Kalin and Son" wrote on the window. Daddy carried the trunk inside and we followed him. It was so dark I couldn't see nothing at first, and it wasn't much warmer inside than it was out. But at least it was dry. A little man with glasses stood behind the counter, and they was a kind of cage around him. The place had a funny smell, like silver polish, and brass and bronze things.

"Don't touch anything," the little man said. He watched us crowding into the dark store, and dripping on the floor.

"I want to sell this," Daddy said, and pointed to the trunk.

"What's inside?" the man said.

"Just some clothes, and pots and pans," Daddy said.

"You want to sell the clothes?"

"I'll sell anything you will take," Daddy said.

"Don't drip on the furniture," the man hollered at Katie. She was standing close to a stuffed chair. Maybe she had started to set down in it. Everything in the store was used. I realized it was a pawnshop. "Let's see what you've got," the man said.

Daddy took out the blouse and stockings, the extra pair of pants, a frying pan and a saucepan, and laid them on the counter. He took out Mama's scissors and thimble, some knitting needles, and the family Bible.

"That's not for sale," Mama said.

"It's worth nothing to me," the man said. Daddy set the Bible aside. Then he lifted the leather trunk up on the counter, and the man looked inside.

"I'll give you two dollars," he said.

"For the trunk?" Daddy said.

"For all of it."

Daddy looked at Mama and back at the pawnbroker. "The scarves are worth five dollars," Mama said.

"Two dollars it is," the man said.

"I'll keep the pants," Daddy said.

"Keep the pants," the man said. "They're worn out anyway."

The man give Daddy two silver dollars and a box to put the Bible and pants in.

It seemed to be raining even harder when we stepped back into the street. It was like the sky was tearing to pieces and falling on us. The rain seemed cold and greasy. We walked past the rest of the stores and we walked past rows of houses that didn't have no paint on them. Wagons went by and splashed us, and we tried to stand aside out of their way. My dress got splattered with mud.

It was such a relief to get out of town finally into the country where they wasn't somebody watching us every step. We stopped at a store the first crossroads we come to. They was men playing checkers by the stove inside and they looked around at us like we had come from the moon. But the warm air felt mighty good.

Daddy bought a box of soda crackers and a can of sardines for each of us. We hadn't had nothing to eat since before Atlanta.

"Where is you all from?" the man at the counter said, looking at our wet dresses and dripping hair. Our boxes was wet and soft.

"We're from Asheville," Daddy said. The men around the stove had quit talking. Daddy walked over and held out his hands to the stove door. They shifted their chairs around to make room for him, and the rest of us moved closer to the stove.

We stood in the dark store and ate our sardines. I tried not to get juice on my dress or spill none on the floor. But I was so hungry I didn't care too much. When I finished the sardines I wiped my hands on the soda crackers before I ate them.

"Where is you all going?" the man at the counter said.

"We're going back to Asheville," Daddy said. "We've done been to Texas."

When Daddy sold our house near Asheville he said he could buy a thousand acres in Texas with the money. He said he would raise cattle in the sunshine, and not have to do no more hardscrabble farming. He wanted to get away from the fussing and backbiting in the Baptist church. He wanted to live in open country, and not in the shadow of a mountain. We went to Brownsville because that is where Great-grand-pappy had been give a square mile of land by the Republic of Texas for fighting in the war against Mexico. That was way back before the Confederate War even. Great-grandpappy had gone out there and fought against Santa Anna, but instead of taking his tract of land he come back to the mountains. The family had talked for years of going out there to Brownsville, and claiming that land.

"I'll bet they's a thousand head of cattle on that property," Uncle Dave would say at Christmas dinner.

"They might be gold on it," Daddy would say. "It's close to Mexico and they's gold in Mexico."

But when we got to Texas, after riding on the train for almost a week, Daddy went to the courthouse in Brownsville and they said they didn't have no record of Great-grandpappy ever owning any land grant. They asked him if he had any receipt for taxes paid on the land. Daddy didn't have no records at all except what he had been told by Grandpappy. They asked if he had any deed, or any charter from the Lone Star Republic.

So Daddy give up trying to claim the square mile of land and tried to buy a place. We had spent some of the money going out to Texas, but he still had about eight hundred dollars. We lived in a boardinghouse, and every day we went out looking for property to buy. But he found all the good ranch land and all the farmland wasn't for sale. Most of the places for sale wasn't fit for nothing. It was the poorest soil you ever seen. Wasn't nothing but a little brush growing on it. And it was too dry, even by the river, to do any real farming. People growed little gardens, but they had to carry water to them in buckets.

The place Daddy finally bought wasn't neither a farm nor a ranch. It was about a hundred acres outside town. Somebody had tried to grow cotton on it at one time. Daddy was going to try to raise cotton and some wheat. He bought an old horse and he put all us girls to hoeing cotton and carrying water for the garden. The water there tasted awful. We drawed it from a well and carried it in buckets to sprinkle on the peas and corn and potatoes.

It was like that ground had no life in it. The soil was dead, and had no grease at all. It was flat and starved of water. In Carolina you put a seed in the ground and it springs right up. In the hot bare soil at Brownsville the seeds went to sleep, and when they did sprout they made the sorriest corn you ever seen. I doubt we got five bushels to the acre.

Daddy kept spending his money and couldn't get none back. Times got leaner and leaner. We lived on cornbread, and we lived on taters. We lived on whatever we had. We run plumb out of money. They wasn't no money in Brownsville except what the big cattlemen brought in, the people with big ranches. They wasn't no jobs, and what they was was took by Mexicans. Mama and me done sewing, but they wasn't much of that to take in.

Every week they was less to eat. Daddy sold off his shotgun, and he sold off his horse, and he sold off his tools. We lived on grits, and then one week we lived on tomatoes because we had a few bushes that come in. It was always hot and dusty, or cold and wet, in Brownsville. They wasn't no in-between times. Maybe we was so hungry and worried we didn't enjoy the pretty weather when it come. I just remember mud, and I remember dust.

When you fall off your dresses don't fit no more. They hang on you like sacks. You wonder how you ever filled up your clothes. And when you're worried you get weak and lazy. You sleep late in the morning and you go to bed early at night. You fall asleep in the afternoon. You want to sleep and forget how bad things is. If you close your eyes and fall asleep, maybe you will dream things is better. You get to where you don't want to go any place or do anything. It all winds down, like you want to stop living, to stop the worry of living. I dreamed the world was a breast we sucked from, and sometimes the breast went dry.

Daddy tried to borrow money, and he tried to find work. He worked a few days for a blacksmith helping to shoe horses. But mostly they hired Mexicans because they didn't have to pay them nothing.

"The Lord is punishing us for leaving Asheville," Mama said.

Finally the sheriff come and throwed all our things out of the house.

When we left the store it was beginning to get dark. I felt some better after eating the sardines and soda crackers. But I hated to leave the warm stove and go back out in the rain. My box was so wet it was about to crumble.

"Where we going to sleep?" Katie said.

"Hush up," Mama said. "We'll find a place."

The road beyond the store was nothing but mud, and we walked along the edge in weeds and grass. The grass was getting green, but they wasn't nothing else putting out in upper South Carolina. We met a man in a wagon coming back from mill. He had several meal sacks in the bed behind the wagon seat. He looked at all us girls like we was something from a circus.

"How do," he said.

"How do," Daddy said.

They wasn't any houses that seemed friendly. Most was set way back from the road, and big dogs barked in the yards. You'd see a lantern or a lamp around some. Others was dark but had smoke coming out the chimney. I knowed Daddy was looking for an empty house. We was too many to stop and ask for hospitality. Or maybe we was too wet and discouraged to stop and ask anybody to take us in. If we'd had plenty of money, we'd have stopped at the biggest house and asked for room and board, and they would have took us in. And when we offered to pay like as not they wouldn't have took our money. It's all a matter of how you're feeling, and what people think of you. We was too wet and wore out to have any pride, or confidence.

Daddy had coughed in the store two or three times. I thought he must have got a cracker crumb caught in his throat, or the smoke from the stove was bothering him. But he coughed again several times while we was walking up the road.

It was almost dark when we seen the churchhouse ahead. They was tombstones in the yard, some of them leaning everywhich way like they was drunk. The church was just a little building, all dark and set back in the woods. They was a damp smell of wet leaves and oak trees all around.

"Let's stop here," Daddy said.

"This is a graveyard," Ella Mae said.

"Hush up," Mama said.

The meeting house door was unlocked, and we all climbed the board steps and slipped inside. It was so dark we couldn't see a thing.

"It smells musty," Rita said.

"It's colder than outside," Callie said, her teeth chattering. Daddy searched through his pockets and then struck a match. The churchhouse wasn't no bigger than a regular living room. It had benches and a platform up front for an altar. They was a barn lantern hanging from a rafter. The little stove at the side didn't look no bigger than a coal bucket with a pipe coming out of the top. They was a pile of cobs and kindling beside the stove.

"I'll start us a fire," Daddy said, and begun coughing again.

"I ain't sleeping in no church," Rita said. "Not with all the graves outside."

"Me neither," Shirley said.

"Hush up," Mama said.

"The Lord said he would provide," Daddy said. "And what he has provided is his own house."

"You can't sleep in a church," Callie said. "It would be a sin."

"Ain't no sin," Mama said.

The churchhouse was so cold we was all shivering and chattering our teeth. It seemed twice as cold inside as out in the rain. Daddy put some kindling and cobs in the stove and lit them. We crowded close to the light of the fire.

"Ain't we going to light the lantern?" Katie said.

"A light might attract attention," Daddy said. None of us argued, because none of us wanted anybody to see us in the church. We might not be doing anything wrong, but we didn't want anybody to catch us there either.

Daddy left the door on the little stove open, and as the fire caught it begun to throw out light and warmth. We moved two of the benches up to the stove and set down. We had been standing up and walking since Atlanta. It felt sweet in my bones to set down and hold my hands out to the fire.

Daddy started coughing again. I guess the dampness had sunk into his chest.

"You need something hot to drink," Mama said.

"Be alright," Daddy said. "Once I warm up."

Mama untied the box she had been carrying and tilted it toward the firelight. She looked through the combs and brushes and packets of needles and took out a crumpled paper sack. "This is the last of our coffee," she said. "I ground it before we left."

I could smell the coffee. It had been ground for three days, but still smelled good. Mama got up and started looking around the meeting house. She felt her way among the benches and around the edge of the church. Behind the altar she found a bucket and dipper. It was for the preacher to drink from when he got all hot and sweaty preaching. The bucket was about half full of water. Mama set the bucket on the stove and poured the coffee in.

"I hope that water's clean," Daddy said, and coughed again.

"It smells fresh," Mama said. "It was brought in on Sunday, I reckon,"

As the water begun to simmer and the bucket rattled on the stove it filled the church house with the smell of coffee. The water started to boil and Mama stirred the coffee with the dipper. It was like the fumes theirselves made us feel better. My face begun to tingle from getting warmed up after being cold and wet so long. My fingers started itching as I held them out to the stove.

After the coffee had boiled about five minutes Mama set the bucket off the stove. We didn't have nothing to drink out of but the dipper. We'd have to drink the coffee scalding hot. Of course Daddy always drunk his coffee that way anyway. Mama dipped out about a third of a dipper full and handed it to Daddy. "Sorry I don't have any cream," she said.

"And no sugar neither," Daddy said.

"And no crumpets at all," Mama said. She laughed, and Daddy laughed. We all started laughing. It felt so good to get warm, and to be setting down in the privacy of the church, we all felt a little lightheaded.

"Would you like some coffee, ma'am?" Mama said to me, after Daddy had drunk from the dipper.

"After you, ma'am," I said and giggled. We all laughed again. That's the way we drunk the coffee, passing the dipper around with exaggerated politeness.

"Coffee, ma'am?" I said to Rita.

"Please," she said, and took the dipper.

The coffee made us feel happy and silly. It warmed the mud inside our bones, and the soil in our blood. We laughed and drunk coffee, and then Daddy started coughing again.

"You need some pneumony salve," Mama said.

"I just need some sleep, and a day in the sunshine," Daddy said.

After we finished the coffee we pushed eight benches close as we could to the stove, and we laid down on them to sleep. I was so tired I must have dropped off, bang. As I slept I heard Daddy coughing, and I dreamed it was raining. I dreamed again the world was a great breast from which we sucked milk and coffee and time. Everybody sucked all they could, and sometimes the breast went dry. It was a long hard dream, like I was walking and working. When I woke the fire had died down in the stove and Daddy was still coughing.

We didn't have nothing to eat in the morning, and we didn't have no more coffee. And all the wood and cobs by the stove had been burned up too. We didn't even need to get dressed since we had slept in our clothes. Daddy said we had best get out of the church before it got completely light. "The Lord has shared his house with us," he said. "But some of the deacons may not be as kind."

Daddy was coughing bad, and his face was flushed like he had a fever.

"You ain't in no shape to walk," Mama said to him.

"I'm in better shape to walk than to set here and freeze to death," he said.

It had quit raining in the night, but it was wet outside, and they was a fog over everything. You couldn't even see the road from the church door. I was so stiff from sleeping on the bench, and so sore from walking the day before, it felt like I had to walk sideways. I needed to stretch and rest, and I needed to wash my face. But they wasn't nothing to do but start walking.

"I never thought I would sleep in a church," Rita said as we stepped onto the wet grass.

"It's bad luck to sleep near a graveyard," Callie said.

"Hush up," Mama said. "We've got a long way to walk and you might as well save your breath."

We walked through the fog up the muddy road. Daddy's coughing made dogs bark from houses we couldn't see. He would cough and we could hear echoes. We tried to surround the puddles and walk on the grass when we could. Men on horses passed us, and wagons passed us. But nobody offered us a ride. They was too many of us.

My feet was sore and my shoes was still wet from the day before. My right shoe had broke open down where the lace started. I had to favor that foot or I'd get more mud in the shoe. It was the grit in the mud that hurt. The grains of sand cut into my toe, making a blister.

But we couldn't walk fast anyway. Daddy had always walked ahead and the rest of us had to keep up with him. But that morning he walked slow, and he took little steps. Sometimes he coughed so hard he had to bend over holding to his knees.

By the middle of the morning it begun to clear up. The fog opened in places and you could see the sun. And then the fog just seemed to melt into itself and disappear. It was a clear morning, with everything wet and shining. You could see the blue mountains ahead. At first I thought they was clouds, but they went all the way across the world to the north. The fields everywhere was plowed and red and the pastures and yards dark green. You could see buds on the maples and oak trees looking red and light green.

As we kept walking Daddy's cough got worser. We come over a long hill and down beside a branch where they was a line of sycamore trees. Daddy coughed until he was red in the face, and he leaned over holding to a sapling. It was like he couldn't hardly get his breath. They was a house about a hundred yards ahead.

"You run down there and get a dipper of water," Mama said to me. "Ask them for a dipper of water."

I told Katie to come with me. We hurried on, trying not to step in puddles. In some places the branch had washed right across the road, and we had to jump across the muddy water. They was a big cur dog in the yard and it come growling out at us.

"Anybody home?" I hollered from the road. "We just want a dipper of water." They was smoke over to the side of the house and I walked around the edge of the yard till I seen this old woman bent over a washpot.

"Could we borrow a dipper of water?" I hollered. The dog growled and come toward me. But the woman looked up and called the dog to be quiet. I walked over to her.

"My daddy's took sick," I said, "and we need to borrow a cup of water."

"Where's your daddy?" the woman said. She had a snuff stick in her mouth and didn't take it out to talk.

"He's down at the road," I said.

"Why lord a mercy child," the woman said. "You bring him to the house. I don't want nobody sick out on the muddy road."

The woman called to the cur dog, and Katie and me went back to get Daddy and the rest of them. The old woman stood in the door watching us walk across her yard. The house was a big frame house, but it looked like it had never been painted.

"You all come right in and set down," the woman said. She had us set down around this big table in the kitchen. We must have been a sight in our wrinkled clothes. "Where you all from?" she said.

"We're going back to Asheville," Mama said. "We been to Texas."

"Lord a mercy, you mean you walked all the way from Texas?"

"We rode the train to Greenville," I said. I knowed we looked awful from being rained on and sleeping in our clothes. I wished I could wash my face and comb my hair.

The woman's name was Mrs. Lindsay. She said her man had gone to mill. He always went to mill when she done her washing. That way he didn't have to help carry water from the spring. She give Daddy a drink of water, and she made a pot of fresh coffee and served us biscuits with jelly. She give Daddy a spoon of sourwood honey for his cough.

I drunk the hot coffee but I couldn't eat the biscuits. They must have been cooked for breakfast for they was cold and greasy and the jelly made them seem slimy. I must have been half sick myself. I set there trying to be polite and watching Mama and my sisters eating biscuits and jelly, and I thought my stomach was going to turn. But the coffee made me feel better. And the honey seemed to help Daddy's cough.

"The roads is terrible this time of year," Mrs. Lindsay said. "A wagon will sink almost up to its axles." I knowed she was hoping we'd tell her what we had done in Texas, and why we was out on the road with just the clothes on our back and our little cardboard boxes. But they really wasn't no mystery to it. We was broke. Else why would a man and woman and half a dozen half-grown girls be out walking the muddy road? She was trying to be neighborly, but I could see she was curious.

After we drunk the coffee and they ate some biscuits it was time to start again. Mrs. Lindsay give us some sweet taters to take with us. Daddy was the quietest I'd ever seen him. He wheezed when he breathed, but he wasn't coughing so bad. "Much obliged," he said.

"It's turning off cold," Mrs. Lindsay said as we stepped out on the porch. And sure enough, the sky was bright and clear, and the wind had picked up a chill. It was coming from the north, right where we was headed.

Daddy used to tell us stories about way back yonder when he was a boy. He said they was a time, after the Texas war, when near about everybody wanted to go to Texas, because of all the free land. People that lived on little scratch-farms squeezing a living from rocks and trying to put in crops beside branches would just up and disappear. People left their little washed-out farms by the dozen. Sometimes they burned the barn and house down to get the nails. But most of the time they just left, took their horse and mule and wrote "GTT" on the doorpost, "Gone to Texas." Sometimes they might be going to Arkansas or even Indian Territory, but they still wrote "GTT" because Texas meant the West, which was a big place.

When Daddy got tired of farming his wore-out acres over in West Asheville, and after they had a big fuss and falling out at the church over who was to be the new preacher, and then when Grandma died and Mama and her sister Hettie got in this awful feud about who was to heir the silverware, Daddy just up and sold his little dab of land on the creek and we headed out for the west. "Gone to Texas" he would say to hisself and smile, like he had a secret, like he had found an answer to his troubles. I just wish it hadn't been so different from the way he planned.

After the coffee and Mrs. Lindsay's hot kitchen the wind felt fresh and thrilling in my face. After about a mile we come across the top of a hill and the air hit me smack in the face. It was getting colder, and we didn't really have no winter clothes. The mountains rose ahead, black and far away.

I buttoned my little jacket tighter around my neck and we all walked closer together. The sun was still warm on our backs. If we stayed closer together, those in the middle and back could keep warm. But whoever walked in front had to take the cold wind.

"You walk in front," Mama said to me. I knowed she would say that cause I was younger than her and Daddy and older than the other girls. It was my job to take the brunt of the cold air. I wished then I'd ate some of the greasy biscuits. When you're out in the cold without much clothes on you have to think yourself warm. It's like you make extra heat with your will to push the cold back. You make your whole body tense and alert and you meet the cold air with the heat of determination.

I got out in front and walked like I was shoving the cold air ahead of me. I was breaking trail through drifts and shoals of sharp wind. The road was drying and the lips of ruts was firm enough to walk on in places. The wind was drying a crust on the clay. Daddy started coughing again.

"Don't hurry so," Mama said.

We had to slow down and stop while Daddy coughed. The honey that soothed his throat was wearing off. Daddy must have coughed for five minutes, and then throwed up the coffee and biscuits. When we started walking again he was slower. He still carried the box with the Bible and pants in it. But he let the box dangle on its string while he coughed.

"We ought to find a place to stop, where you can lay down," Mama said.

"No, I'll be alright," he said.

I didn't see no hope but to keep walking. If we didn't get to Uncle Dave's soon it looked like we would all die on the road. I didn't feel no pride anymore about going back to Uncle Dave's with nothing. We was flat, and it didn't do no good to deny it.

The road was getting steeper, up and around hills. We crossed a creek on a shackly footlog. I noticed Daddy's hands was trembling as he held onto the rail. He had always been the strongest one of us, but he had lost his get up and go. Seemed like every house and cabin we passed had a woman doing her washing in the yard. Must have been raining for weeks, and the first clear day they was trying to catch up. You could smell the smoke from fires by the branch. The smoke got knocked around by wind and smelled like ashes and lye soap.

Finally the road went into a deep holler. They wasn't any more hills, and it seemed the tracks disappeared into the side of the mountain.

"This is Chestnut Springs," Mama said. And we all knowed what she meant. Chestnut Springs was at the heart of Dark Corner, where most of the blockaders, the whiskey men, lived and carried on their business. What she meant was it was getting toward the middle of the evening and we had to climb up the mountain and cross into North Carolina before night come. We didn't want to be caught in Dark Corner after dark.

"Girls ain't safe in this country," Mama said. "Ain't nobody safe after dark."

I tried to walk as fast as I could but not get ahead of the others. Daddy was wheezing and walking with a limp. His face had red splotches on it, like people's with a fever does. He limped not like he was crippled, but like he didn't have the strength to take regular steps.

The houses we passed looked like ordinary houses, except they was little. Every place had a dog that run out to bark and sniff at us. I knowed it was better to ignore dogs, or if one seemed mean you could reach out your hand and it would wag its tail. People come out on their porches and called their dogs back. They said "Howdy" and they watched us walk up the holler like they'd never seen such a big bunch of girls hoofing up the road. None of my sisters said nothing all evening. They was too tired, and too embarrassed.

The creek looked like it had red paint spilling into it from the patches behind the houses. It must have been raining for a long time for all the slant ground seemed full of wet weather springs bleeding muddy water.

We come to this place where the road went right up the side of the mountain, swinging back and forth. It was called the Winding Stairs and they must have been fifty switchbacks. I didn't see how a team with a wagon could make it around the sharp curves. It was more like climbing steps than a road.

Mama was helping Daddy to walk, and Katie started holding his arm too. They got on either side of him and held him up. There against the face of the mountain we was out of the worst wind. I begun to sweat a little. But Daddy was out of breath. We had to stop to let him rest. Nobody said nothing. We was all thinking the same thing, that we had to get up the mountain before nightfall.

When we finally reached the top of the Winding Stairs I seen it wasn't the top of the mountain at all, but just the lip of a valley floor. They was poplars growing along the branch and little houses set back on the sides of the ridge.

"Where is this?" I said to Mama.

"This is Chestnut Springs," she said.

They was several taverns clustered along the road at the place where spring water was piped down off the mountain into a trough. Horses was tied to rails and you could hear people laughing in all the places. In one house they was fiddle music. A woman that was only half dressed come to the door of a tavern and looked at us go by.

"Let's hurry on," Mama said. But she didn't need to say nothing. We was all afraid. I had always heard about the shooting and knife fights at Chestnut Springs. It was said somebody was killed about every week there.

A man wearing clean overalls and a fine gray hat stood on the porch of one of the houses. He tipped his hat to us and said, "How do."

I answered back, but not so as to seem too friendly. I didn't want to invite any attention to us. Just then Daddy started coughing again. He took the worst coughing fit he had yet, and Mama and Katie had to stop and hold him up. It was like every inch of his body heaved and shook with the coughs. He wasn't strong enough to take deep breaths anymore.

"Give him a drink of water," the man in overalls said. He brought a dipper from the spring. Mama waited a second, like she didn't want to have nothing to do with the strange man, and then she took the dipper. But Daddy was coughing so bad he almost choked when he took a sip from the dipper. He tried to swallow and coughed all the water out, spraying some of it on Katie's dress.

"Maybe he needs some medicine," the man said. He pulled a flat whiskey bottle from the pocket of his overalls. Other men had come to the door of the tavern and was watching us.

"He don't need none," Mama said.

"Might help him breathe," the man said. "It's the best medicine they is." The man's face was red, like he had had a lot of liquor hisself. But he didn't seem drunk. He was just calm and helpful. He held out the bottle and Daddy reached for it.

Daddy took a little swallow and held it in his mouth, like he was holding his breath to keep from coughing. And then he took a longer swallow. He coughed, but only after the liquor had gone down. "Much obliged," he said, wheezing.

"You folks need to find a place to stay," the man said.

"We'll be on our way," Mama said. We started walking on up the road. It was getting late, and the valley was in shadow. The music had stopped in the tavern and everybody in Chestnut Springs seemed to be gathered on the porches watching us. The sun was still bright way up on the peaks, but it would be dark in another hour. They would be frost that night; you could feel it in the air.

"I could find you a room," the man said. "My name is Zander Gosnell. I don't believe your husband should be out in this wind."

"We'll be on our way," Mama said. "We have to get to the top of the mountain by dark."

We started walking again. The man stood by the side of the road watching us. He had on the cleanest overalls I had ever seen. They even had a crease ironed in each leg. His hat did not have a wide brim, but it looked finer than any hat I had seen in Texas.

When we got further up the road the fiddle music started again. I didn't look but guessed the men drifted back into the taverns. I wanted to hurry, but they was no way Daddy could walk faster. They was nothing ahead but the holler in deep shadows.

"Where are we going to stay tonight?" Rita said.

"Hush up," Mama said. "We'll find a place."

"Daddy still has a dollar," Callie said.

"He has a dollar and twenty cents," Ella Mae said.

"He don't neither," Shirley said. "It's only a dollar and fifteen cents."

"Hush up," Mama said.

Daddy wasn't coughing as bad, but he seemed even weaker. It was like the liquor made him slow and sleepy. His eyes shined with the fever. Part of the time he walked with his eyes closed. "Are we home?" he said. That was the first time I knowed he was out of his head.

"We ain't home," Mama said. "We still got to cross the mountain."

"I want to stop," he said.

"We can't stop yet," Mama said. "We've got to climb over the mountain."

The road ahead looked so dark I wondered if that was why this place was called Dark Corner, because the mountain was so black and the holler so deep. I could hear wind high up on the ridge, but by the creek they was spring peepers chirping. I shivered, and I knowed Daddy must be cold.

I took Katie's place on the other side of Daddy, but he was having trouble standing up, much less walking. They was a crackling in his throat, and his breath come in quick pants. The sun was gone now and the cove looked cold and shadowy.

We got Daddy about a mile up the road, to where they was a steep turn over a little branch. Mama said it wasn't much more than a mile to the state line. I don't know what we would have done if we had got to the state line, for we was still thirty miles from Asheville, but it seemed to us desperate to get to North Carolina and out of Dark Corner by nightfall.

But Daddy wasn't able to go no further. We was almost carrying him. He was so sick and fevered he didn't know where he was no more. And I don't reckon he much cared either. He wasn't paying no attention, and he was hot as a stove. He would have fell down in the road if we hadn't held him up.

When the worst things happen to you it's like you know how bad they are, but you don't quite feel it. So many bad things had happened since we got to Brownsville that maybe I couldn't feel anything anymore. I was so worried I had quit shivering, for I knowed this was the worst we had seen. But it was like the Lord was protecting me by giving me something to do. Mama was wore out, and my sisters was tired and scared.

"You help hold Daddy," I said to Callie. She took him under his arm. He was leaning over now, breathing short and hard.

It was getting dark quick. I followed the branch from where it crossed the road. Laurel bushes growed almost in the water, and they was no clear place at all. We couldn't let Daddy lay down in the muddy road. I squeezed my eyes to see in the dark, and remembered you could see most at night by looking out of the corner of your eyes.

About fifty feet up the branch they was a little open place among the laurels. It was a kind of shelf of ground above the branch. I went back to the road and we almost carried Daddy up there through the bushes. It took all of us to help. Rita and Ella Mae brought the boxes, and they was crying. Mama didn't even tell them to hush up.

After we laid Daddy down in the leaves and put what scarves and clothes we had over him I looked in his pockets for the matches. He had a little box with not more than five or six matches in it. They was a hard wind on the ridge above, but by the branch we felt only gusts. I heaped up some leaves and little sticks, and after striking four of the matches finally got a fire going. Me and Callie felt around in the dark for more sticks, bigger sticks that wasn't too damp.

When the fire got brighter we could see Daddy had took even worser. He had the kind of pneumony that chokes you up and smothers you fast. His breath come in quicker and shorter pants, like his lungs was full of water. The fire lit his face and the laurel bushes like some terrible dream. Mama set by Daddy and held his hand. She didn't say nothing.

To keep from looking at Daddy smothering I went out in the dark to gather more sticks. It was going to be a long cold night. I built the fire higher to warm us. The flames crackled and the branch splashed below us. Up on the ridge the wind roared like a train in a tunnel. I lost track of time, but sometime during the night I heard this voice and woke up. There at the edge of the laurels was Zander Gosnell. He held a blanket and jug.

"I thought you might need these," he said.

We wrapped Daddy in the blanket and give him a drink from the jug. Zander helped me gather more sticks for the fire. My sisters was still asleep, and Mama just set by Daddy and wouldn't say nothing. Zander and me bent over Daddy, giving him drinks from the jug. I watched our shadows move on the laurel bushes. They stretched like some kind of puppets in a story you couldn't make any sense of.

Sometime before daylight Daddy quit breathing. He gasped harder and shorter, harder and shorter, and then he just stopped. I don't think he knowed a thing after it got dark. I don't think he knowed where he was. He kept talking all night about farming and planting corn. He said it was time to plant the corn.

After Daddy was dead and turning cold in the dawn, we was all so washed out we didn't know what to do. I can't guess what would have happened if it hadn't been for Zander Gosnell. I suppose we would have buried Daddy with our own hands. But Zander got some of his friends from Chestnut Springs and they carried Daddy down to one of the taverns. They laid the body out and made a coffin for him. Mama said Daddy wanted to be buried in North Carolina.

Some of the women there at Chestnut Springs, some of the bad women, helped us clean our clothes and even give us some new things to wear. They was bright and silky things.

Then they put the coffin in a wagon and drove us to the top of the mountain, to the Double Springs Cemetery. And the liquor people had even got a preacher to preach the funeral by the grave. I don't know what we would have done without them.

We stood there in the cold wind while they funeraled Daddy. We must have looked like beggars and vagabonds in our odd pieces of clothes. The people of the community come out to see us. That's why I'm glad nobody knows I was one of that family. I didn't dream I would marry some day and come back here. I always wanted to thank those people in Chestnut Springs, but was afraid to give myself away. I've put flowers on Daddy's grave over at Double Springs many a time, but I'm glad people never knowed I was one of that family of girls. It was hard enough to live through that time, without having to live it down.

🐦 🐦 🐦

Suggestions for Discussion

1. Which details help create the reality of a past time? Which lines of dialogue?
2. Identify descriptions of setting or weather that reflect the narrator's emotion.

Retrospect

3. How do dialect and first-person narration enhance this story?
4. The author has said of this story, "My experience has been that the disreputable, and those living slightly beyond the law, are as apt to help you when you are in real trouble as the more respectable members of the community." How does he show this without spelling it out?

☐

Which Is More Than I Can Say About Some People

LORRIE MOORE

It was a fear greater than death, according to the magazines. Death was number four. After mutilation, three, and divorce, two. Number one, the real fear, the one death could not even approach, was public speaking. Abby Mallon knew this too well. Which is why she had liked her job at American Scholastic Tests: she got to work with words in a private way. The speech she made was done in the back, alone, like little shoes cobbled by an elf: spider is to web as weaver is to *blank*. That one was hers. She was proud of that.

Also, *blank* is to heartache as forest is to bench.

But then one day the supervisor and the AST district coordinator called her upstairs. She was good, they said, but perhaps she had become *too* good, too *creative*, they suggested, and gave her a promotion out of the composing room and into the high school auditoriums of America. She would have to travel and give speeches, tell high school faculty how to prepare students for the entrance exams, meet separately with the juniors and seniors and answer their questions unswervingly, with authority and grace. "You may have a vacation first," they said, and handed her a check.

"Thank you," she said doubtfully. In her life, she had been given the gift of solitude, a knack for it, but now it would be of no professional use. She would have to become a people person.

"A *peeper* person?" queried her mother on the phone from Pittsburgh.

"*People*," said Abby.

"Oh, those," said her mother, and she sighed the sigh of death, though she was strong as a brick.

Of all Abby's fanciful ideas for self-improvement (the inspirational video, the breathing exercises, the hypnosis class), the Blarney Stone, with its whoring barter of eloquence for love—O GIFT OF GAB, read the T-shirts—was perhaps the most extreme. Perhaps. There had been, after all, her marriage to Bob, her boyfriend of many years, after her dog, Randolph, had died of kidney failure and marriage to Bob seemed the only way to overcome her grief. Of course, she had always admired the idea of marriage, the citizenship and public speech of it, the innocence rebestowed, and Bob was big and comforting. But he didn't have a lot to say. He was not a verbal man. Rage gave him syntax—but it just wasn't enough! Soon Abby had begun to keep him as a kind of pet, while she quietly looked for distractions of depth and consequence. She looked for words. She looked for ways with words. She worked hard to befriend a lyricist from New York—a tepid, fair-haired, violet-eyed bachelor—she and most of the doctors' wives and arts administrators in town. He was newly arrived, owned no car, and wore the same tan blazer every day. "Water, water everywhere but not a drop to drink," said the bachelor lyricist once, listening wanly to the female chirp of his phone messages. In his apartment, there were no novels or book-cases. There was one chair, as well as a large television set, the phone machine, a rhyming dictionary continuously renewed from the library, and a coffee table. Women brought him meals, professional introductions, jingle commissions, and cash grants. In return, he brought them small piebald stones from the beach, or a pretty weed from the park. He would stand behind the coffee table and recite his own songs, then step back and wait fearfully to be seduced. To be lunged at and de-voured by the female form was, he believed, something akin to applause. Sometimes he would produce a rented lute and say, "Here, I've just composed a melody to go with my Creation verse. Sing along with me."

And Abby would stare at him and say, "But I don't know the tune. I haven't heard it yet. You just made it up, you said."

Oh, the vexations endured by a man of poesy! He stood paralyzed behind the coffee table, and when Abby did at last step forward, just touch him, to take his pulse, perhaps, *to capture one of his arms in an invisible blood-pressure cuff!* he crum-pled and shrank. "Please don't think I'm some kind of emotional Epstein-Barr," he said, quoting from other arguments he'd had with women. "I'm not indifferent or dispassionate. I'm calm. I'm romantic, but I'm calm. I have appetites, but I'm very calm about them."

When she went back to her husband—"Honey, you're home!" Bob exclaimed—she lasted only a week. Shouldn't it have lasted longer—the mix of loneliness and lust and habit she always felt with Bob, the mix that was surely love, for it so often felt like love, how could it not be love, surely nature intended it to be, surely nature with its hurricanes and hail was counting on this to suffice? Bob smiled at her and said nothing. And the next day, she booked a flight to Ireland.

How her mother became part of the trip, Abby still couldn't exactly recall. It had something to do with a stick shift: how Abby had never learned to drive one. "In my day and age," said her mother, "everyone learned. We all learned. Women had skills. They knew how to cook and sew. Now women have no skills."

The stick shifts were half the rental price of the automatics.

"If you're looking for a driver," hinted her mother, "I can still see the road."

"That's good," said Abby.

"And your sister Theda's spending the summer at your aunt's camp again." Theda had Down's syndrome, and the family adored her. Every time Abby visited, Theda would shout, "Look at you!" and throw her arms around her in a terrific hug. "Theda's, of course, sweet as ever," said her mother, "which is more than I can say about some people."

"That's probably true."

"I'd like to see Ireland while I can. Your father, when he was alive, never wanted to. I'm Irish, you know."

"I know. One-sixteenth."

"That's right. Of course, your father was Scottish, which is a totally different thing."

Abby sighed. "It seems to me that *Japanese* would be a totally different thing."

"*Japanese?*" hooted her mother. "Japanese is close."

And so in the middle of June, they landed at the Dublin airport together. "We're going to go all around this island, every last peninsula," said Mrs. Mallon in the airport parking lot, revving the engine of their rented Ford Fiesta, "because that's just the kind of crazy Yuppies we are."

Abby felt sick from the flight; and sitting on what should be the driver's side but without a steering wheel suddenly seemed emblematic of something.

Her mother lurched out of the parking lot and headed for the nearest roundabout, crossing into the other lane only twice. "I'll get the hang of this," she said. She pushed her glasses farther up on her nose and Abby could see for the first time that her mother's eyes were milky with age. Her steering was jerky and her foot jumped around on the floor, trying to find the clutch. Perhaps this had been a mistake.

"Go straight, Mom," said Abby, looking at her map.

They zigged and zagged to the north, up and away from Dublin, planning to return to it at the end, but now heading toward Drogheda, Abby snatching up the guidebook and then the map again and then the guidebook, and Mrs. Mallon shouting, "What?" or "Left?" or "This can't be right; let me see that thing." The Irish countryside opened up before them, its pastoral patchwork and stone walls and its chimney aroma of turf fires like some other century, its small stands of trees, abutting fields populated with wildflowers and sheep dung and cut sod and cows with ear tags, beautiful as women. Perhaps fairy folk lived in the trees! Abby saw immediately that to live amid the magic feel of this place would be necessarily to believe in magic. To live here would make you superstitious, warm-hearted with secrets, unrealistic. If you were literal, or practical, you would have to move—or you would have to drink.

They drove uncertainly past signs to places unmarked on the map. They felt lost—but not in an uncharming way. The old narrow roads with their white side markers reminded Abby of the vacations the family had taken when she was little, the cow-country car trips through New England or Virginia—in those days before there were interstates, or plastic cups, or a populace depressed by asphalt and French fries. Ireland was a trip into the past of America. It was years behind, unmarred, like a story or a dream or a clear creek. I'm a child again, Abby thought. I'm back. And just as when she was a child, she suddenly had to go to the bathroom.

"I have to go to the bathroom," she said. To their left was a sign that said ROAD WORKS AHEAD, and underneath it someone had scrawled, "No, it doesn't."

Mrs. Mallon veered the car over to the left and slammed on the brakes. There were some black-faced sheep haunch-marked in bright blue and munching grass near the road.

"Here?" asked Abby.

"I don't want to waste time stopping somewhere else and having to buy something. You can go behind that wall."

"Thanks," said Abby, groping in her pocketbook for Kleenex. She missed her own apartment. She missed her neighborhood. She missed the plentiful U-Pump-Itt's, where, she often said, at least they spelled *pump* right! She got out and hiked back down the road a little way. On one of the family road trips thirty years ago, when she and Theda had had to go to the bathroom, their father had stopped the car and told them to "go to the bathroom in the woods." They had wandered through the woods for twenty minutes, looking for the bathroom, before they came back out to tell him that they hadn't been able to find it. Her father had looked perplexed, then amused, and then angry—his usual pattern.

Now Abby struggled over a short stone wall and hid, squatting, eyeing the sheep warily. She was spacey with jet lag, and when she got back to the car, she realized she'd left the guidebook back on a stone and had to turn around and retrieve it.

"There," she said, getting back in the car.

Mrs. Mallon shifted into gear. "I always feel that if people would just be like animals and excrete here and there rather than a single agreed-upon spot, we wouldn't have any pollution."

Abby nodded. "That's brilliant, Mom."

"Is it?"

They stopped briefly at an English manor house, to see the natural world cut up into moldings and rugs, wool and wood captive and squared, the earth stolen and embalmed and shellacked. Abby wanted to leave. "Let's leave," she whispered.

"What is it with you?" complained her mother. From there, they visited a neo-lithic passage grave, its floor plan like a birth in reverse, its narrow stone corridor spilling into a high, round room. They took off their sunglasses and studied the Celtic curlicues. "Older than the pyramids," announced the guide, though he failed to address its most important feature, Abby felt: its deadly maternal metaphor.

"Are you still too nervous to cross the border to Northern Ireland?" asked Mrs. Mallon.

"Uh-huh." Abby bit at her thumbnail, tearing the end off it off like a tiny twig.

"Oh, come on," said her mother. "Get a grip."

And so they crossed the border into the North, past the flak-jacketed soldiers patrolling the neighborhoods and barbed wire of Newry, young men holding automatic weapons and walking backward, block after block, their partners across the street, walking forward, on the watch. Helicopters flapped above. "This is a little scary," said Abby.

"It's all show," said Mrs. Mallon breezily.

"It's a scary show."

"If you get scared easily."

Which was quickly becoming the theme of their trip—Abby could see that already. That Abby had no courage and her mother did. And that it had forever been that way.

"You scare too easily," said her mother. "You always did. When you were a child, you wouldn't go into a house unless you were reassured there were no balloons in it."

"I didn't like balloons."

"And you were scared on the plane coming over," said her mother.

Abby grew defensive. "Only when the flight attendant said there was no coffee because the percolator was broken. Didn't you find that alarming? And then after all that slamming, they still couldn't get one of the overhead bins shut." Abby remembered this like a distant, bitter memory, though it had only been yesterday. The plane had taken off with a terrible shudder, and when it proceeded with the rattle of an old subway car, particularly over Greenland, the flight attendant had gotten on the address system to announce there was nothing to worry about, especially when you think about "how heavy air really is."

Now her mother thought she was Tarzan. "I want to go on that rope bridge I saw in the guidebook," she said.

On page 98 in the guidebook was a photograph of a rope-and-board bridge slung high between two cliffs. It was supposed to be for fishermen, but tourists were allowed, though they were cautioned about strong winds.

"Why do you want to go on the rope bridge?" asked Abby.

"Why?" replied her mother, who then seemed stuck and fell silent.

For the next two days, they drove east and to the north, skirting Belfast, along the coastline, past old windmills and sheep farms, and up out onto vertiginous cliffs that looked out toward Scotland, a pale sliver on the sea. They stayed at a tiny stucco bed-and-breakfast, one with a thatched roof like Cleopatra bangs. They slept lumpily, and in the morning in the breakfast room with its large front window, they ate their cereal and rashers and black and white pudding in an exhausted way, going through the motions of good guesthood—"Yes, the troubles," they agreed, for who could say for certain whom you were talking to? It wasn't like race-riven America, where you always knew. Abby nodded. Out the window, there was a breeze, but she couldn't hear the faintest rustle of it. She could only see it silently moving the dangling branches of the sun-sequined spruce, just slightly, like objects hanging from a rearview mirror in someone else's car.

She charged the bill to her Visa, tried to lift both bags, and then just lifted her own.

"Goody-bye! Thank you!" she and her mother called to their host. Back in the car, briefly, Mrs. Mallon began to sing "Toora-loora-loora." "'Over in Killarney, many years ago,'" she warbled. Her voice was husky, vibrating, slightly flat, coming in just under each note like a saucer under a cup.

And so they drove on. The night before, a whole day could have shape and design. But when it was upon you, it could vanish tragically to air.

They came to the sign for the rope bridge.

"I want to do this," said Mrs. Mallon, and swung the car sharply right. They crunched into a gravel parking lot and parked; the bridge was a quarter-mile walk from there. In the distance, dark clouds roiled like a hemorrhage, and the wind was picking up. Rain mizzled the windshield.

"I'm going to stay here," said Abby.

"You are?"

"Yeah."

"Whatever," said her mother in a disgusted way, and she got out, scowling, and trudged down the path to the bridge, disappearing beyond a curve.

Abby waited, now feeling the true loneliness of this trip. She realized she missed Bob and his warm, quiet confusion; how he sat on the rug in front of the fireplace, where her dog, Randolph, used to sit; sat there beneath the five Christmas cards they'd received and placed on the mantel—five, including the one from the paperboy—sat there picking at his feet, or naming all the fruits in his fruit salad, remarking life's great variety! Or asking what was wrong (in his own silent way), while poking endlessly at a smoldering log. She thought, too, about poor Randolph, at the vet, with his patchy fur and begging, dying eyes. And she thought about the pale bachelor lyricist, how he had once come to see her, and how he hadn't even placed enough pressure on the doorbell to make it ring, and so had stood there waiting on the porch, holding a purple coneflower, until she just happened to walk by the front window and see him standing there. *O poetry!* When she invited him in, and he gave her the flower and sat down to decry the coded bloom and doom of all things, decry as well his own unearned deathlessness, how everything hurtles toward oblivion, except words, which assemble themselves in time like molecules in space, for God was an act—an act!—of language, it hadn't seemed silly to her, not really, at least not *that* silly.

The wind was gusting. She looked at her watch, worried now about her mother. She turned on the radio to find a weather report, though the stations all seemed to be playing strange, redone versions of American pop songs from 1970. Every so often, there was a two-minute quiz show—Who is the president of France? Is a tomato a vegetable or a fruit?—questions that the caller rarely if ever answered correctly, which made it quite embarrassing to listen to. Why did they do it? Puzzles, quizzes, game shows. Abby knew from AST that a surprising percentage of those taking the college entrance exams never actually applied to college. People just loved a test. Wasn't that true? People loved to put themselves to one.

Her mother was now knocking on the glass. She was muddy and wet. Abby unlocked the door and pushed it open. "Was it worth it?" Abby asked.

Her mother got in, big and dank and puffing. She started the car without looking at her daughter. "What a bridge," she said finally.

The next day, they made their way along the Antrim coast, through towns bannered with Union Jacks and Scottish hymns, down to Derry with its barbed wire and IRA scrawlings on the city walls—"John Major is a Zionist Jew" ("Hello," said a British officer when they stopped to stare)—and then escaping across bandit country, and once more down across the border into the south, down the Donegal coast, its fishing villages like some old, never-was Cape Cod. Staring out through the windshield, off into the horizon, Abby began to think that all the beauty and ugliness and turbulence one found scattered through nature, one could also find in people themselves, all collected there, all together in a single place. No matter what terror or loveliness the earth could produce—winds, seas—a person could produce the same, lived with the same, lived with all that mixed-up nature swirling inside, every bit. There was nothing as complex in the world—no flower or stone—as a single hello from a human being.

Once in a while, Abby and her mother broke their silences with talk of Mrs. Mallon's job as office manager at a small flashlight company—"I had to totally rearrange our insurance policies. The dental and Major Medical were eating our lunch!"—or with questions about the route signs, or the black dots signifying the auto deaths. But mostly, her mother wanted to talk about Abby's shaky marriage and what she was going to do. "Look, another ruined abbey," she took to saying every time they passed a heap of medieval stones.

"When you going back to Bob?"

"I went back," said Abby. "But then I left again. Oops."

Her mother sighed. "Women of your generation are always hoping for some other kind of romance than the one they have," said Mrs. Mallon. "Aren't they?"

"Who knows?" said Abby. She was starting to feel a little tight-lipped with her mother, crammed into this space together like astronauts. She was starting to have a highly inflamed sense of event: a single word rang and vibrated. The slightest movement could annoy, the breath, the odor. Unlike her sister, Theda, who had always remained sunny and cheerfully intimate with everyone, Abby had always been darker and left to her own devices; she and her mother had never been very close. When Abby was a child, her mother had always repelled her a bit—the oily smell of her hair, her belly button like a worm curled in a pit, the sanitary napkins in the bathroom wastebasket, horrid as a war, then later strewn along the curb by raccoons who would tear them from the trash cans at night. Once at a restaurant, when she was little, Abby had burst into an unlatched ladies' room stall, only to find her mother sitting there in a dazed and unseemly way, peering out at her from the toilet seat like a cuckoo in a clock.

There were things one should never know about another person.

Later, Abby decided that perhaps it hadn't been her mother at all.

Yet now here she and her mother were, sharing the tiniest of cars, reunited in a wheeled and metal womb, sharing small double beds in bed-and-breakfasts, waking up with mouths stale and close upon each other, or backs turned and rocking in angry-seeming humps. *The land of ire!* Talk of Abby's marriage and its possible demise trotted before them on the road like a herd of sheep, insomnia's sheep, and it made Abby want to have a gun.

"I never bothered with conventional romantic fluff," said Mrs. Mallon. "I wasn't the type. I always worked, and I was practical, put myself forward, and got things done and over with. If I liked a man, I asked him out myself. That's how I met your father. I asked him out. I even proposed the marriage."

"I know."

"And then I stayed with him until the day he died. Actually, three days after. He was a good man." She paused. "Which is more than I can say about some people."

Abby didn't say anything.

"Bob's a good man," added Mrs. Mallon.

"I didn't say he wasn't."

There was silence again between them now as the countryside once more unfolded its quilt of greens, the old roads triggering memories as if it were a land she had traveled long ago, its mix of luck and unluck like her own past; it seemed stuck in time, like a daydream or a book. Up close the mountains were craggy, scabby with rock and green, like a buck's antlers trying to lose their fuzz. But distance filed the gaps with moss. Wasn't that the truth? Abby sat quietly, glugging Ballygowan water from a plastic bottle and popping Extra Strong Mints. Perhaps she should turn on the radio, listen to one of the call-in quizzes or to the news. But then her mother would take over, fiddle and retune. Her mother was always searching for country music, songs with the words *devil woman*. She loved those.

"Promise me one thing," said Mrs. Mallon.

"What?" said Abby.

"That you'll try with Bob."

At what price? Abby wanted to yell, but she and her mother were too old for that now.

Mrs. Mallon continued, thoughtfully, with the sort of pseudowisdom she donned now that she was sixty. "Once you're with a man, you have to sit still with him. As scary as it seems. You have to be brave and learn to reap the benefits of inertia," and here she gunned the motor to pass a tractor on a curve. LOOSE CHIPPINGS said the sign. HIDDEN DIP. But Abby's mother drove as if these were mere cocktail party chatter. A sign ahead showed six black dots.

"Yeah," said Abby, clutching the dashboard. "Dad was inert. Dad was inert, except that once every three years he jumped up and socked somebody in the mouth."

"That's not true."

"It's basically true."

In Killybegs, they followed the signs for Donegal City. "You women today," Mrs. Mallon said. "You expect too much."

"If it's Tuesday, this must be Sligo," said Abby. She had taken to making up stupid jokes. "What do you call a bus with a soccer team on it?"

"What?" They passed a family of gypsies, camped next to a mountain of car batteries they hoped to sell.

"A football coach." Sometimes Abby laughed raucously, and sometimes not at all. Sometimes she just shrugged. She was waiting for the Blarney Stone. That was all she'd come here for, so everything else she could endure.

They stopped at a bookshop to get a better map and inquire, perhaps, as to a bathroom. Inside, there were four customers: two priests reading golf books, and a mother with her tiny son, who traipsed after her along the shelves, begging, "Please, Mummy, just a wee book, Mummy. Please just a wee book." There was no better map. There was no bathroom. "Sorry," the clerk said, and one of the priests glanced up quickly. Abby and her mother went next door to look at the Kinsale smocks and wool sweaters—tiny cardigans that young Irish children, on sweltering summer days of seventy-one degrees, wore on the beach, over their bathing suits. "So cute," said Abby, and the two of them wandered through the store, touching things. In the back by the wool caps, Abby's mother found a marionette hanging from a ceiling hook and began to play with it a little, waving its arms to the store music, which was a Beethoven concerto. Abby went to pay for a smock, ask about a bathroom or a good pub, and when she came back, her mother was still there, transfixed, conducting the concerto with the puppet. Her face was arranged in a girlish joy, luminous, as Abby rarely saw it. When the concerto was over, Abby handed her a bag. "Here," she said, "I bought you a smock."

Mrs. Mellon let go of the marionette, and her face darkened. "I never had a real childhood," she said, taking the bag and looking off into the middle distance. "Being the oldest, I was always my mother's confidante. I always had to act grown-up and responsible. Which wasn't my natural nature." Abby steered her toward the door. "And then when I really was grown up, there was Theda, who needed all my time, and your father of course, with his demands. But then there was you. You I liked. You I could leave alone."

"I bought you a smock," Abby said again.

They used the bathroom at O'Hara's pub, bought a single mineral water and split it, then went on to the Drumcliff cemetery to see the dead Yeatses. Then they sped on toward Sligo City to find a room, and the next day were up and out to Knock to watch lame women, sick women, women who wanted to get pregnant ("Knocked up," said Abby) rub their rosaries on the original stones of the shrine. They drove down to Clifden, around Connemara, to Galway and Limerick—"There once were two gals from America, one named Abby and her mother named Erica. . . ." They sang, minstrel speed demons around the Ring of Kerry, its palm trees and blue and pink hydrangea like a set from an operetta. "Playgirls of the Western World!" exclaimed her mother. They came to rest, at dark, near Ballylickey, in a bed-and-breakfast, a former hunting lodge, in a glen just off the ring. They ate a late supper of toddies and a soda bread their hostess called "Curranty Dick."

"Don't I know it," said Mrs. Mallon. Which depressed Abby, like a tacky fixture in a room, and so she excused herself and went upstairs, to bed.

It was the next day, through Ballylickey, Bantry, Skibbereen, and Cork, that they entered Blarney. At the castle, the line to kiss the stone was long, hot, and frightening. It jammed the tiny winding stairs of the castle's suffocating left tower, and people pressed themselves against the dark wall to make room for others who had lost their nerve and were coming back down.

"This is ridiculous," said Abby. But by the time they'd reached the top, her annoyance had turned to anxiety. To kiss the stone, she saw, people had to lie on their backs out over a parapet, stretching their necks out to place their lips on the underside of a supporting wall where the stone was laid. A strange-looking leprechaunish man was squatting at the side of the stone, supposedly to help people arch back, but he seemed to be holding them too loosely, a careless and sadistic glint in his eyes, and some people were changing their minds and going back downstairs, fearful and inarticulate as ever.

"I don't think I can do this," said Abby hesitantly, tying her dark raincoat more tightly around her.

"Of course you can," said her mother. "You've come all this way. This is why you came." Now that they were at the top of the castle, the line seemed to be moving quickly. Abby looked back, and around, and the view was green and rich, and breathtaking, like a photo soaked in dyes.

"Next!" she heard the leprechaun shouting.

Ahead of them, a German woman was struggling to get back up from where the leprechaun had left her. She wiped her mouth and made a face. "That vuz awfhul," she grumbled.

Panic seized Abby. "You know what? I don't want to do this," she said again to her mother. There were only two people ahead of them in line. One of them was now getting down on his back, clutching the iron supports and inching his hands down, arching at the neck and waist to reach the stone, exposing his white throat. His wife stood above him, taking his picture.

"But you came all this way! Don't be a ninny!" Her mother was bullying her again. It never gave her courage; in fact, it deprived her of courage. But it gave her bitterness and impulsiveness, which could look like the same thing.

"Next," said the leprechaun nastily. He hated these people; one could see that. One could see he half-hoped they would go crashing down off the ledge into a heap of raincoats, limbs, and traveler's checks.

"Go on," said Mrs. Mallon.

"I can't," Abby whined. Her mother was nudging and the leprechaun was frowning. "I can't. You go."

"No. Come on. Think of it as a test." Her mother gave her a scowl, unhinged by something lunatic in it. "You work with tests. And in school, you always did well on them."

"For tests, you have to study."

"You studied!"

"I didn't study the right thing."

"Oh, Abby."

"I can't," Abby whispered. "I just don't think I can." She breathed deeply and moved quickly. "Oh—okay." She threw her hat down and fell to the stone floor fast, to get it over with.

"Move back, move back," droned the leprechaun, like a train conductor.

She could feel now no more space behind her back; from her waist up, she was out over air and hanging on only by her clenched hands and the iron rails. She bent her head as far back as she could, but it wasn't far enough.

"Lower," said the leprechaun.

She slid her hands down farther, as if she were doing a trick on a jungle gym. Still, she couldn't see the stone itself, only the castle wall.

"Lower," said the leprechaun.

She slid her hands even lower, bent her head back, her chin skyward, could feel the vertebrae of her throat pressing out against the skin, and this time she could see the stone. It was about the size of a microwave oven and was covered with moisture and dirt and lipstick marks in the shape of lips—lavender, apricot, red. It seemed very unhygienic for a public event, filthy and wet, and so now instead of giving it a big smack, she blew a peck at it, then shouted, "Okay, help me up, please," and the leprechaun helped her back up.

Abby stood and brushed herself off. Her raincoat was covered with whitish mud. "Eeyuhh," she said. But she had done it! At least sort of. She put her hat back on. She tipped the leprechaun a pound. She didn't know how she felt. She felt nothing. Finally, these dares one made oneself commit didn't change a thing. They were all a construction of wish and string and distance.

"Now my turn," said her mother with a kind of reluctant determination, handing Abby her sunglasses, and as her mother got down stiffly, inching her way toward the stone, Abby suddenly saw something she'd never seen before: her mother was terrified. For all her bullying and bravado, her mother was proceeding, and proceeding badly, through a great storm of terror in her brain. Abby, now privy to her bare face, saw that this fierce bonfire of a woman had gone twitchy and melancholic—it was a ruse, all her formidable display. She was only trying to prove something, trying pointlessly to defy and overcome her fears—instead of just learning to live with them, since, hell, you were living with them anyway. "Mom, you okay?" Mrs. Mallon's face was in a grimace, her mouth open and bared. The former auburn of her hair had descended, Abby saw, to her teeth, which she'd let rust with years of coffee and tea.

Now the leprechaun was having to hold her more than he had the other people. "Lower, now lower."

"Oh, God, not any lower," cried Mrs. Mallon.

"You're almost there."

"I don't see it."

"There you got it?" He loosened his grip and let her slip farther.

"Yes," she said. She let out a puckering, spitting sound. But then when struggled to come back up, she seemed to be stuck. Her legs thrashed out before her; her shoes loosened from her feet; her skirt rode up, revealing the brown tops of her panty hose. She was bent too strangely, from the hips, it seemed, and she was plump and didn't have the stomach muscles to lift herself back up. The leprechaun seemed to be having difficulty.

"Can someone here help me?"

"Oh my God," said Abby, and she and another man in line immediately squatted next to Mrs. Mallon to help her. She was heavy, stiff with fright, and when they had finally lifted her and gotten her sitting, then standing again, she seemed stricken and pale.

A guard near the staircase volunteered to escort her down.

"Would you like that, Mom?" and Mrs. Mallon simply nodded.

"You get in front of us," the guard said to Abby in the singsong accent of County Cork, "just in case she falls." And Abby got in front, her coat taking the updraft and spreading to either side as she circled slowly down into the dungeon-dark of the stairwell, into the black like a bat new to its wings.

In a square in the center of town, an evangelist was waving a Bible and shouting about "the brevity of life," how it was a thing grabbed by one hand and then gone, escaped through the fingers. "God's word is quick!" he called out.

"Let's go over there," said Abby, and she took her mother to a place called Brady's Public House for a restorative Guinness. "Are you okay?" Abby kept asking. They still had no place to stay that night, and though it remained light quite late, and the inns stayed open until ten, she imagined the two of them temporarily homeless, sleeping under the stars, snacking on slugs. Stars the size of Chicago! Dew like a pixie bath beneath them! They would lick it from their arms.

"I'm fine," she said, waving Abby's questions away. "What a stone!"

"Mom," said Abby, frowning, for she was now wondering about a few things. "When you went across that rope bridge, did you do that okay?"

Mrs. Mallon sighed. "Well, I got the idea of it," she said huffily. "But there were some gusts of wind that caused it to buck a little, and though some people thought that was fun, I had to get down and crawl back. You'll recall there was a little rain."

"You crawled back on your hands and knees?"

"Well, yes," she admitted. "There was a nice Belgian man who helped me." She felt unmasked, no doubt, before her daughter and now gulped at her Guinness.

Abby tried to take a cheerful tone, switching the subject a little, and it reminded her of Theda; Theda somehow living in her voice, her larynx suddenly a summer camp for the cheerful and slow. "Well, look at you!" said Abby. "Do you feel eloquent and confident, now that you've kissed the stone?"

"Not really." Mrs. Mallon shrugged.

Now that they had kissed it, or sort of, would they become self-conscious? What would they end up talking about?

Movies, probably. Just as they always had at home. Movies with scenery, movies with songs.

"How about you?" asked Mrs. Mallon.

"Well," said Abby, "mostly I feel like we've probably caught strep throat. And yet, and yet. . ." Here she sat up and leaned forward. No tests, or radio quizzes, or ungodly speeches, or songs brain-dead with biography, or kooky prayers, or shouts, or prolix conversations that with drink and too much time always revealed how stupid and mean even the best people were, just simply this: "A toast. I feel a toast coming on."

"You do?"

"Yes, I do." No one had toasted Abby and Bob at their little wedding, and that's what had been wrong, she believed now. No toast. There had been only thirty guests and they had simply eaten the ham canapés and gone home. How could a marriage go right? It wasn't that such ceremonies were important in and of themselves. They were nothing. They were zeros. But they were zeros as placeholders; they held numbers and equations intact. And once you underwent them, you could move on, know the empty power of their blessing, and not spend time missing them.

From here on in, she would believe in toasts. One was collecting itself now, in her head, in a kind of hesitant philately. She gazed over at her mother and took a deep breath. Perhaps her mother had never shown Abby affection, not really, but she had given her a knack for solitude, with its terrible lurches outward, and its smooth glide back to peace. Abby would toast her for that. It was really the world that was one's brutal mother, the one that nursed and neglected you, and your own mother was only your sibling in that world. Abby lifted her glass. "May the worst always be behind you. May the sun daily warm your arms. . . ." She looked down at her cocktail napkin for assistance, but there was only a cartoon of a big-chested colleen, two shamrocks over her breasts. Abby looked back up. *God's word is quick!* "May your car always start—" But perhaps God might also begin with tall, slow words; the belly bloat of a fib; the distended tale. "And may you always have a clean shirt," she continued, her voice growing gallant, public and loud, "and a holding roof, healthy children and good cabbages—and may you be with me in my heart, Mother, as you are now, in this place; always and forever—like a flaming light."

There was noise in the pub.

Blank is to childhood as journey is to lips.

"Right," said Mrs. Mallon, looking into her stout in a concentrated, bright-eyed way. She had never been courted before, not once in her entire life, and now she blushed, ears on fire, lifted her pint, and drank.

🖎 🖎 🖎

Suggestions for Discussion

1. Where is Abby shown to be in harmony or in conflict with the Irish landscape?

2. Find a passage of setting description that reflects Abby's emotions or concerns.

Retrospect

3. Why is indirect dialogue used to cover much of the early scene between Abby and her supervisors? Why are the lines "You may have a vacation first," and "Thank you" in direct dialogue?

4. How is the minor character of the Blarney Stone attendant created through speech, appearance, and action?

Bullet in the Brain

TOBIAS WOLFF

Anders couldn't get to the bank until just before it closed, so of course the line was endless and he got stuck behind two women whose loud, stupid conversation put him in a murderous temper. He was never in the best of tempers anyway, Anders—a book critic known for the weary, elegant savagery with which he dispatched almost everything he reviewed.

With the line still doubled around the rope, one of the tellers stuck a "POSITION CLOSED" sign in her window and walked to the back of the bank, where she leaned against a desk and began to pass the time with a man shuffling papers. The women in front of Anders broke off their conversation and watched the teller with hatred. "Oh, that's nice," one of them said. She turned to Anders and added, confident of his accord, "One of those little human touches that keep us coming back for more."

Anders had conceived his own towering hatred of the teller, but he immediately turned it on the presumptuous crybaby in front of him. "Damned unfair," he said. "Tragic, really. If they're not chopping off the wrong leg, or bombing your ancestral village, they're closing their positions."

She stood her ground. "I didn't say it was tragic," she said. "I just think it's a pretty lousy way to treat your customers."

"Unforgivable," Anders said. "Heaven will take note."

She sucked in her cheeks but stared past him and said nothing. Anders saw that the other woman, her friend, was looking in the same direction. And then the tellers stopped what they were doing, and the customers slowly turned, and silence came over the bank. Two men wearing black ski masks and blue business suits were standing to the side of the door. One of them had a pistol pressed against the guard's neck. The guard's eyes were closed, and his lips were moving. The other man had a sawed-off shotgun. "Keep your big mouth shut!" the man with the pistol said, though no one had spoken a word. "One of you tellers hits the alarm, you're all dead meat. Got it?"

The tellers nodded.

"Oh, bravo," Anders said. *"Dead meat."* He turned to the woman in front of him. "Great script, eh? The stern, brass-knuckled poetry of the dangerous classes."

She looked at him with drowning eyes.

The man with the shotgun pushed the guard to his knees. He handed the shotgun to his partner and yanked the guard's wrists up behind his back and locked them to-gether with a pair of handcuffs. He toppled him onto the floor with a kick between the shoulder blades. Then he took his shotgun back and went over to the security gate at the end of the counter. He was short and heavy and moved with peculiar slowness, even torpor. "Buzz him in," his partner said. The man with the shotgun opened the gate and sauntered along the line of tellers, handing each of them a Hefty bag. When he came to the empty position he looked over at the man with the pistol, who said, "Whose slot is that?"

Anders watched the teller. She put her hand to her throat and turned to the man she'd been talking to. He nodded. "Mine," she said.

"Then get your ugly ass in gear and fill that bag."

"There you go," Anders said to the woman in front of him. "Justice is done."

"Hey! Bright boy! Did I tell you to talk?"

"No," Anders said.

"Then shut your trap."

"Did you hear that?" Anders said. "'Bright boy.' Right out of 'The Killers.'"

"Please be quiet," the woman said.

"Hey, you deaf or what?" The man with the pistol walked over to Anders. He poked the weapon into Anders' gut. "You think I'm playing games?"

"No," Anders said, but the barrel tickled like a stiff finger and he had to fight back the titters. He did this by making himself stare into the man's eyes, which were clearly visible behind the holes in the mask: pale blue and rawly red-rimmed. The man's left eyelid kept twitching. He breathed out a piercing, ammoniac smell that shocked Anders more than anything that had happened, and he was beginning to develop a sense of unease when the man prodded him again with the pistol.

"You like me, bright boy?" he said. "You want to suck my dick?"

"No," Anders said.

"Then stop looking at me."

Anders fixed his gaze on the man's shiny wing-tip shoes.

"Not down there. Up there." He stuck the pistol under Anders' chin and pushed it upward until Anders was looking at the ceiling.

Anders had never paid much attention to that part of the bank, a pompous old building with marble floors and counters and pillars, and gilt scrollwork over the tellers' cages. The domed ceiling had been decorated with mythological figures whose fleshy, toga-draped ugliness Anders had taken in at a glance many years ear-lier and afterward declined to notice. Now he had no choice but to scrutinize the painter's work. It was even worse than he remembered, and all of it executed with the utmost gravity. The artist had a few tricks up his sleeve and used them again and again—a certain rosy blush on the underside of the clouds, a coy backward glance on the faces of the cupids and fauns. The ceiling was crowded with various dramas, but the one that caught Anders' eye was Zeus and Europa—portrayed, in this rendition, as a bull ogling a cow from behind a haystack. To make the cow sexy, the painter had canted her hips suggestively and given her long, droopy eyelashes through which she gazed back at the bull with sultry welcome. The bull wore a smirk and his eyebrows were arched. If there'd been a bubble coming out of his mouth, it would have said, "Hubba hubba."

"What's so funny, bright boy?"

"Nothing."

"You think I'm comical? You think I'm some kind of clown?"

"No."

"You think you can fuck with me?"

"No."

"Fuck with me again, you're history. *Capiche?*"

Anders burst out laughing. He covered his mouth with both hands and said, "I'm sorry, I'm sorry," then snorted helplessly through his fingers and said, "*Capiche*—oh, God, *capiche*," and at that the man with the pistol raised the pistol and shot Anders right in the head.

The bullet smashed Anders' skull and ploughed through his brain and exited behind his right ear, scattering shards of bone into the cerebral cortex, the corpus callosum, back toward the basal ganglia, and down into the thalamus. But before all this occurred, the first appearance of the bullet in the cerebrum set off a crackling chain of iron transports and neuro-transmissions. Because of their peculiar origin these traced a peculiar pattern, flukishly calling to life a summer afternoon some forty years past, and long since lost to memory. After striking the cranium the bullet was moving at 900 feet per second, a pathetically sluggish, glacial pace compared to the synaptic lightning that flashed around it. Once in the brain, that is, the bullet came under the mediation of brain time, which gave Anders plenty of leisure to contemplate the scene that, in a phrase he would have abhorred, "passed before his eyes."

It is worth noting what Anders did not remember, given what he did remember. He did not remember his first lover, Sherry, or what he had most madly loved about her, before it came to irritate him—her unembarrassed carnality, and especially the cordial way she had with his unit, which she called Mr. Mole, as in, "Uh-oh, looks like Mr. Mole wants to play," and, "let's hide Mr. Mole!" Anders did not remember his wife, whom he had also loved before she exhausted him with her predictability, or his daughter, now a sullen professor of economics at Dartmouth. He did not remember standing just outside his daughter's door as she lectured her bear about his naughtiness and described the truly appalling punishments Paws would receive unless he changed his ways. He did not remember a single line of the hundreds of poems he had committed to memory in his youth so that he could give himself the shivers at will—not "Silent, upon a peak in Darien," or "My God, I heard this day," or "All my pretty ones? Did you say all? O hell-kite! All?" None of these did he remember; not one. Anders did not remember his dying mother saying of his father, "I should have stabbed him in his sleep."

He did not remember Professor Josephs telling his class how Athenian prisoners in Sicily had been released if they could recite Aeschylus, and then reciting Aeschylus himself, right there, in the Greek. Anders did not remember how his eyes had burned at those sounds. He did not remember the surprise of seeing a college classmate's name on the jacket of a novel not long after they graduated, or the respect he had felt after reading the book. He did not remember the pleasure of giving respect.

Nor did Anders remember seeing a woman leap to her death from the building opposite his own just days after his daughter was born. He did not remember shouting, "Lord have mercy!" He did not remember deliberately crashing his father's car into a tree, or having his ribs kicked in by three policemen at an anti-war rally, or waking himself up with laughter. He did not remember when he began to regard the heap of books on his desk with boredom and dread, or when he grew angry at writers for writing them. He did not remember when everything began to remind him of something else.

This is what he remembered. Heat. A baseball field. Yellow grass, the whirr of insects, himself leaning against a tree as the boys of the neighborhood gather for a pickup game. He looks on as the others argue the relative genius of Mantle and Mays. They have been worrying this subject all summer, and it has become tedious to Anders: an oppression, like the heat.

Then the last two boys arrive, Coyle and a cousin of his from Mississippi. Anders has never met Coyle's cousin before and will never see him again. He says hi with the rest but takes no further notice of him until they've chosen sides and someone asks the cousin what position he wants to play. "Shortstop," the boy says. "Short's the best position they is." Anders turns and looks at him. He wants to hear Coyle's cousin repeat what he's just said, but he knows better than to ask. The others will think he's being a jerk, ragging the kid for his grammar. But that isn't it, not at all—it's that Anders is strangely roused, elated, by those final two words, their pure unexpectedness and their music. He takes the field in a trance, repeating them to himself.

The bullet is already in the brain; it won't be outrun forever, or charmed to a halt. In the end it will do its work and leave the troubled skull behind, dragging its comet's tail of memory and hope and talent and love into the marble hall of commerce. That can't be helped. But for now Anders can still make time. Time for the shadows to lengthen on the grass, time for the tethered dog to bark at the flying ball, time for the boy in right field to smack his sweat-blackened mitt and softly chant, *They is, they is, they is*.

🐾 🐾 🐾

Suggestions for Discussion

1. Half of this story is set in a bank and half in a brain. How does the author orient readers to each setting?

2. What Anders "did not remember" amounts to a flashback of three paragraphs that covers three generations and introduces at least eight people. Which specifics capture the core of a character or relationship? What keeps the accumulation of memories from being confusing?

Retrospect

3. Why has the author given Anders the profession of book critic? How does the author telegraph Anders's change of feeling about literature and language over time?

🐋 🐋 🐋

Writing Exercises

INDIVIDUAL

1. Through the eyes of a character, describe a setting that has changed over time—a family home sold to remodelers, a forest or farm turned housing development, a city block demolished for a freeway. Focus on the details of the place, including weather, geography, people, and machines, letting these details imply the character's feelings about the change. Or, describe a setting that has remained the same, but let readers see how the observer's description of it reflects changes that have occurred in that observer over time.

2. Write a scene, involving only one character, who is uncomfortable in his or her surroundings: socially inept, frightened, revolted, homesick, or the like. Using active verbs in your description of the setting, build forceful conflict between the person and the place.

3. Write a scene with two characters in conflict over the setting: One wants to go and one wants to stay. The more interesting the setting you choose, the more interesting the conflict will inevitably be.

4. Describe a setting that is likely to be quite familiar to your readers (supermarket, dormitory, classroom, movie theater, suburban house, etc.) but that is unfamiliar, strange, outlandish, or outrageous to the central character. Let us feel the strangeness through the character's eyes.

5. Write the first page of a story set in a strange, exotic place or a time far distant either in the past or the future, in which the setting is quite familiar to the central character. Convince us of the ordinariness of the place.

DEVELOPMENT/REVISION

6. List ten objects found in a story character's bedroom, car, locker, or other self-designed place. Make these objects as specific as possible, giving titles of books, contents of photographs, kind of junk food, and so on. Three of these objects should be connected with the story; one should be an object the character would not want anyone else to see. Using that list, write a half-page description of the character's space, mentioning the objects or other elements of the decor (such as paint color) that will give readers clues to character.

7. Write a scene containing a flashback in which information revealed about the past is crucial to an understanding of the present.

8. Choose a moment from a story-in-progress that could benefit from intensification of a character's emotional and/or physical experience.

- Focus on the place: the sights, sounds, smells, and weather.
- For three minutes, freewrite sensory details as rapidly as possible in present tense.
- Look back and select the most striking or significant sensory details. Look for places they might fit into the original passage.
- *Rewrite* the original paragraph, moving slowly, incorporating some of these details.

COLLABORATIVE

9. (Adapted from John Gardner's *The Art of Fiction*) In five minutes, write a description of one of the following settings. Do not mention the circumstances or emotion:
   - A description of a barn as seen by an old man or woman whose son has just been killed in a war.
   - A description of a lake as seen by someone who has just committed a murder.
   - A description of a grocery story as seen by a mother or father of three small children. The parent is away from the children for the first time in a week.

   Read the descriptions in small groups. Readers need not guess the circumstances; rather, the point is to give feedback on the mood evoked in the description and to identify the details that reflect that mood.

   Follow-Up: Write one paragraph to fit a story-in-progress in which the main character's emotion or mood is reflected in his or her perception of a particular setting.

10. With a partner, choose a photograph of a distinctive character from a magazine advertisement.
    a. Invent a name and some background for the character. Then choose a dominant trait, such as Anders's cynicism in "Bullet in the Brain."
    b. One partner should write a list, using specifics, of things "He or she did not remember. . . ."
    c. The other partner should write a paragraph describing a single memory that may seem random but is actually central to the person the character has become. Begin the paragraph: "This is what he/she remembered." Follow it with three details that set the place, then write a slow-motion version of the memory.
    d. Read the character sketches to the rest of the class. The point of this exercise is first, to invent a character, and second, to mirror the economical style that Wolff uses to sketch Anders's life up to its final point.

7

CALL ME ISHMAEL
Point of View, Part I

+ *Who Speaks?*

+ *To Whom?*

+ *In What Form?*

Point of view is the most complex element of fiction. Although it may be labeled and analyzed, it is finally a question of relationship among writer, characters, and reader. We can define person, omniscience, narrative voice, tone, authorial distance, and reliability; but none of these concepts will ever pigeonhole a work in such a way that any other work may be placed in the exact same pigeonhole.

The first thing to do is to set aside the common use of the phrase "point of view" as synonymous with "opinion," as in *It's my point of view that they all ought to be shot.* An author's view of the world will ultimately be revealed by the way that author manipulates the technique of point of view. However, the reverse does not hold true, for identifying the author's beliefs will not describe the point of view, meaning the controlling perspective, of the work. Rather than thinking of point of view as an opinion or belief, begin instead with the more literal synonym of "vantage point." *Who* is standing *where* to watch the scene?

Better, since we are dealing with a verbal medium, these questions might be translated: *Who speaks? To whom? In what form? At what distance from the action? With what limitations?* All these issues go into the determination of the point of view. Because the author *inevitably wants to convince us to share the same perspective*, the answers will also help reveal her or his final opinion, judgment, attitude, or message.

This chapter deals with the first three questions: Who speaks? To whom? In what form? Distance and limitations are considered in chapter 8.

POINT OF VIEW

Who Speaks?

The Author	*The Author*	*A Character*
In: *Third Person*	In: *Second Person*	In: *First Person*
Editorial Omniscient	You as Character	Central Narrator
Limited Omniscient	You as Reader-	Peripheral Narrator
Objective	Turned-Character	

To Whom?

The Reader	*Another Character or Characters*	*The Self*

In What Form?

---

*Story, Monologue, Letter, Journal, Interior Monologue,
Stream of Consciousness, etc.*

At What Distance?

Complete Identification	Complete Opposition

With What Limitations?

Reliable Narrator (or Author)	Unreliable Narrator (or Author)

CONSISTENCY: A PRELIMINARY CAUTION

In establishing the story's point of view, you make your own rules, but having made them, you must stick to them. Your position as a writer is analogous to that of a poet who may choose whether to write free verse or a ballad stanza. If the poet chooses the stanza, then he or she is obliged to rhyme. Beginning writers of prose fiction are often tempted to shift viewpoint when it is both unnecessary and disturbing.

> Leo's neck flushed against the prickly weave of his uniform collar. He concentrated on his buttons and tried not to look into the face of the bandmaster, who, however, was more amused than angry.

This is an awkward point-of-view shift because, having felt Leo's embarrassment with him, we are suddenly asked to leap into the bandmaster's feelings. The shift can be corrected by moving instead from Leo's mind to an observation that he might make.

Leo's neck flushed against the prickly weave of his uniform collar. He concentrated on his buttons and tried not to look into the face of the bandmaster, who, however, was astonishingly smiling.

The rewrite is easier to follow because we remain with Leo's mind as he observes that the bandmaster is not angry. It further serves the purpose of implying that Leo fails to concentrate on his buttons, and so intensifies his confusion.

Apart from the use of significant detail, there is no more important skill for a writer of fiction to grasp than this, the control of point of view. Sometimes it may be hard simply to recognize that your narrative has leapt from one point of view to another—often, in workshop, students are troubled by a point-of-view shift in someone else's story but can't spot one in their own. In other cases there's a healthy desire to explore every possibility in a scene, and a mistaken sense that this can't be done without changing point of view. Indeed, no writing rule is so frequently broken to such original and inventive effect as *consistency in point of view*, as several stories in this volume attest. Yet the general rule of consistency holds, and a writer signals amateurism in the failure to make a point-of-view contract and stick to it.

Who Speaks?

The primary point-of-view decision that you as author must make before you can set down the first sentence of the story is *person*. This is the simplest and crudest subdivision that must be made in deciding who speaks. The story can be told . . .

- in the third person (*she walked out into the harsh sunlight*),
- the second person (*you walked out into the harsh sunlight*),
- or the first person (*I walked out into the harsh sunlight*).

Third- and second-person stories are told by an author; first-person stories, by a character.

THIRD PERSON

Third person, in which the author is telling the story, can be subdivided again according to the degree of knowledge, or *omniscience*, the author assumes. As an author you are free to decide how much you know: You may know every universal and eternal truth; you may know what is in the mind of one character but not what is in the mind of another; or you may know only what can be observed by a witness. You decide, and very early in the story you signal to the reader what degree of omniscience you have chosen.

Once given, this signal constitutes a "contract" between author and reader, and it will be difficult to break the contract gracefully. Returning to the notion of consistency, if you have restricted yourself to the mind of James Lordly for five pages, as he observes the actions of Mrs. Grumms and her cats, you will violate the contract by suddenly dipping into Mrs. Grumms's mind to let us know what she thinks of James

Lordly. We are likely to feel misused, and likely to cancel the contract altogether, if you suddenly give us the thoughts of the cats.

OMNISCIENCE

The *omniscient author* has total knowledge and tells us directly what we are supposed to think. As omniscient author you are God. You can:

1. Objectively report what is happening;
2. Go into the mind of any character;
3. Interpret for us that character's appearance, speech, actions, and thoughts, even if the character cannot do so;
4. Move freely in time or space to give us a panoramic, telescopic, microscopic, or historical view; tell us what has happened elsewhere or in the past or what will happen in the future; and
5. Provide general reflections, judgments, and truths.

In all these aspects, we will accept what the omniscient author tells us. If you tell us that Ruth is a good woman, that Jeremy doesn't really understand his own motives, that the moon is going to explode in four hours, and that everybody will be better off for it, we will believe you. Here is a paragraph that blatantly exhibits all five of these areas of knowledge.

(1) Joe glared at the screaming baby. (2) Frightened by his scowl, the baby gulped and screamed louder. I hate that thing, Joe thought. (3) But it was not really hatred that he felt. (4) Only two years ago he himself had screamed like that. (5) Children can't tell hatred from fear.

This illustration is awkwardly compressed, but authors well in control of their craft can move easily from one area of knowledge to another. In the first scene of *War and Peace*, Tolstoy describes Anna Scherer.

To be an enthusiast had become her social vocation, and sometimes even when she did not feel like it, she became enthusiastic in order not to disappoint the expectations of those who knew her. The subdued smile which, though it did not suit her faded features, always played around her lips, expressed as in a spoiled child, a continual consciousness of her charming defect, which she neither wished, nor could, nor considered it necessary to correct.

In two sentences Tolstoy tells us what is in Anna's mind, what the expectations of her acquaintances are, what she looks like, what suits her, what she can and cannot do; and he offers a general reflection on spoiled children.

The omniscient voice is the voice of the classical epic ("And Meleager, far-off, knew nothing of this, but felt his vitals burning with fever"), of the Bible ("So the

Lord sent a pestilence upon Israel; and there fell seventy thousand men"), and of most nineteenth-century novels ("Tito put out his hand to help him, and so strangely quick are men's souls that in this moment, when he began to feel that his atonement was accepted, he had a darting thought of the irksome efforts it entailed"). But it is one of the manifestations of modern literature's movement downward in class from heroic to common characters, from external action to the psychological action of the mind, that authors of realistic fiction have largely avoided the godlike stance of the omniscient author and have chosen to restrict themselves to fewer areas of knowledge.

LIMITED OMNISCIENCE

The *limited omniscient* viewpoint is one in which the author may move with some, but not all, of the omniscient author's freedom. The most commonly used form of the limited omniscient point of view is one in which the author can see events objectively and also grants himself or herself access to the mind of one character, but *not* to the minds of the others, nor to any explicit powers of judgment. This point of view is particularly useful for the short story because it very quickly establishes the point-of-view character or *means of perception*. The short story is so compressed a form that there is rarely time or space to develop more than one consciousness. Staying with external observation and one character's thoughts helps control the focus and avoid awkward point-of-view shifts. A further advantage of limited omniscience is that it mimics our individual experience of life, that is, our own inability to penetrate the minds and motivations of others, which can lead to the kinds of conflicts or struggles for connection that inspire much fiction.

Limited omniscience is also frequently used for the novel, as in Gail Godwin's *The Odd Woman*.

> It was ten o'clock on the evening of the same day, and the permanent residents of the household on the mountain were restored to routines and sobriety. Jane, on the other hand, sat by herself in the kitchen, a glass of Scotch before her on the cleanly wiped table, going deeper and deeper into a mood she could recognize only as unfamiliar. She could not describe it; it was both frightening and satisfying. It was like letting go and being taken somewhere. She tried to trace it back. When, exactly, had it started?

It is clear here that the author has limited her omniscience. She is not going to tell us the ultimate truth about Jane's soul, nor is she going to define for us the unfamiliar mood that the character herself cannot define. The author has the facts at her disposal, and she has Jane's thoughts, and that is all.

The advantage of the limited omniscient voice is immediacy. Here, because we are not allowed to know more than Jane does about her own thoughts and feelings, we grope *with* her toward understanding. In the process, a contract has been made between the author and the reader, and this contract must not now be broken. If at this point the author should step in and answer Jane's question "When, exactly, had

There should be the illusion that it's the character's point of view, when in fact it isn't; it's really the narrator who is there but who doesn't make herself . . . known in that role. . . . What I really want is that intimacy in which the reader is under the impression that he isn't really reading this; that he is participating in it as he goes along.

Toni Morrison

it started?" with "Jane was never to remember this, but in fact it had started one afternoon when she was two years old," we would feel it as an abrupt and uncalled-for *authorial intrusion*. Nevertheless, within the limits the author has set herself, there is fluidity and a range of possibilities.

THE OPAQUE CHARACTER

If you choose the one-mind limited omniscient (or the first-person narrator, discussed below), it may at first seem difficult, sometimes impossible, to let the reader know what she or he needs to know without the thoughts of the *opaque character* (the one whose mind we cannot see into). In fact this is one of the tests, and the joys, of skill—a limitation that can become an opportunity for invention and imagination. For whether or not that opaque character is willing to speak truly, he or she can betray real feelings, intentions, or reactions with a gesture, actions, expressions, even clothing. Diane Schoemperlen takes advantage of the phenomenon in the story "Body Language," which is told in the limited omniscient from the viewpoint of the husband:

> Or (on a good day) she would have been in the kitchen starting supper with the radio on, humming and chopping and stirring . . . In the kitchen he joyfully discovers that she has already changed out of her work clothes and is wearing her black silk kimono with the red dragon on the back. She greets him with a kiss. . . .
> On a bad day she doesn't exactly push him away but turns, gracefully, out of his embrace, like a ring once stuck on a finger magically removed with soap. Both her skin and her kimono are slippery and he cannot hold on.

THE OBJECTIVE AUTHOR

The *objective author* is not omniscient but impersonal. As an objective author, you restrict your knowledge to the external facts that might be observed by a human witness; to the senses of sight, sound, smell, taste, and touch. In the chapter 5 story "Hills Like White Elephants," Ernest Hemingway reports what is said and done by a quarreling couple, both without any direct revelation of the characters' thoughts and without comment.

> The American and the girl with him sat at a table in the shade, outside the building. It was very hot and the express from Barcelona would come in forty minutes. It stopped at this junction for two minutes and went on to Madrid.
> "What should we drink?" the girl asked. She had taken off her hat and put it on the table.
> "It's pretty hot," the man said.
> "Let's drink beer."
> "Dos cervezas," the man said into the curtain.
> "Big ones?" a woman asked from the doorway.
> "Yes. Two big ones."
> The woman brought two glasses of beer and two felt pads. She put the felt pads and the beer glasses on the table and looked at the man and the girl. The girl was looking off at the line of hills. They were white in the sun and the country was brown and dry.

In the course of this story we learn, entirely by inference, that the girl is pregnant and that she feels herself coerced by the man into having an abortion. Neither pregnancy nor abortion is ever mentioned. The narrative remains clipped, austere, and external. What does Hemingway gain by this pretense of objective reporting? The reader is allowed to discover what is really happening. The characters avoid the subject, prevaricate, and pretend, but they betray their real meanings and feelings through gestures, repetitions, and slips of the tongue. The reader, focus directed by the author, learns by inference, as in life, so that we finally have the pleasure of knowing the characters better than they know themselves.

SECOND PERSON

First and third persons are most common in literature; the second person remains an idiosyncratic and experimental form, but it is worth mentioning because several contemporary authors have been attracted to its possibilities.

Person refers to the basic mode of a piece of fiction. In the third person, all the characters will be referred to as *he, she,* or *they.* In the first person, the character telling the story will refer to himself or herself as *I* and to other characters as *he, she,* or *they.* The second person is the basic mode of the story *only when a character* is referred to as *you.* When one character addresses "you" in letter or monologue, that narrative is still told by the "I" character. When an omniscient author addresses the reader as *you* (*You will remember that John Doderring was left dangling on the cliff at Dover*), this is called "direct address" and does not alter the basic third-person mode of the piece. Only when "you" become an actor in the drama, so designated by the author, is the story or novel written in second person.

Lorrie Moore's story "How to Become a Writer" illustrates how a reader is made into a character through second person.

First, try to be something, anything, else. A movie star/astronaut. A movie star/missionary. A movie star/kindergarten teacher. President of the World. Fail miserably. It is best if you fail at an early age—say, fourteen. Early, critical disillusionment is necessary so that at fifteen you can write long haiku sentences about thwarted desire. It is a pond, a cherry blossom, a wind brushing against sparrow wing leaving for mountain. Count the syllables. Show it to your mom.

Here the author assigns you, the reader, specific characteristics and reactions, and thereby—assuming that you go along with her characterization of you—pulls you deeper and more intimately into the story.

Some writers choose second person to depict trauma, as its slight sense of detachment mutes possible melodrama and mirrors the sense of shock; others may use it to make a highly individual experience feel more universal, as in M. Evelina Galang's story "Lectures on How You Never Lived Back Home," which comes at the end of this chapter. While it is unlikely that the second person will ever become a major mode of narration as the first and third person are, for precisely that reason you may find it an attractive experiment.

FIRST PERSON

A story is told in the first person when it is a character who speaks. The term "narrator" is sometimes loosely used to refer to any teller of a tale, but strictly speaking a story has a narrator only when it is told in the first person by one of the characters. This character may be the protagonist, the *I* telling *my* story, in which case that character is a *central narrator* ("American History"); or the character may be telling a story about someone else, in which case he or she is a *peripheral narrator* ("Silver Water").

In either case it's important to indicate early which kind of narrator we have so that we know who the story's protagonist is, as in the first paragraph of Alan Sillitoe's "The Loneliness of the Long-Distance Runner."

> As soon as I got to Borstal they made me a long-distance cross-country runner. I suppose they thought I was just the build for it because I was long and skinny for my age (and still am) and in any case I didn't mind it much, to tell you the truth, because running had always been made much of in our family, especially running away from the police.

The focus here is immediately thrown on the *I* of the story, and we expect that *I* to be the central character whose desires and decisions impel the action. But from the opening lines of Amy Bloom's "Silver Water" (in chapter 2), it is the sister, Rose, who is brought alive through the description of her marvelous singing voice, while the narrator, Violet, is established as an observer and protector of her subject.

> My sister's voice was like mountain water in a silver pitcher; the clear, blue beauty of it cools you and lifts you up beyond your heat, beyond your body. After

we went to see *La Traviata*, when she was fourteen and I was twelve, she elbowed me in the parking lot and said, "Check this out." And she opened her mouth unnaturally wide and her voice came out, so crystalline and bright, that all the departing operagoers stood frozen by their cars, unable to take out their keys or open their doors until she had finished and then they cheered like hell.

That's what I like to remember and that's the story I told to all of her therapists. I wanted them to know her, to know that who they saw was not all there was to see.

The central narrator is always, as the term implies, at the center of the action; the peripheral narrator may be in virtually any position that is not the center. He or she may be the second most important character in the story ("Gryphon"), or may appear to be a bystander for much of the story. It is even possible to make the first-person narrator plural, as William Faulkner does in "A Rose for Emily," where the story is told by a narrator identified only as one of "us," the people of the town in which the action has taken place.

That a narrator may be either central or peripheral, that a character may tell either his or her own story or someone else's, is both commonly assumed and obviously logical. But the author and editor Rust Hills, in his book *Writing in General and the Short Story in Particular*, takes interesting and persuasive exception to this idea. When point of view fails, Hills argues, it is always because the perception we are using for the course of the story is different from that of the character who is moved or changed by the action. Even when a narrator seems to be a peripheral observer and the story is "about" someone else, in fact it is the narrator who is changed, and must be, in order for us to be satisfied by our emotional identification with him or her.

This, I believe, is what will always be the case in successful fiction: that either the character moved by the action will be the point-of-view character, or else the point of view character will *become* the character moved by the action. Call it Hills' Law.

Obviously, this view does not mean that we have to throw out the useful fictional device of the peripheral narrator. Hills uses the familiar examples of *The Great Gatsby* and *Heart of Darkness* to illustrate his meaning. In the former, Nick Carroway as a peripheral narrator observes and tells the story of Jay Gatsby, but by the end of the book it is Nick's life that has been changed by what he has observed. In the latter, Marlow purports to tell the tale of the ivory hunter Kurtz, even protesting that "I don't want to bother you much with what happened to me personally." By the end of the story, Kurtz (like Gatsby) is dead, but it is not the death that moves us so much as what, "personally," Marlow has learned through Kurtz and his death. The same can be said of "Silver Water": the focus of the action is on Rose, but the ultimate responsibility for her death falls on the narrator, her sister Violet. Even in "A Rose for Emily," where the narrator is a collective "we," it is the implied effect of Miss Emily on the town that moves us, the emotions of the townspeople that we share. Because we tend to identify with the means of perception in a story, we are moved with that perception; even when the overt action of the story is elsewhere, it is often the act of observation itself that provides the epiphany. Anton Chekhov (as paraphrased by Tobias Wolff) cautioned, "The narrator cannot escape the *consequences* of the story he is telling. If he does, it's not a story. It's an anecdote, a tale, or something else."

Central or peripheral, a first-person narrator is a character, so it's vital to remember that she or he has all the limitations of a human being and cannot be omniscient. The narrator is confined to reporting what she or he could realistically know. More than that, although the narrator may certainly interpret actions, deliver dictums, and predict the future, these remain the fallible opinions of a human being; we are not bound to accept them as we are bound to accept the interpretations, truths, and predictions of the omniscient author. You may want us to accept the narrator's word, and then the most difficult part of your task, and the touchstone of your story's success, will be to convince us to trust and believe the narrator. On the other hand, it may be an important part of your purpose that we should reject the narrator's opinions and form our own. In the latter case, the narrator is "unreliable," a phenomenon that will be taken up in chapter 8.

To Whom?

In choosing a point of view, the author implies an identity not only for the teller of the tale, but also for the audience.

THE READER

Most fiction is addressed to a literary convention, "the reader." When we open a book, we tacitly accept our role as a member of this unspecified audience. If the story begins, "I was born of a drunken father and an illiterate mother in the peat bogs of Galway during the Great Potato Famine," we are not, on the whole, alarmed. We do not face this clearly deceased Irishman who has crossed the Atlantic to take us into his confidence and demand, "Why are you telling me all this?" After all, the most common assumption of the tale-teller, whether omniscient author or narrating character, is that the reader is an amenable and persuasible Everyman, and that the telling needs no justification.

ANOTHER CHARACTER

More specifically, the story may be told to *another character*, or *characters*, in which case we as readers "overhear" it; the teller of the tale does not acknowledge us even by implication.

In the *epistolary* novel or story, the narrative consists entirely of letters written from one character to another, or between characters. The recipient of the letter may be a relative stranger or a close friend or relative, like the near-annual readers of *The Christmas Letters*, by Lee Smith.

First, my apologies for not writing a Christmas letter last year (for not returning calls, for not returning letters, etc.). The fact is, for a long time I couldn't do anything. Not a damn thing. Nothing. I was shell-shocked, immobilized. This was followed by a period when I did *too many things*. Marybeth, who has been through it, wrote to me about this time, saying, "Don't make any big decisions" —very good advice, and I wish I'd followed it. Instead, I agreed to a separation agreement, then to a quick no-fault divorce, then to Sandy's plan of selling the house P.D.Q. I just wanted everything *over with*—the way you feel that sudden irresistible urge to clean out your closet sometimes.

Or the convention of the story may be that of a monologue, spoken aloud by one character to another.

May I, *monsieur*, offer my services without running the risk of intruding? I fear you may not be able to make yourself understood by the worthy ape who presides over the fate of this establishment. In fact, he speaks nothing but Dutch. Unless you authorize me to plead your case, he will not guess that you want gin.

Albert Camus, *The Fall*

Again, the possible variations are infinite: the narrator may speak in intimate confessional to a friend or lover, or may present his case to a jury or a mob; she may be writing a highly technical report of the welfare situation, designed to hide her emotions; he may be pouring out his heart in a love letter he knows (and we know) he will never send.

In any of these cases, the convention employed is the opposite of that employed in a story told to "the reader." The listener as well as the teller is involved in the action; the assumption is not that we readers are there but that we are not. We are eavesdroppers, with all the ambiguous intimacy that position implies.

THE SELF

An even greater intimacy is implied if the character's story is as secret as a diary or as private as a mind, addressed to *the self* and not intended to be heard by anyone inside or outside the action.

In a *diary* or *journal*, the convention is that the thoughts are written but not expected to be read by anyone except the writer.

Tuesday 3 January

130 lbs. (terrifying slide into obsesity—why? why?), alcohol units 6 (excellent), cigarettes 23 (v.g.), calories 2472.

9 a.m. Ugh. Cannot face thought of going to work. Only thing which makes it tolerable is thought of seeing Daniel again, but even that is inadvisable since I am fat, have spot on chin, and desire only to sit on cushion eating chocolate and

watching Xmas specials. It seems wrong and unfair that Christmas, with its stressful and unmanageable financial and emotional challenges, should first be forced upon one wholly against one's will, then rudely snatched away just when one is starting to get into it. Was really beginning to enjoy the feeling that normal service was suspended and it was OK to lie in bed as long as you want, put anything you fancy into your mouth, and drink alcohol whenever it should chance to pass your way, even in the mornings. Now suddenly we are all supposed to snap into self-discipline like lean teenage greyhounds.

Helen Fielding, Bridget Jones's Diary

The protagonist here is clearly using her diary to vent her feelings and does not intend it to be read by anyone else. Still, she has deliberately externalized her secret thoughts in a journal.

INTERIOR MONOLOGUE

Because the author has the power to enter a character's mind, the reader also has the power to eavesdrop on thoughts, read what is not written, hear what is not spoken, and share what cannot be shared. Overheard thoughts are generally of two kinds, of which the more common is *interior monologue*, the convention being that we follow that character's thoughts in their sequence, though in fact the author, for our convenience, sets out those thoughts with a coherence and logic that no human mind ever possessed.

I must organize myself. I must, as they say, pull myself together, dump this cat from my lap, stir—yes, resolve, move, do. But do what? My will is like the rosy dustlike light in this room: soft, diffuse, and gently comforting. It lets me do . . . anything . . . nothing. My ears hear what they happen to; I eat what's put before me; my eyes see what blunders into them; my thoughts are not thoughts, they are dreams. I'm empty or I'm full . . . depending; and I cannot choose. I sink my claws in Tick's fur and scratch the bones of his back until his rear rises amorously. Mr. Tick, I murmur, I must organize myself, I must pull myself together. And Mr. Tick rolls over on his belly, all ooze.

William H. Gass, "In the Heart of the Heart of the Country"

This interior monologue ranges, as human thoughts do, from sense impression to self-admonishment, from cat to light to eyes and ears, from specific to general and back again. But the logical connections between these things are all provided; the mind "thinks" logically and grammatically as if the character were trying to express himself.

STREAM OF CONSCIOUSNESS

Stream of consciousness acknowledges the fact that the human mind does not operate with the order and clarity of the monologue just quoted. Even what little we know of its operations makes clear that it skips, elides, makes and breaks images, leaps faster and further than any mere sentence can suggest. Any mind at any moment is simultaneously accomplishing dozens of tasks that cannot be conveyed simultaneously. As you read this sentence, part of your mind is following the sense of it; part of your mind is directing your hand to hold the book open; part of it is twisting your spine into a more comfortable position; part of it is still lingering on the last interesting image of this text, Mr. Tick rolling over on his belly, which reminds you of a cat you had once that was also *all ooze*, which reminds you that you're nearly out of milk and have to finish this chapter before the store closes—and so forth.

In *Ulysses*, James Joyce tried to catch the speed and multiplicity of the mind with the technique that has come to be known as stream of consciousness. The device is difficult and in many ways thankless: Since the speed of thought is so much faster than that of writing or speaking, and stream of consciousness tries to suggest the process as well as the content of the mind, *it requires a more, not less, rigorous selection and arrangement* than ordinary grammar requires. But Joyce and a very few other writers have handled stream of consciousness as an ebullient and exciting way of capturing the mind.

> Yes because he never did a thing like that before as ask to get his breakfast in bed with a couple of eggs since the City Arms hotel when he used to be pretending to be laid up with a sick voice doing his highness to make himself interesting to that old faggot Mrs. Riordan that he thought he had a great leg of and she never left us a farthing all for masses for herself and her soul greatest miser ever was actually afraid to lay out 4d for her methylated spirit telling me all her ailments she had too much old chat in her about politics and earthquakes and the end of the world let us have a bit of fun first God help the world if all the women were her sort . . .
>
> James Joyce, *Ulysses*

The preceding two examples, of interior monologue and stream of consciousness, respectively, are written in the first person, so that we overhear the minds of narrator characters. We may also overhear the thoughts of the characters through the third-person omniscient and limited omniscient authors, as in John Edgar Wideman's *tour de force* story "The Tambourine Lady." Here, Wideman succeeds in the challenging fusion of third-person narrative and stream of consciousness, so that although the answer to the question "who speaks?" is technically "the author," nevertheless we are aware of the point-of-view character speaking to herself in rapid-fire associative thought:

> . . . She thinks about how long it takes to get to the end of your prayers, how the world might be over and gone while you still saying the words to yourself. Words her mama taught her, words her mama said her mother had taught her so somebody would always be saying them world without end amen. So God would not forget his children . . .

In What Form?

The form of the story also contributes to the overall point of view. That form may announce itself as a generalized *story*, either *written* or *spoken;* or it may suggest *reportage, confessional, interior monologue,* or *stream of consciousness;* or it may be overtly identified as *monologue, oratory, journal,* or *diary.* This list is not exhaustive; you can tell your story in the form of a catalogue or a television commercial as long as you can also contrive to give it the form of a story.

Here are the opening paragraphs from Lorrie Moore's short story "People Like That Are the Only People Here," in which the form blurs traditional lines, as fiction appears to masquerade as third-person memoir, or perhaps the reverse, and the point of view is extremely complex. An adequate understanding of it will require—more than a definition or a diagram—a series of *yes but*'s and *but also*'s.

A beginning, an end: there seems to be neither. The whole thing is like a cloud that just lands, and everywhere inside it is full of rain. A start: the Mother finds a blood clot in the Baby's diaper. What is the story? Who put this here? It is big and bright, with a broken, khaki-colored vein in it. Over the weekend, the Baby had looked listless and spacy, clayey and grim. But today he looks fine—so what is this thing, startling against the white diaper, like a tiny mouse heart packed in snow? Perhaps it belongs to someone else. Perhaps it is something menstrual, something belonging to the Mother or the Babysitter, something the Baby has found in a wastebasket and for his own demented reasons stowed away here. (Babies—they're crazy! What can you do?) In her mind, the Mother takes this away from his body and attaches it to someone else's. There. Doesn't that make more sense?

Still, she phones the children's hospital and the clinic. Blood in the diaper, she says, and sounding alarmed and perplexed, the woman on the other end says, "Come in now."

Such pleasing instant service! Just say "blood." Just say "diaper." Look what you get.

In the examination room, the pediatrician, the nurse, and the head resident all seem less alarmed and perplexed than simply perplexed. At first, stupidly, the Mother is calmed by this. But soon, besides peering and saying "Hmm," the doctor, the nurse, and the head resident are all drawing their mouths in, bluish and tight—morning glories sensing noon. They fold their arms across their white-coated chests, unfold them again, and jot things down. They order an ultrasound. Bladder and kidneys. Here's the card. Go downstairs, turn left.

In Radiology, the Baby stands anxiously on the table, naked against the Mother, as she holds him still against her legs and waist, the Radiologist's cold scanning disk moving about the Baby's back. The Baby whimpers, looks up at the Mother. *Let's get out of here,* his eyes beg. *Pick me up!*

Who speaks? The opening is so tentative and perplexed that this seems to be some character's speculation, and we think we are in the presence of a first-person narrator. But no. By the third sentence it's clear the passage is written in the third person—"the Mother finds"—and that we are in the limited omniscient, privy to the Mother's thoughts, sometimes overhearing them directly: "Who put this here?" Yet this central character whose thoughts we share calls herself and others by the names of types: the Mother, the Baby, the Babysitter. No one would think of herself or her baby in this way. Even her babysitter would have a name. And this Mother's thoughts are sometimes colder, more distant than the things anyone would say out loud in this situation. She talks in literary terms, striking metaphors. She is sarcastic. She fires off jokes. All the same, when she enters the baby's mind—"*Let's get out of here*"—we trust her.

To whom? The narrative clearly addresses the convention of "the reader." Yet because the narrative is at one and the same time so closely fused with the mother's thoughts and so deliberately distanced, the effect is that the Mother is talking to herself and also saying things to herself that she doesn't mean, bucking herself up, distracting herself with one-liners, denying. ("Babies—they're crazy! What can you do?")

In what form? Again, the form is the convention of "a story" and, indeed, this is insisted on by the familiar opening reference to Aristotle's *beginning, middle,* and *end,* and the Mother's cry, "What is the story?" We are not surprised later to find out that the protagonist is a short-story writer—who, moreover, disdains the form of the memoir and refuses to take notes on the baby's illness—the "notes," of course, that we are reading. (In the original publication of this story, *The New Yorker* compounded the paradox by labeling it "Fiction" but publishing a picture of the author in the middle of the first page, captioned with a quotation from the story in which the Mother says "This isn't fiction.") The bleak rhythm and the starkness of the images, whether visceral ("mouse heart packed in snow") or gratingly pretty ("morning glories sensing noon") betray the desperation of the Writer even as the Mother protects herself with blunt jokes.

The amazing thing is that the complexities of the point of view do not in the least confuse us! We do not feel that the author is inept at point of view, but on the contrary that she has captured with great precision the paradoxes and contradictions of the protagonist's emotional state. We feel no awkward point-of-view shift because all the terms of the contract—those same paradoxes and contradictions—are laid out for us in the opening paragraph.

In order to deal with a viewpoint as complex as this, it will be necessary to deal not only with who speaks to whom in what form, but also with *distance* and *limitation,* subjects treated in chapter 8.

Orientation

DANIEL OROZCO

Those are the offices and these are the cubicles. That's my cubicle there, and this is your cubicle. This is your phone. Never answer your phone. Let the Voicemail System answer it. This is your Voicemail System Manual. There are no personal phone calls allowed. We do, however, allow for emergencies. If you must make an emergency phone call, ask your supervisor first. If you can't find your supervisor, ask Phillip Spiers, who sits over there. He'll check with Clarissa Nicks, who sits over there. If you make an emergency phone call without asking, you may be let go.

These are your IN and OUT boxes. All the forms in your IN box must be logged in by the date shown in the upper left-hand corner, initialed by you in the upper right-hand corner, and distributed to the Processing Analyst whose name is numerically coded in the lower left-hand corner. The lower right-hand corner is left blank. Here's your Processing Analyst Numerical Code Index. And here's your Forms Processing Procedures Manual.

You must pace your work. What do I mean? I'm glad you asked that. We pace our work according to the eight-hour workday. If you have twelve hours of work in your IN box, for example, you must compress that work into the eight-hour day. If you have one hour of work in your IN box, you must expand that work to fill the eight-hour day. That was a good question. Feel free to ask questions. Ask too many questions, however, and you may be let go.

That is our receptionist. She is a temp. We go through receptionists here. They quit with alarming frequency. Be polite and civil to the temps. Learn their names, and invite them to lunch occasionally. But don't get close to them, as it only makes it more difficult when they leave. And they always leave. You can be sure of that.

The men's room is over there. The women's room is over there. John LaFountaine, who sits over there, uses the women's room occasionally. He says it is accidental. We know better, but we let it pass. John LaFountaine is harmless, his forays into the forbidden territory of the women's room simply a benign thrill, a faint blip on the dull flat line of his life.

Russell Nash, who sits in the cubicle to your left, is in love with Amanda Pierce, who sits in the cubicle to your right. They ride the same bus together after work. For Amanda Pierce, it is just a tedious bus ride made less tedious by the idle nattering of Russell Nash. But for Russell Nash, it is the highlight of his day. It is the highlight of his life. Russell Nash has put on forty pounds, and grows fatter with each passing month, nibbling on chips and cookies while peeking glumly over the partitions at Amanda Pierce, and gorging himself at home on cold pizza and ice cream while watching adult videos on TV.

Amanda Pierce, in the cubicle to your right, has a six-year-old son named Jamie, who is autistic. Her cubicle is plastered from top to bottom with the boy's crayon artwork—sheet after sheet of precisely drawn concentric circles and ellipses, in black and yellow. She rotates them every other Friday. Be sure to comment on them. Amanda Pierce also has a husband, who is a lawyer. He subjects her to an escalating array of painful and humiliating sex games, to which Amanda Pierce reluctantly submits. She comes to work exhausted and freshly wounded each morning, wincing from the abrasions to her breasts, or the bruises on her abdomen, or the second-degree burns on the backs of her thighs.

But we're not supposed to know any of this. Do not let on. If you let on, you may be let go.

Amanda Pierce, who tolerates Russell Nash, is in love with Albert Bosch, whose office is over there. Albert Bosch, who only dimly registers Amanda Pierce's existence, has eyes only for Ellie Tapper, who sits over there. Ellie Tapper, who hates Albert Bosch, would walk through fire for Curtis Lance. But Curtis Lance hates Ellie Tapper. Isn't the world a funny place? Not in the ha-ha sense, of course.

Anika Bloom sits in that cubicle. Last year, while reviewing quarterly reports in a meeting with Barry Hacker, Anika Bloom's left palm began to bleed. She fell into a trance, stared into her hand, and told Barry Hacker when and how his wife would die. We laughed it off. She was, after all, a new employee. But Barry Hacker's wife is dead. So unless you want to know exactly when and how you'll die, never talk to Anika Bloom.

Colin Heavey sits in that cubicle over there. He was new once, just like you. We warned him about Anika Bloom. But at last year's Christmas Potluck, he felt sorry for her when he saw that no one was talking to her. Colin Heavey brought her a drink. He hasn't been himself since. Colin Heavey is doomed. There's nothing he can do about it, and we are powerless to help him. Stay away from Colin Heavey. Never give any of your work to him. If he asks to do something, tell him you have to check with me. If he asks again, tell him I haven't gotten back to you.

This is the Fire Exit. There are several on this floor, and they are marked accordingly. We have a Floor Evacuation Review every three months, and an Escape Route Quiz once a month. We have our Biannual Fire Drill twice a year, and our Annual Earthquake Drill once a year. These are precautions only. These things never happen.

For your information, we have a comprehensive health plan. Any catastrophic illness, any unforeseen tragedy is completely covered. All dependents are completely covered. Larry Bagdikian, who sits over there, has six daughters. If anything were to happen to any of his girls, or to all of them, if all six were to simultaneously fall victim to illness or injury—stricken with a hideous degenerative muscle disease or some rare toxic blood disorder, sprayed with semiautomatic gunfire while on a class field trip, or attacked in their bunk beds by some prowling nocturnal lunatic—if any of this were to pass, Larry's girls would all be taken care of. Larry Bagdikian would not have to pay one dime. He would have nothing to worry about.

We also have a generous vacation and sick leave policy. We have an excellent disability insurance plan. We have a stable and profitable pension fund. We get group discounts for the symphony, and block seating at the ballpark. We get commuter ticket books for the bridge. We have Direct Deposit. We are all members of Costco.

This is our kitchenette. And this, this is our Mr. Coffee. We have a coffee pool, into which we each pay two dollars a week for coffee, filters, sugar, and CoffeeMate. If you prefer Cremora or half-and-half to CoffeeMate, there is a special pool for three dollars per week. If you prefer Sweet'n Low to sugar, there is a special pool for two-fifty a week. We do not do decaf. You are allowed to join the coffee pool of your choice, but you are not allowed to touch the Mr. Coffee.

This is the microwave oven. You are allowed to *heat* food in the microwave oven. You are not, however, allowed to *cook* food in the microwave oven.

We get one hour for lunch. We also get one fifteen-minute break in the morning, and one fifteen-minute break in the afternoon. Always take your breaks. If you skip a break, it is gone forever. For your information, your break is a privilege, not a right. If you abuse the break policy, we are authorized to rescind your breaks. Lunch, however, is a right, not a privilege. If you abuse the lunch policy, our hands will be tied, and we will be forced to look the other way. We will not enjoy that.

This is the refrigerator. You may put your lunch in it. Barry Hacker, who sits over there, steals food from this refrigerator. His petty theft is an outlet for his grief. Last New Year's Eve, while kissing his wife, a blood vessel burst in her brain. Barry Hacker's wife was two months pregnant at the time, and lingered in a coma for half a year before dying. It was a tragic loss for Barry Hacker. He hasn't been himself since. Barry Hacker's wife was a beautiful woman. She was also completely covered. Barry Hacker did not have to pay one dime. But his dead wife haunts him. She haunts all of us. We have seen her, reflected in the monitors of our computers, moving past our cubicles. We have seen the dim shadow of her face in our photocopies. She pencils herself in in the receptionist's appointment book with the notation: To see Barry Hacker. She has left messages in the receptionist's Voicemail box, messages garbled by the electronic chirrups and buzzes in the phone line, her voice echoing from an immense distance within the ambient hum. But the voice is hers. And beneath her voice, beneath the tidal *whoosh* of static and hiss, the gurgling and crying of a baby can be heard.

In any case, if you bring a lunch, put a little something extra in the bag for Barry Hacker. We have four Barrys in this office. Isn't that a coincidence?

This is Matthew Payne's office. He is our Unit Manager, and his door is always closed. We have never seen him, and you will never see him. But he is here. You can be sure of that. He is all around us.

This is the Custodian's Closet. You have no business in the Custodian's Closet.

And this, this is our Supplies Cabinet. If you need supplies see Curtis Lance. He will log you in on the Supplies Cabinet Authorization Log, then give you a Supplies Authorization Slip. Present your pink copy of the supplies Authorization Slip to Ellie Tapper. She will log you in on the Supplies Cabinet Key Log, then give you the key. Because the Supplies Cabinet is located outside the Unit Manager's office, you must be very quiet. Gather your supplies quietly. The Supplies Cabinet is divided into four sections. Section One contains letterhead stationery, blank paper and envelopes, memo and note pads, and so on. Section Two contains pens and pencils and typewriter and printer ribbons, and the like. In Section Three we have erasers, correction fluids, transparent tapes, glue sticks, et cetera. And in Section Four we have paper clips and push pins and scissors and razor blades. And here are the spare blades for the shredder. Do not touch the shredder, which is located over there. The shredder is of no concern to you.

Gwendolyn Stich sits in that office there. She is crazy about penguins, and collects penguin knickknacks: penguin posters and coffee mugs and stationery, penguin stuffed animals, penguin jewelry, penguin sweaters and T-shirts and socks. She has a pair of penguin fuzzy slippers she wears when working late at the office. She has a tape cassette of penguin sounds which she listens to for relaxation. Her favorite colors are black and white. She has personalized license plates that read PEN GWEN. Every morning she passes through all the cubicles to wish each of us a *good* morning.

She brings Danish on Wednesdays for Hump Day morning break, and doughnuts on Fridays for TGIF afternoon break. She organizes the Annual Christmas Potluck, and is in charge of the Birthday List. Gwendolyn Stich's door is always open to all of us. She will always lend an ear, and put in a good word for you; she will always give you a hand, or the shirt off her back, or a shoulder to cry on. Because her door is always open, she hides and cries in a stall in the women's room. And John LaFountaine—who, enthralled when a woman enters, sites quietly in his stall with his knees to his chest—John LaFountaine has heard her vomiting in there. We have come upon Gwendolyn Stich huddled in the stairwell, shivering in the updraft, sipping a Diet Mr. Pibb and hugging her knees. She does not let any of this interfere with her work. If it interfered with her work, she might have to be let go.

Kevin Howard sits in that cubicle over there. He is a serial killer, the one they call the Carpet Cutter, responsible for the mutilations across town. We're not supposed to know that, so do not let on. Don't worry. His compulsion inflicts itself on strangers only, and the routine established is elaborate and unwavering. The victim must be a white male, a young adult no older than thirty, heavyset, with dark hair and eyes, and the like. The victim must be chosen at random, before sunset, from a public place; the victim is followed home, and must put up a struggle; et cetera. The carnage inflicted is precise: the angle and direction of the incisions; the layering of skin and muscle tissue; the rearrangement of the visceral organs; and so on. Kevin Howard does not let any of this interfere with his work. He is, in fact, our fastest typist. He types as if he were on fire. He has a secret crush on Gwendolyn Stich, and leaves a red-foil-wrapped Hershey's Kiss on her desk every afternoon. But he hates Anika Bloom, and keeps well away from her. In his presence, she has uncontrollable fits of shaking and trembling. Her left palm does not stop bleeding.

In any case, when Kevin Howard gets caught, act surprised. Say that he seemed like a nice person, a bit of a loner, perhaps, but always quiet and polite.

This is the photocopier room. And this, this is our view. It faces southwest. West is down there, toward the water. North is back there. Because we are on the seventeenth floor, we are afforded a magnificent view. Isn't it beautiful? It overlooks the park, where the tops of those trees are. You can see a segment of the bay between those two buildings over there. You can see this building reflected in the glass panels of that building across the way. There. See? That's you, waving. And look there. There's Anika Bloom in the kitchenette, waving back.

Enjoy this view while photocopying. If you have problems with the photocopier, see Russell Nash. If you have any questions, ask your supervisor. If you can't find your supervisor, ask Phillip Spiers. He sits over there. He'll check with Clarissa Nicks. She sits over there. If you can't find them, feel free to ask me. That's my cubicle. I sit in there.

𝒫 𝒫 𝒫

Suggestions for Discussion

1. Who is the implied listener? Why isn't the listener's dialogue included?

2. Why is no background given on the speaker or the listener?

Retrospect

3. The absurdities of this office environment progress from the mundane to the surreal. How does the repetition of elements and phrases (such as "we," "you may be let go," and "never") help to build tension? What else creates a looming sense of trouble?

4. Where does the soothing rhythm of the speaker contrast with the disturbing content of his/her speech? What effect is achieved by this contrast?

The Comedian

JOHN L'HEUREUX

Corinne hasn't planned to have a baby. She is thirty-eight and happy and she wants to get on with it. She is a stand-up comedian with a husband, her second, and with no thought of a child, and what she wants out of life now is a lot of laughs. To give them, and especially to get them. And here she is, by accident, pregnant.

The doctor sees her chagrin and is surprised, because he thinks of her as a competent and sturdy woman. But that's how things are these days and so he suggests an abortion. Corinne says she'll let him know; she has to do some thinking. A baby.

"That's great," Russ says. "If you want it, I mean. I want it. I mean, I want it if you do. It's up to you, though. You know what I mean?"

And so they decide that, of course, they will have the baby, of course they want the baby, the baby is just exactly what they need.

In the bathroom mirror that night, Russ looks through his eyes into his cranium for a long time. Finally he sees his mind. As he watches, it knots like a fist. And he continues to watch, glad, as that fist beats the new baby flat and thin, a dead slick silverfish.

Mother. Mother and baby. A little baby. A big baby. Bouncing babies. At once Corinne sees twenty babies, twenty pink basketball babies, bouncing down the court and then up into the air and—whoosh—they swish neatly through the net. Babies.

Baby is its own excuse for being. Or is it? Well, Corinne was a Catholic right up until the end of her first marriage, so she thinks maybe it is. One thing is sure: the only subject you can't make a good joke about is abortion.

Yes, they will have the baby. Yes, she will be the mother. Yes.

But the next morning, while Russ is at work, Corinne turns off the television and sits on the edge of the couch. She squeezes her thighs together, tight; she contracts her stomach; she arches her back. This is no joke. This is the real thing. By an act of will, she is going to expel this baby, this invader, this insidious little murderer. She pushes and pushes and nothing happens. She pushes again, hard. And once more she pushes. Finally she gives up and lies back against the sofa, resting.

After a while she puts her hand on her belly, and as she does so, she is astonished to hear singing.

It is the baby. It has a soft reedy voice and it sings slightly off-key. Corinne listens to the words: "Some of these days, you'll miss me, honey. . . ."

Corinne faints then, and it is quite some time before she wakes up.

When she wakes, she opens her eyes only a slit and looks carefully from left to right. She sits on the couch, vigilant, listening, but she hears nothing. After a while she says three Hail Marys and an Act of Contrition, and then, confused and a little embarrassed, she does the laundry.

She does not tell Russ about this.

Well, it's a time of strain, Corinne tells herself, even though in California there isn't supposed to be any strain. Just surfing and tans and divorce and a lot of interfacing. No strain and no babies.

Corinne thinks for a second about interfacing babies, but forces the thought from her mind and goes back to thinking about her act. Sometimes she does a very funny set on interfacing, but only if the audience is middle-aged. The younger ones don't seem to know that interfacing is laughable. Come to think of it, *nobody* laughs much in California. Everybody smiles, but who laughs?

Laughs: that's something she can use. She does Garbo's laugh: "I am so hap-py." What was that movie? "I am so happy." She does the Garbo laugh again. Not bad. Who else laughs? Joe E. Brown. The Wicked Witch of the West. Who was she? Somebody Hamilton. Will anybody remember these people? Ruth Buzzi? Goldie Hawn? Yes, that great giggle. Of course, the best giggle is Burt Reynolds's. High and fey. Why does he do that? Is he sending up his own image?

Corinne is thinking of images, Burt Reynolds's and Tom Selleck's when she hears singing: "Cal-i-for-nia, here I come, Right back where I started from. . . ." Corinne stops pacing and stands in the doorway to the kitchen—as if I'm waiting for the earthquake, she thinks. But there is no earthquake; there is only the thin sweet voice, singing.

Corinne leans against the doorframe and listens. She closes her eyes. At once it is Easter, and she is a child again at Sacred Heart Grammar School, and the thirty-five members of the children's choir, earnest and angelic, look out at her from where they stand, massed about the altar. They wear red cassocks and white surplices, starched, and they seem to have descended from heaven for this one occasion. Their voices are pure, high, untouched by adolescence or by pain; and, with a conviction born of absolute innocence, they sing to God and to Corinne, "Cal-i-for-nia, here I come."

Corinne leans against the doorframe and listens truly now. Imagination aside, drama aside—she listens. It is a single voice she hears, thin and reedy. So, she did not imagine it the first time. It is true. The baby sings.

That night, when Russ comes home, he takes his shower, and they settle in with their first martini and everything is cozy.

Corinne asks him about his day, and he tells her. It was a lousy day. Russ started his own construction company a year ago just as the bottom fell out of the building business, and now there are no jobs to speak of. Just renovation stuff. Cleanup after fires. Sometimes Victorian restorations down in the gay district. But that's about it. So whatever comes his way is bound to be lousy. This is Russ's second marriage, though, so he knows not to go too far with a lousy day. Who needs it?

"But I've got you, babe," he says, and pulls her toward him, and kisses her.

"We've got each other," Corinne says, and kisses him back. "And the baby," she says.

He holds her close then, so that she can't see his face. She makes big eyes like an actor in a bad comedy—she doesn't know why; she just always sees the absurd in everything. After a while they pull away, smiling, secret, and sip their martinis.

"Do you know something?" she says. "Can I tell you something?"

"What?" he says. "Tell me."

"You won't laugh?"

"No," he says, laughing. "I'm sorry. No, I won't laugh."

"Okay," she says. "Here goes."

There is a long silence, and then he says, "Well?"

"It sings."

"It sings?"

"The baby. The fetus. It sings."

Russ is stalled, but only for a second. Then he says, "Rock and roll? Or plain-chant?" He begins to laugh, and he laughs so hard that he chokes and sloshes martini onto the couch. "You're wonderful," he says. "You're really a funny, funny girl. Woman." He laughs some more. "Is that for your act? I love it."

"I'm serious," she says. "I mean it."

Corinne puts her hand on her stomach and thinks she has never been so alone in her life. She looks at Russ, with his big square jaw and all those white teeth and his green eyes so trusting and innocent, and she realizes for one second how corrupt she is, how lost, how deserving of a baby who sings; and then she pulls herself together because real life has to go on.

"Let's eat out," she says. "Spaghetti. It's cheap." She kisses him gently on the left eyelid, on his right. She gazes into his eyes and smiles, so that he will not guess she is thinking: Who is this man? Who am I?

Corinne has a job, Fridays and Saturdays for the next three weeks, at the Ironworks. It's not The Comedy Shop, but it's a legitimate gig, and the money is good. More-over, it will give her something to think about besides whether or not she should go through with the abortion. She and Russ have put that on hold.

She is well into her third month, but she isn't showing yet, so she figures she can handle the three weekends easily. She wishes, in a way, that she were showing. As it is, she only looks. . . . She searches for the word, but not for long. The word is *fat*. She looks fat.

She could do fat-girl jokes, but she hates jokes that put down women. And she hates jokes that are blue. Jokes that ridicule husbands. Jokes that ridicule the joker's looks. Jokes about nationalities. Jokes that play into audience prejudice. Jokes about the terrible small town you came from. Jokes about how poor you were, how ugly, how unpopular. Phyllis Diller jokes. Joan Rivers jokes. Jokes about small boobs, wrinkles, sexual inadequacy. Why is she in this business? She wonders. She hates jokes.

She thinks she hears herself praying: Please, please.

What should she do at the Ironworks? What should she do about the baby? What should she do?

The baby is the only one who's decided what to do. The baby sings.

Its voice is filling out nicely and it has enlarged its repertoire considerably. It sings a lot of classical melodies Corinne thinks she remembers from somewhere, churchy stuff, but it also favors golden oldies from the forties and fifties, with a few real old-timers thrown in when they seem appropriate. Once, right at the beginning, for instance, after Corinne and Russ had quarreled, Corinne locked herself in the bathroom to sulk and after a while was surprised, and then grateful, to hear the baby crooning, "Oh, my man, I love him so." It struck Corinne a day or so later that this could be a baby that would sell out for *any* one-liner . . . if indeed she decided to have the baby . . . and so she was relieved when the baby turned to more classical pieces.

The baby sings only now and then, and it sings better at some times than at others, but Corinne is convinced it sings best on weekend evenings when she is preparing for her gig. Before she leaves home, Corinne always has a long hot soak in the tub. She lies in the suds with her little orange bath pillow at her head and, as she runs through the night's possibilities, preparing ad-libs, heckler put-downs, segues, the baby sings to her.

There is some connection, she is sure, between her work and the baby's singing, but she can't guess what it is. It doesn't matter. She loves this: just she and the baby, together, in song.

Thank you, thank you, she prays.

The Ironworks gig goes extremely well. It is a young crowd, mostly, and so Corinne sticks to her young jokes: life in California, diets, dating, school. The audience laughs, and Russ says she is better than ever, but at the end of the three weeks the manager tells her, "You got it, honey. You got all the moves. You really make them laugh, you know? But they laugh from here only"—he taps his head—"not from the gut. You gotta get gut. You know? Like feeling."

So now the gig is over and Corinne lies in her tub trying to think of gut. She's gotta get gut, she's gotta get feeling. Has she ever *felt?* Well, she feels for Russ; she loves him. She felt for Alan, that bastard; well, maybe he wasn't so bad; maybe he just wasn't ready for marriage, any more than she was. Maybe it's California; maybe nobody *can* feel in California.

Enough about feeling, already. Deliberately, she puts feeling out of her mind, and calls up babies instead. A happy baby, she thinks, and at once the bathroom is crowded with laughing babies, each one roaring and carrying on like Ed McMahon.

A fat baby, and she sees a Shelley Winters baby, an Elizabeth Taylor baby, an Orson Welles baby. An active baby: a mile of trampolines and babies doing quadruple somersaults, back flips, high dives. A healthy baby: babies lifting weights, swimming the Channel. Babies.

But abortion is the issue, not babies. Should she have it, or not?

At once she sees a bloody mess, a crushed-looking thing, half animal, half human. Its hands open and close. She gasps. "No," she says aloud, and shakes her head to get rid of the awful picture. "No," and covers her face.

Gradually she realizes that she has been listening to humming, and now the humming turns to song—"It ain't necessarily so," sung in a good clear mezzo.

Her eyes hurt and she has a headache. In fact, her eyes hurt all the time.

Corinne has finally convinced Russ that she hears the baby singing. Actually, he is convinced that Corinne is halfway around the bend with worry, and he is surprised, when he thinks about it, to find that he loves her anyway, crazy or not. He tells her that as much as he hates the idea, maybe she ought to think about having an abortion.

"I've actually gotten to like the singing," she says.

"Corinne," he says.

"It's the things I see that scare me to death."

"What things? What do you see?"

At once she sees a little crimson baby. It has been squashed into a mason jar. The tiny eyes almost disappear into the puffed cheeks, the cheeks into the neck, the neck into the torso. It is a pickled baby, ancient, preserved.

"Tell me," he says.

"Nothing," she says. "It's just that my eyes hurt."

It's getting late for an abortion, the doctor says, but she can still have one safely.

He's known her for twenty years, all through the first marriage and now through this one, and he's puzzled that a funny and sensible girl like Corinne should be having such a tough time with pregnancy. He had recommended abortion right from the start, because she didn't seem to want the baby and because she was almost forty, but he hadn't really expected her to take him up on it. Looking at her now, though, it is clear to him that she'll never make it. She'll be wacko—if not during the pregnancy, then sure as hell afterward.

So what does she think? What does Russ think?

Well, first, she explains in her new, sort of wandering way, there's something else she wants to ask about; not really important, she supposes, but something, well, kind of different she probably should mention. It's the old problem of the baby . . . well, um, singing.

"Singing?" he asks.

"Singing?" he asks again.

"And humming," Corinne says.

They sit in silence for a minute, the doctor trying to decide whether or not this is a joke. She's got this great poker face. She really is a good comic. So after a while he laughs, and then when she laughs, he knows he's done the right thing. But what a crazy sense of humor!

"You're terrific," he says. "Anything else? How's Russ? How was the Ironworks job?"

"My eyes hurt," she says. "I have headaches."

And so they discuss her vision for a while, and stand-up comedy, and she makes him laugh. And that's that.

At the door he says to her, "Have an abortion, Corinne. Now, before it's too late."

They have just made love and now Russ puts off the light and they lie together in the dark, his hand on her belly.

"Listen," he says. "I want to say something. I've been thinking about what the doctor said, about an abortion. I hate it, I hate the whole idea, but you know, we've got to think of you. And I think this baby is too much for you, I think maybe that's why you've been having those headaches and stuff. Don't you think?"

Corinne puts her hand on his hand and says nothing. After a long while Russ speaks again, into the darkness.

"I've been a lousy father. Two sons I never see. I never see them. The stepfather's good to them, though; he's a good father. I thought maybe I'd have another chance at it, do it right this time, like the marriage. Besides, the business isn't always going to be this bad, you know; I'll get jobs; I'll get money. We could afford it, you know? A son. A daughter. It would be nice. But what I mean is, we've got to take other things into consideration, we've got to consider your health. You're not strong enough, I guess. I always think of you as strong, because you do those gigs and you're funny and all, but, I mean, you're almost forty, and the doctor thinks that maybe an abortion is the way to go, and what do I know. I don't know. The singing. The headaches. I don't know."

Russ looks into the dark, seeing nothing.

"I worry about you, you want to know the truth? I do. Corinne?"

Corinne lies beside him, listening to him, refusing to listen to the baby, who all this time has been singing. Russ is as alone as she is, even more alone. She is dumbfounded. She is speechless with love. If he were a whirlpool, she thinks, she would fling herself into it. If he were . . . but he is who he is, and she loves only him, and she makes her decision.

"You think I'm losing my mind," she says.

Silence.

"Yes."

More silence.

"Well, I'm not. Headaches are a normal part of lots of pregnancies, the doctor told me, and the singing doesn't mean anything at all. He explained what was really going on, why I thought I heard it sing. You see," Corinne says, improvising freely now, making it all up, for him, her gift to him, "you see, when you get somebody as high-strung as me and you add pregnancy right at the time I'm about to make it big as a stand-up, then the pressures get to be so much that sometimes the imagination can take over, the doctor said, and when you tune in to the normal sounds of your body, you hear them really loud, as if they were amplified by a three-thousand-watt PA system, and it can sound like singing. See?"

Russ says nothing.

"So you see, it all makes sense, really. You don't have to worry about me."

"Come on," Russ says. "Do you mean to tell me you never heard the baby singing?"

"Well, I heard it, sort of. You know? It was really all in my mind. I mean, the *sound* was in my body physiologically, but my hearing it as *singing* was just . . ."

"Just your imagination."

Corinne does not answer.

"Well?"

"Right," she says, making the total gift. "It was just my imagination."

And the baby—who has not stopped singing all this time, love songs mostly—stops singing now, and does not sing again until the day scheduled for the abortion.

The baby has not sung in three weeks. It is Corinne's fifth month now, and at last they have been able to do an amniocentesis. The news is bad. One of the baby's chromosomes does not match up to anything in hers, anything in Russ's. What this means, they tell her, is that the baby is not normal. It will be deformed in some way; in what way, they have no idea.

Corinne and Russ decide on an abortion.

They talk very little about their decision now that they have made it. In fact, they talk very little about anything. Corinne's face grows daily more haggard, and Corinne avoids Russ's eyes. She is silent much of the time, thinking. The baby is silent all the time.

The abortion will be by hypertonic saline injection, a simple procedure, complicated only by the fact that Corinne has waited so long. She has been given a booklet to read and she has listened to a tape, and so she knows about the injection of the saline solution, she knows about the contractions that will begin slowly and then get more and more frequent, and she knows about the dangers of infection and excessive bleeding.

She knows moreover that it will be a formed fetus she will expel.

Russ has come with her to the hospital and is outside in the waiting room. Corinne thinks of him, of how she loves him, of how their lives will be better, safer, without this baby who sings. This deformed baby. Who sings. If only she could hear the singing once more, just once.

Corinne lies on the table with her legs in the thigh rests, and one of the nurses drapes the examining sheet over and around her. The other nurse, or someone—Corinne is getting confused; her eyesight seems fuzzy—takes her pulse and her blood pressure. She feels someone washing her, the careful hands, the warm fluid. So, it is beginning.

Corinne closes her eyes and tries to make her mind a blank. Dark, she thinks. Dark. She squeezes her eyes tight against the light, she wants to remain in this cool darkness forever, she wants to cease being. And then, amazingly, the dark does close in on her. Though she opens her eyes, she sees nothing. She can remain this way forever if she wills it. The dark is cool to the touch, and it is comforting somehow; it invites her in. She can lean into it, give herself up to it, and be safe, alone, forever.

She tries to sit up. She will enter this dark. She will do it. Please, please, she hears herself say. And then all at once she thinks of Russ and the baby, and instead of surrendering to the dark, she pushes it away.

With one sweep of her hand she pushes the sheet from her and flings it to the floor. She pulls her legs from the thigh rests and manages to sit up, blinded still, but fighting.

"Here now," a nurse says, caught off guard, unsure what to do. "Hold on now. It's all right. It's fine."

"Easy now. Easy," the doctor says, thinking Yes, here it is, what else is new.

Together the nurses and the doctor make an effort to stop her, but they are too late, because by this time Corinne has fought free of any restraints. She is off the examining couch and, naked, huddles in the corner of the small room.

"No," she shouts. "I want the baby. I want the baby." And later, when she has stopped shouting, when she has stopped crying, still she clutches her knees to her chest and whispers over and over, "I want the baby."

So there is no abortion after all.

By the time she is discharged, Corinne's vision has returned, dimly. Moreover, though she tells nobody, she has heard humming, and once or twice a whole line of music. The baby has begun to sing again.

Corinne has more offers than she wants: The Hungry I, The Purple Onion, The Comedy Shop. Suddenly everybody decides it's time to take a look at her, but she is in no shape to be looked at, so she signs for two weeks at My Uncle's Bureau and lets it go at that.

She is only marginally pretty now, she is six months pregnant, and she is carrying a deformed child. Furthermore, she can see very little, and what she does see, she often sees double.

Her humor, therefore, is spare and grim, but audiences love it. She begins slow: "When I was a girl, I always wanted to look like Elizabeth Taylor," she says, and glances down at her swollen belly. Two beats. "And now I do." They laugh with her, and applaud. Now she can quicken the pace, sharpen the humor. They follow her; they are completely captivated.

She has found some new way of holding her body—tipping her head, thrusting out her belly—and instead of putting off her audience, or embarrassing them, it charms them. The laughter is *with* her, the applause *for* her. She could do anything out there and get away with it. And she knows it. They simply love her.

In her dressing room after the show she tells herself that somehow, magically, she's learned to work from the heart instead of just from the head. She's got gut. She's got feeling. But she knows it's something more than that.

By the end of the two weeks she is convinced that the successful new element in her act is the baby. This deformed baby, the abnormal baby she has tried to get rid of. And what interests her most is that she no longer cares about success as a stand-up.

Corinne falls asleep that night to the sound of the baby's crooning. She is trying to pray, Please, please, but with Russ's snoring and the baby's lullaby, they all get mixed up together in her mind—God, Russ, the baby—and she forgets to whom she is praying or why. She sleeps.

The baby sings all the time now. It starts first thing in the morning with a nice soft piece by Telemann or Brahms; there are assorted lullabies at bedtime; and throughout the day it is bop, opera, ragtime, blues, a little rock and roll, big-band stuff—the baby never tires.

Corinne tells no one about this, not even Russ.

She and Russ talk about almost everything now: their love for each other, their hopes for the baby, their plans. They have lots of plans. Russ has assured Corinne that whatever happens, he's ready for it. Corinne is his whole life, and no matter how badly the baby is deformed, they'll manage. They'll do the right thing. They'll survive.

They talk about almost everything, but they do not talk about the baby's singing.

For Corinne the singing is secret, mysterious. It contains some revelation, of course, but she does not want to know what that revelation might be.

The singing is somehow tied up with her work; but more than that, with her life. It is part of her fate. It is inescapable. And she is perfectly content to wait.

Corinne has been in labor for three hours, and the baby has been singing the whole time. The doctor has administered a mild anesthetic and a nurse remains at bedside, but the birth does not seem imminent, and so for Corinne it is a period of pain and waiting. And for the baby, singing.

"These lights are so strong," Corinne says, or thinks she says. "The lights are blinding."

The nurse looks at her for a moment and then goes back to the letter she is writing.

"Please," Corinne says, "thank you."

She is unconscious, she supposes; she is imagining the lights. Or perhaps the lights are indeed bright and she sees them as they really are *because* she is unconscious. Or perhaps her sight has come back, as strong as it used to be. Whatever the case, she doesn't want to think about it right now. Besides, for some reason or other, even though the lights are blinding, they are not blinding her. They do not even bother her. It is as if light is her natural element.

"Thank you," she says. To someone.

The singing is wonderful, a cappella things Corinne recognizes as Brahms, Mozart, Bach. The baby's voice can assume any dimension it wants now, swelling from a single thin note to choir volume; it can take on the tone and resonance of musical instruments, violin, viola, flute; it can become all sounds; it enchants.

The contractions are more frequent; even unconscious, Corinne can tell that. Good. Soon the waiting will be over and she will have her wonderful baby, her perfect baby. But at once she realizes hers will not be a perfect baby; it will be deformed. "Please," she says, "please," as if prayer can keep Russ from being told—as he will be soon after the birth—that this baby has been born dumb. Russ, who has never understood comedians.

But now the singing has begun to swell in volume. It is as if the baby has become a full choir, with many voices, with great strength.

The baby will be fine, however it is, she thinks. She thinks of Russ, worried half to death. She is no longer worried. She accepts what will be.

The contractions are very frequent now and the light is much brighter. She knows the doctor has come into the room, because she hears his voice. There is another nurse too. And soon there will be the baby.

The light is so bright that she can see none of them. She can see into the light, it is true; she can see the soft fleecy nimbus glowing beyond the light, but she can see nothing in the room.

The singing. The singing and the light. It is Palestrina she hears, in polyphony, each voice lambent. The light envelops her, catches her up from this table where the doctor bends over her and where already can be seen the shimmering yellow hair of the baby. The light lifts her, and the singing lifts her, and she says, "Yes," she says, "Thank you."

She accepts what will be. She accepts what is.

The room is filled with singing and with light, and the singing is transformed into light, more light, more lucency, and still she says, "Yes," until she cannot bear it, and she reaches up and tears the light aside. And sees.

Suggestions for Discussion

1. How is the point-of-view contract for omniscience established in the first two paragraphs?
2. Where and why does the point of view shift?

Retrospect

3. Why has the author made Corinne a comedian—and one who "hates jokes"?
4. How is the baby's singing used to reflect Corinne's concerns at different points throughout the story?
5. In what ways is the transcendence of the ending earned by the story itself?

Lectures on How You Never Lived Back Home

M. EVELINA GALANG

You grew up hearing two languages—one you can pull apart, name, slap a series of rules to, twist like clay-dough in a child's hand—the other you cannot explain, you listen and you know. It is a language you understand intuitively—like being able to read the sunrise, the strips of pink and orange, the clumps of uneven clouds, a thin patch of grey and the moon and somehow, without thinking twice, you know what kind of day it will be. You understand like this because you are the first born. First generation. First American. First cousin. First hope.

Back home, one of your grandmothers sewed children's clothing by hand, and sold them in an open-air market. The other grandmother raised seven children on her own, gathering them up, hiding them away in the provinces along the sea, away from Japanese soldiers, away from American fighters. Away from war. Your grandmother feared the safety of all her children, especially her young ladies. Your mother survived wartime. She was smart and well-read and ambitious, skipped grades, travelled across the oceans, met your father in Milwaukee, gave up her princess status to be your mother. As a boy, your dad farmed fish out of monsoon-swollen rice paddies, cut school to hitchhike from Pampanga to Rizal just to see MacArthur. Somewhere in his youth, he spied on American GIs and caught on to this notion of democracy, this notion of rights. His rights, his family's rights, the rights of his countrymen. The rights taken first by three hundred years of Spanish rule, then Japanese terror and war, then of course, there were the Americans and their intentions. After sneaking about soldier camps, making friends with a GI from Atlanta, bumming cigarettes from another one from Pasadena, your father worked his way out of those provinces, studied hard at school. He passed his boards, passed immigration, slipped into that ballroom on Racine and Wisconsin, and charmed his way into your mother's life.

They raised you to understand that back home, a young girl serves her parents, lives to please them, fetches her father's slippers and her mother's cups of tea. Back home a young girl learns to embroider fine stitches, learns parlor dances, wears white uniforms at all-girl schools, convent schools. She never crosses her legs or wears skirts above the knee. Back home a girl does not date. She is courted. And when there is a young man present, there is always a chaperon. Young ladies grow up to be young housewives, good mothers, and in their old age, they still behave like obedient daughters.

You, on the other hand, have never had to obey a curfew because of war, never had to tiptoe through your own house, never had to read your books underneath a blanket where no soldier would see. As far as you knew, your curfew was your curfew because Mom and Dad said so. You were raised in suburbia in a split-level house, always in fashion, even when you were only two, dressed in your white lace and pink ribbons, toting your very own parasol. You've never been without heat, without food, without parents. All your life your worries consisted of boys and pimples and overdue books. You had your first boy-girl party when you were five years old, played Pin-the-Tail-on-the-Donkey and kissed Timmy Matasaki underneath the dining room table. You had a bad habit of talking back. You learned how to scream no to your parents, and it didn't matter if you were punished, slapped across the face, sent away to sulk, banished to the kitchen, you still opened your mouth and the words came out.

You grew up pouring chicken soy sauce dishes over beds of steamed rice, never mashing potatoes until you were on your own, eating your meals with a spoon in your right hand, a fork in the left, marvelling at the Americans and how they could balance entire meals on one fork, or the Chinese who could eat bowls of rice with two sticks. Your family roasted pigs on a spit, while next door, the neighbors cooked brats and burgers on electric grills.

From the start, you were a piece that did not fit, never given the chance to be like the rest—the ones with blond hair and red hair and something someone called strawberry. The ones with eyes that change like the ocean—green to blue to seafoam, depending on the color of their sweater. Your eyes have always been black. Your hair dark. Straight. No variety. To the kids at school, you were no different from the other Oriental girl, the one who spoke English with a chopped-up accent. To your aunts and uncles you were turning into a *bratty Americana*, loose like those blond children, mouthy like the kids who ran the streets wild. They worried you might grow up too indelicate for marriage.

Now you are well over twenty-five and still single. The old aunts raise one eyebrow and say, See? But you know, it's because you refuse to settle for less than best. Anyone can get married, you say. You not only tell men off, you ask them out. Recently, you've considered having a child without a father. This attitude bangs up against your mother's heart like the bumpers of two cars when she's parallel parking and the car doesn't fit. Sometimes she looks at you and sighs.

Your home is in Bucktown, Wicker Park, Ravenswood, Illinois, and because you won't admit the fact that what your parents call "back home" has made a place in your house, because you are not white, and still you are not one of them—the foreigners—you continue to displease everyone. Your father's headache is mostly just you. He has been known to throw his hands up, call you stubborn, say *Bahala na!* It's up to you. Your choice. Your responsibility.

Still, in the privacy of your kitchen, you admit you cannot live without your family, your history, this ideal called "your people." You cannot divorce yourself from yourself. You know you are the hyphen in American-born. Your identity scrawls the length and breadth of the page, American-born-girl. American-born-Filipina. Because you have always had one foot planted in the Midwest, one foot floating on the islands, and your arms have stretched across the generations, barely kissing your father's province, your children's future, the dreams your mother has for you. Because you were meant for the better life, whatever that is, been told you mustn't forget where you come from, what others have done for you. Because all your life you've simply been told. Just told. Because a council of ancestors—including a few who are not yet dead, who are not even related to you—haunt you, you do your best. You try. You struggle. And somehow, when you stand in the center of a room, and the others look on, you find yourself acting out your role. Smart American girl, beautiful Filipina, dutiful daughter.

ク ク ク

Suggestions for Discussion

1. Why is second person an effective point-of-view choice for this story? What would change if the story were told in first person?

Retrospect

2. How do the descriptions of language in the first paragraph reflect the daughter's character?

3. Find a metaphor used to describe "your" situation and explain why it is effective.

Writing Exercises

INDIVIDUAL

1. Select a tense situation such as an auto accident, a potentially violent encounter, or a disintegrating love affair, and describe it four times from four different points of view:
   a. first person
   b. third-person *limited* omniscient
   c. third-person objective
   d. third-person omniscient

   Analyze which point of view works best for this material and why.

2. Think back to your last significant argument and write out the dialogue as well as you can recall it, trying to be fair and objective. Then, using that dialogue as a framework, write the scene from the point of view of the other person (using third-person limited omniscience, with access to thoughts, sensory perceptions and memories), trying to let readers see why that person feels justified in his or her position.

3. Write about a recent dream, using the viewpoint of the objective author. Without any comment or interpretation whatsoever, report the events (the more bizarre, the better) as they occur.

COLLABORATIVE

4. Brainstorm a list of characters who might be given how-to instructions (for example, a new waiter, a band member, a bride, a sorority or a fraternity pledge, a student teacher, a mother-to-be, a dog, a baby). These instructions should come *from* another character who thinks the recipient is sure to be incompetent (from a boss, bandleader, mother-in-law, etc.).
   a. Write one set of such instructions.
   b. Read the pieces back to the class, identifying the speaker and implied listener. Discuss whether or not class members would classify each piece as a short-short story and why.

5. In groups of five, choose either a Bible story (for example, Lazarus raised from the dead), a well-known historical or news event (the Kennedy assassination), or a fairy tale (Hansel and Gretel).

   a. List five characters who have some role in the story, including minor characters and perhaps even inanimate objects (the gingerbread house) or animals (the birds that eat Hansel's scattered crumbs).

   b. After choosing one central event to depict, each group member should write about that moment from one of the five characters' points of view. Try to exaggerate that character's concerns or private agenda so that we see how his or her view colors the story.

   c. Decide on the most dramatic order in which to present the monologues.

   d. Read the series of monologues back to the class.

   e. *Class Feedback:* How does each character's perspective alter the commonly known story?

8

ASSORTED LIARS
Point of View, Part II

• *At What Distance?*

• *With What Limitations?*

A reader's experience of fiction is influenced by person, tone, distance, reliability, and other aspects of point of view. The good news for novice writers feeling overwhelmed by these considerations is that point-of-view choices, like plot and theme, are seldom calculated and preplanned. Rather, point of view tends to evolve organically as a story develops, and you can usually trust intuition to guide you through several drafts. It is when a story is well underway that analysis of its specific point-of-view issues becomes most useful for the writer ready to refine or refocus the work. Gaining control over *distance*, a major topic of this chapter, becomes especially relevant once readers' feedback reveals a mismatch between the author's intention and the reader's reception of a character or situation.

As with the chemist at her microscope and the lookout in his tower, fictional point of view always involves the *distance*, close or far, of the perceiver from the thing perceived. Often involving not only space but time, distance may also arise from tone and involve a judgment—moral, intellectual, and/or emotional. More complicated still, the narrator or characters or both may view the action from one distance, the author and reader from another.

At What Distance?

Authorial distance, sometimes called *psychic distance*, is the degree to which we as readers feel on the one hand intimacy and identification with, or on the other hand detachment and alienation from, the characters in a story. Choosing and *controlling* the psychic distance that best suits a given story is one of the most elusive challenges a writer faces, and it is an area in which the feedback of other workshop members may be of particular value.

When desired, a sense of distance may be increased through the use of abstract nouns, summary, typicality, and apparent objectivity. Such techniques, which in other contexts might be seen as writing flaws, are employed in the following passage purposely to detach readers from characters.

> It started in the backyards. At first the men concentrated on heat and smoke, and on dangerous thrusts with long forks. Their wives gave them aprons in railroad stripes, with slogans on the front—*Hot Stuff, The Boss*—to spur them on. Then it began to get mixed up who should do the dishes, and you can't fall back on paper plates forever, and around that time the wives got tired of making butterscotch brownies and jello salads with grated carrots in them and wanted to make money instead, and one thing led to another.
>
> Margaret Atwood, "Simmering"

Conversely, closeness and sympathy can be achieved by concrete detail, scene, a character's thoughts, and so forth.

> She dreams she does not already have three children. A squeeze around the flowers in her hands chokes off three and four and five years of breath. Instantly she is ashamed and frightened in her superstition. She looks for the first time at the preacher, forces humility into her eyes, as if she believes he is, in fact, a man of God. She can imagine God, a small black boy, timidly pulling the preacher's coattail.
>
> Alice Walker, "Roselily"

Or a combination of techniques may make us feel simultaneously sympathetic and detached—a frequent effect of comedy—as in this example:

> I'm a dishwasher in a restaurant. I'm not trying to impress anybody. I'm not bragging. It's just what I do. It's not the glamorous job people make it out to be. Sure, you make a lot of dough and everybody looks up to you and respects you, but then again there's a lot of responsibility. It weighs on you. It wears on you. Everybody wants to be a dishwasher these days, I guess, but they've got an idealistic view of it.
>
> Robert McBrearty, "The Dishwasher"

As author you may ask us to identify completely with one character and totally condemn another. One character may judge another harshly while you as author suggest that we should qualify that judgment. If there is also a narrator, that narrator may think himself morally superior while behind his back you make sure that we will think him morally deficient. Further, the four members of the author-reader-charac-ter-narrator relationship may operate differently in various areas of value: A character calls the narrator stupid and ugly; the narrator thinks herself ugly but clever; the author and the reader know that she is both intelligent and beautiful.

Any complexity or convolution in the relationship among author, narrator, and characters can make successful fiction. The one relationship in which there must not be any distance, however, is between author and reader. We may find the characters and/or the narrator bad, stupid, and tasteless and still applaud the book as just, brilliant, and beautiful. But if the hero's agony strikes us as ridiculous, if the comedy leaves us cold—if we say that the *book* is bad, stupid, or tasteless—then we are in opposition to the author's values and reject his or her "point of view" in the sense of "opinion." Ultimately, the reader must accept the essential attitudes and judgments of the author, even if only provisionally, if the fiction is going to work.

I can think of no exception to this rule, and it is not altered by experimental plays and stories in which the writer's purpose is to embarrass, anger, or disgust us. Our acceptance of such experiments rests on our understanding that the writer did want to embarrass, anger, or disgust us, just as we accept being frightened by a horror story because we know that the writer set out to frighten us. If we think the writer is disgusting by accident, ineptitude, or moral depravity, then we are "really" disgusted and the fiction does not work.

It is a frustrating experience for many beginning (and established) authors to find that, whereas they meant the protagonist to appear sensitive, their readers find him self-pitying; whereas the author meant her to be witty, the readers find her vulgar. When this happens there is a failure of authorial or psychic distance: The author did not have sufficient perspective on the character to convince us to share his or her judgment. I recall one class in which a student author had written, with excellent use of image and scene, the story of a young man who fell in love with an exceptionally beautiful young woman, and whose feelings turned to revulsion when he found out she had had a mastectomy. The most vocal feminist in the class loved this story, which she described as "the exposé of a skuzzwort." This was not, from the author's point of view, a successful reading of his story.

When writers are self-conscious about themselves as writers they often keep a great distance from their characters, sounding as if they were writing encyclopedia entries instead of stories. Their hesitancy about physical and psychological intimacy can be a barrier to vital fiction.

Conversely, a narration that makes readers hear the characters' heavy breathing and smell their emotional anguish diminishes distance. Readers feel so close to the characters that, for those magical moments, they *become* those characters.

Jerome Stern

TEMPORAL DISTANCE

The author's or narrator's attitude may involve distance in time or space or both. When a story begins "Long ago and far away," we are instantly transported by a tone we recognize as belonging to fairy tale, fantasy, and neverland. Any time you (or your narrator) begin by telling us that the events you are relating took place in the far past, you distance us, making a submerged promise that the events will come to an end, since they "already have."

> That spring, when I had a great deal of potential and no money at all, I took a job as a janitor. That was when I was still very young and spent money very freely, and when, almost every night, I drifted off to sleep lulled by sweet anticipation of that time when my potential would suddenly be realized and there would be capsule biographies of my life on the dust jackets of many books.
>
> James Alan McPherson, "Gold Coast"

Here a distance in time indicates the attitude of the narrator toward his younger self, and his indulgent, self-mocking tone (*lulled by sweet anticipation of that time when my potential would suddenly be realized*) invites us as readers to identify with the older, narrating self. We know that he is no longer lulled by such fantasies, and, at least for the duration of the story, neither are we. That is, we are close to the narrator, distanced from him as a young man, so that the distance in time also involves distance in attitude.

By contrast, the young protagonist of Frederick Busch's *Sometimes I Live in the Country* is presented in perceptions, vocabulary, and syntax that, *even though in the third person*, suggest we are inside the child's mind, close to the time at which these events occurred. At the same time, these techniques distance us psychically, since we are aware of the difference between our own perceptions and way of speaking, and the child's.

> The sky sat on top of their hill. He was between the grass and the black air and the stars. Pop's gun was black too and it was colder than the ground. It filled his mouth. It was a small barrel but it filled his mouth up. He gagged on the gun that stuffed up into his head. He decided to close his eyes. Then he opened them. He didn't want to miss anything. He pulled the trigger but nothing happened. He didn't want to pull the trigger but he did.

SPATIAL DISTANCE

In crafting spatial distance, a writer may find it helpful to imagine filming the scene: Where is the camera? Is it at the far back of the room, looking *at* the characters? Or is it on one character's shoulder, looking *through* him? The closer the camera, the greater the scene's emotional intensity and immediacy, as is contrasted by the spatially distant and close-up passages below.

In the first example, the author makes use of space to establish an impersonal and authoritative tone.

> An unassuming young man was traveling, in midsummer, from his native city of Hamburg, to Davos-Platz in the Canton of Grisons, on a three weeks' visit.
>
> From Hamburg to Davos is a long journey—too long, indeed, for so brief a stay. It crosses all sorts of country; goes up hill and down dale, descends from the plateau of Southern Germany to the shore of Lake Constance, over its bounding waves and on across marshes once thought to be bottomless.
>
> Thomas Mann, *The Magic Mountain*

Here Mann distances us from the young man by characterizing him perfunctorily, not even naming him, and describes the place travelogue style, inviting us to take a panoramic view. This choice of tone establishes a remoteness that is emotional as well as geographical, and would do so even if the reader happened to be a native of Grisons. (Eventually we will become intimately involved with Davos and the unassuming young man, who is in for a longer stay than he expects.)

But by moving in the "camera" to close the literal distance between the reader and the subject, the intangible distance can be closed as well.

> Her face was half an inch from my face. The curtain flapped at the open window and her pupils pulsed with the coming and going of the light. I know Jill's eyes; I've painted them. They're violent and taciturn, a ring of gas-blue points like cold explosion to the outside boundary of iris, the whole held back with its brilliant lens. A detonation under glass.
>
> Janet Burroway, *Raw Silk*

In the extreme closeness of this focus, we are brought emotionally close, invited to share the narrator's perspective of Jill's explosive eyes.

In *Making Shapely Fiction*, Jerome Stern contrasts the extremes of distance by showing two versions of the same story opening. Says Stern,

> A story that starts "A young man and a young woman sat morosely under a green parasol. They seemed mutually peeved" has its readers looking at the characters from the outside, almost as if they were animals being observed in a human zoo. But if the story starts "Philip stared unhappily across the table. The honeymoon was not going well at all," readers are virtually inside the character.

Note, furthermore, how the language changes from formal and stiff when distant to conversational and concrete in the "close-up" version. Again, the point is that creation of any degree of distance should be a matter of choice, not chance, on the writer's part.

TONE

Spatial and temporal distance, then, can imply distance in the attitude of the teller toward his or her material. But authorial distance may also be implied through *tone*.

The word *tone*, applied to fiction, is a metaphor derived from music and also commonly—and metaphorically—used to describe color and speech. When we speak of a "tone of voice" we mean that an attitude is conveyed, and this attitude is determined by the situation and by the relation of the persons involved in the situation. Tone can match, emphasize, alter, or contradict the meaning of the words.

Tone in dialogue is relatively easily reinforced through posture, gesture, and facial expressions. Yet the tone of the narrator or author in telling the story must do without these helpful signs. The narrator's tone must convey identification or distance, sympathy or judgment, with words chosen and arranged so as to match, emphasize, alter, or contradict their inherent meaning.

Tone itself is an intangible, but in literature as in life, we generally will trust a choice of words that seems appropriate in intensity or value to the meaning conveyed. For example, in Cynthia Ozick's "The Shawl," the narrator's tone of urgency, fear, and sorrow invite our belief in and sympathy with the dilemma of a mother who is being marched to a Nazi death camp.

> Rosa, floating, dreamed of giving Magda away in one of the villages. She could leave the line for a minute and push Magda into the hands of any woman on the side of the road. But if she moved out of line they might shoot. And even if she fled the line for half a second and pushed the shawl-bundle at a stranger, would the woman take it?

Yet if the intensity or value of tone seems *inappropriate*, we will start to read between the lines. Another story with the same concentration camp setting, deliberately uses a tone of scientific, numbed detachment to ask readers to question and morally distance themselves from the prisoner-turned-guard who narrates "This Way for the Gas, Ladies and Gentlemen."

> Twenty-eight thousand women have been stripped naked and driven out of the barracks. Now they swarm around the large yard between the blockhouses.
>
> The heat rises, the hours are endless. We are without even our usual diversion: the wide roads leading to the crematoria are empty. For several days now, no new transports have come in. Part of "Canada" has been liquidated and detailed to a labour Kommando—one of the very toughest—at Harmenz. For there exists in the camp a special brand of justice based on envy: when the rich and mighty fall, their friends see to it that they fall to the very bottom.
>
> Tadeusz Borowski

As author, you manipulate intensity and value in your choice of language, sometimes matching meaning, sometimes contradicting, sometimes overstating, sometimes understating, to indicate your attitude to the reader.

IRONY

Discrepancies of intensity and value are ironic. Any time there is a discrepancy between what is said and what we are to accept as the truth, we are in the presence of an irony. There are three basic types of irony.

Verbal irony is a rhetorical device in which the author (or character) says one thing and means another. The passage from "The Dishwasher" at the beginning of this chapter displays verbal irony, where the "glamour" and "responsibility" of the job point up the opposite. On an extended scale, Carter Revard's "Report to the Nation: Claiming Europe" uses irony to satirize the self-justifying narratives of Old World conquerors and colonizers:

> It may be impossible to civilize the Europeans. When I claimed England for the Osage Nation, last month, some of the English chiefs objected. They said the Thames is not the Thames until it's past Oxford; above Oxford, it is two streams, the Isis and the Cherwell. So even though I'd taken a Thames Excursions boat and on the way formally proclaimed from the deck, with several Germans and some Japanese tourists for witnesses, that all the land this river drained was ours, these Oxford chiefs maintained our title was not good, except below their Folly Bridge at most. At least that leaves us Windsor Palace and some other useful properties, and we can deal with the legal hitches later. . . .
>
> So I said the hell with England for this trip and went to France and rented a little Renault in Paris and drove down past the chateaux to Biarritz, stopping only to proclaim that everything the Loire and Seine flowed past was ours. I did this from the filling stations, and I kept the sales-slips for evidence. . . .The people there talk differently from those in London, but their signs are much the same—they use a lingua franca so to speak—and they recognized my VISA card and gave the Renault gasoline much like that in Oklahoma, so they aren't completely benighted. Whether they understood that France belongs to us now was not clear, but they were friendly and they fed me well, accepting in return some pretty paper and some metal discs with which they seemed very pleased; if they are this credulous we shouldn't have much trouble bargaining with them when we come to take the rest of France. It was so easy that I headed on down to Spain.

Dramatic irony is a device of plot in which the reader or audience knows more than the character does. The classical example of dramatic irony is *Oedipus Rex*, where the audience knows that Oedipus himself is the murderer he seeks. There is dramatic irony in "Bullet in the Brain," where the reader (and other characters) realize the seriousness of Anders's situation when he does not. In the novel *Time's Arrow*, time and its every component action run in reverse, and while readers understand that they are reading the history of a Nazi war criminal, the naive narrator, growing ever younger, mistakes his life of destruction for one of healing as his dead victims return to life.

> There was usually a long wait while the gas was invisibly introduced by the ventilation grills. The dead look so dead. Dead bodies have their own dead body language. It says nothing. I always felt a gorgeous stirring of relief at the moment of the first stirring. Then it was ugly again. Well, we cry and twist and are naked at both ends of life. We cry at both ends of life, while the doctor watches. It was I, Odilo Unverdorben, who personally removed the pellets of Zyklon B and entrusted them to the pharmacist in his white coat. Next, the facade of the Sprinkleroom, the function of whose spouts and nozzles . . . was merely to reassure and not, alas, to cleanse; and the garden path beyond.
> Clothes, spectacles, hair, spinal braces, and so on—these came later. Entirely intelligibly, though, to prevent needless suffering, the dental work was usually completed while the patients were not yet alive . . . Hair for the Jews came courtesy of Filzfabrik A.G. of Roth, near Nuremberg. Freight cars full of it. Freight car after freight car.

> Martin Amis

Cosmic irony is an all-encompassing attitude toward life, a grand-scale reversal of expectations that takes into account the contradictions inherent in the human condition. For example, the environmentalist slogan "Nature Bats Last" puts cosmic irony on a bumper sticker. A more literary form of cosmic irony is the cautionary teaching of many fairy tales: watch what you wish for because you might get it, but not in the way you were expecting. We see this at work in the realistic story "Where Are You Going, Where Have You Been?", in which Connie's contemptuous desire to get away from her family is fulfilled but destroys her. The narrator of the story "Jealous Husband Returns in Form of Parrot," which comes at the end of this chapter, is agonizingly aware of the cosmic irony of his reincarnation and wonders if his fellow pet store parrots are also "paying some kind of price for living their life in a certain way." There is irony too at the end of the story as he resolves to make a break for emotional freedom that he knows is bound to kill him.

Any of these types of irony will inform the author's attitude toward the material and will be reflected in his or her tone. Any of them will involve authorial distance, since the author means, knows, or wishes to take into account—and also intends the reader to understand—something not wholly conveyed by the literal meaning of the words.

With What Limitations?

In stories such as "The Use of Force," "The Things They Carried," and "Gryphon," we trust the teller of the tale. We may find ourselves in opposition to characters perceived or perceiving, but we identify with the attitudes, straightforward or ironic, of the authors and narrators who present us these characters. We share, at least for the duration of the narrative, their norms.

THE UNRELIABLE NARRATOR

It is also possible to mistrust the teller. Authorial distance may involve not a deliberate attitude taken by the speaker, but distance on the part of the author from the narrator. The answer to the question *Who speaks?* may itself necessitate a judgment, and again this judgment may imply opposition of the author (and reader) on any scale of value—moral, intellectual, aesthetic, physical, educational, and experiential.

If the answer to *Who speaks?* is *a child, a bigot, a jealous lover, an animal, a schizophrenic, a murderer, a liar*, the implications may be that the narrator speaks with limitations we do not necessarily share. To the extent that the narrator displays and betrays such limitations, she or he is an *unreliable narrator*; and the author, without a word to call his or her own, must let the reader know that the story is not to be trusted.

Here is a woman, imperious and sour, who tells her own story.

> I have always, always, tried to do right and help people. It's a part of my community duty and my duty to God. But I can tell you right now, you don't never gets no thanks for it! . . .
>
> Use to be a big ole fat sloppy woman live cross the street went to my church. She had a different man in her house with her every month! She got mad at me for tellin the minister on her about all them men! Now, I'm doin my duty and she got mad! I told her somebody had to be the pillar of the community and if it had to be me, so be it! She said I was the pill of the community and a lotta other things, but I told the minister that too and pretty soon she was movin away. Good! I like a clean community!

> J. California Cooper, "The Watcher"

We mistrust every judgment this woman makes, but we are also aware of an author we do trust, manipulating the narrator's tone to expose her. The outburst is fraught with ironies, but because the narrator is unaware of them, they are directed against herself. We can hear that interference is being dressed up as duty. When she brags in cliché, we agree that she's more of a pill than a pillar. When she appropriates biblical language—"so be it!"—we suspect that even the minister might agree. Punctuation itself, the self-righteous overuse of the exclamation point, suggests her inappropriate intensity. It occurs to us we'd probably like the look of that "big ole fat sloppy" neighbor; and we know for certain why that neighbor moved away.

In this case the narrator is wholly unreliable, and we're unlikely to accept any judgment she could make. But it is also possible for a narrator to be reliable in some areas of value and unreliable in others. Mark Twain's Huckleberry Finn is a famous case in point. Here Huck has decided to free his friend Jim, and he is astonished that Tom Sawyer is going along with the plan.

> Here was a boy that was respectable, and well brung up; and had a character to lose; and folks at home that had characters; and he was bright and not leather-headed; and knowing and not ignorant; and not mean, but kind; and yet here he was, without any more pride, or rightness, or feeling, than to stoop to this business, and make himself a shame, and his family a shame, before everybody. I couldn't understand it, no way at all.

The extended irony in this excerpt is that slavery should be defended by the respectable, the bright, the knowing, the kind, and those of character. We reject Huck's assessment of Tom as well as the implied assessment of himself as worth so little that he has nothing to lose by freeing a slave. Huck's moral instincts are better than he himself can understand. (Notice, incidentally, how Huck's lack of education is communicated by word choice and syntax and how sparse the misspellings are.) So author and reader are in intellectual opposition to Huck the narrator, but morally identify with him. Similarly reliable "unreliable" narrators, whose distorted views reveal a strangely accurate portrait of the social institutions that confine them, include Chief Bromden, the narrator of Ken Kesey's *One Flew Over the Cuckoo's Nest*, and the "hysterical" wife and patient, forbidden to write, who relates Charlotte Perkins Gilman's 1892 story "The Yellow Wallpaper."

The unreliable narrator—who has become one of the most popular characters in modern fiction—is far from a newcomer to literature and in fact predates fiction. Every drama contains characters who speak for themselves and present their own cases, and from whom we are partly or wholly distanced in one area of value or another. So we admire Oedipus's intellect but are exasperated by his lack of intuition, we identify with Othello's morality but mistrust his logic, we trust Mr. Spock's brain but not his heart, we count on Bridget Jones's wit but not her judgment. As these examples suggest, the unreliable narrator often presents us with an example of consistent inconsistency and always presents us with dramatic irony, because we always "know" more than he or she does about the characters, the events, and the significance of both.

The truth is not distorted here, but rather a certain distortion is used to get at the truth.

Flannery O'Connor

AN EXERCISE IN UNRELIABILITY

The following three passages represent narrations by three relatively mad madmen and one relatively mad madwoman. How mad is each? To whom does each speak? In what form? Which of their statements are reliable? Which are unreliable? Which of them admit to madness? Is the admission reliable? What ironies can you identify, and against whom is each directed? What is the attitude of the author behind the narrator? By what choice and arrangement of words do you know this?

True—nervous—very, very dreadfully nervous I had been and am; but why *will* you say that I am mad? The disease had sharpened my senses—not destroyed—not dulled them. Above all was the sense of hearing acute. I heard all things in the heaven and in the earth. I heard many things in hell. How, then, am I mad? Hearken! And observe how healthily—how calmly I tell you the whole story.

Edgar Allan Poe, "The Tell-Tale Heart"

Madrid, Februarius the thirtieth
So I'm in Spain. It all happened so quickly that I hardly had time to realize it. This morning the Spanish delegation finally arrived for me and we all got into the carriage. I was somewhat bewildered by the extraordinary speed at which we traveled. We went so fast that in half an hour we reached the Spanish border. But then, nowadays there are railroads all over Europe and the ships go so fast too. Spain is a strange country. When we entered the first room, I saw a multitude of people with shaven heads. I soon realized, though, that these must be Dominican or Capuchin monks because they always shave their heads. I also thought that the manners of the King's Chancellor, who was leading me by the hand, were rather strange. He pushed me into a small room and said: "You sit quiet and don't you call yourself King Ferdinand again or I'll beat the nonsense out of your head." But I knew that I was just being tested and refused to submit.

Nikolai Gogol, *The Diary of a Madman*

There is one marked peculiarity about this paper, a thing nobody seems to notice but myself, and that is that it changes as the light changes.

When the sun shoots in through the east window—I always watch for that first long, straight ray—it changes so quickly that I never can quite believe it.

That is why I watch it always.

By moonlight—the moon shines in all night when there is a moon—I wouldn't know it was the same paper.

At night in any kind of light, in twilight, candlelight, lamplight, and worst of all by moonlight, it becomes bars! The outside pattern I mean, and the woman behind it is as plain as can be.

I didn't realize for a long time what the thing was that showed behind, that dim sub-pattern, but now I am quite sure it is a woman.

By daylight she is subdued, quiet. I fancy it is the pattern that keeps her so still. It is so puzzling. It keeps me quiet by the hour.

Charlotte Perkins Gilman, "The Yellow Wallpaper"

UNRELIABILITY IN OTHER VIEWPOINTS

Although the "unreliable narrator" is generally taken to mean a first-person speaker, it is possible to indicate unreliability through virtually any point of view. If, for example, you have chosen a limited omniscient viewpoint including only external observation and the thoughts of one character, then it may be that the character's thoughts are unreliable and that he or she misrepresents external facts. Then you must make us aware through tone that you know more than you have chosen to present. William Golding, in *The Inheritors*, tells his story in the third person, but through the eyes and thoughts of a Neanderthal who has not yet developed the power of deductive reasoning.

The man turned sideways in the bushes and looked at Lok along his shoulder. A stick rose upright and there was a lump of bone in the middle. Suddenly Lok understood that the man was holding the stick out to him but neither he nor Lok could reach across the river. He would have laughed if it were not for the echo of screaming in his head. The stick began to grow shorter at both ends. Then it shot out to full length again.

The dead tree by Lok's ear acquired a voice.

"Clop!"

His ears twitched and he turned to the tree. By his face there had grown a twig: a twig that smelt of other, and of goose, and of the bitter berries that Lok's stomach told him he must not eat.

The imaginative problem here, imaginatively embraced, is that we must supply the deductive reasoning of which our point of view character is incapable. Lok has no experience of bows or poison arrows, nor of "men" attacking each other, so his conclusions are unreliable. "Suddenly Lok understood" is an irony setting us in opposition to the character's intellect; at the same time, his innocence makes him morally sympathetic. Since the author does not intervene to interpret for us, the effect is very near that of an unreliable narrator.

THE AUTHOR'S VIEWPOINT

I'm conscious that this discussion of point of view contains more analysis than advice, and this is because very little can be said to be right or wrong about point of view *as long as the reader ultimately identifies with the author*; as long, that is, as you make it work. Virtually any story can be told from virtually any point of view and convey the same attitude.

Suppose, for example, that you are going to write this story: Two soldiers, one a seasoned corporal and the other a newly arrived private, are sent on a mission in a Balkan "police action" to kill a sniper. They track, find, and capture the sniper, who turns out to be a fifteen-year-old boy. The corporal offers to let the private pull the trigger, but he cannot. The corporal kills the sniper and triumphantly cuts off his ear for a trophy. The young soldier vomits; ashamed of himself, he pulls himself together and vows to do better next time.

Your attitude as author of this story is that war is inhumane and dehumanizing.

You may write the story from the point of view of the editorial omniscient, following the actions of the hunters and the hunted, going into the minds of corporal, private, and sniper, ranging the backgrounds of each and knowing the ultimate pointlessness of the death, telling us, in effect, that war is inhumane and dehumanizing.

Or you may write it from the point of view of the corporal as an unreliable narrator, proud of his toughness and his expertise, condescending to the private, certain the local people are animals, glorying in his trophy, betraying his inhumanity.

Between these two extremes of total omniscience and total unreliability, you may take any position of the middle ground. The story might be written in the limited omniscient, presenting the thoughts only of the anxious private and the external actions of the others. It might be written objectively, with a cold and detached accuracy of military detail. It might be written by a peripheral narrator, a war correspondent, from interviews and documents; as a letter home from the private to his girl; as a field report from the corporal; as an interior monologue of the young sniper during the seconds before his death.

Any of these modes could contain your meaning, any of them fulfill your purpose. Your central problem as a writer might prove to be the choosing. But whatever your final choice of point of view in the technical sense, your point of view in the sense of *opinion*—that war is inhumane and dehumanizing—could be revealed.

Story

LYDIA DAVIS

I get home from work and there is a message from him: that he is not coming, that he is busy. He will call again. I wait to hear from him, then at nine o'clock I go to where he lives, find his car, but he's not home. I knock at his apartment door and then at all the garage doors, not knowing which garage door is his—no answer. I write a note, read it over, write a new note, and stick it in his door. At home I am restless and all I can do, though I have a lot to do, since I'm going on a trip in the morning, is play the piano. I call again at 10:45 and he's home, he has been to the movies with his old girlfriend, and she's still there. He says he'll call back. I wait. Finally I sit down and write in my notebook that when he calls me either he will then come to me, or he will not and I will be angry, and so I will have either him or my own anger, and this might be all right, since anger is always a great comfort, as I found with my husband. And then I go on to write, in the third person and the past tense, that clearly she always needed to have a love even if it was a complicated love. He calls back before I have time to finish writing all this down. When he calls, it is a little after 11:30. We argue until nearly twelve. Everything he says is contradiction: for example, he says he did not want to see me because he wanted to work and even more because he wanted to be alone, but he has not worked and he has not been alone. There is no way I can get him to reconcile any of his contradictions and when this conversation begins to sound too much like many I had with my husband I say goodbye and hang up. I finish writing down what I started to write down even though by now it no longer seems true that anger is any great comfort.

I call him back five minutes later to tell him that I am sorry about all this arguing, and that I love him, but there is no answer. I call again five minutes later, thinking he might have walked out to his garage and walked back, but again there is no answer. I think of driving to where he lives again and looking for his garage to see if he is in there working, because he keeps his desk there and his books and that is where he goes to read and write. I am in my nightgown, it is after twelve and I have to leave the next morning at five. Even so, I get dressed and drive the mile or so to his place. I am afraid that when I get there I will see other cars by his house that I did not see earlier and that one of them will belong to his old girlfriend. When I drive down the driveway I see two cars that weren't there before, and one of them is parked as close as possible to his door, and I think that she is there. I walk around the small building to the back where his apartment is, and look in the window: the light is on, but I can't see anything clearly because of the half closed venetian blinds and the steam on the glass. But things inside the room are not the same as they were earlier in the evening, and before there was no steam. I open the outer screen door and knock. I wait. No answer. I let the screen door fall shut and I walk away to check the garages. Now the door opens behind me as I am walking away and he comes out. I can't see him very well because it is dark in the narrow lane beside his door and he is wearing dark clothes and whatever light there is is behind him. He comes up to me and puts his arms around me without speaking, and I think he is not speaking not because he is feeling so much but because his is preparing what he will say. He lets go of me and walks around me and ahead of me out to where the cars are parked by the garage doors.

As we walk out there he says "Look," and my name, and I am waiting for him to say that she is here and also that it's all over between us. But he doesn't, and I have the feeling he did intend to say something like that, at least say that she was here, and that he then thought better of it for some reason. Instead, he says that everything that went wrong tonight was his fault and he's sorry. He stands with his back against a garage door and his face in the light and I stand in front of him with my back to the light. At one point he hugs me so suddenly that the fire of my cigarette crumbles against the garage door behind him. I know why we're out here and not in his room, but I don't ask him until everything is all right between us. Then he says, "She wasn't here when I called you. She came back later." He says the only reason she is there is that something is troubling her and he is the only one she can talk to about it. Then he says, "You don't understand, do you."

I try to figure it out.

So when they went to the movies and then came back to his place and then I called and then she left and he called back and we argued and then I called back twice but he had gone out to get a beer (he says) and then I drove over and in the meantime he had returned from buying beer and she had also come back and she was in his room so we talked by the garage doors. But what is the truth? Could he and she both really have come back in that short interval between my last phone call and my arrival at his place? Or is the truth really that during his call to me she waited outside or in his garage or in her car and that he then brought her in again, and that when the phone rang with my second and third calls he let it ring without answering, because he was fed up with me and with arguing? Or is the truth that she did leave and did come back later but that he remained and let the phone ring without answering? Or did he perhaps bring her in and then go out for the beer while she waited there and listened to the phone ring? The last is the least likely. I don't believe anyway that there was any trip out for beer.

The fact that he does not tell me the truth all the time makes me not sure of his truth at certain times, and then I work to figure out for myself if what he is telling me is the truth or not, and sometimes I can figure out that it's not the truth and sometimes I don't know and never know, and sometimes just because he says it to me over and over again I am convinced it is the truth because I don't believe he would repeat a lie so often. Maybe the truth does not matter, but I want to know it if only so that I can come to some conclusions about such questions as: whether he is angry at me or not; if he is, then how angry; whether he still loves her or not; if he does, then how much; whether he loves me or not; how much; how capable he is of deceiving me in the act and after the act in the telling.

🍂 🍂 🍂
Suggestions for Discussion

1. To whom does the story seem to be told? In what form?
2. First-person narration is used, yet the psychic distance is often more typical of third-person narration. How and why does the author create this effect?

Retrospect

3. Does "Story" fit the traditional definition of a story? Why or why not?
4. Where is a character's speech at odds with his or her actions? How does this increase dramatic tension?

Snow

JULIA ALVAREZ

Our first year in New York we rented a small apartment with a Catholic school nearby, taught by the Sisters of Charity, hefty women in long black gowns and bonnets that made them look peculiar, like dolls in mourning. I liked them a lot, especially my grandmotherly fourth grade teacher, Sister Zoe. I had a lovely name, she said, and she had me teach the whole class how to pronounce it. *Yo-lan-da*. As the only immigrant in my class, I was put in a special seat in the first row by the window, apart from the other children so that Sister Zoe could tutor me without disturbing them. Slowly, she enunciated the new words I was to repeat: *laundromat, cornflakes, subway, snow*.

Soon I picked up enough English to understand holocaust was in the air. Sister Zoe explained to a wide-eyed classroom what was happening in Cuba. Russian missiles were being assembled, trained supposedly on New York City. President Kennedy, looking worried too, was on the television at home, explaining we might have to go to war against the Communists. At school, we had air-raid drills: an ominous bell would go off and we'd file into the hall, fall to the floor, cover our heads with our coats, and imagine our hair falling out, the bones in our arms going soft. At home, Mami and my sisters and I said a rosary for world peace. I heard new vocabulary: *nuclear bomb, radioactive fallout, bomb shelter*. Sister Zoe explained how it would happen. She drew a picture of a mushroom on the blackboard and dotted a flurry of chalkmarks for the dusty fallout that would kill us all.

The months grew cold, November, December. It was dark when I got up in the morning, frosty when I followed my breath to school. One morning as I sat at my desk daydreaming out the window, I saw dots in the air like the ones Sister Zoe had drawn—random at first, then lots and lots. I shrieked, "Bomb! Bomb!" Sister Zoe jerked around, her full black skirt ballooning as she hurried to my side. A few girls began to cry.

But then Sister Zoe's shocked look faded. "Why, Yolanda dear, that's snow!" She laughed. "Snow."

"Snow," I repeated. I looked out the window warily. All my life I had heard about the white crystals that fell out of American skies in the winter. From my desk I watched the fine powder dust the sidewalk and parked cars below. Each flake was different, Sister Zoe said, like a person, irreplaceable and beautiful.

Suggestions for Discussion

1. Why is this event more effectively told from the child's point of view than the teacher's?

2. Find word choices or images that help to re-create a child's perceptions. Experiment with changing some words to more adult language to see how that alters the effect of the narration.

Retrospect

3. Fear of nuclear attack spanned decades. What narrative purpose is served by tying the story to the specific event of the Cuban missile crisis?

Beautiful My Mane in the Wind

CATHERINE PETROSKI

I am a horse, perhaps the last mustang.

This is my yard, this is my pasture. And I told her I hate her. My dam-mother. She does not understand horses. She doesn't even try. There are many things she doesn't notice about me.

Horses move their feet like this.

Horses throw their heads like this, when they are impatient, about to dash away to some shady tree. See how beautiful my mane in the wind.

Horses snort.

Horses whinny.

Horses hate her.

I am a girl horse. I am building a house under the loquat tree. It is taking me a long time.

My house is made of logs, logs that Daddy doesn't want. That is because our fireplace goes nowhere. It is just a little cave in the wall because this is Texas and it is mostly hot here. Our fireplace has a permanent fake log. I am six.

I will be six next month.

Anyway that is why I got the real logs when our weeping willow died and Mama pushed it over one Sunday afternoon. The bottom of the trunk was rotten and the tree just fell over and Mama laughed and the baby laughed and I didn't laugh. I hate her.

I hate also the baby who is a Botherboy.

Daddy cut the willow tree into pieces I could carry and gave them to me and now I am building a horsehouse under the loquat and waiting for a man horse to come along, which is the way it is supposed to happen.

I saw a picture of one and its name was Centaur.

Of a Sunday afternoon, in her stable

My room I also hate. Bother loves it best and squeals when he gets to its door, because he thinks it's nicer than his own room, nicer than the bigroom, nicer than anyplace at all. He likes best all the blocks and the toy people. I build temples and bridges sometimes but then he comes along. He throws blocks when he plays because he's just a baby. And a boy. And not a horse.

What I hate most about this room is picking up pieces of the lotto game when he throws it all over, picking up pieces of jigsaw puzzles that he has thrown all over. Picking up the spilled water, the blocks, the people. I hate the messes. I know that horses are not this messy. Mama says it is our fate to be left with the mess, but I don't think she likes it any more than I do.

She pays very little attention to me actually. She thinks I just read and I'm pretty sure she doesn't realize about the change. To a horse. She acts as though I'm still a girl. She doesn't observe closely.

Administering herself first aid

The fact is there is a fossil in my hoof.

At school we have a hill that is called Fossilhill because there are a lot of fossils to be found there. Actually the fossils are very easy to find. You just pick up a handful of dirt and you come up with fossils. The trick is to find big fossils. I can always find the biggest fossils of anybody, snails and funny sea snakes and shells of all kinds.

The boys run up and down Fossilhill and don't look where they're going. It's no wonder they don't find many fossils. They come and pull Horse's mane. They scruff through where Horse is digging with her hoof. They sometimes try to capture Horse, since she is perhaps the last mustang of great value. But mostly they are silly, these boys. They don't make much sense, just a mess.

Today I was trotting on the side of the hill and found the biggest fossil I have ever found in my life, which in horse is I think twelve or maybe twenty-four years old. Then I found more and more fossils and other children came to the hill, even the girlygirls who never look for fossils because they always play games I don't know how to play. House and Shopping and Bad Baby. But they tried to find fossils today and asked me if this was a fossil or that, and they found many, many fossils. And we all had a good time. And when we had found all the fossils we had time to find, our teacher said, Put them in your pockets, children, and if you don't have pockets put them in your socks. And we did, and that's why there is a fossil in my hoof.

Girlygirls vs. Boyannoys vs. Horse

In my kindergarten there is a girl whose name is Larch. It is a funny name for a girl. It might not be such a funny name for a horse, but Larch isn't a horse because she is in fact the girl leader because she decides what games are going to be played and will let the boys tie her up. And the other girls too. When they tie people up they don't use real rope because our teacher wouldn't allow that. If they tie me up with their pretend rope it doesn't work. They think I just don't want to play, but the truth is I'm a horse and stronger than a girl and can break their girlygirl rope.

It's more fun being a horse. More fun than being a girl too, because they just play Housekeeping Area and none of them really knows yet how to read even though they pretend to. I can tell because they can't get the hard words. So they don't let me play with them. My mother says it's all right because they wish they could enjoy stories themselves and next year they will all read and everything will be all right.

The reading is the real problem between the horse and the girls, I guess. But sometimes they do let me play with them, if they need a victim or a hostage or an offering.

Herself among the others

Horses are I think lucky. They do not seem to have friends, such as people, you know, for they do not to need friends. They have enemies – the snakes, the potholes, the cougars, the fancy-booted cowboys who don't know the difference between a canter and a hand gallop. What friends they have are on a very practical basis. Other horses with the same problems.

The wind.

A talk with herself

If I tell her what I am she will not believe me.

If I tell the others what I am they may rope me and tell me to pull their wagon.

If I tell a boy what I am he will invade my loquat house, and maybe it will be good and maybe it will be bad.

If I tell Daddy what I am he will act interested for a minute and then drink some beer and start reading again.

And if I tell Bother he will not understand even the words but will grab my mane and pull it until he has pulled some of it out.

What does it matter? What does it all matter? I will whinny and run away.

Who could blame me? Horses should not be abused, ignored, or made fun of.

Discussing the weather or nothing at all

Just a little while ago, when I needed to go out to race a bit and throw my head in the wind, she stopped me, my dam-mother, and asked me who I thought I was. A girl? A horse? My name? I know what she's thinking. The others at school ask me the same questions.

So I said, A girl, because I know that's what I'm supposed to think. One thing I know, not a girlygirl, which would be stupid playing games talking teasing being tied to the junglegym. I won't. Sometimes it's hard not telling her what I really think, what I know. That sometimes I'm a girl, sometimes I'm a horse. When there are girl-things to do, like read, which a horse never does, or go in the car to the stockshow or for ice cream or any of those things, I have to be a girl, but when there are hillsides of grass and forests with lowhanging boughs and secret stables in loquat trees, I am a horse.

Maybe someday there will be no changing back and forth and I will be stuck a horse. Which will be all right with me. Because horses think good easy things, smooth green and windy things, without large people or Bothers or other kids or school, and they have enough grass to trot in forever and wind to throw their manes high to the sky and cool sweet stream water to drink, and clover.

🐦 🐦 🐦

Suggestions for Discussion

1. In which areas is the narrator reliable? In which is she unreliable?
2. How do the third-person section headings affect your reading of the story?

Retrospect

3. What kinds of power struggle do you see in this story?

🐦

Jealous Husband Returns in Form of Parrot

ROBERT OLEN BUTLER

I never can quite say as much as I know. I look at other parrots and I wonder if it's the same for them, if somebody is trapped in each of them paying some kind of price for living their life in a certain way. For instance, "Hello," I say, and I'm sitting on a perch in a pet store in Houston and what I'm really thinking is Holy shit. It's you. And what's happened is I'm looking at my wife.

"Hello," she says, and she comes over to me and I can't believe how beautiful she is. Those great brown eyes, almost as dark as the center of mine. And her nose—I don't remember her for her nose but its beauty is clear to me now. Her nose is a little too long, but it's redeemed by the faint hook to it.

She scratches the back of my neck.

Her touch makes my tail flare. I feel the stretch and rustle of me back there. I bend my head to her and she whispers, "Pretty bird."

For a moment I think she knows it's me. But she doesn't, of course. I say "Hello" again and I will eventually pick up "pretty bird." I can tell that as soon as she says it, but for now I can only give her another hello. Her fingertips move through my feathers and she seems to know about birds. She knows that to pet a bird you don't smooth his feathers down, you ruffle them.

But of course she did that in my human life, as well. It's all the same for her. Not that I was complaining, even to myself, at that moment in the pet shop when she found me like I presume she was supposed to. She said it again, "Pretty bird," and this brain that works like it does now could feel that tiny little voice of mine ready to shape itself around these sounds. But before I could get them out of my beak there was this guy at my wife's shoulder and all my feathers went slick flat like to make me small enough not to be seen and I backed away. The pupils of my eyes pinned and dilated and pinned again.

He circled around her. A guy that looked like a meat packer, big in the chest and thick with hair, the kind of guy that I always sensed her eyes moving to when I was alive. I had a bare chest and I'd look for little black hairs on the sheets when I'd come home on a day with the whiff of somebody else in the air. She was still in the same goddamn rut.

A "hello" wouldn't do and I'd recently learned "good night" but it was the wrong suggestion altogether, so I said nothing and the guy circled her and he was looking at me with a smug little smile and I fluffed up all my feathers, made myself about twice as big, so big he'd see he couldn't mess with me. I waited for him to draw close enough for me to take off the tip of his finger.

But she intervened. Those nut-brown eyes were before me and she said, "I want him."

And that's how I ended up in my own house once again. She bought me a large black wrought-iron cage, very large, convinced by some young guy who clerked in the bird department and who took her aside and made his voice go much too soft when he was doing the selling job. The meat packer didn't like it. I didn't either. I'd missed a lot of chances to take a bite out of this clerk in my stay at the shop and I regretted that suddenly.

But I got my giant cage and I guess I'm happy enough about that. I can pace as much as I want. I can hang upside down. It's full of bird toys. That dangling thing over there with knots and strips of rawhide and a bell at the bottom needs a good thrashing a couple of times a day and I'm the bird to do it. I look at the very dangle of it and the thing is rough, the rawhide and the knotted rope, and I get this restlessness back in my tail, a burning thrashing feeling, and it's like all the times when I was sure there was a man naked with my wife. Then I go to this thing that feels so familiar and I bite and bite and it's very good.

I could have used the thing the last day I went out of this house as a man. I'd found the address of the new guy at my wife's office. He'd been there a month in the shipping department and three times she'd mentioned him. She didn't even have to work with him and three times I heard about him, just dropped into the conversation. "Oh," she'd say when a car commercial came on the television, "that car there is like the one the new man in shipping owns. Just like it." Hey, I'm not stupid. She said another thing about him and then another and right after the third one I locked myself in the bathroom because I couldn't rage about this anymore. I felt like a damn fool whenever I actually said anything about this kind of feeling and she looked at me like she could start hating me real easy and so I was working on saying nothing, even if it meant locking myself up. My goal was to hold my tongue about half the time. That would be a good start.

But this guy from shipping. I found out his name and his address and it was one of her typical Saturday afternoons of vague shopping. So I went to his house, and his car that was just like the commercial was outside. Nobody was around in the neighborhood and there was this big tree in the back of the house going up to a second floor window that was making funny little sounds. I went up. The shade was drawn but not quite all the way. I was holding on to a limb with arms and legs wrapped around it like it was her in those times when I could forget the others for a little while. But the crack in the shade was just out of view and I crawled on along till there was no limb left and I fell on my head. Thinking about that now, my wings flap and I feel myself lift up and it all seems so avoidable. Though I know I'm different now. I'm a bird.

Except I'm not. That's what's confusing. It's like those times when she would tell me she loved me and I actually believed her and maybe it was true and we clung to each other in bed and at times like that I was different. I was the man in her life. I was whole with her. Except even at that moment, holding her sweetly, there was this other creature inside me who knew a lot more about it and couldn't quite put all the evidence together to speak.

My cage sits in the den. My pool table is gone and the cage is sitting in that space and if I come all the way down to one end of my perch I can see through the door and down the back hallway to the master bedroom. When she keeps the bedroom door open I can see the space at the foot of the bed but not the bed itself. That I can sense to the left, just out of sight. I watch the men go in and I hear the sounds but I can't quite see. And they drive my crazy.

I flap my wings and I squawk and I fluff up and I slick down and I throw seed and I attack that dangly toy as if it was the guy's balls, but it does no good. It never did any good in the other life either, the thrashing around I did by myself. In that other life I'd have given anything to be standing in this den with her doing this thing with some other guy just down the hall and all I had to do was walk down there and turn the corner and she couldn't deny it anymore.

But now all I can do is try to let it go. I sidestep down to the opposite end of the cage and look out the big sliding glass doors to the backyard. It's a pretty yard. There are great placid maple trees with good places to roost. There's a blue sky that plucks at the feathers on my chest. There are clouds. Other birds. Fly away. I could just fly away.

I tried once and I learned a lesson. She forgot and left the door to my cage open and I climbed beak and foot, beak and foot, along the bars and curled around to stretch sideways out the door and the vast scene of peace was there at the other end of the room. I flew.

And a pain flared through my head and I fell straight down and the room whirled around and the only good thing was she held me. She put her hands under my wings and lifted me and clutched me to her breast and I wish there hadn't been bees in my head at the time so I could have enjoyed that, but she put me back in the cage and wept awhile. That touched me, her tears. And I looked back to the wall of sky and trees. There was something invisible there between me and that dream of peace. I remembered, eventually, about glass, and I knew I'd been lucky, I knew that for the little fragile-boned skull I was doing all this thinking in, it meant death.

She wept that day but by the night she had another man. A guy with a thick Georgia truck-stop accent and pale white skin and an Adam's apple big as my seed ball. This guy has been around for a few weeks and he makes a whooping sound down the hallway, just out of my sight. At times like that I want to fly against the bars of the cage, but I don't. I have to remember how the world has changed.

She's single now, of course. Her husband, the man that I was, is dead to her. She does not understand all that is behind my "hello." I know many words, for a parrot. I am a yellow-nape Amazon, a handsome bird, I think, green with a splash of yellow at the back of my neck. I talk pretty well, but none of my words are adequate. I can't make her understand.

And what would I say if I could? I was jealous in life. I admit it. I would admit it to her. But it was because of my connection to her. I would explain that. When we held each other, I had no past at all, no present but her body, no future but to lie there and not let her go. I was an egg hatched beneath her crouching body, I entered as a chick into her wet sky of a body, and all that I wished was to sit on her shoulder and fluff my feathers and lay my head against her cheek, my neck exposed to her hand. And so the glances that I could see in her troubled me deeply, the movement of her eyes in public to other men, the laughs sent across a room, the tracking of her mind behind her blank eyes, pursuing images of others, her distraction even in our bed, the ghosts that were there of men who'd touched her, perhaps even that very day. I was not part of all those other men who were part of her. I didn't want to connect to all that. It was only her that I would fluff for but these others were there also and I couldn't put them aside. I sensed them inside her and so they were inside me. If I had the words, these are the things I would say.

But half an hour ago there was a moment that thrilled me. A word, a word we all knew in the pet shop, was just the right word after all. This guy with his cowboy belt buckle and rattlesnake boots and his pasty face and his twanging words of love trailed after my wife, through the den, past my cage, and I said, "Cracker." He even flipped his head back a little at this in surprise. He'd been called that before to his face, I realized. I said it again. "Cracker." But to him I was a bird and he let it pass. "Cracker," I said. "Hello, cracker." That was even better. They were out of sight through the hall doorway and I hustled along the perch and I caught a glimpse of them before they made the turn to the bed and I said, "Hello, cracker," and he shot me one last glance.

It made me hopeful. I eased away from that end of the cage, moved toward the scene of peace beyond the far wall. The sky is chalky blue today, blue like the brow of the blue-front Amazon who was on the perch next to me for about a week at the store. She was very sweet, but I watched her carefully for a day or two when she first came in. And it wasn't long before she nuzzled up to a cockatoo named Gordo and I knew she'd break my heart. But her color now in the sky is sweet, really. I left all those feelings behind me when my wife showed up. I am a faithful man, for all my suspicions. Too faithful, maybe. I am ready to give too much and maybe that's the problem.

The whooping began down the hall and I focused on a tree out there. A crow flapped down, his mouth open, his throat throbbing, though I could not hear his sound. I was feeling very odd. At least I'd made my point to the guy in the other room. "Pretty bird," I said, referring to myself. She called me "pretty bird" and I believed her and I told myself again, "Pretty bird."

But then something new happened, something very difficult for me. She appeared in the den naked. I have not seen her naked since I fell from the tree and had no wings to fly. She always had a certain tidiness in things. She was naked in the bedroom, clothed in the den. But now she appears from the hallway and I look at her and she is still slim and she is beautiful, I think—at least I clearly remember that as her husband I found her beautiful in this state. Now, though, she seems too naked. Plucked. I find that a sad thing. I am sorry for her and she goes by me and she disappears into the kitchen. I want to pluck some of my own feathers, the feathers from my chest, and give them to her. I love her more in that moment, seeing her terrible nakedness, than I ever have before.

And since I've had success in the last few minutes with words, when she comes back I am moved to speak. "Hello," I say, meaning, You are still connected to me, I still want only you. "Hello," I say again. Please listen to this tiny heart that beats fast at all times for you.

And she does indeed stop and she comes to me and bends to me. "Pretty bird," I say and I am saying, You are beautiful, my wife, and your beauty cries out for protection. "Pretty." I want to cover you with my own nakedness. "Bad bird," I say. If there are others in your life, even in your mind, then there is nothing I can do. "Bad." Your nakedness is touched from inside by the others. "Open," I say. How can we be whole together if you are not empty in the place that I am to fill?

She smiles at this and she opens the door to my cage. "Up," I say, meaning, Is there no place for me in this world where I can be free of this terrible sense of others?

She reaches in now and offers her hand and I climb onto it and I tremble and she says, "Poor baby."

"Poor baby," I say. You have yearned for wholeness too and somehow I failed you. I was not enough. "Bad bird," I say. I'm sorry.

And then the cracker comes around the corner. He wears only his rattlesnake boots. I take one look at his miserable, featherless body and shake my head. We keep our sexual parts hidden, we parrots, and this man is a pitiful sight. "Peanut," I say. I presume that my wife simply has not noticed. But that's foolish, of course. This is, in fact, what she wants. Not me. And she scrapes me off her hand onto the open cage door and she turns her naked back to me and embraces this man and they laugh and stagger in their embrace around the corner.

For a moment I still think I've been eloquent. What I've said only needs repeating for it to have its transforming effect. "Hello," I say. "Hello. Pretty bird. Pretty. Bad bird. Bad. Open. Up. Poor baby. Bad bird." And I am beginning to hear myself as I really sound to her. "Peanut." I can never say what is in my heart to her. Never.

I stand on my cage door now and my wings stir. I look at the corner to the hallway and down at the end the whooping has begun again. I can fly there and think of things to do about all this.

But I do not. I turn instead and I look at the trees moving just beyond the other end of the room. I look at the sky the color of the brow of a blue-front Amazon. A shadow of birds spanks across the lawn. And I spread my wings. I will fly now. Even though I know there is something between me and that place where I can be free of all these feelings, I will fly. I will throw myself there again and again. Pretty bird. Bad bird. Good night.

🎔 🎔 🎔

Suggestions for Discussion

1. What contract is made with the reader in the opening paragraph? How does the author signal the narrator's degree of reliability? What might limit his reliability?

2. What aspects of being a parrot ironically parallel his former life as a jealous husband?

Retrospect

3. What techniques does the author use to make this fantastic reality believable?

Who's Irish?

GISH JEN

In China, people say mixed children are supposed to be smart, and definitely my granddaughter Sophie is smart. But Sophie is wild, Sophie is not like my daughter Natalie, or like me. I am work hard my whole life, and fierce besides. My husband always used to say he is afraid of me, and our restaurant, busboys and cooks all afraid of me too. Even the gang members come for protection money, they try to talk to my husband. When I am there, they stay away. If they come by mistake, they pretend they are come to eat. They hide behind the menu, they order a lot of food. They talk about their mothers. Oh, my mother have some arthritis, need to take herbal medicine, they say. Oh, my mother getting old, her hair all white now.

I say, Your mother's hair used to be white, but since she dye it, it become black again. Why don't you go home once in a while and take a look? I tell them, Confucius say a filial son knows what color his mother's hair is.

My daughter is fierce too, she is vice president in the bank now. Her new house is big enough for everybody to have their own room, including me. But Sophie take after Natalie's husband's family, their name is Shea. Irish. I always thought Irish people are like Chinese people, work so hard on the railroad, but now I know why the Chinese beat the Irish. Of course, not all Irish are like the Shea family, of course not. My daughter tell me I should not say Irish this, Irish that.

How do you like it when people say the Chinese this, the Chinese that, she say.

You know, the British call the Irish heathen, just like they call the Chinese, she say.

You think the Opium War was bad, how would you like to live right next door to the British, she say.

And that is that. My daughter have a funny habit when she win an argument, she take a sip of something and look away, so the other person is not embarrassed. So I am not embarrassed. I do not call anybody anything either. I just happen to mention about the Shea family, an interesting fact: four brothers in the family, and not one of them work. The mother, Bess, have a job before she got sick, she was executive secretary in a big company. She is handle everything for a big shot, you would be surprised how complicated her job is, not just type this, type that. Now she is a nice woman with a clean house. But her boys, every one of them is on welfare, or so-called severance pay, or so-called disability pay. Something. They say they cannot find work, this is not the economy of the fifties, but I say, Even the black people doing better these days, some of them live so fancy, you'd be surprised. Why the Shea family have so much trouble? They are white people, they speak English. When I come to this country, I have no money and do not speak English. But my husband and I own our restaurant before he die. Free and clear, no mortgage. Of course, I understand I am just lucky, come from a country where the food is popular all over the world. I understand it is not the Shea family's fault they come from a country where everything is boiled. Still, I say.

She's right, we should broaden our horizons, say one brother, Jim, at Thanksgiving. Forget about the car business. Think about egg rolls.

Pad thai, say another brother, Mike. I'm going to make my fortune in pad thai. It's going to be the new pizza.

I say, You people too picky about what you sell. Selling egg rolls not good enough for you, but at least my husband and I can say, We made it. What can you say? Tell me. What can you say?

Everybody chew their tough turkey.

I especially cannot understand my daughter's husband John, who has no job but cannot take care of Sophie either. Because he is a man, he say, and that's the end of the sentence.

Plain boiled food, plain boiled thinking. Even his name is plain boiled: John. Maybe because I grew up with black bean sauce and hoisin sauce and garlic sauce, I always feel something is missing when my son-in-law talk.

But, okay: so my son-in-law can be man, I am baby-sitter. Six hours a day, same as the old sitter, crazy Amy, who quit. This is not so easy, now that I am sixty-eight, Chinese age almost seventy. Still, I try. In China, daughter take care of mother. Here it is the other way around. Mother help daughter, mother ask, Anything else I can do? Otherwise daughter complain mother is not supportive. I tell daughter, We do not have this word in Chinese, *supportive*. But my daughter too busy to listen, she has to go to meeting, she has to write memo while her husband go to the gym to be a man. My daughter say otherwise he will be depressed. Seems like all his life he has this trouble, depression.

No one wants to hire someone who is depressed, she say. It is important for him to keep his spirits up.

Beautiful wife, beautiful daughter, beautiful house, oven can clean itself automatically. No money left over, because only one income, but lucky enough, got the baby-sitter for free. If John lived in China, he would be very happy. But he is not happy. Even at the gym things go wrong. One day, he pull a muscle. Another day, weight room too crowded. Always something.

Until finally, hooray, he has a job. Then he feel pressure.

I need to concentrate, he say. I need to focus.

He is going to work for insurance company. Salesman job. A paycheck, he say, and at least he will wear clothes instead of gym shorts. My daughter buy him some special candy bars from the health-food store. They say THINK! on them, and are supposed to help John think.

John is a good-looking boy, you have to say that, especially now that he shave so you can see his face.

I am an old man in a young man's game, say John.

I will need a new suit, say John.

This time I am not going to shoot myself in the foot, say John.

Good, I say.

She means to be supportive, my daughter say. Don't start the send her back to China thing, because we can't.

Sophie is three years old American age, but already I see her nice Chinese side swallowed up by her wild Shea side. She looks like mostly Chinese. Beautiful black hair, beautiful black eyes. Nose perfect size, not so flat looks like something fell down, not so large looks like some big deal got stuck in wrong face. Everything just right, only her skin is a brown surprise to John's family. So brown, they say. Even John say it. She never goes in the ·sun, still she is that color, he say. Brown. They say. Nothing the matter with brown. They are just surprised. So brown. Nattie is not that brown, they say. They say, It seems like Sophie should be a color in between Nattie and John. Seems funny, a girl named Sophie Shea be brown. But she is brown, maybe her name should be Sophie Brown. She never go in the sun, still she is that color, they say. Nothing the matter with brown. They are just surprised.

The Shea family talk is like this sometimes, going around and around like a Christmas-tree train.

Maybe John is not her father, I say one day, to stop the train. And sure enough, train wreck. None of the brothers ever say the word *brown* to me again.

Instead, John's mother, Bess, say, I hope you are not offended.

She say, I did my best on those boys. But raising four boys with no father is no picnic.

You have a beautiful family, I say.

I'm getting old, she say.

You deserve a rest, I say. Too many boys make you old.

I never had a daughter, she say. You have a daughter.

I have a daughter, I say. Chinese people don't think a daughter is so great, but you're right. I have a daughter.

I was never against the marriage, you know, she say. I never thought John was marrying down. I always thought Nattie was just as good as white.

I was never against the marriage either, I say. I just wonder if they look at the whole problem.

Of course you pointed out the problem, you are a mother, she say. And now we both have a granddaughter. A little brown granddaughter, she is so precious to me.

I laugh. A little brown granddaughter, I say. To tell you the truth, I don't know how she came out so brown.

We laugh some more. These days Bess need a walker to walk. She take so many pills, she need two glasses of water to get them all down. Her favorite TV show is about bloopers, and she love her bird feeder. All day long, she can watch that bird feeder, like a cat.

I can't wait for her to grow up, Bess say. I could use some female company.

Too many boys, I say.

Boys are fine, she say. But they do surround you after a while.

You should take a break, come live with us, I say. Lots of girls at our house.

Be careful what you offer, say Bess with a wink. Where I come from, people mean for you to move in when they say a thing like that.

Nothing the matter with Sophie's outside, that's the truth. It is inside that she is like not any Chinese girl I ever see. We go to the park, and this is what she does. She stand up in the stroller. She take off all her clothes and throw them in the fountain.

Sophie! I say. Stop!

But she just laugh like a crazy person. Before I take over as baby-sitter, Sophie has that crazy-person sitter, Amy the guitar player. My daughter thought this Amy very creative—another word we do not talk about in China. In China, we talk about whether we have difficulty or no difficulty. We talk about whether life is bitter or not bitter. In America, all day long, people talk about creative. Never mind that I cannot even look at this Amy, with her shirt so short that her belly button showing. This Amy think Sophie should love her body. So when Sophie take off her diaper, Amy laugh. When Sophie run around naked, Amy say she wouldn't want to wear a diaper either. When Sophie go *shu-shu* in her lap, Amy laugh and say there are no germs in pee. When Sophie take off her shoes, Amy say bare feet is best, even the pediatrician say so. That is why Sophie now walk around with no shoes like a beggar child. Also why Sophie love to take off her clothes.

Turn around! say the boys in the park. Let's see that ass!

Of course, Sophie does not understand. Sophie clap her hands, I am the only one to say, No! This is not a game.

It has nothing to do with John's family, my daughter say. Amy was too permissive, that's all.

But I think if Sophie was not wild inside, she would not take off her shoes and clothes to begin with.

You never take off your clothes when you were little. I say, All my Chinese friends had babies, I never saw one of them act wild like that.

Look, my daughter say. I have a big presentation tomorrow.

John and my daughter agree Sophie is a problem, but they don't know what to do.

You spank her, she'll stop, I say another day.

But they say, Oh no.

In America, parents not supposed to spank the child.

It gives them low self-esteem, my daughter say. And that leads to problems later, as I happen to know.

My daughter never have big presentation the next day when the subject of spanking come up.

I don't want you to touch Sophie, she say. No spanking, period.

Don't tell me what to do, I say.

I'm not telling you what to do, say my daughter. I'm telling you how I feel.

I am not your servant, I say. Don't you dare talk to me like that.

My daughter have another funny habit when she lose an argument. She spread out all her fingers and look at them, as if she like to make sure they are still there.

My daughter is fierce like me, but she and John think it is better to explain to Sophie that clothes are a good idea. This is not so hard in the cold weather. In the warm weather, it is very hard.

Use your words, my daughter say. That's what we tell Sophie. How about if you set a good example.

As if good example mean anything to Sophie. I am so fierce, the gang members who used to come to the restaurant all afraid of me, but Sophie is not afraid.

I say, Sophie, if you take off your clothes, no snack.

I say, Sophie, if you take off your clothes, no lunch.

I say, Sophie, if you take off your clothes, no park.

Pretty soon we are stay home all day, and by the end of six hours she still did not have one thing to eat. You never saw a child stubborn like that.

I'm hungry! She cry when my daughter come home.

What's the matter, doesn't your grandmother feed you? My daughter laugh.

No! Sophie say. She doesn't feed me anything!

My daughter laugh again. Here you go, she say.

She say to John, Sophie must be growing.

Growing like a weed, I say.

Still Sophie take off her clothes, until one day I spank her. Not too hard, but she cry, and when I tell her if she doesn't put her clothes back on I'll spank her again, she put her clothes back on. Then I tell her she is good girl, and give her some food to eat. The next day we go to the park and, like a nice Chinese girl, she does not take off her clothes.

She stop taking off her clothes, I report. Finally!

How did you do it? my daughter ask.

After twenty-eight years experience with you, I guess I learn something, I say.

It must have been a phase, John say, and his voice is suddenly like an expert.

His voice is like an expert about everything these days, now that he carry a leather briefcase, and wear shiny shoes, and can go shopping for a new car. On the company, he say. The company will pay for it, but he will be able to drive it whenever he want.

A free car, he say. How do you like that.

It's good to see you in the saddle again, my daughter say. Some of your family patterns are scary.

At least I don't drink, he say. He say, And I'm not the only one with scary family patterns.

That's for sure, say my daughter.

Everyone is happy. Even I am happy, because there is more trouble with Sophie, but now I think I can help her Chinese side fight against her wild side. I teach her to eat food with fork or spoon or chopsticks, she cannot just grab into the middle of a bowl of noodles. I teach her not to play with garbage cans. Sometimes I spank her, but not too often, and not too hard.

Still, there are problems. Sophie like to climb everything. If there is a railing, she is never next to it. Always she is on top of it. Also, Sophie like to hit the mommies of her friends. She learn this from her playground best friend, Sinbad, who is four. Sinbad wear army clothes every day and like to ambush his mommy. He is the one who dug a big hole under the play structure, a foxhole he call it, all by himself. Very hardworking. Now he wait in the foxhole with a shovel full of wet sand. When his mommy come, he throw it right at her.

Oh, it's all right, his mommy say. You can't get rid of war games, it's part of their imaginative play. All the boys go through it.

Also, he like to kick his mommy, and one day he tell Sophie to kick his mommy too.

I wish this story is not true.

Kick her, kick her! Sinbad say.

Sophie kick her. A little kick, as if she just so happened was swinging her little leg and didn't realize that big mommy leg was in the way. Still I spank Sophie and make Sophie say sorry, and what does the mommy say?

Really, it's all right, she say. It didn't hurt.

After that, Sophie learn she can attack mommies in the playground, and some will say, Stop, but others will say, Oh, she didn't mean it, especially if they realize Sophie will be punished.

This is how, one day, bigger trouble come. The bigger trouble start when Sophie hide in the foxhole with that shovel full of sand. She wait, and when I come look for her, she throw it at me. All over my nice clean clothes.

Did you ever see a Chinese girl act this way?

Sophie! I say. Come out of there, say you're sorry.

But she does not come out. Instead, she laugh. Naaah, naah-na, naaa-naaa, she say.

I am not exaggerate: millions of children in China, not one act like this.

Sophie! I say. Now! Come out now!

But she know she is in big trouble. she know if she come out, what will happen next. So she does not come out. I am sixty-eight, Chinese age almost seventy, how can I crawl under there to catch her? Impossible. So I yell, yell, yell, and what happen? Nothing. A Chinese mother would help, but American mothers, they look at you, they shake their head, they go home. And, of course, a Chinese child would give up, but not Sophie.

I hate you! she yell. I hate you, Meanie!

Meanie is my new name these days.

Long time this goes on, long long time. The foxhole is deep, you cannot see too much, you don't know where is the bottom. You cannot hear too much either. If she does not yell, you cannot even know she is still there or not. After a while, getting cold out, getting dark out. No one left in the playground, only us.

Sophie, I say. How did you become stubborn like this? I am go home without you now.

I try to use a stick, chase her out of there, and once or twice I hit her, but still she does not come out. So finally I leave. I go outside the gate.

Bye-bye! I say. I'm go home now.

But still she does not come out and does not come out. Now it is dinnertime, the sky is black. I think I should maybe go get help, but how can I leave a little girl by herself in the playground? A bad man could come. A rat could come. I go back in to see what is happen to Sophie. What if she have a shovel and is making a tunnel to escape?

Sophie! I say.

No answer.

Sophie!

I don't know if she is alive. I don't know if she is fall asleep down there. If she is crying, I cannot hear her.

So I take the stick and poke.

Sophie! I say. I promise I no hit you. If you come out, I give you a lollipop.

No answer. By now I worried. What to do, what to do, what to do? I poke some more, even harder, so that I am poking and poking when my daughter and John suddenly appear.

What are you doing? What is going on? say my daughter.

Put down that stick! say my daughter.

You are crazy! say my daughter.

John wiggle under the structure, into the foxhole, to rescue Sophie.

She fell asleep, say John the expert. She's okay. That is one big hole.

Now Sophie is crying and crying.

Sophia, my daughter say, hugging her. Are you okay, peanut? Are you okay?

She's just scared, say John.

Are you okay? I say too. I don't know what happen, I say.

She's okay, say John. He is not like my daughter, full of questions. He is full of answers until we get home and can see by the lamplight.

Will you look at her? he yell then. What the hell happened?

Bruises all over her brown skin, and a swollen-up eye.

You are crazy! say my daughter. Look at what you did! You are crazy!

I try very hard, I say.

How could you use a stick? I told you to use your words!

She is hard to handle, I say.

She's three years old! You cannot use a stick! say my daughter.

She is not like any Chinese girl I ever saw, I say.

I brush some sand off my clothes. Sophie's clothes are dirty too, but at least she has her clothes on.

Has she done this before? ask my daughter. Has she hit you before?

She hits me all the time, Sophie say, eating ice cream.

Your family, say John.

Believe me, say my daughter.

A daughter I have, a beautiful daughter. I took care of her when she could not hold her head up. I took care of her before she could argue with me, when she was a little girl with two pigtails, one of them always crooked. I took care of her when we have to escape from China, I took care of her when suddenly we live in a country with cars everywhere, if you are not careful your little girl get run over. When my husband die, I promise him I will keep the family together, even though it was just two of us, hardly a family at all.

But now my daughter take me around to look at apartments. After all, I can cook, I can clean, there's no reason I cannot live by myself, all I need is a telephone. Of course, she is sorry. Sometimes she cry, I am the one to say everything will be okay. She say she have no choice, she doesn't want to end up divorced. I say divorce is terrible, I don't know who invented this terrible idea. Instead of live with a telephone, though, surprise, I come to live with Bess. Imagine that. Bess make an offer and, sure enough, where she come from, people mean for you to move in when they say things like that. A crazy idea, go to live with someone else's family, but she like to have some female company, not like my daughter, who does not believe in company. These days when my daughter visit, she does not bring Sophie. Bess say we should give Nattie time, we will see Sophie again soon. But seems like my daughter have more presentation than ever before, every time she come she have to leave.

I have a family to support, she say, and her voice is heavy, as if soaking wet. I have a young daughter and a depressed husband and no one to turn to.

When she say no one to turn to, she mean me.

These days my beautiful daughter is so tired she can just sit there in a chair and fall asleep. John lost his job again, already, but still they rather hire a baby-sitter than ask me to help, even they can't afford it. Of course, the new baby-sitter is much younger, can run around. I don't know if Sophie these days is wild or not wild. She call me Meanie, but she like to kiss me too, sometimes. I remember that every time I see a child on TV. Sophie like to grab my hair, a fistful in each hand, and then kiss me smack on the nose. I never see any other child kiss that way.

The satellite TV. has so many channels, more channels than I can count, including a Chinese channel from the Mainland and a Chinese channel from Taiwan, but most of the time I watch bloopers with Bess. Also, I watch the bird feeder—so many, many kinds of birds come. The Shea sons hang around all the time, asking when will I go home, but Bess tell them, Get lost.

She's a permanent resident, say Bess. She isn't going anywhere.

Then she wink at me, and switch the channel with the remote control.

Of course, I shouldn't say Irish this, Irish that, especially now I am become honorary Irish myself, according to Bess. Me! Who's Irish? I say, and she laugh. All the same, if I could mention one thing about some of the Irish, not all of them of course, I like to mention this: Their talk just stick. I don't know how Bess Shea learn to use her words, but sometimes I hear what she say a long time later. *Permanent resident. Not going anywhere.* Over and over I hear it, the voice of Bess.

☙ ☙ ☙
Suggestions for Discussion

1. Find three places where the narrator's perception seems unreliable. What is the author trying to show us in those places?
2. How does the author make the narrator sympathetic or endearing? How does she make her aggravating? What keeps you interested in this character?

Retrospect

3. Compare the grandmother's struggles with Sophie with the doctor's struggle with the sick child in "The Use of Force" (page 48). How is each pair matched in power? Who triumphs in each adult-child conflict?
4. How is the narrator's dialect suggested?

☙

Screentime

STEPHEN JONES

We had all seen the yellow and black vans line into town, sit outside the drugstore for about ten minutes, then drive bee straight out to the old drive-in, but it was Cheryl who found the ad in the paper, misplaced under Legal Notices.

"Wanted," she read, laid across the hood of my truck, "a kissing boy."

I smiled and she talked me into it.

Lynn at the drugstore said the van people were from the movies, that they'd rented the old drive-in for seven hundred and fifty dollars a day, and still needed directions.

"Does he look like a kissing boy?" Cheryl asked Lynn, framing my face with her hands, and Lynn said I sure looked like something. I stole a pack of dusty rubbers off the wall while Lynn looked away politely, and then the cowbell was a brass ringing thing and we were gone, weaving in my truck off into our last summer, trying to redo everything one last time before whatever was coming came.

We were just out of high school and hadn't learned yet about how hard you had to watch, not to let ten years get behind you.

That next morning I was one of four who showed up at the drive-in, to be a kissing boy, and the only one who'd had a Cheryl to pick my button-up shirt, tuck it in right, and wash under my fingernails with a toothbrush and bleach. Of the three others, two were Tim and Jim, twin linebackers from six years back, when I'd been playing touch football during sixth grade recess, my helmet overbalancing me, making me faster than I was. They were still drunk from the night before, leaning on each other and blinking their eyes too fast. One night my freshman year they'd stuffed me in a plastic trashcan and sat on the lid smoking dope and waving at people who drove by. The other of the three was Old Chester from the gas station, who didn't even make it under the tarp before he ran his finger down the hollow line of the clipboard girl's back and was asked to leave.

I felt like John Schneider for some reason.

When I looked back the last time before stepping in, Cheryl was posing like a poster, her legs crossed at the shins, her lace-up boots skylined out the driver's side window of my truck. She was posing on purpose, to make me keep all my promises. We'd practiced for my audition deep into the night.

Still though, when I walked under the tarp I wasn't ready for Charley, with her hair too black and dull to be natural, her eyes green like she was from another world altogether. She was sitting to the right of the little man who turned out to be her uncle, who was introduced as Herr Director; she was smoking a cigarette fast and angry and balanced the ashes straight up, flirting with gravity.

Later that year I would find in a catalogue all the bit parts she'd played, and have the tapes shipped to me COD. In one of the music videos she would dance around for a few seconds in a black bra and flared-out skirt. For discipline, I would only let myself watch that part after watching all of the other four videos, including the one we shot that week at the old drive-in, a place my dad always said held special significance for me and my beginnings, if I knew what he meant.

I watched them without sound, because somehow that made it all last longer.

That first day under the tarp we didn't test-run kiss, either, me and Charley. I did get in a fight though, with Tim and Jim, after Tim kneeled in front of Charley, took her hand, and held it to his unshaved cheek. He started singing some slow, fake song to her and she just smiled with her mouth and ashed behind the table. Herr Director rested his chin on the back of his laced fingers, hands bent at the wrists, elbows held close to his ribs, and watched. He had laryngitis or something and I never heard his voice, just followed his white-tipped baton all week.

Meaning I did get the job.

But that was in a few minutes. Right then, what was happening was Jim covered his hand with his mouth and elbowed me soft in the side, so I'd notice the fool his brother was making of himself, for her. When he touched me the second time I came back with a shoulder pushing him away, and when his big hand caressed the back of my neck like he was my father or something I was already punching and we were on the ground together in the sharp-stalked white weeds, rolling, Tim kicking both of us and finally diving in too. By the time the clipboard girl separated us her bikini top was most of the way pulled off and Tim and Jim were laughing, elbowing me in the side again.

That fight with them was one of the last things I'd meant to redo anyways, even if nobody won, or if they said they did.

It didn't matter.

The first thing Charley asked me was was I local?

I nodded.

The second thing was did I think I was a knight in shining armor or something.

I shrugged, then signed on for seventy dollars a day, and was probably standing in the exact same spot where my dad had unhooked my mom's bra eighteen years ago and told her not to worry, everything was going to be alright, some blue and white love scene burning into the screen for all time.

That night I had a handful of cash, too.

Cheryl asked were my lips tired. She used the flat side of her voice and I told her it was her idea after all, my new job.

"So then, what're you going to buy me?" she asked.

I told her anything, because it was eight o'clock and all the stores were closed and we were going to eat at the Texaco anyways, like every night when we didn't want to get tied up with her parents or mine. I did buy her a huge candy wedding ring though, which stained her mouth blue and made her look like a little girl, nothing like Charley.

Parked out at the end of the old airstrip with our friends and the beer I'd bought, we played Bob Seger in my tape deck and let our headlights feel out into the scrub. I didn't know what song the video was going to be yet, but I knew it was going to be Bob Seger. One of the van drivers had told me that much earlier when we were both packed into the old projection booth, rigging up the camera they'd brought. My job was to keep the spiders off him. We were both sweating and drinking lemonade from pointy-bottomed cups we couldn't set down.

"That Charley girl," he said, whistling in without noise, and I nodded and looked away from the spiderweb bridge caught between his hair and the low ceiling.

Outside our booth the parking lot was filling with people, with old car club cars that Herr Director positioned mutely between the speakers with his baton, then repositioned. The clipboard girl showed me the car I would be performing in, third row back. It was a long low Impala with rally rims, and me and Charley were going to be in the backseat, the second base crowd, no lines to remember, only motions to follow.

"Just pretend she's your girlfriend," she said, and that night when the headlights were off and no planes were coming I closed my eyes to Cheryl's blue candy mouth and drove us into San Angelo, where we rented a motel room for the first time in our five years together. Cheryl rang her sister's house once to let her know she was safe. We ate at a Chinese restaurant with chopsticks I sharpened under the table with my knife, skewering the chicken and pork and feeding each other like lovers.

I never meant to marry her.

It was all make believe.

That next morning they cut my hair, because I didn't look like I was from sixty-two. The hair guy asked me was I the token local, and I didn't answer him. Charley watched as he cut and finally just took over, holding the comb in her teeth, touching sometimes on a shoulder or a knee.

"Bob's coming tomorrow," she said, then followed with "Bob *Seger*, you know."

I smiled and told her I knew.

The haircut took longer than most, because I kept moving at every last second. Finally she had to get out the shears and give me a flat top. Punishment, she called it, and hit me lightly with the comb. My wet hair was all around us. She told me I looked like I should be an extra in a movie about malt shops, and then led me by the hand to our Impala. She opened the passenger door and bent over, looking in. Behind us one of the van drivers clapped and whistled.

She shook her head and lit a cigarette. "We can't smoke in the cars, you know. Leather seats. Rules."

I told her I didn't smoke much anyways, and then we stood there with nothing to say, my white skin sideburns and back of the neck burning wonderfully in the sun. Later that night, another seventy dollars in hand, Cheryl rubbed lotion into my small burns as I drove, and said she missed my hair.

That night in San Angelo it was custom-ordered pizza at some dark place we'd been to for prom, and when the waiter wasn't around I looked away and told Cheryl I liked my hair better like this, it was easier. That night one more of the dusty rubbers broke in the motel room, and one more night I opened my eyes and said don't worry.

When my son Rick gets old enough I plan on drinking hard one night and then lying to him that he was conceived out at the old drive-in, in a lowslung Impala, Bob Seger's mouth moving with no noise, his guitar deep like the sound of thunder.

He'll never ask his mom about it.

Two days later Cheryl was on the set with me, holding my arm with both her hands. I was already calling it the set, not the old drive-in. She made fun of me, asked what was I going to do when the video was over. I shrugged, stood by the Impala, talked to the bearded accountant leaning under his hood, who said I was lucky, this car was a home run car if there ever was one. He offered us beer and we sat in the shade of a van and drank and talked about where the rest of our class had wound up after graduation, where we might be winding up ourselves. She was already saying we, too, we both were. I didn't notice.

Instead I was watching the helicopter with Bob Seger approach, a day late.

They had to set it down a half mile off, to keep the dust off the cars; a yellow VW van picked him up and buzzed back, and when he stepped out he was a star and Cheryl was squeezing bruises into my arm and I was even getting a lump in my throat. In the floorboard of my truck were all the old 8-tracks my uncle wanted him to sign, even though his 8-track player was long dead.

The rest of the day we spent doing dry runs, Bob Seger straddling the hood of some car, pool table felt glued to the bottom of his boots, me and Charley sitting in the backseat stage-kissing, the clipboard girl telling me what to do with my right arm, since that's mostly what would be seen when the windows were fogged. A lot of the time I was alone in the car, too, since Charley was the backseat girl in four other cars in different rows. Once a blonde girl poked her head into my backseat and said oops, wiped her mouth, and then was gone.

When we finally shot the video it would take two nights. Cheryl would be sitting out at the road in my truck, the parking lights on, waiting for life to begin. We'd spend the days between the nights at her sister's empty house, and her sister was nice enough to ring once before coming home from work.

I never got Bob Seger's autograph, either. I did talk to him, though, the day after the shoot, when everybody was gone, when he came back on his own time with a small video camera, to stand in the old drive-in and look around and find me sitting in the third row.

I told him I was the kissing boy, and he smiled and said aren't we all.

The other day Rick asked me why I liked that old video so much. I told him it was a good song, but had the volume turned all the way down, too. He shook his head and left on his bicycle, to wherever nine-year olds go in the summer heat. Cheryl was in the kitchen on the phone, trying to organize the class reunion, trying to get everybody together one more time. I was pushing play, rewind, play, rewind, no discipline at all, remembering that second night of shooting, when the firetrucks were there to make the rain, when the camera crane hovered impossibly over our Impala and Charley climbed on top of me and made me kiss her hard and deep. She was out of breath from running from the first three cars, and her shirt was wet. In the front seat the battery-driven humidifier was turned up to 10 and the windows were impenetrable, and somewhere one of the yellow vans was playing Bob Seger at full tilt, and Bob Seger himself was leaning back into the fans, singing, his voice getting pulled behind him to lose itself on the drive-in screen, where there were spliced together love scenes in blue, all turning into each other.

In the video my right arm curves around Charley Waine's lower back, pulls her close, and her too-black hair is falling all over the both of us, her hands on my shoulder, both pushing away and not letting go.

Blink and you'll miss me.

🖎 🖎 🖎

Suggestions for Discussion

1. What do the flash-forwards reveal about the events of the story?

2. How would you describe the older narrator's attitude toward his younger self?

Retrospect

3. Find examples of indirect dialogue. Why do you think the author chose to use indirect rather than direct dialogue for these exchanges?

4. The author manages major time shifts without the use of such blatant transitions as "many years before" or "later." What makes the time changes apparent?

🖎 🖎 🖎

Writing Exercises

INDIVIDUAL

1. Choose a significant incident from a child's life (your own or invented) and in first person write about the incident from the temporally distanced perspective of an adult narrator. Then rewrite the same incident in the child's language in present tense, from the child's point of view.

2. Write a gossipy monologue from the point of view of one family member who passes scathing judgments on another, but let readers know that the speaker really loves or envies the other. Alternatively, have the speaker loudly praise the other family member, but let readers hear harsh criticism implied.

3. Write a description of a current custom or news event as seen from the perspective of a time traveler who comes from either one hundred years in the past or one hundred years in the future.

DEVELOPMENT/REVISION

4. Take any scene or assignment you have previously written and recast it from a different character's point of view (either first- or third-person limited omniscient). Give readers an entirely different perspective on the same events, but let your attitude as author remain the same.

COLLABORATIVE

5. After reading "Jealous Husband Returns in Form of Parrot," which comes from the author's story collection *Tabloid Dreams*, bring a few current issues of a supermarket tabloid like *The Weekly World News* or *The National Enquirer* to class. Divide the more fantastic pieces—or even simply the headlines—among class members.
   a. Write fifteen-minute, first-person drafts of stories suggested by the tabloid pieces. Use as much detail and emotional honesty as possible to make the stories convincing.
   b. Read the pieces in small groups and discuss:
   • What common wish or fear the story might reflect
   • Why this character needs or deserves this miraculous event
   • The chain of cause and effect that leads from one event to the next
   • Whether the character has a crisis decision to make

6. Write a two- to three-page piece from a domestic animal's perspective depicting either of the following:
   a. Any human ritual done at home, such as getting ready for a date, making dinner, or working out.
   b. A holiday, such as the Fourth of July, Thanksgiving, or Halloween.

   Making use of the animal's sensory perceptions and natural behaviors, let the animal's account offer an indirect comment on the human activity.

9

IS AND *IS NOT*
Comparison

- *Types of Metaphor and Simile*
- *Metaphoric Faults to Avoid*
- *Allegory*
- *Symbol*

Every reader reading is a self-deceiver: We simultaneously "believe" a story and know that it is a fiction, a fabrication. Our belief in the reality of the story may be so strong that it produces physical reactions—tears, trembling, sighs, gasps, a headache. At the same time, as long as the fiction is working for us, we know that our submission is voluntary; that we have, as Samuel Taylor Coleridge pointed out, suspended disbelief. "It's just a movie," says the exasperated father as he takes his shrieking six-year-old out to the lobby. For the father the fiction is working; for the child it is not.

Simultaneous belief and awareness of illusion are present in both the content and the craft of literature, and what is properly called artistic pleasure derives from the tension of this *is* and *is not*. The content of a plot, for instance, tells us that something happens that does not happen, that people who do not exist behave in such a way, and that the events of life—which we know to be random, unrelated, and unfinished—are necessary, patterned, and come to closure. Pleasure in artistry comes precisely when the illusion rings true without destroying the knowledge that it is an illusion.

In the same way, the techniques of every art offer us the tension of things that are and are not alike. This is true of poetry, in which rhyme is interesting because *tend* sounds like *mend* but not exactly like; it is also true of music, whose interest lies in

325

variations on a theme. And it is the fundamental nature of metaphor, from which literature derives.

Metaphor is the literary device by which we are told that something is, or is like, something that it clearly is not, or is not exactly, like. What a good metaphor does is surprise us with the unlikeness of the two things compared while at the same time convincing us of the truth of the likeness. In the process it may also illuminate the meaning of the story and its theme. A bad metaphor fails to surprise or convince or both—and so fails to illuminate.

Types of Metaphor and Simile

The simplest distinction between kinds of comparison, and usually the first one grasped by beginning students of literature, is between *metaphor* and *simile*. A simile makes a comparison with the use of *like* or *as*, a metaphor without. Though this distinction is technical, it is not entirely trivial, for a metaphor demands a more literal acceptance. If you say, "a woman is a rose," you ask for an extreme suspension of disbelief, whereas "a woman is like a rose" acknowledges the artifice in the statement.

In both metaphor and simile, the resonance of comparison is in the essential or abstract quality that the two objects share. When a writer speaks of "the eyes of the houses" or "the windows of the soul," the comparison of eyes to windows contains the idea of transmitting vision between the inner and the outer. When we speak of "the king of beasts," we don't mean that a lion wears a crown or sits on a throne (although in children's stories the lion often does precisely that, in order to suggest a primitive physical likeness); we mean that king and lion share abstract qualities of power, position, pride, and bearing.

In both metaphor and simile a physical similarity can yield up a characterizing abstraction. So if "a woman" is either "a rose" or "like a rose," the significance lies not in the physical similarity but in the essential qualities that such similarity implies: slenderness, suppleness, fragrance, beauty, color—and perhaps the hidden threat of thorns.

Every metaphor and simile I have used so far is either a cliché or a dead metaphor (a metaphor so familiar that it has lost its original meaning). Each of them may at one time have surprised by their aptness, but by now each has been used so often that the surprise is gone. I wished to use familiar examples in order to clarify that *resonance of comparison depends on the abstractions conveyed in the likeness of the things compared.* A good metaphor reverberates with the essential; this is the writer's principle of choice.

So Flannery O'Connor, in "A Good Man Is Hard to Find," describes the mother as having "a face as broad and innocent as a cabbage." A soccer ball is roughly the same size and shape as a cabbage; so is a schoolroom globe; so is a street lamp. But if the mother's face had been as broad and innocent as any of these things, she would be a different woman altogether. A cabbage is also rural, heavy, dense, and cheap, and so it conveys a whole complex of abstractions about the woman's class and mentality. There is, on the other hand, no innocence in the face of Shrike, in Nathanael West's *Miss Lonelyhearts*, who "buried his triangular face like a hatchet in her neck."

Sometimes the aptness of a comparison is achieved by taking it from an area of reference relevant to the thing compared. In *Dombey and Son*, Charles Dickens describes the ships' instrument maker, Solomon Gills, as having "eyes as red as if they had been small suns looking at you through a fog." The simile suggests a seascape, whereas in *One Flew Over the Cuckoo's Nest*, Ken Kesey's Ruckly, rendered inert by shock therapy, has eyes "all smoked up and gray and deserted inside like blown fuses." But the metaphor may range further from its original, in which case the abstraction conveyed must strike us as strongly and essentially appropriate. William Faulkner's Emily Grierson in "A Rose for Emily" has "haughty black eyes in a face the flesh of which was strained across the temple and about the eyesockets as you imagine a lighthouse-keeper's face ought to look." Miss Emily has no connection with the sea, but the metaphor reminds us not only of her sternness and self-sufficiency, but also that she has isolated herself in a locked house. The same character as an old woman has eyes that "looked like two pieces of coal pressed into a lump of dough," and the image domesticates her, robs her of her light.

Both metaphors and similes can be *extended,* meaning that the writer continues to present aspects of likeness in the things compared.

> There was a white fog . . . standing all around you like something solid. At eight or nine, perhaps, it lifted as a shutter lifts. We had a glimpse of the towering multitude of trees, of the immense matted jungle, with the blazing little ball of sun hanging over it—all perfectly still—and then the shutter came down again, smoothly, as if sliding in greased grooves.
>
> Joseph Conrad, *Heart of Darkness*

Notice that Conrad moves from a generalized image of "something solid" to the specific simile "as a shutter lifts"; reasserts the simile as a metaphor, "then the shutter came down again"; and becomes still more specific in the extension "as if sliding in greased grooves."

Also note that Conrad emphasizes the dumb solidity of the fog by comparing the larger natural image with the smaller manufactured object. This is a technique that contemporary writers have used to effects both comic and profound, as when Frederick Barthelme in *The Brothers* describes a young woman "with a life stretching out in front of her like so many unrented videos" or a man's head "bobbing like an enormous Q-Tip against the little black sky."

In a more usual metaphoric technique, the smaller or more ordinary image is compared with one more significant or intense, as in this example from Louise Erdrich's "Machimanito," where the narrator invokes the names of Anishinabe Indians dead of tuberculosis:

> Their names grew within us, swelled to the brink of our lips, forced our eyes open in the middle of the night. We were filled with the water of the drowned, cold and black—airless water that lapped against the seal of our tongues or leaked slowly from the corners of our eyes. Within us, like ice shards, their names bobbed and shifted.

A *conceit*, which can be either metaphor or simile, is a comparison of two things radically and startlingly unlike—in Samuel Johnson's words, "yoked by violence together." A conceit is as far removed as possible from the purely sensuous comparison of "the eyes of the potato." It compares two things that have very little or no immediately apprehensible similarity; and so it is the nature of the conceit to be long. The author must explain to us, sometimes at great length, why these things can be said to be alike. When John Donne compares a flea to the Holy Trinity, the two images have no areas of reference in common, and we don't understand. He must explain to us that the flea, having bitten both the poet and his lover, now has the blood of three souls in its body.

The conceit is more common to poetry than to prose because of the density of its imagery, but it can be used to good effect in fiction. In *The Day of the Locust*, Nathanael West uses a conceit in an insistent devaluation of love. The screenwriter Claude Estee says:

> Love is like a vending machine, eh? Not bad. You insert a coin and press home the lever. There's some mechanical activity inside the bowels of the device. You receive a small sweet, frown at yourself in the dirty mirror, adjust your hat, take a firm grip on your umbrella and walk away, trying to look as though nothing had happened.

"Love is like a vending machine" is a conceit; if the writer didn't explain to us in what way love is like a vending machine, we'd founder trying to figure it out. So he goes on to develop the vending machine in images that suggest not "love" but seamy sex. The last image—"trying to look as though nothing had happened"—has nothing to do with the vending machine; we accept it because by this time we've fused the two ideas in our minds.

Deborah Galyan employs conceit in "The Incredible Appearing Man," in a playfully self-conscious description of the overpowering effect of a new baby's presence.

> A baby transforms you, body and soul. The moment you give birth, your mind is instantaneously filled with Styrofoam peanuts. Your past is trash-compacted to make room for all the peanuts. As the baby grows, you add more peanuts, and the little tin can of your past gets more compressed. But it is still there, underneath all the peanuts. The smashed cans of your past never entirely disappear.

The comparison of a mind and a trash compactor is a conceit because their physical or sensuous similarity is not the point. Rather, the similarity is in the abstract idea of material (metal cans or memories) that once loomed large being crushed and all but crowded out by the volume of daily experience.

Metaphoric Faults to Avoid

Comparison is not a frivolity. It is, on the contrary, the primary business of the brain. Some eighteenth-century philosophers spoke of the human mind as a *"tabula rasa,"* a blank slate on which sense impressions were recorded, compared, and grouped. Now we're more likely to speak of the mind as a "computer" "storing" and "processing" "data." What both metaphors acknowledge is that comparison is the basis of all learning and all reasoning. When a child burns his hand on the stove and hears his mother say, "It's hot," and then goes toward the radiator and again hears her say, "It's hot," the child learns not to burn his fingers. The implicit real-life comparison is meant to convey a fact, and it teaches a mode of behavior. By contrast, the goal of literary comparison is to convey not a fact but a perception, and thereby to enlarge our scope of understanding. When we speak of "the flames of torment," our impulse is comprehension and compassion.

Nevertheless, metaphor is a dirty word in some critical circles, because of the strain of the pursuit. Clichés, mixed metaphors, and similes that are inept, unapt, obscure, or done to death mar good prose and tax the patience of the most willing reader. After eyes have been red suns, burnt-out fuses, lighthouse keepers, and lumps of coal, what else can they be?

The answer is, always something. But because by definition metaphor introduces an alien image into the flow of the story, metaphor is to some degree always self-conscious. Badly handled, it calls attention to the writer rather than the meaning and produces a sort of hiccup in the reader's involvement. A good metaphor fits so neatly that it fuses to and illuminates the meaning. Generally speaking, where metaphors are concerned, less is more and, if in doubt, don't.

Certainly, there are more *don'ts* than *dos* to list for the writing of metaphor and simile, because every good comparison is its own justification by virtue of being apt and original.

To study good metaphor, read. In the meantime, avoid the following:

Cliché metaphors are metaphors so familiar that they have lost the force of their original meaning. They are inevitably apt comparisons; if they were not, they wouldn't have been repeated often enough to become clichés. But such images fail to surprise, and we blame the writer for this expenditure of energy without a payoff. Or, to put it a worse way:

> Clichés are *the last word* in bad writing, and *it's a crying shame* to see all you *bright young things* spoiling your *deathless prose* with phrases as *old as the hills*. You must *keep your nose to the grindstone*, because *the sweet smell of success* only comes to those who *march to the tune of a different drummer*.

It's a sad fact that at this stage of literary history, you may not say that eyes are like pools or stars, and you should be very wary of saying that they flood with tears. These have been so often repeated that they've become shorthand for emotions (attractions in the first and second instances, grief in the third) without the felt force of those emotions. Anytime you as writer record an emotion without convincing us to feel that emotion, you introduce a fatal distance between author and reader. Therefore, neither may your characters be hawk-eyed nor eagle-eyed; nor may they have ruby lips or pearly teeth or peaches-and-cream complexions or necks like swans or thighs like hams. Let them not shed single tears or freeze like deer caught in headlights. If you sense—and you may—that the moment calls for the special intensity of metaphor, you may have to sift through a whole stock of clichés that come readily to mind. Or it may be time for freewriting, clustering, and giving the mind room to play. Sometimes your internal critic may reject as fantastic the comparison that, on second look, proves fresh and apt.

In any case, *pools* and *stars* have become clichés for *eyes* because they capture and manifest something essential about the nature of eyes. As long as eyes continue to contain liquid and light, there will be a new way of saying so.

Cliché can be useful as a device, however, for establishing authorial distance from a character or narrator. If the author tells us that Rome wasn't built in a day, we're likely to think the author has little to contribute to human insight; but if a character says so, in speech or thought, the judgment attaches to the character rather than to the author.

> The door closed and he turned to find the dumpy figure, surmounted by the atrocious hat, coming toward him. "Well," she said, "*you only live once* and paying a little more for it, I at least won't *meet myself coming and going.*"
>
> "Some day I'll start making money . . ."
>
> "I think you're doing fine," she said, drawing on her gloves. "You've only been out of school a year. *Rome wasn't built in a day.*"

Flannery O'Connor, "Everything That Rises Must Converge"(italics added)

Far-fetched metaphors are the opposite of clichés: They surprise but are not apt. As the dead metaphor *far-fetched* suggests, the mind must travel too far to carry back the likeness, and too much is lost on the way. When such a comparison does work, we speak laudatorily of a "leap of the imagination." But when it does not, what we face is in effect a failed conceit: The explanation of what is alike about these two things does not convince. Very good writers in the search for originality sometimes fetch too far. Ernest Hemingway's talent was not for metaphor, and on the rare occasions that he used a metaphor, he was likely to strain. In this passage from *A Farewell to Arms*, the protagonist has escaped a firing squad and is fleeing the war.

> You had lost your cars and your men as a floorwalker loses the stock of his department in a fire. There was, however, no insurance. You were out of it now. You had no more obligation. If they shot floorwalkers after a fire in the department store because they spoke with an accent they had always had, then certainly the floorwalkers would not be expected to return when the store opened again for business. They might seek other employment; if there was any other employment and the police did not get them.

Well, this doesn't work. We may be willing to see the likeness between stock lost in a department store fire and men and cars lost in a military retreat; but "they" *don't* shoot floorwalkers as the Italian military shot defeated line officers. And although a foreign accent might be a disadvantage in a foreign war, it's hard to see how a floorwalker could be killed because of one, although it might make it hard for him to get hired in the first place, if. . . . The mind twists trying to find any illuminating or essential logic in the comparison of a soldier to a floorwalker, and fails, so that the protagonist's situation is trivialized in the attempt.

Mixed metaphors are so called because they ask us to compare the original image with things from two or more different areas of reference: *As you walk the path of life, don't founder on the reefs of ignorance.* Life can be a path or a sea, but it cannot be both at the same time. The point of the metaphor is to fuse two images in a single tension. The mind is adamantly unwilling to fuse three.

Separate metaphors or similes too close together, especially if they come from areas of reference very different in value or tone, disturb in the same way the mixed metaphor does. The mind doesn't leap; it staggers.

> They fought like rats in a Brooklyn sewer. Nevertheless her presence was the axiom of his heart's geometry, and when she was away you would see him walking up and down the street dragging his cane along the picket fence like an idle boy's stick.

Any of these metaphors or similes might be acceptable by itself, but rats, axioms, and boys' sticks connote three different areas and tones, and two sentences cannot contain them all. Pointed in too many directions, a reader's attention follows none.

Obscure and *overdone metaphors* falter because the author has misjudged the difficulty of the comparison. The result is either confusion or an insult to the reader's intelligence. In the case of obscurity, a similarity in the author's mind isn't getting onto the page. One student described the spines on a prickly pear cactus as being "slender as a fat man's fingers." I was completely confused by this. Was it ironic, that the spines weren't slender at all? Ah no, he said, hadn't I noticed how startling it was when someone with a fleshy body had bony fingers and toes? The trouble here was that the author knew what he meant but had left out the essential abstraction in the comparison, the startling quality of the contrast: "the spines of the fleshy prickly pear, like slender fingers on a fat man."

In this case, the simile was underexplained. It's probably a more common impulse—we're so anxious to make sure the reader gets it—to explain the obvious. In the novel *Raw Silk,* I had the narrator describe quarrels with her husband, "which I used to face with my dukes up in high confidence that we'd soon clear the air. The air can't be cleared now. We live in marital Los Angeles. This is the air—polluted, poisoned." A critic friend pointed out to me that anybody who didn't know about L.A. smog wouldn't get it anyway, and that all the last two words did was ram the comparison down the reader's throat. He was right. "The air can't be cleared now. We live in marital Los Angeles. This is the air." The rewrite is much stronger because it neither explains nor exaggerates; and the reader enjoys supplying the metaphoric link.

Metaphors using *topical references,* including brand names, esoteric objects, or celebrity names, can work as long as a sense of the connection is given; don't rely for effect on knowledge that the reader may not have. To write, "The sisters looked like the Dixie Chicks" is to make the trio do your job; and if the reader happens to be a Beethoven buff, or Hungarian, or reading your story twenty years from now, there may be no way of knowing what the reference refers to. "They had the blindingly blond, in-your-face exuberance of the Dixie Chicks" will convey the sense even for someone who doesn't watch country music cable. Likewise, "She was as beautiful as Theda Bara" may not mean much to you, whereas if I say, "She had the saucer eyes and satin hair of Theda Bara," you'll get it, close enough.

Allegory

Allegory is a fictional form in which the action of the story represents a different action or a philosophical idea. The simplest illustration of an allegory is a fable, in which, for example, the race between the tortoise and the hare is used to illustrate the philosophical notion that "the race is not always to the swift." Such a story can be seen as an extended simile, with the original figure of the comparison suppressed: The tortoise and the hare represent types of human beings, but people are never mentioned and the comparison takes place in the reader's mind. George Orwell's *Animal Farm* is a less naive animal allegory, exploring ideas about corruption in a democratic society. Children may read *The Lion, the Witch, and the Wardrobe* without seeing the Christian allegory clear to adults; *The Lord of the Flies* has long been taught to adolescents to illustrate how impulses toward evil and goodness become manifest in groups. The plots of such stories are self-contained, but their significance lies in the reference to outside events or ideas.

In the hands of Dante, John Bunyan, Franz Kafka, Samuel Beckett, and such contemporary authors as John Edgar Wideman, Ursula K. Le Guin, and Charles Johnson (whose story "Menagerie" comes at the end of this chapter), the allegory has yielded works of serious philosophical and political insight. But it is a tricky form and can seem to smirk. A naive philosophical fable leads to a simpleminded idea that can be stated in a single phrase; a social satire rests on our familiarity with the latest Washington sex scandal, sports lockout, or celebrity brouhaha, and so appeals to a limited and insular readership.

Symbol

A *symbol* is an object or event that represents something beyond itself. Unlike metaphor and simile, it need not contain a comparison. Sometimes an object is invested arbitrarily with such meaning, as a flag represents a nation and patriotism. Sometimes a single event stands for a whole complex of events, as the crucifixion of Christ stands as well for resurrection and redemption. Such events and attendant qualities in turn may become invested in an object like the cross. These symbols are not metaphor: the cross represents redemption but is not similar to redemption, which cannot be said to be wooden or T-shaped. In Flannery O'Connor's 1965 story "Everything That Rises Must Converge," the protagonist's mother encounters a black woman wearing the same absurd hat of which she has been so proud. The hat can in no way be said to "resemble" desegregation, but in the course of the story it comes to represent the tenacious nostalgia of gentility and the aspirations of the new black middle class, and therefore the unacknowledged "converging" of equality.

Nevertheless, most literary symbols, including this one, do in the course of the action derive their extra meaning from some sort of likeness on the level of emotional or ideological abstraction. The hat is not "like" desegregation, but the action of the story reveals that both women are able to buy such a hat and choose it; this is a concrete example of equality, and so represents the larger concept of equality.

Margaret Drabble's novel *The Garrick Year* recounts the disillusionment of a young wife and mother who finds no escape from her situation. The book ends with a family picnic in an English meadow and the return home.

On the way back to the car, Flora dashed at a sheep that was lying in the path, but unlike all the others it did not get up and move: it stared at us instead with a sick and stricken indignation. Flora passed quickly on, pretending for pride's sake that she had not noticed its recalcitrance; but as I passed, walking slowly, supported by David, I looked more closely and I saw curled up and clutching at the sheep's belly a real snake. I did not say anything to David: I did not want to admit that I had seen it, but I did see it, I can see it still. It is the only wild snake that I have ever seen. In my book on Herefordshire it says that that part of the country is notorious for its snakes. But "Oh, well, so what," is all that one can say, the Garden of Eden was crawling with them too, and David and I managed to lie amongst them for one whole pleasant afternoon. One just has to keep on and to pretend, for the sake of the children, not to notice. Otherwise one might just as well stay at home.

The sheep is a symbol of the young woman's emotional situation. It does resemble her, but only on the level of the abstractions: sickness, indignation, and yet resignation at the fatal dangers of the human condition. There is here a metaphor that could be expressed as such (*she was as sick and resigned as the sheep*), but the strength of the symbol is that such literal expression does not take place: We let the sheep stand in the place of the young woman while we reach out to the larger significance.

The truer the symbol, the deeper it leads you, the more meaning it opens up.

Flannery O'Connor

Fiction is better experienced than interpreted. . . . To fully understand a symbol is to kill it.

Ron Hansen

A symbol may also begin as and grow from a metaphor, so that it finally contains more qualities than the original comparison. In John Irving's novel *The World According to Garp*, the young Garp mishears the word "undertow" as "under toad" and compares the danger of the sea to the lurking fantasies of his childish imagination. Throughout the novel the "under toad" persists, and it comes symbolically to represent all the submerged dangers of ordinary life, ready to drag Garp under just when he thinks he is swimming under his own power.

One important distinction in the use of literary symbols is between those symbols of which the character is aware, and therefore "belong" to him or her, and those symbols of which only writer and reader are aware, and therefore belong to the work. This distinction is often important to characterization, theme, and distance. In the passage quoted from *The Garrick Year*, the narrator is clearly aware of the import of the sheep, and her awareness suggests her intelligence and the final acceptance of her situation, so that we identify with her in recognizing the symbol. In "Everything That Rises Must Converge," the adult son recognizes the symbolism implied as

> the vision of the two hats, identical, broke upon him with the radiance of a brilliant sunrise. His face was suddenly lit with joy. He could not believe that Fate had thrust upon his mother such a lesson.

His mother, on the other hand, does not recognize the hat as a symbol of equality, and this distances us from her perception.

Symbols are subject to all the same faults as metaphor: cliché, strain, obscurity, obviousness, and overwriting. For these reasons (and because the word "Symbolism" also describes a particular late-nineteenth-century movement in French poetry, with connotations of obscurity, dream, and magical incantation), *symbolism* as a method has sometimes been treated with scorn in the hard-nosed postmodern world. Flannery O'Connor attributed this attitude in part to a reductive manner of reading.

> . . . the word *symbol* scares a good many people off, just as the word *art* does. They seem to feel that a symbol is some mysterious thing put in arbitrarily by the writer to frighten the common reader—sort of a literary Masonic grip that is only for the initiated . . . they approach it as if it were a problem in algebra. Find *x*. And when they do find or think they find this abstraction, *x*, then they go off with an elaborate sense of satisfaction and the notion that they have "understood" the story. Many students confuse the *process* of understanding a thing with understanding it.
>
> *Mystery and Manners*

THE SYMBOLIC MIND

It seems to me incontrovertible that the writing process is inherently and by definition symbolic. In the structuring of plot, the creation of character and atmosphere, the choice of object, detail, and language, you are selecting and arranging elements to signify more than their literal existence. If this were not so, then you would have no unifying principle of choice and might just as well write about any other sets of events, characters, and objects.

People constantly function symbolically. By night our dreaming minds fuse their own symbols, merging the eternally missed exam or public nakedness with the current anxieties of the dreamer's life. By day, in speaking, we leap past unwieldy words with intuition, body language, tone, and symbol. "Is the oven supposed to be on?" he asks. He is only peripherally curious about whether the oven is supposed to be on. He is really complaining: *You're scatterbrained and extravagant with the money I go out and earn.* "If I don't preheat it, the muffins won't crest," she says, meaning: *You didn't catch me this time! You're always complaining about the food, and God knows I wear myself out trying to please you.* "We used to have salade niçoise in the summertime," he recalls, meaning: *Don't be so damn triumphant. You're still extravagant, and you haven't got the class you used to have when we were young.* "We used to keep a garden," she says, meaning: *You're always away on weekends and never have time to do anything with me because you don't love me anymore; I think you have a mistress.* "What do you expect of me!" he explodes, and neither of them is surprised that ovens, muffins, salads, and gardens have erupted. When people say "we quarreled over nothing," this is what they mean—through the subtext of their dialogue, they quarreled over symbols.

When a literary symbol fails, it is most often because it has not been integrated into the texture of the story. As Bonnie Friedman puts it in *Writing Past Dark:* "Before a thing can be a symbol it must be a thing. It must do its job as a thing in the world before and during and after you have projected all your meaning all over it." In a typical example, we begin the story in a room of a dying woman alone with her collection of perfume bottles. The story ranges back over her rich and sensuous life, and at the end we focus on an empty perfume bottle. It is meant to move us at her death, but it does not. Yet the fault is not in the perfume bottle itself. Presumably a perfume bottle may express mortality as well as a hat may express racial equality. The fault is rather that we need to be convinced of the importance this woman placed on scent as essence, need to know how the collection has played a part in the conflicts of her life, need to see her fumbling now toward her favorite, so that we could emotionally equate the spilling or evaporation of the scent with the death of her own spirit.

Good description is symbolic not because the writer plants symbols in it but because . . . he forces symbols still largely mysterious to him up into his conscious mind where, little by little as his fiction progresses, he can work with them and finally understand them.

John Gardner

A symbolic object, situation, or event may err because it seems to have been imposed upon the story, existing for its own sake rather than emanating naturally from the characters' lives. Or it may err because it is too heavy or heavy-handed; that is, the author keeps pushing the symbol at us, nudging us in the ribs to say: Get it? In any of these cases we will say that the symbol is *artificial*—a curious word in the critical vocabulary, analogous to the charge of a *formula* plot, since *art*, like *form*, is a word of praise. All writing is "artificial," and when we charge it with being so, we mean that it isn't artificial enough, that the artifice has not concealed itself so as to give the illusion of the natural, and that the artificer must go back to work.

San

LAN SAMANTHA CHANG

My father left my mother and me one rainy summer morning, carrying a new umbrella of mine. From our third-floor window I watched him close the front door and pause to glance at the sky. Then he opened my umbrella. I liked the big red flower pattern—it was *fuqi*, prosperous—but in the hands of a man, even a handsome man like my father, the umbrella looked gaudy and ridiculous. Still, he did not hunch underneath but carried it high up, almost jauntily.

As I watched him walk away, I remembered a Chinese superstition. The Mandarin word for umbrella, *san*, also means "to fall apart." If you acquire an umbrella without paying for it, your life will fall apart. My father had scoffed at such beliefs. The umbrella had been a present from him. Now I stood and watched it go, bright and ill-fated like so many of his promises.

Later that morning the roof of our apartment sprang a leak. Two tiles buckled off the kitchen floor, revealing a surprising layer of mud, as if my mother's mopping over the years had merely pushed the dirt beneath the tiles and all along we'd been living over a floor of soot.

My mother knelt with a sponge in one hand. She wouldn't look at me. Her heavy chignon had come undone and a thick lock of hair wavered down her neck.

"Can I help?" I asked, standing over her. She did not answer but stroked the tiles with her sponge.

I put the big rice cooker underneath the leak. Then I went to my room. All morning, I studied problems for my summer school math class. I heard my mother, in the kitchen, start to sob. I felt only fear—a dense stone in my chest—but I put even this aside so I could study. My father had taught me to focus on the equations in front of me, and so I spent the hours after he left thinking about trigonometry, a subject he had loved.

My mathematical talent had sprung from an early backwardness. As a child I could not count past three: my father, my mother, and me.

"Caroline is making progress in her English lessons, but she remains baffled by the natural numbers," read an early report card. "She cannot grasp the *countability* of blocks and other solid objects. For this reason I am recommending that she repeat the first grade."

This comment left my father speechless. He believed I was a brilliant child. And mathematics had been his favorite subject back in China, before political trouble had forced him to quit school and, eventually, the country.

"*Counting*," he said in English, when he was able to talk again. His dark eyebrows swooped over the bridge of his aquiline nose. Despite his drastic ups and downs, bad news always caught him by surprise. But he recovered with typical buoyancy. "Don't worry, Lily," he told my mother. "It's those western teachers. *I'll* teach her how to count."

And so my father, himself an unreliable man, taught me to keep track of things. We counted apples, bean sprouts, grains of rice. I learned to count in pairs, with ivory chopsticks. We stood on the corner of Atlantic Avenue, counting cars to learn big numbers. We spent a lovely afternoon in Prospect Park, counting blades of grass aloud until we both had scratchy throats.

"Keep going," he urged me on as the shadows lengthened. "I want you to be able to count all the money I'm going to make, here in America."

By the time I was seven I had learned the multiplication tables to twenty-times-twenty. In the following year I learned to recite the table of squares and the table of cubes, both so quickly that the words blended together into a single stream, almost meaningless: "Oneeighttwentysevensixtyfouronetwentyfivetwosixteenthree-fortythree . . ."

As I chanted, my father would iron the white shirt and black trousers he wore to his waiter's job, a "temporary" job. Or he stood in the kitchen, Mondays off, with three blue balls and one red ball, juggling expertly beneath the low tin ceiling. Each time the red ball reached his hand I was ordered to stress a syllable. Thus "One, *eight*, twenty-seven, sixty-*four*."

"Pronounce," said my father, proud of his clear r's. To succeed in America, he was sure, required good pronunciation as well as math. He often teased my mother for pronouncing my name *Calorin*, "like a diet formula," he said. They had named me Caroline after Caroline Kennedy, who was born shortly before their arrival in the States. After all, my father's name was Jack. And if the name was good enough for a president's daughter, then certainly it was good enough for me.

After I learned to count I began, belatedly, to notice things. Signs of hard luck and good fortune moved through our apartment like sudden storms. A pale stripe on my father's tanned wrist revealed where his watch had been. A new pair of aquamarine slippers shimmered on my mother's feet. A beautiful collection of fourteen cacti, each distinct, bloomed on our fire escape for several summer months and then vanished.

I made careful explorations of our apartment. At the back of the foyer closet, inside the faded red suitcase my mother had brought from China, I discovered a cache of little silk purses wrapped in a cotton shirt. When I heard her footsteps I instinctively closed the suitcase and pretended I was looking for a pair of mittens. Then I went to my room and shut the door, slightly dizzy with anticipation and guilt.

A few days later when my mother was out, I opened one purse. Inside was a swirling gold pin with pearl and coral flowers. I made many secret visits to the closet, a series of small sins. Each time I opened one more treasure. There were bright green, milky white, and carmine bracelets. Some of the bracelets were so small I could not fit them over my hand. There was a ring with a pearl as big as a marble. A strand of pearls, each the size of a large pea. A strand of jade beads carved in the shape of small buddhas. A rusty key.

"Do you still have keys to our old house in China?" I asked my father.

"That's the past, Caroline," he said. "*Wanle*. It is gone."

Surrounded by questions, I became intrigued by the answers to things. My report cards showed that I became a good student, a very good student, particularly in math. At twelve, I was the only person from my class to test into a public school for the gifted in Manhattan. My father attended the school event where this news was announced. I remember his pleased expression as we approached the small, crowded auditorium. He had piled all of our overcoats and his fedora over one arm, but with the other he opened the door for my mother and me. As I filed past he raised his eyebrows and nodded—proud, but not at all surprised by my achievement.

He believed in the effortless, in splurging and quick riches. While I studied, bent and dogged, and my mother hoarded things, my father strayed from waitering and turned to something bigger. He had a taste for making deals, he said to us. A nose for good investments. Some friends were helping him. He began to stay out late and come home with surprises. On good nights, he brought us presents: a sewing kit, a pink silk scarf. Once he climbed out of a taxicab with a hundred silver dollars in my old marble bag.

On bad nights, my father whistled his way home. I sometimes woke to his high music floating from the street. I sat up and spied at him through the venetian blind. He no longer wore his waiter's clothes; his overcoat was dark. I could just make out the glitter of his shiny shoes. He stepped lightly, always, on bad nights, although he'd whistled clear across the bridge to save on subway fare. He favored Stephen Foster tunes and Broadway musicals. He flung his head back on a long, pure note. When he reached our door he stood still for a moment and squared his shoulders.

My mother, too, knew what the whistling meant.

"Stayed up for me?"

"I wasn't tired."

I crept to my door to peek at them. My mother staring at her feet. My father's hopeful face, his exaggerated brightness. My mother said, "Go to sleep, Caroline."

But I had trouble sleeping. I could feel him slipping away from us, drifting far in search of some intoxicating music. Each time he wandered off, it seemed to take more effort to recall us. He began to speak with his head cocked, as if listening for something. He often stood at the living room window, staring at the street.

"Does Baba have a new job?" I asked my mother.

"No." She looked away.

I felt sorry I'd asked. Questions caused my mother pain. But I was afraid to ask my father. In his guarded face he held a flaming knowledge: a kind of faith, a glimpse of opportunities that lay beyond my understanding.

All that year I hunted clues, made lists of evidence.

> *Missing on February 3:*
>> *carved endtable*
>> *painting of fruit (from front hallway)*
>> *jade buddha*
>> *camera (mine)*

I followed him. One evening after I missed my camera, I heard the front door slam. I grabbed my coat and bolted down the stairs. I dodged across the street half a block back, peering around pedestrians and traffic signs, my eyes fixed on his overcoat and fedora. At the subway station I waited by the token booth and dashed into the bright car behind him, keeping track of his shiny shoes through the swaying windows. I almost missed him when he left the train. Outside it was already dusk. The tall, cold shapes of City Hall and the courthouses loomed over us and I followed at a distance. I felt light as a puff of silk, breathing hard, excited, almost running.

Past the pawn shops, the off-track betting office with its shuffling line of men in old overcoats, toward the dirty, crowded streets of Chinatown, its neon signs winking on for the night. Groups of teenagers, chattering in Cantonese, looked strangely at me and kept walking.

"Incense, candles, incense, *xiaojie?*" A street vendor held a grimy handful toward me.

"No thanks," I panted. I almost lost him but then ahead I recognized his elegant stride. He turned into a small, shabby building, nodding to an old man who stood at the door. I hung around outside, stamping my shoes on the icy sidewalk.

After a minute the old man walked over to me. "Your father does not know you followed him," he told me in Chinese. "You must go home. Go home, and I will not tell him you were here."

For a minute I couldn't move. He was exactly my height. His short hair was white but his forehead strangely unlined, his clothes well-made. It was his expensive tweed overcoat that made me turn around. That and the decaying, fetid odor of his teeth, and the fact that he knew my father well enough to recognize my features, knew he would not have wanted me to follow him. I reboarded the train at the Canal Street station. Back in the apartment, I stayed up until well past midnight, but I didn't hear him come home.

I didn't need to follow him. I should have known that eventually he would show his secret to me, his one pupil. A few months later, on the night before my fourteenth birthday, he motioned me to stay seated after supper. The hanging lamp cast a circle of light over the worn kitchen table.

"I'm going to teach you some math," he said.

I glanced at his face, but his eyes glowed black and expressionless in their sockets, hollow in the lamplight.

Over his shoulder I saw my mother check to see that we were occupied. Then she walked into the foyer and opened the closet door, where the jewelry was. I felt a tingle of fear, even though I had concealed my visits perfectly.

"Concentrate," said my father. "Here is a penny. Each penny has two sides: heads and tails. You understand me, Caroline?"

I nodded. The dull coin looked like a hole in his palm.

"*Hao*," he said: good. His brown hand danced and the penny flipped onto the table. Heads. "Now, if I throw this coin many many times, how often would I get heads?"

"One-half of the time."

He nodded.

"*Hao*," he said. "That is the *huo ran lu*. The *huo ran lu* for heads is one-half. If you know that, you can figure out the *huo ran lu* that I will get two heads if I throw twice in a row." He waited a minute. "Think of it as a limiting of possibilities. The first throw cuts the possibilities in half."

I looked into the dark tunnel of my father's eyes and, following the discipline of his endless drilling, I began to understand where we had been going. Counting, multiplication, the table of squares. "Half of the half," I said. "A quarter."

He set the coins aside and reached into his shirt pocket. Suddenly, with a gesture of his hand, two dice lay in the middle of the yellow circle of light. Two small chunks of ivory, with tiny black pits in them.

"Count the sides," he said.

The little cube felt cold and heavy. "Six."

My father's hand closed over the second die. "What is the *huo ran lu* that I will get a side with only two dots?"

My mind wavered in surprise at his intensity. But I knew the answer. "One-sixth," I said.

He nodded. "You are a smart daughter," he said.

I discovered that I had been holding onto the table leg with my left hand, and I let go. I heard the creak of the hall closet door but my father did not look away from the die in his hand.

"What is the *huo ran lu* that I can roll the side with two dots twice in a row?" he said.

"One thirty-sixth."

"Three times in a row?"

"One two-hundred-and-sixteenth."

"That is very good!" he said. "Now, the *huo ran lu* that I will be able to roll a two is one-sixth. Would it be a reasonable bet that I will not roll a two?"

I nodded.

"We could say, if I roll a two, you may have both pennies."

I saw it then, deep in his eyes—a spark of excitement, a piece of joy particularly his. It was there for an instant and disappeared. He frowned and nodded toward the table as if to say: pay attention. Then his hand flourished and the die trickled into the light. I bent eagerly over the table, but my father sat perfectly still, impassive. Two dots.

When I looked up at him in astonishment I noticed my mother, standing in the doorway, her two huge eyes burning in her white face.

"Jack."

My father started, but he didn't turn around to look at her. "Yes, Lily," he said. The die grew wet in my hand.

"What are you doing?"

"Giving the child a lesson."

"And what is she going to learn from this?" My mother's voice trembled but it did not rise. "Where will she go with this?"

"Lily," my father said.

"What will become of us?" my mother almost whispered. She looked around the kitchen. Almost all of the furniture had disappeared. The old kitchen table and the three chairs, plus our rice cooker, were virtually the only things left in the room.

I grabbed the second die and left the table. In my room as I listened to my parents next door in the kitchen I rolled one die two hundred and sixteen times, keeping track by making marks on the back of a school notebook. But I failed to reach a two more than twice in a row.

"The suitcase, Jack. Where is it?"

After a moment my father muttered, "I'll get it back. Don't you believe me?"

"I don't know." She began to cry so loudly that even though I pressed my hands against my ears I could still hear her. My father said nothing. I hunched down over my knees, trying to shut them out.

"You promised me, you promised me you'd never touch them!"

"I was going to bring them back!"

"We have nothing for Caroline's birthday . . ."

Something crashed against the other side of my bedroom wall. I scuttled to the opposite wall and huddled in the corner of my bed.

For a long period after I heard nothing but my mother's sobbing. Then they left the kitchen. The house was utterly silent. I realized I had wrapped my arms around my knees to keep from trembling. I felt strange and light-headed: oh, but I understood now. My father was a gambler, a *dutu*, an apprentice of chance. Of course.

With the understanding came a desperate need to see both of them. I stood up and walked through the living room to my parents' bedroom. The door was ajar. I peered in.

The moonlight, blue and white, shifted and flickered on the bed, on my mother's long black hair twisting over her arm. Her white fingers moved vaguely. I felt terrified for her. He moved against her body in such a consuming way, as if he might pass through her, as if she were incorporeal. I watched for several minutes before my mother made a sound that frightened me so much I had to leave.

The next morning my eyes felt sandy and strange. We strolled down Atlantic Avenue, holding hands, with me in the middle because it was my birthday. My mother's stride was tentative, but my father walked with the calculated lightness and unconcern of one who has nothing in his pockets. Several gulls flew up before us, and he watched with delight as they wheeled into the cloudy sky. The charm of Brooklyn, this wide shabby street bustling with immigrants like ourselves, was enough to make him feel lucky.

He squeezed my hand, a signal that I should squeeze my mother's for him. We'd played this game many times over the years, but today I hesitated. My mother's hand did not feel like something to hold onto. Despite the warm weather her fingers in mine were cold. I squeezed, however, and she turned. He looked at her over the top of my head, and my mother, seeing his expression, lapsed into a smile that caused the Greek delivery boys from the corner pizza parlor to turn their heads as we passed. She and my father didn't notice.

We walked past a display of furniture on the sidewalk—incomplete sets of dining chairs, hat stands, old sewing tables—and I stared for a minute, for I thought I saw something standing behind a battered desk: a rosewood dresser my parents had brought from Taiwan; it used to be in my own bedroom. I once kept my dolls in the bottom left drawer, the one with the little scar where I had nicked it with a roller skate. . . . Perhaps it only had a similar shape. But it could very well be our dresser. I knew better than to point it out. I turned away.

"Oh, Jack, the flowers!" my mother exclaimed in Chinese. She let go of my hand and rushed to DeLorenzio's floral display, sank down to smell the potted gardenias with a grace that brought my father and me to a sudden stop.

My father's black eyebrows came down over his eyes. "Ni qu gen ni mama tan yi tan, go talk to your mother," he said, giving me a little push. I frowned. "Go on."

She was speaking with Mr. DeLorenzio, and I stood instinctively on their far side, trying to act cute despite my age in order to distract them from what my father was doing. He stood before the red geraniums. He picked up a plant, considered it, and set it down with a critical shake of his head.

"And how are you today sweetheart?" Mr. DeLorenzio bent toward me, offering me a close-up of his gray handlebar moustache. Behind him, my father disappeared from view.

"She's shy," said my mother proudly. After a few minutes I tugged her sleeve, and she said goodbye to the florist. We turned, continued walking down the street.

"Where is your father?"

"I think he's somewhere up there."

I pulled her toward the corner. My father stepped out from behind a pet store, smiling broadly, holding the pot of geraniums.

"It's going to rain," he proclaimed, as if he'd planned it himself.

The drops felt light and warm on my face. We ran to the nearest awning, where my mother put on her rain bonnet. Then my father disappeared, leaving us standing on the sidewalk. I didn't notice him leave. All of a sudden he was just gone.

"Where's Baba?" I asked my mother.

"I don't know," she said, calmly tucking her hair into the plastic bonnet. The geraniums stood at her feet. I looked around us. The sidewalks had become slick and dark; people hurried along. The wind blew cool in my face. Then the revolving doors behind us whirled and my father walked out.

"There you are," my mother said.

"Here, Caroline," said my father to me. He reached into his jacket and pulled out the umbrella. It lay balanced on his palm, its brilliant colors neatly furled, an offering.

I wanted to refuse the umbrella. For a moment I believed that if I did, I could separate myself from both of my parents, and our pains, and everything that bound me to them.

I looked up at my father's face. He was watching me intently. I took the umbrella. "Thanks," I said. He smiled. The next day, he was gone.

My mother had her hair cut short and dressed in mourning colors; this attitude bestowed on her a haunting, muted beauty. She was hired for the lunch shift at a chic Manhattan Chinese restaurant. Our lives grew stable and very quiet. In the evenings I studied while my mother sat in the kitchen, waiting, cutting carrots and mushroom caps into elaborate shapes for our small stir-frys, or combining birdseed for the feeder on the fire escape in the exact proportions that my father had claimed would bring the most cardinals and the fewest sparrows. I did the homework for advanced placement courses. I planned to enter Columbia with the academic standing of a sophomore. We spoke gently to each other about harmless, tactful things. "Peanut sauce," we said. "Shopping." "Homework." "Apricots."

I studied trigonometry. I grew skillful in that subject without ever liking it. I learned calculus, linear algebra, and liked them less and less, but I kept studying, seeking the comfort that arithmetic had once provided. Things fall apart, it seems, with terrible slowness. I could not see that true mathematics, rather than keeping track of things, moves toward the unexplainable. A swooping line descends from nowhere, turns, escapes to some infinity. Centuries of scholars work to solve a single puzzle. In mathematics, as in love, the riddles matter most.

In the months when I was failing out of Columbia, I spent a lot of my time on the subway. I rode to Coney Island, to the watery edge of Brooklyn, and stayed on the express train as it changed directions and went back deep under the river, into Manhattan. Around City Hall or 14th Street a few Chinese people always got on the train, and I sometimes saw a particular kind of man, no longer young but his face curiously unlined, wearing an expensive but shabby overcoat and shiny shoes. I would watch until he got off at his stop. Then I would sit back and wait as the train pulsed through the dark tunnels under the long island of Manhattan, and sometimes the light would blink out for a minute and I would see blue sparks shooting off the tracks. I was waiting for the moment around 125th Street where the express train rushed up into daylight. This sudden openness, this coming out of darkness into a new world, helped me understand how he must have felt. I imagined him bent over a pair of dice that glowed like tiny skulls under the yellow kitchen light. I saw him walking out the door with my flowery umbrella, pausing to look up at the sky and the innumerable, luminous possibilities that lay ahead.

𝒫 𝒫 𝒫

Suggestions for Discussion

1. Follow the extended metaphor of mathematics through the story. How do the elements of mathematics mirror and enhance the emotions of the characters?

2. What is the significance of the word *san*? How does it play out through the story?

Retrospect

3. How is the apartment setting symbolic in the story's third paragraph? How is the subway setting symbolic in the final paragraph?

Menagerie

CHARLES JOHNSON

Among watchdogs in Seattle, Berkeley was known generally as one of the best. Not the smartest, but steady. A pious German shepherd (Black Forest origins, probably), with big shoulders, black gums, and weighing more than some men, he sat guard inside the glass door of Tilford's Pet Shoppe, watching the pedestrians scurry along First Avenue, wondering at the derelicts who slept ever so often inside the foyer at night, and sometimes he nodded when things were quiet in the cages behind him, lulled by the bubbling of the fishtanks, dreaming of an especially fine meal he'd once had, or the little female poodle, a real flirt, owned by the aerobic dance teacher (who was no saint herself) a few doors down the street; but Berkeley was, for all his woolgathering, never asleep at the switch. He took his work seriously. Moreover, he knew exactly where he was at every moment, what he was doing, and why he was doing it, which was more than can be said for most people, like Mr. Tilford, a real gumboil, whose ways were mysterious to Berkeley. Sometimes he treated the animals cruelly, or taunted them; he saw them not as pets but profit. Nevertheless, no vandals, or thieves, had ever brought trouble through the doors or windows of Tilford's Pet Shoppe, and Berkeley, confident of his power but never flaunting it, faithful to his master though he didn't deserve it, was certain that none ever would.

At closing time, Mr. Tilford, who lived alone, as most cruel men do, always checked the cages, left a beggarly pinch of food for the animals, and a single biscuit for Berkeley. The watchdog always hoped for a pat on his head, or for Tilford to play with him, some sign of approval to let him know he was appreciated, but such as this never came. Mr. Tilford had thick glasses and a thin voice, was stubborn, hot-tempered, a drunkard and a loner who, sliding toward senility, sometimes put his shoes in the refrigerator, and once—Berkeley winced at the memory—put a Persian he couldn't sell in the Mix Master during one of his binges. Mainly, the owner drank and watched television, which was something else Berkeley couldn't understand. More than once he'd mistaken gunfire on screen for the real thing (a natural error, since no one told him violence was entertainment for some), howled loud enough to bring down the house, and Tilford booted him outside. Soon enough, Berkeley stopped looking for approval; he didn't bother to get up from biting fleas behind the counter when he heard the door slam.

But it seemed one night too early for closing time. His instincts on this had never been wrong before. He trotted back to the darkened storeroom; then his mouth snapped shut. His feeding bowl was as empty as he'd last left it.

"Say, Berkeley," said Monkey, whose cage was near the storeroom. "What's goin' on? Tilford didn't put out the food."

Berkeley didn't care a whole lot for Monkey, and usually he ignored him. He was downright wicked, a comedian always grabbing his groin to get a laugh, throwing feces, or fooling with the other animals, a clown who'd do anything to crack up the iguana, Frog, Parrot, and the Siamese, even if it meant aping Mr. Tilford, which he did well, though Berkeley found this parody frightening, like playing with fire, or literally biting the hand that fed you. But he, too, was puzzled by Tilford's abrupt departure.

"I don't know," said Berkeley. "He'll be back, I guess."

Monkey, his head through his cage, held onto the bars like a movie inmate. "Wanna bet?"

"What're you talking about?"

"Wake *up*," said Monkey. "Tilford's sick. I seen better faces on dead guppies in the fishtank. You ever see a pulmonary embolus?" Monkey ballooned his cheeks, then started breathing hard enough to hyperventilate, rolled up both red-webbed eyes, then crashed back into his cage, howling.

Not thinking this funny at all, Berkeley padded over to the front door, gave Monkey a grim look, then curled up against the bottom rail, waiting for Tilford's car to appear. Cars of many kinds, and cars of different sizes, came and went, but that Saturday night the owner did not show. Nor the next morning, or the following night, and on the second day it was not only Monkey but every beast, bird, and fowl in the Shoppe that shook its cage or tank and howled at Berkeley for an explanation—an ear-shattering babble of tongues, squawks, trills, howls, mewling, bellows, hoots, blorting, and belly growls because Tilford had collected everything from baby alligators to zebra-striped fish, an entire federation of cultures, with each animal having its own distinct, inviolable nature (so they said), the rows and rows of counters screaming with a plurality of so many backgrounds, needs, and viewpoints that Berkeley, his head splitting, could hardly hear his own voice above the din.

"Be patient!" he said. "Believe me, he's comin' back!"

"Come *off* it," said one of three snakes. "Monkey says Tilford's *dead*. Question is, what're we gonna *do* about it?"

Berkeley looked, witheringly, toward the front door. His empty stomach gurgled like a sewer. It took a tremendous effort to untangle his thoughts. "If we can just hold on a—"

"We're *hungry*!" shouted Frog. "We'll starve before old Tilford comes back!"

Throughout this turmoil, the shouting, beating of wings, which blew feathers everywhere like confetti, and an angry slapping of fins that splashed water to the floor, Monkey simply sat quietly, taking it all in, stroking his chin as a scholar might. He waited for a space in the shouting, then pushed his head through the cage again.

His voice was calm, studied, like an old-time barrister before the bar. "Berkeley? Don't get mad now, but I think it's obvious that there's only one solution."

"What?"

"Let us out," said Monkey. "Open the cages."

"No!"

"We've got a crisis situation here." Monkey sighed like one of the elderly, tired lizards, as if his solution bothered even him. "It calls for courage, radical decisions. You're in charge until Tilford gets back. That means you gotta feed us, but you can't do that, can you? Only one here with hands is *me*. See, we all have different talents, unique gifts. If you let us out, we can pool our resources. I can *open* the feed bags!"

"You can?" The watchdog swallowed.

"Uh-huh." He wiggled his fingers dexterously, then the digits on his feet. "But somebody's gotta throw the switch on this cage. I can't reach it. Dog, I'm asking you to be democratic! Keeping us locked up is fascist!"

The animals clamored for release; they took up Monkey's cry, "Self-determination!" But everything within Berkeley resisted this idea, the possibility of chaos it promised, so many different, quarrelsome creatures uncaged, set loose in a low ceilinged Shoppe where even he had trouble finding room to turn around between the counters, pens, displays of paraphernalia, and heavy, bubbling fishtanks. The chances for mischief were incalculable, no question of that, but slow starvation was certain if he didn't let them in the storeroom. Furthermore, he didn't want to be called a fascist. It didn't seem fair, Monkey saying that, making him look bad in front of the others. It was the one charge you couldn't defend yourself against. Against his better judgement, the watchdog rose on his hindlegs and, praying this was the right thing, forced open the cage with his teeth. For a moment Monkey did not move. He drew breath loudly and stared at the open door. Cautiously, he stepped out, stood up to his full height, rubbed his bony hands together, then did a little dance and began throwing open the other cages one by one.

Berkeley cringed. "The tarantula, too?"

Monkey gave him a cold glance over one shoulder. "You should get to know him, Berkeley. Don't be a bigot."

Berkeley shrank back as Tarantula, an item ordered by a Hell's Angel who never claimed him, shambled out—not so much an insect, it seemed to Berkeley, as Pestilence on legs. ("Be fair!" he scolded himself. "He's okay, I'm okay, we're all okay.") He watched helplessly as Monkey smashed the ant farm, freed the birds, and then the entire troupe, united by the spirit of a bright, common future, slithered, hopped, crawled, bounded, flew, and clawed its way into the storeroom to feed. All except crankled, old Tortoise, whom Monkey hadn't freed, who, in fact, didn't want to be released and snapped at Monkey's fingers when he tried to open his cage. No one questioned it. Tortoise had escaped the year before, remaining at large for a week, and then he returned mysteriously on his own, his eyes strangely unfocused, as if he'd seen the end of the world, or a vision of the world to come. He hadn't spoken in a year. Hunched inside his shell, hardly eating at all, Tortoise lived in the Shoppe, but you could hardly say he was part of it, and even the watchdog was a little leery of him.

Berkeley, for his part, had lost his hunger. He dragged himself, wearily, to the front door, barked frantically when a woman walked by, hoping she would stop, but after seeing the window sign, which read—DESOLC—from his side, she stepped briskly on. His tail between his legs, he went slowly back to the storeroom, hoping for the best, but what he found there was no sight for a peace-loving watchdog.

True to his word, Monkey had broken open the feed bags and boxes of food, but the animals, who had always been kept apart by Tilford, discovered as they crowded into the tiny storeroom and fell to eating that sitting down to table with creatures so different in their gastronomic inclinations took the edge off their appetites. The birds found the eating habits of the reptiles, who thought eggs were a delicacy, disgusting and drew away in horror; the reptiles, who were proud of being cold-blooded, and had an elaborate theory of beauty based on the aesthetics of scales, thought the body heat of the mammals cloying and nauseating, and refused to feed beside them, and this was fine for the mammals, who, led by Monkey, distrusted anyone odd enough to be born in an egg, and dismissed them as lowlifes on the evolutionary scale; they were shoveling down everything—bird food, dog biscuits, and even the thin wafers reserved for the fish.

"Don't touch that!" said Berkeley. "The fish have to eat, too! They can't leave the tanks!"

Monkey, startled by the watchdog, looked at the wafers in his fist thoughtfully for a second, then crammed them into his mouth. "That's their problem."

Deep inside, Berkeley began a rumbling bark, let it build slowly, and by the time it hit the air it was a full-throated growl so frightening that Monkey jumped four, maybe five feet into the air. He threw the wafers at Berkeley. "Okay—okay, give it to 'em! But remember one thing, dog: You're a mammal, too. It's unnatural to take sides against your own kind."

Scornfully, the watchdog turned away, trembling with fury. He snuffled up the wafers in his mouth, carried them to the huge, man-sized tanks, and dropped them in amongst the sea horses, guppies, and jellyfish throbbing like hearts. Goldfish floated toward him, his voice and fins fluttering. He kept a slightly startled expression. "What the hell is going on? Where's Mr. Tilford?"

Berkeley strained to keep his voice steady. "Gone."

"For good?" asked Goldfish. "Berkeley, we heard what the others said. They'll let us starve—"

"No," he said. "I'll protect you."

Goldfish bubbled relief, then looked panicky again. "What if Tilford doesn't come back ever?"

The watchdog let his head hang. The thought seemed too terrible to consider. He said, more to console himself than Goldfish, "It's his Shoppe. He has to come back."

"But suppose he *is* dead, like Monkey says." Goldfish's unblinking, lidless eyes grabbed at Berkeley and refused to release his gaze. "Then it's our Shoppe, right?"

"Eat your dinner."

Goldfish called, "Berkeley, wait—"

But the watchdog was deeply worried now. He returned miserably to the front door. He let fly a long, plaintive howl, his head tilted back like a mountaintop wolf silhouetted by the moon in a Warner Brothers cartoon—he did look like that—his insides hurting with the thought that if Tilford was dead, or indifferent to their problems, that if no one came to rescue them, then they were dead, too. True, there was a great deal of Tilford inside Berkeley, what he remembered from his training as a pup, but this faint sense of procedure and fair play hardly seemed enough to keep order in the Shoppe, maintain the peace, and more important provide for them as the old man had. He'd never looked upon himself as a leader, preferring to attribute his distaste for decision to a rare ability to see all sides. He was no hero like Old Yeller, or the legendary Gellert, and testing his ribs with his teeth, he wondered how much weight he'd lost from worry. Ten pounds? Twenty pounds? He covered both eyes with his black paws, whimpered a little, feeling a failure of nerve, a soft white core of fear like a slug in his stomach. Then he drew breath and, with it, new determination. The owner couldn't be dead. Monkey would never convince him of that. He simply had business elsewhere. And when he returned, he would expect to find the Shoppe as he left it. Maybe even running more smoothly, like an old Swiss watch that he had wound and left ticking. When the watchdog tightened his jaws, they creaked at the hinges, but he tightened them all the same. His eyes narrowed. No evil had visited the Shoppe from outside. He'd seen to that. None, he vowed, would destroy it from within.

But he could not be everywhere at once. The corrosion grew day by day. Cracks, then fissures began to appear, it seemed to Berkeley, everywhere, and in places where he least expected them. Puddles and pyramidal plops were scattered underfoot like traps. Bacterial flies were everywhere. Then came maggots. Hamsters gnawed at electrical cords in the storeroom. Frog fell sick with a genital infection. The fish, though the gentlest of creatures, caused undertow by demanding day-and-night protection, claiming they were handicapped in the competition for food, confined to their tanks, and besides, they were from the most ancient tree; all life came from the sea, they argued, the others owed *them*.

Old blood feuds between beasts erupted, too, grudges so tired you'd have thought them long buried, but not so. The Siamese began to give Berkeley funny looks, and left the room whenever he entered. Berkeley let him be, thinking he'd come to his senses. Instead, he jumped Rabbit when Berkeley wasn't looking, the product of this assault promising a new creature—a cabbit—with jackrabbit legs and long feline whiskers never seen in the Pet Shoppe before. Rabbit took this badly. In the beginning she sniffed a great deal, and with good reason—rape was a vicious thing—but her grief and pain got out of hand, and soon she was lost in it with no way out, like a child in a dark forest, and began organizing the females of every species to stop cohabiting with the males. Berkeley stood back, afraid to butt in because Rabbit said that it was none of his damned business and he was as bad as all the rest. He pleaded reason, his eyes burnt-out from sleeplessness, with puffy bags beneath them, and when that did no good, he pleaded restraint.

"The storeroom's half-empty," he told Monkey on the fifth day. "If we don't start rationing the food, we'll starve."

"There's always food."

Berkeley didn't like the sound of that. "Where?"

Smiling, Monkey swung his eyes to the fishtanks.

"Don't you go near those goldfish!"

Monkey stood at bay, his eyes tacked hatefully on Berkeley, who ground his teeth, possessed by the sudden, wild desire to bite him, but knowing, finally, that he had the upper hand in the Pet Shoppe, the power. In other words, bigger teeth. As much as he hated to admit it, his only advantage, if he hoped to hold the line, his only trump, if he truly wanted to keep them afloat, was the fact that he outweighed them all. They were afraid of him. Oddly enough, the real validity of his values and viewpoint rested, he realized, on his having the biggest paw. The thought fretted him. For all his idealism, truth was decided in the end by those who could be bloodiest in fang and claw. Yet and still, Monkey had an arrogance that made Berkeley weak in the knees.

"Dog," he said, scratching under one arm, "you got to sleep *sometime.*"

And so Berkeley did. After hours of standing guard in the storeroom, or trying to console Rabbit, who was now talking of aborting the cabbit, begging her to reconsider, or reassuring the birds, who crowded together in one corner against, they said, threatening moves by the reptiles, or splashing various medicines on Frog, whose sickness had now spread to the iguana—after all this, Berkeley did drop fitfully to sleep by the front door. He slept greedily, dreaming of better days. He twitched and woofed in his sleep, seeing himself schtupping the little French poodle down the street, and it was good, like making love to lightning, she moved so well with him; and then of his puppyhood, when his worst problems were remembering where he'd buried food from Tilford's table, or figuring out how to sneak away from his mother, who told him all dogs had cold noses because they were late coming to the Ark and had to ride next to the rail. His dream cycled on, as all dreams do, with greater and greater clarity from one chamber of vision to the next until he saw, just before waking, the final drawer of dream-work spill open on the owner's return. Splendidly dressed, wearing a bowler hat and carrying a walking stick, sober, with a gentle smile for Berkeley (Berkeley was sure), Tilford threw open the Pet Shoppe door in a blast of wind and burst of preternatural brilliance that rayed the whole room, evaporated every shadow, and brought the squabbling, the conflict of interpretations, mutations, and internecine battles to a halt. No one dared move. They stood frozen like fish in ice, or a bird caught in the crosswinds, the colorless light behind the owner so blinding it obliterated their outlines, blurred their precious differences, as if each were a rill of the same ancient light somehow imprisoned in form, with being-formed itself the most preposterous of conditions, outrageous, when you thought it through, because it occasioned suffering, meant separation from other forms, and the illusion of identity, but even this ended like a dream within the watchdog's dream, and only he and the owner remained. Reaching down, he stroked Berkeley's head. And at last he said, like God whispering to Samuel: *Well done.* It was all Berkeley had ever wanted. He woofed again, snoring like a sow, and scratched in his sleep; he heard the owner whisper *begun*, which was a pretty strange thing for him to say, even for Tilford, even in a dream. His ears strained forward; *begun*, Tilford said again. And for an instant Berkeley thought he had the tense wrong, intending to say, "Now we can begin," or something prophetically appropriate like that, but suddenly he was awake, and Parrot was flapping his wings and shouting into Berkeley's ear.

"The gun," said Parrot. "Monkey has it."

Berkeley's eyes, still phlegmed by sleep, blearily panned the counter. The room was swimming, full of smoke from a fire in the storeroom. He was short of wind. And, worse, he'd forgotten about the gun, a Smith and Wesson, that Tilford had bought after pet shop owners in Seattle were struck by thieves who specialized in stealing exotic birds. Monkey had it now. Berkeley's water ran down his legs. He'd propped the pistol between the cash register and a display of plastic dog collars, and his wide, yellow grin was frighteningly like that of a general Congress had just given the go-ahead to on a scorched-earth policy.

"Get it!" said Parrot. "You promised to protect us, Berkeley!"

For a few fibrous seconds he stood trembling paw-deep in dung, the odor of decay burning his lungs, but he couldn't come full awake, and still he felt himself to be on the fringe of a dream, his hair moist because dreaming of the French poodle had made him sweat. But the pistol . . . There was no power balance now. He'd been out-played. No hope unless he took it away. Circling the counter, head low and growl-ing, or trying to work up a decent growl, Berkeley crept to the cash register, his chest pounding, bunched his legs to leap, then sprang, pretending the black explosion of flame and smoke was like television gunfire, though it ripped skin right off his ribs, sent teeth flying down his throat, and blew him back like an empty pelt against Tor-toise's cage. He lay still. Now he felt nothing in his legs. Purple blood like that deep-est in the body cascaded to the floor from his side, rushing out with each heartbeat, and he lay twitching a little, only seeing now that he'd slept too long. Flames licked along the floor. Fish floated belly up in a dark, unplugged fishtank. The females had torn Siamese to pieces. Spackled lizards were busy sucking baby canaries from their eggs. And in the holy ruin of the Pet Shoppe the tarantula roamed free over the corpses of Frog and Iguana. Beneath him, Berkeley heard the ancient Tortoise stir, clearing a nasty throat clogged from disuse. Only he would survive the spreading fire, given his armor. His eyes burning from the smoke, the watchdog tried to explain his dream before the blaze reached them. "We could have endured, we had enough in common—for Christ's sake, we're *all* animals."

"Indeed," said Tortoise grimly, his eyes like headlights in a shell that echoed cav-ernously. "Indeed."

🐾 🐾 🐾

Suggestions for Discussion

1. Find several clichés. Whose clichés are they? What function do they serve in the story?
2. Find three places where the animals display human qualities through their ac-tions. Why is this story better told allegorically rather than realistically, and with animal characters rather than human ones?

Retrospect

3. Examine the breakdown of society in the pet shop. How do events escalate so that "each battle is bigger than the last"?

4. How are the animals characterized through their speech?

5. How is the perspective of a dog established immediately?

Eyes of a Blue Dog

GABRIEL GARCÍA MÁRQUEZ

TRANSLATED BY GREGORY RABASSA

Then she looked at me. I thought that she was looking at me for the first time. But then, when she turned around behind the lamp and I kept feeling her slippery and oily look in back of me, over my shoulder, I understood that it was I who was looking at her for the first time. I lit a cigarette. I took a drag on the harsh, strong smoke, before spinning in the chair, balancing on one of the rear legs. After that I saw her there, as if she'd been standing beside the lamp looking at me every night. For a few brief minutes that's all we did: look at each other. I looked from the chair, balancing on one of the rear legs. She stood, with a long and quiet hand on the lamp, looking at me. I saw her eyelids lighted up as on every night. It was then that I remembered the usual thing, when I said to her: "Eyes of a blue dog." Without taking her hand off the lamp she said to me: "That. We'll never forget that." She left the orbit, sighing: "Eyes of a blue dog. I've written it everywhere."

I saw her walk over to the dressing table. I watched her appear in the circular glass of the mirror looking at me now at the end of a back and forth of mathematical light. I watched her keep on looking at me with her great hot-coal eyes: looking at me while she opened the little box covered with pink mother of pearl. I saw her powder her nose. When she finished, she closed the box, stood up again, and walked over to the lamp once more, saying: "I'm afraid that someone is dreaming about this room and revealing my secrets." And over the flame she held the same long and tremulous hand that she had been warming before sitting down at the mirror. And she said: "You don't feel the cold." And I said to her: "Sometimes." And she said to me: "You must feel it now." And then I understood why I couldn't have been alone in the seat. It was the cold that had been giving me the certainty of my solitude. "Now I feel it," I said. "And it's strange because the night is quiet. Maybe the sheet fell off." She didn't answer. Again she began to move toward the mirror and I turned again in the chair, keeping my back to her. Without seeing her, I knew what she was doing. I knew that she was sitting in front of the mirror again, seeing my back, which had had time to reach the depths of the mirror and be caught by her look, which had also had just enough time to reach the depths and return—before the hand had time to start the second turn—until her lips were anointed now with crimson, from the first turn of her hand in front of the mirror. I saw, opposite me, the smooth wall, which was like another blind mirror in which I couldn't see her—sitting behind me—but could imagine her where she probably was as if a mirror had been hung in place of the wall. "I see you," I told her. And on the wall I saw what was as if she had raised her eyes and had seen me with my back turned toward her from the chair, in the depths of the mirror, my face turned toward the wall. Then I saw her lower her eyes again and remain with her eyes always on her brassiere, not talking. And I said to her again: "I see you." And she raised her eyes from her brassiere again. "That's impossible," she said. I asked her why. And she, with her eyes quiet and on her brassiere again: "Because your face is turned toward the wall." Then I spun the chair around. I had the cigarette clenched in my mouth. When I stayed facing the mirror she was back by the lamp. Now she had her hands open over the flame, like the two wings of a hen, toasting herself, and with her face shaded by her own fingers. "I think I'm going to catch cold," she said. "This must be a city of ice." She turned her face to profile and her skin, from copper to red, suddenly became sad. "Do something about it," she said. And she began to get undressed, item by item, starting at the top with the brassiere. I told her: "I'm going to turn back to the wall." She said: "No. In any case, you'll see me the way you did when your back was turned." And no sooner had she said it than she was almost completely undressed, with the flame licking her long copper skin. "I've always wanted to see you like that, with the skin of your belly full of deep pits, as if you'd been beaten." And before I realized that my words had become clumsy at the sight of her nakedness she became motionless, warming herself on the globe of the lamp, and she said: "Sometimes I think I'm made of metal." She was silent for an instant. The position of her hands over the flame varied slightly. I said: "Sometimes in other dreams, I've thought you were only a little bronze statue in the corner of some museum. Maybe that's why you're cold." And she said: "Sometimes, when I sleep on my heart, I can feel my body growing hollow and my skin is like plate. Then, when the blood beats inside me, it's as if someone were calling by knocking on my stomach and I can feel my own copper sound in the bed. It's like—what do you call it—laminated metal." She drew closer to the lamp. "I would have liked to hear you," I said. And she said: "If we find each other sometime, put your ear to my ribs when I sleep on the left side and you'll hear me echoing. I've always wanted you to do it sometime." I heard her breathe heavily as she talked. And she said that for years she'd done nothing different. Her life had been dedicated to finding me in reality, through that identifying phrase: "Eyes of a blue dog." And she went along the street saying it aloud, as a way of telling the only person who could have understood her:

"I'm the one who comes into your dreams every night and tells you: 'Eyes of a blue dog.'" And she said that she went into restaurants and before ordering said to the waiters: "Eyes of a blue dog." But the waiters bowed reverently, without remembering ever having said that in their dreams. Then she would write on the napkins and scratch on the varnish of the tables with a knife: "Eyes of a blue dog." And on the steamed-up windows of hotels, stations, all public buildings, she would write with her forefinger: "Eyes of a blue dog." She said that once she went into a drug-store and noticed the same smell that she had smelled in her room one night after having dreamed about me. "He must be near," she thought, seeing the clean, new tiles of the drugstore. Then she went over to the clerk and said to him: "I always dream about a man who says to me: 'Eyes of a blue dog.'" And she said the clerk had looked at her eyes and told her: "As a matter of fact, miss, you do have eyes like that." And she said to him: "I have to find the man who told me those very words in my dreams." And the clerk started to laugh and moved to the other end of the counter. She kept on seeing the clean tile and smelling the odor. And she opened her purse and on the tiles with her crimson lipstick, she wrote in red letters: "Eyes of a blue dog." The clerk came back from where he had been. He told her: "Madam, you have dirtied the tiles." He gave her a damp cloth, saying: "Clean it up." And she said, still by the lamp, that she had spent the whole afternoon on all fours, washing the tiles and saying: "Eyes of a blue dog," until people gathered at the door and said she was crazy.

Now, when she finished speaking, I remained in the corner, sitting, rocking in the chair. "Every day I try to remember the phrase with which I am to find you," I said. "Now I don't think I'll forget it tomorrow. Still, I've always said the same thing and when I wake up I've always forgotten what the words I can find you with are." And she said: "You invented them yourself on the first day." And I said to her: "I invented them because I saw your eyes of ash. But I never remember the next morning." And she, with clenched fists, beside the lamp, breathed deeply: "If you could at least re-member now what city I've been writing it in."

Her tightened teeth gleamed over the flame. "I'd like to touch you now," I said. She raised the face that had been looking at the light; she raised her look, burning, roasting, too, just like her, like her hands, and I felt that she saw me, in the corner where I was sitting, rocking in the chair. "You'd never told me that," she said. "I tell you now and it's the truth," I said. From the other side of the lamp she asked for a cigarette. The butt had disappeared between my fingers. I'd forgotten I was smoking. She said: "I don't know why I can't remember where I wrote it." And I said to her: "For the same reason that tomorrow I won't be able to remember the words." And she said sadly: "No. It's just that sometimes I think that I've dreamed that too." I stood up and walked toward the lamp. She was a little beyond, and I kept on walking with the cigarettes and matches in my hand, which would not go beyond the lamp. I held the cigarette out to her. She squeezed it between her lips and leaned over to reach the flame before I had time to light the match. "In some city in the world, on all the walls, those words have to appear in writing: 'Eyes of a blue dog,'" I said. "If I remembered them tomorrow I could find you." She raised her head again and now the lighted coal was between her lips. "Eyes of a blue dog," she sighed, remembered, with the cigarette drooping over her chin and one eye half closed. The she sucked in the smoke with the cigarette between her fingers and exclaimed: "This is something else now. I'm warming up." And she said it with her voice a little lukewarm and fleeting, as if she hadn't really said it, but as if she had written it on a piece of paper and had brought the paper close to the flame while I read: "I'm warming," and she had continued with the paper between her thumb and forefinger, turning it around as it was being consumed and I had just read ". . . up," before the paper was completely consumed and dropped all wrinkled to the floor, diminished, converted into light ash dust. "That's better," I said. "Sometimes it frightens me to see you that way. Trembling beside a lamp."

We had been seeing each other for several years. Sometimes, when we were already together, somebody would drop a spoon outside and we would wake up. Little by little we'd been coming to understand that our friendship was subordinated to things, to the simplest of happenings. Our meetings always ended that way, with the fall of a spoon early in the morning.

Now, next to the lamp, she was looking at me. I remembered that she had also looked at me in that way in the past, from that remote dream where I made the chair spin on its back legs and remained facing a strange woman with ashen eyes. It was in that dream that I asked her for the first time: "Who are you?" And she said to me: "I don't remember." I said to her: "But I think we've seen each other before." And she said, indifferently: "I think I dreamed about you once, about this same room." And I told her: "That's it. I'm beginning to remember now." And she said: "How strange. It's certain that we've met in other dreams."

She took two drags on the cigarette. I was still standing, facing the lamp, when suddenly I kept looking at her. I looked her up and down and she was still copper; no longer hard and cold metal, but yellow, soft, malleable copper. "I'd like to touch you," I said again. And she said: "You'll ruin everything." I said: "It doesn't matter now. All we have to do is turn the pillow in order to meet again." And I held my hand out over the lamp. She didn't move. "You'll ruin everything," she said again before I could touch her. "Maybe, if you come around behind the lamp, we'd wake up frightened in who knows what part of the world." But I insisted: "It doesn't matter." And she said: "If we turned over the pillow, we'd meet again. But when you wake up you'll have forgotten." I began to move toward the corner. She stayed behind, warming her hands over the flame. And I still wasn't beside the chair when I heard her say behind me: "When I wake up at midnight, I keep turning in bed, with the fringe of the pillow burning my knee, and repeating until dawn: 'Eyes of a blue dog.'"

Then I remained with my face toward the wall. "It's already dawning," I said without looking at her. "When it struck two I was awake and that was a long time back." I went to the door. When I had the knob in my hand, I heard her voice again, the same, invariable. "Don't open that door," she said. "The hallway is full of difficult dreams." And I asked her: "How do you know?" And she told me: "Because I was there a moment ago and I had to come back when I discovered I was sleeping on my heart." I had the door half opened. I moved it a little and a cold, thin breeze brought me the fresh smell of vegetable earth, damp fields. She spoke again. I gave the turn, still moving the door, mounted on silent hinges, and I told her: "I don't think there's any hallway outside here. I'm getting the smell of country." And she, a little distant, told me: "I know that better than you. What's happening is that there's a woman outside dreaming about the country." She crossed her arms over the flame. She continued speaking: "It's that woman who always wanted to have a house in the country and was never able to leave the city." I remembered having seen the woman in some previous dream, but I knew, with the door ajar now, that within half an hour I would have to go down for breakfast. And I said: "In any case, I have to leave here in order to wake up."

Outside the wind fluttered for an instant, then remained quiet, and the breathing of someone sleeping who had just turned over in bed could be heard. The wind from the fields had ceased. There were no more smells. "Tomorrow I'll recognize you from that," I said. "I'll recognize you when on the street I see a woman writing 'Eyes of a blue dog' on the walls." And she, with a sad smile—which was already a smile of surrender to the impossible, the unreachable—said: "Yet you won't remember anything during the day." And she put her hands back over the lamp, her features darkened by a bitter cloud. "You're the only man who doesn't remember anything of what he's dreamed after he wakes up."

🐦 🐦 🐦

Suggestions for Discussion

1. Is there any significance to the phrase "eyes of a blue dog"? What effect is created by its frequent repetitions?
2. Discuss the metallic imagery used by and about the woman.

Retrospect

3. How does the author use elements such as pacing, details, dialogue, and prose rhythm to create a dreamlike atmosphere?
4. What effect is achieved by the last line? How?

🐦 🐦 🐦

Writing Exercises

INDIVIDUAL

1. Look back at the discussion of metaphors that begins on page 326. Then choose a page from an anthologized story and alter its metaphors to see how the meaning changes.
2. List all the clichés you can think of to describe a pair of blue eyes. Then write a paragraph in which you find a fresh, new metaphor for blue eyes.
3. Make a list of clichés, then write a short-short story in which one or several clichés are made literally and freshly accurate.

4. Take any dead metaphor and write a comic or serious scene that reinvests the metaphor with its original comparative force. Here are a few sample suggestions:
   - Sifting the evidence. (The lawyer uses a colander, a tea strainer, two coffee filters, and a garlic press to decide the case.)
   - Speakeasy. (Chicago, 1916. A young libertine tricks a beautiful but repressed young woman into an illegal basement bar. He thinks the drink will loosen her up. What it loosens is not her sensuality but her tongue, and what she says he doesn't want to hear.)
   - Peck on the cheek. (Alfred Hitchcock has done this one already, perhaps?)
   - Bus terminal.
   - Breakup.
   - Fraternity hazing.
   - Broken home.
   - Don't spoil your lunch.

5. Write a dialogue scene involving conflict between two people over an object. Let the object take on symbolic significance. It may have the same significance to the two people, or a different significance to each.

DEVELOPMENT/REVISION

6. In an earlier piece you have written, identify a few clichés. Cut them. Replace them with concrete details or more original similes or metaphors.

10

I GOTTA USE WORDS
WHEN I TALK TO YOU
Theme

* *Idea and Morality in Theme*

* *How Fictional Elements Contribute to Theme*

* *Developing Theme as You Write*

How does a fiction mean?

Most literature textbooks begin a discussion of theme by warning that theme is not the *message*, not the *moral*, and that the *meaning* of a piece cannot be paraphrased. Theme contains an idea but cannot be stated as an idea. It suggests a morality but offers no moral. Then what is theme, and how as a writer can you pursue that rich resonance?

First of all, theme is what a story is about. But that is not enough, because a story may be "about" a dying Samurai or a quarreling couple or two kids on a trampoline, and those would not be the themes of those stories. A story is also "about" an abstraction, and if the story is significant, that abstraction may be very large; yet thousands of stories are about love, other thousands about death, and still other thousands about both love and death, and to say this is to say little about the theme of any of them.

We might better understand theme if we ask the question: *What about what it's about?* What does the story have to say about the idea or abstraction that seems to be contained in it? What attitudes or judgments does it imply? Above all, how do the elements of fiction contribute to our experience of those ideas and attitudes in the story?

Idea and Morality in Theme

Literature is stuck with ideas in a way other arts are not. Music, paradoxically the most abstract of the arts, creates a logical structure that need make no reference to the world outside itself. It may express a mood, but it need not draw any conclusions. Shapes in painting and sculpture may suggest forms in the physical world, but they need not represent the world, and they need not contain a message. But words mean, and the grammatical structure of even the simplest sentence contains a concept.

Yet those who choose to deal in the medium of literature consistently discourage focus on concepts and insist on the value of the particular instance. Here is Flannery O'Connor's advice to writers:

> People have a habit of saying, "What is the theme of your story?" and they expect you to give them a statement: "The theme of my story is the economic pressure of the machine on the middle class"—or some such absurdity. And when they've got a statement like that, they go off happy and feel it is no longer necessary to read the story.
>
> Some people have the notion that you read the story and then climb out of it into the meaning, but for the fiction writer himself the whole story is the meaning, because it is an experience, not an abstraction.

What this passage suggests is that a writer of fiction approaches concepts, abstract ideas, generalizations, and truths through their particular embodiments—showing, not telling. "Literature," says John Ciardi, "is never only about ideas, but about the experience of ideas." T. S. Eliot points out that the creation of this experience is itself an intellectual feat.

> We talk as if thought was precise and emotion was vague. In reality there is precise emotion and there is vague emotion. To express precise emotion requires as great intellectual power as to express precise thought.

The value of the literary experience is that it allows us to judge an idea at two levels of consciousness, the rational and the emotional, simultaneously. The kind of

---

> The kind of vision the fiction writer needs to have, or to develop . . . is the kind of vision that is able to see different levels of reality in one image or situation.
>
> Flannery O'Connor

"truth" that can be told through thematic resonance is many-faceted and can acknowledge the competing of many truths, exploring paradox and contradiction.

There is a curious prejudice built into our language that makes us speak of
telling *the* truth but telling *a* lie. No one supposes that all conceivable falsehood
can be wrapped up in a single statement called "the lie"; lies are manifold, varied,
and specific. But truth is supposed to be absolute: the truth, the whole truth, and
nothing but the truth. This is, of course, impossible nonsense, and *telling a lie* is a
truer phrase than *telling the truth*. Fiction does not have to tell *the* truth, but *a*
truth.

Anton Chekov wrote that "the writer of fiction should not try to solve such questions as those of God, pessimism and so forth." What is "obligatory for the artist," he
said, is not "solving a problem," but "stating a problem correctly." John Keats went
even further, defining genius itself as *negative capability*, "that is when a man is capable of being in uncertainties, mysteries and doubts, without any irritable reaching
after fact and reason."

A story, then, speculates on a possible truth. It is not an answer or a law but a sup-
position, an exploration. Every story reaches in its climax and resolution an interim
solution to a specifically realized dilemma. But it offers no ultimate solution.

The idea that is proposed, supposed, or speculated about in a fiction may be simple and idealistic, like the notion in "Cinderella" that the good and beautiful will
triumph. Or it may be profound and unprovable, like the theme in *Oedipus Rex* that
man cannot escape his destiny but may be ennobled in the attempt. Or it may be deliberately paradoxical and offer no guidelines that can be used in life, as in Jane
Austen's *Persuasion*, where the heroine, in order to adhere to her principles, must
follow advice given on principles less sound than her own.

In any case, while exploring an idea the writer conveys an attitude toward that
idea. Rust Hills puts it this way:

> . . . coherence in the world [an author] creates is constituted of two concepts he
> holds, which may be in conflict: one is his world view, his sense of the way the
> world is; and the other is his sense of morality, the way the world ought to be.

Literature is a persuasive art, and no writer who fails to convince us of the validity of his or her vision of the world can convince us of his or her greatness. The
writer, of course, may be powerfully impelled to impose a limited vision of the world
as it ought to be, and even to tie that vision to a political stance, wishing not only to
persuade and convince but also to propagandize. But because the emotional force of
literary persuasion is in the realization of the particular, the writer is doomed to fail.
The greater the work, the more it refers us to some permanent human impulse rather
than an easy slogan or a given institutional embodiment of that impulse. Fine writing expands our scope by continually presenting a new way of seeing, a further possibility of emotional identification; it flatly refuses to become a law. I am not a Roman
Catholic like Gerard Manley Hopkins and cannot be persuaded by his poetry to become one; but in a moment near despair I can drive along an Illinois street in a
Chevrolet station wagon and take strength from the lines of a Jesuit in the Welsh

Your beliefs will be the light by which you see, but they will not be what you see and they will not be a substitute for seeing.

Flannery O'Connor

wasteland. I am not a communist as Bertolt Brecht was and cannot be convinced by his plays to become one; but I can see the hauteur of wealth displayed on the Gulf of Mexico and recognize, from a parable of the German Marxist, the difference between a possession and a belonging.

In the human experience, emotion, logic, and judgment are inextricably mixed, and we make continual cross-references between and among them. *You're just sulking.* (I pass judgment on your emotion.) *What do you think of this idea?* (How do you judge this logic?) *Why do I feel this way?* (What is the logic of this emotion?) *It makes no sense to be angry about it.* (I pass judgment on the logic of your emotion.) Literature attempts to fuse three areas of experience organically, denying the force of none of them, positing that no one is more real than the others. This is why I have insisted throughout this book on detail and scene (immediate felt experience), the essential abstractions conveyed therein (ideas), and the attitude implied thereby (judgment).

Not all experience reveals, but all revelation comes through experience. Books aspire to become a part of that revelatory experience, and the books that are made in the form of fiction attempt to do so by re-creating the experience of revelation.

How Fictional Elements Contribute to Theme

Whatever the idea and attitudes that underlie the theme of a story, that story will bring them into the realm of experience through its particular and unique pattern. Theme involves emotion, logic, and judgment, all three—but the pattern that forms the particular experience of that theme is made up of every element of fiction this book has discussed: the arrangement, shape, and flow of the action, as performed by the characters, realized in their details, seen in their atmosphere, from a unique point of view, through the imagery and the rhythm of the language.

This book, for example, contains at least nine stories that may be said to have "the generation gap" as a major theme: "How Far She Went," "Girl," "Where Are You Going, Where Have You Been?", "Gryphon," "Aren't You Happy for Me?", "Beautiful My Mane in the Wind," "Who's Irish?", "San," and (at the end of this chapter) "Ralph the Duck." It could also be argued that "The Use of Force" and "No One's a Mystery" share the theme. Some of these are written from the point of view of a member of the older generation, some from the point of view of the younger. In some, conflict is resolved by bridging the gap; in others, it is not. The characters are variously poor, middle-class, rural, urban, male, female, adolescent, middle-aged, old, Asian, black, white. The imagery variously evokes food, schooling, landscape, religion, gambling, music, painting, horses, sex, speed, and death. It is in the different uses of the elements of fiction that each story makes unique what it has to say about, and what attitude it takes toward, the idea of "the generation gap."

What follows is as short a story as you are likely to encounter in print. It is spare in the extreme—almost, as its title suggests, an outline. Yet the author has contrived in this minuscule compass to direct every fictional element we have discussed toward the exploration of several large themes.

A Man Told Me the Story of His Life

GRACE PALEY

Vicente said: I wanted to be a doctor. I wanted to be a doctor with my whole heart.

I learned every bone, every organ in the body. What is it for? Why does it work?

The school said to me: Vicente, be an engineer. That would be good. You understand mathematics.

I said to the school: I want to be a doctor. I already know how the organs connect. When something goes wrong, I'll understand how to make repairs.

The school said: Vicente, you will really be an excellent engineer. You show on all the tests what a good engineer you will be. It doesn't show whether you'll be a good doctor.

I said: Oh, I long to be a doctor. I nearly cried. I was seventeen. I said: But perhaps you're right. You're the teacher. You're the principal. I know I'm young.

The school said: And besides, you're going into the army.

And then I was made a cook. I prepared food for two thousand men.

Now you see me. I have a good job. I have three children. This is my wife, Consuela. Did you know I saved her life?

Look, she suffered pain. The doctor said: What is this? Are you tired? Have you had too much company? How many children? Rest overnight, then tomorrow we'll make tests.

The next morning I called the doctor. I said: She must be operated on immediately. I have looked in the book. I see where her pain is. I understand what the pressure is, where it comes from. I see clearly the organ that is making trouble.

The doctor made a test. He said: She must be operated at once. He said to me: Vicente, how did you know?

I think it would be fair to say this story is about the waste of Vicente's talent through the bad guidance of authority. I'll start by staying, then, that *waste* and *power* are its central themes. How do the elements of fiction illuminate these themes?

The *conflict* is between Vicente and the figures of authority he encounters: teacher, principal, army, doctor. His desire at the beginning of the story is to become a doctor (in itself a figure of authority), and this desire is thwarted by persons of increasing power. In the *crisis action* what is at stake is his wife's life. In this "last battle" he succeeds as a doctor, so that the *resolution* reveals the *irony* of his having been denied in the first place.

The story is told from the *point of view* of a *first-person central narrator*, but with an important qualification. The title, "A Man Told Me the Story of His Life," and the first two words, *"Vicente said,"* posit a *peripheral narrator* reporting what Vicente said. If the story was titled "My Life" and began, "I wanted to be a doctor," Vicente might be making a public appeal, a boast of how wronged he has been. As it is, he told his story privately to the barely sketched author who now wants it known, and this leaves Vicente's modesty intact.

The modesty is underscored by the simplicity of his *speech*, a *rhythm* and *word choice* that suggest educational *limitations* (perhaps that English is a second language). At the same time, that simplicity helps us *identify* with Vicente morally. Clearly, if he has educational limitations, it is not for want of trying to get an education! His credibility is augmented by *understatement*, both as a youth—"But perhaps you're right. You're the teacher"—and as a man—"I have a good job. I have three children." This apparent acceptance makes us trust him at the same time as it makes us angry on his behalf.

It's consistent with the spareness of the language that we do not have an accumulation of minute or vivid details, but the degree of *specificity* is nevertheless a clue to where to direct our sympathy. In the title Vicente is just "A Man." As soon as he speaks he becomes an individual with a name. "The school," collective and impersonal, speaks to him, but when he speaks it is to single individuals, "the teacher," "the principal," and when he speaks of his wife she is personalized as "Consuela."

Moreover, the *sensory details* are so arranged that they relate to each other in ways that give them *metaphoric* and *symbolic significance*. Notice, for example, how Vicente's desire to become a doctor "with my whole heart" is immediately followed by, "I learned every bone, every organ in the body." Here the factual anatomical study refers us back to the heart that is one of those organs, suggesting by implication that Vicente is somebody who knows what a heart is. He knows how things "connect."

An engineer, of course, has to know how things connect and how to make repairs. But so does a doctor, and the authority figures of the school haven't the imagination to see the connection. The army, by putting him to work in a way that involves both connections and anatomical parts, takes advantage of his by-now clear ability to order and organize things—he feeds two thousand men—but it is too late to repair the misdirection of such talents. We don't know what his job is now; it doesn't matter, it's the wrong one.

As a young man, Vicente asked, "What is it for? Why does it work?", revealing a natural fascination with the sort of question that would, of course, be asked on an anatomy test. But no such test is given, and the tests that are given are irrelevant.

Break up the larger story into its components, make sure you understand the exact function of each component (a story is like a machine with numerous gears: it should contain no gear that doesn't turn something), and after each component has been carefully set in place, step back and have a look at the whole. Then rewrite until the story flows as naturally as a river, each element so blending with the rest that no one, not even yourself two years from now, can locate the separate parts.

John Gardner

Stories . . . do not so much resist interpretation as survive its scrutiny.

Editor C. Michael Curtis

His wife's doctor will "make tests," but like the school authorities he knows less than Vicente does, and so asks insultingly personal questions. In fact you could say that all the authorities of the story fail the test.

This analysis, which is about two and a half times as long as the story, doesn't begin to exhaust the possibilities for interpretation, and you may disagree with any of my suggestions. But it does indicate how the techniques of characterization, plot, detail, point of view, image, and metaphor all reinforce the themes of waste and power. The story is so densely conceived and developed that it might fairly be titled "Connections," "Tests," "Repairs," "What Is It For?", or "How Did You Know?"—any one could lead us toward the themes of waste and the misguidance of authority.

Not every story is or needs to be as intensely interwoven in its elements as "A Man Told Me the Story of His Life," but the development of theme always involves such interweaving to a degree. It is a standard to work toward.

Developing Theme as You Write

In an essay, your goal is to say as clearly and directly as possible what you mean. In fiction, your goal is to make people and make them do things, and, ideally, never to "say what you mean" at all. Theoretically, an outline can never harm an essay: This is what I have to say, and I'll say it through points A, B, and C. But if a writer sets out to write a story to illustrate an idea, the fiction will almost inevitably be thin. Even if you begin with an outline, as many writers do, it will be an outline of the action and not of your "points." You may not know the meaning of the story until the characters begin to tell you what it is. You'll begin with an image of a person or a situation that seems vaguely to embody something important, and you'll learn as you go what that something is. Likewise, what you mean will emerge in the reading experience and take place in the reader's mind, "not," as the narrator says of Marlow's tales in *Heart of Darkness*, "inside like a kernel but outside, enveloping the tale which brought it out."

But at some point in the writing process, you may find yourself impelled by, under pressure of, or interested primarily in your theme. It will seem that you have set yourself this lonely, austere, and tortuous task because you do have something to say. At this point you will, and you should, begin to let that sorting-comparing-cataloging neocortex of your brain go to work on the stuff of your story. John Gardner describes the process in *The Art of Fiction*.

> Theme, it should be noticed, is not imposed on the story but evoked from within it—initially an intuitive but finally an intellectual act on the part of the writer. The writer muses on the story idea to determine what it is in it that has attracted him, why it seems to him worth telling. Having determined . . . what interests him—and what chiefly concerns the major character . . . he toys with various ways of telling his story, thinks about what has been said before about (his theme), broods on every image that occurs to him, turning it over and over, puzzling it, hunting for connections, trying to figure out—before he writes, while he writes, and in the process of repeated revisions—what it is he really thinks. . . . Only when he thinks out a story in this way does he achieve not just an alternative reality or, loosely, an imitation of nature, but true, firm art—fiction as serious thought.

This process—worrying a fiction until its theme reveals itself, connections occur, images recur, a pattern emerges—is more conscious than readers know, beginning writers want to accept, or established writers are willing to admit. It has become a popular—cliché—stance for modern writers to claim that they haven't the faintest idea what they meant in their writing. *Don't ask me; read the book. If I knew what it meant, I wouldn't have written it. It means what it says.* When an author makes such a response, it is well to remember that an author is a professional liar. What he or she means is not that there are no themes, ideas, or meanings in the work but that these are not separable from the pattern of fictional experience in which they are embodied. It also means that, having done the difficult writerly job, the writer is now unwilling also to do the critic's work. But beginning critics also resist. Students irritated by the analysis of literature often ask, "How do you know she did that on purpose? How do you know it didn't just happen to come out that way?" The answer is that you don't. But what is on the page is on the page. An author no less than a reader or critic can see an emerging pattern, and the author has both the possibility and the obligation of manipulating it. When you have put something on the page, you have two possibilities, and only two: You may cut it or you are committed to it. Gail Godwin asks:

> But what about the other truths you lost by telling it that way?
>   Ah, my friend, this is my question too. The choice is always a killing one. One option must die so that another may live. I do little murders in my workroom every day.

Often the choice to commit yourself to a phrase, an image, a line of dialogue will reveal, in a minor convulsion of understanding, what you mean. I have written no story or novel in which this did not occur in trivial or dramatic ways. I once sat bolt upright at 4 A.M. in a strange town with the realization that my sixty-year-old narrator, in a novel full of images of hands and manipulation, had been lying to me for two hundred pages. Sometimes the realistic objects or actions of a work will begin to take on metaphoric or symbolic associations with your theme, producing a crossing of references, or what Richmond Lattimore calls a "symbol complex." In a novel about a woman who traveled around the world, I employed images of dangerous water and the danger of losing balance, both physically and mentally. At some point I came up with—or, as it felt, was given—the image of a canal, the lock in which water finds its balance. This unforeseen connection gave me the purest moment of pleasure I had in writing that book. Yet I dare say no reader could identify it as a moment of particular intensity; nor, I hope, would any reader be consciously aware that the themes of danger and balance joined there.

Such an unpredictable moment of recognition is what Robert Morgan calls "the point beside the point" of the story—"the surprise that seems inevitable once it occurs. The truest vision of a story is probably the peripheral," Morgan explains. "What is going on off to the side may seem marginal at first, but central as the story comes to a climax and resolution. That curvature, the surprising convergence, is definitive in the really good short story."

The fusion of elements into a unified pattern is the nature of creativity, a word devalued in latter years to the extent that it has come to mean a random gush of self-expression. God, perhaps, created out of the void; but in the world as we know it, all creativity, from the sprouting of an onion to the painting of *Guernica*, is a matter of selection and arrangement. At the conception of an embryo or a short story, there occurs a conjunction of two unlike things, whether cells or ideas, that have never been joined before. Around this conjunction other cells, other ideas accumulate in a deliberate pattern. That pattern is the unique personality of the creature, and if the pattern does not cohere, it miscarries or is stillborn.

The organic unity of a work of literature cannot be taught—or, if it can, I have not discovered a way to teach it. I can suggest from time to time that concrete image

---

When we dream we make connections that astound us later. . . . The same thing happens on the page when we forget ourselves and as it were, watch our own waking dream. . . . Later we can make sense of what we've created and craft it accordingly. That's when we appreciate the poetry of our unconscious mind.

Tom Batt

---

is not separate from character, which is revealed in dialogue and point of view, which may be illuminated by simile, which may reveal theme, which is contained in plot as water is contained in an apple. But I cannot tell you how to achieve this; nor, if you achieve it, will you be able to explain very clearly how you have done so. Analysis separates in order to focus; it assumes that an understanding of the parts contributes to an understanding of the whole, but it does not produce the whole. Scientists can determine with minute accuracy the elements, in their proportions, contained in a piece of human skin. They can gather these elements, stir and warm them, but the result will not be skin. A good critic can show you where a metaphor does or does not illuminate character, where the character does or does not ring true in an action. But the critic cannot tell you how to make a character breathe; the breath is talent and can be neither explained nor produced. No one can tell you what to mean, and no one can tell you how.

In the unified pattern of a fiction there is something to which the name of magic may be given, where one empty word is placed upon another and tapped with a third, and a flaming scarf or a long-eared hope is pulled out of the tall black heart. The most magical thing about this magic is that once the trick is explained, it is not explained, and the better you understand how it works, the better it will work again.

Birth, death, work, and love continue to occur. Their meanings change from time to time and place to place, and new meanings engender new forms, which capture and create new meanings until they tire, while birth, death, work, and love continue to recur. Something to which we give the name of "honor" seems to persist, though in one place and time it is embodied in choosing to die for your country, in another, choosing not to. A notion of "progress" survives, though it is expressed now in technology, now in ecology, now in the survival of the fittest, now in the protection of the weak; "love" takes its form now in tenacious loyalty, now in letting go.

Ideas are not new, but the form in which they are expressed is constantly renewed, and new forms give life to what used to be called (in the old form) the "eternal verities." An innovative writer tries to forge, and those who follow try to perfect, forms that so fuse with meaning that form itself expresses.

Ralph the Duck

FREDERICK BUSCH

I woke up at 5:25 because the dog was vomiting. I carried seventy-five pounds of heaving golden retriever to the door and poured him onto the silver, moonlit snow. "Good boy," I said because he'd done his only trick. Outside he retched, and I went back up, passing the sofa on which Fanny lay. I tiptoed with enough weight on my toes to let her know how considerate I was while she was deserting me. She blinked her eyes. I swear I heard her blink her eyes. Whenever I tell her that I hear her blink her eyes, she tells me I'm lying; but I can hear the damp slap of lash after I have made her weep.

In bed and warm again, noting the red digital numbers (5:29) and certain that I wouldn't sleep, I didn't. I read a book about men who kill each other for pay or for their honor. I forget which, and so did they. It was 5:45, the alarm would buzz at 6:00, and I would make a pot of coffee and start the wood stove; I would call Fanny and pour her coffee into her mug; I would apologize because I always did, and then she would forgive me if I hadn't been too awful—I didn't think I'd been that bad— and we would stagger through the day, exhausted but pretty sure we were all right, and we'd sleep that night, probably after sex, and then we'd awaken in the same bed to the alarm at 6:00, or the dog, if he returned to the frozen deer carcass he'd been eating in the forest on our land. He loved what made him sick. The alarm went off, I got into jeans and woolen socks and a sweatshirt, and I went downstairs to let the dog in. He'd be hungry, of course.

I was the oldest college student in America, I thought. But of course I wasn't. There were always ancient women with their parchment for skin who graduated at seventy-nine from places like Barnard and the University of Georgia. I was only forty-two, and I hardly qualified as a student. I patrolled the college at night in a Bronco with a leaky exhaust system, and I went from room to room in the classroom buildings, kicking out students who were studying or humping in chairs—they'd do it anywhere— and answering emergency calls with my little blue light winking on top of the truck. I didn't carry a gun or a billy, but I had a flashlight that took six batteries and I'd used it twice on some of my overprivileged northeastern-playboy part-time classmates. On Tuesdays and Thursdays I would awaken at 6:00 with my wife, and I'd do my homework, and work around the house, and go to school at 11:30 to sit there for an hour and a half while thirty-five stomachs growled with hunger and boredom, and this guy gave instruction about books. Because I was on the staff, the college let me take a course for nothing every term. I was getting educated, in a kind of slow-motion way— it would have taken me something like fifteen or sixteen years to graduate, and I would no doubt get an F in gym and have to repeat—and there were times when I respected myself for it. Fanny often did, and that was fair incentive.

I am not unintelligent. *You are not an unintelligent writer*, my professor wrote on my paper about Nathaniel Hawthorne. We had to read short stories, I and the other students, and then we had to write little essays about them. I told how I saw Kafka and Hawthorne in similar light, and I was not unintelligent, he said. He ran into me at dusk one time, when I answered a call about a dead battery and found out it was him. I jumped his Buick from the Bronco's battery, and he was looking me over, I could tell, while I clamped onto the terminals and cranked it up. He was a tall, handsome guy who never wore a suit. He wore khakis and sweaters, loafers or sneaks, and he was always talking to the female students with the brightest hair and best builds. But he couldn't get a Buick going on an ice-cold night, and he didn't know enough to look for cells going bad. I told him he was going to need a new battery and he looked me over the way men sometimes do with other men who fix their cars for them.

"Vietnam?"

I said, "Too old."

"Not at the beginning. Not if you were an adviser. So-called. Or one of the Phoenix Project fellas?"

I was wearing a watch cap made of navy wool and an old Marine fatigue jacket. Slick characters like my professor like it if you're a killer or at least a onetime middleweight fighter. I smiled like I knew something. "Take it easy," I said, and I went back to the truck to swing around the cemetery at the top of the campus. They'd been known to screw in down-filled sleeping bags on horizontal stones up there, and the dean of students didn't want anybody dying of frostbite while joined at the hip to a matriculating fellow resident of our northeastern camp for the overindulged.

He blinked his high beams at me as I went. "You are not an unintelligent driver," I said.

Fanny had left me a bowl of something with sausages and sauerkraut and potatoes, and the dog hadn't eaten too much more than his fair share. He watched me eat his leftovers and then make myself a king-sized drink composed of sourmash whiskey and ice. In our back room, which is on the northern end of the house, and cold for sitting in that close to dawn, I sat and watched the texture of the sky change. It was going to snow, and I wanted to see the storm come up the valley. I woke up that way, sitting in the rocker with its loose right arm, holding a watery drink, and thinking right away of the girl I'd convinced to go back inside. She'd been standing outside her dormitory, looking up at a window that was dark in the midst of all those lighted panes—they never turned a light off, and often left the faucets run half the night—crying onto her bathrobe. She was barefoot in shoe-pacs, the brown ones so many of them wore unlaced, and for all I know she was naked under the robe. She was beautiful, I thought, and she was somebody's red-headed daughter, standing in a quadrangle how many miles from home weeping.

"He doesn't love anyone," the kid told me. "He doesn't love his wife—I mean his ex-wife. And he doesn't love the ex-wife before that, or the one before that. And you know what? He doesn't love me. I don't know anyone who *does!*"

"It isn't your fault if he isn't smart enough to love you," I said, steering her toward the truck.

She stopped. She turned. "You know him?"

I couldn't help it. I hugged her hard, and she let me, and then she stepped back, and of course I let her go. "Don't you *touch* me! Is this sexual harassment? Do you know the rules? Isn't this sexual harassment?"

"I'm sorry," I said at the door to the truck. "But I think I have to be able to give you a grade before it counts as harassment."

She got in. I told her we were driving to the dean of students' house. She smelled like marijuana and something very sweet, maybe one of those coffee-with-cream liqueurs you don't buy unless you hate to drink.

As the heat of the truck struck her, she started going kind of clay-gray-green, and I reached across her to open the window.

"You touched my breast!" she said.

"It's the smallest one I've touched all night, I'm afraid."

She leaned out the window and gave her rendition of my dog.

But in my rocker, waking up, at whatever time in the morning in my silent house, I thought of her as someone's child. Which made me think of ours, of course. I went for more ice, and I started on a wet breakfast. At the door of the dean of students' house, she'd turned her chalky face to me and asked, "What grade would you give me, then?"

It was a week composed of two teachers locked out of their offices late at night, a Toyota with a flat and no spare, an attempted rape on a senior girl walking home from the library, a major fight outside a fraternity house (broken wrist and significant concussion), and variations on breaking-and-entering. I was scolded by the director of nonacademic services for embracing a student who was drunk; I told him to keep his job, but he called me back because I was right to hug her, he said, and also wrong, but what the hell, and would I please stay. I thought of the fringe benefits—graduation in only sixteen years—so I went back to work.

My professor assigned a story called "A Rose for Emily," and I wrote him a paper about the mechanics of corpse fucking, and how, since she clearly couldn't screw her dead boyfriend, she was keeping his rotten body in bed because she truly loved him. I called the paper "True Love." He gave me a B and wrote *See me, pls.* In his office after class, his feet up on his desk, he trimmed a cigar with a giant folding knife he kept in his drawer.

"You got to clean the hole out," he said, "or they don't draw."

"I don't smoke," I said.

"Bad habit. Real *habit*, though. I started in smoking 'em in Georgia, in the service. My C.O. smoked 'em. We collaborated on a brothel inspection one time, and we ended up smoking these with a couple of women." He waggled his eyebrows at me, now that his malehood was established.

"Were the women smoking them too?"

He snorted laughter through his nose while the greasy smoke came curling off his thin, dry lips. "They were pretty smoky, I'll tell ya!" Then he propped his feet—he was wearing cowboy boots that day—and he sat forward. "It's a little hard to explain. But—hell. You just don't say *fuck* when you write an essay for a college prof. Okay?" Like a scoutmaster with a kid he'd caught in the outhouse jerking off: "All right? You don't wanna do that."

"Did it shock you?"

"Fuck, no, it didn't shock me. I just told you. It violates certain proprieties."

"But if I'm writing it to you, like a letter—"

"You're writing it for posterity. For some mythical reader someplace, not just me. You're making a *statement*."

"Right. My statement said how hard it must be for a woman to fuck with a corpse."

"And a point worth making. I said so. Here."

"But you said I shouldn't say it."

"No. Listen. Just because you're taking about fucking, you don't have to say *fuck*. Does that make it any clearer?"

"No."

"I wish you'd lied to me just now," he said.

I nodded. I did too.

"Where'd you do your service?" he asked.

"Baltimore. Baltimore, Maryland."

"What's in Baltimore?"

"Railroads. I liaised on freight runs of army matériel. I killed a couple of bums on the rod with my bare hands, though."

He snorted again, but I could see how disappointed he was. He'd been banking on my having been a murderer. Interesting guy in one of my classes, he must have told some terrific woman at an overpriced meal: I just *know* the guy was a rubout specialist in the Nam, he had to have said. I figured I should come to work wearing my fatigue jacket and a red bandana tied around my head. Say "Man" to him a couple of times, hang a fist in the air for grief and solidarity, and look terribly worn, exhausted by experiences he was fairly certain that he envied me. His dungarees were ironed, I noticed.

On Saturday we went back to the campus because Fanny wanted to see a movie called *The Seven Samurai*. I fell asleep, and I'm afraid I snored. She let me sleep until the auditorium was almost empty. Then she kissed me awake. "Who was screaming in my dream?" I asked her.

"Kurosawa," she said.

"Who?"

"Ask your professor friend."

I looked around, but he wasn't there. "Not an un-weird man," I said.

We went home and cleaned up after the dog and put him out. We drank a little Spanish brandy and went upstairs and made love. I was fairly premature, you might say, but one way and another by the time we fell asleep we were glad to be there with each other, and glad that it was Sunday coming up the valley toward us, and nobody with it. The dog was howling at another dog someplace, or at the moon, or maybe just his moon-thrown shadow on the snow. I did not strangle him when I opened the back door and he limped happily past me and stumbled up the stairs. I followed him into our bedroom and groaned for just being satisfied as I got into bed. You'll notice I didn't say fuck.

He stopped me in the hall after class on a Thursday, and asked me How's it goin, just one of the kickers drinking sour beer and eating pickled eggs and watching the tube in a country bar. How's it goin. I nodded. I wanted a grade from the man, and I did want to learn about expressing myself. I nodded and made what I thought was a smile. He'd let his mustache grow out and his hair grow longer. He was starting to wear dark shirts with lighter ties. I thought he looked like someone in *The Godfather*. He still wore those light little loafers or his high-heeled cowboy boots. His corduroy pants looked baggy. I guess he wanted them to look that way. He motioned me to the wall of the hallway, and he looked and said, "How about the Baltimore stuff?"

I said, "Yeah?"

"Was that really true?" He was almost blinking, he wanted so much for me to be a damaged Vietnam vet just looking for a bell tower to climb into and start firing from.

The college didn't have a bell tower you could get up into, though I'd once spent an ugly hour chasing a drunken ATO down from the roof of the observatory. "You were just clocking through boxcars in Baltimore?"

I said, "Nah."

"I thought so!" He gave a kind of sigh.

"I killed people," I said.

"You know, I could have sworn you did," he said.

I nodded, and he nodded back. I'd made him so happy.

The assignment was to write something to influence somebody. He called it Rhetoric and Persuasion. We read an essay by George Orwell and "A Modest Proposal" by Jonathan Swift. I liked the Orwell better, but I wasn't comfortable with it. He talked about "niggers," and I felt him saying it two ways.

I wrote "Ralph the Duck."

Once upon a time, there was a duck named Ralph who didn't have any feathers on either wing. So when the cold wind blew, Ralph said, Brr, and shivered and shook.

What's the matter? Ralph's mommy asked.

I'm cold, Ralph said.

Oh, the mommy said. Here. I'll keep you warm.

So she spread her big, feathery wings, and hugged Ralph tight, and when the cold wind blew, Ralph was warm and snuggly, and fell fast asleep.

The next Thursday, he was wearing canvas pants and hiking boots. He mentioned kind of casually to some of the girls in the class how whenever there was a storm he wore his Lake District walking outfit. He had a big, hairy sweater on. I kept waiting for him to make a noise like a mountain goat. But the girls seemed to like it. His boots made a creaky squeak on the linoleum of the hall when he caught up with me after class.

"As I told you," he said, "it isn't unappealing. It's just—not a college theme."

"Right," I said. "Okay. You want me to do it over?"

"No," he said. "Not at all. The D will remain your grade. But I'll read something else if you want to write it."

"This'll be fine," I said.

"Did you understand the assignment?"

"Write something to influence someone—Rhetoric and Persuasion."

We were at his office door and the redheaded kid who had gotten sick in my truck was waiting for him. She looked at me like one of us was in the wrong place, which struck me as accurate enough. He was interested in getting into his office with the redhead, but he remembered to turn around and flash me a grin he seemed to think he was known for.

Instead of going on shift a few hours after class, the way I'm supposed to, I told my supervisor I was sick, and I went home. Fanny was frightened when I came in, because I don't get sick and I don't miss work. She looked at my face and she grew sad. I kissed her hello and went upstairs to change. I always used to change my clothes when I was a kid, as soon as I came home from school. I put on jeans and a flannel shirt and thick wool socks, and I made myself a dark drink of sourmash. Fanny poured herself some wine and came into the cold northern room a few minutes later. I was sitting in the rocker, looking over the valley. The wind was lining up a lot of rows of cloud so that the sky looked like a baked trout when you lift the skin off. "It'll snow," I said to her.

She sat on the old sofa and waited. After a while, she said, "I wonder why they always call it a mackerel sky?"

"Good eating, mackerel," I said.

Fanny said, "Shit! You're never that laconic unless you feel crazy. What's wrong? Who'd you punch out at the playground?"

"We had to write a composition," I said.

"Did he like it?"

"He gave me a D."

"Well, you're familiar enough with D's. I never saw you get this low over a grade."

"I wrote about Ralph the Duck."

She said, "You did?" She said, "Honey." She came over and stood beside the rocker and leaned into me and hugged my head and neck. "Honey," she said. "Honey."

It was the worst of the winter's storms, and one of the worst in years. That afternoon they closed the college, which they almost never do. But the roads were jammed with snow over ice, and now it was freezing rain on top of that, and the only people working at the school that night were the operator who took emergency calls and me. Everyone else had gone home except the students, and most of them were inside. The ones who weren't were drunk, and I kept on sending them in and telling them to act like grown-ups. A number of them said they were, and I really couldn't argue. I had the bright beams on, the defroster set high, the little blue light winking, and a thermos of sourmash and hot coffee that I sipped from every time I had to get out of the truck or every time I realized how cold all that wetness was out there.

About eight o'clock, as the rain was turning back to snow and the cold was worse, the roads impossible, just as I was done helping a country sander on the edge of the campus pull a panel truck out of a snowbank, I got the emergency call from the college operator. We had a student missing. The roommates thought the kid was heading for the quarry. This meant I had to get the Bronco up on a narrow road above the campus, above the old cemetery, into all kinds of woods and rough track that I figured would be choked with ice and snow. Any kid up there would really have to want to be there, and I couldn't go in on foot, because you'd only want to be there on account of drugs, booze, or craziness, and either way I'd be needing blankets and heat, and then a fast ride down to the hospital in town. So I dropped into four-wheel drive to get me up the hill above the campus, bucking snow and sliding on ice, putting all the heater's warmth up onto the windshield because I couldn't see much more than swarming snow. My feet were still cold from the tow job, and it didn't seem to matter that I had on heavy socks and insulated boots I'd coated with waterproofing. I shivered, and I thought of Ralph the Duck.

I had to grind the rest of the way, from the cemetery, in four-wheel low, and in spite of the cold I was smoking my gearbox by the time I was close enough to the quarry—they really did take a lot of rocks for the campus buildings from there—to see I'd have to make my way on foot to where she was. It was a kind of scooped-out shape, maybe four or five stories high, where she stood—well, wobbled is more like it. She was as chalky as she'd been the last time, and her red hair didn't catch the light anymore. It just lay on her like something that had died on top of her head. She was in a white nightgown that was plastered to her body. She had her arms crossed as if she wanted to be warm. She swayed, kind of, in front of the big, dark, scooped-out rock face, where the trees and brush had been cleared for trucks and earthmovers. She looked tiny against all the darkness. From where I stood, I could see the snow driving down in front of the lights I'd left on, but I couldn't see it near her. All it looked like around her was dark. She was shaking with the cold, and she was crying.

I had a blanket with me, and I shoved it down the front of my coat to keep it dry for her, and because I was so cold. I waved. I stood in the lights and I waved. I don't know what she saw—a big shadow, maybe. I surely didn't reassure her, because when she saw me she backed up, until she was near the face of the quarry. She couldn't go any farther.

I called, "Hello! I brought a blanket. Are you cold? I thought you might want a blanket."

Her roommates had told the operator about pills, so I didn't bring her the coffee laced with mash. I figured I didn't have all that much time, anyway, to get her down and pumped out. The booze with whatever pills she'd taken would make her die that much faster.

I hated that word. Die. It made me furious with her. I heard myself seething when I breathed. I pulled my scarf and collar up above my mouth. I didn't want her to see how close I might come to wanting to kill her because she wanted to die.

I called, "Remember me?"

I was closer now. I could see the purple mottling of her skin. I didn't know if it was cold or dying. It probably didn't matter much to distinguish between them right now, I thought. That made me smile. I felt the smile, and I pulled the scarf down so she could look at it. She didn't seem awfully reassured.

"You're the sexual harassment guy," she said. She said it very slowly. Her lips were clumsy. It was like looking at a ventriloquist's dummy.

"I gave you an A," I said.

"When?"

"It's a joke," I said. "You don't want me making jokes. You want me to give you a nice warm blanket, though. And then you want me to take you home."

She leaned against the rock face when I approached. I pulled the blanket out, then zipped my jacket back up. The snow had stopped, I realized, and that wasn't really a very good sign. It felt like an arctic cold descending in its place. I held the blanket out to her, but she only looked at it.

"You'll just have to turn me in," I said. "I'm gonna hug you again."

She screamed, "No more! I don't want any more hugs!"

But she kept her arms on her chest, and I wrapped the blanket around her and stuffed a piece into each of her tight, small fists. I didn't know what to do for her feet. Finally, I got down on my haunches in front of her. She crouched down too, protecting herself.

"No," I said. "No. You're fine."

I took off the woolen mittens I'd been wearing. Mittens keep you warmer than gloves because they trap your hand's heat around the fingers and palms at once. Fanny had knitted them for me. I put a mitten as far onto each of her feet as I could. She let me. She was going to collapse, I thought.

"Now, let's go home," I said. "Let's get you better."

With her funny, stiff lips, she said, "I've been very self-indulgent and weird and I'm sorry. But I'd really like to die." She sounded so reasonable that I found myself nodding in agreement as she spoke.

"You can't just die," I said.

"Aren't I dying already? I took all of them," and then she giggled like a child, which of course is what she was. "I borrowed different ones from other people's rooms. See, this isn't some teenage cry for like help. Understand? I'm seriously interested in death and I have to like stay out here a little longer and fall asleep. All right?"

"You can't do that," I said. "You ever hear of Vietnam?"

"I saw that movie," she said. "With the opera in it? Apocalypse? Whatever."

"I was there!" I said. "I killed people! I helped to kill them! And when they die, you see their bones later on. You dream about their bones and blood on the ends of the splintered ones, and this kind of mucous stuff coming out of their eyes. You probably heard of guys having dreams like that, didn't you? Whacked-out Vietnam vets? That's me, see? So I'm telling you, I know about dead people and their eyeballs and everything falling out. And people keep dreaming about the dead people they knew, see? You can't make people dream about you like that! It isn't fair!"

"You dream about me?" She was ready to go. She was ready to fall down, and I was going to lift her up and get her to the truck.

"I will," I said. "If you die."

"I want you to," she said. Her lips were hardly moving now. Her eyes were closed. "I want you all to."

I dropped my shoulder and put it into her waist and picked her up and carried her down to the Bronco. She was talking, but not a lot, and her voice leaked down my back. I jammed her into the truck and wrapped the blanket around her better and then put another one down around her feet. I strapped her in with the seat belt. She was shaking, and her eyes were closed and her mouth open. She was breathing. I checked that twice, once when I strapped her in, and then again when I strapped myself in and backed hard into a sapling and took it down. I got us into first gear, held the clutch in, leaned over to listen for breathing, heard it—shallow panting, like a kid asleep on your lap for a nap—and then I put the gear in and howled down the hillside on what I thought might be the road.

We passed the cemetery. I told her that was a good sign. She didn't respond. I found myself panting too, as if we were breathing for each other. It made me dizzy, but I couldn't stop. We passed the highest dorm, and I dropped the truck into four-wheel high. The cab smelled like burnt oil and hot metal. We were past the chapel now, and the observatory, the president's house, then the bookstore. I had the blue light winking and the V-6 roaring, and I drove on the edge of out-of-control, sensing the skids just before I slid into them, and getting back out of them as I needed to. I took a little fender off once, and a bit of the corner of a classroom building, but I worked us back on course, and all I needed to do now was negotiate the sharp left turn around the Administration Building past the library, then floor it for the straight run to the town's main street and then the hospital.

I was panting into the mike, and the operator kept saying, "Say again?"

I made myself slow down some, and I said we'd need stomach pumping, and to get the names of the pills from her friends in the dorm, and I'd be there in less than five or we were crumpled up someplace and dead.

"Roger," the radio said. "Roger all that." My throat tightened and tears came into my eyes. They were helping us, they'd told me: Roger.

I said to the girl, whose head was slumped and whose face looked too blue all through its whiteness, "You know, I had a girl once. My wife, Fanny. She and I had a small girl one time."

I reached over and touched her cheek. It was cold. The truck swerved, and I got my hands on the wheel. I'd made the turn past the Ad Building using just my left. "I can do it in the dark," I sang to no tune I'd ever learned. "I can do it with one hand." I said to her, "We had a girl child, very small. Now, I do *not* want you dying."

I came to the campus gates doing fifty on the ice and snow, smoking the engine, grinding the clutch, and I bounced off a wrought iron fence to give me the curve going left that I needed. On a pool table, it would have been a bank shot worth applause. The town cop picked me up and got out ahead of me and let the street have all the lights and noise I could want. We banged up to the emergency room entrance and I was out and at the other door before the cop on duty, Elmo St. John, could loosen his seat belt. I loosened hers, and I carried her into the lobby of the ER. They had a gurney, and doctors, and they took her away from me. I tried to talk to them, but they made me sit down and do my shaking on a dirty sofa decorated with drawings of little spinning wheels. Somebody brought me hot coffee, I think it was Elmo, but I couldn't hold it.

"They won't," he kept saying to me. "They won't."

"What?"

"You just been sitting there for a minute and a half like St. Vitus dancing, telling me, Don't let her die. Don't her her die."

"Oh."

"You all *right*?"

"How about the kid?"

"They'll tell us soon."

"She better be all right."

"That's right."

"She—somebody's gonna have to tell me plenty if she isn't."

"That's right."

"She better not die this time," I guess I said.

Fanny came downstairs to look for me. I was at the northern windows, looking through the mullions down the valley to the faint red line along the mounds and little peaks of the ridge beyond the valley. The sun was going to come up, and I was looking for it.

Fanny stood behind me. I could hear her. I could smell her hair and the sleep on her. The crimson line widened, and I squinted at it. I heard the dog limp in behind her, catching up. He panted and I knew why his panting sounded familiar. She put her hands on my shoulders and arms. I made muscles to impress her with, and then I let them go, and let my head drop down until my chin was on my chest.

"I didn't think you'd be able to sleep after that," Fanny said.

"I brought enough adrenaline home to run a football team."

"But you hate being a hero, huh? You're hiding in here because somebody's going to call, or come over, and want to talk to you—her parents for shooting sure, sooner or later. Or is that supposed to be part of the service up at the playground? Saving their suicidal daughters. Almost dying to find them in the woods and driving too fast for any weather, much less what we had last night. Getting their babies home. The bastards." She was crying. I knew she would be, sooner or later. I could hear the soft sound of her lashes. She sniffed and I could feel her arm move as she felt for the tissues on the coffee table.

"I have them over here," I said. "On the windowsill."

"Yes." She blew her nose, and the dog thumped his tail. He seemed to think it one of Fanny's finer tricks, and he had wagged for her for thirteen years whenever she'd done it. "Well, you're going to have to talk to them."

"I will," I said. "I will." The sun was in our sky now, climbing. We had built the room so we could watch it climb. "I think that jackass with the smile, my prof? She showed up a lot at his office, the last few weeks. He called her 'my advisee,' you know? The way those guys sound about what they're achieving by getting up and shaving and going to work and saying the same thing every day? Every year? Well, she was his advisee, I bet. He was shoving home the old advice."

"She'll be okay," Fanny said. "Her parents will take her home and love her up and get her some help." She began to cry again, then she stopped. She blew her nose, and the dog's tail thumped. She kept a hand between my shoulder and my neck. "So tell me what you'll tell a waiting world. How'd you talk her out?"

"Well, I didn't, really. I got up close and picked her up and carried her is all."

"You didn't say *anything*?"

"Sure I did. Kid's standing in the snow outside of a lot of pills, you're gonna say something."

"So what'd you *say?*"

"I told her stories," I said. "I did Rhetoric and Persuasion."

Fanny said, "Then you go in early on Thursday, you go in half an hour early, and you get that guy to jack up your grade."

🦆 🦆 🦆
Suggestions for Discussion

1. Briefly summarize this story's plot. Then, in a phrase, describe what the story is about. Compare your phrase with those of other readers to see how these descriptions of theme resemble and differ from one another.

2. Find a line that implies more than its literal meaning, such as "Ralph the Duck"; "He loved what made him sick"; "I was getting educated, in a kind of slow-motion way"; "Rhetoric and Persuasion"; or "She better not die this time." How does your chosen line help illuminate the theme of the story?

Retrospect

3. Find a slow-motion passage in the story. Why do you think the author chose this technique to depict this particular moment?

4. Many connections are left to the reader to make throughout this story rather than explained directly. What does this reticence reflect about the narrator's character? How does it affect your participation in the story as a reader?

Wave

JOHN HOLMAN

Sometimes because of traffic Ray cut through a neighborhood that emptied out behind the hotel where he worked. He operated a wait-staff service that was contracted to a small hotel in Research Triangle Park. It was a quiet street, twenty miles per hour, though fairly busy just before school in the mornings and in the afternoons when school got out. At one house about half-way in, there was a man who sat on his porch and waved. The man waved no matter who was passing by. He waved every time, at every car, at everybody. He was always on the porch, unless the weather was bad, and then he sat on a tall stool inside the glass storm door and waved.

Ray had recently discovered this alternate route, finally found a way around the clogged stretch of expressway. Lately the usual wrecks and congestion were caused by sandbags in the lanes, and chickens, lumber, or wet paint. The oddities seemed to compete, to Ray's amusement and frustration. There had been roofing shingles, cats, loaves of bread, golf balls, and a washing machine blocking the way. The hazards of the thriving economy. So Ray needed the short cut. After the first two greetings from the man, when Ray realized the man was not simply friendly but somehow stunned into a compulsion to wave, his dilemma was whether or not to wave back. If he was in a rush, Ray sometimes noticed too late and threw up his hand at the neighbor's porch, as if his wave might trail backward like a ribbon and flutter at the man before snapping forward to catch up. He felt silly waving to a possible idiot. It made Ray feel like an idiot, making an empty gesture at an empty-headed old white man who waved because he couldn't help it. It was like talking to a doll. He couldn't fully pretend it was meaningful. Yet, if he did not wave, he felt guilty. Sometimes, traffic or no, he stayed on the main road to the front of the hotel, only to chastise himself for preferring the stress of traffic to the stress of simply waving.

Occasionally, policemen pulled over cars for exceeding the street's speed limit, drivers late for school or work, or maybe rushing because of fear of the waving man. The man's house was small and blue, with a neat little yard. Azalea bushes trimmed the border along the porch. A clean concrete walkway led to three porch steps. The porch was fenced by a painted wooden rail, and the man sat on a rocking chair and waved. He was a big man, as chubby as an infant, with an infant's bald head and an infant's dimpled smile. He had gleaming small teeth and silver-rimmed glasses. In cool weather he wore a dove gray cardigan, and when the temperature was warm he wore pressed, pale-colored sport shirts. He was neat, clean, with plump soft-looking hands. Sometimes he leaned forward from his chair and waved. When he was behind the glass door, as he was this morning, and Ray had to make an effort to find him, the man would also be ducking and leaning in an effort to be seen.

Desperate optimism, Ray thought. This on a bleak, wet, early March morning when, the rainy night before, Ray had discovered someone lying drunk and crying in his backyard, trapped in the narrow space between his back hedges and rusting chain-link fence. Hearing the cry, Ray had gone out in the downpour and aimed a flashlight on him, a ruddy-looking man with soaked dark hair streaking his face— some kind of Indian maybe, in sopping denim shirt and pants and wearing the weight of wet black cowboy boots. Ray asked if he was all right, what's wrong, tried and failed to pull him up by his limp heavy arm. Shivering, Ray held the umbrella over the man for a while. This man was inordinately sad, eyes closed, speaking no language but despair. Sobbing and moaning. Rhythm and lilt.

So Ray covered him with a blanket and a bunched sheet of blue plastic tarpaulin. Ray's friend Alma was visiting, standing at the opened back door and looking out. She wanted to call the police, or an ambulance. "He'll freeze, catch pneumonia and die," she pleaded when Ray came inside.

"Catch pneumonia, maybe. He can't freeze out there tonight." He talked Alma into waiting. The police would be more trouble for the man, and an ambulance didn't seem warranted; he was just depressed, breathing well, not hemorrhaging. But they watched the Weather Channel to check the forecast for the night. The temperature would stay in the forties and rain would persist. Then they turned off the kitchen light and stared out the back window, but they couldn't see the man where he lay. He still sobbed loudly now and then, and his intermittent wails reassured them.

Standing there in the dark, sharing a bottle of red wine, was awkward. Alma was not exactly Ray's girlfriend although he had thought she was, or could be. When she first moved to town, months ago, he was all for some romance, and she had a flirty way of being friendly that sustained anticipation. And that night he still hoped for her affection, except the presence of the sad man was an impediment. No way to talk of love, and no sign from her other than her being there. She had come with a betting sheet for the NCAA basketball tournament, wanting Ray's help choosing winners for her office pool. The paper with the names of the hopeful teams in their starting brackets was held by a magnet to his refrigerator, where it semi-glowed in the weak tree-filtered light from a neighbor's back porch. Ray went over and pretended to study it in the near-dark.

"Maybe we should take him something to eat, or some coffee," Alma said. So Ray opened the refrigerator and realized the uselessness of taking food out there. "He's not going to eat anything. He's too . . . disconsolate." He pulled out lunch meat anyway. And mustard and mayo and lettuce. "Are you hungry?" he asked Alma.

The man outside moaned. "A sandwich would disintegrate in this rain," Ray said.

"Oh I can't bear this," Alma said. "Either that guy goes, or I do. I mean, get him inside or something, which is not really what I want while I'm here."

"Well, you're not going anywhere just yet."

"But he's out there like a wounded dog, or deer, or bear. What moans like that? There's nothing human about any of this."

Ray turned to look at her. She was making gestures of frustration and impatience, flexing her fingers and pivoting in her hiking boots, performing in the fan of refrigerator light, her short braids lifting slightly, like tentacles.

"I can't put him out of his misery. Besides, a wounded animal is the most dangerous kind, they say."

She stopped pivoting. "You're not making jokes about this, are you? You're using that poor person to make fun of me?"

Ray closed the refrigerator. But Alma was still dimly visible in front of him. "Sorry. It's just a way of being patient, of passing time here. No offense to you or him. I mean, if I were heartbroken and lost, drunk on the ground in the dark rain of somebody's raggedy back yard, I'd want to be left alone. I wouldn't want anybody to know I was even there. I'd want to suffer until I was through without some do-gooder guy and his happy young friend meddling with delusions of rescue."

"Then you ought to shut the hell up instead of moaning and crying to high heaven. And who the hell you calling happy?"

Ray laughed at that. "All right. Damn. Sorry about that, too. I thought you were happy. Why aren't you happy?"

"None of your business." She turned away, and when she turned back, in the semi-darkness, he thought she held her wineglass. There was a glint of light at the position of her heart.

"Aw, you're happy. You're just ashamed to say it."

"If I were happy, you'd know it."

"How?"

She didn't say anything. She raised her glint of light and drank from it. She'd had some troubles he knew about, the job for one—struggling a little bit when she first came to town to be Assistant Director of Special Programs at the college library; she was young, just out of grad school. And housing for another—such as having to move suddenly when her apartment building caught fire, and then moving in with a co-worker and another roommate who was either on crack or struggling with some other alternate reality. That roommate had taken to wearing Alma's clothes and claiming they were hers, that she and Alma had clothes just alike. But all Alma needed to solve the problem was to move again. In with him, would be nice. She could wear *his* clothes. And they could be amused together at what the roommate's disturbance would cause next.

"What would make you happy?"

"I don't have a clue," she said, cheerlessly. "Maybe the end of all wars, and all people experiencing personal adoration with humility." She looked down at her wine.

"Of course. Well, that's a clue." Ray stepped over beside her and poured more wine into his glass, and then hers, wishing she would ask him that question. Then he could say that she would make him happy, that he was happy with her just being there, but that holding her would work the magic, having her hold him back. Something real rather than pretend or cursory like their cheek-to-cheek kisses when they said hello or goodbye.

The man outside was quiet now. Ray flicked on the flashlight and shined it through the window but it was hard to see through the yellow glare on the glass to the spot of ground the light shined on. He raised the window a little, to the splatter of rain on the soggy earth.

"Well, it's not good for him to spend the night out there," he said finally, because he imagined water rising up around the man, head in a pool, nostrils filling with puddle and silt.

"Maybe he'll just leave," Alma said. She put her glass down and left the kitchen, went to the bathroom Ray thought.

"There's pretty good drainage out there," he called out to her. There had never been any real flooding that he knew about.

Ray took the tournament diagram into the living room where he sat on the blue sofa and laid the sheet of paper on the glass-topped coffee table. There was light from a chrome floor lamp and the TV was still on, *Animal Planet*—leopards lounging in tall dry grass. He watched that a few seconds, the image of the man out back swelling onto it. Dry leopard, wet man; if it was meaningful he didn't know how.

For the first round, he picked the teams he knew about but soon understood that filling all the brackets would take some time, some very considered guesses. Everybody picked Duke to win the whole thing, be the team of the decade—the nineties—but the teams Duke would beat were harder to choose. Among them, somewhere, was the team of the '00s. The zeros. Was anybody even hopeful for that distinction, Ray wondered.

Alma came and sat beside him. She turned up the volume and changed the channel to ESPN in case they were analyzing the teams. But it was hockey night, so she muted the sound.

Ray watched her as she went into the kitchen to bring the wine bottle. He said, "Are you hopeful, then?"

"About what?"

"Hopeful. If not happy?"

"Sure." She slid the betting sheet in front of her and took the pencil from Ray's hand.

While she scanned his guesses, Ray thought to tell her about the man who waved, but his mind skipped over to the subject of his boss, the hotel manager who seemed hopeful *and* happy, but was also mean. He was burly, with a British accent and tight suits. He treated Ray like a servant. Ordered him recently in a room full of his staff to raise their wages (necessitating some struggle not to offend either his staff or the manager, while trying to disguise his anger and humiliation), threatened to hire another serving group within earshot of customers and staff alike, but then pretended to be friendly, as if he'd been only teasing—such an arrogant, meaty thug, in Ray's opinion. So that was a problem, since Ray's contract was up for renewal. His regular staff depended on him, he thought, and he kept a pool of extras active. This contract kept him steady at the one hotel with pretty good money. He was developing a hate for the manager, but he didn't want to quit.

He wasn't ambitious, he chided himself. At thirty-one, he should have already accomplished more than becoming a glorified waiter. This week he was to meet with the manager to discuss contract renewal, terms thereof. Still, he wasn't sure he wanted it—another year of that bull. Except the manager might be leaving, he'd heard from Jamal, the assistant manager, who might take over—a better man altogether. So maybe stick it out—maybe something good could happen—a nice long-term contract eventually, and an employer who treated him like an equal, like another boss.

He knew better than to get into all that with Alma. Those thoughts colliding in his head sounded like complaint, like whining, even more so with a broken-hearted man watering the backyard with tears.

So, "Did I tell you about this guy on my way to work who waves at everybody?" he asked. The way it came out, like mockery, even that sounded like complaint.

"No. Something wrong with that?"

"I don't know."

"People wave, don't they? It's a common, person-like gesture." She tucked her braids behind her ears. She had funny ears. They stuck out, even more with the braids pushing behind them. She didn't seem self-conscious in the least. He found that utterly charming, such a pretty, comical face.

"People don't do it like he does. Not like that," Ray said of the waving. "He's automatic, compelled, troubling."

"You don't like him?"

"Yeah, I like him all right. He makes me feel funny, though. It's like he went crazy and his mind stuck on friendly, which is better than taking the serial killer turn. Still, while you want to feel good about chronic cheerfulness, it doesn't look any more sane than chronic moping, hatred, and murder."

"Ray," she said, leaning to stare facetiously into his eyes. "What's wrong with you?" She held up her hand and wiggled her fingers in his face.

"What's wrong with *you*?"

"Nothing." She leaned away.

"I want it normal. I want that waving son-of-a-bitch to be sane. He's got somebody inside the house to put a sweater on him when it's cold and to sit him inside when it's freezing and wet, to buy his shirts and shave him, maybe."

"The Luckiest Man, you mean."

"You got it. One time I was going by and he was helping some lady bring a couple of small suitcases from a car in his driveway—the first time I'd seen him on his feet—and you should have seen the panic on his smiling face. He couldn't wave 'cause of the suitcases, so he just stood there looking at me passing as if I was an ice cream truck coming to flatten him. You know, something both welcome and troubling. So I waved, and felt perfectly evil, then. It was like he was drowning and those suitcases were concrete blocks tied to his wrists."

"Not waving but drowning."

"Well, I guess."

"It's a poem."

"What is?"

"That line. It's from a poem about somebody seeming to wave when actually he's drowning, and somebody else misreading the gesture. I think that's the reading."

"Oh. Maybe I remember that poem, then. But this guy is just waving. It was like drowning when he couldn't wave."

"You're not evil, Ray," she said, patting his knee. She handed him his wine glass and clinked hers to his. "But speaking of drowning, do you think your boy out back is dead yet?"

"Aw, that guy." Ray glanced back at the dark kitchen window. "What's the matter with him, anyway? How come he gets to do that?"

"He's a drunk man. Desperate. Down on his luck and on the margins of society, lying up against your fence."

"Now you get to make the joke," he said.

He took the flashlight back outside. The rain had eased to a hard drizzle. In the beam of light, rain flashed. The grass was spongy, and Ray stepped over illuminated bare spots of glistening mud. The sound of rain in the trees was enthralling and Ray didn't want to go over to the man. Didn't care to see him lying there passed out or dead, or to hear the sobbing, and the thick splat of blunted rain hitting the slick face and wet clothes.

When Ray walked to the hedges by the fence, the man was gone. The light revealed matted grass, flattened tufts of daffodil stems. He pointed the light through the fence in case the man had climbed over and collapsed there. Nothing. Not even a liquor bottle left behind. Alien abduction, perhaps. Alma, he thought, would be relieved.

She left soon after, the betting sheet thoroughly guessed at. Ray put away the sandwich makings, finished the bottle of wine, and fell asleep on the sofa to the hockey game. The next morning going to work he was waving at the man sitting on the stool in the doorway.

It wasn't until after work that he felt bad about the man in his yard again. He had two lunch meetings to serve and one of his waiters got sick during the shift while another just didn't show up, and still another came in late during the serving with hair limp from rain, her white shirt wet and sticking to her shoulders, which showed pink through the thin fabric. Meanwhile, Ray tried to fill in, going from room to room to keep plates moving, but the hotel manager kept popping in, stupidly commenting on contract points while Ray was hoisting trays of *cordon-bleu*, hustling with pots of coffee and pitchers of tea. Then, still shorthanded, he had to break down both rooms and set up a larger one for a breakfast meeting tomorrow, check with the kitchen to synchronize the head-count because the manager told him late that the number had been increased, and often the kitchen never learned of such changes. While he was there, he had a talk with the dishwasher staff about sending out racks of glasses and cutlery covered with spots that his crew was obliged to wipe away. Then he got on the phone to some of his staff, to leave messages, persuade others to come in very early tomorrow morning to cover the crowd.

Raining all day, a steady, sharp drizzle. Ray had sneaked a couple of moments to stand on the kitchen's loading platform and sip a glass of tea. Then at 5:30, before leaving for the day, he stood there again and looked out on the lushly wet cedar trees that buffered the hotel from the expressway, and at the stretch of green yard through which the jogging trail coursed. He was tired; yet he imagined the insistent rain excited the earth. Flowers were already springing up, opening. Azalea buds dotted the bushes. Daffodils were already everywhere. He was thinking of Alma of course, thinking of how romantic the rain could be—the way it encouraged huddling under umbrellas, as it had when he walked her to her car the night before, and the way it sent people indoors with the options of what to do there; he often imagined the intimacy of the hotel guests in their rented rooms, and envied them. And then the rain became sad again, gray and relentless, falling all night and all day and probably all night again. He and Alma had done nothing much indoors last night. And the image of the man in his backyard returned. "Forlorn," he said aloud, tasting the sour age of the word. Another little something from a poem. Keats. Alma wasn't the only one with an education.

It was time to go home, the deflated mood of low expectation upon him. Alma wouldn't come by again tonight, two nights in a row, and there was no excuse to go see her, and her strange roommate. Surely Alma knew he longed for her, and obviously it didn't matter.

He sat in his car awhile and listened for the traffic report. Incredibly, cattle were loose on the expressway, their transporting truck overturned. The rain slowed a little. Ray circled out of the parking lot and steered onto his alternate route. At a traffic light, he noticed a line of cars behind him, and much of it followed as he turned onto the street through the neighborhood where the waving man lived. He wanted to be alone, not leading a procession through his secret. But maybe it was everybody's secret, and he wondered whether the others imagined a relationship with the waving man, too.

It was then, thinking of the waving man, and the sad man still on his mind, that he felt himself held in a balance, sustained between his own hope and despair, caught between the waving man and the wailing man. He realized that he was afraid to move, to risk sinking under the weight of his pessimism, or rising up too happy and untethered by solemnity, of being lost in space like the waving man. It was why he wouldn't drive over to Alma's and climb through her window and wait for her in her bed—that and her roommate—and why he wouldn't simply leave her alone. To contemplate either one wobbled him, because for her to accept him would mean his giving up his hold on his reality, his suffering, and for her to reject him would send him crashing. It was not a stasis that cheered him.

Maybe, he thought, a similar stasis, a similar fear, kept Alma from being happy. Maybe all it would take was for him to upset the balance, push her off her anchor. And maybe they could soar into a new life, a new decade and new century together. And maybe not.

At the blue house, the man was on his stool behind the storm door and waving. Ray waved back. He looked in his rearview mirror and saw that driver also wave. The driver was wearing a suit and tie, in a soft-gold Lincoln with green tinted windows. A wealthy man, it seemed, the car old and well-kept, water beading on the polished gold surface like wet jewels. Behind the Lincoln, the wet headlights of the other cars filtered through those green windows, creating a gliding capsule of soft-green glimmer, the color of water in an ocean. Ray slowed and kept glancing back to hold the slow float of green headlights, the glimmering green rain on the Lincoln's windows, to ride it around the curves and out beyond the neighborhood to the unobstructed expressway, the wealthy man's car creating a green lens of comfort in the gray day.

On the expressway, the Lincoln pulled around to pass, and Ray waved, thankful for that sustained moment. The man waved back and sped by. Other cars sped by, too, spraying thick rain onto Ray's windshield. Ray quickened his wipers and soon could see well enough to drive safely home.

𝓇 𝓇 𝓇

Suggestions for Discussion

1. Find places where the setting, particularly of roadways, reflects Ray's sense of being connected to or alienated from the community.

2. Where is weather used in a similar way?

Retrospect

3. How is Ray's small step toward change externalized in an action?

4. How could the story be described in terms of making and breaking connections?

𝓇

This Is What It Means To Say Phoenix, Arizona

SHERMAN ALEXIE

Just after Victor lost his job at the BIA, he also found out that his father had died of a heart attack in Phoenix, Arizona. Victor hadn't seen his father in a few years, only talked to him on the telephone once or twice, but there still was a genetic pain, which was soon to be pain as real and immediate as a broken bone.

Victor didn't have any money. Who does have money on a reservation, except the cigarette and fireworks salespeople? His father had a savings account waiting to be claimed, but Victor needed to find a way to get to Phoenix. Victor's mother was just as poor as he was, and the rest of his family didn't have any use at all for him. So Victor called the Tribal Council.

"Listen," Victor said. "My father just died. I need some money to get to Phoenix to make arrangements."

"Now, Victor," the council said. "You know we're having a difficult time financially."

"But I thought the council had special funds set aside for stuff like this."

"Now, Victor, we have some money available for the proper return of tribal members' bodies. But I don't think we have enough to bring your father all the way back from Phoenix."

"Well," Victor said. "It ain't going to cost all that much. He had to be cremated. Things were kind of ugly. He died of a heart attack in his trailer and nobody found him for a week. It was really hot, too. You get the picture."

"Now, Victor, we're sorry for your loss and the circumstances. But we can really only afford to give you one hundred dollars."

"That's not even enough for a plane ticket."

"Well, you might consider driving down to Phoenix."

"I don't have a car. Besides, I was going to drive my father's pickup back up here."

"Now, Victor," the council said. "We're sure there is somebody who could drive you to Phoenix. Or is there somebody who could lend you the rest of the money?"

"You know there ain't nobody around with that kind of money."

"Well, we're sorry, Victor, but that's the best we can do."

Victor accepted the Tribal Council's offer. What else could he do? So he signed the proper papers, picked up his check, and walked over to the Trading Post to cash it.

While Victor stood in line, he watched Thomas Builds-the-Fire standing near the magazine rack, talking to himself. Like he always did. Thomas was a storyteller that nobody wanted to listen to. That's like being a dentist in a town where everybody has false teeth.

Victor and Thomas Builds-the-Fire were the same age, had grown up and played in the dirt together. Ever since Victor could remember, it was Thomas who always had something to say.

Once, when they were seven years old, when Victor's father still lived with the family, Thomas closed his eyes and told Victor this story: "Your father's heart is weak. He is afraid of his own family. He is afraid of you. Late at night he sits in the dark. Watches the television until there's nothing but that white noise. Sometimes he feels like he wants to buy a motorcycle and ride away. He wants to run and hide. He doesn't want to be found."

Thomas Builds-the-Fire had known that Victor's father was going to leave, knew it before anyone. Now Victor stood in the Trading Post with a one-hundred-dollar check in his hand, wondering if Thomas knew that Victor's father was dead, if he knew what was going to happen next.

Just then Thomas looked at Victor, smiled, and walked over to him.

"Victor, I'm sorry about your father," Thomas said.

"How did you know about it?" Victor asked.

"I heard it on the wind. I heard it from the birds. I felt it in the sunlight. Also, your mother was just in here crying."

"Oh," Victor said and looked around the Trading Post. All the other Indians stared, surprised that Victor was even talking to Thomas. Nobody talked to Thomas anymore because he told the same damn stories over and over again. Victor was embarrassed, but he thought that Thomas might be able to help him. Victor felt a sudden need for tradition.

"I can lend you the money you need," Thomas said suddenly. "But you have to take me with you."

"I can't take your money," Victor said. "I mean, I haven't hardly talked to you in years. We're not really friends anymore."

"I didn't say we were friends. I said you had to take me with you."

"Let me think about it."

Victor went home with his one hundred dollars and sat at the kitchen table. He held his head in his hands and thought about Thomas Builds-the-Fire, remembered little details, tears and scars, the bicycle they shared for a summer, so many stories.

Thomas Builds-the-Fire sat on the bicycle, waited in Victor's yard. He was ten years old and skinny. His hair was dirty because it was the Fourth of July.

"Victor," Thomas yelled. "Hurry up. We're going to miss the fireworks."

After a few minutes, Victor ran out of his house, jumped the porch railing, and landed gracefully on the sidewalk.

"And the judges award him a 9.95, the highest score of the summer," Thomas said, clapped, laughed.

"That was perfect, cousin," Victor said. "And it's my turn to ride the bike."

Thomas gave up the bike and they headed for the fairgrounds. It was nearly dark and the fireworks were about to start.

"You know," Thomas said. "It's strange how us Indians celebrate the Fourth of July. It ain't like it was *our* independence everybody was fighting for."

"You think about things too much," Victor said. "It's just supposed to be fun. Maybe Junior will be there."

"Which Junior? Everybody on this reservation is named Junior."

And they both laughed.

The fireworks were small, hardly more than a few bottle rockets and a fountain. But it was enough for two Indian boys. Years later, they would need much more.

Afterwards, sitting in the dark, fighting off mosquitoes, Victor turned to Thomas Builds-the-Fire.

"Hey," Victor said. "Tell me a story."

Thomas closed his eyes and told this story: "There were these two Indian boys who wanted to be warriors. But it was too late to be warriors in the old way. All the horses were gone. So the two Indian boys stole a car and drove to the city. They parked the stolen car in front of the police station and then hitchhiked back home to the reservation. When they got back, all their friends cheered and their parents' eyes shone with pride. *You were very brave,* everybody said to the two Indian boys. *Very brave.*"

"Ya-hey," Victor said. "That's a good one. I wish I could be a warrior."

"Me, too." Thomas said.

They went home together in the dark, Thomas on the bike now, Victor on foot. They walked through shadows and light from streetlamps.

"We've come a long ways," Thomas said. "We have outdoor lighting."

"All I need is the stars," Victor said. "And besides, you still think about things too much."

They separated then, each headed for home, both laughing all the way.

Victor sat at his kitchen table. He counted his one hundred dollars again and again. He knew he needed more to make it to Phoenix and back. He knew he needed Thomas Builds-the-Fire. So he put his money in his wallet and opened the front door to find Thomas on the porch.

"Ya-hey, Victor," Thomas said. "I knew you'd call me."

Thomas walked into the living room and sat down on Victor's favorite chair.

"I've got some money saved up," Thomas said. "It's enough to get us down there, but you have to get us back."

"I've got this hundred dollars," Victor said. "And my dad had a savings account I'm going to claim."

"How much in your dad's account?"

"Enough. A few hundred."

"Sounds good. When we leaving?"

When they were fifteen and had long since stopped being friends, Victor and Thomas got into a fistfight. That is, Victor was really drunk and beat Thomas up for no reason at all. All the other Indian boys stood around and watched it happen. Junior was there and so were Lester, Seymour, and a lot of others. The beating might have gone on until Thomas was dead if Norma Many Horses hadn't come along and stopped it.

"Hey, you boys," Norma yelled and jumped out of her car. "Leave him alone."

If it had been someone else, even another man, the Indian boys would've just ignored the warnings. But Norma was a warrior. She was powerful. She could have picked up any two of the boys and smashed their skulls together. But worse than that, she would have dragged them all over to some tipi and made them listen to some elder tell a dusty old story.

The Indian boys scattered, and Norma walked over to Thomas and picked him up.

"Hey, little man, are you okay?" she asked.

Thomas gave her a thumbs up.

"Why they always picking on you?"

Thomas shook his head, closed his eyes, but no stories came to him, no words or music. He just wanted to go home, to lie in his bed and let his dreams tell his stories for him.

Thomas Builds-the-Fire and Victor sat next to each other in the airplane, coach section. A tiny white woman had the window seat. She was busy twisting her body into pretzels. She was flexible.

"I have to ask," Thomas said, and Victor closed his eyes in embarrassment.

"Don't," Victor said.

"Excuse me, miss," Thomas asked. "Are you a gymnast or something?"

"There's no something about it," she said. "I was first alternate on the 1980 Olympic team."

"Really?" Thomas asked.

"Really."

"I mean, you used to be a world-class athlete?" Thomas asked.

"My husband still thinks I am."

Thomas Builds-the-Fire smiled. She was a mental gymnast, too. She pulled her leg straight up against her body so that she could've kissed her kneecap.

"I wish I could do that," Thomas said.

Victor was ready to jump out of the plane. Thomas, that crazy Indian storyteller with ratty old braids and broken teeth, was flirting with a beautiful Olympic gymnast. Nobody back home on the reservation would ever believe it.

"Well," the gymnast said. "It's easy. Try it."

Thomas grabbed at his leg and tried to pull it up into the same position as the gymnast. He couldn't even come close, which made Victor and the gymnast laugh.

"Hey," she asked. "You two are Indian, right?"

"Full-blood," Victor said.

"Not me," Thomas said. "I'm half magician on my mother's side and half clown on my father's."

They all laughed.

"What are your names?" she asked.

"Victor and Thomas."

"Mine is Cathy. Pleased to meet you all."

The three of them talked for the duration of the flight. Cathy the gymnast complained about the government, how they screwed the 1980 Olympic team by boycotting.

"Sounds like you all got a lot in common with Indians," Thomas said.

Nobody laughed.

After the plane landed in Phoenix and they had all found their way to the terminal, Cathy the gymnast smiled and waved good-bye.

"She was really nice," Thomas said.

"Yeah, but everybody talks to everybody on airplanes," Victor said. "It's too bad we can't always be that way."

"You always used to tell me I think too much," Thomas said. "Now it sounds like you do."

"Maybe I caught it from you."

"Yeah."

Thomas and Victor rode in a taxi to the trailer where Victor's father died.

"Listen," Victor said as they stopped in front of the trailer. "I never told you I was sorry for beating you up that time."

"Oh, it was nothing. We were just kids and you were drunk."

"Yeah, but I'm still sorry."

"That's all right."

Victor paid for the taxi and the two of them stood in the hot Phoenix summer. They could smell the trailer.

"This ain't going to be nice," Victor said. "You don't have to go in."

"You're going to need help."

Victor walked to the front door and opened it. The stink rolled out and made them both gag. Victor's father had lain in that trailer for a week in hundred-degree temperatures before anyone found him. And the only reason anyone found him was because of the smell. They needed dental records to identify him. That's exactly what the coroner said. They needed dental records.

"Oh, man," Victor said. "I don't know if I can do this."

"Well, then don't."

"But there might be something valuable in there."

"I thought his money was in the bank."

"It is. I was talking about pictures and letters and stuff like that."

"Oh," Thomas said as he held his breath and followed Victor into the trailer.

When Victor was twelve, he stepped into an underground wasp nest. His foot was caught in the hole, and no matter how hard he struggled, Victor couldn't pull free. He might have died there, stung a thousand times, if Thomas Builds-the-Fire had not come by.

"Run," Thomas yelled and pulled Victor's foot from the hole. They ran then, hard as they ever had, faster than Billy Mills, faster than Jim Thorpe, faster than the wasps could fly.

Victor and Thomas ran until they couldn't breathe, ran until it was cold and dark outside, ran until they were lost and it took hours to find their way home. All the way back, Victor counted his stings.

"Seven," Victor said. "My lucky number."

Victor didn't find much to keep in the trailer. Only a photo album and a stereo. Everything else had that smell stuck in it or was useless anyway.

"I guess this is all," Victor said. "It ain't much."

"Better than nothing," Thomas said.

"Yeah, and I do have the pickup."

"Yeah," Thomas said. "It's in good shape."

"Dad was good about that stuff."

"Yeah, I remember your dad."

"Really?" Victor asked. "What do you remember?"

Thomas Builds-the-Fire closed his eyes and told this story: "I remember when I had this dream that told me to go to Spokane, to stand by the Falls in the middle of the city and wait for a sign. I knew I had to go there but I didn't have a car. Didn't have a license. I was only thirteen. So I walked all the way, took me all day, and I finally made it to the Falls. I stood there for an hour waiting. Then your dad came walking up. *What the hell are you doing here?* he asked me. I said, *Waiting for a vision.* Then your father said, *All you're going to get here is mugged.* So he drove me over to Denny's, bought me dinner, and then drove me home to the reservation. For a long time I was mad because I thought my dreams had lied to me. But they didn't. Your dad was my vision. *Take care of each other* is what my dreams were saying. *Take care of each other.*"

Victor was quiet for a long time. He searched his mind for memories of his father, found the good ones, found a few bad ones, added it all up, and smiled.

"My father never told me about finding you in Spokane," Victor said.

"He said he wouldn't tell anybody. Didn't want me to get in trouble. But he said I had to watch out for you as part of the deal."

"Really?"

"Really. Your father said you would need the help. He was right."

"That's why you came down here with me, isn't it?" Victor asked.

"I came because of your father."

Victor and Thomas climbed into the pickup, drove over to the bank, and claimed the three hundred dollars in the savings account.

Thomas Builds-the-Fire could fly.

Once, he jumped off the roof of the tribal school and flapped his arms like a crazy eagle. And he flew. For a second, he hovered, suspended above all the other Indian boys who were too smart or too scared to jump.

"He's flying," Junior yelled, and Seymour was busy looking for the trick wires or mirrors. But it was real. As real as the dirt when Thomas lost altitude and crashed to the ground.

He broke his arm in two places.

"He broke his wing," Victor chanted, and the other Indian boys joined in, made it a tribal song.

"He broke his wing, he broke his wing, he broke his wing," all the Indian boys chanted as they ran off, flapping their wings, wishing they could fly, too. They hated Thomas for his courage, his brief moment as a bird. Everybody has dreams about flying. Thomas flew.

One of his dreams came true for just a second, just enough to make it real.

Victor's father, his ashes, fit in one wooden box with enough left over to fill a cardboard box.

"He always was a big man," Thomas said.

Victor carried part of his father and Thomas carried the rest out to the pickup. They set him down carefully behind the seats, put a cowboy hat on the wooden box and a Dodgers cap on the cardboard box. That's the way it was supposed to be.

"Ready to head back home," Victor asked.

"It's going to be a long drive."

"Yeah, take a couple days, maybe."

"We can take turns," Thomas said.

"Okay," Victor said, but they didn't take turns. Victor drove for sixteen hours straight north, made it halfway up Nevada toward home before he finally pulled over.

"Hey, Thomas," Victor said. "You got to drive for a while."

"Okay."

Thomas Builds-the-Fire slid behind the wheel and started off down the road. All through Nevada, Thomas and Victor had been amazed at the lack of animal life, at the absence of water, of movement.

"Where is everything?" Victor had asked more than once.

Now when Thomas was finally driving they saw the first animal, maybe the only animal in Nevada. It was a long-eared jackrabbit.

"Look," Victor yelled. "It's alive."

Thomas and Victor were busy congratulating themselves on their discovery when the jackrabbit darted out into the road and under the wheels of the pickup.

"Stop the goddamn car," Victor yelled, and Thomas did stop, backed the pickup to the dead jackrabbit.

"Oh, man, he's dead," Victor said as he looked at the squashed animal.

"Really dead."

"The only thing alive in this whole state and we just killed it."

"I don't know," Thomas said. "I think it was suicide."

Victor looked around the desert, sniffed the air, felt the emptiness and loneliness, and nodded his head.

"Yeah," Victor said. "It had to be suicide."

"I can't believe this," Thomas said. "You drive for a thousand miles and there ain't even any bugs smashed on the windshield. I drive for ten seconds and kill the only living thing in Nevada."

"Yeah," Victor said. "Maybe I should drive."

"Maybe you should."

Thomas Builds-the-Fire walked through the corridors of the tribal school by himself. Nobody wanted to be anywhere near him because of all those stories. Story after story.

Thomas closed his eyes and this story came to him: "We are all given one thing by which our lives are measured, one determination. Mine are the stories which can change or not change the world. It doesn't matter which as long as I continue to tell the stories. My father, he died on Okinawa in World War II, died fighting for this country, which had tried to kill him for years. My mother, she died giving birth to me, died while I was still inside her. She pushed me out into the world with her last breath. I have no brothers or sisters. I have only my stories which came to me before I even had the words to speak. I learned a thousand stories before I took my first thousand steps. They are all I have. It's all I can do."

Thomas Builds-the-Fire told his stories to all those who would stop and listen. He kept telling them after people had stopped listening.

Victor and Thomas made it back to the reservation just as the sun was rising. It was the beginning of a new day on earth, but the same old shit on the reservation.

"Good morning," Thomas said.

"Good morning."

The tribe was waking up, ready for work, eating breakfast, reading the newspaper, just like everybody else does. Willene LeBret was out in her garden wearing a bathrobe. She waved when Thomas and Victor drove by.

"Crazy Indians made it," she said to herself and went back to her roses.

Victor stopped the pickup in front of Thomas Builds-the-Fire's HUD house. They both yawned, stretched a little, shook dust from their bodies.

"I'm tired," Victor said.

"Of everything," Thomas added.

They both searched for words to end the journey. Victor needed to thank Thomas for his help, for the money, and make the promise to pay it all back.

"Don't worry about the money," Thomas said. "It don't make any difference anyhow."

"Probably not, enit?"

"Nope."

Victor knew that Thomas would remain the crazy storyteller who talked to dogs and cars, who listened to the wind and pine trees. Victor knew that he couldn't really be friends with Thomas, even after all that had happened. It was cruel but it was real. As real as the ashes, as Victor's father, sitting behind the seats.

"I know how it is," Thomas said. "I know you ain't going to treat me any better than you did before. I know your friends would give you too much shit about it."

Victor was ashamed of himself. Whatever happened to the tribal ties, the sense of community? The only real thing he shared with anybody was a bottle and broken dreams. He owed Thomas something, anything.

"Listen," Victor said and handed Thomas the cardboard box which contained half of his father. "I want you to have this."

Thomas took the ashes and smiled, closed his eyes, and told this story: "I'm going to travel to Spokane Falls one last time and toss these ashes into the water. And your father will rise like a salmon, leap over the bridge, over me, and find his way home. It will be beautiful. His teeth will shine like silver, like a rainbow. He will rise, Victor, he will rise."

Victor smiled.

"I was planning on doing the same thing with my half," Victor said. "But I didn't imagine my father looking anything like a salmon. I thought it'd be like cleaning the attic or something. Like letting things go after they've stopped having any use."

"Nothing stops, cousin," Thomas said. "Nothing stops."

Thomas Builds-the-Fire got out of the pickup and walked up his driveway. Victor started the pickup and began the drive home.

"Wait," Thomas yelled suddenly from his porch. "I just got to ask one favor."

Victor stopped the pickup, leaned out the window, and shouted back. "What do you want?"

"Just one time when I'm telling a story somewhere, why don't you stop and listen?" Thomas asked.

"Just once?"

"Just once."

Victor waved his arms to let Thomas know that the deal was good. It was a fair trade, and that was all Victor had ever wanted from his whole life. So Victor drove his father's pickup toward home while Thomas went into his house, closed the door behind him, and heard a new story come to him in the silence afterwards.

🝆 🝆 🝆

Suggestions for Discussion

1. Comment upon a line that seems to reflect a central theme of the story.

2. How does the author use setting, and in particular the Spokane Falls, to help illuminate the story's meaning?

3. Near the story's end, Thomas twice says, "Nothing stops." How does this line of dialogue help reveal the story's theme?

Retrospect

4. What do you find effective—or not—in the way flashbacks are dispersed throughout the story? Can you think of an alternative way to present the background? How would that approach change the story?

5. How is the past felt in the present?

🝆 🝆 🝆

Writing Exercises

INDIVIDUAL

1. As soon as you wake up, make notes about a dream you recall: events; specific images; lines of dialogue. What seemed to be the main concern or theme of the dream? How does each element in some way relate to the main concern?

2. Identify the belief you hold most passionately and profoundly. Write a short story that explores an instance in which this belief is untrue.

3. Write a short story that you have wanted to write all term and have not written because you knew it was too big for you and you would fail. You may fail. Write it anyway.

DEVELOPMENT/REVISION

4. Go through the draft of a story-in-progress, highlighting the images used. Which images have more significance than you first realized? Which of these images resonate with the story's emerging theme?

11

PLAY IT AGAIN, SAM
Revision

- *Re-Vision*

- *Worry It and Walk Away*

- *Criticism and the Story Workshop*

- *Revision Questions*

- *Further Suggestions for Revision*

- *Examples of the Revision Process*

"Talent is a long patience," Anton Chekhov remarked, an acknowledgment that the creative process is not all inventive, and extends far beyond the first heated rush. Partly corrective, critical, nutritive, and fostering, revision is a matter of rendering a story the best that it can be. William C. Knott, in *The Craft of Fiction*, cogently observes that "anyone can write—and almost everyone you meet these days is writing. However, only the writers know how to rewrite. It is this ability alone that turns the amateur into a pro."

While the focus of this chapter is the overall revision of stories and the best use of readers' feedback, the methods of shaping, enriching, and enlivening stories discussed throughout this book implicitly concern the revision of fiction, element by element. We have already visited the process of revision through the discussion of the story workshop in the Preface (a discussion that will continue here); the Development/Revision exercises at the end of most chapters; the chapter 5 review "Character: A Summary"; and in the chapter 6 sections "Revising Summary and Scene" and "Further Thoughts on Openings and Endings." The preceding chapter on theme invites you to seek the true subject of your story-in-progress, and to direct your revision work toward exploring that understanding.

Re-Vision

Revising is a process more dreaded than dreadful. The resistance to rewriting is, if anything, greater than the resistance to beginning in the first place. Yet the chances are that once you have committed yourself to a first draft, you'll be unable to leave it in an unfinished and unsatisfying state. You'll be *unhappy* until it's right. Making it right will involve a second commitment, to seeing the story fresh and creating it again with the advantage of this "re-vision." Alice Munro, in the introduction to her *Selected Stories*, describes the risk, the readiness, and the reward.

> . . . The story, in the first draft, has put on rough but adequate clothes, it is "finished" and might be thought to need no more than a lot of technical adjustments, some tightening here and expanding there, and the slipping in of some telling dialogue and chopping away of flabby modifiers. It's then, in fact, that the story is in the greatest danger of losing its life, of appearing so hopelessly misbegotten that my only relief comes from abandoning it. It doesn't do enough. It does what I intended, but it turns out that my intention was all wrong. . . . I go around glum and preoccupied, trying to think of ways to fix the problem. Usually the right way pops up in the middle of this.
>
> A big relief. Renewed energy. Resurrection.
>
> Except that it isn't the right way. Maybe a way *to* the right way. Now I write pages and pages I'll have to discard. New angles are introduced, minor characters brought center stage, lively and satisfying scenes are written, and it's all a mistake. Out they go. But by this time I'm on the track, there's no backing out. I know so much more than I did, I know what I want to happen and where I want to end up and I just have to keep trying till I find the best way of getting there.

To find the best way of getting there, you may have to "see again" more than once. The process of revision involves external and internal insight; you'll need your conscious critic, your creative instinct, and readers you trust. You may need each of them several times, not necessarily in that order. A story gets better not just by polishing and refurbishing, not by improving a word choice here and an image there, but by taking risks with the structure, reenvisioning, being open to new meaning itself. "In the first draft is the talent," said French poet Paul Valery, "in the second is the art."

Worry It and Walk Away

To write your first draft, you banished the internal critic. Now make the critic welcome. Revision is work, but the strange thing is that you may find you can concentrate on the work for much longer than you could play at freedrafting. It has occurred to me that writing a first draft is very like tennis or softball—I have to be psyched for it. Energy level up, alert, on my toes. A few hours is all I can manage, and at the end of it I'm wiped out. Revision is like careful carpentry, and if I'm under a deadline or just determined to get this thing crafted and polished, I can be good for twelve hours of it.

The first round of rewrites is probably a matter of letting your misgivings surface. Focus for a while on what seems awkward, overlong, undeveloped, flat, or flowery. Tinker. Tighten. Sharpen. More important at this stage than finishing any given page or phrase is that you're getting to know your story in order to open it to new possibilities. You will also get tired of it; you may feel stuck.

Then put it away. Don't look at it for a matter of days or weeks—until you feel fresh on the project. In addition to getting some distance on your story, you're mailing it to your unconscious, not consciously working out the flaws but temporarily letting them go. Rollo May, in *The Courage to Create*, describes what frequently happens next:

> Everyone uses from time to time such expressions as, "a thought pops up," an
> idea comes "from the blue" or "dawns" or "comes as though out of a dream," or
> "it suddenly hit me." These are various ways of describing a common experience:
> the breakthrough of ideas from some depth below the level of awareness.

It is my experience that such realizations occur over and over again in the course of writing a short story or novel. Often I will believe that because I know who my characters are and what happens to them, I know what my story is about—and often I find I'm wrong, or that my understanding is shallow or incomplete.

In the first draft of a recent novel, for instance, I opened with the sentence, "It took a hundred and twelve bottles of champagne to see the young Poindexters off to Arizona." A page later one character whispered to another that the young Mr. Poindexter in question had "consumption." I worked on this book for a year (taking my characters off to Arizona where they dealt with the desert heat, lack of water, alcoholism, loss of religion, and the development of mining interests and the building trade) before I saw the connection between "consumption" and "champagne."

. . . the first impulse in writing is to flood it out, let as much run freely as you possibly can. Then to take a walk or go to the bank . . . and come back in a day or six months later. To read it with a cold eye and say, "This is good. This is not. That sentence works. This is magical. This is crummy." You have to maintain your critical sensibility and not just assume, because it was an extraordinary dream for you, that it will be a dream for other people. Because people need maps to your dreams.

Alan Gurganus

When I understood that simple link, I understood the overarching theme—surely latent in the idea from the moment it had taken hold of me—between tuberculosis, spiritual thirst, consumerism, and addiction, all issues of "consumption."

It might seem dismaying that you should see what your story is about only after you have written it. Try it; you'll like it. Nothing is more exhilarating than the discovery that a complex pattern has lain in your mind ready to unfold.

Note that in the early stages of revision, both the worrying and the walking away are necessary. Perhaps it is bafflement itself that plunges us to the unconscious space where the answer lies.

Criticism and the Story Workshop

Once you have thought your story through, drafted it, and worked on it to the best of your ability, someone else's eyes can help to refresh the vision of your own. Wise professionals rely on the help of an agent or editor at this juncture (although even the wisest still smart at censure); anyone can rely on the help of friends, family, or classmates in a story workshop. The trick to making good use of criticism is to be utterly selfish about it. Be greedy for it. Take it all in. Ultimately you are the laborer, the arbiter, and the boss in any dispute about your story, so you can afford to consider any problem and any solution. Most of us feel not only committed to what we have put on the page, but also defensive on its behalf—wanting, really, to be told only that it is a work of genius or, failing that, to find out that we have gotten away with it. Therefore, the first exigency of revision is that you learn to hear, absorb, and accept criticism.

"Revising is like cutting your own hair," says novelist Robert Stone, for while you may sense the need for improvement, it's hard to get right what you can never entirely see for yourself. This is the major advantage of a workshop—your fellow writers may not be able to tell you how to style the material in the way that best suits the story, but they can at least hold up the mirror and see from a more distanced per-

... you generally start out with some overall idea that you can see fairly clearly, as if you were standing on a dock and looking at a ship on the ocean. At first you can see the entire ship, but then as you begin work you're in the boiler room and you can't see the ship anymore. . . . What you really want in an editor is someone who's still on the dock, who can say, Hi, I'm looking at your ship, and it's missing a bow, the front mast is crooked, and it looks to me as if your propellers are going to have to be fixed.

Michael Crichton

spective. (If you are just beginning the practice of group critiques, you may wish to look back at the description of common workshop procedures in the preface.)

How to assimilate so many opinions, let alone choose what is useful? First, give special consideration to the comments of those two or three workshop members with whose responses you have generally agreed before. However, the best—or at any rate the most useful—criticism, John L'Heureux suggests, simply points out what you had already sensed for yourself but had hoped to get away with. Or as Flannery O'Connor put it, with typical bluntness, in fiction "you can do anything you can get away with, but nobody has ever gotten away with much."

It used to be popular to speak of "constructive criticism" and "destructive criticism," but these are misleading terms suggesting that positive suggestions are useful and negative criticism useless. In practice the opposite is usually the case. You're likely to find that the most constructive thing a reader can do is say *I don't believe this, I don't like this, I don't understand this,* pointing to precisely the passages that made you uneasy. This kind of laying-the-finger-on-the-trouble-spot produces an inward groan, but it's also satisfying; you know just where to go to work. Often the most destructive thing a reader can do is offer you a positive suggestion—*Why don't you have him crash the car?*—that is irrelevant to your vision of the story. Be suspicious of praise that is too extravagant, of blame that is too general. If your impulse is to defend the story or yourself, still the impulse. Behave as if bad advice were good advice, and give it serious consideration. You can reject it after you have explored it for anything of use it may offer.

Workshop members often voice sharply divided responses to a manuscript, a situation that may confuse and frustrate the author. Algonquin Books of Chapel Hill editor Duncan Murrell advises workshop writers "to pay close attention to the parts of their work that make readers stumble, but to disregard most of the solutions those readers suggest. Give a flawed story to ten good readers and they'll accurately find the flawed passages before offering ten wildly varying explanations and a handful of contradictory solutions. Good readers have a gut level understanding that something's wrong in a story, but they're often unclear about what it is, or what to do about it. Yet once pointed to the weak sections, authors almost always come up with better solutions than anything a reader or an editor can offer; they know the story and the characters better. The trick is to bite your lip when readers tell you how to fix your story, while noting the passages that need repair."

Indeed, while the author may or may not benefit from peer suggestions, everyone else in the workshop does, for the practice of thinking through and articulating responses to a story's challenges eventually makes all participants more objective critics of their own work. You will notice that the more specific the criticism you offer—or receive—the more useful it proves and the less it stings; similarly, the more specific the praise of "what works," the more likely it is to reinforce good habits—and to be believed. After a semester's experience of workshopping, you'll find that you can critique a story within your own imagination, knowing who would say what, with whom you would agree, and telling yourself what you already know to be true.

Within a day or two of the workshop, novelist, playwright, and teacher Michelle Carter advises that the author try to "re-hear criticism," that is, to assess what it is readers are responding to, which may not be apparent from the suggested "fix." For example, if a number of readers suggest changing the story's point of view from third person to first, Carter might reinterpret that to mean that the narrator seems overly remote from the characters—not that first-person narration is literally a better choice, but that readers want a more immediate experience of the main character's emotional dilemma.

A second example would be wanting "to know more about Character X." This doesn't necessarily mean sprinkling on some facts and history; rather the reader may be desiring a greater understanding of the character's motivations or a closer rendering of crucial moments.

Additionally, Carter cautions, be tough with yourself, even when you realize that criticism is based on a misreading. Rarely is misinterpretation solely the mistake of the reader: ask what awkwardness of writing or false emphasis might have led to that skewed reading. Novelist Wally Lamb reinforces this point: "Often I think we let the writer get away with too much. If the writing is unclear, we'll read it a second time and make it clear to ourselves and then let the writer off the hook, when, in fact, the writing has to stand for itself . . .You want to work on the writing until it is good enough that the writer doesn't have to be in the room explaining and interpreting."

Kenneth Atchity, in *A Writer's Time*, advises compulsory "vacations" at crucial points in the revising process, in order to let the criticism cook until you feel ready, impatient, to get back to writing. So once again, walk away, and when you feel that you have acquired enough distance from the story to see it anew, go back to work. Make notes of your plans, large and small. Talk to yourself in your journal about what you want to accomplish and where you think you have failed. Let your imagination play with new images or passages of dialogue. Always keep a copy (and/or a document on disk) of the story as it is so that you can go back to the original, and then be ruthless with another copy. Eudora Welty advised cutting sections apart and

---

. . . the writing workshop finally is the one place where you can be sure you and your work are taken seriously, where your writing intentions are honored, where even in a mean-spirited comment you can divine—if you wish—the truth about your writing, its strengths and its weaknesses. It is a place where you are surrounded by people whose chief interest is also yours, where the talk is never anything but writing and writing well and writing better. . . . It is where you somehow pick up the notion that what you're doing is a good and noble thing, and though you may not write as well as you'd like, it is enough and will suffice.

John L'Heureux

pinning them back together so that they can be easily rearranged. I like to take the whole surface of the kitchen table as a cut-and-paste board. Some people can keep the story in their heads and do their rearranging directly onto the computer screen—which in any case has made the putting-back-together process less tedious than retyping.

Revision Questions

As you plan the revision and as you rewrite, you will know (and your critics will tell you) what problems are unique to your story. There are also general, almost universal, pitfalls that you can avoid if you ask yourself the following questions:

What is my story about? Another way of saying this is *What is the pattern of change?* Once this pattern is clear, you can check your draft to make sure you've included all the crucial moments of discovery and decision. Is there a crisis action?

Is there unnecessary summary? Remember that it is a common impulse to try to cover too much ground. Tell your story in the fewest possible scenes; cut down on summary and unnecessary flashback. These dissipate energy and lead you to tell rather than show.

Why should the reader turn from the first page to the second? Is the language fresh? Are the characters alive? Does the first sentence, paragraph, page introduce real tension? If it doesn't, you have probably begun at the wrong place. If you are unable to find a way to introduce tension on the first page, you may have to doubt whether you have a story after all.

Is it original? Almost every writer thinks first, in some way or other, of the familiar, the usual, the given. This character is a stereotype, that emotion is too easy, that phrase is a cliché. First-draft laziness is inevitable, but it is also a way of being dishonest. A good writer will comb the work for clichés and labor to find the exact, the honest, and the fresh.

Is it clear? Although ambiguity and mystery provide some of our most profound pleasures in literature, beginning writers are often unable to distinguish between mystery and muddle, ambiguity and sloppiness. You may want your character to be rich with contradiction, but we still want to know whether that character is male or female, black or white, old or young. We need to be oriented on the simplest level of reality before we can share your imaginative world. Where are we? When are we? Who are they? How do things look? What time of day or night is it? What's the weather? What's happening?

Is it self-conscious? Probably the most famous piece of advice to the rewriter is William Faulkner's "kill all your darlings." When you are carried away with the purple of your prose, the music of your alliteration, the hilarity of your wit, the profundity of your insights, then the chances are that you are having a better time writing than the reader will have reading. No reader will forgive you, and no reader should. Just tell the story. The style will follow of itself if you just tell the story.

Where is it too long? Most of us, and even the best of us, write too long. We are so anxious to explain every nuance, cover every possible aspect of character, action, and setting that we forget the necessity of stringent selection. In fiction, and especially in the short story, we want sharpness, economy, and vivid, telling detail. More than necessary is too much. I have been helped in my own tendency to tell all by a friend who went through a copy of one of my novels, drawing a line through the last sentence of about every third paragraph. Then in the margin he wrote, again and again, "Hit it, and get out." That's good advice for anyone.

Where is it undeveloped in character, action, imagery, theme? In any first, second, or third draft of a manuscript there are likely to be necessary passages sketched, skipped, or skeletal. What information is missing, what actions are incomplete, what motives obscure, what images inexact? Where does the action occur too abruptly so that it loses its emotional force? Is the crisis presented as a scene?

Where is it too general? Originality, economy, and clarity can all be achieved through the judicious use of significant detail. Learn to spot general, vague, and fuzzy terms. Be suspicious of yourself anytime you see nouns like *someone* and *everything*, adjectives like *huge* and *handsome*, adverbs like *very* and *really*. Seek instead a particular thing, a particular size, an exact degree.

Although the dread of "starting over" is a real and understandable one, the chances are that the rewards of revising will startlingly outweigh the pains. Sometimes a character who is dead on the page will come to life through the addition of a few sentences or significant details. Sometimes a turgid or tedious paragraph can become sharp with a few judicious cuts. Sometimes dropping page one and putting page seven where page three used to be can provide the skeleton of an otherwise limp story. And sometimes, often, perhaps always, the difference between an amateur rough-cut and a publishable story is in the struggle at the rewriting stage.

Further Suggestions for Revision

- If you have been writing your story on a computer, retype at least one full draft, making both planned and spontaneous changes as you go. The computer's abilities can tempt us to a "fix-it" approach to revision, but jumping in and out of the text to correct problems can result in a revision that reads like patchwork. Rather, the effect of even small changes should ripple through the story, and this is more likely to happen if the writer reenters the story as a whole by literally re-writing it from start to finish.

- Screenwriter Stephen Fischer emphasizes that "writing is not a monolithic process, just as cooking is not a monolithic process. You don't just go in the kitchen and cook—you do a number of very specific things that you focus on one at a time—you peel garlic, you dice garlic, you saute onions—these are separate processes. You don't go into a kitchen and flap your arms and just cook—and in the same way, you don't 'just write.'"

  To put this analogy into practice: Write two or three revisions of a story draft, focusing on a different issue each time. For example, you might zero in on the motivations of a character whose behavior and dialogue don't yet ring true; or you might simply focus on using setting to reflect emotion or threading physical activity through dialogue scenes. Focusing on a single goal lets you concentrate your efforts—yet other developments will naturally occur in response to the single-focus changes.

- In an interview in *Conversations on Writing Fiction,* novelist and teacher Jane Smiley says she asks her student writers to confront their own sets of "evasions," the counterproductive "rituals which don't actually allow them to spend time with or become engaged with their chosen themes or characters." For example, many people find conflict hard to handle in real life and therefore avoid it, often for good reason. Yet many of us sidestep conflict in our fiction too, even knowing its necessity in driving a character toward a defining crisis. If this sounds like an evasion you've experienced, take a look back at places in the story where explosive scenes *should* happen—places where characters ought to confront or defend. Are these, in fact, all-out scenes? Or do your characters neatly sidestep the conflict and retreat to their private thoughts? Does another character too conveniently knock at the door?

  Taking refuge in the making of metaphors, however vivid, rather than clearly depicting what *is,* may be another form of evasion, perhaps reflecting a writer's lack of confidence in the interest of his or her material.

  Spiraling off into the weird and random may reflect a similar lack of confidence or indecision; overly clever, bantering dialogue that strains to entertain may reflect a desire to dazzle, while avoiding the harder search for dialogue that is both realistic and revealing.

  Evasions may be easier to observe in others' work at first, so you might want to ask a trusted workshop friend to help you recognize the evasions in your own stories. As you revise and encounter points of resistance—those places you hesitate to go further or become more specific—ask yourself, Is this right for the story or is it simply my comfortable habit?

Examples of the Revision Process

When reading a polished, published story, it can be difficult to imagine that it once was any other way—difficult to realize that the author made both choices and unplanned connections, difficult to envision the story's history. After all, by the point of publication the writer has likely heeded critic Annie Dillard's admonition: "Process is nothing; erase your tracks. The path is not the work."

Yet a glimpse of these earlier "tracks" may reveal the paths writers forged to final versions of their stories, and this may in turn inspire you to a more thorough reenvisioning of your own work. What follow are authors' accounts of the revision process of some of the stories that appear in this text.

"Dark Corner" (Robert Morgan): This story grew out of a sliver of family rumor. The gossip was that one of my great-aunts by marriage had been taken to Texas as a girl. After her family lost everything there they returned to the mountains of North Carolina on foot. It was supposedly her husband who said, "I'm glad nobody here knows I married one of those girls that came walking through here from Texas." I barely knew the great-aunt and made up the story and her voice from that splinter of an idea. I tried to make the world of upper South Carolina as real as I could.

Two things added in revising "Dark Corner" were the viciousness of the policeman at the train station in Greenville, and the kindness of the bootlegger, Zander Gosnell, in Chestnut Springs. I knew the cruelty of the policeman would deepen the drama. I wanted to show how he enjoys humiliating the helpless family, and how powerless they are to respond. It was a surprise to me that the family would be helped later in the story by the very people they feared most, the moonshiners and whores of Dark Corner. But once I got the idea I saw the truth and significance of it. Those outside the law themselves are more apt to help those in desperate trouble who are also beyond the protection of the law and middle class manners. One of the real pleasures of writing fiction is such surprise and discovery in the process of revision, to see further and deeper, to learn more as the story unfolds, to see the story grow bigger with the addition of just a few details, until the story falls in place and seems inevitable. And you can't believe you hadn't planned it that way from the beginning.

"Wave" (John Holman): One rainy evening when my wife and I were newly married, we found a man sprawled and crying in a hard-to-get-to path beside our house. We were afraid of and for him. Months later I saw him walking by the house during the day. He didn't seem to recognize me and I never saw him again. Years later, along the route I drove my son to school, we passed a man who waved at everybody from his porch. He seemed desperate somehow.

In writing the story, the relationship of Alma and Ray was there from the start, as was Ray's job. I had been working on ways to describe their friendship. But I had also wanted to do the waving man as someone Ray always encountered on his way to work . . . I must have thought of the sad man at the same time as I thought of a way to bring Alma into the story—a way to focus on Ray's life away from work, his longing for Alma. The weather is rainy because my real encounter with the man in my yard was on a rainy night. But I saw that I could use it all the way through to affect mood, and to create images—auditory and visual. It turned out that the opposing moods of the waving man and the sad man helped me to understand Ray and to describe his dilemma concerning Alma.

"The Comedian" (John L'Heureux): Watching a lot of late-night television, I had become fascinated by stand-up comics: delivery, tone, values implicit in that tone, the things they thought were funny. I talked about this to everybody. One day a friend told me her sister-in-law was a stand-up comic who retired because she got pregnant. Bummer, she said.

I shut my office door and within an hour I wrote parts 1 and 3 of "The Comedian." I always mistrust anything easy so I put the story aside for six months; nonetheless, when I returned to it, I finished it in a week. The rewriting was just a matter of getting the comic bits to seem less flat. I sent it to a famous New York magazine that kept it three months and finally said they'd publish it with just one revision: they wanted me to remove the transcendence at the end and "leave Corinne just lying there, pondering the light and the music, thinking this isn't so bad."

I always listen to advice, especially about revision, but I knew this was wrong, dead wrong. I was lucky. *The Atlantic* took the story without any revisions at all.

"The Visible Man" (Elizabeth Stuckey-French): Early drafts of the story were bloated with flashbacks—mostly backstory about Max and Althea. I described how they met and how he proposed (on a Ferris Wheel) and included several scenes of them together. I also had Althea think about Max throughout the story and even, at times, hear his voice telling her what to do. Gradually I realized (why does it always take so long?) that the real focus of the story was the friendship between Rona and Althea, and all the stuff about Max, even though Althea misses him very much, slowed the story down and made the present conflict between the two women less intense. (My friend Mary Helen Stefaniak, when writing a short story, pictures a highway worker waving her on. Keep it moving!) The only surviving flashback is Max and Althea dancing above the Arthur Murray Studio. I must say, however, that even though I ended up tossing most of the backstory out, writing it really helped me get to know Althea better.

In earlier drafts of the story I couldn't get past the seance scene. My husband suggested that maybe Seth should come in and interrupt them, and he was, as usual, absolutely right. I wanted Althea, by the end, to be the one in charge, and I wanted her to be physically active. After writing and rejecting many endings, it came to me that having her "teach" Rona how to dance was a good way to show how she'd changed and how their roles had been reversed.

"Screentime" (Stephen Jones): I wrote "Screentime" one afternoon in 1997. It's my Pop-Up Video story, a direct result of VH1's little wet bubbles telling me that the video for "Night Moves" was shot in southern California, a place not wholly real for me, or not real in the way Texas is at least, home. So I moved it all over to this little town called Bronte, just outside San Angelo, where I'd stood in the back of the auditorium once, watching one of my cousins graduate high school. There had been music (Garth Brooks) and roses (hand-delivered) and I instantly became sad I hadn't lived there. Which is to say nostalgic for something that never was. That main guy in "Screentime," more or less.

As for how the story's told—flashing forward, catching up, all that—I've just always thought those were the most effective scenes, jumping from high point to high point across time, never getting bogged down in the boring stuff—how we're supposed to get from A to E. Anyway, if you can disorder the sequence some and still retain a sense of causality, you can delay all the "meaning" until the end. Sometimes. Which is what it's all about for me: trying to sum everything up in five oblique words, exit with a little grace before anybody even knew you were eyeing the door. It's the difference between craft and art—between asking yourself what *should* come next, and what *does*. Every once in a while you stumble upon something that "does." The rest of the time you just limp along.

In her book-length essay "The Writing Life," Annie Dillard uses the metaphor of knocking out "a bearing wall" for the revising writer's sacrifice of the very aspect of the story that inspired its writing. Strange as it sounds, this is an experience familiar to many accomplished writers: "The part you must jettison," says Dillard, "is not only the best-written part; it is also, oddly, that part which was to have been the very point. It is the original key passage, the passage on which the rest was to hang, and from which you yourself drew the courage to begin."

Joyce Carol Oates describes this phenomenon—and more—in her essay "Smooth Talk: Short Story into Film." Readers of "Where Are You Going, Where Have You Been?", one of the most famous American stories of the late twentieth century, may be surprised to learn that the author's initial impulse to write the story disappeared in the drafting process. Recounts Oates:

Some years ago in the American Southwest, there surfaced a tabloid psychopath known as "The Pied Piper of Tucson." I have forgotten his name, but his specialty was the seduction and occasional murder of teen-aged girls. He may or may not have had actual accomplices, but his bizarre activities were known among a circle of teenagers in the Tucson area; for some reason they kept his secret, deliberately did not inform parents or police. It was this fact, not the fact of the mass murderer himself, that struck me at the time. And this was a pre-Manson time, early or mid-1960s.

The Pied Piper mimicked teenagers in their talk, dress, and behavior, but he was not a teenager—he was a man in his early thirties. Rather short, he stuffed rags in his leather boots to give himself height. (And sometimes walked unsteadily as a consequence: did none among his admiring constituency notice?) He charmed his victims as charismatic psychopaths have always charmed their victims, to the bewilderment of others who fancy themselves free of all lunatic attractions. The Pied Piper of Tucson: a trashy dream, a tabloid archetype, sheer artifice, comedy, cartoon—surrounded, however improbably, and finally tragically, by real people. You think that, if you look twice, he won't be there. But there he is.

I don't remember any longer where I first read about this Pied Piper—very likely in *Life* Magazine. I do recall deliberately not reading the full article because I didn't want to be distracted by too much detail. It was not after all the mass murderer himself who intrigued me, but the disturbing fact that a number of teenagers—from "good" families—aided and abetted his crimes. This is the sort of thing authorities and responsible citizens invariably call "inexplicable" because they can't find explanations for it. *They* would not have fallen under this maniac's spell, after all.

An early draft of my short story, "Where Are You Going, Where Have You Been?" —from which the film *Smooth Talk* was adapted by Joyce Chopra and Tom Cole—had the rather too explicit title "Death and the Maiden." It was cast in a mode of fiction to which I am still partial—indeed, every third or fourth story of mine is probably in this mode— "realistic allegory," it might be called. It is Hawthornean, romantic, shading into parable. Like the medieval German engraving from which my title was taken, the story was minutely detailed yet clearly an allegory of the fatal attractions of death (or the devil). An innocent young girl is seduced by way of her own vanity; she mistakes death for erotic romance of a particularly American/trashy sort.

In subsequent drafts the story changed its tone, its focus, its language, its title. It became "Where Are You Going, Where Have You Been?" Written at a time when the author was intrigued by the music of Bob Dylan, particularly the hauntingly elegiac song "It's All Over Now, Baby Blue," it was dedicated to Bob Dylan. The charismatic mass murderer drops into the background and his inno-cent victim, a fifteen-year-old, moves into the foreground. She becomes the true protagonist of the tale, courting and being courted by her fate, a self-styled 1950s pop figure, alternately absurd and winning. There is no suggestion in the pub-lished story that "Arnold Friend" has seduced and murdered other young girls, or even that he necessarily intends to murder Connie. Is his interest "merely" sexual? (Nor is there anything about the complicity of other teenagers. I saved that yet more provocative note for a current story, "Testimony.") Connie is shal-low, vain, silly, hopeful, doomed—but capable nonetheless of an unexpected ges-ture of heroism at the story's end.

Saving the abandoned idea for another story is the point upon which Annie Dil-lard concludes the section of her essay: "So it is that a writer writes many books. In each book, he intended several urgent and vivid points, many of which he sacrificed as the book's form hardened . . . The writer returns to these materials, these passion-ate subjects, as to unfinished business, for they are his life's work."

Dud

PAMELA PAINTER

I've watched it three times and each time I reach the same conclusion: this movie's a dud. It's a dud in spite of the medium-big stars playing network mogul, reporter on the story, mafia patsy, and the TV talking head who spouts the evening's news—the Peter Jennings type. My job's making the trailer. Dark and crowded with expensive equipment, my editing room is plastered with posters of *Casablanca*, *Citizen Kane*, *The Unforgiven*—ghosts more alive than the dud running on my screen. Yesterday the boss pulled his glasses down his nose and said over their tops, Eddie there's a lot riding on this trailer. No market surveys. We're only doing one.

Today I take a hike down the hall to tell the boss what he must have suspected. For the past two days he's been running through the latest new-age western, a movie

John Wayne would have shot dead. The boss hits the pause circuit and nods for me to make it fast.

"It's a dud," I say. I tell him I've pieced together ten prelims for the trailer and it's not coming out sweet.

He pulls his tiny glasses to the end of his nose. "Eddie," he says, "who paid you to be a movie critic?" He says with movies a dud is a dud. It's a luxury big directors and rich studios have—making duds—but we don't have that luxury here he says. There's no way the trailer can be a dud.

"Great logic," I say. "The movie's a dud, but the trailer can't be a dud."

He tells me do a preview that will bring the people to the box office before word gets out, before the *real* critics call it a dud. He pushes his glasses up, already back to work before I've left the screening room.

"Eddie," he says. "Rearrange. Deceive. But if you want to keep your job, don't use the 'dud' word."

I go back to the editing room where the dud is waiting like a corpse. What with two sets of alimony and child support payments, keeping my job is top priority, so I need a resurrection. I run the dud through again ready to stop at any even slightly promising moments. I make myself forget the plot. The dud doesn't have a plot. I hit the switch and take it in. It's me and the dud.

I look for sex, action; I look for bodies and blood; I look for weapons.

There's a spot near the end of the movie where they're having a fractious meeting and someone pulls a gun and shoots in order to get everyone's attention. Believe it or not, that's the only role the gun has in the story. I write 112:34 to 112:59 to let the cutter know to start with these frames. Then I think: OK I have a gun. Now it's got to go off big. I try to recall any falling bodies, any blood. There's a scene right at the beginning where the talking head slips on a banana peel and ends up flat on his stomach with a bloody nose, a fat lip. I rewind fast. I look for the banana peel. Bingo! I can actually show the fall happening after the gun goes off and there are sixteen seconds where the banana peel does not show. One clip done—a body almost dead from the gun going off. Chekhov would be proud.

Sex. I fast forward to the network mogul's office where he is yelling "No, no, no," into a high-tech laser phone. He's trying to drown out his wife who's called to complain about another fancy dinner party he is going to miss. He looks frantic to get off the phone. His Chinese take out just arrived and he has a fetish about eating food hot. I write 15:15 to 15:32.

Inspired, I fast forward to the nude scene in the hot tub, where the talking head and the reporter are refreshing themselves after screwing. A phone beside the hot tub is ringing but they ignore it. I do not. I reverse the order and feed forty seconds of hot tub, wet flesh and ringing phone into ten seconds of the mogul screaming "no" into another phone. Who says they have to be the same call. I'm feeling lucky about this dud.

Next I remember a low-key chase scene in the shopping mall where the reporter is hysterically hunting for the right trench coat for her first big story. I splice it together with the mafia patsy's shakedown of a liquor store in a seedy part of town. I relocate the liquor store in the mall. So it's a slight change of neighborhood, but hey. Time flies as I make notes of where to cut and splice.

When I finish, it's a winner. My dud has a new story. My dud almost cons me into thinking the movie's worth seeing.

Why did I think this would be so hard?

Who says the story you tell has to be the story that happened?

Cut and splice. It's what I do every night warming a bar stool at The Last Reel: exaggerate, lie, edit. Hey Eddie, someone will say and then I'm off on another story before I head for home. It's what I do most nights when I can't sleep. It's what I do with my life.

🖋 🖋 🖋

Suggestions for Discussion

1. What is the effect of the last line of the story?

2. How might this story be read as a metaphor for the revision process?

Retrospect

3. Like Margaret Atwood's "Happy Endings," and Sherman Alexie's "This Is What It Means to Say Phoenix, Arizona," "Dud" deals with the way stories and lives are constructed. Which comes closest to describing your view of story-telling? What would be an apt metaphor for your writing process?

🖋 🖋 🖋

Writing Exercises

INDIVIDUAL

1. Pick any story in this book that dissatisfied you. Imagine that you are the editor of a magazine that is going to publish it. What suggestions for revision would you make to the author?

2. If you did assignment 1 in chapter 2 (the postcard short story), rewrite your story, making it at least three times as long so that the development enriches the action and the characters.

3. Choose any other story you wrote this term; rewrite it, improving it any way you can, but also either cutting or expanding its original length by at least one-fourth.

4. Choose a published story you like and highlight the direct dialogue in one color and all indirect discourse or summarized dialogue in another color. Do the same for your most recent story. Compare the two. Are your most important lines in direct dialogue or summarized? (Generally, these should be direct.) Is information or idle chatter direct or summarized? (Generally, these should be summarized.) Revise to make sure that the most important moments are in direct dialogue.

5. Actors sometimes experiment with changing the background circumstances of a scene to raise the intensity. Apply this technique to a story in progress. Add a new circumstance that makes it more urgent that the protagonist should get his or her way. Do the same for each character in the scene. (Example: a shoplifting scene. The protagonist, who wants to steal, needs an impressive gift for a potential boyfriend. Her reluctant friend spots a security guard.)

DEVELOPMENT/REVISION

6. Following your story workshop, but before starting the next draft, write a "contributor's note" similar to those in the back of the *Best American Short Stories* and *O'Henry* series volumes. In a paragraph, describe how the story first occurred to you. What intrigued you about it? How did the story evolve? Which of your plans changed, and why? What do you hope that readers will think the story is "about"? Read these contributors' notes aloud in class. Do they help you articulate the dramatic and thematic elements you wish to address in the revision process?

7. Spend about half an hour in class writing a scene that involves a conflict between two characters. Make a copy of what you write. Take one copy home and rewrite it. Send the other copy home with another class member for him or her to make critical comments and suggestions. Compare your impulses with those of your reader. On the following day, forgive your reader. On the day after that, rewrite the scene once more, incorporating any of the reader's suggestions that prove useful.

APPENDIX A

KINDS OF FICTION

What follows is a discussion of some kinds of fiction likely to be found in current books and magazines, which are also the kinds of contemporary narrative most likely to show up in a workshop. This is not by any means a comprehensive list, nor does it deal with the forms that represent the history of narrative—myth, tale, fable, allegory, and so forth—some of which are mentioned elsewhere in this book.

Mainstream refers to fiction that deals with subject matter with a broad appeal—situations and emotions common to and of interest to large numbers of readers in the culture for which it is intended. Mainstream fiction is **literary fiction** if its appeal is also lodged in the original, interesting, and illuminating use of the language; the term also implies a degree of care in the psychological exploration of its characters, and an attempt to shed light on the human condition. All of the stories in this volume fall under the general category of literary fiction.

Literary fiction differs from **genre fiction** fundamentally in the fact that the former is character-driven, the latter plot-driven. There is a strong tendency—though it is not a binding rule—of genre fiction to imply that life is fair, and to let the hero or heroine, after great struggle, win out in the end; and of literary fiction to posit that life is not fair, that triumph is partial, happiness tentative, and that the heroine and hero are subject to mortality. Literary fiction also strives to reveal its meaning through the creation of unexpected or unusual characters, through patterns of action and turns of event that will surprise the reader. Genre fiction, on the other hand, tends to develop character stereotypes and set patterns of action that become part of the expectation, the demand, and the pleasure of the readers of that genre.

Readers of the **romance** genre, for example, will expect a plucky-but-down-on-her-luck heroine, a handsome and mysterious hero with some dark secret (usually a dark-haired woman) in his background, a large house, some woods (through which the heroine will at some point flee in scanty clothing), and an eventual happy ending with the heroine in the hero's arms. These elements can be seen in embryo in the literary fiction of the Brontë sisters; by now, in the dozens of Harlequin and Silhouette romances on the supermarket rack, they have become **formulaic**, and the language is similar from book to book.

Like romance, most genres have developed from a kind of fiction that was at one time mainstream and represented a major social problem or concern. Early romance, for example, dealt with the serious question of how a woman was to satisfy the need for both stability and love in married life, how to be both independent and secure in a society with rigid sexual rules. The **detective** story evolved simultaneously with widespread and intense interest in science, an optimistic expectation that violence and mystery could be rationally explained. The **western** dealt with the ambivalence felt by large numbers of westward-traveling Euro-Americans about the civilizing of the wilderness, the desire to rid the West of its brutality, the fear that "taming" it would also destroy its promise of solitude and freedom. **Science fiction,** the most recently developed and still developing genre, similarly deals with ambivalence about technology, the near-miraculous accomplishments of the human race through science, the dangers to human feeling, soul, and environment. The surge in popularity of **fantasy fiction** can probably be attributed to nostalgia for a time even more free of technological accomplishment and threat, since fantasy employs a medieval setting and solves problems through magic, whereas science fiction is set in the future and solves problems through intelligence and technology. It is relevant that science fiction usually deals with some problem that can be seen to have a counterpart in the contemporary culture (space travel, international or interplanetary intrigue, mechanical replacement of body parts, genetic manipulation), whereas the plots of fantasies tend to deal with obsolete or archaic traumas—wicked overlords, demon interlopers, and so forth. Because of this contemporary concern, science fiction seems capable at this point in history of a deployment much more varied and original than other genres, and more often engages the attention of writers (and filmmakers) with literary intentions and ambitions. Among such writers are Octavia Butler, William Gibson, Ursula K. LeGuin, Philip K. Dick, and Doris Lessing.

In any case, the many other genres, including but not confined to **adventure,** **spy, horror,** and **thriller,** each have their own set of conventions of character, language, and events. Note again that the very naming of these kinds of fiction implies a narrowing; unlike mainstream fiction, they appeal to a particular restricted range of interest.

Many—perhaps most—teachers of fiction writing do not accept manuscripts in genre, and I believe there's good reason for this, which is that whereas writing literary fiction can teach you how to write good genre fiction, writing genre fiction does not teach you how to write good literary fiction—does not, in effect, teach you "how to write," by which I mean how to be original and meaningful in words. Further, dealing in the conventions and hackneyed phrases of romance, horror, fantasy, and so forth can operate as a form of personal denial, using writing as a means of avoiding rather than uncovering your real concerns. It may be fine to offer readers an escape through fiction, but it isn't a way to educate yourself as a writer, and it's also fair to say that escape does not represent the goal of a liberal education, which is to pursue, inquire, seek, and extend knowledge of whatever subject is at hand, fiction no less than science.

Partly because many college teachers of creative writing do not welcome genre fiction in the classroom, there has developed a notion of a "workshop story" that is realistic, sensitive, and small. I have never known a teacher who solicited such stories, or any particular sort of story. Leaps of imagination, originality, and genuine experimentation are in my experience welcome to both instructors and students. But it is true that often what seems wild and crazy to the student writer has occurred to others before. Stories set in dreams, outer space, game shows, heaven and hell, may seem strange and wonderful by comparison with daily life, but they are familiar as "experiments" and likely to be less startling to their readers than the author expects, whereas extreme focus on what the author has experienced may seem striking and fresh. **Realism**—the attempt to render an authentic picture of life, in such a way that the reader identifies with one or more characters—is a fair starting point for the pursuit of literary fiction. The writer's attempt at verisimilitude is comparable to the scientific method of observation and verification. Realism is also a convention, and not the only way to begin to write; but like the drawing of still life in the study of painting it can impart skills that will be useful in more sophisticated efforts whether they are realistic or not. Many of the stories in this book are realistic; "How Far She Went," "Wave," and "Ralph the Duck," for example, might be seen as attempts to reveal in recognizable detail the drama of ordinary life.

Experimental fiction is always possible, however. It's more difficult by far to describe what is experimental in fiction than what is cliché, because by definition the experimental is the thing that nobody expects or predicts. There are, however, a number of kinds of experiment that have come to be recognized as subsets of literary fiction, and a few of these are worth mentioning.

Magic realism uses the techniques and devices of realism—verisimilitude, ordinary lives and settings, familiar psychology—and introduces events of impossible or fantastic nature, never leaving the tone and techniques of realism. Whereas fantasy will attempt to bedazzle its readers with the amazing quality of the magic, magic realism works in the opposite direction, to convince the reader that the extraordinary occurs in the context and the guise of the ordinary. David Lodge, in *The Art of Fiction*, interestingly points out that the practitioners of magic realism tend to have lived through some sort of historical upheaval—a political coup or terror, a literal war or gender war. Flight, he points out, is a central image in this fiction, because the defiance of gravity represents a persistent "human dream of the impossible." Gabriel García Márquez, whose "Eyes of a Blue Dog" appears in this volume, is a foremost practitioner of magic realism, and his novel *One Hundred Years of Solitude* is the best known example of the genre. Interested readers might also look for *Labyrinths* by Jorge Luis Borges, who is often considered the father of this experimental mode.

Metafiction takes as its subject matter the writing of fiction, calls attention to its own techniques, and insists that what is happening is that a story is being written and read. Often the writing of the story is used as a metaphor for some other human struggle or endeavor.

Minimalism (also called miniaturism) refers to a flat, spare and subdued style of writing, characterized by an accumulation of (sometimes apparently random) detail that gives an impression of benumbed emotion. The point of view tends to be objective or near-objective, the events accumulating toward a tense, disturbing—and inconclusive—conclusion.

The short-short story or **sudden fiction** is a fiction under 2000 words; **microfictions** is a term sometimes used to distinguish stories under 250 words. Such pieces, according to Nancy Huddleston Packer, "push to the limit the basic elements of all short stories—compression, suggestion, and change. They combine the intensity and lyricism of a poem with the dramatic impact and movement of a short story—these stories are so compressed, they explode." In a short-short story, change is often subtle, taking form as a moment of surprise or a shift in perception. Called a "one-page novel" by Stephen Dunning, the short-short form is represented in this volume by "Girl," "No One's A Mystery," "Linoleum Roses," "Mount Olive," "Snow," "20/20," and other pieces.

It's always comforting to have a good reference book on hand when an unfamiliar literary term comes up. Two I recommend are *The Fiction Dictionary* by Laurie Henry (Cincinnati: Story Press, 1995) and *The Bedford Glossary of Critical and Literary Terms* by Ross Murfin and Supryia M. Ray (Boston and New York: Bedford Books, 1997).

APPENDIX B

SUGGESTIONS FOR FURTHER READING

Like writing programs and writers' conferences, books on writing have proliferated in the last thirty years, and you can probably find a new one on the Internet or the library bookshelf for every week of the year. Browse for your own favorites—don't forget to write meanwhile. Here are some—most of them written by writers for writers—that have struck me as most useful, graceful, or original:

Alvarez, Julia. *Something to Declare*. Chapel Hill, NC: Algonquin Books of Chapel Hill, 1998. Part poetry, part prose, all inspiration, and not in any way a textbook, this beautiful collection of essays about Alvarez's life also includes pieces about the writing life, how paying attention to details can be the springboard for material, and how writing is a different process for everyone.

Aristotle. *The Poetics*. This is the first extant work of literary criticism and the essay from which all later criticism derives. There are numerous good translations.

Atchity, Kenneth. *A Writer's Time: A Guide to the Writer's Process from Vision through Revision*. New York: Norton, 1988. Atchity focuses on the problem every writer complains about most and offers startling perceptions and helpful directions for finding and apportioning time.

Barzun, Jacques. *On Writing, Editing, and Publishing*. Chicago: University of Chicago Press, 1986. Is it possible to be elegant, irascible, practical, and witty, all at the same time, at the full stretch of each? Read it and see.

Baxter, Charles. *Burning Down the House: Essays on Fiction*. St. Paul: Graywolf Press, 1997. Discursive, insightful, and large-minded, Baxter ruminates on craft in its relation to our culture. Some of his best passages convincingly and interestingly challenge traditional ideas laid down in *Writing Fiction*.

Bell, Madison Smartt. *Narrative Design: A Writer's Guide to Structure*. New York: Norton, 1997. Bell begins and ends with the assumption that all the elements of fiction are subservient to narrative form. His close readings of stories show how the authors have gone about making choices that contribute to overall design.

Benson, Angela. *Telling the Tale: The African-American Fiction Writer's Guide*. New York: Berkley Publishing Group, 2000. Wonderful all-around writing advice with helpful examples from African-American writers and culture. The exercises are designed to keep writers writing and are particularly helpful for fleshing out characters.

Bernays, Anne, and Pamela Painter. *What If? Writing Exercises for Fiction Writers*. New York: Harper Collins, 1995. Bernays and Painter identify more than seventy-five situations that a writer may face and provide exercises for each; included are student examples and clear descriptions of objectives. This book is useful and provocative.

Bly, Carol. *The Passionate, Accurate Story*. Minneapolis: Milkweed Editions, 1990. A genuine original, this book makes a thoughtful plea for value in writing and writing from your values. It combines the insights of literary technique, therapy, and ethics.

Brande, Dorothea. *Becoming a Writer*. Los Angeles: J. P. Tarcher, 1981. For those who are overmeticulous, or who have a hard time getting started, Brande's mind-freeing exercises may be enormously helpful.

Brown, Kurt, ed. *Writers on Life and Craft*. Boston: Beacon, 1994–96. This series culls the best of the lectures, talks, and keynote speeches from writing conferences around the country. It is various and thoughtful, and cheaper than travel.

Busch, Frederick. *A Dangerous Profession: A Book about the Writing Life*. New York: St. Martin's Press, 1998. Busch pulls out all the stops as he explores some authors, himself included, driven to write despite the risks and discontents. He has also edited *Letters to a Fiction Writer* (New York: Norton, 1999), a rich compendium of advice from writers living and dead.

Checkoway, Julie. *Creating Fiction*. Cincinnati: Story Press, 1999. This book enables the reader to step into the minds of well-respected authors and teachers of the Associated Writing Programs and includes intelligent essays about the writing process with useful insights into characters including a section on minor characters.

Chiarella, Tom. *Writing Dialogue*. Cincinnati: Story Press, 1998. Including a detailed breakdown of dialogue patterns, Chiarella provides tips and exercises to help re-create them effectively and realistically.

Danford, Natalie, and John Kulka, eds. *Best New American Voices*. New York: Harcourt Brace, ongoing. An ongoing series of short-story collections culled from workshops around the country by more than one hundred writing programs, it gives an opportunity to see what's new and what's best in college and conference writing.

Darnton, John, ed. *Writers on Writing: Collected Essays from* The New York Times. New York: Henry Holt and Company, 2001. A varied selection of essays from the popular weekly feature of *The New York Times Book Review*, which publishes short pieces on craft, inspiration, and the writing process by the country's most respected literary authors.

Dillard, Annie. *The Writing Life*. New York: HarperCollins, 1989. This stunningly written account of "your day's triviality" touches drudgery itself with luminous significance. Every writer should read it. Also recommended is Dillard's *Living by Fiction* (New York: Harper, 1982).

Elbow, Peter. *Writing without Teachers*. New York and Oxford: Oxford, 1973. Elbow is excellent on how to keep going, growing, and cooking when you haven't the goads of teacher and deadline. *Writing with Power* (New York and Oxford: Oxford, 1981) is not aimed specifically at the imaginative writer, but still has useful advice and a good section on revising.

Forster, E. M. *Aspects of the Novel*. New York: Harcourt Brace Jovanovich, 1956. Forster delivered these Clark Lectures at Trinity College, Cambridge, England, in 1927. They are talkative, informal, and informative—still the best analysis of literature from a writer's point of view—a must.

Friedman, Bonnie. *Writing Past Dark*. New York: HarperCollins, 1993. Richly written ruminations on the writer's life illuminate this book. If you think writing is a lonely task, and you can afford only one book, buy this one.

Gardner, John. *The Art of Fiction: Notes on Craft for Young Writers*. New York: Alfred A. Knopf, 1984. *The Art of Fiction* is a new classic among books on writing. Gardner's advice is based on his experience as a teacher of creative writing and is addressed to "the serious beginning writer." The book is clear, practical, and a delight to read. Also recommended is Gardner's *On Becoming a Novelist* (New York: HarperCollins, 1985).

Gass, William. *Fiction and the Figures of Life*. Boston: David R. Godine, 1979. Gass writes of character, language, philosophy, and form, from acute angles in stunning prose—a joy to read.

Goldberg, Natalie. *Writing Down the Bones*. Boston: Shambhala, 1986. Also, *Wild Mind* (New York: Bantam, 1990). Goldberg is the guru of can-do, encouraging the writer with short, pithy, personal, and lively cheerings-on.

Hemley, Robin. *Turning Life into Fiction*. Cincinnati: Story Press, 1994. An excellent resource for turning life's situations into seeds for fiction writing, this book has an easy style with practical exercises to keep writers moving forward.

Hills, Rust. *Writing in General and the Short Story in Particular*. Boston: Houghton Mifflin, 1987. A former literary editor of *Esquire* magazine, Hills has written a breezy, enjoyable guide to fiction technique with good advice on every page.

Huddle, David. *The Writing Habit: Essays*. Layton, UT: Peregrine Smith Books, 1991. Huddle has a level voice and a sound sense of what it is to live with the habit. He is kind without being sentimental; this book is highly recommended.

James, Henry. *The House of Fiction*. Westport, CT: Greenwood, 1973. The master of indirection goes directly to the heart of the house of fiction.

Kaplan, David Michael. *Revision: A Creative Approach to Writing and Rewriting Fiction*. Cincinnati: Story Press, 1997. Kaplan convinces you that writing is revising, and that not only style and structure but meaning itself depends on the seeing-again part of the process.

Lamott, Anne. *Bird by Bird*. New York: Pantheon, 1994. Breezy, easy-reading, and full of witty, good advice, *Bird by Bird* (of which a chapter appears in this book) takes you from shitty first drafts through publication blues.

Le Guin, Ursula K. *Steering the Craft*. Portland, OR: The Eighth Mountain Press, 1998. Written by a master storyteller, this volume has a detailed chapter on point of view that includes helpful and explicit examples.

Lodge, David. *The Art of Fiction*. London: Penguin, 1992. A collection of Lodge's articles for British and American newspapers, this is not a how-to book but a work of short critical analyses. Nevertheless it crackles with insight and advice for writers.

Madden, David. *Revising Fiction: A Handbook for Fiction Writers*. New York: New American Library, 1995. Although it is too weighty to operate as a handbook, this volume shows the revision process convincingly and in full. Also useful as a reference tool is Madden's *A Primer of the Novel for Readers and Writers* (Lanham, MD: Scarecrow Press, 1980).

May, Rollo. *The Courage to Create*. New York: Bantam, 1984. May's book is a philosophic classic on the subject.

Nelson, Victoria. *On Writer's Block: A New Approach to Creativity*. Boston: Houghton Mifflin, 1993. Among the new breed of writers' books that use the insights of psychology and therapy, this is exceptionally helpful. Nelson is sensible as well as sensitive. Her suggestions work.

Olsen, Tillie. *Silences*. New York: Delacorte Press, 1978. *Silences* is comprised of eloquent essays, of which the title piece is a must.

Pack, Robert, and Jay Parini, eds. *Writers on Writing*. Middlebury, VT: Middlebury College Press, 1991. Described by the editors as a "celebration," this volume collects twenty-five eloquent essays by established writers who offer advice and experience that is practical, witty, confessional, flip, and moving and/or profound.

Rhodes, Jewel Parker. *Free Within Ourselves*. New York: Main Street Books, 1999. Encouraging exploration into the rich background of literary ancestors, Rhodes draws on her cultural resources as an African-American writer. In "My Best Advice," she shares her own tools for writing success.

Rico, Gabriele Lusser. *Writing the Natural Way*. Los Angeles: J. P. Tarcher, 1983. Rico describes in full the technique of clustering and offers useful techniques for freeing the imagination.

Seidman, Michael. *The Complete Guide to Editing Your Fiction*. Cincinnati: Writer's Digest Books, 2000. After a quick survey of the basic elements of writing, Seidman emphasizes the importance of revision in quality work and includes before-and-after case studies to illustrate the process of editing.

Shelnutt, Eve. *The Writing Room*. Marietta, GA: Longstreet Press, 1989. This is a wide-ranging, outspoken, often persuasive discussion of the crafts of fiction and poetry, with examples, analyses, and exercises.

Sloane, William. *The Craft of Writing*. Edited by Julia Sloane. New York: Norton, 1983. This book was culled posthumously from the notes of one of the great teachers of fiction writing.

Stafford, William. *Writing the Australian Crawl*. Edited by Donald Hall. Ann Arbor, MI: University of Michigan Press, 1978. The poet has affable and practical advice for fiction writers too. Also, *You Must Revise Your Life* (Ann Arbor, MI: University of Michigan Press, 1986) is an inspiriting potpourri of poems, essays, and interviews regarding writing.

Stern, Jerome. *Making Shapely Fiction*. New York: Norton, 1991. In this witty, useful guide, Stern illustrates various possible shapes for stories; he includes a cogent list of *don'ts* and discusses the elements of good writing in dictionary form so that you can use the book as a handy reference.

Strunk, William C., and E. B. White. *The Elements of Style*. 3rd ed. Boston: Allyn and Bacon, 1979. Strunk provides the rules for correct usage and vigorous writing in this briefest and most useful of handbooks.

Ueland, Barbara. *If You Want to Write*. St. Paul: Graywolf Press, 1987. "Everybody is talented. Everybody is original," Ueland says, and she says it convincingly in this book that holds up very well since its first edition in 1938.

Welty, Eudora. *One Writer's Beginnings*. Cambridge, MA: Harvard Press, 1984. One of the best autobiographies ever offered by a writer, Welty's book is moving, funny, and full of insight.

Willis, Meredith Sue. *Personal Fiction Writing*. Rev. 2nd ed., 2000; *Blazing Pencils*, 1990; and *Deep Revision*, 1993, all published by Teachers & Writers Collaborative, New

York. Willis teaches elementary to college-level and developmental workshops, both fiction and nonfiction, so her advice is a bit diffuse, but on the whole bears out her contention that "the heart of what happens in writing is shared by all writers, professional and avocational, adult and child." *Deep Revision*, especially, has many useful "do this" sections.

Wolitzer, Hilma. *The Company of Writers: Fiction Workshops and Thoughts on the Writing Life*. New York: Penguin Putnam, Inc., 2001. A guide to getting the most out of writing workshops, particularly outside the academic setting. The second half of the book is devoted to "focus sessions" designed to spark discussions of craft among workshop members.

Woodruff, Jay, ed. *A Piece of Work: Five Writers Discuss Their Revisions*. Iowa City, IA: University of Iowa Press, 1993. Poets and fiction writers (including Tobias Wolff and Joyce Carol Oates, whose stories are included in this volume) discuss their drafts, their writing processes, and much more.

Ziegler, Alan. *The Writing Workshop*. 2 vols. New York: Teachers & Writers Collaborative, 1981 and 1984. The author calls these useful books a "survey course" in writing. They are mainly intended for teachers of writing but can be adapted for use as a self-teaching tool; they're full of interesting practical advice.

Zinsser, William, ed. *Inventing the Truth: The Art and Craft of Memoir*. Boston: Houghton Mifflin, 1988. Although this series of talks, originally given at the New York Public Library, is not aimed at the fiction writer, it shines with hints on how to use the subject matter of your life from five fine writers: Annie Dillard, Toni Morrison, Russell Baker, Alfred Kazin, and Lewis Thomas.

Services for Writers

Associated Writing Programs (Tallwood House, Mail Stop 1E3, George Mason University, Fairfax, VA 22030). Those enrolled in the creative writing program of a college or university that is a member of AWP are automatically members; others can join for a reasonable fee. AWP's services include a magazine, *The Writer's Chronicle*, a job placement service, an annual meeting, and a number of awards and publications. The organization can provide contact with other writers, as well as valuable information on prizes, programs, presses, and the ideas current in the teaching of writing. *The AWP Official Guide to Writing Programs* (published bi-annually in cooperation with Dustbooks) is a thorough guide to graduate and undergraduate creative writing programs in the United States, Canada, and the United Kingdom.

Poets & Writers, Inc. (72 Spring St., New York, NY 10012). Poets & Writers issues a bi-monthly magazine of the same name that has articles of high quality and interest to writers; the magazine and organization also provide information on contests and on magazines and publishers soliciting manuscripts. The organization also has a number of useful publications that are periodically revised: the

Directory of American Poets and Fiction Writers; Literary Agents: A Writer's Guide; Author and Audience: A Readings and Workshops Guide; and an annual listing called *Writers' Conferences*.

Writers' Guides

Directory of Small Press/Magazine Editors & Publishers 2000–2001. Edited by Len Fulton. Paradise, CA: Dustbooks, 1999 and ongoing. An exhaustive list of smaller book and magazine publishers for poetry, fiction, and nonfiction, this resource is an easy reference for writers looking for comprehensive information about the small press industry, including helpful subject and regional indexes.

The Portable Publishing Classroom for Fiction and Creative Non-Fiction Writers. Audiocassette produced by Poets & Writers, Inc. Amy Holman describes in detail the most efficient way to publish your writing by matching your style with the appropriate publication.

2001–2002 Writer's Guide to Book Editors, Publishers, and Literary Agents. Edited by Jeff Herman. Rockland, CA: Prima Publishing, 2000 and ongoing. Detailed chapters—about creating the perfect query letter and the drawbacks of sending unsolicited manuscripts as well as question-and-answer sections designed to take the mystery out of the publishing process—help writers understand the business side of writing.

Writer's Market. Cincinnati: Writer's Digest Books, ongoing. A new edition comes out each year with practical advice on how to sell fiction and nonfiction manuscripts as well as lists of book and magazine publishers, agents, foreign markets, and other services for writers.

Credits

Index